DISEASES OF TURFGRASSES

DISEASES OF TURFGRASSES

Third Edition

Houston B. Couch

Professor of Plant Pathology
Virginia Polytechnic Institute
and State University

KRIEGER PUBLISHING COMPANY
MALABAR, FLORIDA
1995

Original Edition 1962
Second Edition 1973
Third Edition 1995

Printed and Published by
KRIEGER PUBLISHING COMPANY
KRIEGER DRIVE
MALABAR, FLORIDA 32950

FROM A DECLARATION OF PRINCIPLES JOINTLY ADOPTED BY A COMMITTEE
OF THE AMERICAN BAR ASSOCIATION AND COMMITTEE OF PUBLISHERS:

This Publication is designed to provide accurate and authoritative information in regard to the subject
matter covered. It is sold with the understanding that the publisher is not engaged in rendering legal,
accounting, or other professional service. If legal advice or other expert assistance is required, the
services of a competent professional person should be sought.

Library of Congress Cataloging-in-Publication Data

Couch, Houston B.
    Diseases of turfgrasses / Houston B. Couch.—3rd ed.
        p.   cm.
    Includes bibliographical references (p.   ) and index.
    ISBN 0-89874-211-0 (acid-free paper)
    1. Turfgrasses—Diseases and pests. 2. Turf management.
I. Title.
SB608.T87C68   1995   94-1649
635.9'64293—dc20   CIP

10   9   8   7   6   5   4   3   2

Contents

PREFACE   xi

PART ONE—INTRODUCTION

CHAPTER ONE   Turfgrass Pathology: Past and Present   3

Historical perspective. Sequence of events in the development of our present understanding of the nature and control of turfgrass diseases. Magnitude of current turfgrass disease control efforts in the golf course and lawn care industries.

CHAPTER TWO   The Nature of Disease   13

Diseases Are Caused by Biotic and Abiotic Entities   13
Biotically-Incited Disease Is a Dynamic Process   14
Terminology   14
    The Terminology of Disease Dynamics   14
    How Names Are Assigned to Individual Diseases   16
    Why It Is Necessary to Maintain a Uniform List of Standard Turfgrass Disease Names   17

PART TWO—DISEASES OF TURFGRASSES CAUSED BY FUNGI

CHAPTER THREE   The Nature of Plant Pathogenic Fungi   21

Distinguishing characteristics of fungi. Morphology and reproduction of fungi. How fungi survive adverse conditions. The nature of fungal pathogenesis using turfgrass disease illustrations.

CHAPTER FOUR   Patch Diseases   25

Spring and Fall Patch Diseases   25
    Necrotic Ring Spot   25
    Take-all Patch   28
    Rhizoctonia Yellow Patch   31
    Rhizoctonia Blight of Warm Season Turfgrasses   33
    Corticium Red Thread   36
    Limonomyces Pink Patch   39
Summer Patch Diseases   42
    Fusarium Blight   42
    Summer Patch   47
    Pythium Blight   51
    Rhizoctonia Blight of Cool Season Turfgrasses   59
    Rhizoctonia Sheath Spot   64

Sclerotinia Dollar Spot 65
Copper Spot 69
Sclerotium Blight 71
Melanotus White Patch 73
Winter Patch Diseases 74
Fusarium Patch 74
Typhula Blight 77
Sclerotinia Patch 79
Cottony Snow Mold 81
Frost Scorch 84
Spring Dead Spot of Bermudagrass 85
Pythium Patch 91

CHAPTER FIVE   Leaf Spots   **93**

Helminthosporium-Incited Diseases 93
Melting-Out of Kentucky Bluegrass 93
Helminthosporium Leaf Spot of Cool Season Turfgrasses 96
Red Leaf Spot of Bentgrass 100
Helminthosporium Blight of Fescue, Ryegrass, and Bluegrass 102
Brown Blight of Ryegrass 104
Drechslera Leaf Blight of Bentgrass 105
Zonate Eyespot of Bentgrass, Bluegrass, and Bermudagrass 106
Leaf Blotch of Bermudagrass 108
Stem and Crown Necrosis of Bermudagrass 109
Additional Helminthosporium Pathogens of Bermudagrass 109
Helminthosporium Crown and Root Rot of Zoysiagrass 110
Gray Leaf Spot 111
Black Leaf Spot 113
Char Spot 115
Septoria Leaf Spots 116
Septoria Leaf Spot of Bluegrasses 116
Septoria Leaf Spot of Bentgrasses 117
Septoria Leaf Spot of Tall Fescue 117
Septoria Leaf Spot of Ryegrasses 118
Stagonospora Leaf Spots 119
Stagonospora Leaf Spot of Kentucky Bluegrass 119
Stagonospora Leaf Spot of Fescues 119
Cercospora Leaf Spots 120
Cercospora Leaf Spot of St. Augustinegrass 120
Cercospora Leaf Spot of Tall Fescue 121
Spermospora Leaf Spots 122
Spermospora Eyespot of Kentucky Bluegrass 122
Spermospora Leaf Spot of Red Fescue 122
Spermospora Leaf Spot of Tall Fescue and Ryegrasses 123
Pseudoseptoria Leaf Spot 124
Ascochyta Leaf Spots 125
Ascochyta Leaf Spot of Ryegrasses 125
Ascochyta Leaf Spot of Tall Fescue 125
Ascochyta Leaf Spot of Kentucky Bluegrass, Fescues, and Perennial Ryegrass ... 126
Rhynchosporium Leaf Blotch 127
Brown Stripe 128
Phleospora Leaf Spot 129
Mastigosporium Leaf Spot 130
Ramularia Leaf Spot 132

CHAPTER SIX   Molds, Mildews, Rusts, and Smuts   135

Slime Molds   135
Downy Mildew (Yellow Tuft)   136
Powdery Mildew   139
Rusts   141
Leaf Smuts   149
    Stripe Smut   149
    Flag Smut   152
    Blister Smut   153

CHAPTER SEVEN   Senectopathic Disorders   155

Anthracnose   156
Curvularia Blight   159
Leptosphaeurlina Leaf Blight   162
Other Incitants of Senectopathic Disorders   163

CHAPTER EIGHT   Root Dysfunctions, Declines, and Rots   165

Anaerobiosis (Black Layer)   165
    Diagnostic Features   165
    Disease Profile   165
    Control   169
Pythium-Incited Root and Crown Diseases   170
    Pythium Root Dysfunction of Creeping Bentgrass   171
    Pythium Decline of Creeping Bentgrass   173
Gaeumannomyces Decline of Bermudagrass   175
Take-all Root Rot of St. Augustinegrass   176
Polymyxa Root Rot   177
Pyrenochaeta Root Rot   178
Pseudocercosporella Basal Rot   179

CHAPTER NINE   Fairy Rings   181

Edaphic Fairy Rings   181
    Disease Profile   182
    Control   184
Lectophilic Fairy Rings   185
    Disease Profile   186
    Control   186

CHAPTER TEN   Seedling Diseases   187

Pythium Damping-Off   187
Fusarium Damping-Off   188
Rhizoctonia Damping-Off   188

CHAPTER ELEVEN   Disease of the Inflorescence   191

Covered Smut   191
Loose Smuts   192
Silver Top (White Heads, White Top)   192
Choke   194
Ergot   195
Blind Seed   197

**PART THREE—DISEASES OF TURFGRASSES
CAUSED BY VIRUSES AND PROKARYOTES**

CHAPTER TWELVE   Diseases of Turfgrasses Caused by Viruses   **203**

The Form and Composition of Viruses   203
How Viruses Affect Plant Growth and Development   203
Control of Virus Diseases   205
St. Augustinegrass/Centipedegrass Decline   205
St. Augustinegrass Leaf Mottle   206
Ryegrass Leaf Mottle   206
Necrotic Mottle of Kentucky Bluegrass and Annual Ryegrass   207
Yellow Dwarf of Cool Season Turfgrasses   207
Leaf Mosaics   208
    Western Ryegrass Mosaic of Tall Fescue and Ryegrasses   208
    Ryegrass Mosaic of Cool Season Turfgrasses   208
    Bromegrass Mosaic of Cool Season Turfgrasses   209

CHAPTER THIRTEEN   Diseases of Turfgrasses Caused by Prokaryotes   **211**

Bacterial Wilt   211
Ryegrass Yellows   213
White Leaf of Bermudagrass   214

PART FOUR—DISEASES OF TURFGRASSES CAUSED BY NEMATODES

CHAPTER FOURTEEN   Diseases of Turfgrasses Caused by Nematodes   **217**

Characteristics of Plant Parasitic Nematodes   217
Floral and Foliar Nematodes   219
    Grass Seed Nematode   219
    Leaf Gall Nematodes   222
Root-Feeding Nematodes   223
    Cyst Nematodes   223
    Cystoid Nematodes   224
    Endoparasitic Nematodes
    Rootknot Nematodes   224
    Root Lesion Nematodes (Meadow Nematodes)   226
    Burrowing Nematodes   227
    Ectoparasitic Nematodes
    Spiral Nematodes   228
    Sting Nematodes   230
    Stunt Nematodes   230
    Ring Nematodes   231
    Pin Nematodes   232
    Stubby Root Nematodes   233
    Dagger Nematodes   233
    Lance Nematodes   234
    Needle Nematodes   234
    Sheath Nematodes   235
    Awl Nematodes   235
    Control of Root-Feeding Nematodes   235

PART FIVE—FUNDAMENTALS OF TURFGRASS DISEASE CONTROL

CHAPTER FIFTEEN   Diagnostic Procedures   **243**

Laboratory Procedures   243
Field Procedures   243
Determining the Cause of Root Declines   246
Collection of Samples for Laboratory Workups   246
Maintaining Records of Diagnoses and Control Procedures   247

CHAPTER SIXTEEN   Developing Integrated Disease Control Strategies   **249**

Cultural Practices   249
    Plant Nutrition and Soil pH   249
    Thatch Management   250
    Mowing Height   251
    Soil Moisture Stress   251
    Leaf Wetness   252
Use of Disease Resistant Genotypes   252
Biological Control   253
    Use of Preparations Containing Known Microbial Antagonists   253
    Use of Natural Organic Products   255
Use of Pesticides   257

CHAPTER SEVENTEEN   Selection and Use of Fungicides   **259**

Fungicide Nomenclature   259
Fungicidal Modes of Action   259
Fungicide Groups   261
Types of Fungicide Formulations   262
Synergistic Fungicide Combinations   263
Fungicidal Resistance   264
Optimum Fungicide Dilution Rates   267
Relationship Between Nozzle Type, Pressure at the Nozzle, and Fungicide Effectiveness 268
Effect of pH of the Preparation and In-Tank Storage Time on Fungicide Stability   270
Guidelines for Tank Mixing Spray Materials   272
Effect of Postspray Rainfall or Sprinkler Irrigation on Fungicide Effectiveness   274
Procedures for Making Accurate and Uniform Fungicide Applications   275
Use of Granular Fungicide Formulations   276
Nontarget Effects of Fungicides on Turfgrasses   278

APPENDIXES

Table I.   Profiles of Basic Fungicides and Nematicides Used for Control of Turfgrass Diseases   285
Table II.   Diseases of Turfgrasses Arranged According to Turfgrass Species Affected   299
Table III. Grass Species Susceptible to Turfgrass Pathogens Listed by Common Name   309
Table IV.   Grass Species Susceptible to Turfgrass Pathogens Listed by Scientific Names   323

COLOR PLATES   **339**

GLOSSARY   Pesticides and Pesticide Usage   **381**

BIBLIOGRAPHY   **389**

INDEX   **411**

To Billie

about whom Proverbs 31
was written

Preface to the Third Edition

Since the preparation of the second edition of this book there has been an accumulation of a significant body of new information on the nature and control of turfgrass diseases. The syndromes for several newly recognized maladies have been described, the epidemiological patterns of many of the commonly known diseases have been more fully defined, the names of several of the fungal pathogens have been changed, and entirely new groups of fungicides have been placed on the market.

The increased understanding of the etiology and epidemiology of certain diseases has led to the development of better diagnostic procedures and more precise timing of fungicidal applications for their control. Specific cultural practices have been identified for use in developing integrated control strategies for individual diseases. Also, the potential for resistance to specific site fungicides has been detected within at least three of the major fungal pathogen groups and systems of fungicide rotation have been developed to minimize its occurrence.

The format for the coverage of specific diseases for this edition is essentially the same as used in the earlier printings. Specifically, the information on each disease is presented as follows: (1) Symptoms, (2) The Pathogen, (3) Turfgrass Hosts, (4) All Known Gramineous Hosts, (5) Disease Profile, and (5) Control. The control sections for many of the diseases are further divided into three sections: (1) Cultural Practices, (2) Use of Resistant Grasses, and (3) Chemical Control. Chemicals suggested for the control of the various diseases are given by coined name. Representative trade names and a profile of each fungicide, including modes of action and procedures for maximizing its effectiveness, is given in Appendix Table I. In order to facilitate laboratory-based diagnostic procedures, the listing for each of the fungal pathogens provides a technical description of the organism and techniques for isolation and culture. Also, photo-micrographs and drawings are provided of many of the species.

The introductory section of this edition includes specific information on the nature of disease and the development of a working vocabulary in disease dynamics. Background information on each biotic group of pathogens is given in the introduction to the section that profiles the diseases it incites. Finally, the disease control section has been expanded to include chapters on diagnostic procedures, developing integrated disease management strategies, and the selection and use of fungicides.

I am very thankful to my colleagues for reviewing the sections of the manuscript and making helpful suggestions. Dr. Philip Larsen reviewed the chapter on leaf spots, Dr. John Hall read the section on anaerobiosis and the chapter on developing integrated disease management strategies, Dr. Jonathan Eisenback made many helpful suggestions on the chapter on diseases incited by nematodes, Dr. Sue Tolin reviewed the chapter on virus diseases, Dr. Bruce Clarke reviewed the material on summer patch diseases, Dr. James Muchovej brought the taxonomic positions of the fairy ring fungi up to date and reviewed the material on senectopathic disorders, Dr. David Chalmers reviewed the chapter on the selection and use of fungicides, and James Snow and James Latham offered many helpful suggestions on the section on anaerobiosis. I am also grateful to Drs. Leon Lucas, Monica Elliott, Clinton Hodges, Bruce Martin and Robert Dunn for advice and input on matters related to the nature of root and crown diseases and nematode dynamics, and to Sandy Jordan who prepared the drawings for this edition.

Houston B. Couch

Blacksburg, Virginia
January 1995

PART ONE

Introduction

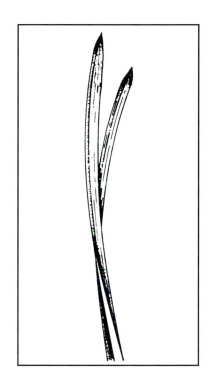

Turfgrass Pathology: Past and Present

Turfgrass pathology is an integration of the concepts and principles of the science of plant pathology with those of the practice of turfgrass culture. The story of the development of turfgrass pathology, then, flows with the events that relate to the development of both of these disciplines.

In Europe, lawns of pure stands of grass were first purposely established in the thirteenth century. By the sixteenth century, lawns had become common features of home grounds in northern Europe. Also by this time, most towns and villages had a turfed "common" or "green." These public greens were the playing sites for the game of bowls and early forms of soccer and cricket. As the popularity of bowls increased, there was a progression of improvements in the quality of the care that was being taken to establish and maintain the bowling greens.

The first disease to be described on cultivated turf was fairy rings. In 1563, an essay by W. Faulke, entitled *A goodly Gallerye with a most pleasant Prospect, into the garden of naturall contemplation, to behold the natuurall causes of all kynde of Meteors,* attributed the formation of "those round circles that ignorant people affirm to be the rings of the Fairies dances" to the effects of lightning. Most of the early writings on fairy rings, however, were not so much concerned with the biology of the formation of the rings as they were with the uniqueness of their appearance. Also, in spite of the objections of Faulke and others, accounts of supernatural activities associated with the occurrence of fairy rings persisted throughout the Middle Ages. The rings of greener grass dotted with mushrooms were said to be the dancing sites of fairies. In Holland, the dead grass in the center of the rings was supposed to mark the place where the devil churned his butter. In France, intentional entrance into one of these rings would result in an encounter with large toads with bulging eyes. If a Scottish farmer tilled an area containing fairy rings, then "wierdless days and weary nights are his to his deein' day." A more optimistic view of the consequences of fairy rings was taken in England, where it was considered a good omen to build a house on land supporting them (Ramsbotton, 1953).

By the eighteenth century, turf maintenance had become fairly sophisticated. Instructions for the proper care of grass walks and bowling greens called for them to be rolled and mowed every 15 days. Many of the gardening books contained instructions on the mowing, rolling, edging and weeding of lawns. The equipment used in turfgrass culture during this period was borrowed from the farm. Cutting the grass, for example, was accomplished with hand scythes and cradles.

In 1754 the Royal and Ancient Golf Club of St. Andrews, Scotland was established. With this, the game that was to become universally known as "golf" received recognition as an established, on-going sport. The widespread popularity of golf through the years, and the various requirements it places on turf for play, has served as a major impetus for the development of the basic procedures now used in turfgrass culture.

Also during the eighteenth century, more serious thought was given to determining what stimulated the plants in fairy rings to grow more rapidly, and what eventually caused them to die. One theory held that fairy rings were caused by insects. Finally, in 1792 it was proposed that these growth patterns were caused by the mushrooms that were present in the rings (Ramsbottom, 1953).

The early part of the nineteenth century brought the invention of the first mowing machine for turf. The device was patented in 1830, and its manufacture began two years later. The capacity to maintain both specified and uniform heights of cut continuously with rather low investments in labor was the innovation needed in order for the unique features of the turfgrass plant to be fully utilized in a wide range of landscape and utilitarian situations. The motivation to exploit these now-recognized potentials led to the development of the systematic programs of research and testing that have established the various concepts and principles that comprise the art of turf-grass management.

As the nineteenth century unfolded, plant pathology developed into a *bona fide* biological science. During this time a continuing series of discoveries firmly reinforced the germ theory of disease causality. Through the course of the century, the fungal incitants of several major plant diseases were identified. In addition to fungi, certain species of bacteria came to be recognized as being pathogenic to plants, and at the close of the century, research was begun on determining the nature of an infectious agent that would eventually become known as a virus.

In 1882, a major breakthrough in chemical control of plant diseases was made. It was discovered that Bordeaux mixture (a blend of copper sulfate and lime) functioned as a very effective, low cost fungicide. With the advent of Bordeaux mixture, the era of systematic research for the purpose of developing programs of plant disease control through the use of pesticides was ushered in.

Corticium red thread has the distinction of being the first foliar disease to be diagnosed on cultivated turfgrass. The fungus that incites red thread (*Laetisaria fuciformis*) had been found on range grasses in Australia in 1854. In 1873, it was determined that this same species was causing a widespread and severe foliar blighting of ryegrass lawns in Great Britain.

In the United States, 1885 stands as a hallmark year for both turfgrass culture and plant pathology. The first official golf club in the country was established in Yonkers, New York in 1885. This was also the year that turf research started in the United States. The location of this work was the Olcott turf gardens in Connecticut. Also in 1885, the United States Department of Agriculture's Division of Botany was established. This unit was to serve as the first administrative base for plant disease research in this country.

By the close of the nineteenth century, there were over 80 golf courses in the United States, and the first games of two other turf-dependent sports, football and baseball, had been played. The United States Golf Association had been formed. Research on turf management was being conducted on a much broader scale, and the nature and control of plant disease was being investigated at many of the state agricultural experiment stations.

By the beginning of the twentieth century, all of the components needed for the establishment of the discipline of turfgrass pathology were in place. Many of the basic methods and techniques of turfgrass culture had been defined, and the science of plant pathology had developed to the extent that it could address itself constructively to identifying the causes of specific diseases and developing programs for their control.

In 1911, frost scorch, a winter patch disease, was reported on Kentucky bluegrass in Wisconsin. In 1913, a warm weather patch disease was observed to be causing extensive damage to the putting greens of a golf course near Philadelphia, Pennsylvania. The following year, what appeared to be the same disease developed on red fescue in a turf garden in Philadelphia. The owner of the garden, F. W. Taylor, was keenly interested in turfgrass culture and was active in both the development of management techniques and in the search for superior strains of grass. Based on its characteristic symptom pattern of foliage blighting and death of the plants in large irregular patches, Taylor named the disease "brown patch." In his efforts to determine the cause of the disease at hand, he enlisted the assistance of Charles V. Piper, a member of the research staff of the United States Department of Agriculture and Director of the Green Section of the United States Golf Association. Isolations from the diseased plants by Piper consistently yielded the fungus *Rhizoctonia solani*. Inoculation experiments conducted in 1917 by Piper and his associate, H. S. Coe, showed conclusively that this fungus was the incitant of the disease (Piper and Coe, 1919) (Figure 1-1).

During the first two decades of the twentieth century, turfgrass disease control programs consisted primarily of removal of free water from leaf surfaces by poling and/or the application of hydrated lime. Once the turf had been damaged by disease, it was thought that copious watering would help the grass make a quicker comeback; therefore, recommendations were made to water the diseased areas heavily at any time of the day.

In 1917, field tests were begun by the United States Golf Association to determine the feasibility of using sprays and dusts of Bordeaux mixture to control brown patch. These experiments showed that this material was toxic to bentgrass after repeated applications, and that it left an unsightly color on the surface of the turf, but it did control the disease, and since there were no alternatives, by 1919 the treatment of putting greens with Bordeaux mixture for the control of brown patch had become a general practice (Figure 1-2) (Carrier, 1922).

During the early part of the 1920s, another turfgrass disease was identified. This malady was first recognized on bentgrass putting greens. Its symptom pattern resembled the early stages of brown patch, and it occurred at about the same time in the growing

During this decade, the incitants were identified and symptom patterns described for melting-out of Kentucky bluegrass, zonate eyespot of bentgrass, red leaf spot of bentgrasses, Helminthosporium blight of fescues, leaf blotch of bermudagrass, Helminthosporium leaf spot, Septoria leaf spot, Ascochyta leaf spot, Cercospora leaf spot, powdery mildew, rust, stripe smut, Pythium blight, and Fusarium patch.

Efforts were also made in the 1920s to discover the cause of yellow tuft and determine the cause and control of a destructive patch disease of Washington bentgrass greens known as "drum-head brown patch." In its early stages of development, drum-head brown patch resembled large brown patch, but as the disease progressed, the roots and stolons developed a dark rot, and a hard crust formed over the surfaces of the affected areas. Attempts to control the disease with Bordeaux mixture and with organic and inorganic mercury compounds failed (Orton and Strazza, 1928). Yellow tuft has since been found to be caused by the fungus *Sclerophthora macrospora*, but drumhead brown patch seems to have been primarily a disease of Washington bentgrass, for it disappeared along with the diminished popularity of this variety, and its cause was never determined.

During the early 1920s, sulfur, formalin, copper stearate, and copper sulfate were tested for brown patch control. Although these materials were found to be fungicidal, their extreme phytotoxicity outweighed their disease control benefits. In 1920, mercuric chloride was used successfully in the Chicago area for control of brown patch. In 1924, the organic

Figure 1-1. Charles V. Piper was a member of the research staff of the United States Department of Agriculture and Director of the Greens Section of the United States Golf Association. His research showing that the fungus *Rhizoctonia solani* was the incitant of the disease known as "large brown patch" marked the beginnings of modern turfgrass pathology. *Courtesy Lee C. Dieter.*

season. However, during the later stages of development of the two diseases, the individual areas of turf blighted by the pathogen of this newly recognized disease were usually lighter in color and much smaller in diameter. The two were distinguished from each other by referring to the disease incited by *Rhizoctonia solani* as "large brown patch", and to the newly recognized malady as "small brown patch" (or "small patch"). "Small patch" eventually became known as "dollar spot," and finally in 1937 its incitant was given the name *Sclerotinia homoeocarpa*.

The 1920s proved to be very productive years for reporting newly recognized diseases of turfgrasses.

Figure 1-2. A common disease control practice in the 1920s was to apply Bordeaux mixture dust to putting greens. *From Bulletin U.S. Golf Association Green Section, Vol. 12, 1932.*

mercury compound Semesan (chlorophenol mercury) was tested in Yonkers, New York for control of Sclerotinia dollar spot on bentgrass putting greens (Godfrey, 1925). In these trials, different rates of Semesan were applied as drenches in 50 gallons of water per 1,000 square feet. While some phytotoxicity was noted at the higher rates, the material provided effective control of the disease.

In 1925, tests were begun at the Arlington Turf Gardens in Arlington, Virginia for control of brown patch and Sclerotinia dollar spot. These trials included Bordeaux mixture, formalin, sulfur, copper sulfate, copper stearate, Semesan, Uspulun (chlorophenol mercury), mercuric oxide, mercuric sulfide, mercuric cyanide, mercurous nitrate, mercuric sulfate, mercurous chloride, and mercuric chloride. The experiments were continued through 1927, at which time the conclusion was drawn that mercury-based products were the most satisfactory for the control of turf diseases.

The Arlington investigations showed that mercuric chloride (corrosive sublimate) was the quicker acting form of mercury for the control of Sclerotinia dollar spot and brown patch. However, the phytotoxic potential of this material was found to be high—particularly during hot weather. Mercurous chloride (calomel) was found to be slower acting than mercuric chloride, but it was less toxic to the grass. These features led to the use of mixes of these two forms of mercury. The most common mixture was 2 parts calomel to 1 part corrosive sublimate (Couch, 1971) (Couch, 1979b) (Ferguson and Grau, 1949) (Monteith and Dahl, 1932).

Mercury-based fungicides were sold as single component products or in combination with a fertilizer—usually ammonium sulfate. Advertisements for these materials in the trade journals focused primarily on their effectiveness in the control of brown patch. One such advertisement informed its readers that "Divot diggers can be reformed but brown patch must be killed." In listing the virtues of the fungicide it was promoting, another advertisement pointed out that the product was odorless and mixed easily, and when used as a preventive, ". . . it keeps greens smooth and relatively free from Brown Patch," and "As a cure, it not only checks the fungus growth immediately, but it quickly brings back a normal stand of turf" (Figure 1-3).

In 1929, a turfgrass research and advisory service was established in Great Britain. The work was conducted under the oversight of the Board of Greenskeeping Research. The name of the organization was later changed to the British Sports Turf Research Institute. From the outset, the staff addressed itself to the solution of a broad range of problems in turfgrass culture—including determining the nature and control of certain diseases. The papers that have been published on the subject of turfgrass pathology in its journal are a valuable addition to the body of knowledge in this field.

The first comprehensive publication on the nature and control of turfgrass diseases was published in 1932. It was released as an entry in the Bulletin of the United States Golf Association under the title *Turf Diseases and Their Control.* The authors, John Monteith, Jr. and Arnold S. Dahl, were the principal researchers in the field of turfgrass pathology in the late 1920s and early 1930s (Figure 1-4).

This publication stands as a classic, both for the thorough manner in which it integrates the principles and concepts of plant pathology with those of the practice of turfgrass culture, and the completeness of detail in its descriptions of the nature of many of the more important diseases of turfgrasses. It covered diseases incited by both biotic and abiotic entities. Control was approached from the standpoint of the use of resistant varieties, the use of cultural practices such as fertilization and irrigation, and the application of fungicides.

As the 1930s began, turfgrass disease control programs were almost entirely dependent on either chlorophenol mercury or the inorganic mercury chlorides. In 1931, however, it was discovered that a non-mercury, organic compound that had been developed for use as an accelerator in the manufacture of rubber, had fungicidal properties. Known by the coined chemical name "thiram," this material was used in the rubber industry under the trade name of "Tuads." Field tests showed that thiram was effective in controlling several of the more important diseases of turfgrasses. Within a few years, thiram was in general use in turfgrass disease control programs.

It was also discovered that thiram in combination with either Semesan or mercuric chloride made a very good tank mixture. In addition to functioning as a fungicide in its own right, thiram reduced the phytotoxicity potential of the mercuries. As the result, the introduction of thiram to golf course use established a new dimension in disease control—greater efficiency with less hazard of injury to the grass. A combination formulation of Semesan and thiram, sold under the trade name "Tersan OM," was a mainstay in turfgrass disease control programs from the mid 1930s until it was removed from the market in 1970.

During this period, the available selection of methods for applying fungicides to stands of turfgrass included (a) diluting them in water and then

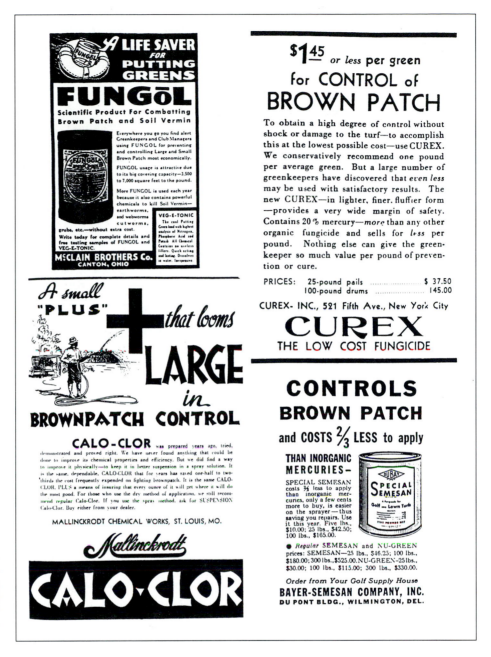

Figure 1-3. Product announcements and advertisements for turfgrass fungicides in the late 1920s and early 1930s promoted the use of organic and inorganic mercuries for the control of brown patch and Sclerotinia dollar spot.

spraying the plants, (b) mixing them in an inert powder and then dusting the mixture over the surface of the greens, and (c) mixing them either in sand, fertilizer or a top dressing and then using drop spreaders to distribute the preparation over the area to be treated (Figure 1-5). Throughout the 1920s, no one method of fungicide application was the most popular. However, during this period, rapid advances were being made in the development of spray equipment and the adaptation of sprayers for use in turfgrass management. As the result, by the mid 1930s, the use of sprayers equipped with either broadcast booms or spray guns had become the most common method for applying fungicides to established stands of turfgrass (Figure 1-6).

Cadmium succinate (Cadminate™) was introduced as a turfgrass fungicide in the mid-1940s. This material was particularly effective in the control of Sclerotinia dollar spot, copper spot, and Corticium red thread. It was also during the 1940s that the era of antibiotics for use in medicine and plant disease control came into being. In 1955, cycloheximide, a member of this new chemical group was introduced into turfgrass disease control programs. Marketed as

Figure 1-4. John Monteith, Jr. (left) and Arnold S. Dahl (right) were the principal researchers in the field of turfgrass pathology during the 1920s and early 1930s. They also authored the first comprehensive publication on the nature and control of turfgrass diseases. *Courtesy Department of Plant Pathology, University of Wisconsin.*

Acti-dione, this particular antibiotic was unique in that it was antifungal rather than antibacterial. Acti-dione not only controlled many of the common turfgrass diseases, such as Rhizoctonia blight, Sclerotinia dollar spot and Helminthosporium leaf spot, but it also provided a level of control of rust and powdery mildew that had never before been realized.

It was during the early part of the 1950s that there developed a full appreciation of the importance of parasitic nematodes as turfgrass pathogens. As the result, assays for the purpose of determination of population levels of ectoparasitic forms of nematodes in the root zones of turfgrasses became commonplace.

The close of the 1950s and the early 1960s was marked by the publication of the first books on the nature and control of turfgrass diseases. In 1959, the British Sports Turf Research Institute issued *Fungal Diseases of Turfgrasses* by J. D. Smith (Smith, 1959b). This book covered the more important diseases of turfgrasses in Great Britain. In 1962, *Diseases of Turfgrasses* by H. B. Couch was printed (Couch, 1962). The scope of this book included all known turfgrass diseases. Its second edition was released in 1973.

Smith's *Fungal Diseases of Turfgrasses* went into its second edition in 1965, with Noel Jackson as a co-author. In 1988 it was revised by J. D. Smith, Noel Jackson and A. R. Woolhouse into a comprehensive treatment of the subject and issued under the new title *Fungal Diseases of Amenity Turfgrasses.* In 1978, a symposium covering research developments in turfgrass pathology was held in Columbus, Ohio. The proceedings from this conference were compiled by B. G. Joyner and P. O. Larsen and published in 1980 under the title *Advances in Turfgrass Pathology* (Joyner and Larsen, 1980).

During the mid 1950s and early 1960s, nine additional fungicides were labeled for use in the control of turfgrass diseases: chloroneb (Tersan SP™), diazoben (Dexon™), ethazole (Koban™), zineb (Parzate C™), maneb (Dithane M-22™), mancozeb (Fore™), quintozene (Terraclor™), phenylmercury acetate (PMAS™), and anilazine (Dyrene™). Also, in the late 1950s the post-planting nematicide DBCP (Nemagon™) came into widespread use in turfgrass management.

In 1963, resistance to anilazine (Dyrene™) by the dollar spot pathogen (*Sclerotinia homoeocarpa*) was reported. This was the first verified instance of the development of field resistance to a fungicide on the part of a turfgrass pathogen. Within a few years, episodes of both anilizene and cadmium resistant *Sclerotinia homoeocarpa* had been reported from several locations in the central and eastern sections of the United States and southeastern Canada.

By the close of the 1960s, the results of assessments of possible harmful side effects of pesticides on the quality of the environment began to impact on

Figure 1-5. During the 1920s and early 1930s, a common method of applying fungicides was to mix them with sand, compost, or similar material. In order to insure even distribution of the materials, all lumps were first broken by use of a roller. The fungicide was then mixed with fine sand on a piece of canvas by lifting the corners (above). The fungicide-sand preparation was then mixed with soil or compost and applied to the turf by means of a drop spreader. *From Bulletin U.S. Golf Association Green Section, Vol. 12, 1932.*

turfgrass disease control programs. More clearly defined restrictions were placed on the use of mercury-based fungicides. In 1970, the manufacturer of Semesan™ and Tersan OM™ voluntarily removed both products from the market. The use of these two formulations as a mainstay in turfgrass disease control programs had spanned four decades.

In 1964, the cause, symptomatology and holopathology of Fusarium blight, a newly recognized warm weather patch disease, was described. During the following twenty years, research was conducted on the nature of ten other newly identified diseases: bacterial wilt of bentgrass, St. Augustinegrass decline, centipedegrass decline, Drechslera leaf blight and crown rot of bentgrass, necrotic ring spot, Rhizoc-

tonia yellow patch, Limonomyces pink patch, Melanotus white patch, Sclerotium blight, and summer patch. Also during this time, the incitants of yellow tuft and spring dead spot of bermudagrass were identified.

In addition to the research on newly reported diseases, during the period from the 1960s through the 1980s several advances were made in our understanding of the nature of the turfgrass diseases that had been identified in the 1920s and 1930s. The influence of nutrition and soil moisture stress on the incidence and severity of Rhizoctonia blight, Sclerotinia dollar spot, Pythium blight, melting-out of Kentucky bluegrass, Helminthosporium leaf spot of bentgrass, rust, and Corticium red thread was defined. A

Figure 1-6. The early power sprayers manufactured for use in turfgrass management were available as tractor-drawn rigs and as self-propelled units. They could be fitted with either broadcast booms or spray guns.

procedure was developed for forecasting outbreaks of Pythium blight, and the relationship between leaf wetness period and air temperature and the incidence and severity of Rhizoctonia blight and Helminthosporium leaf spot was worked out.

The 1970s saw the introduction of a new contact fungicide, chlorothalonil (Daconil 2787™) and a localized penetrant, iprodione (Chipco 26019™). The first commercially available acropetal penetrant fungicides for use on turfgrass were marketed in 1970–71. They were the benzimidazoles, benomyl (Tersan 1991™), thiophanate ethyl (Cleary 3336™), and thiophanate methyl (Fungo 50™). Although these materials provided high levels of control of several turfgrass diseases, within a few years, there came reports

of resistance by the powdery mildew (*Erysiphe graminis*) and Sclerotinia dollar spot pathogens. During the 1980s, seven new turfgrass fungicides became commercially available for use in turfgrass management. This list included a systemic compound, fosetyl Al (Aliette™), two additional localized penetrants, vinclozolin (Vorlan™) and propamocarb (Banol™), and four acropetal penetrants, triadimefon (Bayleton™), propiconazole (Banner™), and fenarimol (Rubigan™), and metalaxyl (Subdue™).

Research on disease control procedures conducted through the 1970s and 1980s (a) compared the relative effectiveness of granular and spray formulations of turfgrass fungicides, (b) defined the optimum dilution rates for several fungicide formulations,

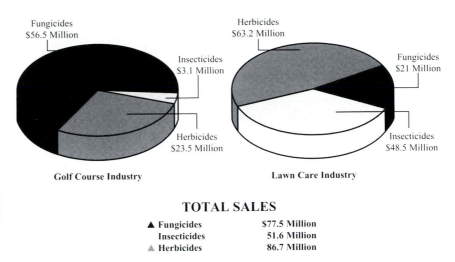

Figure 1-7. 1992 sales of pesticides in the United States to the golf course and lawn care industries by product category. (Based on 1992 Agricultural Chemical Industry Profile).

TOTAL SALES

▲ Fungicides	$77.5 Million
Insecticides	51.6 Million
▲ Herbicides	86.7 Million

(c) determined the appropriate nozzle types and sizes for maximum fungicide effectiveness, and (d) studied the in-tank stability of several turfgrass fungicides. Also during this time, it was found that certain fungicides will bring about an increase in the incidence and severity of non-target diseases in the treated areas, and that when a benzimidazole-resistant strain of the Sclerotinia dollar spot pathogen is present, treatment of these areas with one of the benzimidazoles will cause a significant increase in the incidence and severity of dollar spot.

For several decades prior to 1970, mycologists had been reviewing the taxonomic positions of certain fungi that are pathogenic to turfgrasses. As the result of these studies, from the mid 1970s through the early 1980s, several of the fungi that incite the turfgrass diseases were renamed. During this time,

the consensus was reached that the incitants of Fusarium blight should be called *Fusarium culmorum* and *Fusarium poae* instead of *Fusarium roseum* f. sp. *cerealis* 'Culmorum' and *Fusarium tricinctum* f. sp. *poae*. Also, certain of the Helminthosporium species were moved to the genera Drechslera and Bipolaris, the long standing proposal the incitant of Corticium red thread be placed in the genus Laetisaria was accepted, the organism that causes the low temperature disease Sclerotinia patch was reclassified as a Myriosclerotinia, and the incitant of Fusarium patch was placed in the genus Microdochium. In addition, after three decades of being called "unidentified Basidiomycete", in 1984 the fungus that causes cottony snow mold was finally assigned a name, *Coprinus psychromorbidus*.

Eight viruses, 3 prokaryotes, 62 species of nema-

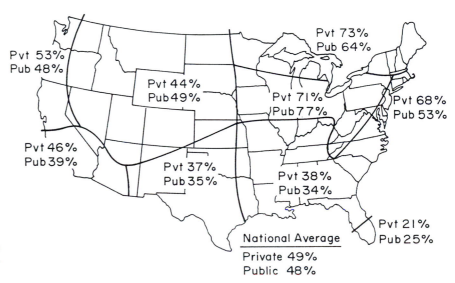

Figure 1-8. Fungicide portion of annual pesticide expenditures for private (Pvt) and public (Pub) 18 hole golf courses in the United States. *Based on 1987 Golf Course Superintendents Association of America-National Golf Foundation Survey.*

todes, and some 157 species of fungi are now known to be capable of inciting diseases of turfgrasses. Even though all of these entities do not occur in the same locality, during any season of the year in any given region of the world there is at least one known disease that can cause severe damage to turfgrass. This means that throughout the world, the maintenance of turfgrass stands within acceptable performance limits for either landscape or recreational purposes requires the carrying out of successful programs of disease diagnosis and control.

The list of pesticides now available for the con-trol of turfgrass diseases is made up of eight contacts, three localized penetrants, eight acropetal pene-trants, one systemic fungicide, and two post planting nematicides. The annual sales of turfgrass fungicides in the United States exceed those for any other agri-cultural commodity (Figure 1-7) (Couch and Smith, 1991b). Within the turfgrass management industry, golf courses rank number one in the total expendi-tures for fungicides. Also, for the average private golf course in the United States, fungicide purchases comprise 49 percent of the total pesticide budget (Figure 1-8).

§ § §

2

The Nature of Disease

DISEASES ARE CAUSED BY BIOTIC AND ABIOTIC ENTITIES

From the first century on through the Middle Ages, disease was thought to be caused by the internal disorganization of the nutrition process of the plant, and had its origin in a lack of certain chemical constituents of the sap. This was known as the autogenetic concept of disease causality.

Autogenesis was an outgrowth of the theory of spontaneous generation of life. It promoted the idea that the associated microorganisms were essentially transformed sap of diseased tissues, that they came into being as the result of exudation of morbid sap into intercellular spaces, where, under the influence of the live cells, it was converted into this new life-form. The fungi found in association with various diseases were thought to be the results, rather than the causes of these maladies.

Because the autogenetic concept considered certain diseases to be brought on by an accumulation of excess cell sap, a common approach to the control of these maladies consisted of "bleeding" the plants to allow an escape of the excess fluids. In these instances, the treatment was often more life-threatening to the plant than the original disease had been. In fact, death of the plant due to the therapy was not uncommon.

Research during the early part of the nineteenth century gave support to an emerging idea that the cause of disease was actually allogenic. The concept of **allogenesis** holds to the idea that the biotic incitants of disease originate from without, rather than from within the plant. As the century progressed, the tempo of these investigations increased. In 1853, the parasitic nature of the rust and smut fungi was proved conclusively and the allogenic concept of disease causality finally began to receive widespread acceptance in the scientific community (Large, 1962).

With allogenesis as the guiding principle in investigations to determine the cause of various diseases, the science of plant pathology developed at a rapid rate. In 1858, the first book on the nature and control of plant diseases based entirely on the allogenic concept of disease causality was published (Kuhn, 1858). At the close of the nineteenth century, effective control measures had been devised for several major plant diseases, including the use of fungicides and crop rotation (Schneiderhan, 1935). Also during this time, conclusive proof was given that certain bacteria were parasitic to plants, the capacity of insects to spread pathogenic microorganisms had been demonstrated, and successful transmission of a virus from a diseased to a healthy plant had been accomplished (Ainsworth, 1981; Burrill, 1881; Ivanowski, 1892; Mayer, 1886).

By the turn of the twentieth century, research on the dynamics of disease development had provided the insights needed to accept the fact that various abiotic factors, such as air pollutants, extremes in plant nutrient levels, extremes in atmospheric and soil temperatures, and soil moisture stresses not only alter the susceptibility of plants to disease, but that they can also function as agents of disease in their own right (Table 2-1).

Table 2-1. Examples of biotic and abiotic incitants of disease in plants.

Biotic Entities	Abiotic Entities
Fungi	Air Temperature Extremes
Nematodes	Soil Temperature Extremes
Viruses	Plant Nutrient Extremes
Bacteria	Anaerobic Soil Conditions
Rickettsia	Pruning Tools
Spiroplasma	Mowing Equipment
Mycoplasma	Air Pollutants
Insects	Wind Desiccation of Foliage
Mistletoe	Lightning Damage
Dodder	Pesticide Injury
Witchweed	Soil Moisture Stress

BIOTICALLY-INCITED DISEASE IS A DYNAMIC PROCESS

Biotically incited disease is directly dependent on an intricately balanced relationship between the suscept, the incitant, and the environment. The physical environment can alter the form of a disease by changing the susceptibility of the plant or by modifying the pathogenic capabilities of the associated microorganism. The result can be a significant change in either the incidence or the severity of the disease, or in its symptom patterns. For example, with each biotically incited foliar disease of turfgrass, in order for leaf infection to occur there are specific air temperature and durations of leaf wetness conditions that must be met. Also, once infection has been accomplished, the extent of tissue colonization by the invading microorganism is governed by such factors as air temperatures, the degree of availability of soil moisture, levels of fertilization, and various mowing practices. The conditions that are ideal for infection are not necessarily the same as those that are optimum for colonization of the plant tissue by the invading microorganism.

The impact of weather patterns and management practices on disease development have been worked out in detail for several of the major turfgrass diseases. For example, with Helminthosporium leaf spot of Kentucky bluegrass (incited by *Bipolaris sorokiniana*), when the leaf surface temperature is 70°F (21°C), the leaves must be continually wet for 48 hours in order for a high incidence of infections to develop. However, when leaf surface temperatures are in the 80–90°F (26–32°C) range, the same amplitude of infections occurs within 24 hours (Couch and Smith, 1987). At air temperatures of 70–80°F (21–26°C), the primary symptom pattern for the disease is leaf lesioning. When the air temperatures are in the 90–95°F (32–35°C) range, the predominant symptom pattern is overall blighting of the leaves (Weihing, Jenson and Hamilton, 1957). Helminthosporium leaf spot is more severe on grass that is mowed to a height to 2 inches (5 cm) rather than 1½ inches (3.8 cm). Also, the disease is more severe when the grass is growing under high soil moisture stress or at high nitrogen fertilization (Couch, Moore and Shoulders, 1974).

Information on optimum threshold temperatures and leaf wetness periods for leaf infections is used to develop systems for predicting disease outbreaks and the scheduling of fungicide programs. Knowledge of how cultural practices affect the development of a disease is utilized in developing fertilization, watering, and mowing programs designed to minimize the severity of the problem.

TERMINOLOGY

The preciseness of the terminology of any academic discipline is a good measure of the depth of understanding its researchers have concerning the various phenomena they are researching and its teachers have of the concepts they are teaching. Also, the ability of a student to properly use the terms of an academic discipline is a direct reflection of the extent of his or her knowledge of the subject. Developing a working vocabulary in a particular field of study, then, is not an empty exercise in semantics, it is a necessary learning experience if the subject is to be mastered.

In the following sections, we will first consider the meanings of the basic terms used to identify the various aspects of disease dynamics. Then we will review the procedures used to develop standard names for turfgrass diseases.

The Terminology of Disease Dynamics

All of the terms used to identify the various phases of disease development stem from two foundational concepts: **disease** and **health**. In order to develop a working knowledge of the vocabulary of disease dynamics, one must first understand these two concepts.

Disease is an absolute condition. **Disease** is defined as an aberrant form of metabolism, incited by components of the biological and/or physical environments, and manifested by the altered physiological activity of one or more cells.

Disease is an absolute condition. Since it is the inability of the cells to metabolize properly, the baselines from which it begins and ends are clearly defined. A state of disease is initiated the moment either a metabolic pathway or the rate of metabolism within a single cell is disrupted, and it ceases when all of the normal functions of the cell's metabolic systems are restored.

Depending on whether or not the situation at hand favors disease development, the process may be a transitory episode that is limited to a few cells for a brief period of time, or it may be a long term activity that results in a series of vital changes in several of the plant's tissue systems. Also, since the condition of disease is determined by the existence of abnormal metabolism rather than the amount of harm that is done to the plant, the fact of its being is not dependent on how long the state of abnormal metabolism lasts, or by how severe its impact is on the growth and development of the plant.

Health is a relative condition. The measure of the severity of the impact of disease on the growth and development of a plant is referred to as **health**. Health is a relative condition. A diseased plant is considered to be in good health as long as its growth pattern conforms to a set of prescribed standards. If the diseased condition increases to the point that the plant can no longer satisfy these requirements, then it is said to be in poor health. For example, it is possible for all of the plants on a bentgrass golf green to be afflicted with Pythium blight, but the state of disease in each plant not be severe. The plants respond well to mowing and foot traffic and the playing quality of the green is good; therefore, even though they are diseased, they are considered to be in good health. However, if the severity of the disease increases to the degree that it takes a heavy toll of the leaves, crowns and roots, these same plants are then said to be in poor health.

The terminology of disease dynamics identifies interlocking events. A **pathogenic condition** is initiated in a plant by a disruption of the metabolism of its cells. A **pathogen** is any agent, biotic or abiotic, that can bring about this change. An organism that obtains nutrients from, and at the expense of the metabolism of another living organism is called a **parasite**. A **saprophyte**, on the other hand, is an organism that obtains its nutrients from dead organic matter.

Certain microorganisms can only function as either a parasite or a saprophyte. Those that can only obtain nutrients from living cells are called **obligate parasites**. The rusts and powdery mildews are examples of this type of parasitism. Organisms that can only live on dead organic matter are called **obligate saprophytes**. These life forms play an important role in the decomposition of thatch and the breakdown of organic matter in the soil.

The majority of fungi that incite diseases of turfgrasses can alternate between parasitic and saprophytic growth patterns. The fungi that cause Pythium blight, Rhizoctonia blight and Fusarium blight are examples of organisms that can live as either parasites or saprophytes. These organisms can incite a diseased condition in the plant and then obtain nutrients from the dying tissue, or they can use the dead organic matter that is already present in the thatch and soil as a source of nutrients.

Infection of plant tissue is a dynamic process that progresses through a sequence of three events: (a) deposition of the propagules of the pathogen on the surface of the host, (b) entry of the pathogen into the underlying host tissue, and (c) the initiation of parasitism. When the **deposition** (**placement**) of the **propagules** (reproductive units) of the parasite occurs on its surface, the plant is said to be **infested**. **Entry** (**penetration**) of the plant surface by the parasite may be by active means (direct action of the invading organism), or by passive means (the propagules of the parasite are carried into wounds or natural plant openings by water or by cutting tools or on the mouth parts of feeding insects). When the invading organism finally comes into intimate contact with the underlying plant cell and the first steps of the parasitic relationship between it and the donor organism (**host**) are established, the plant is then said to be **infected**. If all three of these activities have not been completed, the event of infection has not occurred.

Certain turfgrass pathogens are capable of inciting disease without infecting the plant. This phenomenon is referred to as **pathogenesis without parasitism**. The activities of slime molds and several species of the fungi that cause fairy rings are examples of this type of pathogenesis. The slime molds grow freely over the surface of the grass leaves but do not infect them. However, if they remain on the leaves for an extended period of time, they can exclude enough sunlight to cause chlorosis and death of the underlying leaf cells.

Pathogenesis by several of the fungi that cause fairy rings is the consequence of the saprophytic growth of these organisms on the dead organic matter in the soil. They breakdown the organic matter, which eventually forms into nitrogenous compounds that promote rapid plant growth. In addition, they grow extensively through the soil in the root zones making it water resistant. Since the moisture in these fungus-permeated zones is depleted at a faster rate than in areas in which the plants have not been stimulated to more rapid growth, and since it cannot be replaced in quantities sufficient to sustain growth, death of the plants results.

The growth and development of an organism either in or on the surface of a substratum is called **colonization**. With plant pathogenic microorganisms, the area of colonization may be internal to the plant, on the surface of the plant, or in the soil adjacent to the root system of the plant.

The **process** of colonization involves three basic activities on the part of the pathogen: (a) obtaining nutrition, (b) a period of growth and development, and (c) the production of propagules (reproductive units). If all three of these activities have not been completed, the event of colonization has not occurred.

The **extent** of colonization may be (a) **localized**: limited to tissue within proximity to the site of infection and thus cause small necrotic spots or lesions to develop, such as with Helminthosporium leaf spot, (b) **generalized**: extending to large areas of tissue and thereby be seen as blotches or withered areas, such as with Rhizoctonia blight, or (c) **systemic** to varying degrees throughout the plant, such as with St. Augustinegrass decline.

The terminology used to describe the various **forms** of colonization of the host relate to whether the major portion of the body of the invading pathogen remains largely on the surface of the host or whether it is primarily internal. If the major portion of the body of the pathogen is confined largely to the surface of the plant, the process is referred to as **ectotropic colonization** and the pathogen is called an **ectoparasite**. The powdery mildews are ectoparasites. If the major portion of the body of the pathogen is internal to the plant, then the process is called **endophytic colonization**, and the invading pathogen is referred to as an **endoparasite**. The vast majority of the microorganisms that are pathogenic to turfgrasses are endoparasites.

The visible evidence of the presence of the pathogenic organism on the host is called a **sign**. The various changes in function and appearance of a plant brought on by disease are called **symptoms**. Death of cells or tissue is referred to as **necrosis**. Dead tissue is referred to as **necrotic** tissue. A localized area of necrotic tissue is known as a **lesion**. If the lesion has distinct margins, it is called a **spot**. If the margins of the lesion are irregular, it is referred to as a **blotch**. A **blight**, is a nonrestricted necrotic symptom characterized by the ultimate death of tissues throughout the entire organ. For example, when an entire leaf dies due to the colonization of the plant by a biotic pathogen, it is said to be **blighted**. Yellowing of tissue due to loss of chlorophyll is called **chlorosis**. The development of a reddish purple color in tissues that are normally green is called **anthocyanescence**.

The collective group of symptoms that characterize a specific disease are referred to as its **syndrome**. While two or more diseases may have certain symptoms that are similar, no two diseases have all symptoms in common. In other words, no two diseases have exactly the same syndrome. For example, although the syndromes of the spring and summer patch diseases, Rhizoctonia yellow patch, necrotic ring spot, Pythium blight, Fusarium blight, Rhizoctonia blight, Sclerotium blight, and summer patch, have certain symptoms in common, not all of their symptoms are similar, each has its own distinctive syndrome (Couch, 1985a).

Working from the concept of health as a measure of the impact of disease on the growth and development of the plant, we use the term **disease incidence** to refer to the number of plants within a population that are diseased, and **disease severity** to designate the extent of the damage done by disease. It is possible for a disease to be (a) high in incidence and low in severity, (b) high in incidence and high in severity, (c) low in incidence and low in severity, or (d) low in incidence and high in severity. For example, with Helminthosporium leaf spot, Pythium blight, and Rhizoctonia blight, the optimum environmental conditions for infection are different from those for colonization; therefore, it is possible for any one of these diseases to be high in incidence long before it is high in severity.

How Names Are Assigned to Individual Diseases

The biological sciences follow a well-defined procedure for the development of a codified system of names for all known life forms. The method includes preparing a description of the organism in Latin. After this, it is given a Latinized, two-part name (binomial). The results of this effort are then reviewed by the scientific community. If there is general agreement, the name is considered to be valid, and it is then used universally to designate the organism in question.

In addition to a scientific name, a great many of the various life forms are also known by a so-called "common name." For any given organism, its common name may vary from one locality to the next, or it may be uniform throughout the geographic location in which the species is found. *Poa pratensis*, for example, is most commonly referred to as "Kentucky bluegrass" in North America, while in Europe it is known as "smooth-stalked meadowgrass" or "Junegrass." *Poa annua* is "annual bluegrass" in North America and "annual meadowgrass" or "low speargrass" in Europe. In North America, *Agropyron repens* is known as "quackgrass," while in Great Britain it is referred to as "Couchgrass."

The highly methodical approach used to assign scientific names to pathogenic microorganisms is not followed when it comes to naming the diseases they incite. There are no scientific names for plant diseases, only common names. The origins of the names of the various turfgrass diseases are very diverse.

They range all the way from folklore surrounding the disease ("fairy rings") to a systematically devised construction based on a combination of the season in which the disease appears with a term that describes the primary symptom pattern ("spring dead spot," "winter crown rot," "summer patch").

The use of primary symptoms.   The ideal system for developing a common name for a turfgrass disease is one in which the primary symptom of the disease is described. The problem with this approach, however, is that several of the more important diseases of turfgrasses sometimes have key symptoms in common. For example, nine of the patch diseases of turfgrasses are known to cause both a general dying-out of large irregularly shaped areas of grass as well as the death of grass in discretely outlined circles with patches of unaffected plants in the centers ("frogeyes").

Another problem in using only primary symptoms for the name of the disease is that these features may vary with different climatic conditions. For example, "downy mildew" of St. Augustinegrass in the humid areas of the southernmost section of the United States is incited by the same fungus that causes "yellow tuft" of the cool season grasses in the northern areas of the United States and southern Canada. This striking difference in symptom patterns is brought on by the higher rainfall and warmer air temperatures in the South.

Disease names that are based on the appearance of individual plant parts sometimes refer to the color of the affected tissue ("red leaf spot"). The more frequently used terms, however, identify the shape and extent of tissue breakdown. These employ such expressions as "spot," "streak," "stripe," "blight," and "wilt." When the overall appearance of the affected areas is being incorporated into the name of the disease, the terms "patch," "spot," and "decline" are commonly used.

Making reference to the pathogen.   A commonly used approach to naming turfgrass diseases is to make reference to the pathogen. One way in which this is accomplished is to call attention to the pathogen's presence (e.g., "rust," "smut," "powdery mildew," "slime mold," "downy mildew"). In these cases, instead of assigning a name to the associated disease,

the common name of the pathogen is used to designate the condition.

Another way of utilizing the name of the pathogen in disease nomenclature is the combination of the name of the genus to which it belongs with a term that describes a primary feature of the symptoms. "Rhizoctonia blight," "Melanotus white patch," "Helminthosporium leaf spot," and "Corticium red thread" are examples of names that have been coined by this method. Since this system of naming is not subject to the rules of nomenclature laid down for the establishment of Latin binomials, in cases where the genus name of the pathogen is renamed it is neither necessary nor appropriate to change the name of the disease.

Why It Is Necessary to Maintain a Uniform List of Standard Turfgrass Disease Names

Although the present group of turfgrass disease names is largely a patchwork of terms that have been developed in a variety of ways, it is fairly functional. For the most part, the same names are being used universally to refer to the same diseases. For the sake of accurate communications, it is important that there be a uniform list of standard turfgrass disease names.

Unless it can be demonstrated that there is a clear and present need for a change, the names of turfgrass diseases in widespread use should not be replaced with new terms. Changing the names of turfgrass diseases, or the failure to use the same names in different locations for the same diseases, can cause problems in the selection of the proper fungicides for their control. In the preparation of control recommendations, the disease names given in the advisory agency's reports on diagnosis to its clients must be the same names as those listed for those diseases on the labels of the pesticides that control the problems. Also, the disease names listed in turfgrass disease control guides must coincide with those on the pesticide labels. If this is not the case, improper selection of fungicides can result. When changes are made in disease names, the former name should be listed in synonymy with the new name for at least three years (Couch, 1984).

PART TWO

Diseases of Turfgrasses Caused by Fungi

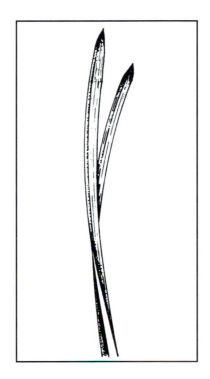

The Nature of Plant Pathogenic Fungi

There are over 40,000 known species of fungi. Fungi are used for food, and for medical and industrial purposes. Also, certain species of fungi cause diseases of human beings, animals, and plants. Together with bacteria, the fungi are the principal agents of decay of organic matter. Through the decomposition of organic matter into basic nutrient elements, and the infection and colonization of the cortical cells of roots, they play an essential role in promoting the nutrition of green plants.

The first conclusive experimental proof that fungi are capable of inciting diseases of plants was given in 1807. Through a series of experiments, it was shown that the spores of *Tilletia caries*, a fungus always found associated with bunt of wheat, were able to cause the disease. Since then, more than 8,000 species of fungi have been found to be pathogenic to higher plants. Of this group, some 127 species cause diseases of turfgrasses.

Fungi are defined as nongreen plants that do not produce true seeds, and whose bodies lack true roots, stems and leaves. The body of a fungus is a very simple structure. It is either made up of a single cell or a series of cells arranged linearly into tube-like strands. These individual strands or filaments are called **hyphae**. An aggregation or group of hyphae is called a **mycelium**. The hyphae of individual species of fungi may vary from 0.5μm (.00001968 inch) to 100μm (.003937 inch) in diameter. If strands of hyphae measuring 100μm thick were laid side by side, it would take 24,500 individual units to cover an area one inch (2.54 cm) wide (Figure 3-1).

Hyphae contain cytoplasm and nuclei. The hyphal strands of most fungus species are divided into cells by cross walls (septae). Some species, such as the members of the genus *Pythium*, do not have septate hyphae. This condition is referred to as **nonseptate** or **coenocytic**.

Reproduction of fungi is usually carried out by **spores**. Spores are analogous to seeds in higher plants. They differ from seeds, however, in that they do not contain embryonic tissue. Some spores have smooth outer surfaces, some are spiny, and others are highly sculptured. Also, some spores may consist of only one cell while others may be highly septate. The numbers of cells and the relative sizes and shapes of spores are a primary means of distinguishing species of fungi from each other (Figure 3-2).

Fungus spores are of two general types, those produced through sexual reproduction, and those formed by asexual processes. The portion of the life cycle of a fungus in which sexual reproduction occurs is called the **perfect stage**. The phase of the life cycle in which the asexual state is produced is called the **imperfect stage**. Many fungi possess the ability to produce both a perfect and an imperfect stage of growth. Some fungi are known to generate only the perfect stage, while others can only reproduce by asexual means. Fungi that have a sexual growth stage are able to hybridize and thus have a greater potential for producing new strains that are more pathogenic or are more resistant to fungicides than do those that do not have a sexual stage. On the other hand, plant pathogenic fungi that produce spores asexually are usually able to generate large numbers of spores more rapidly than those with only a sexual stage. Therefore, they have a greater potential for causing explosive epidemics.

Certain fungi, such as the mushrooms and puffballs which cause fairy rings, produce their spores within massive fruiting bodies that are formed by the aggregation of numerous hyphae. Most of the fungus species that are pathogenic to turfgrasses, however, do not produce highly conspicuous fruiting structures. Instead, the spores are either borne in very small, specialized bodies, or are scattered openly over the surface of the mycelium.

With some fungi, the hyphae may clump together to form rounded or flattened scaly hard masses ranging from ⅛ inch (3.2 mm) to 1 inch (25.4 mm) or more in diameter called **sclerotia** (sing. = **sclerotium**). Depending on the species, their color will range from light to dark brown to black (Plates 20-F and 21-F). Sclerotia serve as resting bodies by which

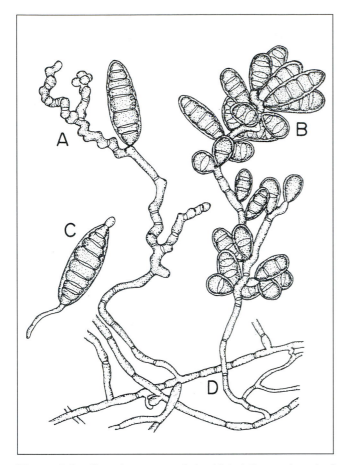

Figure 3-1. Growth pattern of the Helminthosporium leaf spot pathogen, *Bipolaris sorokiniana*. A) Denuded spore-bearing structure (conidiophore) showing former places of attachment of spores. B) Cluster of spores still attached to the hypha. C) Spore germinating by the production of germ tubes from the two terminal cells. D) Hyphal strands. *After Drechsler, 1923*.

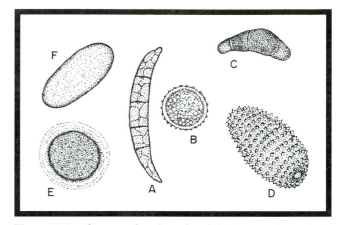

Figure 3-2. Spores of various fungi that are pathogenic to turfgrasses. (A) Conidiospore of the Fusarium blight pathogen, *Fusarium culmorum*. (B) Chlamydospore of stripe smut fungus, *Ustilago striiformis*. (C) Conidiospore of *Curvularia lunata*, the incitant of Curvularia blight. (D) Urediospore of leaf rust fungus, *Puccinia graminis*. (E) Oospore of Pythium blight pathogen, *Pythium ultimum*. (F) Conidiospore of powdery mildew fungus, *Erysiphe graminis*.

the fungus survives adverse environmental conditions. The sclerotia of certain fungus species can remain viable for 20–30 years. The fungi that incite Rhizoctonia blight, Corticium red thread, Typhula blight, Sclerotinia dollar spot, Sclerotinia patch, and Sclerotium blight all produce sclerotia.

Since the fungi lack chlorophyll, they cannot synthesize their own food base; therefore, they must obtain their nutrients from organic matter that has been produced by other organisms. Fungi that live on dead organic matter are called **saprophytes**, and fungi that obtain their nutrients directly from living organisms are called **parasites.** Some species can only live on dead organic matter. These organisms are called **obligate saprophytes**. The thatch and soil of turfgrass stands is replete with species of fungi that are obligate saprophytes.

Some of the fungi that are pathogenic to turfgrasses can only utilize nutrients they have obtained directly from living host cells. If the host cell dies, they can no longer use it as a source of nutrition. When their method for obtaining nutrients is being described, these organisms are called **obligate parasites**. However, when their role as a pathogen is being characterized, then they are called **biotrophs**. By definition, a **biotroph** is a parasite that can only obtain its nutrients from a living cell. The rust and powdery mildew fungi are biotrophs.

The vast majority of fungi that are pathogenic to turfgrasses are capable of living as either saprophytes or parasites. In their saprophytic growth stage, these organisms live on the dead organic matter in the thatch and soil. During their parasitic phase, they kill the host's cells rapidly during the process of colonization, and then utilize the various breakdown products as nutrients. This form of pathogenesis is called **necrotrophy**, and the organisms that function in this manner are referred to as **necrotrophs**.

In order for a parasitic fungus to obtain nutrients from the plant, it must first gain access to the tissue in question. The process by which it enters the host's tissue and begins functioning as a parasite is referred to as **infection**. Many of the fungi that are pathogenic to turfgrass infect the plants by directly penetrating the surfaces of intact epidermal cells. As the hyphae of these organisms grow over the surface of the plant, they either form infection cushions or

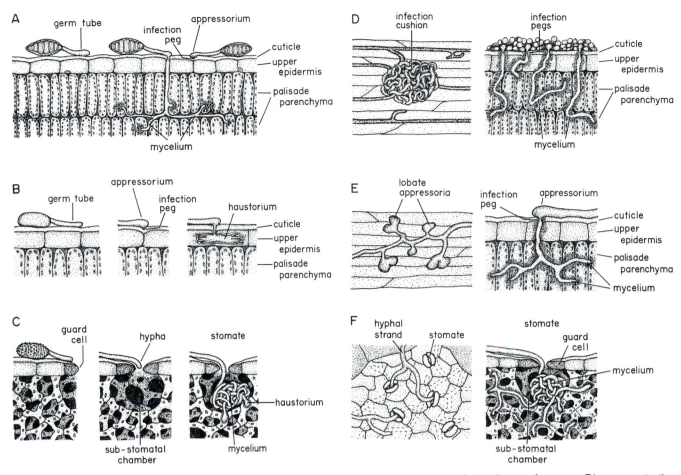

Figure 3-3. Mechanisms of penetration of intact plant surface cells by fungi that are pathogenic to turfgrasses. Direct penetration of leaf surface by means of appressoria by (A) Helminthosporium blight and (B) powdery mildew fungi. Penetration of intact leaf and leaf sheath surfaces by Rhizoctonia blight fungus by means of (D) infection cushion and (E) appressoria. Penetration of leaf surfaces by entry through stomatal chambers by (C) rust and (F) Rhizoctonia blight fungi.

specialized penetration structures known as **appressoria**. In the cases of leaf infections, the appressoria become attached to the cuticle and produce **infection pegs**. Then by a combination of direct physical pressure and the activity of fungus-produced enzymes that degrade cutin and cellulose, these **infection pegs** move through the epidermis and into the underlying host tissue. The fungi that incite the Helminthosporium diseases of turfgrasses are examples of turfgrass pathogens that infect the plant by directly penetrating intact leaf surfaces (Figure 3-3 A, B, D).

Some leaf-infecting fungi cannot penetrate intact cuticles, they can only gain access to the underlying tissue by first entering open stomates. Once they are in the stomatal chamber, the mycelium fills space available. Hyphal growth from the mass of mycelium penetrates the wall of the substomatal chamber and the fungus then begins parasitizing the host tissue. The rust and Rhizoctonia blight fungi are examples of turfgrass pathogens that penetrate the leaf in this manner. (Figure 3-3 C, F).

Certain of the fungi that are pathogenic to turfgrasses can only enter the plant through open wounds. Aerification procedures and vertical and lateral mowing operations provide infection courts for these organisms. The fungus that incites Curvularia blight is an example of a turfgrass pathogen that can only invade leaf tissue through open wounds. Wounds produced by mowing are also a commonly used entry court by the Rhizoctonia blight pathogen, *Rhizoctonia solani*.

Once the hypha of an invading fungus comes in contact with susceptible plant cells and starts to remove nutrients, the infection process is completed and colonization (active parasitism of the host tissue and growth and development of the fungus) begins. During colonization, biotrophs remove nutrients from the individual cells of the host plant by means of specialized absorption structures known as **haustoria**. Rather than piercing directly into the cytoplasm, the haustorium invaginates it by allowing the cell's plasma membrane to wrap around it as it moves into the cell. A delicate physiological balance is then established between the invading parasite and the cytoplasm of the host. Under this form of parasitism, nutrients are withdrawn by the invading symbiont without the rapid death of the donor cell.

Necrotrophic fungi are not as specific as biotrophs in their nutrient requirements. They can utilize both primary plant constituents and breakdown products as sources of nutrition. As the result, necrotrophs tend to kill the host tissue outright. They produce enzymes that degrade the cell walls and plasma membranes of the host plant, and secrete compounds that are toxic to the cytoplasm and organelles (nuclei, chloroplasts, mitochondria, etc). These fungal secretions may be restricted to the immediate area of colonization, or in some instances they may spread through the tissue and kill cells well ahead of the advancing mycelium.

The means by which fungi are able to survive during unfavorable weather conditions are highly varied:

- Those fungi that produce sclerotia are able to survive for several years in the absence of a suitable host.
- The enclosed sexual and asexual fruiting structures produced by certain species of pathogenic fungi serve as a primary means of protecting the spores against unfavorable weather conditions.

- Several of the fungi that are pathogenic to turfgrass survive off seasons for disease development as dormant mycelium in the perennial portion of a diseased plant.
- Fungi with a strong saprophytic capability are able to survive during adverse conditions for infecting and colonizing the host by growing on the thatch and on dead organic matter in the soil.
- The spores of certain fungi are either thick-walled or are embedded in a gelatinous material. These features protect them from desiccation and the harmful effects of extremes in temperature.

Both the means of dispersal from one location to the next and the climatic conditions most favorable for growth and development of plant pathogenic fungi can vary widely among different species. The spores of some species are wind disseminated, while with other forms they can only be dislodged and moved to new locations by splashing water. The spores of some species of fungi will germinate when the relative humidity is as low as 96 percent, however, others must be in direct contact with free water before they will germinate. Also, each fungus species has its own set of temperature requirements for growth and development. For example, *Coprinus psychromorbidus*, the fungus that incites cottony snow mold, will grow at temperatures as low as 25 °F (−4 °C), but has an optimum growth temperature of 55 °F (13 °C), while *Bipolaris sorokiniana*, the Helminthosporium leaf spot pathogen, grows best at 81 °F (27 °C), and will not grow at temperatures less than 50 °F (10 °C).

§ § §

Patch Diseases

The classic "patch" disease symptom pattern in turf-grasses is one in which the overall appearance of the affected area is characterized by a blighting of the majority of the leaves of the plants in a section of otherwise green turf. This group of diseases makes up a large and important segment of the major diseases of turfgrasses. Throughout the world there is a patch disease for every cultivated warm- and cool-season turfgrass species for every season of the year.

Several of the patch diseases are difficult to diagnose in the field. One of the reasons for this is that some of the more dramatic symptoms associated with these diseases can also be incited by a variety of causes other than the pathogenic activity of microorganisms. For example, plant stress caused by extremes in air temperatures, deficient or excessive soil moisture levels, improper mowing, or improper fertilization practices can also bring about a browning of turfgrass in irregularly shaped patches (Couch, 1988).

Diagnosis of certain patch diseases can be further complicated by the fact that although their total syndromes are different, they often have certain individual symptoms in common. For example, the so-called frogeye symptom (circular patches of blighted grass with center tufts of green, apparently healthy plants) is common to 10 members of this group: necrotic ring spot, Rhizoctonia yellow patch, Fusarium patch, spring dead spot of bermudagrass, take-all patch, Pythium blight, Rhizoctonia blight, Fusarium blight, summer patch, and Sclerotium blight. Proper field diagnosis of these diseases requires that the diagnostician be familiar with all of their primary and secondary field symptoms as well as the features that are unique to each disease.

The various patch diseases described in this chapter are grouped according to the season of the year in which they are usually most severe: Spring and Fall Patch Diseases, Summer Patch Diseases, and Winter Patch Diseases (Table 4-1).

SPRING AND FALL PATCH DISEASES

Necrotic Ring Spot

Necrotic ring spot was first described in Wisconsin in 1986 (Worf, Stewart and Avenius, 1986) and since been reported from the Pacific northwest, northeast, and north central sections of the United States. This disease affects all of the commonly cultivated cool season turfgrasses, but is particularly destructive to Kentucky bluegrass, creeping red fescue, and annual bluegrass. The fungus species that incites necrotic ring spot is also one of the four root and crown pathogens that cause spring dead spot of bermudagrass in various sections of the United States and Australia.

Symptoms

In the early stages of disease development, necrotic ring spot is seen as irregular patches of grass that have a general appearance of drought injury. The plants are often stunted or discolored, turning various shades of red, yellow or tan. These areas become dull tan to brown as the disease progresses.

The shapes of the individual patches of dead grass are usually more or less circular in outline. They may range in size from 2–3 inches (5–8 cm) to 2–6 feet (0.6–2 meters) in diameter. At first, leaf death is usually uniform throughout the affected area. However, as the disease progresses, many of the patches may develop center tufts of apparently disease-free grass. This combination produces a distinct frogeye effect. During weather conditions that are particularly favorable for outbreaks of necrotic ring spot, reddish-brown borders may develop between the patches of dead plants and the adjacent healthy grass. The diseased plants can be easily lifted from the soil. Eventually, the initial sites of disease development may coalesce to form large, irregularly shaped zones of blighted grass (Plate 1).

Table 4-1.   Patch diseases of turfgrasses.

Disease and Season of Occurrence	Susceptible Grasses	Incitant
I. Spring and Fall		
Corticium Red Thread	bentgrass, bermudagrass, Kentucky bluegrass, red fescue, tall fescue, ryegrass, annual bluegrass	*Laetisaria fuciformis*
Limonomyces Pink Patch	red fescue, ryegrass, Kentucky bluegrass, annual bluegrass, bermudagrass	*Limonomyces roseipellis*
Necrotic Ring Spot	Kentucky bluegrass fine fescues, annual bluegrass	*Leptosphaeria korrae*
Rhizoctonia Yellow Patch	bentgrass, bermudagrass, Kentucky bluegrass, tall fescue, zoysiagrass	*Rhizoctonia cerealis*
Take-all Patch	bentgrass, Kentucky bluegrass, red fescue, tall fescue, ryegrass	*Gaeumannomyces graminis* var. *avenae*
Pythium Blight	creeping bentgrass, Colonial bentgrass, red fescue	*Pythium torulosum* *Pythium vanterpoolii*
Rhizoctonia Blight (Warm Season Grasses)	bermudagrass, buffalograss, centipedegrass, St. Augustinegrass, zoysiagrass, bahiagrass	*Rhizoctonia solani*
II. Summer		
Fusarium Blight	bentgrass, bermudagrass, centipedegrass, Kentucky bluegrass, red fescue, tall fescue, ryegrass	*Fusarium culmorum* *Fusarium poae*
Melanotus White Patch	tall fescue, red fescue, Chewings fescue, creeping bentgrass	*Melanotus phillipsii*
Pythium Blight	annual bluegrass, Kentucky bluegrass, bermudagrass, creeping bentgrass, Colonial bentgrass, tall fescue, red fescue	*Pythium aphanidermatum*
	Kentucky bluegrass, tall fescue, red fescue, St. Augustinegrass	*Pythium arrhenomanes*
	creeping bentgrass, Colonial bentgrass, Kentucky bluegrass, tall fescue, red fescue, perennial ryegrass, St. Augustinegrass	*Pythium graminicola*
	annual bluegrass, creeping bentgrass, perennial ryegrass	*Pythium myriotylum*
	annual bluegrass, Kentucky bluegrass, creeping bentgrass, Colonial bentgrass, tall fescue, red fescue, annual ryegrass, perennial ryegrass	*Pythium ultimum*
Rhizoctonia Blight (Cool Season Grasses)	bentgrass, Kentucky bluegrass, red fescue, tall fescue, ryegrass	*Rhizoctonia solani*
Rhizoctonia Sheath Spot	bentgrass, Kentucky bluegrass, centipedegrass, tall fescue, ryegrass, zoysiagrass, annual bluegrass	*Rhizoctonia zeae* *Rhizoctonia oryzae*
Sclerotinia Dollar Spot	bentgrass, bermudagrass, Kentucky bluegrass, red fescue, centipedegrass, zoysiagrass, annual bluegrass	*Sclerotinia homoeocarpa*
Sclerotium Blight	bentgrass, bermudagrass, Kentucky bluegrass, annual bluegrass, perennial ryegrass	*Sclerotium rolfsii*
Summer Patch	Kentucky bluegrass, annual bluegrass, fine fescues	*Magnaporthe poae*
III. Winter		
Frost Scorch	Kentucky bluegrass	*Sclerotium rhizodes*
Fusarium Patch	annual bluegrass, bentgrass, bermudagrass Kentucky bluegrass, red fescue, tall fescue, ryegrass	*Microdochium nivale*
Sclerotinia Patch	Kentucky bluegrass, red fescue, perennial ryegrass	*Myrioclerotinia borealis*
Spring Dead Spot	bermudagrass	*Leptosphaeria korrae* *Leptosphaeria namari* *Gaeumannomyces graminis* var. *graminis* *Ophiosphaerella herpotricha*
Cottony Snow Mold	bentgrass, Kentucky bluegrass, red fescue, tall fescue, annual bluegrass	*Coprinus psychromorbidus*

In the advanced stages of disease development, a dark brown to black discoloration develops on the roots, lower stems, and nodes of the affected plants. Examination of the surface of the lower stems and roots with a microscope often reveals the presence of dark fungal runner hyphae. Also, short-necked, black fruiting bodies (pseudothecia) are sometimes found on the colonized crowns and roots (Plate 1-E, F).

The Fungus

Leptosphaeria korrae Walker and Smith

Description

Pseudothecia erumpent, usually closely packed, 400–600 μm long (including the neck), 300–500 μm wide, flask-shaped, with a globose body and a thick neck 50–150 μm long and 200 μm wide, often with thickened ridges around it. Pseudothecial wall 80–120 μm thick at the base, 40–80 μm at the sides, and 60–80 μm at the junction with the neck, composed of several layers of flattened brown cells 10–18 μm × 4–7 μm. Neck canal up to 80–100 μm wide, lined with hyaline upwardly pointing periphyses, and, in young pseudothecia, often colored reddish-brown by some material between the periphyses (Plate 1-F).

Asci cylindrical to clavate, narrowed towards the foot-like base, 150–185 μm × 10–13 μm, bitunicate, eight-spored. Ascospores filiform, slightly twisted in a bundle and parallel to one another, pale brown, septate, 140–170 μm × 4–5 μm, an occasional very long spore to 210 μm, widest in the middle and tapering more towards the base than the apex, rounded at the ends. Pseudoparaphyses hyaline, septate, numerous, 1.5–2.0 μm wide. Hyphae on the host brown, septate, branched, 2.5–5.0 μm wide, often in strands of three or four and forming flattened dark sclerotia 50–400 μm in diameter (Walker and Smith, 1972).

Procedures for Isolation and Culture

Leptosphaeria korrae grows on a variety of supplemented agar-based media. Isolation attempts should be made only from crown and root tissue. Surface sterilization of the specimens should be accomplished by soaking them for one hour in sterile distilled water, then transferring them to a 1% NaOCl-95% ethanol solution (1:1) for 30 seconds, and then soaking them in sterile distilled water for one hour before plating. Supplementing the culture medium with 100 mg of streptomycin per liter aids in the reduction of secondary organisms.

The optimum growth temperature range for the fungus is 20–25 °C. A small amount of growth is usually evident about 7 days after plating and becomes easily identifiable after another 10 days. On potato dextrose agar, the colonies are at first colorless, then off-white to light gray and somewhat floccose. As growth continues, both the media and older mycelium become almost black. The aerial growth of the fungus maintains some gray color. The reverse side of the culture is always black. The advancing hyphal margin sometimes shows a trace of curling back toward the center (Worf, Stewart and Avenius, 1986; Crahay, Dernoeden and O'Neill, 1988).

The production of pseudothecia of the fungus can be induced by either (a) growing the fungus on sterile oat grains (Jackson, 1984), (b) incubating it in tubes containing wheat leaf agar medium (irradiated wheat leaf sections embedded in slants of water agar) (Smiley and Craven-Fowler, 1984), or (c) inducing their formation on already colonized plant tissue. This latter procedure consists of immersing crowns or roots showing the characteristic dark brown runner hyphae on their surfaces in running tap water for 30 minutes. They should then be placed on plugs of moistened, gauze-covered, cotton, in sterile test tubes and incubated at 22 °C in an alternating 12-hour day-night light cycle. Care should be taken throughout the incubation period to keep the cotton and gauze moistened. Under these conditions, ascocarps will be produced in approximately six weeks (Crahay, Dernoeden and O'Neill, 1988).

Hosts

1. **Turfgrasses**—annual bluegrass (*Poa annua*), creeping bentgrass (*Agrostis palustris*), bermudagrass (*Cynodon dactylon*), Kentucky bluegrass (*Poa pratensis*), chewings fescue (*Festuca rubra* var. *commutata*), red fescue (*Festuca rubra*), and perennial ryegrass (*Lolium perenne*).
2. **All Known Gramineous Hosts**—A listing of common names for the following species is given in Appendix Table IV. *Agrostis palustris* Huds., *Avena sativa* L., *Axonopus compressus* (Swartz) Beauv., *Cynodon dactylon* (L.) Pers., *Eremochloa ophiuroides* (Munro) Hack., *Festuca rubra* L., *Festuca rubra* var. *commutata* Gaud., *Lolium perenne* L., *Oryza sativa* L., *Poa annua* L., *Poa pratensis* L., *Triticum aestivum* L. (Walker and Smith, 1972; Worf, Stewart and Avenius, 1986).

Disease Profile

Leptospheaeia korrae is primarily a colonizer of root and crown tissue. Isolates of this organism have shown a wide range of variability in their pathogenic capabilities (Chastagner, 1986).

Development of necrotic ring spot is generally most active during the cool, wet weather of spring and fall. During April and May, heavy outbreaks of the disease have been noted after prolonged periods of rainfall. The severity of necrotic ring spot is not affected by soil pH's in the 5.0 to 8.0 range; however, the disease is usually more destructive in stands of turfgrass under high nitrogen fertilization. Development of necrotic ring spot is usually most prominent in 3–4 year old turfs. Spread of the pathogen to new sites is accomplished primarily by the transport of infested soil and diseased crown and root tissue on coring, vertical mowing, and power raking equipment.

Control

Cultural Practices

Of the cool-season turfgrasses, necrotic ring spot is most severe on Kentucky bluegrass, annual bluegrass, and creeping red fescue. This means that during the months of spring and early fall, golf or bowling greens with high populations of annual bluegrass should be carefully monitored for outbreaks of this disease. Management practices that promote deep rooting of the turfgrass during periods of new root growth (spring and fall), will aid materially in reducing the severity of outbreaks of necrotic ring spot.

Use of Fungicides

Fenarimol, thiophanate methyl, cyproconazole, and propiconazole have been reported to control necrotic ring spot. In order to obtain maximum disease control with these materials, while the leaves are still wet with the spray the treated areas should be watered to a soil penetration depth of 1 inch (2.5 cm). Spiking or coring can help facilitate movement of the fungicide into the root zone. Also, the fungicide will move more readily through the soils that are initially moist than through soils that are dry at the time of application. Timing of the initial fungicide application is important to maximum control of the disease. Treatments should begin when the soil temperature at the 3 inch (7.5 cm) depth reaches 60 °F (16 °C) and continue at 30-day intervals for as long as weather conditions continue to be favorable for disease development (Chastagner, 1987; Shane, 1991). See Appendix Table I for a profile of each of these fungicides and a listing of representative trade names and manufacturers.

Take-all Patch

Take-all patch was first diagnosed on putting greens and landscape turf in Holland in 1931 (Schoevers, 1937). It has since been described as a major disease of cool-season turfgrasses in many parts of Western Europe, the British Isles, Canada, the United States, and Australia (Gould, Goss and Eglitis, 1961; Smith, 1956).

Symptoms

The initial symptoms of take-all patch develop during the months of early spring and late fall. The disease is first seen as depressed, circular patches of blighted turfgrass 2–3 inches (5–8 cm) in diameter. At first, the color of the patches may range from to bronze to a bright reddish bronze. Eventually, the color fades dull brown to tan, and during the winter it is usually gray.

The affected areas may enlarge as much as 6 inches (18 cm) per year and eventually reach a diameter of 2 feet (0.6 meter) or larger. With the outward movement of the pathogen, the centers of the patches frequently fill-in with resistant species, thus creating a "frog-eye" appearance of a green patch of grass, surrounded by a ring of bronze-colored, blighted plants. Often the individual patches will coalesce to form large irregularly-shaped areas of dead turf (Figure 4-1, Plate 2). Diseased roots at first develop internal dark brown necrotic streaks. With the advent of warm, dry weather, the affected roots turn dark brown and become brittle. At this time, the plants can easily be pulled loose from the soil. Individual strands of dark brown runner hyphae, and slender dark brown rhizomorph-like structures formed from five or more strands of hyphae, develop on the surfaces of diseased rhizomes, stolons, and roots, and on the culms under the basal leaf sheaths. Also, in late fall, very small, dark brown to black, flask-shaped structures (perithecia) may develop on the culms of affected plants (Plate 2-F).

The Fungus

Gaeumannomyces graminis (Sacc.) von Arx and Oliver var. *avenae* (E. M. Turner) Dennis; syn. *Ophiobolus graminis* Sacc.

Description

Mycelium comprising a limited growth of fine, grayish hyphae, and an abundant development of coarse, thick-walled, brown to black, irregular hyphae. Perithecia round to oblong, black, about 400 μm in diameter, formed in or beneath the leaf sheath with strands of mycelium associated with the base and the cylindrical curved beaks extending through the sheath tissues (Plate 2-F). Asci 10–15 μm × 100–

Figure 4-1. Take-all patch of bentgrass under fairway management. *Courtesy British Sports Turf Research Institute.*

165 μm, numerous, elongate, clavate, straight or curved, with numerous thread-like paraphyses in the young perithecia. Mature asci ejected from perithecia during periods of abundant moisture. Ascus wall degenerates in contact with free water, liberating the ascospores. Ascospores 8, hyaline, slender, tapering toward the ends, 3 μm × 75–138 μm; 5–7 septate at maturity. Under some conditions, minute falcate conidia are produced upon the germination of ascospores.

Procedures for Isolation and Culture

In standard laboratory procedures for maintaining cultures, the organism grows well on potato-dextrose agar at 21 °C (Smith, 1956). However, where direct isolation from diseased roots and crowns is concerned, *Gaeumannomyces graminis* develops slowly in culture; therefore, it is often overgrown by other, faster growing, plant tissue and soil-inhabiting microorganisms. This problem can be alleviated to some extent by use of the modified Juhnke selective medium (Elliott, 1991). This medium contains 39 g Difco dehydrated potato dextrose agar, 100 mg of streptomycin, 10 mg of dichloran, 10 mg of metalaxyl, 50 mg of vinclozolin, 500 mg a.i. of L-DOPA (L-B-3,4-dihydroxyphenylalanine), and 1 mg of CGA-173506 (a phenylpyrolle available from CIBA-GEIGY Corp, Agricultural Div., Greensboro, NC 27419). Add dehydrated potato dextrose agar to distilled water and autoclave at 15 psi (120 °C) for 20 minutes, and then cool to 50 °C. The remaining compounds should first be placed in 10 ml sterile distilled water and this suspension added to the molten potato dextrose agar just prior to pouring the plates. On Juhnke medium, isolates of *Gaeumannomyces*-type fungi are distinguished by the diffusion of a dark brown pigment (melanin) into the agar (Juhnke, Mathre and Sands, 1983).

Hosts

1. **Turfgrasses**—annual bluegrass (*Poa annua*), Colonial bentgrass (*Agrostis tenuis*), velvet bentgrass (*Agrostis canina*), creeping bentgrasses (*Agrostis palustris*), Kentucky bluegrass (*Poa pratensis*), creeping red fescue (*Festuca rubra*), tall fescue (*Festuca arundinacea*), and perennial ryegrass (*Lolium perenne*).

2. **All Known Gramineous Hosts**—A listing of common names for the following species is given in Appendix Table IV. *Agropyron caninum* (L.) Beauv., *A. cristatum* (L.) Gaertn., *A. intermedium* (Host) Beauv., *A. repens* (L.) Beauv., *A. smithii* Rydb., *A. trachycaulum* (Link) Malte, *Agrostis alba* L., *A. canina* L., *A. palustris* Huds., *A. stolonifera* L., *A. tenuis* Sibth., *Anthoxanthum odoratum* L., *Arrhenatherum elatius* (L.) J. & L. Presl, *Avena byzantina* K. Koch, *A. sativa* L., *A. sterilis* L., *Bromus arvensis* L., *B. carinatus* Hook. and Arn., *B. ciliatus* L., *B. erectis* Huds., *B. inermis* Leyss., *B. japonicus* Thunb., *B. madritensis* L., *B. orcuttianus* Vasey, *B. racemosus* L., *B. secalinus* L., *B. sterilis* L. *B. tectorum* L., *B. vulgaris* (Hook.) Shear, *Deschampsia caespitosa* (L.) Beauv., *D. danthoniodes* (Trin.) Munro, *Elymus*

canadensis L., *E. glaucus* Buckl., *E. villosus* Muhl., *E. virginicus* L., *E. virginicus* var. *australis* (Scribn. and Ball) Hitchc., *Festuca arundinacea* Schreb., *F. dertonensis* (All.) Aschers. and Graebn., *F. megalura* Nutt., *F. myuros* L., *F. octoflora* Walt., *F. rubra* L., *Holcus lanatus* L., *Hordeum distichon* L., *H. jubatum* L., *H. murinum* L., *H. pusillum* Nutt., *H. vulgare* L., *Hystrix patula* Moench, *Lolium multiflorum* Lam., *L. perenne* L., *Phalaris arundinacea* L., *Phleum pratense* L., *Poa annua* L., *P. canbyi* (Scribn.) Piper, *P. compressa* L., *P. pratensis* L., *P. trivialis* L., *Secale cereale* L., *Setaria geniculata* (Lam.) Beauv., *Triticum aestivum* L., (Kirby, 1922; Smith, 1956; Index Plant Dis., 1960).

Disease Profile

The pathogen can survive adverse conditions as perithecia embedded in crown and culm tissue. Germinating ascospores can penetrate root hairs and root epidermal cells but they do not infect leaves or leaf sheaths. The principal means of survival of *Gaeumannomyces graminis* is as a saprophyte on debris from the previous season's host plant growth, and as dormant mycelium in the perennial portions of plants. The major means of primary infections is mycelium from either of these later two sources penetrating the root, crown, and culm tissues of actively growing plants. Penetration of the roots by *Gaeumannomyces graminis* is accomplished by hyphopodia (specialized infection structures) and direct growth of the fungus from masses of hyphae known as "infection cushions" (Figure 3-3).

Two forms of hyphae are produced during the process of infection and colonization of root tissue: (a) brown or colorless hyphae that branch and form the hyphopodia and colonize the cortex and stele, and (b) dark brown runner hyphae that grow over the surface of the roots. Death of the epidermal and outer cortical cells of the roots does not usually occur during the early stages of colonization. However, as the colonization process continues, the vascular tissue becomes plugged with fungal hyphae, and dark brown necrotic streaks develop in the stele and adjacent cortical tissue. Eventually, all tissues in the affected roots turn dark brown.

Root infection by *Gaeumannomyces graminis* is favored by moist soil conditions and soil temperatures in the 50–65 °F (10–19 °C) range. The primary stages in the development of take-all patch occur during the cool, wet months of early spring and late fall. However, severe root damage and death of the plants may not develop until plant stress occurs from hot, dry weather. Take-all patch is more severe when the pH of the upper one inch (2.54 cm) of the soil is 6.5 and above (Smith, 1956).

Maintaining adequate levels of soil phosphorus and potassium has been shown to have a suppressive effect on development of the disease. Types and rates of application of nitrogen-based fertilizers also impact on the severity of take-all patch. High rates of urea will enhance its development; however, marked recovery from the disease has been reported with applications of either ammonium sulfate or ammonium chloride. There appears to be no relationship between degree of thatch accumulation and the severity of take-all patch (Smith, 1956; Goss and Gould, 1967; Dernoeden, 1987).

Localized spread of *Gaeumannomyces graminis* is accomplished by outward growth of the organism from plant to plant. The fungus does not grow through the soil, but, rather over roots, rhizomes, and other plant parts. Spread of the organism for greater distances is accomplished by the transport of infested soil and diseased crown and root tissue on coring, vertical mowing, and raking equipment.

Control

Cultural Practices

Recovery of grass from take-all patch is slow; therefore, when small areas have been affected on golf and bowling greens, the most practical immediate remedy is to remove the diseased turf and resod. On aprons, collars and similar locations, the patches can be raked and reseeded.

Where the overall approach to control of take-all patch is concerned, management practices should be employed that establish and maintain acid soil conditions. Applications of sulfur and either ammonium sulfate or ammonium chloride in the early spring will reduce the severity of the disease. It is also important that a balanced fertilization program be followed. The potassium and phosphorous levels in the soil should not be allowed to become deficient. Since depletions in nutrient element contents can occur very rapidly in light, sandy soils and high sand-content greens, these soils should be checked frequently for levels of available phosphorous and potassium (Smith, 1956; Goss and Gould, 1967; Dernoeden, 1987).

Use of Resistant Grasses

Gaeumannomyces graminis shows a high degree of host specificity. Some isolates are more pathogenic on certain turfgrasses than others. As a general rule, however, (a) creeping bentgrass (*Agrostis palustris*),

Colonial bentgrass (*Agrostis tenuis*), velvet bentgrass (*Agrostis canina*), and perennial ryegrass (*Lolium perenne*) are all highly susceptible to *Gaeumannomyces graminis*, (b) annual bluegrass (*Poa annua*), Chewings fescue (*Festuca rubra* var. *commutata*), and rough bluegrass (*P. trivialis*) are moderately susceptible, and (c) creeping red fescue (*Festuca rubra*) and Kentucky bluegrass (*Poa pratensis*) are highly resistant (Sampson and Western, 1954; Smith, 1956; Dernoeden and O'Neil, 1983).

Use of Fungicides

Phenyl mercuric acetate drenches have been used successfully for control of take-all patch (Smith, 1956; Jackson, 1958; Dernoeden, 1987). However, the use of this fungicide is prohibited in some areas.

Rhizoctonia Yellow Patch

Rhizoctonia yellow patch is particularly destructive to annual bluegrass (*Poa annua*) and Kentucky bluegrass (*Poa pratensis*). The disease was originally thought to be a cool temperature variation of Rhizoctonia brown patch. For over four decades, plant pathologists in Canada and the United States reported that they were isolating *Rhizoctonia solani* from the foliage of turfgrasses showing disease symptoms during cool, wet weather. Since these isolates were considered to be the same species as the Rhizoctonia brown patch pathogen, the disease they were observing was generally referred to as "cool weather brown patch" (Broadfoot, 1936; Sprague, 1950; Gould, 1976).

In the late 1970s, studies conducted on Kentucky bluegrass at the Plant Diagnostics Laboratories of the Chemlawn Corporation and at the Ohio State University, on tall fescue at the Pennsylvania State University, and on zoysiagrass (*Zoysia japonica*) at the University of Arkansas showed that the fungus isolated from leaves that had become diseased during cool wet weather was a species of *Rhizoctonia* other than *R. solani* (Joyner, Partyka and Larsen, 1977; Sanders, Burpee and Cole, 1977; Dale, 1978). Additional research with these cool temperature isolates of *Rhizoctonia* demonstrated that they were also pathogenic to bermudagrass, perennial ryegrass, and creeping bentgrass (Burpee *et al.*, 1980). A further study of their comparative growth features showed that they all were the taxonomic species *Rhizoctonia cerealis*. In addition to identifying the taxonomic position of the pathogen, the report from this later research also recommended that the disease it incited be given the descriptive name "yellow patch" (Burpee, 1980b).

Symptoms

The symptoms of Rhizoctonia yellow patch can develop suddenly during cool, moist weather. The severity of the disease and types of symptom expression will vary somewhat depending on the turfgrass species involved and prevailing climatic conditions.

Rhizoctonia yellow patch is usually first seen as yellow, tan, or straw colored patches ranging from 1 inch to 3 feet (2.5 cm–0.9 meters) in diameter. The grass in the center of the larger patches may recover, leading to the formation of a frogeye pattern of areas of green plants with 1–2 inch light yellow to tan outer rings. The patches often merge to form an overall mosaic pattern (Plate 3-A, B, C). On warm season grasses, the development of the disease is usually limited to leaf yellowing. However, on cool season grasses, in the advanced stages of disease development the individual patches may develop a pronounced sunken appearance that has been brought on by the decomposition of the thatch in the affected area (Plate 3-D).

The most frequent individual leaf symptom of Rhizoctonia yellow patch is a yellow to light tan discoloration that begins at the tips and progresses downward. Also, grayish-tan, mottled lesions may develop on the lower portions of the leaves. With Kentucky bluegrass, the leaves of plants at the margins of the patches often develop a characteristic reddish or reddish purple appearance (Plate 3-F).

During extended periods of cool, humid weather, the white mycelium of the pathogen can often be detected around the crowns and lower leaves of diseased plants. Also, on cool season grasses, the lower crowns and roots of the affected plants may become brown or black.

On cool season as well as warm season grasses, very commonly with outbreaks of Rhizoctonia yellow patch, the leaves of the plants in the affected areas may remain light yellow in appearance for several weeks without becoming necrotic. With the advent of warmer air temperatures, all of the plants in these areas may completely recover. On the other hand, with the cool season grasses, if weather conditions remain favorable for the development of Rhizoctonia yellow patch for an extended period of time, death of the leaves may occur.

In instances of field diagnosis on warm season grasses during cool, wet weather, it is important that one be able to distinguish between the symptom patterns of Rhizoctonia yellow patch and Rhizoctonia blight. With the warm season grasses, both diseases produce distinctively yellowed leaves and yellow patches of affected turf. However, patches of turf affected by the yellow patch pathogen lack the marginal, purplish borders ("smoke rings") that are often found associated with outbreaks of Rhizoctonia blight. Also, with Rhizocotnia blight, there will usually be a high incidence of leaves showing extensive necrosis on the sheaths. For a detailed display of the comparative and contrasting symptoms of Rhizoctonia blight on warm season grasses see Plates 11, 12, and 13.

The Fungus

Rhizoctonia cerealis Van der Hoeven; telemorph *Ceratobasidium cereale* Murray and Burpee

Description

On potato dextrose agar, the colonies grow comparatively slowly and are colorless to dirty white with little white aerial mycelium. The main hyphae are 3.8–6.2 μm wide, side branch hyphae 5.1–8.7 μm and aerial hyphae 2.8–5.3 μm. The hyphae generally branch at right angles, with a constriction at the point of origin and the first septum placed a few microns beyond this. The hyphal branches sometimes anastomose. All hyphal cells are binucleate (Figure 4-2).

Monilioid hyphae of irregular length, consisting of doliform cells, 17–30 μm × 7–15 μm. Sclerotia produced after 10 days on potato dextrose agar are first white to yellow, later brown, globose to irregular, 0.3–1.2 mm in diameter. They consist of loosely arranged doliform cells with little differentiated superficial layer. In older cultures, aggregations of dark brown sclerotia occur (Boerema and Verhoven, 1977).

Procedures for Isolation and Culture

Rhizoctonia cerealis grows well on potato dextrose agar. Its optimum growth temperature is 23 °C. At this temperature, radial growth rates on potato dextrose agar range from 3.3 mm to 5 mm per day. On potato dextrose agar, during the first 3 weeks the mycelium is at first cff-white then may become buff-colored. Hyphal pigmentation may continue to increase with time, resulting in a distinctive buff to light brown mycelium after 8 weeks of growth (Burpee, 1980b).

The cells of the vegetative hyphae of *Rhizoctonia cerealis* are predominately binucleate. This is in contrast with *Rhizoctonia solani* and *Rhizoctonia zeae* which produce vegetative hyphae with predominantly multinucleate cells. A simple procedure for determining the nuclear number of the hyphal cells consists of culturing the isolate in question on 2

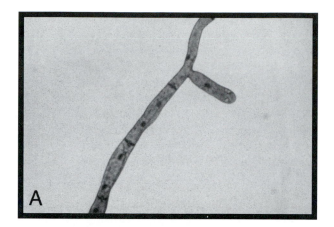

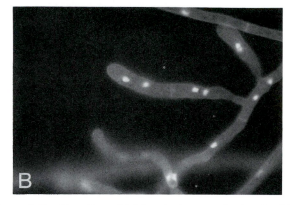

Figure 4-2. Mycelium of *Rhizoctonia cerealis* showing binucleate cells and constriction in hyphal branch at the point of origin as seen with (A) bright field microscopy and (B) fluorescence microscopy. *Courtesy Leon Burpee.*

percent water agar in petri plates in the dark at 25 °C until the hyphal growth has almost reached the periphery of the plates. At this time, a drop of 0.05 percent trypan blue in lactophenol should be placed directly onto the agar surface approximately 2 cm inside the area of advancing hyphal tips. A cover slip can then be placed over the drop of stain and the hyphae examined in place for nuclear numbers with a microscope at 400×. Or the agar can be cut around the cover slips and the squares placed on microscope slides for the examination. This procedure can also be used to determine if the hyphae have dolipore septa (Burpee, 1980a).

Hosts

1. **Turfgrasses**—bermudagrass (*Cynodon dactylon*), creeping bentgrass (*Agrostis palustris*), annual bluegrass (*Poa annua*), Kentucky bluegrass (*Poa pratensis*), tall fescue (*Festuca arundiinacea*), perennial ryegrass (*Lolium perenne*), and zoysiagrass (*Zoysia japonica*).

2. **All Known Gramineous Hosts**—A listing of common names for the following species is given in Appendix Table IV. *Agrostis palustris* Huds., *Avena sativa* L., *Cynodon dactylon* (L.) Pers., *Festuca arundinacea* Schreb., *Lolium perenne* L., *Poa annua* L., *P. pratensis* L., *Triticum aestivum* L., *Zoysia japonica* Steud. (Joyner, Partyka and Larsen, 1977; Dale, 1978; Sanders, Burpee and Cole, 1977; Burpee, 1980b; Burpee *et al.*, 1980; Martin and Lucas, 1984).

Disease Profile

The development of Rhizoctonia yellow patch is favored by cool, wet weather. The optimum air temperature range for disease development is 50–65 °F (10–18 °C) (Burpee, 1980b). When the leaf symptoms are at the light yellow stage of development, the plants will recover if the air temperatures drop below 45 °F (5 °C) or go above 75 °F (24 °C). However, during times of extended rainfall, if the temperatures stay within the 50–65 °F range, foliar blighting will occur (Couch, 1986).

Rhizoctonia cerealis survives adverse weather conditions in the form of sclerotia in the thatch and soil. Also, the organism is capable of active growth as a saprophyte in both the thatch and soil. The earliest infections of the plants occur on the crowns and roots. However, the primary damage from the disease results from the direct infection and colonization of the foliage. During periods of prolonged leaf wetness, *Rhizoctonia cerealis* mycelium in the thatch grows over the leaf sheaths and onto the lower surfaces of the leaves. It then penetrates the underlying cells by hyphal growth from masses of mycelium known as "infection cushions" (Figure 3.3). The leaf yellowing symptom of the disease begins in the very early stages of tissue colonization by the pathogen.

Control

Cultural Practices

The influence of fertilization practices on the development of this disease has not been fully researched. However, it has been observed that the severity of Rhizoctonia yellow patch does not appear to be affected by rates of fertilization, but a properly balanced fertilization program will facilitate more rapid recovery of the grass when the climatic conditions are no longer favorable for development of the disease (Shurtleff, 1983).

Good surface and subsurface drainage will reduce the severity of Rhizoctonia yellow patch by lowering the humidity within the canopy. Management practices that decrease the length of time the leaves are wet will aid in reducing the incidence of the disease. One such practice is the early morning removal of dew and guttation water from putting greens by poling or by dragging a water hose across them. The duration of the periods of daily leaf wetness can also be reduced by two to four hours by following a nighttime watering schedule in which the irrigation system is set to begin at least three hours after sunset and programmed to be completed before sunrise (see Chapter 16, Figure 16-2).

Use of Resistant Grasses

Research at the Ohio State University has shown that the Kentucky bluegrass cultivars Adelphi, Cheri, and Touchdown are highly resistant to Rhizoctonia yellow patch (Philip Larsen, *personal communication*).

Use of Fungicides

Flutolanil is registered for the control of Rhizoconia yellow patch. For a profile of flutolanil and a listing of representative trade name and manufacturer, see Appendix Table I.

Rhizoctonia Blight of Warm Season Turfgrasses

Rhizoctonia blight was referred to in the early literature on turfgrass diseases, as "large patch," "large brown patch," "brown patch," and "Rhizoctonia brown patch" (Monteith and Dahl, 1932; Couch, 1984). The disease was first observed in 1913 on bentgrass putting greens on a golf course near Philadelphia, Pennsylvania. Its incitant (*Rhizoctonia solani*) is now known to be pathogenic on all the major warm season and cool season turfgrasses.

The epidemiology and descriptive pathology of Rhizoctonia blight varies with the turfgrass type. With the warm season turfgrasses (bermudagrass, zoysiagrass, centipedegrass, St. Augustinegrass), the disease is most destructive during the spring and fall. However, with the cool season turfgrasses (bentgrasses, bluegrasses, fescues, ryegrasses), the severity of Rhizoctonia blight is greatest during the summer months.

This section covers the nature and control of Rhizoctonia blight as a spring and fall patch disease of warm season turfgrasses. Additional background information on Rhizoctonia blight and its nature and control on cool season grasses is given in the section, Summer Patch Diseases.

Symptoms

On warm season grasses in the fall, Rhizoctonia blight is first seen in overall view as light green patches ranging from 2 inches (5 cm) to 2 feet (0.9 meter) wide. Under conditions favorable for development of the disease, the color of theses areas changes rapidly to a distinctive bright yellow and then to brown (Plate 11- A, B, C, D; Plate 12-A, B). In cases of prolonged outbreaks of Rhizoctonia blight, the diameter of diseased sections of turf may extend to 20 feet (6 meters) or more (Plate 13-A, B, D, E). During extended periods of humid weather, these patches may develop dark purplish borders 2–6 inches (5–15 cm) wide (Plate 11-F). In the spring, large yellow patches become visible as the grasses resume growth from winter dormancy. These areas may rapidly turn to brown and continue to enlarge as long as relatively cool, wet weather persists.

A primary diagnostic feature of Rhizoctonia blight on zoysiagrass, bermudagrass, centipedegrass and St. Augustinegrass is a soft, dark brown to purplish rot of the lower portion of the leaf sheaths (Plate 12-B, C, D; Plate 13-C). This symptom pattern is most prevalent when the leaves are continuously wet for 48 hours or more. When periods of relatively dry weather follow major outbreaks of Rhizoctonia blight, a dry, reddish brown necrosis envelopes the base of the leaf sheaths and extends into the stem tissue (Plate 12-E, F).

In the advanced stages of disease development, an extensive soft rot will develop at the bases of the fascicles and the stems. When this happens, the dying plants at the edges of the patches can be easily pulled off the stolons.

As a general rule, bermudagrass will recover from Rhizoctonia blight during favorable growing conditions in the summer. Zoysiagrass and centipedegrass, however, recover slowly, and the initial patches may be visible throughout the summer and into the following growing season.

The Fungus

Rhizoctonia solani Kuhn; telemorph *Thanatephorous cucumeris* (Frank) Donk; syn. *Pellicularia filamentosa* (Pat.) D. P. Rogers

The strains of *Rhizoctonia solani* parasitizing warm season grasses are usually constituents of anastamosis group AG-2-2 (Hurd and Grisham, 1983; Martin and Lucas, 1984; Haygood and Martin, 1990).

Description

Mycelium tan to brown, 4–15 μm in diameter, with right-angled branching and characteristic constriction at the septa and the formation of a septum in the branch near the point of origin. Hyphal cells multinucleate, with doliform septae. Produces monilioid cells (often called barrel-shaped cells or chlamydospores) in chains or aggregates sometimes referred to as sporodochia. Clamp connections are absent. Sclerotia generally dark brown to black, sometimes off white or pale buff, spherical to irregular, aggregated or crust-like, never differentiated into rind and medulla, and 1–10 mm in diameter (Parmeter and Whitney, 1985).

Procedures for Isolation and Culture

Attempts at isolation of *Rhizoctonia solani* from the warm season grasses are more successful when platings are made from sheath and crown tissue rather than leaf blades. The organism grows well on a wide range of media. Its optimum growth temperature is 28 °C. At this temperature, radial growth rates on potato dextrose agar vary among isolates, but usually range from 2–3 cm per day (Sherwood, 1965). On potato dextrose agar, the mycelium is pale to dark brown (Parmeter and Whitney, 1965).

The cells of actively growing vegetative hyphae of *Rhizoctonia solani* are predominately multinucleate. This is in contrast with *Rhizoctonia cerealis* which produces vegetative hyphae with predominately binucleate cells. A simple procedure for determining the nuclear number of the hyphal cells consists of culturing the isolate in question on 2 percent water agar in petri plates in the dark at 27 °C until the hyphal growth has almost reached the periphery of the plates. At this time, a drop of 0.05 percent trypan blue in lactophenol should be placed directly onto the agar surface approximately 2 cm inside the area of advancing hyphal tips. A cover slip can then be placed over the drop of stain, and after approximately 30 minutes the hyphae examined in place for nuclear numbers with a microscope at 400×. Or the agar can be cut around the cover slips and the squares placed on microscope slides for the examination. This procedure can also be used to determine if the hyphae have dolipore septa (Burpee, 1980a).

Hosts

1. **Turfgrasses**—annual bluegrass (*Poa annua*), buffalograss (*Buchloe dactyloides*), creeping bentgrass (*Agrostis palustris*), Colonial bentgrass (*Agrostis tenuis*), velvet bentgrass (*Agrostis canina*), bermudagrass (*Cynodon dactylon*), centipedegrass (*Eremochloa ophiuroides*), Kentucky bluegrass (*Poa pratensis*), red fescue (*Festuca rubra*), tall fescue (*Festuca arundinacea*), annual ryegrass (*Lolium multiflorum*), perennial rye-

grass (*Lolium perenne*), sheep fescue (*Festuca ovina*), Chewings fescue (*Festuca rubra* var. *commutata*), St. Augustinegrass (*Stenotaphrum secundatum*), and zoysiagrass (*Zoysia japonica*).

2. **All Known Gramineous Hosts**—A listing of common names for the following species is given in Appendix Table IV. *Agropyron angustiglume* Nevski, *A. cristatum* (L.) Gaertn., *A. dasystachyum* (Hook.) Scribn., *A. desertorum* (Fisch.) Schult., *A. intermedium* (Host) Beauv., *A. mongolicum* Keng, *A. repens* (L.) Beauv., *A. rigidum* Beauv., *A. riparium* Scribn. and Smith, *A. sibiricum* (Willd.) Beauv., *A. smithii* Rydb., *A. subsecundum* (Link) Hitchc., *A. trachycaulum* (Link) Malte, *A. trichophorum* (Link) Richt., *Agrostis alba* L., *A. canina* L., *A. exarata* Trin., *A. halli* Vasey, *A. palustris* Huds., *A . stolonifera* L., *A. tenuis* Sibth., *Arrhenatherum elatius* (L.) Presl, *Avena byzantina* K. Koch, *A. fatua* L., *A. sativa* L., *A. sterilis* L., *Axonopus affinis* Chase, *Bouteloua curtipendula* (Michx.) Torr., *B. gracilis* (H. B. K.) Lag., *Bromus arvensis* L., *B. carinatus* Hook. and Arn., *B. catharticus* Vahl, *B. erectus* Huds., *B. inermis* Leyss., *B. japonicus* Thunb., *B. madritensis* L., *B. mollis* L., *B. pumpellianus* Scribn. *B. racemosus* L., *B. rigidus* Roth, *B. secalinus* L., *B. tectorum* L., *Buchloe dactyloides* (Nutt.) Engelm., *Calamagrostis montanensis* Scribn., *Cenchrus pauciflorus* Benth., *Cynodon dactylon* (L.) Pers., *Dactylis glomerata* L., *Danthonia californica* Boland, *Deschampsia atropurpurea* (Wahl.) Scheele, *Digitaria sanguinalis* (L.) Scop., *Echinochloa colonum* (L.) Link, *E. crusgalli* (L.) Beauv., *Eleusine indica* (L.) Gaertn., *Elymus antarticus* Hook., *E. canadensis* L., *E. dahuricus* Turcz., *E. giganteus* Vahl, *E. glaucus* Buckl., *E. interruptus* Buckl., *E. junceus* Fisch., *E. macounii* Vasey, *E. sibiricus* L., *Eragrostis curvula* (Schrad.) Nees, *E. trichodes* (Nutt.) Wood, *Eremochloa ophiuroides* (Munro) Hack., *Festuca arundinacea* Schreb., *F. dertonensis* (All.) Aschers and Graebn., *F. idahoensis* Elmer, *F. megalura* Nutt., *F. myuros* L., *F. octoflora* Walt., *F. ovina* L., *F. rubra* L., *F. rubra* var. *commutata* Gaud., *Hierochloe odorata* (L.) Beauv., *Holcus lanatus* L., *Hordeum brachyantherum* Nevski, *H. distichon* L., *H. hystrix* Roth, *H. jubatum* L., *H. murinum* L., *H. nodosum* L., *H. secalinum* Guss., *H. vulgare* L., *Koeleria cristata* (L.) Pers., *Lolium multiflorum* Lam., *L. perenne* L., *Muhlenbergia racemosa* (Michx.) B. S. P., *M. richardsonis* (Trin.) Rydb., *Oryza sativa* L., *Oryzopsis hymenoides* (Roem. and Schult.) Ricker, *Panicum capillare* L., *P. miliaceum* L., *P. tennesseense* Ashe, *P. virgatum* L., *Phalaris arundinacea* L., *P. tuberosa* L., *Phleum pratense* L., *Poa ampla* Merr.,

P. annua L., *P. bulbosa* L., *P. compressa* L., *P. nemoralis* L., *P. palustris* L., *P. pratensis* L., *P. secunda* Presl, *P. trivialis* L., *Redfieldia flexuosa* (Thurb.) Vasey, *Saccharum officinarum* L., *Schedonnardus paniculatus* (Nutt.) Trel., *Secale cereale* L., *Setaria lutescens* (Weigel) Hubb., *S. viridis* (L.) Beauv., *Sitanion hystrix* (Nutt.) J. G. Smith, *Sorghum sudanense* (Piper) Stapf, *S. vulgare* Pers., *Sporobolus cryptandrus* (Torr.) A. Gray, *S. neglectus* Nash, *Stenotaphrum secundatum* (Walt.) Kuntze, *Stipa comata* Trin., and Rupr., *S. sibirica* Lam., *S. spartea* Trin., *S. viridula* Trin., *Trisetum canescens* Buckl., *Triticum aestivum* L., *T. dicoccum* Schrank, *T. durum* Desf., *T. monococcum* L., *T. spelta* L., *T. timopheevi* (Zhukov.) Zhukov., *Zea mays* L., *Zoysia japonica* Steud. (Sprague, 1950; Index Plant Dis., 1960; Haygood and Martin, 1990).

Disease Profile

The bases of leaf sheaths are the primary infection sites for *Rhizoctonia solani* on the warm season grasses. Penetration of the plant surface is by means of appressoria produced on freely growing hyphae and on hyphae within infection cushions (Figure 3-3). During colonization, the vascular bundles remain intact but maceration of the parenchymatous tissue of the sheaths is usually extensive, causing the tissue to become soft and slimy. If conditions remain favorable for disease development, the colonization process eventually involves the sheaths of entire clusters of leaves. At this stage, these fascicles are easily broken off from the stolons (Zummo and Plakidas, 1958; Hurd and Grisham, 1983).

With the warm season grasses, Rhizoctonia blight is most destructive spring and fall months. The conditions that favor major outbreaks of the disease are extended periods of leaf wetness as the plants are going into dormancy in late fall or early winter, or are coming out of dormancy in the spring. The incidence of the disease is usually greater on turfgrass growing in low wet areas or on poorly drained soil. The susceptibility of plants to colonization by *Rhizoctonia solani* is greater under conditions of high nitrogen fertilization (Haygood *et al.*, 1989; Couch, Lucas and Haygood, 1990).

Control

Cultural Practices

The maintenance of good drainage will reduce the incidence and severity of Rhizoctonia blight. Also, management practices that decrease the length of time the leaves are wet will aid in lowering the intensity of the disease. One procedure for reducing the leaf wetness periods is the early morning removal of water from bermudagrass putting greens by dragging a water hose across them or by poling. The practice of poling simply involves brushing the surface of the turf with long, limber bamboo poles.

The duration of the daily leaf wetness period can also be decreased two to four hours by following a nighttime watering schedule. Rather than irrigating immediately after sunrise or during late afternoon hours, the watering routine should be set to begin at least three hours after sunset and programmed to be completed before sunrise (see Chapter 16, Figure 16-2).

Use of Fungicides

The use of fungicides for the control of Rhizoctonia blight of warm season turfgrasses has met with varying degrees of success. Research conducted at North Carolina State University has shown that presently available fungicides applied after the appearance of Rhizoctonia blight in the spring will not provide satisfactory control of the disease. The most effective fungicide programs are those that (a) begin the treatments with the first outbreak of the disease in the fall and continue the application schedule until the grass is into winter dormancy, and (b) initiate a fungicide application program in the same areas as the plants are coming out of dormancy in the spring (Couch, Lucas and Haygood, 1990).

Fungicides labeled for the control of Rhizoctonia blight include flutolanil, chlorothalonil, iprodione, and quintozene. For a profile of these fungicides and a listing of representative trade names and manufacturers, see Appendix Table I.

Corticium Red Thread

Corticium red thread has the distinction of being the first reported foliar disease of a turfgrass species. The fungus that incites this disease was first observed on ryegrass in Australia in 1854 (Berkeley, 1873). Corticium red thread was reported occurring on ryegrass lawns in England in 1873 (Wallis, 1873). By the late 1920s it had been diagnosed on creeping red fescue in the United States (Erwin, 1941). At the present time, Corticium red thread is known to occur on bermudagrass, Kentucky bluegrass, creeping red fescue, tall fescue, and perennial ryegrass in the humid areas of the United States, Canada, Northern Europe, the United Kingdom, New Zealand, and Australia (Figure 4-3) (Erwin, 1941; Smith, 1953a; Hims, Dickinson and Fletcher, 1984; Bahuon, 1985; O'Neill and Murray, 1985).

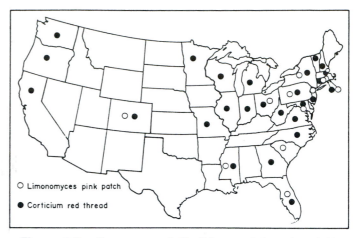

Figure 4-3. Occurrence of Corticium red thread and Limonomyces pink patch in the United States from 1980–1984. *After O'Neill and Murray, 1985.*

For many years, the total group of symptoms associated with outbreaks of Corticium red thread were thought to be caused by a single species of fungi. Recently, however, research has shown that what has been considered to be the syndrome of one disease is actually an aggregate of the symptoms of two diseases, Corticium red thread and Limonomyces pink patch. Either disease can occur separately, or both can develop simultaneously in the same stand of turfgrass. Although their symptom patterns have features in common, they also have certain characteristics that distinguish them from each other. Also, even though both incitants are in the same major taxonomic group of fungi and produce pink mycelia, they are clearly distinguishable from each other.

Symptoms

In overall view, red thread is seen as irregularly shaped patches of blighted turfgrass, ranging in size from 2 inches (5 cm) to 3 feet (0.9 meter) in diameter. In cases of evolvement of large areas of grass, the patches often have a general ragged appearance due to a fairly high population of unaffected leaves (Plate 4-B, D).

The disease is confined to the leaves and leaf sheaths only. Small, water-soaked spots develop within 24–48 hours from the time of infection. Under favorable weather conditions, these lesions enlarge rapidly. As colonization of the leaf progresses, there begins a general drying-out of the affected tissue. Under favorable weather conditions, the affected leaves may be completely covered with the pink gelatinous growth of the pathogen.

A key feature for field diagnosis of Corticium red

thread on tall cut grass is the presence of fine, thread-like, coral-pink structures (sclerotia) ¹⁄₁₆–¹⁄₄ inch (1–6 mm) in length at the terminal portions of the leaves (Plate 4-C, E, F; Figure 4-4). These structures are never present in cases of Limonomyces pink patch. Therefore, in field diagnosis, if reddish sclerotia are not present, one can be reasonably certain that only Limonomyces pink patch is present. However, since many of the other field diagnostic features of the two diseases are similar, if the reddish sclerotia have formed at the tips of the leaves, one cannot be certain that pink patch is not also present. This determination can be made by a laboratory-based examination of the fungi colonizing the leaves. The mycelium of the incitant of Limonomyces pink patch (*Limonomyces roseipellis*) has clamp connections and the cells are binucleate (Figure 4-7). The mycelium of the Corticium red thread pathogen (*Laetisaria fuciformis*) does not have clamp connections and the cells have more than two nuclei.

Under the close mowing conditions of golf greens and bowling greens, the symptom pattern for Corticium red thread is somewhat different from that of taller cut grass. The affected areas range from 2–6 inches (5–15 cm) in diameter and are irregular in outline. The leaves are tan, and a cursory examination of the area can result in a misdiagnosis of the problem as being an atypical case of Sclerotinia dollar spot (Plate 4-A). If the disease is Corticium red thread, however, close examination of leaves from the affected areas will usually reveal the presence of a

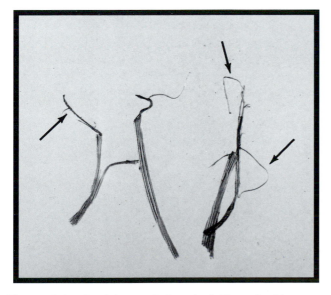

Figure 4-4. Corticium red thread of Kentucky bluegrass (*Poa pratensis*) showing formation of thread-like tendrils at terminal portions of leaves.

light reddish tinge to the sheaths. Also, although the number of sclerotia will be low because of the close mowing, the 'red threads' that characterize the disease on tall cut grass can also be found in these areas.

The Fungus

Laetisaria fuciformis (McAlpine) Burds.; syn. *Corticium fuciforme* (McAlpine) Wakef.

Description

Growth consists of variously shaped sterile mycelium and (if present) an effused basidiocarp. Sterile mycelium weblike, pale reddish, surrounding and connecting leaf blades, or simple or branched, forming pink flocks and antlerlike processes; threadlike processes simple or branched, occurring at tips of grass blades, typically acuminate, up to 10 mm long (up to 50 mm mentioned in some literature), when fresh gelatinous, pale pink, pale orange, or nearly hyaline, when dry ceraceous and bright pink, orange, or red; flocks brittle, pink, up to 10 mm, consisting of a mass of arthroconidia. Basidiocarps resupinate, effused, adnate, ceraceous to membranaceous, pruinose when dry, up to 120 µm thick. Hymeneal surface even, pinkish when fresh, cream colored to nearly invisible when dry. Hyphal strands often present. Hyphal system monomitic. Hyphae hyaline to lightly pink, 3–7.5 (–10) µm wide, lacking clamp connections, thin to thick walled (0.4–2.3 um), multinucleate (up to 11 nuclei per cell). Hyphidia simple, hyaline, thin walled, 20–45 µm × 2–4 µm, not abundant. Basidia urniform, originating from probasidia, 30–56 µm × 6–8.5 µm, with 4 sterigmata. Probasidia irregular to sphaeropedunculate, 12.5–20 µm × 5.5–9 µm. Sterigmata up to 6 µm long, rarely becoming septate. Basidiospores hyaline, thin walled, smooth, ellipsoid to pip shaped, 8–12 µm × 6–6 (–6.5) µm, distinctly apiculate, not amyloid. Hyphae of threadlike processes arranged in textura porrecta, hyaline, thin walled, 3.5 µm × 8 µm wide. Arthroconidia hyaline, thin walled, ellipsoid to cylindrical or irregularly shaped, 10–47 (–90) µm × 5–17 µm, containing up to 32 nuclei, often separated by small, thin-walled cells, which finally disintegrate (Stalpers and Loerakker, 1982).

Procedures for Isolation and Culture

Laetisaria fuciformis grows well on acidified potato dextrose agar and on malt extract agar. Two growth types have been described on malt extract agar, depending on the source of the isolate. A fast growing type is derived from the antlerlike processes (basidiocarps). It produces scanty aerial mycelium, and at 20–22 °C reaches a radius of 70 mm in 12–14 days. A slow growing type is derived from the brittle flocks. The mycelium of the slow growing form is floccose (aerial), and at 20–22 °C, the cultures reach a diameter of 10–25 mm in 14 days (Stalpers and Loerakker, 1982). The types that produce aerial mycelium in culture vary from very faint pink to a marked eosin pink. The more resupinate types are usually distinctly eosin pink. The pink coloration is darker if the fungus is grown in bright light (Smith, 1954).

Hosts

1. **Turfgrasses**—annual bluegrass (*Poa annua*), creeping bentgrass (*Agrostis palustris*), Colonial bentgrass (*Agrostis tenuis*), bermudagrass (*Cynodon dactylon*), Kentucky bluegrass (*Poa pratensis*), hard fescue (*Festuca ovina* var. *duriuscula*), red fescue (*Festuca rubra*), sheep fescue (*Festuca ovina*), tall fescue (*Festuca arundiinacea*), annual ryegrass (*Lolium multiflorum*), and perennial ryegrass (*Lolium perenne*).

2. **All Known Gramineous Hosts**—A listing of common names for the following species is given in Appendix Table IV. *Agropyron repens* (L.) Beauv., *Agrostis alba* L., *A. canina* L., *A. palustris* Huds., *A. stolonifera* L., *A. tenuis* Sibth., *Briza media* L., *Bromus mollis* L., *B. sterilis* L., *Cynodon dactylon* (L.) Pers., *Festuca dertonensis* (All.) Aschers. and Graebn., *F. myuros* L., *F. ovina* L., *F. ovina* var. *duriuscula* (L.) Koch, *F. rubra* L., *F. rubra* var. *commutata* Gaud., *Holcus lanatus* L., *Lolium perenne* L., *Poa annua* L., *P. pratensis* L. (Erwin, 1941; Sprague, 1950; Smith, 1953a; Howard *et al.*, 1951; Filer, 1966b).

Disease Profile

Laetisaria fuciformis survives adverse climatic conditions in the form of the sclerotia that have been formed at the terminal portions of the leaves, and as mycelium in the debris of previously diseased plants. The sclerotia are known to retain their viability for at least two years (Bennett, 1935; Libbey, 1938).

The Corticium red thread pathogen penetrates the leaves through stomata and cut tips. The mycelium moves intercellularly and spreads rapidly through all the tissue groups (Erwin, 1941; Bahuon, 1985). Enlargement of individual patches is accomplished by growth of mycelium from leaf to leaf. Under favorable weather conditions this form of spread can be very rapid.

Laetisaria fuciformis is dispersed to new locations within a stand of turfgrass by sclerotia and diseased leaf tissue adhering to the surfaces of maintenance equipment. Also, when the sclerotia dry out, they become brittle and are easily broken loose from the leaves and can be carried in wind currents. Hymenium of *Laetisaria fuciformis* have been found on perennial ryegrass seed (McAlpine, 1906). This raises the possibility that turfgrass seed might serve to introduce the pathogen into new locations. Long distance spread of the pathogen in the field is probably accomplished most commonly by wind-borne arthroconidia. These spore types are formed in the tufts of pinkish mycelium that develop on the leaves of diseased plants.

Although air temperatures in the 65–75 °F (18–24 °C) range are usually considered to be most conducive to the development of Corticium red thread, the length of time the surfaces of the leaves are wet appears to be an overriding factor in the epidemiology of the disease (Bennett, 1935). Corticium red thread can develop on unfrozen turf under snow cover and during winter months that are marked by extended periods of rainfall. In addition, major outbreaks of the disease can occur in warm summer months during prolonged rainfall.

Application of plant growth retardants to the turf will bring about an increase in the incidence of Corticium red thread (Chastagner and Vassey, 1979). The incidence of the disease is lower on creeping red fescue turf cut at 1.5 inches (3.8 cm) than when mowed at 0.75 inch (1.9 cm) (Goss and Gould, 1973) (Figure 4-5).

Calcium, potassium, and nitrogen fertilization have been shown to influence the development of Corticium red thread. Low soil calcium levels increase the susceptibility of creeping red fescue to the disease (Muse and Couch, 1965). Increased potassium fertilization has been shown to reduce the severity of the disease on red fescue, bentgrass, and perennial ryegrass (Goss and Gould, 1971; Cahill *et al.*, 1983). Laboratory and greenhouse-based studies have shown that nitrogen nutrition does not alter the susceptibility of creeping red fescue to Corticium red thread (Couch and Muse, 1965). However, application of nitrogenous fertilizers often alleviate the field symptoms of the disease (Erwin, 1941; Smith, 1953a; Goss, 1968; Goss and Gould, 1971; Cahill *et al.*, 1983). The observed reductions of incidence of the disease under high nitrogen fertilization are probably the result of more rapid plant recovery during periods of lessened activity on the part of the pathogen.

The Rainier variety of creeping red fescue has been shown to be more resistant to *Laetisaria fucifor-*

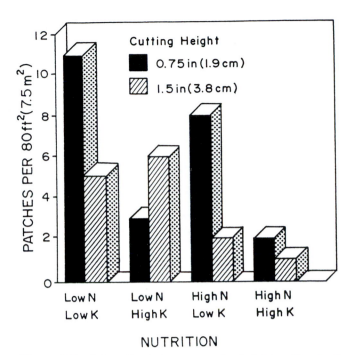

Figure 4-5. Interaction between mowing height and levels of nitrogen (N) and potassium (K) fertilization and the incidence and severity of Corticium red thread on 'Rainier' creeping red fescue. *After Goss and Gould, 1971.*

mis when grown under conditions of low soil moisture content. The susceptibility of the variety Pennlawn does not appear to be affected by soil moisture content (Muse and Couch, 1965).

Control

Cultural Practices

If the stand of turfgrasses is under either low nitrogen or low potassium fertility, the application of muriate of potash and a readily available form of nitrogen fertilizer during the periods of high disease incidence will aid in offsetting disease damage as well as facilitate faster plant recovery when the weather conditions are no longer favorable for the development of the disease.

Use of Resistant Grasses

The comparative susceptibility of various cultivars of Kentucky bluegrass, perennial ryegrass, and tall fescue to Corticium red thread are given in Table 4-2.

Use of Fungicides

Treatment of perennial ryegrass with benomyl at 1 oz a.i. per 1,000 ft^2 (28.4 gm per 93 m^2) has been

shown to increase the incidence of Corticium red thread (Dernoeden, O'Neill and J. J. Murray, 1985).

Corticium red thread may be controlled by the use of either triadimefon, propiconazole, cyproconazole, iprodione, chlorothalonil, flutolanil, or vinclozolin (Ashbugh and Larsen, 1983; Clarke, et al., 1985; Dernoeden, O'Neill and Murray, 1985; Couch and Smith, 1990). Preventive fungicidal applications should be started when the daytime air temperatures stabilize in the 60–70 °F (16–21 °C) range, and continued at 10–14 day intervals as long as wet weather persists. Curative applications should be made at 4–5 day intervals until recovery is affected, and then a 10–14 day program should be followed.

For a profile of these fungicides and a listing of representative trade names and manufacturers, see Appendix Table I.

Limonomyces Pink Patch

The symptoms of Limonomyces pink patch were first described in The Netherlands in 1982. Since then, the disease has been diagnosed on perennial ryegrass, bentgrass, Kentucky bluegrass, annual bluegrass, creeping red fescue, and bermudagrass in the United Kingdom, Canada, and the United States (Figure 4-3) (Stalpers and Loerakker, 1982; Kaplan and Jackson, 1982; Couch, 1983; O'Neill and Murray, 1985).

Symptoms

Limonomyces pink patch and Corticium red thread can occur concurrently in the same stand of turfgrass. The symptom patterns of the two diseases have many features in common. Also, both incitants are in the same major taxonomic group of fungi and produce pink mycelia. It wasn't until a detailed study was carried out on the taxonomic positions of isolates of fungi found in association with outbreaks of the disease that it was discovered that the syndrome of what was thought to be Corticium red thread was actually a composite of two diseases (Stalpers and Loerakker, 1982).

Limonomyces pink patch is confined to the aboveground plant parts. Symptoms are usually seen first along the margins of the leaves as small, irregularly shaped blotches of pink color bordered by light green to yellow bands of discolored leaf tissue. Eventually, the entire width of the leaf takes on a distinctive pinkish cast. When this occurs, a light brown to tan tip dieback of the leaves then develops. A thin, pink layer of fungal growth is often present on the surfaces of the leaves of affected plants. Also, there may be distinctive pink-colored tufts of mycelium produced

Table 4-2. Comparative susceptibility of cultivars of Kentucky bluegrass, perennial ryegrass, and tall fescue to Corticium red thread. *After O'Neill and Murray, 1985.*

Most Resistant	Intermediate		Most Susceptible
A. Kentucky Bluegrass:			
Bonnieblue	Adelphi	Baron	Piedmont
Harmony	Nugget	Trenton	Cello
Plush	Admiral	Vanessa	Apart
Monopoly	Aspen	Shasta	Glade
Challenger	Welcome	Merion	Vantage
Victa	Fylking	Columbia	Mystic
Bristol	Holiday	Charlotte	Argyle
Eclipse	Midnight	America	Kenblue
Merit	Barblue	Rugby	S. D. Common
Cheri	Birka	Touchdown	Sydsport
Geronimo	Somerset	Parade	
	Enoble	Wabash	
B. Perennial Ryegrass:			
Pennant	Omega	Barry	Blazer
Pennfine	Cowboy	Premier	Birdie II
Yorktown II	Acclaim	Dasher	Prelude
Palmer	Tara	Ranger	Derby
Fiesta	Manhattan	Repell	
	Regal	Manhattan II	
	Linn	All Star	
	Birdie	Citation II	
C. Tall Fescue:			
Falcon	Clemfine	Galway	Alta
	Kennmont	Kenhyy	
	Kenwell	Rebel	
	Ky 31	Goar	
	Monaco		

by extensive colonization of stems and the sheaths of leaves that are in advanced senescence (Figure 4-6).

The patches often assume an overall pinkish tinge (Plate 5-A). On stands of grass that are mowed frequently and are growing under optimum nitrogen fertilization, the affected areas seldom reach more than 20 inches (0.6 m) in diameter. Also, the severity of the disease within the individual patches is minimal. Consequently, under these management conditions, Limonomyces pink patch is generally regarded to be of minor importance. However, on turf that is mowed infrequently and is under low nitrogen fertilization, damage from the disease may be severe. In these instances, all of the above-ground plant parts may become completely blighted.

The fine, thread-like coral pink tendrils (sclerotia) that develop on leaves affected with Corticium red thread are never present in cases of Limonomyces pink patch. Therefore, if reddish sclerotia are not present, one can be reasonably certain that only Limonomyces pink patch is present. However, since many of the other field diagnostic features of the two diseases are similar, if the reddish sclerotia have

formed at the tips of the leaves, one cannot be certain that pink patch is not also present. This determination can be made by a laboratory-based examination of the fungi colonizing the leaves. The mycelium of the of the incitant of Limonomyces pink patch (*Limonomyces roseipellis*) has clamp connections and the cells are binucleate. The mycelium of the Corticium red thread pathogen (*Laetisaria fuciformis*) does not have clamp connections and the cells have more than two nuclei.

The Fungus

Limonomyces roseipellis Stalpers and Loerakker

Description

Fungus consisting of an effused, ceraceous, pink to reddish film, 18–350 μm thick, which is originally agglutinated onto the grass leaf, but may become detached and fissured after drying, often showing the pattern of the leaf surface on the under side. Sometimes sterile, cream colored to pale pink or reddish mycelium present, forming dots which surround and

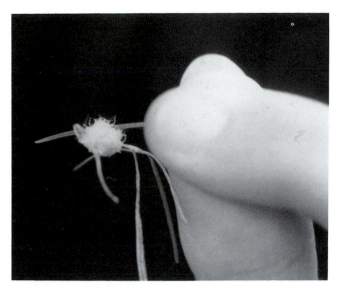

Figure 4-6. Tuft of mycelium of Limonomyces pink patch fungus on leaf sheath of perennial ryegrass (*Lolium perenne*). *Courtesy Nicole O'Neil.*

connect leaf blades. Basidiocarps resupinate, effused, adnate, ceraceous when fresh, pruinose when dry, 50–350 μm thick. Hymeneal surface even, pink (shrimp pink) to reddish pink to orange red when wet, pale orange (salmon orange) to pale ochraceous or cream colored when dry. Hyphal system monomitic. Hyphae hyaline, thin to rarely somewhat thick walled, binucleate conglutinate, 2–7 μm wide, with clamp connections at nearly all primary septa (Figure 4-7). Basidia typically urniform, originating from probasidia, 27–60 (−70) × 6.5–8.5 μm, sometimes clavate without probasidial swelling, bearing 4 sterigmata. Probasidia irregular to somewhat ovoid, 11–28 × (4.5-) 6.5–13 μm, metabasidia basally 2.5–3.5 μm wide, often arising laterally from the probasidia. Sterigmata stout, curved, 4.5–5.5 (−9) μm long. Basidiospores hyaline, ellipsoid to subcylindrical or pip shaped, (8-) 9–12 (−14) × (4.5-) 5–6 (−6.5) μm, somewhat ovoid from above and then 6–7 μm broad, distinctly apiculate, not amyloid. Sterile mycelium consisting of conglutinate hyphae, which are arranged in fascicles consisting of loosely interwoven hyphae. Hyphae hyaline, thin to thick walled, septate, septa with or without clamps (Stalpers and Loerakker, 1982).

Procedures for Isolation and Culture

Limonomyces roseipellis grows well on a wide range of artificial media. It grows in culture at a temperature range of 4–31 °C, with an optimum of 21–23 °C. On 2 percent malt agar, colonies reach a radius of 70 mm in 7–10 days. In Petri dish cultures, the marginal hyphae are appressed to submerged and even in outline. About 10 mm from the margin, a zone of pink, cottony to sometimes plumose aerial mycelium develops. This growth diminishes in height towards the center of the culture. The aerial hyphae is hyaline with clamps at most of the septa. Also, the hyphal cells are binucleate (Figure 4-7).

The area immediately around the center of the culture is typically appressed, except in strains that have been plated for a long period of time. In these instances, the texture of the colony may be low cottony or wooly, and finally become nearly felt-like. After 6 weeks, the mat is appressed, but the pink mycelium typically grows against the lid of the Petri dish. Arthroconidia are rarely produced. When the cultures are stored in the dark at 5 °C, irregularly shaped, reddish ceraceous bodies up to 10 mm in diameter may develop (Stalpers and Loerakker, 1982).

Hosts

1. **Turfgrasses**—bentgrass (*Agrostis* sp.), perennial ryegrass (*Lolium perenne* L.), Kentucky bluegrass (*Poa pratensis* L.), annual bluegrass (*Poa annua* L.), creeping red fescue (*Festuca rubra* L.), and bermudagrass (*Cynodon dactylon* (L.) Pers.
2. **All Known Gramineous Hosts**—The turfgrass species listed above constitute the presently known host range of *Limonomyces roseipellis*.

Disease Profile

Limonomyces roseipellis grows saprophytically on turfgrass debris. The fungus survives adverse climatic conditions by means of dormant mycelium

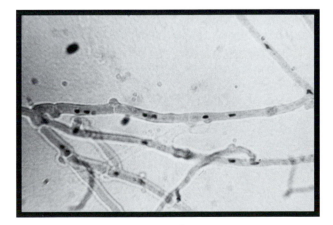

Figure 4-7. Mycelium of *Limonomyces roseipellis* showing binucleate condition of cells and clamp connections. *Courtesy Nicole O'Neil.*

in colonized turfgrass debris, and as small, reddish, waxy pads of mycelium on the surfaces of leaves and stems. It penetrates the leaf surfaces directly by hyphae from mycelial strands. Leaves in advanced stages of senescence are more vulnerable to infection and colonization than young, actively growing leaves. As the disease progresses, the older leaves often become bleached and matted together, while the younger leaves maintain their integrity.

The enlargement of individual patches is accomplished by the direct growth of mycelium from leaf to leaf. Unlike the Corticium red thread pathogen, *Limonomyces roseipellis* does not produce arthroconidia or leaf-borne sclerotia; therefore, its means of spread to new sites within a stand of turfgrass is limited to diseased leaf tissue and colonized turfgrass debris adhering to the surfaces of maintenance equipment. It is possible that long distance spread of the fungus may be accomplished by basidiospores carried by wind currents, but this aspect of the epidemiology of the disease has not yet been studied.

The development of Limonomyces pink patch is favored by extended periods of leaf wetness and air temperatures in the 60–70 °F (16–21 °C) range. Also, the disease is more severe under low nitrogen fertilization. Typically, Limonomyces pink patch is considered to be a minor disease; however, on semidormant turf, during extended periods of rainfall the above ground plant parts can be killed back to the tillers. In addition, during prolonged periods of wet weather, Limonomyces pink patch can be very severe on infrequently mowed grass growing under low nitrogen fertilization (Stalpers and Loerakker, 1982).

Control

Successful control of Limonomyces pink patch has been reported with preventive applications of either propiconazole, triadimefon, iprodione, vinclozolin, flutolanil, or fenarimol (Clarke *et al.*, 1985). For a profile of these fungicides and a listing of representative trade names and manufacturers, see Appendix Table I.

SUMMER PATCH DISEASES

Fusarium Blight

Fusarium blight is an important and widespread warm weather disease of cool season turfgrasses in the United States and Canada. The disease was first observed in 1959 in stands of 'Merion' Kentucky bluegrass (*Poa pratensis*) in southeastern Pennsylvania. In addition to Kentucky bluegrass, outbreaks of Fusarium blight have since been reported on bentgrasses (*Agrostis* spp.), red fescue (*Festuca rubra*), tall fescue (*Festuca arundinacea*), perennial ryegrass (*Lolium perenne*), and centipedegrass (*Eremochloa ophiuroides*) (Couch, 1964; Couch and Bedford, 1966; Subirats and Self, 1972; Endo *et al.*, 1973).

Symptoms

The holopathology of Fusarium blight is highly complex. Infection and colonization of turfgrass plants can include the roots, rhizomes, crowns, and leaves. The total syndrome for the disease involves the physical appearance of all of these plant parts. This means that the procedure for field diagnosis of Fusarium blight should include both an assessment of the overall appearance of the turf and the condition of each plant part.

Foliar symptoms

1. *Tall cut grass*—Lesions can originate at both the cut tip and at random over the entire leaf. These first appear as irregularly-shaped, dark green blotches. They rapidly fade to a light green, then assume a reddish brown hue, and finally become dull tan. Individual lesions often involve the entire width of the leaf blade and may extend up to ½ inch (6 mm) in length (Plate 6-F).

   In overall view, affected turfgrass stands first show scattered light green patches 2–6 inches (5–15 cm) in diameter. Under environmental conditions favorable for disease development, the color of these patches changes in a 36–48 hour period to a dull reddish brown, then to tan, and finally to a light straw color. Initially, the shapes of the patches are elongate streaks, crescents, or circular patches. The most characteristic feature of the gross symptomatology is seen in the later stages of disease development. At these times, there are present more or less circular patches of blighted turfgrass 1–3 feet (0.9 meter) in diameter. Light tan to straw colored, they often have reddish brown margins 1–2 inches (3–5 cm) wide and contain center tufts of green, apparently unaffected grass. This combination produces a distinctive frogeye effect. When optimum conditions for disease development exist for an extended period of time, these affected areas coalesce. As a result, large areas of turfgrass may be blighted (Plate 6-A, B, C, D and Plate 7-E).

2. *Golf greens*—Fusarium blight can be very destructive to bentgrass under golf green management. The frogeye pattern of overall symptom development that sometimes appears on taller cut

grass is usually not present in these situations. Instead, the disease first appears on golf greens as tan to light brown, irregularly shaped areas 2–3 inches (5–7.5 cm) in diameter. Under favorable weather conditions, these patches will develop into irregularly-shaped areas of blighted grass up to 3 feet (0.9 meter) wide. During periods of relatively high soil moisture brought on by frequent rainfalls, the pinkish growth of the pathogen can be seen on the root and crown tissue near the soil surface (Plate 7-A, B, C, D)

Root, Crown and Basal Stem Symptoms

A problem in diagnosis of the root and crown rot aspect of Fusarium blight centers around the fact that the foliar blight phase of the disease is more commonly known. As the result, in instances where root and crown rot is the predominant condition, the possibility of the problem at hand being Fusarium blight can be easily overlooked.

In semiarid climates, basal stem and root rot is frequently the predominant phase of Fusarium blight on Kentucky bluegrass (Endo and Colbaugh, 1974). This is also the case for the development of Fusarium blight on perennial ryegrass and tall fescue in areas characterized by higher rainfall. Where the production of tall fescue sod is concerned, situations can develop in which even though the root rot phase of Fusarium blight is not having a visible effect on above ground plant growth, the extent of root deterioration will still be severe enough to reduce the binding quality of the sod to the extent that it shatters when the cutting and lifting operation is attempted (Couch, 1976).

Plants affected primarily by the root rot phase of Fusarium blight are often stunted, pale green in color, and do not readily recover from mowing or adverse weather conditions. Their roots and crowns develop a brown to reddish brown dry rot. This is in contrast with the dark purple to black rot characteristic of root and crown tissue affected by summer patch. As the disease progresses, these affected areas on the crowns turn dark brown and become very difficult to cut, even with a sharp knife (Plate 7-F) (Endo et al., 1973). During periods of relatively high soil moisture brought on by frequent rainfalls, the pinkish growth of the pathogen can be seen on the root and crown tissue near the soil surface.

Positive diagnosis of Fusarium blight always requires determination that the causal fungus is present in the diseased tissue. Certain of the field symptoms of Fusarium blight are similar to those of summer patch, necrotic ring spot, Rhizoctonia blight, and

Pythium blight. Also, in addition to the two species that incite Fusarium blight, 16 nonpathogenic species of Fusarium have been found in close association with decomposing turfgrass leaves, crowns, roots and thatch (Table 4-3) (Smiley and Craven, 1979).

If the diagnosis of these diseases is to be accurate, it is essential that a laboratory examination be made to determine which incitant is present. If Fusarium spores are found on the decomposing tissue, it then becomes necessary to determine if the species present is the one that actually incites Fusarium blight or if it is one of the saprophytic species that commonly inhabit decomposing turfgrass debris (Couch and Bedford, 1966; Couch, 1988).

The Fungi

A. *Fusarium culmorum* (W. G. Smith) Sacc.; syn. *Fusarium roseum* (Lk.) emend Snyder and Hanson f. sp. *cerealis* (Cke.) 'Culmorum'

Description

Mycelium loosely cottony, carmine red with buff or off-white mycelium scattered throughout; sporodochial masses golden to ocher, later darker; conidia thick, curved, bluntly pointed apex, slightly more tapering at the base with prominent, well marked foot cell; 3–9 (usually 5) septate, 4.5–6.5 μm × 30–60 μm (Figure 4-8) (Sprague, 1950).

Procedures for Isolation and Culture

Fusarium culmorum grows well on potato dextrose agar at 21°C. After 2–3 days growth, the mycelium becomes yellow at the point of transfer and spreads gradually throughout the colony. At the same time, a red pigmentation develops on the surface of the medium. This material is eventually diffused into the medium and becomes a dark reddish-brown. Microconidia are not produced, but abundant macroconidia develop after a few days (Booth, 1971).

Table 4-3. Fusarium species nonpathogenic to turfgrass found in association with decomposing turfgrass leaves, crowns, roots and thatch. *After Smiley and Craven, 1979.*

Fusarium avanaceum	Fusarium semitectum
Fusarium robustum	Fusarium heterosporum
Fusarium solani	Fusarium merismoides
Fusarium equiseti	Fusarium moniliforme
Fusarium sporotrichoides	Fusarium concolor
Fusarium sambucinum	Fusarium oxysporum
Fusarium sambucinum var. coreuleum	Fusarium tricinctum

Figure 4-8. Conida of *Fusarium culmorum. Courtesy Paul E. Nelson.*

Hosts

1. **Turfgrasses**—creeping bentgrass (*Agrostis palustris*), Colonial bentgrass (*Agrostis tenuis*), annual bluegrass (*Poa annua*), Kentucky bluegrass (*Poa pratensis*), centipedegrass (*Eremochloa ophiuroides*), Chewings fescue (*Festuca rubra* var. *commutata*), red fescue (*Festuca rubra*), tall fescue (*Festuca arundinacea*), annual ryegrass (*Lolium multiflorum*), perennial ryegrass (*Lolium perenne*).

2. **All Known Gramineous Hosts**—A listing of common names for the following species is given in Appendix Table IV. *Agropyron cristatum* (L.) Gaertn., *A. desertorum* (Fisch.) Schult., *A. inerme* (Scribn. and Smith) Rydb., *A. sibiricum* (Willd.) Beauv., *A. smithii* Rydb., *A. trachycaulum* (Link) Malte, *Agrostis palustris* Huds., *A. stolonifera* L., *A. tenuis* Sibth., *Avena byzantina* K. Koch, *A. fatua* L., *A. sativa* L., *Bromus carinatus* Hook. and Arn., *B. inermis* Leyss., *B. mollis* L., *B. tectorum* L., *Dactylis glomerata* L., *Echinochloa crusgalli* (L.) Beauv., *E. crusgalli* var. *frumentacea* (Roxb.) Wight, *Elymus condensatus* Presl, *Eremochloa ophiuroides* (Munto) Hack., *Festuca arundinacea* Schreb., *F. rubra* L., *F. rubra* var. *commutata* Gaud., *Hordeum distichon* L., *H. jubatum* L., *H. vulgare* L., *Lolium multiflorum* Lam., *L. perenne* L., *Poa annua* L., *P. juncifolia* Scribn., *P. pratensis* L., *Secale cereale* L., *Sorghum halepense* (L.) Pers., *Triticum aestivum* L., *T. dicoccum* Schrank, *T. durum* Desf., *T. monococcum* L., *T. spelta* L., *Zea mays* L. (Couch and Bedford, 1966; Sprague, 1950; Subirats and Self, 1972).

The Fungi

B. *Fusarium poae* (Peck.) Wollenweber; syn. *Fusarium tricinctum* f. sp. *poae* (Peck) Snyder and Hansen

Description

Fusarium poae grows well on potato dextrose agar at 21 °C. Microconidia begin forming after about 3 days from the time of single sporing. On potato dextrose agar, the mycelium is cobwebby, carmine rose or buff—becoming powdery with the formation of microconidia. Microconidia are citron shaped, 0–1 septate, 8–12 μm × 7–10 μm. Macroconidia are 3–5 septate, 3.0–4.2 μm × 18–36 μm, narrowly sickle-shaped, and pointed at both ends; the foot cell is not prominent (Figure 4-9) (Sprague, 1950; Booth, 1971).

Hosts

1. **Turfgrasses**—creeping bentgrass (*Agrostis palustris*), Colonial bentgrass (*Agrostis tenuis*), annual bluegrass (*Poa annua*), Kentucky bluegrass (*Poa pratensis*), Chewings fescue(*Festuca rubra* var. *commutata*), hard fescue (*Festuca ovina* var. *duriuscula*), red fescue (*Festuca rubra*), tall fescue (*Festuca arundinacea*), annual ryegrass (*Lolium multiflorum*), and perennial ryegrass (*Lolium perenne*).

2. **All Known Gramineous Hosts**—A listing of common names for the following species is given in Appendix Table IV. *Agrostis palustris* Huds., *A. stolonifera* L., *A. tenuis* Sibth., *Avena byzantina*

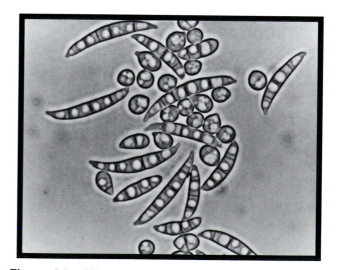

Figure 4-9. Microconidia and macroconidia of *Fusarium poae. Courtesy Paul E. Nelson.*

K. Koch, *A. sativa* L., *Bouteloua curtipendula*
(Michx.) Torr., *B. gracilis* (H. B. K.) Lag., *Bromus
inermis* Leyss., *Dactylis glomerata* L., *Elymus
junceus* Fisch., *Festuca arundinacea* Schreb., *F.
octoflora* Walt., *F. ovina* L., *F. ovina* var. *duriuscula*
(L.) Koch, *F. rubra* L., *F. rubra* var. *commutata*
Gaud., *Hordeum jubatum* L., *H. vulgare* L.,. *Lolium multiflorum* Lam., *L. perenne* L., *Muhlenbergia racemosa* (Michx.) B. S. P., *Panicum capillare* L., *P. miliaceum* L., *Phleum pratense* L., *Poa
annua* L., *Poa nemoralis* L., *P. palustris* L., *P.
pratensis* L., *P. trivialis* L., *Setaria lutescens* (Weigel) Hubb., *S. viridis* (L.) Beauv., *Triticum aestivum* L., *T. durum* Desf., *Zea mays* L. (Couch and
Bedford, 1966; Keil, 1946; Sprague, 1950).

Disease Profile

Fusarium culmorum and *Fusarium poae* can
both be transmitted on turfgrass seed (Cole, Braverman and Duich, 1968). They are also known to be
capable of surviving as saprophytes in the soil (Couch
and Bedford, 1966). These two sources constitute the
main reservoirs of primary inoculum for the development of the disease in newly seeded stands of turfgrass. In established turfgrass, the main sources of
inoculum for new outbreaks of Fusarium blight are
dormant mycelium in crown and root tissue infected
during the previous growing season and thatch that
has been colonized by the pathogens (Couch and
Bedford, 1966; Bean, 1966; Bean, 1969).

Infection of the leaves is accomplished by both
germinating macroconidia and mycelium from the
saprophytic growth of the pathogens on the thatch
and other organic matter. The highest frequency of
primary infections probably originates from the latter source. Macroconidia germinate 12 hours from
the onset of favorable environmental conditions. Penetration of intact leaf surfaces occurs at the junction
of epidermal cells. At the points of direct leaf penetration, there are no observable changes in hyphae
morphology, nor is degradation of the host cell walls
evident.

The most common area of penetration of foliage
by *Fusarium culmorum* and *Fusarium poae* appears
to be the cut ends of the leaves. In either the instance
of direct penetration of epidermal calls or entry
through cut leaf tips, mycelial movement in the leaf
tissue is intercellular over an area of 12 or more cells
and then it becomes intracellular. Penetration of individual parenchymatous cells is usually characterized by a pronounced constriction of the mycelium
at the point of passage through the cell wall (Couch
and Bedford, 1966).

Air and soil temperatures have been shown to be
important environmental factors in the development
of severe outbreaks of Fusarium blight. In home
lawns or grounds situations, the first part of the
sward to show visible symptoms of the disease is
usually sloping land that is close to a paved walk,
driveway or parking lot (Plate 6). Turf on south-
facing slopes will usually show symptoms of Fusarium blight earlier and become more severely diseased than sod on slopes with northern exposures.
Also, there is a tendency for the disease to grade in
severity in proportion to the intensity and duration of
sunlight. Areas in full sunlight throughout the daytime hours will usually be more severely affected by
Fusarium blight than those in which there is shading
from the sun during the noon to 4 p.m. period of
the day.

Certain isolates of *Fusarium culmorum* and *Fusarium poae* have been shown to vary in their temperature requirements for optimum pathogenicity.
As a general rule, however, the foliar phase of Fusarium blight is most severe during prolonged periods
of high atmospheric humidity with daytime air temperatures of 80–95 °F (27–35 °C) and night air temperatures of 70 °F (21 °C) or above (Couch and Bedford, 1966).

Soil temperatures can also have a significant
effect on the development of Fusarium blight. It has
been found that its severity on Kentucky bluegrass
growing at soil temperatures of 85 °F (30 °C) is much
greater than when the root system is at 70 °F (21 °C)
(Cutright and Harrison, 1970).

Fusarium blight is more severe on turf under
high nitrogen nutrition. Also, development of the disease is greater when the grass is grown at low levels
of available calcium (Figure 4-10) (Couch and Bedford, 1966; Bean, 1969; Cutright and Harrison, 1970).

Severe outbreaks of Fusarium blight have been
correlated with thick layers of thatch (Couch, 1976;
Partyka, 1976; Bean, 1976). It is generally thought
that this is primarily due to the buildup of inoculum
levels in the additional organic matter. However, it
has also been suggested that the various biochemical
and environmental changes that take place in the
crown and root zones during the decomposition of the
thatch could be predisposing the plants to more extensive colonization by the Fusarium blight pathogen (Smiley, Craven and Bruhn, 1980).

Organic matter buildup from clippings can also
bring about an increase in the incidence of Fusarium
blight. It has been found that under conditions of
very high nitrogen fertilization, the incidence of Fusarium blight in turf is much higher when the clippings are not removed (Turgeon, 1976).

Figure 4-10. Nutrition-induced changes in the relative susceptibility of (A) 'Highland' bentgrass and (B) 'Merion' Kentucky bluegrass to Fusarium blight.
1.0 H = normal balanced nutrition; 0.1 N = low nitrogen imbalanced nutrition; 0.1 Ca = low calcium imbalanced nutrition; 0.1 H = low balanced nutrition; 3.0 N = high nitrogen imbalanced nutrition. *After Couch, 1966.*

Soil moisture stress also has a significant effect on the development of Fusarium blight.

- The incidence and severity of Fusarium blight is greater when the soil moisture content is low (Keohane, 1967; Endo and Colbaugh, 1974).
- The impact of low soil moisture content on increasing the severity of Fusarium blight is even greater when the plants are growing at high nitrogen levels (Figure 4-11) (Cutright and Harrison; 1970).

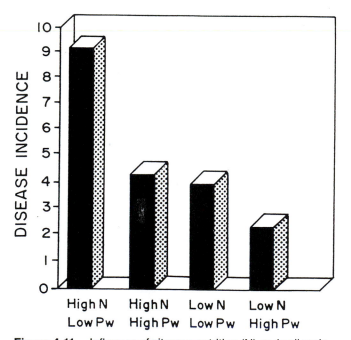

Figure 4-11. Influence of nitrogen nutrition (N) and soil moisture levels (Pw) in the readily available range on the incidence of Fusarium blight of 'Merion' Kentucky bluegrass. *After Cutright and Harrison, 1970.*

- When thatch remains air dry for an extended period of time, it contains a greater number of Fusarium spores than when it is kept moist (Endo and Colbaugh, 1974). Periods of low rainfall, therefore, not only make the plants more susceptible to Fusarium blight, they also create an ideal environment for the production of increased amounts of inoculum, thus increasing the number of infections.

The form of atmospheric moisture is also important to the development of severe outbreaks of Fusarium blight. The presence of free water on the leaf surfaces provides the condition that is necessary for germination of Fusarium spores; therefore, the length of time the leaves are wet is a principal factor in determining the number of leaf infections that will occur in any given period of time. The atmospheric conditions that result in the maximum development of Fusarium blight are an extended period of low rainfall combined with ground fogs or heavy dews which establishes and maintains free water on the leaf surfaces until late morning hours.

Control

Cultural Practices

Maximum effectiveness in the control of Fusarium blight can only be achieved through an integrated management program that combines certain cultural practices with the use of fungicides. The cultural practices should include operations that maintain the thatch at or below ½ inch (1.3 cm) thickness. Areas in which soil compaction is a problem should be subjected to core cultivation. Where feasible, clippings should be removed. During periods of high air temperatures, irrigation should be employed frequently enough to maintain the soil at field capacity (−0.033 MPa). High applications of nitrogen in the spring should be avoided. Also, in semiarid climates, seeding ratios of 15 percent or more of fine textured perennial ryegrasses and 85 percent Kentucky bluegrass by weight can bring about a decrease in the severity of Fusarium blight in established turf (Gibeault *et al.*, 1980).

As important as these various cultural practices are to the effective control of Fusarium blight, they will not in themselves provide a fully acceptable level of disease control. If a high level of Fusarium blight control is desired, then these operations must be used in conjunction with a fungicide program.

Use of Resistant Grasses

Ranked in order of susceptibility to Fusarium blight, the bentgrasses are the most prone to the disease. The Kentucky bluegrasses are next in susceptibility, with the fescues and perennial ryegrass being most resistant. Among certain varieties of Kentucky bluegrass, the range of susceptibility to *F. roseum* and *F. tricinctum* is determined by a complex interaction of air temperature and pathogen and host genotypes (Couch and Bedford, 1966). These types of interactions are illustrated in Table 4-4.

Use of Fungicides

Fusarium blight may be controlled by the use of either triadimefon, fenarimol, benomyl, or thiophanate methyl (Couch, Garber and Fox, 1979; Muse, 1971). For a profile of these fungicides and a listing of representative trade names and manufacturers, see Appendix Table I.

The most efficient use of these materials is made when they are applied on a preventive schedule. A simple rule of thumb for determining when to begin a preventive spray program for Fusarium blight control is based on night air temperatures. In areas with a history of recurring Fusarium blight, the fungicide application should be made immediately after the first occurrence of night temperatures that do not drop below 70 °F (21 °C) and continued on a 10–12 day schedule as long as these conditions persist.

Summer Patch

Summer patch is a destructive warm weather disease of Kentucky bluegrass (*Poa pratensis*), annual bluegrass (*Poa annua*) and fine fescues (*Festuca* spp.) in the United States. The disease was first observed in New York state in the late 1970's. Outbreaks of summer patch have since been reported from other north-eastern and certain mid-Atlantic states, throughout the Midwest, California, and Washington State.

The initial research on summer patch concentrated on its similarities and dissimilarities with Fusarium blight, and the possibility that the soil inhabiting fungi *Leptosphaeria korrae* and a species first thought to be *Phialophora graminicola* might be the incitants of the disease. During the late 1970s and early 1980s, researchers at Cornell University isolated numerous nonpathogenic species of Fusarium from the thatch and dead tissue of diseased plants collected from sites exhibiting circular patches of dead grass with tufts of apparently healthy plants in the centers (frogeyes) (Table 4-3). In several of these locations, they were unable to isolate either of the two Fusarium blight pathogens (*Fusarium culmorum*, *Fusarium poae*) (Couch, 1985b; Smiley and Craven, 1979; Smiley and Fowler, 1984a).

Further isolation efforts from Kentucky bluegrass turf exhibiting what the Cornell group was at that time calling the "Fusarium blight syndrome" yielded *Leptosphaeria korrae* and a species they were identifying as *Phialophora graminicola*. The Cornell workers then conducted a series of field and laboratory-based experiments testing the pathogenic potential of these two fungi. In 1984, and again in 1985, they reported that both species were capable of causing a warm weather patch disease of Kentucky bluegrass (Smiley and Fowler, 1984b; Smiley and Fowler, 1985).

Prior to the publication of the Cornell reports, researchers in Australia had reported that *Leptosphaeria korrae* could incite a cold weather patch disease of bermudagrass (*Cynodon dactylon*) (Walker and Smith, 1972). Where the pathogenic potential of *Phialophora graminicola* is concerned, earlier re-

Table 4-4. Relative pathogenicity of one isolate of *Fusarium poae* and two isolates of *Fusarium culmorum* to eight varieties of Kentucky bluegrass at three air temperatures. *After Couch and Bedford, 1966.*

Air Temperature	Fusarium Isolate[a]	Comparative Resistance[b]
75 °F (24 °C)	E-5	Delta = Newport = Troy = Park = Newport C-1 = Merion = Arboretum > Common
	E-24	Delta = Park = Merion = Newport C-1 = Troy = Common = Newport > Arboretum
	E-35	Merion = Newport = Newport C-1 > Common = Park = Arboretum = Delta = Troy
83 °F (28 °C)	E-5	Delta = Common = Troy = Park = Arboretum = Newport = Merion > Newport C-1
	E-24	Delta = Park = Newport = Troy = Newport C-1 = Merion = Common > Arboretum
	E-35	Park = Arboretum = Newport C-1 = Newport = Merion = Common > Delta = Troy
95 °F (35 °C)	E-5	Merion = Newport C-1 > Arboretum = Newport = Common > C-1 = Common > Merion
	E-24	Newport = Park = Arboretum > Delta > Troy = Newport C-1 = Common > Merion
	E-35	Newport C-1 = Merion = Newport > Common = Delta = Arboretum > Park = Troy

[1]E-5 = *Fusarium culmorum* isolated from Seaside bentgrass foliage.
E-24 = *Fusarium poae* isolated from Pennlawn red fescue seed.
E-35 = *Fusarium culmorum* isolated from Merion Kentucky bluegrass foliage.
[b]Comparative degrees of resistance based on Duncan's multiple range groups (p = .01).

search in Great Britain had shown that this species does not function as a primary parasite of turfgrass. Instead, the British researchers found that the colonization of roots by *Phialophora graminicola* is beneficial to the growth and development of turfgrass. These benefits include enhancing nutrient uptake by the plants and cross protecting the roots against infection and colonization by the take-all patch pathogen, *Gaeumannomyces graminis* (Scott, 1970; Deacon, 1973a; Deacon, 1973b).

In 1986, the Cornell workers reported that they had conducted additional research on the pathogenic potential of their isolates of *Phialophora graminicola* and had found that this fungus could only colonize Kentucky bluegrass roots that had been weakened by drought stress or high soil temperatures. As the result, they concluded that the organism they were testing was incapable of functioning as a primary pathogen on Kentucky bluegrass (Smiley and Giblin, 1986). That same year, researchers at the University of Wisconsin reported that *Leptosphaeria korrae* is the incitant of necrotic ring spot, a spring and fall patch disease of cool season turfgrasses (Worf, Stewart and Avenius, 1986).

While the Cornell studies were underway, a parallel investigation on the cause of summer patch was being conducted at the University of Rhode Island. The scope of the Rhode Island study included evaluations of the pathogenic potential of two fungal species they were isolating from the roots of Kentucky bluegrass afflicted with the disease, *Phialophora graminicola* and *Magnaporthe poae*. Their investigation corroborated the British findings that *Phialophora graminicola* is not a primary root pathogen. The tests with *Magnaporthe poae*, on the other hand, showed conclusively that it is the incitant of summer patch (Landschoot and Jackson, 1987).

During the course of their investigations, the Rhode Island researchers examined a culture of the fungus being used in the Cornell studies. They found that this organism was not *Phialophora graminicola*, as the Cornell group had supposed, but was instead an isolate of the summer patch pathogen, *Magnaporthe poae* (Landschoot and Jackson, 1987; Landschoot and Jackson, 1988).

In summary, by the end of the 1980s (a) the earlier research findings that only two species of Fusarium (*Fusarium culmorum* and *Fusarium poae*) incite Fusarium blight had been confirmed, (b) additional evidence had been given in support of previous research that had shown *Phialophora graminicola* is not a primary pathogen of turfgrass roots, (c) it had been determined that *Leptosphaeria korrae* is the incitant of necrotic ring spot, a spring and fall patch disease of cool season turfgrasses, and (d) it had been shown conclusively that the soil-borne fungus *Magnaporthe poae* is the incitant of summer patch. The establishment of these points on the etiology of this group of patch diseases provided the background needed to conduct definitive research on the comparative pathology and control of summer patch.

Symptoms

There are no distinctive leaf lesions associated with summer patch, however, during the early stages of disease development, white transverse heat stress bands are sometimes present on the leaves. Also, the leaves usually die back from the tip.

In overall view, summer patch is first seen on fairways and landscape turf as gray green, wilted patches 4–6 inches (10–15 cm) in diameter. These areas fade rapidly to a light brown color as the leaves wither and then die. The individual patches may expand up to 12 inches (30 cm). These areas often coalesce, involving large sections of turf. There may be locations within affected stands that exhibit the basic frogeye pattern of more or less circular patches of dead grass with center tufts of apparently unaffected plants. Crater pits (depressed circular patches) are common in diseased red fescue and sometimes in Kentucky bluegrass (Plate 8).

On golf greens with high populations of annual bluegrass, summer patch is usually first seen as more or less circular, reddish brown patches 2–3 inches (5–8 cm) in diameter. When conditions are favorable for the development of the disease, these individual patches may progress to 10–12 inches (25–30 cm). Bentgrasses typically grow in the centers of the patches, creating a frogeye pattern. When conditions are particularly favorable for the development of the disease, the individual patches will coalesce and envelope large areas of turf. Occasionally, large areas of dead grass will suddenly appear, with no previous indication of disease activity (Landschoot, Clarke and Jackson, 1989).

The roots and crowns of diseased plants often contain blackened, necrotic tissue. In advanced stages of disease development, entire roots and crowns may be blackened (Plate 8-F). This is in contrast with the reddish brown coloration that is characteristic of root and crown tissue affected by Fusarium blight (Plate 7-F).

Many of the field symptoms of summer patch are similar to those of Fusarium blight, necrotic ring spot, Rhizoctonia blight, and Pythium blight; therefore, positive diagnosis requires that a total laboratory work-up be performed on the root and crown tissue of the affected plants. If the condition is summer patch, the vascular tissue of the roots will often be discolored. Also, dark brown so-called "runner hyphae" is often present on the surface of the crowns and roots (Figure 4-12). The use of runner hyphae in diagnosis has its limitations. The incitant can grow within root tissue without producing extensive runner hyphae on the root surface. In addition, there are species of non-pathogenic fungi that also produce dark brown runner hyphae on grass roots. This means that using runner hyphae as the only criterion for diagnosing summer patch can lead to an incorrect conclusion.

Identification of *Magnaporthe poae* in culture is complicated by the fact that this species is a member of a group of fungi that have many asexual growth characteristics in common. Precise identification can only be accomplished by examination of its sexual fruiting structures (perithecia). The laboratory procedures used to produce perithecia requires several weeks.

The Fungus

Magnaporthe poae Landschoot and Jackson

Description

Perithecia gregarious or single, immersed, sometimes superficial, black; body globose, 252–556 µm in diameter; neck cylindrical, 357–756 µm long and 95–179 µm at widest point. Perithecial wall up to 47 µm thick composed of several layers of brown, radially compressed or isodiametric cells. External cells epidermoidal. Neck canal up to 40 µm in diameter, lined with hyaline upwardly pointed periphyses in

Figure 4-13. Perithecia of *Magnaporthe poae. Courtesy Noel Jackson.*

canal (Figure 4-13). Asci numerous, clavate, 63–108 µm long and 7–15 µm at widest point, cylindrical, short-stalked, straight or slightly curved, 8-spored, unitunicate, apex tapering but rounded, apical pore with nonamyloid refractive ring. Ascospores fusoid, 23–42 µm long and 4–6 µm in diameter, 3-septate at maturity, end cells hyaline, intermediate cells dark brown thick-walled and germinating from one or both hyaline cells (Figure 4-14). Paraphyses arising from hymenium between asci, hyaline, septate, sometimes branched, 64–112 µm long, 5–12 µm in diameter, near base tapering to 2–3 µm at tip. Superficial hyphae on host roots sparse, brown, septate, 2–5 µm in diameter, often with septa delimiting the lateral branches, single or in strands of 2–3 (Figure 4-12). Infection hyphae hyaline, slender, permeating root tissue. Swollen hyphal cells often fill cortical cells. Hyphopodia globose, occurring singly or in aggre-

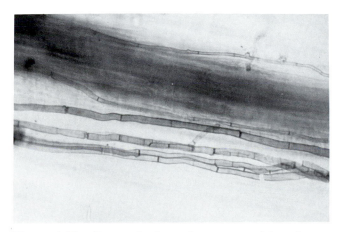

Figure 4-12. Runner hyphae of summer patch pathogen (*Magnaporthe poae*) on surface of turfgrass root. *Courtesy Noel Jackson.*

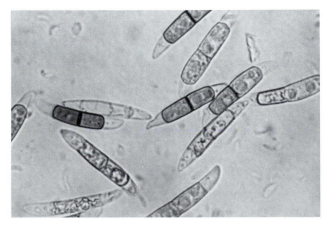

Figure 4-14. Ascospores of *Magnaporthe poae. Courtesy Noel Jackson.*

gates on stem bases or on roots, 6–12 μm in diameter (Landschoot and Jackson, 1989).

Procedures for Isolation and Culture

1. *Direct isolation*—The success rate of isolations of *Magnaporthe poae* is much greater when recently colonized tissue is used. Segments of young, recently colonized tissue should be placed in cheese cloth and washed in running tap water for 6 hours before plating. When possible, just prior to transferring the material to the agar plate, the cortical cells should be removed and the isolation performed directly from the underlying stele (Smiley, Kane and Craven-Fowler, 1985).

Magnaporthe poae grows well on half-strength potato dextrose agar (PDA) at 28–30 °C. On PDA, the mycelium is first appressed, initially hyaline, and then turns gray or olivaceous brown with dark, thick strands of mycelium radiating from the center of the colony. The hyphae at the periphery are wavy, and curl back toward the center of the colony. Older cultures (7–8 weeks) appear olivaceous brown or black. The conidia are hyaline, 3–8 μm long and 1–3 μm wide. Most are slightly curved, some are straight, and commonly rounded at both ends (Landschoot and Jackson, 1989).

Where direct isolation from diseased roots and crowns is concerned, *Magnaporthe poae* is often overgrown by other, faster growing, plant tissue and soil-inhabiting microorganisms. This problem can be alleviated to some extent by use of the modified Juhnke selective medium (Elliott, 1991). This medium contains 39 g Difco dehydrated potato dextrose agar, 100 mg of streptomycin, 10 mg of dichloran, 10 mg of metalaxyl, 50 mg of vinclozolin, 500 mg a.i. of L-DOPA (L-B-3,4-dihydroxyphenylalanine), and 1 mg of CGA-173506 (a phenylpyrolle available from CIBA-GEIGY Corp, Agricultural Div., Greensboro, NC 27419). Add dehydrated potato dextrose agar to distilled water and autoclave at 14 psi (120 °C) for 20 minutes, and then cool to 50 °C. The remaining compounds should first be placed in 10 ml sterile distilled water and this suspension added to the molten potato dextrose agar just prior to pouring the plates. On Juhnke medium, isolates of *Gaeumannomyces*-type fungi are distinguished by the diffusion of a dark brown pigment (melanin) into the agar (Juhnke, Mathre and Sands, 1983).

The telemorph of *Magnaporthe poae* is required for accurate identification of this species. Perithecia can be produced on acidified PDA by the use of paired compatible mating types (Landschoot and Jackson, 1989), or by the trap crop bioassay procedure described below.

2. *Indirect isolation*—This procedure consists of employing a trap crop bioassay. Trap cropping is a particularly useful method for isolating *Magnaporthe poae* when only plant tissue in advanced stages of deterioration is available.

The trap crop procedure is performed by placing several segments of diseased plant tissue at a depth of ½ inch (1 cm) in a pot of coarse sand and then planting a small number of wheat and red fescue seeds on the surface of the sand above the material to be assayed. The seed is then covered with a ½ inch (1 cm) layer of sand, and the pots incubated at 60–70 °F (15–20 °C). Growth of the fungus can usually be detected on the roots and tiller bases of the developing plants within 3–5 weeks from the time of seeding. The fungus can be isolated onto acidified PDA at this time (Scott, 1970; Smiley, Kane and Craven-Fowler, 1985).

Hosts

1. **Turfgrasses**—annual bluegrass (*Poa annua*), creeping bentgrass (*Agrostis palustris*), Kentucky bluegrass (*Poa pratensis*), hard fescue (*Festuca ovina* var. *duriuscula*), red fescue (*Festuca rubra*), Chewings fescue (*Festuca rubra* var. *commutata*), and perennial ryegrass (*Lolium perenne*).

2. **All Known Gramineous Hosts**—A listing of common names for the following species is given in Appendix Table IV. *Agrostis palustris* Huds., *Avena sativa* L., *Festuca ovina* var. *duriuscula* (L.) Koch, *F. rubra* L., *F. rubra* var. *commutata* Gaud., *Lolium perenne* L., *Poa annua* L., *Poa pratensis* L., *Triticum aestivum* L.

Disease Profile

The development of summer patch is favored by hot humid weather. Active colonization of turfgrass roots and crowns by *Magnaporthe poae* begins at soil temperatures in the 65–70 °F (18–21 °C) range, however, visible symptoms usually do not become evident until the air temperatures reach 85 °F (30 °C). The severity of the disease is greatest at air temperatures between 85–95 °F (30–35 °C). The optimum temperature range for the growth of the pathogen is 82–86 °F (28–30 °C). The strong impact of high temperatures on the development of summer patch is twofold. The temperatures that are ideal for the growth of the pathogen are also those that place heavy stress on the development of the roots of cool season turfgrasses. The increased growth rate of the fungus combined with the greater susceptibility of the root systems of the grass host to infection and colonization creates ideal conditions for increasing the severity of the disease (Landschoot, Clarke and Jackson, 1989).

It has been observed that summer patch is more severe on compacted soils and in areas receiving more foot traffic—such as the margins of golf greens and small greens. Turfgrasses with restricted root systems are also more prone to severe outbreaks of summer patch than turf with well developed roots (Landschoot, Clarke and Jackson, 1989).

The development of summer patch is also affected by mowing height. The disease has been found to be more severe on Kentucky bluegrass cut at 1½ inches (4 cm) than at 2¼ inches (6 cm) (Davis and Dernoeden, 1991). Nitrogen source also impacts on the development of the disease. It has been reported that summer patch is less severe in Kentucky bluegrass fertilized with sulfur coated urea than with urea, ammonium chloride, or sodium nitrate (Davis and Dernoeden, 1991). Unlike Fusarium blight, the development of summer patch is not favored by drought conditions—instead, the severity of summer patch is usually greater at high soil moisture levels (Kackley et al., 1990a; Kackely et al., 1990b).

Control

Cultural Practices

Since summer patch is primarily a root disease, management practices that permit good root development will aid in reducing its severity. Core aerification and improving drainage on compacted and poorly drained soils will lessen the intensity of the disease. Low mowing heights often result in shallower rooting; therefore, raising the height of cut can result in less summer patch injury. In areas where summer patch is a recurring problem, when use conditions permit, Kentucky bluegrass should be cut at 2¼ inches (6 cm) rather than 1½ inches (4 cm). Also, at the appearance of drought symptoms, irrigation schedules should be implemented that maintain adequate moisture to the depth of rooting (Davis and Dernoeden, 1991; Landschoot, Clarke and Jackson, 1989).

Reducing population levels of annual bluegrass and promoting the establishment and growth of bentgrass or perennial ryegrass will also result in less summer patch injury. In annual bluegrass-dependent situations, during periods of heat stress, summer patch damage can be lessened to some extent by syringing and raising the cutting height (Landschoot, Clarke and Jackson, 1989).

Use of Resistant Grasses

In general, annual bluegrass (*Poa annua*) and Kentucky bluegrass (*Poa pratensis*) are very susceptible to summer patch. The fine fescues (*Festuca* spp.) are moderately susceptible, and creeping bentgrass (*Agrostis palustris*) and perennial ryegrass (*Lolium perenne*) are highly resistant to the disease.

Use of Fungicides

Propiconozole, triadimefon, cyproconazole, fenarimol, benomyl, and thiophanate methyl have been reported to control summer patch (Landschoot and Clarke, 1989). For a profile of these fungicides and a listing of representative trade names and manufacturers, see Appendix Table I.

Summer patch often causes significant damage to the root system from four to six weeks before the appearance of above ground symptoms. For this reason, fungicide applications must be made at least one month before patch formation is evident. A simple method for determining when to begin a preventive fungicide program for summer patch control is based on daytime soil temperatures. In areas with a history of recurring summer patch, in the spring the soil temperature should be monitored at a depth of 2–4 inches (5–10 cm) during the hottest part of the day (2:00–3:00 p.m.). The first treatment should be made when this temperature reaches 65 °F (18 °C) on two consecutive days. This application should be followed with two additional treatments at four week intervals.

In order to obtain maximum control, the fungicide must be applied in 5 to 10 gallons (19–38 liters) of water per 1,000 ft² (93 m²) (Figures 4-15, 4-16). If the application is made at 5 gallons (19 liters) or less per 1,000 ft² (93 m²), the turf should then be syringed or irrigated with ¼–½ inches (10–20 cm) water before the leaves dry.

Spiking or coring can help facilitate movement of the fungicide into the root zone. Also, the fungicide will move more readily through soils that are initially moist (but not saturated) than through soils that are dry at the time of application (Landschoot, Clarke and Jackson, 1989).

Pythium Blight

Pythium blight is a major disease of warm season and cool season turfgrass in United States, Canada, Germany, France, and Japan. Under favorable environmental conditions, the Pythium blight pathogen(s) may bring about the destruction of all of the foliage of an established stand of grass within 24 hours from the first appearance of visible disease symptoms. In

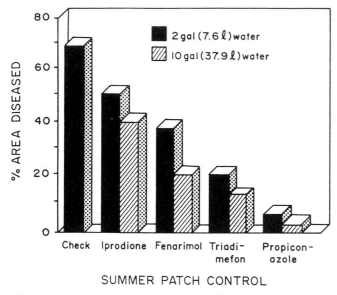

SUMMER PATCH CONTROL

Figure 4-15. Relationship between dilution rate and the effectiveness of propiconazole, triadimefon, fenarimol, and iprodione in the control of summer patch. *After Landschoot and Clarke, 1989.*

the aftermath of a severe outbreak of Pythium blight, it is often necessary to completely re-establish the desired turfgrass species.

Symptoms

In overall view, Pythium blight is first seen as small, irregularly shaped, purplish areas ranging from 1–4 inches (2.5–10 cm) in diameter. The individual leaves in these patches have a dark, water-soaked appearance As colonization by the fungus progresses, they become soft and slimy, and when they come in contact with each other, they mat together.

In the early morning hours, or if conditions of high humidity exist throughout the day, the leaves of diseased plants may be covered with the white, cobwebby, mycelium of the pathogen. Also during these times the older patches often develop dark purplish borders up to 1 inch (2.5 cm) wide (Plate 15).

The color of the affected leaves soon changes to light brown or reddish brown, and they become dry and shriveled. In the event the growth of the pathogen is checked before the entire leaf is colonized, distinct straw-colored lesions of varying size will develop. In general appearance, these lesions are similar to those incited by the Sclerotinia dollar spot pathogen, with the exception that the reddish margins characteristic of the latter disease are absent.

The blighting of the foliage within the developing patches may be uniform, or the affected areas

may develop as frogeyes—circles of blighted grass with centers of green, apparently healthy plants. As the disease progresses, individual patches of affected grass frequently coalesce to envelop sections of turf ranging from 1–10 feet (0.3–3 meters) in diameter (Plate 14). At times, rather than being circular to ovular in shape, the affected areas may develop as elongate streaks. Those streaks may or may not be serpentine in outline. Development of this pattern of blighting is apparently the result of the pathogen being washed over the surface of the soil. Consequently, the presence and general conformity of these streaks are determined for the most part by the surface water drainage pattern of the area.

The Fungi

A. *Pythium aphanidermatum* (Edson) Fitzpatrick; Syn. *P. butleri* Subrm.

Description

Mycelium well developed on cornmeal agar; hyphae branched, 2–8 μm in diameter; sporangia filamentous, composed of a moderately lobulated, inflated mass of branches cut off by cross walls from the remainder of the mycelium, with long or short discharge tubes. Zoospores averaging 9 μm, reniform, difficult to induce on artificial substrate. Oogonia

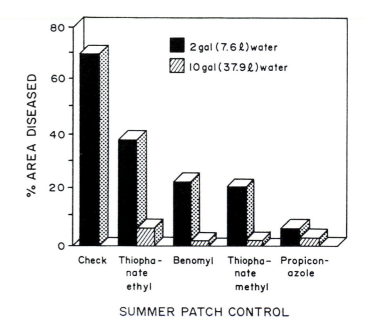

SUMMER PATCH CONTROL

Figure 4-16. Relationship between dilution rate and the effectiveness of propiconazole, benomyl, thiophanate ethyl, and thiophanate methyl in the control of summer patch. *After Landschoot and Clarke, 1989.*

smooth, spherical, terminal, averaging 22 µm in diameter; oospores spherical, smooth, not filling the oogonium 12–25 µm in diameter, averaging about 17.5 µm. Broadly appressed, moderately swollen antheridia frequently produced immediately adjacent to oogania but often an adjacent antheridium fertilizes some more distant oogonium.

Hosts

1. **Turfgrasses**—annual bluegrass (*Poa annua*), Kentucky bluegrass (*Poa pratensis*), bermudagrass (*Cynodon dactylon*), creeping bentgrass (*Agrostis palustrus*), Colonial bentgrass (*Agrostis tenuis*), tall fescue (*Festuca arundinacea*), red fescue (*Festuca rubra*).
2. **All Known Gramineous Hosts**—A listing of common names for the following species is given in Appendix Table IV. *Agrostis alba* L., *A. canina* L., *A. palustris* Huds., *A. tenuis* Sibth., *Cynodon dactylon* (L.) Pers., *C. magennisii* Hurcombe, *C. transvaalensis* Burtt-Davy, *Festuca arundinacea* Schreb., *F. rubra* L., *Lolium perenne* L., *L. multiflorum* Lam., *Poa annua* L., *Poa pratensis* L., *P. trivialis* L., *Saccharium officinarum* L., *Zea mays* L. (Freeman and Horn, 1963; Index Plant Dis., 1960).

The Fungi

B. *Pythium arrhenomanes* Drechsl.

Description

Mycelium intra-and intercellular, hyphae measuring 2.0–5.5 µm in diameter. Sporangia inflated, filamentous, lobulate, forming complexes of elements up to 20 µm or more in diameter, zoospores 20–50 or more in a vesicle borne on an evacuation tube usually 3–4 µm in diameter and of variable length, up to 75 µm, biciliate, measuring approximately 12 µm in diameter upon encystment. Oogonia subspherical to spherical, occasionally intercalary, walls smooth and thin, measuring 17.3–56.3 µm, mean 30.1 µm, in diameter. Antheridia of dielinous origin, numerous, 15–25 often visible, usually borne terminally though occasionally laterally on 4–8 branches each usually contributing up to 4 antheridia, antheridial cells are crook-necked, 6–9 µm wide and 12–15 µm long, making narrow contact with the oogonium. Oospores plerotic, 15.5–54.2 µm, mean 28.2 µm in diameter, wall 1.2–2.0 µm, (usually 1.6 µm) thick, containing a single reserve globule.

Hosts

1. **Turfgrasses**—Kentucky bluegrass (*Poa pratensis*), tall fescue (*Festuca arundinacea*), red fescue (*Festuca rubra*), St. Augustinegrass (*Stenotaphrum secundatum*).
2. **All Known Gramineous Hosts**—A listing of the common names for the following species is given in Appendix Table IV. *Aegilops triuncialis* L., *Agropyron angustiglume* Nevksi, *A. ciliare* (Trin.) Franch, *A. cristatum* (L.) Gaertn., *A. elongatum* (Host) Beauv., *A. inerme* (Scribn and Sm.) Rydb., *A. intermedium* (Host) Beauv., *A. michnoi* Roshev., *A. mongolicum* Keng, *A. orientale* var. *lasianthum* (Boiss) Boiss, *A. repens* (L.) Beauv., *A. riparium* Scribn. and Smith, *A. semicostatum* (Steud.) Nees, *A. sibiricum* (Willd.) Beauv., *A. spicatum* (Pursh) Scribn. amd Smith, *A. trachycaulum* (Lk.) Malte, *A. trichophorum* (Lk.) Richt., *Agrostis alba* L., *Ammophila arenaria* (L.) Lk., *Andropogon furcatus* Muhl., *Aristida purpurea* Nutt., *Arrhenatherum elatius* (L) Presl, *Avena byzantina* K. Koch, *A. fatua* L., *A. nuda* L., *A. sativa* L., *Bouteloua curtipendula* (Michx.) Torr., *B. gracilis* (H.B.K.) Lag., *Bromus arvensis* L., *B. brizaeformis* Fisch. and Mey., *B. carinatus* Hook and Arn., *B. erectus* Huds., *B. inermis* Leyss., *B. japonicus* Thunb., *B. madritensis* L., *B. pumpellianus* Scribn., *B. tectorum* L., *Calamovilfa longifolia* (Hook.) Scribn., *Cenchrus pauciflorus* Benth., *Dactylis glomerata* L., *Echinochloa crusgalli* (L.) Beauv., *Elymus canadensis* L., *E. condensatus* Presl, *E. dahuricus* Turcz, *E. glaucus* Buckl., *E. interruptus* Buckl., *E. junceus* Fisch., *E. macounii* Vasey, *E. sibiricus* L., *E. virginicus* L., *Eragrostis cilianensis* (All.) Lutati, *E. curvula* (Schrad.) Nees, *Festuca arundinacea* Schreb., *F. idahoensis* Elmer, *F. kingii* (S. Wats.) Casidy, *F. octoflora* Walt., *F. rubra* L., *Hordeum brevisubulatum* (Trin.) Lk., *H. distichon* L., *H. jubatum* L., *H. murinum* L., *H. vulgare* L., *Melica scabrosa* Trin., *Muhlenbergia racemosa* (Michx.) B.S.P., *Oryza sativa* L., *Oryzopsis hymenoides* (Roem. and Schult.) Rick., *Panicum capillare* L., *P. miliaceum* L., *P. purpurascens* Raddi, *P. subvillosum* Ashe, *P. virgatum* L., *Phalaris arundinacea* L., *Phleum pratense* L., *Poa compressa* L., *P. juncifolia* Scribn., *P. nevadensis* Vasey, *P. palustris* L., *P. pratensis* L, *P. secunda* Presl, *Redfieldia flexuosa* (Thurb.) Vassey, *Saccharum barberi* Jesweit, *S. officinarum* L., *S. spontaneum* L., *Schedonnardus paniculatus* (Nutt.) Trel., *Scolochloa festucacea* Willd., *Secale cereale* L., *Setaria italica* (L.) Beauv., *S. lutescens* (Weigel) Hubb., *Sorghastrum nutans* (L.) Nash, *Sorghum vulgare* Pers., *S. valgare* var. *sudanense* (Piper) Hitchc., *Sphenopholis obtusata* (Michx.) Scribn., *Sporobolus cryptandrus* (Torr.) A. Gray, *Stenotaphrum secundatum* (Walt.) Kuntze, *Stipa*

baicalensis Roshev., *S. comata* Trin. and Rupr., *S. sibririca* (L.) Lam., *S. spartea* Trin., *Triticum aestivum* L.,*T. dicoccum* Schrank, *T. durum* Desf., *T. timopheevi* Zhukov., *Uniola latifolia* Michx., *Zea mays* L. (Sprague, 1950; Index Plant Dis., 1960; Middleton, 1943).

The Fungi

C. *Pythium graminicola* Subrum.

Description

Antheridia are monoclinous, arising rather close to (within 60 μm) to the oogonium, antheridial cells few, 1–6, usually 2–4, and irregularly arranged about the oogonium. This is in contrast with *Pythium arrhenomanes* in which the antheridia are diclinous and have no discernible connection with the oogonial stalk, and the antheridial cells are numerous, 1–25 (usually in excess of 8) and fairly regularly arranged about the oogonium. *Pythium graminicolum* usually fruits in culture in moderate abundance on ordinary culture media, the antheridia and oogonia retaining their identity many weeks after fecundation has occurred. *Pythium arrhenomanes*, on the other hand, fruits sparingly on ordinary culture media, the antheridia and oogonia losing their identity soon after fecundation has taken place.

Hosts

1. **Turfgrasses**—creeping bentgrass (*Agrostis palustris)*, Colonial bentgrass (*Agrostis tenuis*), Kentucky bluegrass (*Poa pratensis*), tall fescue (*Festuca arundinacea*), red fescue (*Festuca rubra*), perennial ryegrass (*Lolium perenne*), St. Augustinegrass (*Stenotaphrum secundatum*).
2. **All Known Gramineous Hosts**—A listing of the common names for the following species is given in Appendix Table IV. *Aegilops triuncialis* L., *Agropyron angustiglume* Nevski, *A. ciliare* (Trin.) Franch, *A. cristatum* (L.) Gaertn., *A. elongatum* (Host) Beauv., *A. inerme* (Scribn. and Smith) Rydb., *A. intermedium* (Host) Beauv., *A. michnoi* Roshev., *A. mongolicum* Keng, *A. orientale* var. *lasianthum* (Boiss) Boiss, *A. repens* (L.) Beauv., *A. riparium* Scribn. and Smith, *A. semicostatum* (Steud.) Nees, *A. sibiricum* (Willd.) Beauv., *A. spicatum* (Pursh) Scribn. and Smith, *A. trachycaulum* (Lk.) Malte, *A. trichophorum* (Lk.) Richt., *Agrostis alba* L., *A. palustris* Huds., *A. tenuis* Sibth.,*Ammophila arenaria* (L.) Lk., *Andropogon furcatus* Muhl., *Aristida purpurea* Nutt., *Arrhenatherum elatius* (L.) Presl, *Avena byzantina* K.

Koch, *A. fatua* L., *A. nuda* L., *A. sativa* L., *Bouteloua curtipendula* (Michx.) Torr., *B. gracilis* (H.B.K.) Lag., *Bromus arvensis* L., *B. brizaeformis* Fisch. and Mey., *B. carinatus* Hook. and Arn., *B. erectus* Huds., *B. inermis* Leyss., *B. japonicus* Thunb., *B. madritensis* L., *B. pumpellianus* Scribn., *B. tectorum* L., *Calamovilfa longifolia* (Hook.) Scribn., *Cenchrus pauciflorus* Benth., *Dactylis glomerata* L., *Echinochloa crusgalli* (L.), Beauv., *Elymus canadensis* L., *E. condensatus* Presl, *E. dahuricus* Turcz., *E. glaucus* Buckl., *E. interruptus* Buckl., *E. junceus* Fisch., *E. mauconii* Vasey, *E. sibiricus* L., *E. virginicus* L., *Eragrostis cilianensis* (All.) Lutati, *Festuca kingii* (S. Wats.) Casidy. *F. octoflora* Walt., *F. rubra* L., *Hordeum brevisubulatum* (Trin.) Lk., *H. distichon* L., *H. jubatum* L., *H. murinum* L., *H. vulgare* L., *Lolium perenne* L., *Melica scabrosa* Trin., *Muhlenbergia racemosa* (Michx.) B.S.P., *Orysa sativa* L., *Oryzopsis hymenoides* (Roem. and Schult.) Rick., *Panicum capillare* L., *P. miliaceum* L., *P. purpurascens* Raddi, *P. subvillosum* Ashe, *P. virgatum* L., *Phalaris arundinacea* L., *Phleum pratense* L., *Poa compressa* L., *P. juncifolia* Scribn., *P. nevadensis* Vasey, *P. palustris* L., *P. pratensis* L., *P. secunda* Presl, *Redfieldia flexuosa* (Thurb.) Vasey, *Saccharum barberi* Jesweit, *S. officinarum* L., *S. spontaneum* L., *Schedonnardus paniculatus* (Nutt.) Trel., *Scolochloa festucacea* Willd., *Secale cereale* L., *Setaria italica* (L.) Beauv., *S. lutescens* (Weigel) Hubb., *Sorghastrum nutans* (L.) Nash, *Sorghum vulgare* Pers., *S. vulgare* var. *sudanense* (Piper) Hitchc., *Sphenopholis obtusata* (Michx.) Scribn., *Sporobolus cryptandrus* (Torr.) A. Gray, *Stenotaphrum secundatum* (Walt.) Kuntze, *Stipa baicalensis* Roshev., *S. comata* Trin. and Rupr., *S. sibirica* Lam., *S. spartea* Trin., *Triticum aestivum* L., *T. durum* Desf., *T. timopheevi* Zhukov., *Uniola latifolia* Michx., *Zea mays* L. (Middleton, 1943; Saladini and White, 1975; Saladini, Schmitthenner and Larsen, 1983; Muse, Schmitthenner and Partyka, 1974; Sprague, 1950).

The Fungi

D. *Pythium myriotylum* Drechsler

Description

Hyphae measuring 2.5–8.5 μm in diameter, when young mostly 3–4 μm, when old mostly 7–8.5 μm in diameter forming numerous clavate or knob-like appressoria measuring 7–11 μm in diameter. Sporangia terminal or intercalary, sometimes undifferentiated though generally including an inflated filamentous lobulate or digitate lateral element, the undifferentiated portions measuring 0.1–0.5 mm long and 3–7 μm in diameter, the inflated portions of variable size, 10–175 μm in length and 12 μm in diameter; evacuation tube arising either from the undifferentiated or inflated portion, 10–100 μm and 2–3.5 μm wide; 3–40 zoospores formed in the apical vesicle, reniform and laterally biciliate, 9–16 μm, average 11 μm, in diameter, germinating by a single germ tube. Oogonia spherical to subsperical, wall smooth and thin, terminal or interclary, measuring 15–44 μm, average 26.5 μm, in diameter. Antheridia typically diclinous, when monoclinous usually originating in excess of 100 μm from the oogonium, 1–10, usually 3–6, per oogonium, the antheridial cell terminally expanded, clavate, crook-necked, arched, measuring 8–30 μm long and 4–8 μm wide, the apex making narrow apical contact with the oogonial wall, the middle arched upward and the proximal end frequently contacting the oogonial wall. Oospores apleorotic, single, with a wall 1–2 μm thick, containing a single reserve globule and a subspherical or strongly flattened refringent body, oospores measuring 12–37 μm, average 20.8 μm, in diameter.

Hosts

1. **Turfgrasses**—creeping bentgrass (*Agrostis palustris*), perennial ryegrass (*Lolium perenne*), annual ryegrass (*Lolium multiflorum*).
2. **All Known Gramineous Hosts**—A listing of common names for the following species is given in Appendix Table IV. *Agrostis palustris* Huds., *Avena sativa* L., *Lolium multiflorum* Lam., *L. perenne* L., *Secale cereale* L., *Triticum aestivum* L. (Farr *et al.*, 1989; McCarter and Litrell, 1968; Saladini, 1980).

The Fungi

E. *Pythium ultimum* Trow.

Description

Mycelium well developed on media, branched, septate in old cultures, 1.7–6.5 μm (average 3.8 μm). Conidia usually terminal and spherical 12–28 μm in diameter (average 20 μm), intercalary, barrel-shaped forms, 14–22.9 μm × 17–27.8 μm, also formed in cultures; conidial germination direct, zoospores not formed. Oogonia smooth, usually terminal, rarely intercalary, spherical, 19.6–22.9 μm in diameter (average 20.6 μm). Oospores not filling the oogonium, spherical 14.7–18.3 μm in diameter (average 16.3

μm), in mature stage with a heavy wall and a central reserve globule surrounded by a granular layer of protoplasm in which a small refractive body is embedded; germination is directed by 1 or more germ tubes. Antheridia usually 1 to an oogonium arising from the oogonial stalk immediately below the oogonium.

Hosts

1. **Turfgrasses**—annual bluegrass (*Poa annua*), Kentucky bluegrass (*Poa pratensis*), creeping bentgrass (*Agrostis palustris*), velvet bentgrass (*Agrostis canina*), Colonial bentgrass (*Agrostis tenuis*), tall fescue (*Festuca arundinacea*), red fescue (*Festuce rubra*), annual ryegrass (*Lolium multiflorum*), perennial ryegrass (*Lolium perenne*).
2. **All Known Gramineous Hosts**—A listing of the common names for each of the following species is geven in Appendix Table IV. *Agropyron caninum* (L) Beauv., *A. cristatum* (L.) Gaertn., *A. desertorum* (Fisch.) Schult., *A. inerme* (Scribn. and Smith) Rydb., *A. intermedium* (Host) Beauv., *A. repens* (L.) Beauv., *A. semicostatum* (Steud.) Nees, *A. smithii* Rydb., *A. trachycaulum* (Link) Malte, *A. trichophorum* (Link) Richt., *Agrostis alba* L., *A. canina* L., *A. palustris* Huds., *A. tenuis* Sibth., *Alopecurus pratensis* L. *Arrhenatherum elatius* (L.) Presl, *Avena sativa* L., *Axonopus affinis* Chase, *Bouteloua curtipendula* (Michx.) Torr., *Bromus arvensis* L., *B. carinatus* Hook. and Arn., *B. erectus* Huds., *B. inermis* Leyss., *B. mollis* L., *Cynodon dactylon* (L.) Pers., *Dactylis glomerata* L., *Elymus canadensis* L., *E. dahuricus* Turcz., *E. junceus* Fisch., *E. virginicus* L., *Eragrostis chloromelas* Steud., *E. curvula* (Schrad.) Nees, *E. lehmanniana* Nees, *E. superba* Peyr., *Festuca arundinacea* Schreb., *F. rubra* L. *Hordeum vulgare* L., *Lolium multiflorum* Lam., *L. perenne* L., *L. subulatum* Vis., *Oryza sativa* L., *Oryzopsis miliacea* (L.) Benth. and Hook., *Panicum antidotale* Retz., *P. miliaceum* L., *P. virgatum* L., *Phleum pratense* L., *Phragmites communis* Trin., *Poa annua* L., *P. canbyi* (Scribn.) Piper, *P. compressa* L., *P. pratensis* L., *P. secunda* Presl. *Saccharum officinarum* L., *Secale cereale* L., *Setaria glauca* Beauv., *S. italica* (L.) Beavu., *Sorghum almum* L., *S. halepense* (L.) Pers., *S. sudanense* (Piper) Stapf, *S. vulgare* Pers., *Sporobolus airoides* (Torr.) Torr., *S. cryptandrus* (Torr.) A. Gray, *Stipa cernua* Stebbins and Love, *S. viridula* Trin., *Triticum aestivum* L., *T. durum* Desf., *Zea mays* L., (Freeman and Horn, 1963; Index Plant Dis., 1960; Middleton, 1943; Monteith, 1933; Moore and Couch, 1961).

Procedures for Isolation and Culture

1. **Isolation from plant tissue**—Sodium hypochlorite is highly toxic to Pythium; therefore, it should not be used in the washing solution. Instead, prior to plating, the affected tissue should either be washed with water containing a nontoxic wetting agent, such as Tween-20™, or wrapped in cheese cloth and immersed in freely running tap water for 4–6 hours.

   Pythium species grow well on nutritionally weak media such as water agar or dilute synthetic sucrose-asparagine agar (Table 4-5). The use of rich media such as potato dextrose agar or cornmeal agar for the initial plating of the tissue will maximize the incidence of fungal and bacterial contaminations in the plates. Also, Pythium does not sporulate well on nutritionally rich media. Therefore, by using nutritionally weak media for the initial platings, it is often possible to identify species directly on the isolation plates (Schmitthenner, 1980).

   The optimum *in vitro* growth temperature for each species is as follows: *Pythium aphanidermatum*, 34°C; *Pythium arrhenomanes*, 28°C; *Pythium graminicolum*, 28°C; *Pythium myriotylum*, 34°C; *Pythium torulosum*, 28°C; *Pythium ultimum*, 28°C; *Pythium vanterpooli*, 25°C (Middleton, 1943; Kouyeas and Kouyeas, 1963).

2. **Procedures for inducing sporulation**—Media that are nutritionally deficient are best suited for the development of sporangia and oospores. Liquid or semi-solid media are better than solid media for the development of sporangia. Semi-solid media are prepared by using 3 g of plain agar (Difco) per liter of formulation.

Among the nutritionally deficient formulations, Schmitthenner's grass leaf-salt medium is favorable to sporulation by several Pythium species. This medium is prepared by autoclaving 2-cm sections of Kentucky bluegrass (*Poa pratensis*) or creeping bentgrass (*Agrostis palustris*) leaves for 10 minutes in test tubes containing 20 ml salt solution (Table 4-6) and 0.06 g Difco agar.

Another procedure for inducing oospore formation consists of placing 15 gm of fresh Kentucky bluegrass leaves in a 1000 ml Erlenmeyer flask and then adding 500 ml of distilled water. The flask is then autoclaved for 45 minutes under 20 psi (121°C), allowed to cool for 24 hours and then re-autoclaved as before. The cooled supernatant is then decanted into flasks or bottles to give a large surface area-volume ratio. Discs 1 cm in diameter of *Pythium* mycelium growing on corn meal agar are then placed in the bluegrass broth and incubated in the dark at 22°C. Oospores will usually develop in about 3–4 weeks (Kobriger and Hagedorn, 1981).

Disease Profile

The species of *Pythium* that incite Pythium blight grow saprophytically in the thatch and soil of stands of turfgrass. However, under adverse climatic conditions, the mycelia and zoospores are short lived. After active growth ceases, long term survival is achieved by means of dormant oospores and/or sporangia in the thatch and soil, and in the tissue of living plants that had become infected and colonized during the previous growing season (Hall, Larsen and Schmitthenner, 1980; Schmitthenner, 1980).

The primary means of local spread of the Pythium blight pathogens is by growth of mycelium

Table 4-5. Selective medium for isolation of Pythium species. *After Schmitthenner, 1980.*

Component	Amount
Sucrose	2.40 g
Asparagine	0.27 g
KH_2PO_4	0.15 g
K_2HPO_4	0.15 g
$MgSO_4 7H_2$	0.10 g
Cholesterol (2 ml N, N-Dimethyl formamide solution)	0.01 g
Benlate™ (50% benomyl)	0.02 g
Terraclor™ (75% PCNB)	0.027 g
Neomycin sulfate	0.10 g
Chloramphenicol	0.01 g
Agar (Difco™)	20.00 g
Distilled water	1,000 ml

Table 4-6. Grass leaf-salt medium for inducing *in vitro* sporulation of Pythium species. *After Schmitthenner, 1980.*

Component	Amount
Solution A:	
Distilled water	950 ml
KH_2PO_4	0.075 g
K_2HPO_4	0.075 g
$MgSO_4 7H_2O$	0.050 g
$FeSO_4 7H_2O$	0.0005 g
Solution B:	
Distilled Water	50 ml
$Ca(NO_3)_2 2H_2O$	0.100 g

Prepare solutions A and B separately and mix before using.

from plant to plant. Under conditions favorable for disease development, the rate of this movement can be very rapid. Dissemination over greater distances is accomplished by the relocation of infested thatch and soil and diseased plant parts on maintenance equipment, and by the passive movement of mycelial fragments and zoospores in freely flowing surface water.

The infection of leaf, crown and root tissue is accomplished by direct mycelial penetration. The highest frequency of infections occur during extended periods of leaf wetness brought on by either rainfall, high atmospheric humidity in the foliar zone, dew formation, or night and morning ground fogs. Infections begin when the air temperature reaches 65 °F (18 °C) and increase in incidence as the temperature rises, reaching their maximum at 85–90 °F (29–32 °C). Foliar blighting develops most rapidly when the air temperatures are in the 85–95 °F (29–35 °C) range (Table 4-7) (Freeman, 1960; Moore, Couch and Bloom, 1963; Saladini, 1980).

Weather conditions that normally precede outbreaks of severe Pythium blight are (a) daytime air temperatures of 86 °F (30 °C) or greater and (b) nighttime air temperatures of 68 °F (20 °C) or above in combination with fifteen or more consecutive hours in which the relative humidity is 90 percent or higher (Nutter, Cole and Schein, 1983).

The susceptibility of bentgrass to *Pythium aphanidermatum* increases significantly when the plants are being grown at high soil salinity. Because of this increased susceptibility, under conditions of high soil salinity, outbreaks of Pythium blight can occur at air temperatures and atmospheric humidities much lower than those thought to be favorable for disease development. Salinity levels in turfgrass management rarely are static. Instead, they may fluctuate considerably during the course of a year, depending on frequency and duration of irrigations, water quality, soil permeability, and syringing cycles. As the result, in arid climates, these periods of high soil salinity can bring about sporadic outbreaks of Pythium blight during weather conditions that would not normally be considered conducive to the development of the disease (Rasmussen and Stanghellini, 1988).

Bentgrass is more susceptible to *Pythium ultimum* when grown at low soil moisture contents, as compared with plants held near field capacity (−0.033 MPa) by more frequent irrigations (Figure 4-17). When compared with plants grown under normal-balanced or high nitrogen fertility at pH 5.6, those produced at low-balanced fertility are more resistant to the pathogen. Calcium nutrition greatly influences disease development. Plants grown under conditions of deficient calcium are more susceptible to *Pythium ultimum* than when the element is in inadequate supply. With normal or high balanced fertility, disease development is greater at alkaline soil conditions; however, when the overall fertility is low, soil reaction does not alter susceptibility (Moore, Couch and Bloom, 1963).

Four pectolytic enzymes are involved in the blighting of bentgrass foliage by *Pythium ultimum*. These are polymethylgalacturonase, a polygalacturonase, a pectin methyl-*trans*-eliminase, and a polygalacturonate-*trans*-eliminase. It also has been found that pectolytic enzyme activity was greater in the leaves of bentgrass grown under low calcium nutrition (Moore, Couch and Bloom, 1968). This explains in part at least the increased susceptibility bentgrass to *Pythium ultimum* at low calcium levels.

The colonization of ryegrass by *Pythium aphanidermatum* is more severe on ryegrass in the seedling stage of growth. While studies have shown that older plants are more resistant to the pathogen than are juvenile plants, its limitation to the seedling phase of

Table 4-7.   Principal air temperatures for maximum blighting of turfgrass leaves by various Pythium species

Pythium Species	Grasses Affected
A. Cool Weather (55–65 °F; 13–18 °C)	
Pythium torulosum	creeping bentgrass, Colonial bentgrass, red fescue
Pythium vanterpoolii	creeping bentgrass, Colonial bentgrass, red fescue
B. Warm Weather (85–95 °F; 30–35 °C)	
Pythium aphanidermatum	annual bluegrass, Kentucky bluegrass, bermudagrass, creeping bentgrass, Colonial bentgrass, tall fescue, red fescue
Pythium arrhenomanes	Kentucky bluegrass, tall fescue, red fescue, St. Augustinegrass
Pythium graminicola	creeping bentgrass, Colonial bentgrass, Kentucky bluegrass, tall fescue, red fescue, perennial ryegrass, St. Augustinegrass
Pythium myriotylum	creeping bentgrass, annual ryegrass, perennial ryegrass
Pythium ultimum	annual bluegrass, Kentucky bluegrass, Colonial bentgrass, creeping bentgrass, tall fescue, red fescue, annual ryegrass, perennial ryegrass

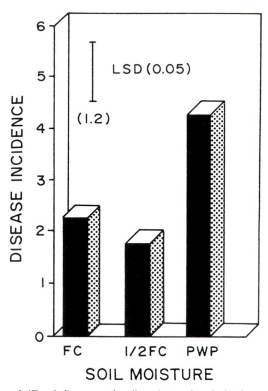

Figure 4-17. Influence of soil moisture levels in the readily available range on the development of Pythium blight [FC = field capacity (−0.033 MPa), PWP = permanent wilting percentage (−1.5 MPa)]. *After Moore, Couch and Bloom, 1963.*

ryegrass growth in certain locations is actually caused by changing climatic conditions that limit disease development (Freeman, 1963).

Control

Cultural Practices

A management program that brings about the highest level of resistance to Pythium blight on the part of the turfgrass suscept is one that (a) provides irrigations with short enough intervening time intervals to hold the soil in the root zone near field capacity levels, (b) maintains satisfactory, but not luxuriant, plant growth through the use of balanced fertilizer applications, and (c) holds the soil reaction in the acid range. It is important to remember, however, that in the absence of treatment of the affected areas with fungicides, this program will not provide total control of the disease.

Management practices that decrease the length of time the leaves are wet will aid in reducing the incidence of Pythium blight. One such practice is the early morning removal of dew and guttation water from putting greens by poling or by dragging a water hose across them. The duration of the periods of daily leaf wetness can also be reduced by two to four hours by following a nighttime watering schedule in which the irrigation system is set to begin at least three hours after sunset and programmed to be completed before sunrise (see Chapter 16, Figure 16-2).

Use of Fungicides

Since significant alterations in incidence and severity of Pythium blight can be brought on by various levels of soil fertility, if a fungicide program for the control of the disease is to be consistent in its effectiveness, it must be worked out in close concert with the fertilizer program. Also, once the overall program is in place, it may become necessary to adjust the fungicide program to compensate for nutritionally-induced changes in the plants vulnerability to the disease. For example, short term increases in the nitrogen fertilization of a bentgrass putting green during weather conditions that are conducive to outbreaks of Pythium blight may also call for an increase in the dosage levels and frequency of application of fungicides.

Applications of the non-Pythium active fungicides benomyl and thiophanate methyl have been shown to increase the susceptibility of creeping bentgrass to *Pythium aphanidermatum* (Warren, Sanders and Cole, 1976).

Pythium blight may be controlled by single component applications of either metalaxyl, propamocarb, fosetyl Al, ethazole, chloroneb, or mancozeb. The following two-component fungicide combinations have been shown to be synergistic in the control of Pythium blight incited by *Pythium aphanidermatum*: (a) mancozeb + metalaxyl, (b) mancozeb + propamocarb, (c) propamocarb + fosetyl Al, and (d) metalaxyl + propamocarb (Table 4-8). For a review of the nature of synergy among pesticides and how this concept applies to the control of Pythium blight, see Chapter 17, Selection and Use of Fungicides.

A mixture of mancozeb and chloroneb is antagonistic, with its disease control effectiveness being approximately 30 percent less than that which would have been provided by either of the components used singly. This combination should not be used in Pythium blight control programs (see Chapter 17, Table 17-3) (Couch and Smith, 1991a).

Sporadic instances of resistance of *Pythium aphanidermatum* to metalaxyl have been reported in golf course turf in the United States (Sanders, 1984). The possibility of the development of resistance to Pythium-active fungicides can be reduced significantly by the use of spray programs that alternate

Table 4-8. Synergistic combinations of fungicides for increased effectiveness in the control of Pythium blight incited by *Pythium aphanidermatum. After Couch and Smith, 1991a.*

| Fungicide Combination[a,b] | Rate per 1000 ft² (93 m²) | |
	Formulated Product	Active Ingredient
Mancozeb (80 WP)	4.0 oz (113.4 g)	3.2 oz (90.7 g)
+ Metalaxyl (2 EC)	1.0 oz (29.6 ml)	0.25 oz (7.09 g)
Mancozeb (80 WP)	4.0 oz (113.4 g)	3.2 oz (90.7 g)
+ Propamocarb (6F)	1.3 oz (38.5 ml)	1.0 oz (28.4 g)
Fosetyl Al (80 WP)	4.0 oz (113.4 g)	3.2 oz (90.7 g)
+ Propamocarb (6 F)	1.3 oz (38.5 ml)	1.0 oz (28.4 g)
Fosetyl Al (80 WP)	4.0 oz (113.4 g)	3.2 oz (90.7 g)
+ Metalaxyl (2 EC)	1.0 oz (29.6 ml)	0.25 oz (7.09 g)

[a]For a listing of trade names for each of these fungicides, refer to Appendix Table I.
[b]The information given in parenthesis after each fungicide indicates formulation type and amount of active ingredient. For an explanation of this terminology, refer to the section Types of Fungicide Formulations in Chapter 17—Selection and Use of Fungicides.

among materials with different modes of action, and/or the use of the synergistic combinations listed above. Also, it has been shown that metalaxyl resistant strains of *Pythium aphanidermatum* can be controlled by the use of combination sprays of metalaxyl and mancozeb (see Chapter 17, Table 17-4) (Couch and Smith, 1991a).

A preventive fungicide program is essential for the most effective control of Pythium blight. In stands of turfgrass with a history of this disease, the first treatment should be made immediately after the first occurrence of night temperatures that do not drop below 65 °F (18 °C) and the relative humidity during the nighttime period under consideration is 85 percent or higher.

A profile of each of the fungicides listed above and the names of representative manufacturers is given in Appendix Table I.

Rhizoctonia Blight of Cool Season Turfgrasses

Rhizoctonia blight is one of the most important diseases of turfgrasses in the continental United States and Canada. The early research on the nature and control of this disease marked the beginnings of modern turfgrass pathology.

Symptoms of the disease that is now known as Rhizoctonia blight were first observed in 1913 on bentgrass putting greens of a golf course near Philadelphia, Pennsylvania. The following year, what appeared to be the same disease caused extensive damage to bentgrass in a turf garden in Philadelphia. The owner of the turf garden, F. W. Taylor, called the disease to the attention of Charles V. Piper, a member of the research staff of the United States Department of Agriculture and Director of the United States Golf Association. By 1917, Piper had identified *Rhizoctonia solani* as the pathogen (Piper and Coe, 1919; Oakley, 1924).

Taylor assigned the disease the name "brown patch." By the mid-1920s, however, the term brown patch was also being used for several other grass diseases, including two newly recognized warm weather patch diseases. In their 1932 turf disease bulletin, Monteith and Dahl called for more precision in the naming of patch diseases. They pointed out, "Any casual student of turf knows that when turfgrassses are killed by any means they usually turn to some shade of brown; therefore, if a sufficient percentage of grass is killed in an area it is likely to form a browned patch. Consequently a great many injuries which produced brown patches of turf have been designated brown patch." They recommended that the name brown patch be limited to the turfgrass disease incited by *Rhizoctonia solani*.

The dilemma of developing an appropriate name for this disease wasn't resolved until 1984. In August of that year, the American Phytopathological Society convened a meeting of turfgrass pathologists. Their assignment was to prepare a working list of standard names for turfgrass diseases. In their consideration of the most appropriate name for the disease incited by *Rhizoctonia solani*, the pathologists agreed with Monteith and Dahl's observation that the term brown patch was much too general. They concluded that the name for this disease should be more definitive. To accomplish this objective, they combined the description of one its primary symptoms on all grasses, foliar blighting, with the genus name of the pathogen and assigned this disease the name "Rhizoctonia blight" (Couch, 1985).

The epidemiology and descriptive pathology of Rhizoctonia blight varies with the turfgrass species affected. With the cool season turfgrasses (bentgrasses, bluegrasses, fescues, ryegrasses), the severity of Rhizoctonia blight is greatest during the summer months. However, with the warm season turfgrasses (bermudagrass, zoysiagrass, centipedegrass, St. Augustinegrass), the disease is most destructive during the spring and fall.

This section covers the nature and control of Rhizoctonia blight as a summer patch disease of cool season turfgrasses. Information on the nature and control of Rhizoctonia blight on warm season grasses is given in the section, Spring and Fall Patch Diseases.

Symptoms

The symptom patterns of Rhizoctonia blight will vary with the turfgrass type, height of cut and prevailing weather conditions. Under close mowing, as practiced for golf greens and bowling greens, Rhizoctonia blight appears as irregularly shaped patches of blighted turfgrass ranging from 2 inches (5 cm) to 2 feet (0.6 meter) or more in diameter. The initial color of these patches is usually a purplish green, but this soon fades to light brown. During periods of warm, humid weather, dark, purplish 'smoke rings' 0.5 to 2 inches (1–6 cm) may border the individual patches. The purple tint of these rings is brought about by a consolidation of the color of the newly colonized leaves with the hue of the dark mycelium of *Rhizoctonia solani* on the leaf surfaces. It is usually most distinctive during early morning hours (Plate 10-A, B, C).

Under conditions of high mowing, i.e., home lawns, park lawns, and golf course fairways, Rhizoctonia blight is first seen as irregularly shaped areas of blighted grass ranging from a few inches to several feet in diameter. During the early stages of patch development, leaf death is usually uniform throughout the affected areas. However, as the disease progresses, many of these may take on the form of circular patches of dull tan to brown grass 1 to 3 feet (0.3–1 meter) in diameter, with center sections of green, unaffected plants. Eventually, the individual sites of disease development may coalesce to form irregularly shaped areas of uniformly blighted grass up to 50 feet (15 meters) in diameter (Plate 9-A, B, C).

The individual leaf symptoms of Rhizoctonia blight on Kentucky bluegrass, tall fescue and ryegrass first show as small, dull tan lesions. Under favorable weather conditions these lesions continue to enlarge and develop reddish brown margins. Individual lesions may expand to envelop large sections of the leaf. At this stage of disease development, the entire leaf may become necrotic and take on a light brown appearance. Also at this time, the affected leaves take on a dry, more-or-less brittle texture, but they usually retain their original shape. This latter symptom pattern is in sharp contrast with the water-soaked, softened, twisted and matted condition that commonly occurs with Pythium blight (Plate 9-A, B, C, D, E; Plate 10-D, E, F).

The Fungus

Rhizoctonia solani Kuhn; telemorph *Thanatephorous cucumeris* (Frank) Donk; syn. *Pellicularia filamentosa* (Pat.) D. P. Rogers

Description

Mycelium tan to brown, 4–15 μm in diameter, with right-angled branching and characteristic constriction at the septa and the formation of a septum in the branch near the point of origin. Hyphal cells multinucleate, with doliform septae (Figure 4-18). Produces monilioid cells (often called barrel-shaped cells or chlamydospores) in chains or aggregates sometimes referred to as sporodochia. Clamp connections are absent. Sclerotia generally dark brown to black, sometimes off white or pale buff, spherical to irregular, aggregated or crust-like, never differentiated into rind and medulla, and 1–10 mm in diameter (Parmeter and Whitney, 1985).

Procedures for Isolation and Culture

The organism grows well on a wide range of media. Its optimum growth temperature is 28 °C. At this temperature, radial growth rates on potato dextrose agar vary among isolates, but usually range from 2–3 cm per day (Sherwood, 1965). On potato dextrose agar, the mycelium is pale to dark brown (Parmeter and Whitney, 1965).

The cells of actively growing vegetative hyphae of *Rhizoctonia solani* are predominately multinucleate. This is in contrast with *Rhizoctonia cerealis* which produces vegetative hyphae with predominately binucleate cells. A simple procedure for determining the nuclear number of the hyphal cells consists of culturing the isolate in question on 2 percent water agar in petri plates in the dark at 27 °C until the hyphal growth has almost reached the periphery of the plates. At this time, a drop of 0.05

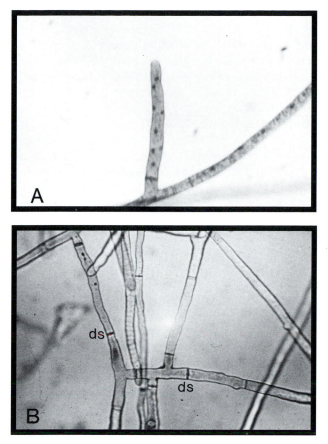

Figure 4-18. Mycelium of *Rhizoctonia solani* showing (A) multinucleate condition of cells, and (B) doliform septae (ds) and right angle branching with formation of septum in a branch near its point of origin. *Courtesy Leon Lucas and Leon Burpee.*

percent trypan blue in lactophenol should be placed directly onto the agar surface approximately 2 cm inside the area of advancing hyphal tips. A cover slip can then be placed over the drop of stain, and after approximately 30 minutes the hyphae examined in place for nuclear numbers with a microscope at 400×. Or the agar can be cut around the cover slips and the squares placed on microscope slides for the examination. This procedure can also be used to determine if the hyphae have dolipore septa (Burpee, 1980a).

For information on the comparative cytological features and growth patterns of colonies of *Rhizoctonia solani* with those of *Rhizoctonia zeae* and *Rhizoctonia oryzae*, see Rhizoctonia Sheath Spot.

Hosts

1. **Turfgrasses**—annual bluegrass (*Poa annua*), creeping bentgrass (*Agrostis palustris*), Colonial bentgrass (*Agrostis tenuis*), velvet bentgrass (*Ag-*

rostis caniana), bermudagrass (*Cynodon dactylon*), buffalograss (*Buchloe dactyloides*), centipedegrass (*Eremochloa ophiuroides*), Kentucky bluegrass (*Poa pratensis*), Chewings fescue (*Festuca rubra* var. *commutata*), red fescue (*Festuca rubra*), sheep fescue (*Festuca ovina*), tall fescue (*Festuca arundinacea*), annual ryegrass (*Lolium multiflorum*), perennial ryegrass (*Lolium perenne*), St. Augustinegrass (*Stenotaphrum secundatum*), and zoysiagrass (*Zoysia japonica*).

2. **All Known Gramineous Hosts**—A listing of common names for the following species is given in Appendix Table IV. *Agropyron angustiglume* Nevski, *A. cristatum* (L.) Gaertn., *A. dasystachyum* (Hook.) Scribn., *A. desertorum* (Fisch.) Schult., *A. intermedium* (Host) Beauv., *A. mongolicum* Keng, *A. repens* (L.) Beauv., *A. rigidum* Beauv., *A. riparium* Scribn. and Smith, *A. sibiricum* (Willd.) Beauv., *A. smithii* Rydb., *A. subsecundum* (Link) Hitchc., *A. trachycaulum* (Link) Malte, *A. trichophorum* (Link) Richt., *Agrostis alba* L., *A. canina* L., *A. exarata* Trin., *A. hallii* Vasey, *A. palustris* Huds., *A . stolonifera* L., *A. tenuis* Sibth., *Arrhenatherum elatius* (L.) Presl, *Avena byzantina* C. Koch, *A. fatua* L., *A. sativa* L., *A. sterilis* L., *Axonopus affinis* Chase, *Boutleoua curtipendula* (Michx.) Torr., *B. gracilis* (H. B. K.) Lag., *Bromus arvensis* L., *B. carinatus* Hook. and Arn., *B. catharticus* Vahl, *B. erectus* Huds., *B. inermis* Leyss., *B. japonicus* Thunb., *B. madritensis* L., *B. mollis* L., *B. pumpellianus* Scribn. *B. racemosus* L., *B. rigidus* Roth, *B. secalinus* L., *B. tectorum* L., *Buchloe dactyloides* (Nutt.) Engelm., *Calamagrostis montanensis* Scribn., *Cenchrus pauciflorus* Benth., *Cynodon dactylon* (L.) Pers., *Dactylis glomerata* L., *Danthonia californica* Boland, *Deschampsia atropurpurea* (Wahl.) Scheele, *Digitaria sanguinalis* (L.) Scop., *Echinochloa colonum* (L.) Link, *E. crusgalli* (L.) Beauv., *Eleusine indica* (L.) Gaertn., *Elymus antarcticus* Hook., *E. canadensis* L., *E. dahuricus* Turcz., *E. giganteus* Vahl, *E. glaucus* Buckl., *E. interruptus* Buckl., *E. junceus* Fisch., *E. macounii* Vasey, *E. sibiricus* L., *Eragrostis curvula* (Schrad.) Nees, *E. trichodes* (Nutt.) Wood, *Eremochloa ophiuroides* (Munro) Hack., *Festuca arundinacea* Schreb., *F. dertonensis* (All.) Aschers and Graebn., *F. elatior* L., *F. idahoensis* Elmer, *F. megalura* Nutt., *F. myuros* L., *F. octoflora* Walt., *F. ovina* L., *F. rubra* L., *F. rubra* var. *commutata* Gaud., *Hierochloe odorata* (L.) Beauv., *Holcus lanatus* L., *Hordeum brachyantherum* Nevski, *H. distichon* L., *H. hystrix* Roth, *H. jubatum* L., *H. murinum* L., *H. nodosum* L., *H. secalinum* Guss., *H. vulgare* L., *Koeleria cristata* (L.) Pers., *Lolium*

multiflorum Lam., *L. perenne* L., *Muhlenbergia racemosa* (Michx.) B. S. P., *M. richardsonis* (Trin.) Rydb., *Oryza sativa* L., *Oryzopsis hymenoides* (Roem. and Schult.) Ricker, *Panicum capillare* L., *P. miliaceum* L., *P. tennesseense* Ashe, *P. virgatum* L., *Phalaris arundinacea* L., *P. tuberosa* L., *Phleum pratense* L., *Poa ampla* Merr., *P. annua* L., *P. bulbosa* L., *P. compressa* L., *P. nemoralis* L., *P. palustris* L., *P. pratensis* L., *P. secunda* Presl, *P. trivialis* L.,. *Redfieldia flexuosa* (Thurb.) Vasey, *Saccharum officinarum* L., *Schedonnardus paniculatus* (Nutt.) Trel., *Secale cereale* L., *Setaria lutescens* (Weigel) Hubb., *S. viridis* (L.) Beauv., *Sitanion hystrix* (Nutt.) J. G. Smith, *Sorghum sudanense* (Piper) Stapf, *S. vulgare* Pers., *Sporobolus cryptandrus* (Torr.) A. Gray, *S. neglectus* Nash, *Stenotaphrum secundatum* (Walt.) Kuntze, *Stipa comata* Trin. and Rupr., *S. sibirica* Lam., *S. spartea* Trin., *S. viridula* Trin., *Trisetum canescens* Buckl., *Triticum aestivum* L., *T. dicoccum* Schrank, *T. durum* Desf., *T. monococcum* L., *T. spelta* L., *T. timopheevi* (Zhukov.) Zhukov., *Zea mays* L., *Zoysia japonica* Steud. (Sprague, 1950; Index Plant Dis., 1960; Haygood and Martin, 1990).

Disease Profile

Rhizoctonia solani survives adverse seasons in the form of sclerotia — either embedded in plant tissue or on the surface of the soil. Also, in the absence of suitable host plants, the organism is capable of existing as a soil saprophyte for long periods of time.

Resumption of growth of the pathogen from the sclerotial stage occurs when air temperatures reach 64–68 °F (18–20 °C). Under these conditions, mycelial growth extends for only a short distance, and the sclerotium serves as the primary nutrient source for the fungus. At this stage of development, if the air temperature drops below 62 °F (17 °C), death of the mycelium may result.

Initial infections of leaves by *Rhizoctonia solani* occurs when the average daily air temperature reaches 73 °F (23 °C). The mechanism of infection is determined by prevailing air temperatures. In the low to high 70s F, invasion of leaf tissue is accomplished primarily through stomates and wounds produced by mowing. When air temperatures are in the 80–85 °F (27–29 °C) range, the predominant form of infection is by means of direct penetration of intact epidermal cells. At 90 °F (32 °C), the capacity of the fungus to infect intact leaf surfaces virtually ceases (Dickinson, 1932).

Infection of intact leaf epidermal cells is accomplished by the formation of infection cushions and the production of appressoria. Penetration pegs develop from the terminal portions of the appressoria and from lobed formations in infection cushions. The penetration process is accomplished by a combination of mechanical pressure and enzymatic degradation of the cuticle and epidermal cell wall (Bateman, 1970). The entry of hyphae into substomatal chambers can occur in the absence of infection structures on the leaf surface. Once the substomatal chamber has been entered, a mycelial pad is formed, which then facilitates hyphal penetration of the adjacent cell walls (Figure 3-3). During colonization, mycelial growth is both intercellular and intracellular. The degradation of grass tissue during the process of colonization by *Rhizoctonia solani* is brought about by the production of extracellular enzymes and the formation of toxins (Nishimura and Sabaki, 1963).

Severe outbreaks of Rhizoctonia blight of cool season turfgrasses are favored by high air temperatures in conjunction with extended periods of leaf wetness. The optimum conditions for a high frequency of infections are continuously wet leaves for 48 hours or more and air temperatures in the high 70s to low 80s F. Colonization of infected leaf tissue by *Rhizoctonia solani* is most rapid at 85–90 °F (29–32 °C) (Table 4-9). Soil moisture levels in the readily available range [field capacity (−0.033 MPa) to permanent wilting percentage (−1.5 MPa)] do not influence the development of Rhizoctonia blight (Couch, 1992). However, development of the disease is significantly affected by certain soil fertility and pH levels. The severity of Rhizoctonia blight is much greater in

Table 4-9. Relationship between leaf wetness, time, air temperature and infection and colonization of tall fescue (*Festuca arundinacea*) leaves by *Rhizoctonia solani. After Couch, 1992.*

Infection Parameters			
Air Temperature	Leaf Wetness	Colonization Temperature	Disease Severity[a,b]
79 °F (26 °C)	48 hours	90 °F (32 °C)	8.4 a
79 °F (26 °C)	48 hours	79 °F (26 °C)	7.1 b
90 °F (32 °C)	48 hours	79 °F (26 °C)	5.9 c
79 °F (26 °C)	48 hours	70 °F (21 °C)	5.7 c
90 °F (32 °C)	48 hours	70 °F (21 °C)	5.3 cd
70 °F (21 °C)	48 hours	79 °F (26 °C)	4.7 de

[a]Disease rating based on 0–10 scale. 0 = no blighting, 10 = 100 percent of foliage blighted.
[b]Means followed by the same letter are not significantly different (p = 0.05) from each other according to Duncan's multiple range test.

turfgrass grown at high nitrogen with normal phosphorous and potassium levels than when the plants are grown at normal, balanced fertility. On the other hand, when phosphorous and potassium levels are increased concurrently with nitrogen, there is no increase in disease development. At low nitrogen fertility, with normal levels of phosphorous and potassium, Rhizoctonia blight is much less severe than when the plants are grown at normal, balanced fertility. When nitrogen, phosphorous, and potassium levels are reduced simultaneously, however, disease severity is greater than when the plants are grown at normal, balanced nutrition (Bloom and Couch, 1960).

Under low nitrogen fertility, pH apparently does not influence disease development. With normal, balanced nutrition, Rhizoctonia blight is more severe in the acid range; while at high nitrogen fertility, development of the disease is greater in the basic, or alkaline, range (Bloom and Couch, 1960).

Rhizoctonia blight has been observed to occur most frequently, and with greater severity, on short cut turfgrasses. This is thought to be due primarily to the more abundant and uniform supply of wound-type infection courts as the result of frequent mowings (Rowell, 1951).

Control

Cultural Practices

Since significant alterations in incidence and severity of Rhizoctonia blight can be brought on by various levels of soil fertility and pH, if a fungicide program for the control of the disease is to be consistent in its effectiveness, it must be worked out in close concert with the fertilizer program. Also, once the overall program is in place, it may become necessary to adjust the fungicide program to compensate for nutritionally-induced changes in the plants vulnerability to the disease. For example, short term increases in the nitrogen fertilization of a bentgrass golf green during weather conditions that are conducive to outbreaks of Rhizoctonia blight, may also call for an increase in the dosage levels and frequency of application of fungicides.

Management practices that decrease the length of time the leaves are wet will aid in reducing the incidence of Rhizoctonia blight. One such practice is the early morning removal of dew and guttation water from golf greens by poling or by dragging a water hose across them. The duration of the periods of daily leaf wetness can also be reduced by two to four hours by following a nighttime watering schedule in which the irrigation system is set to begin at least

three hours after sunset and programmed to be completed before sunrise (see Chapter 16, Figure 16-2).

Since frequent mowing is apparently conducive to the development of Rhizoctonia blight, where the management program has been altered so as to call for less time intervals between cuttings, the turfgrass should be examined more often for indications of early outbreaks of the disease.

Use of Resistant Grasses

The various bentgrass species show different levels of susceptibility to Rhizoctonia blight. Colonial bentgrass (*Agrostis tenuis*) is the most susceptible, velvet bentgrass (*Agrostis canina*) ranks second in vulnerability to the disease, and creeping bentgrass (*Agrostis palustris*) is the most resistant (Shurtleff, 1953). Variability in resistance to Rhizoctonia blight has been reported among selections of St. Augustinegrass (*Stenotaphrum secundatum*) (Allen, Kilpatrick and Bashaw, 1966). Burpee (1992) has ranked the comparative susceptibility of cultivars of tall fescue (*Festuca arundinacea*) to Rhizoctonia blight based on their initial vulnerability to infection and colonization and infection by the pathogen and rate of recovery from the disease when environmental conditions no longer favor disease development. This listing is given in Table 4-10.

Use of Fungicides

Rhizoctonia blight of cool season turfgrasses may be controlled by the use of either triadimefon, anilazine, propiconazole, cyproconazole, iprodione, chlorothalonil, flutolanil, or mancozeb (Couch, Lucas and Haygood, 1990). A preventive fungicide program is essential for the most effective control of this disease. In stands of turfgrass with a history of Rhizoctonia blight, the first fungicide treatment should be

Table 4-10. Comparative susceptibility of cultivars of tall fescue to *Rhizoctonia solani* based on combination of initial vulnerability of plants to infection and colonization and rate of recovery when environmental conditions no longer favor disease development. *After Burpee, 1992.*

Most Resistant		Most Susceptible	
Houndog	Crossfire	Twilight	Shortstop
Mustang	Rebel Jr.	Mojave	Bonsai Dwarf
Falcon	Olympic	Tarus	Finelawn I
Wrangler	Maverick II	Pacer	Mesa
Gala	Titan	Trident	Maurietta
Rebel	Finelawn	Silverado	
Tribute	Arid	Adventure	
Rebel II		Penngrazer	

made immediately after the first occurrence of night temperatures that do not drop below 70 °F (21 °C) and the relative humidity during the nighttime period under consideration is 85 percent or higher.

For a profile of each of the fungicides listed above and the names of representative manufacturers, see Appendix Table I.

Rhizoctonia Sheath Spot

Rhizoctonia sheath spot affects both warm season and cool season turfgrasses. The disease is known to occur in New Zealand and in the southeastern and southwestern sections of the United States (Burpee and Martin, 1992; Christensen, 1979).

Symptoms

The symptom patterns of Rhizoctonia sheath spot vary with the turfgrass type, height of cut and prevailing weather conditions.

On Kentucky bluegrass, perennial ryegrass, and tall fescue, Rhizoctonia sheath spot is first seen in overall view as diffuse, irregularly shaped patches of yellowish green to brown leaves interspersed with green, apparently healthy leaves. The individual leaf symptoms first develop as small, water soaked blotches on the leaf sheaths and the base of blades. As these enlarge, they bleach to dull tan lesions with reddish brown borders. Single lesions can expand to envelop large sections of the leaf. At this stage of disease development, the entire leaf becomes necrotic and takes on a light brown appearance.

On creeping bentgrass and annual bluegrass maintained at golf green mowing height, the disease is seen as dark gray brown or yellow arcs or circles. In contrast with Rhizoctonia blight, a narrow band ("smoke ring") of dark purplish grass does not develop at the outer edges of the patches during periods of extended leaf wetness.

During extended periods of high air temperatures, white to cream-colored mycelia can occasionally be observed growing from the foliage of colonized cool-season grasses. In these cases, Rhizoctonia sheath spot may be mistaken for Pythium blight.

The individual leaf symptoms on zoysiagrass, bermudagrass, centipedegrass and St. Augustinegrass first develop as a soft, dark brown to purplish rot of the lower portion of the leaf sheaths. This part of the syndrome is most prevalent when the leaves are continuously wet for an extended period of time. With the return of relatively dry weather, a reddish brown necrosis will envelop the base of the leaf sheaths and extend into the stem tissue (Burpee and Martin, 1992).

The Fungi

A. *Rhizoctonia zeae* Voorhees; telemorph *Waitea circinata* Warcup and Talbot

Description

Sclerotia superficial and submerged when grown in pure culture—hyaline, white, granulate when young, gradually becoming clear when old. The main mycelial strands are 6 to 10 μm wide, branched at an acute angle with a slight constriction at the point of branching, and with a septation a short distance from the point of constriction. The main hyphae is also septate a short distance above the branch. Later short-celled, much branching hyphae emerge at right angles from the main branches and ramify through the substrate, sometimes forming barrel-shaped cells. Individual cells multinucleate (Figure 4-19). Forms salmon-colored sclerotial masses (Ryker and Gooch, 1938).

Hosts

1. **Turfgrasses**—bermudagrass (*Cynodon dactylon*), annual bluegrass (*Poa annua*), Kentucky bluegrass (*Poa pratensis*), creeping bentgrass (*Agrostis palustris*), centipedegrass (*Eremochloa ophiuroides*), tall fescue (*Festuca arundinacea*), St. Augustinegrass (*Stenotaphrum secundatum*), and zoysiagrass (*Zoysia japonica*).
2. **All Gramineous Hosts**—A listing of common names for the following species is given in Appen-

Figure 4-19. Mycelium of *Rhizoctonia zeae* showing multinucleate condition of cells and hyphal branching at an acute angle. *Courtesy Leon Lucas.*

dix Table IV. *Agrostis palustris* Huds., *Avena sativa* L., *Bromus tectorum* L., *Cynodon dactylon* (L.) Pers., *Eremochloa ophiuroides* (Munro) Hack., *Festuca arundinacea* Schreb., *Hordeum vulgare* L., *Oryza sativa* L., *Poa annua* L., *P. pratensis* L., *Stenotaphrum secundatum* (Walt.) Kuntze, *Triticum aestivum* L., *Zoysia japonica* Steud. (Burpee and Martin, 1991; Haygood and Martin, 1990; Ryker and Gooch, 1938; Sprague, 1950).

The Fungi

B. *Rhizoctonia oryzae* Ryker and Gooch; telemorph *Waitea circinata* Warcup and Talbot

Description

Mycelium superficial and submerged when grown in pure culture—hyaline, white, granulate when young, gradually becoming clear when old. The main mycelial strands are 6 to 10 μm wide, branched at an acute angle with a slight constriction at the point of branching, and with a septation a short distance from the point of constriction. The main hyphae is also septate a short distance above the branch. Later short-celled, much branching hyphae emerge at right angles from the main branches and ramify through the substrate, sometimes forming barrel-shaped cells. Forms salmon-colored sclerotial masses (Ryker and Gooch, 1938).

Hosts

1. **Turfgrasses**—bermudagrass (*Cynodon dactylon*), centipedegrass (*Eremochloa ophiuroides*), St. Augustinegrass (*Stenotaphrum secundatum*), and zoysiagrass (*Zoysia japonica*).
2. **All Known Gramineous Hosts**—A listing of common names for the following species is given in Appendix Table IV. *Avena sativa* L., *Bromus tectorum* L., *Cynodon dactylon* (L.) Pers., *Eremochloa ophiuroides* (Munro) Hack., *Hordeum vulgare* L, *Oryza sativa* L., *Stenotaphrum secundatum* (Walt.) Kuntze, *Triticum aestivum* L., *Zoysia japonica* Steud. (Burpee and Martin, 1991; Haygood and Martin, 1990; Ryker and Gooch, 1938; Sprague, 1950).

Comparative Features in Culture

Rhizoctonia zeae and *Rhizoctonia oryzae* grow well in culture at 32 °C. Colonies of both species on potato dextrose agar are white to buff to salmon colored. The sclerotia of *Rhizoctonia oryzae* are salmon colored, 1 to 3 mm in diameter, and variable in shape. They are usually formed on the agar surface. The sclerotia of *Rhizoctonia zeae*, on the other hand, are smaller (0.5 to 1.0 mm in diameter), more uniformly spherical, white when young, then turning orange, to red, and finally, dark brown. Also, they are commonly formed submerged in the agar rather than on the surface (Burpee and Martin, 1991).

The cells of actively growing vegetative hyphae of *Rhizoctonia zeae* and *Rhizoctonia oryzae* are predominately multinucleate. For a description of the procedure for determining nuclear number of the hyphal cells, and a comparison of the cytological features and growth patterns in culture of these two species with those of *Rhizoctonia solani* and *Rhizoctonia cerealis*, refer to the sections on Rhizoctonia Blight of Cool Season Grasses and Rhizoctonia Yellow Patch.

Disease Profile

Rhizoctonia sheath spot is a warm wet weather disease. The optimum environmental conditions for its development are extended periods of leaf wetness combined with nighttime air temperatures of 78 °F (28 °C) or higher, and daytime air temperatures ranging from the low 80s to the low 90s F (28–33 °C).

Rhizoctonia zeae and *Rhizoctonia oryzae* are both capable of surviving as sclerotia and by growing saprophytically in the thatch (Martin et al., 1983; Burpee and Martin, 1991). The descriptive pathology of Rhizoctonia sheath spot has not been studied in sufficient detail to describe the mechanisms of infection and colonization of host tissue, however, it would seem reasonable to assume that these processes closely parallel those of Rhizoctonia blight of warm season turfgrasses.

Control

At present, there are no fungicides registered for control of Rhizoctonia sheath spot.

Sclerotinia Dollar Spot

Sclerotinia dollar spot is a widespread and major disease of turfgrasses in North America, Central America, Australia, New Zealand, Japan, the British Isles, and continental Europe. In Britain, the disease is confined almost entirely to red fescue (Smith, 1955). However, in the other areas of the world, it affects all commonly cultivated turfgrass species (Bosewinkel, 1977; Hosotsuji, 1977; Reilly, 1969). With the exception of western Canada and the Pacific Northwest section of the United States, Sclerotinia dollar spot is the most commonly occurring turfgrass disease on the North American continent.

Symptoms

Affected individual leaves at first show yellow green blotches, which progress to a water-soaked appearance, and finally bleach to a straw-colored tan with reddish brown borders. Entire leaves are commonly blighted, but, in some cases, only portions of leaves may become necrotic (Plates 17-D, E, F; 18-C, D).

In overall view, the symptom pattern for Sclerotinia dollar spot varies with management practices. Under close mowing, as with golf greens and bowling greens, the disease is first seen as very small spots of blighted turfgrass. These develop into circular, straw-colored patches 2–3 inches (5–7.5 cm) in diameter. The affected areas are usually sharply outlined against the surrounding, healthy turfgrass (Plate 17-A, B). In the early morning hours, while dew is still present on the leaves, a white growth of mycelium may sometimes be seen covering the affected leaves (Plate 17-C). If progress of the disease is unchecked by fungicide applications, the individual patches frequently coalesce and involve large areas of turf.

With the high mowing practices generally employed for home lawns, general purpose park areas, and golf course fairways, the rather small, sharply outlined patches on putting and bowling greens are replaced by irregularly shaped, straw-colored areas of blighted turfgrass, ranging from 6 inches to 12 feet (15 cm–3.5 meters) in diameter (Plates 17-E; 18-A, B, E). In this form, the disease is sometimes erroneously diagnosed on landscape turf as drought injury, dull rotary mower injury, female dog injury, or fertilizer damage. During extended periods of high atmospheric humidity, the white mycelium of the pathogen will grow freely over the surface of the leaves and extend from leaf to leaf in a dense, cottony-type of formation (Plate 18-F).

The Fungus

Sclerotinia homoeocarpa F. T. Bennett

Description

Apothecia cupulate 0.5–0.8 mm. to disk or funnel shaped 1–1.5 mm. in diameter, pale cinnamon to dark brown, with prosenchymatic exciples, arising from microsclerotia or expansive sclerotial flakes or patches. Stalk cylindrical, slender, flexuous, 5–10 mm., or more, long, arising singly or in clusters, simple or branches in the upper part. Asci cylindro-clavate, inoperculate, 10.4–11.5 μm × 140–170 μm, commonly 10.4 μm × 150–165 μm. Ascospores 8, uniserate, hyaline, oblong-elliptical, bi-guttulate, unicellular, a delicate median septum often during germination, 5.2–6.5 μm × 15.6–16.9 μm, commonly 5.5 μm × 16.0 μm. Paraphyses few, cylindro-clavate, sparsely septate, 2.0–2.2 μm × 80–120 μm.

Conidial fructification cupulate, 0.4–0.6 mm. in diameter, light brown; stalk 4–6 mm. long, pale cinnamon. Conidia borne singly on hyphae within the cup, hyaline, one-septate, constricted at the septum, apex either rounded or narrowing to a blunt point; 4.5–5.2 μm. Microconidia spherical, hyaline, 1.5–2.0 μm, in minute cream-colored pustules; not known to germinate.

On potato-dextrose agar, mycelium floccose, at first white, later becoming reddish brown to bluish green, depending on strain. Sclerotia black, from small flakes to expansive patches, parchment-like, formed by conversion of superficial hyphae of the white mycelium into a mosaic of small, thick-walled cells.

The taxonomic position of the incitant of Sclerotinia dollar spot has been in question since the disease was first described. Originally, the fungus was thought to be a species of *Rhizoctonia*, and in the early 1920s, the disease was referred to as "small brown patch" to distinguish it from "large brown patch" incited by *Rhizoctonia solani* (Monteith and Dahl, 1932). A comprehensive study conducted by F. T. Bennett in the 1930s with isolates collected from Britain, Australia, and the United States showed that the incitant of the disease we now refer to as Sclerotinia dollar spot existed as distinct strains: (a) a "perfect strain" of British origin that produced ascospores and conidia, (b) an "ascigerous strain" of British origin that produced ascospores and microconidia, and (c) "nonsporing strains" of British, American, and Australian origin which were sterile in culture, but occasionally produced rudimentary apothecial initials. Working from a broad concept of the genus, Bennett considered the fungus to be a *Sclerotinia*, and because of its unusual conidial state, he assigned it the species name *homoeocarpa* (Bennett, 1935).

Studies with isolates of *Sclerotinia homoeocarpa* from North America have failed to induce the formation of fully mature ascocarps in culture. In some instances, apothecial initials and immature apothecia have developed, but conidia or ascospores have not been observed (Fenstermacher, 1970, 1980).

In recent years, mycologists with a more restricted view of what constitutes the parameters for the genus *Sclerotinia* have called into question Bennett's designation for this fungus. Jackson (1973) studied the mature apothecia of a British "conidial strain" he isolated from diseased red fescue and concluded that it was not a *Sclerotinia*. The characteristics of the fungus he examined were similar to those described by Bennett. This led him to conclude that Bennett had incorrectly placed the fungus in the genus *Sclerotinia*. Kohn (1979) agreed with Jackson that this fungus is not a *Sclerotinia* and suggested that it will probably eventually be placed in either *Lanzia* Sacc. or *Mollerodiscus* Henn. Evidence collected more recently from studies conducted on the characteristics of the sclerotia of isolates of *Sclerotinia homoeocarpa* from the United States and Canada has also supported the view that this fungus does not belong in the genus *Sclerotinia* (Kohn and Greenville, 1989; Novak and Kohn, 1991).

Jackson (1973) recommended that no name changes be made in the designation for this organism until broader questions concerning genus nomenclature within the family Sclerotiniaceae have been resolved and further studies have been conducted on the telemorph of this species. However, a few writers have elected to use the composite expression "*Lanzia* and *Mollerodiscus*" in lieu of *Sclerotinia homoeocarpa* as an interim designation for the incitant of Sclerotinia dollar spot. This action only exacerbates the existing taxonomic dilemma, for although it is possible that *Sclerotinia homoeocarpa* may not say much concerning the appropriate taxonomic location of the fungus, it is certain that the abstruseness of "*Lanzia* and/or *Mollerodiscus*" says even less. Therefore, until the body of information on the characteristics of the telemorph is sufficient to properly evaluate the validity of its present classification, this fungus should continue to be referred to as *Sclerotinia homoeocarpa*.

Sclerotinia homoeocarpa grows well on potato dextrose agar. The optimum growth temperatures for individual biotypes range from 20–30 °C. All strains of the fungus are reported to grow well on artificial media from pH 5 to pH 7 (Endo, 1963; Fenstermacher, 1970).

Hosts

1. **Turfgrasses**—bahiagrass (*Paspalum notatum*), Colonial bentgrass (*Agrostis tenuis*), creeping bentgrass (*Agrostis palustris*), velvet bentgrass (*Agrostis canina*), bermudagrass (*Cynodon dactylon*), annual bluegrass (*Poa annua*), Kentucky bluegrass (*Poa pratensis*), centipedegrass (*Eremochloa ophiuroides*), sheep fescue (*Festuca ovina*), red fescue (*Festuca rubra*), tall fescue (*Festuca*

arundinacea), and zoysiagrass (*Zoysia japonica* and *Zoysia tenuifolia*).

2. **All Known Gramineous Hosts**—A listing of common names for the following species is given in Appendix Table IV. *Agrostis alba* L, *Agrostis canina* L., *Agrostis palustris* Huds., *Agrostis tenuis* Sibtn., *Cynodon dactylon* (L.) Pers., *Festuca ovina* L., *Festuca rubra* L., *Holcus lanatus* L., *Paspalum notatum* Flugge, *Poa annua* L., *Poa pratensis* L., *Zoysia japonica* Steud., *Zoysia tenuifolia* Willd. (Index Plant Dis., 1960; Smith, 1955; Sprague, 1950).

Disease Profile

Sclerotinia homoeocarpa overwinters in the form of sclerotia and as dormant mycelium in the crowns and roots of infected plants. When the microclimate temperature reaches 60 °F (16 °C), the organism resumes growth, and it reaches its peak when the temperature in this zone ranges from 70° to 80 °F (21°–27 °C) and the nighttime atmospheric humidity is 85 percent or higher.

Conidia and ascospores appear to be of minor importance in the spread of the fungus in nature. Distribution of the pathogen to new areas is brought about by relocation of diseased and/or infested plant material with mowers, traveling sprinklers, and other maintenance equipment. Localized movement of the fungus to healthy foliage in proximity to active colonization sites is accomplished by mycelial growth from leaf-to-leaf.

Infection of leaves is achieved by mycelium growing through cut tips and stomates, and by the direct penetration of intact leaf surfaces (Endo, 1966; Monteith and Dahl, 1932)). In addition to its pathogenic effects on foliage, it has been shown that during periods of active growth in the thatch and soil *Sclerotinia homoeocarpa* produces a metabolite that is toxic to the roots of bentgrass. Roots affected by the toxin cease elongating, become thicker, show a decrease in root hair formation and an increase in the development of adventitious roots. The cells of the terminal regions of these roots show hypertrophy and a suppression of mitosis. As these cells degenerate, the cytoplasm disintegrates and largely disappears. At this point, the characteristic organization and structure of the root apex is lost and the apical meristem becomes nonfunctional. No new root-cap cells are produced to replace those lost by sloughing; consequently, the roots assume a pronounced truncate appearance. As root degeneration progresses, there is a gradual increase in amount of cell wall degeneration and loss of cohesion between cells of the

the epidermis and cortex. In the final stages of colonization, the affected roots become light brown and take on a withered appearance (Endo et al., 1964, Endo and Malca, 1965; Malca and Endo, 1965).

Conditions of heavy thatch [thickness greater than ½ inch (13 mm)] are conducive to severe outbreaks of Sclerotinia dollar spot (Wagner and Halisky, 1981). Soil pH does not affect the severity of the disease (Couch and Bloom, 1960).

Turfgrass growing under low soil moisture conditions is more susceptible to *Sclerotinia homoeocarpa* than that which is maintained at field capacity (−0.033 MPa). This increase in susceptibility can be detected when the soil moisture content reaches ¾ field capacity (Figure 4-20) (Couch and Bloom, 1960). The pronounced increase in disease proneness under conditions of low soil moisture possibly explains the sometimes high incidence of Sclerotinia dollar spot in seasons of low rainfall.

The resistance of Kentucky bluegrass to infection and colonization by *Sclerotinia homoeocarpa* has been found to be lower when the plants are growing under high nitrogen fertility (Couch and Bloom, 1960) (Figure 4-21). However, there are instances when increased nitrogen fertility may bring about a decrease in the incidence of Sclerotinia dollar spot

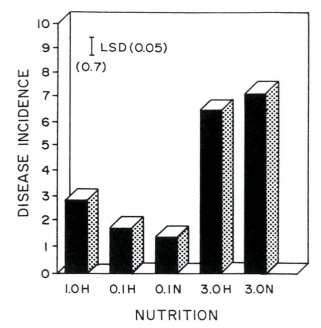

Figure 4-21. Influence of nutrition on the incidence and severity of Sclerotinia dollar spot of Kentucky bluegrass (1.0 H = normal N, P, K; 0.1 H = 1X N, P, K; 3.0 H = 3X N, P, K; 0.1 N = 0.1X N, 1.0X P, K; 3.0 N = 3X N, 1X P, K). *After Couch and Bloom, 1960.*

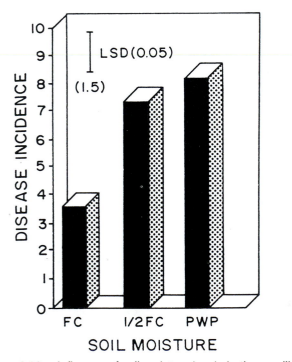

Figure 4-20. Influence of soil moisture levels in the readily available range on the development of Sclerotinia dollar spot [FC = field capacity (−0.033 MPa), PWP = permanent wilting percentage (−1.5 MPa)]. *After Couch and Bloom, 1960.*

(Burpee and Goulty, 1986; Endo, 1966); Freeman, 1963; Markland et al., 1969).

These episodes of lowered disease incidence are probably due to the phenomenon known as "disease escape." Under favorable conditions for the development of Sclerotinia dollar spot, the mycelium of the pathogen grows abundantly on necrotic leaf tissue and protrudes to adjacent, unaffected foliage (Plate 17-C). This type of growth is dependent on extended periods of leaf wetness in combination with optimum microclimate temperatures, and the uniform distribution of necrotic tissue in the foliar area of the turf to serve as a primary nutrient base for the fungus (Endo, 1966). The observed decreases in the incidence of Sclerotinia dollar spot under high nitrogen fertilization, then, are probably brought on by more rapid leaf growth, and thus a more frequent removal of affected (necrotic) leaf tissue by mowings during times in which the microclimate is less favorable for the growth the fungus.

Control

Cultural Practices

Removal of dew and guttation water by mowing or poling during early morning hours will significantly reduce the incidence and severity of Sclerotinia dollar spot (Williams, Powell and Vincelli, 1993). Also, during periods of high incidence of Sclerotinia dollar spot, employment of a high nitrogen fertility program, and irrigation practices to hold the soil near field capacity (−0.033 MPa), will aid in the reduction of disease severity. It is important that one bear in mind, however, that the nitrogen effect is a highly transient condition, and that neither of these practices in the absence of a suitable fungicide program will provide satisfactory level of disease control.

Use of Fungicides

Occurrences have been reported of resistance of the Sclerotinia dollar spot fungus to anilazine, iprodione, benzimidazoles (benomyl, thiophanate methyl), and sterol biosynthesis inhibitors (triadimefon, propiconazole, fenarimol) (Massie et al., 1968; Cole et al, 1974; Warren et al., 1974, 1977; Detweiler et al., 1983). The benzimidazole resistant strains of *Sclerotinia homoeocarpa* are strong competitors with other microbes in the biosphere; therefore, once a high level of resistance to either benomyl or thiophanate methyl becomes established in a stand of turfgrass, it remains constant for several years. On the other hand, the strains of *Sclerotinia homoeocarpa* that are resistant to the sterol biosynthesis inhibitors (SBIs) are not strong competitors with the SBI-sensitive forms, consequently, after an absence of 12 months, propiconazole, triadimefon or fenarimol can usually be included in the Sclerotinia dollar spot control program again.

Applications of either benomyl, thiophanate-methyl, or thiophanate-ethyl to a stand of turfgrass in which a strain of *Sclerotinia homoeocarpa* resistant to these fungicides is already at a high population level will bring about a significant increase in the incidence and severity of Sclerotinia dollar spot (Table 4-11) (Couch and Smith, 1991b).

The likelihood of a buildup in the population level of resistant strains of *Sclerotinia homoeocarpa* can be minimized by following a spray schedule that alternates among fungicides with different modes of action and by applying fungicide combinations that are synergistic. For a review of the nature of fungicide resistance and a more detailed listing of the basic principles for reducing the possibility of its development, refer to Chapter 17, Selection and Use of Fungicides.

Sclerotinia dollar spot may be controlled by single component applications of either triadimefon, anilazine, propiconazole, cyproconazole, thiophanate-methyl, benomyl, iprodione, fenarimol, or chlorothalonil. Also fractional low label rate combinations of the following fungicides have been shown to be synergistic in the control of this disease: (a) triadimefon + propiconazole, (b) triadimefon + chlorothalonil, (c) triadimefon + iprodione, (d) triadimefon + vinclozolin, and (e) triadimefon + anilazine (Couch and Smith, 1989). A listing of these combinations at rates that provide synergy levels equivalent in disease control effectiveness to that of the most effective component at full rate is given in Table 4-12. For a review of the concept of synergy among pesticides and additional information on the use of synergistic fungicide combinations in the control of Sclerotinia dollar spot, refer to Chapter 17—Selection and Use of Fungicides.

In a stand of turfgrass with a known history of Sclerotinia dollar spot occurrence, a preventive spray program at the lower label rate of the fungicide of choice should be initiated when the daytime air temperature stabilizes at approximately 70 °F (21 °C), and, depending on the fungicide being used, continued at either 7–10 day or 14–21 day intervals. If the program is initiated after the appearance of symptoms, the first application should be made at the high label rate of the fungicide of choice. This should then be followed in 5–7 days with a second high label rate application, after which a low label rate of the fungicide of choice. This should then be followed in 5–7 days with a second high label rate application, after which a low label rate application schedule may be employed.

For a profile of each of the fungicides listed above and the names of representative manufacturers, See Appendix Table I.

Copper Spot

Copper spot is presently known to occur on bentgrasses in the northeastern and southwestern costal areas of the United States. The fungus that incites this disease (*Gloeocercospora sorghi*) also parasitizes bermudagrass (*Cynodon dactylon*), and functions as a major foliar pathogen of sorghum (*Sorghum vulgare*) in the Gulf coast and south central sections of the country (Bain and Edgerton, 1943; Luttrell, 1951); therefore, it is highly possible that as the use of bentgrass for golf greens becomes more common in this region, positive diagnoses of copper spot will result.

Symptoms

Copper spot first appears as small light brown to reddish leaf lesions. As these spots enlarge, they become darker red. Under conditions favorable for

Table 4-11. Benomyl, thiophanate-methyl, and thiophanate-ethyl induced increase in incidence of Sclerotinia dollar spot of creeping bentgrass incited by a benzimidazole-resistant strain of *Sclerotinia homoeocarpa. After Couch and Smith, 1991b.*

Fungicide[a]	Active Ingredient per 1000 ft² (93 m²)	Percent Disease Increase[b]	
		July 29	August 4
Non-treated control	—	0 a	0 a
Benomyl	2.0 oz (56.7 g)	22 a	136 b
Thiophanate methyl	2.0 oz (56.7 g)	56 b	136 b
Thiophanate ethyl	2.0 oz (56.7 g)	67 b	163 b
Benomyl	0.5 oz (14.2 g)	67 b	118 b
Thiophanate ethyl	0.5 oz (14.2 g)	78 b	172 b
Thiophanate methyl	0.5 oz (14.2 g)	83 b	172 b

[a]For a listing of trade names for each of these fungicides, refer to Appendix Table I.
[b]Last fungicide application date, July 21. Means followed by the same letter are not significantly different (p = 0.05) from each other according to Duncan's multiple range test.

disease development, the individual lesions often coalesce, thus blighting the entire leaf.

In the overall view, the disease is seen as patches of salmon pink, or copper-colored turfgrass, ranging from 1 to 3 inches (2.5–7.5 cm) in diameter. The intensity of coloration increases during wet weather due to the development of gelatinous, pink spore masses of the pathogen on the surface of the leaves.

Copper spot and Sclerotinia dollar spot sometimes occur simultaneously in the same stand of turfgrass. The two diseases can be distinguished from each other by differences in color and in sharpness of outline of the individual patches. Instead of a reddish brown hue, the Sclerotinia dollar spot patches have a bleached, straw-colored appearance. Also, Sclerotinia dollar spot patches usually have clearly defined borders, while the margins of copper spot patches tend to be diffuse (Plate 5-F).

The Fungus

Gloeocercospora sorghi Bain and Edgerton

Description

Vegetative hyphae septate, hyaline, branching; sporodochium between guard cells and above stomatal aperture; conidiophores hyaline, septate, simple or short branched, 5–10 μm; conidia hyaline, elongate to filiform, or variable length, to longer one tapering 1.4–3.2 μm × 20–195 μm, average 2.4 μm × 82.5 μm, borne in a slimy matrix, salmon color in mass; sclerotia 0.1.0.2 mm. in diameter, lenticular to spherical, black, occurring inside the necrotic tissue of the host, abundant.

Procedures for Isolation and Culture

Gloeocercospora sorghi sporulates well on oatmeal agar, with optimum growth being obtained at 28°–30°C (Bain and Edgerton, 1943).

Table 4-12. Fractional rate combinations of fungicides for the control of Sclerotinia dollar spot with synergy levels equivalent to that of the most effective component at its full label rate. *After Couch and Smith, 1989.*

Fungicide Combination[a,b]	Rate per 1000 ft² (93 m²)	
	Formulated Product	Active Ingredient
Propiconazole (1.1 EC)	0.25 oz (7.4 ml)	0.035 oz (0.99 g)
+ Triadimefon (25 WDG)	0.25 oz (7.1 g)	0.0625 oz (1.77 g)
Propiconazole (1.1 EC)	0.25 oz (7.4 ml)	0.035 oz (0.99 g)
+ Iprodione (2 F)	0.75 oz (22.2 ml)	0.1875 oz (5.32 g)
Propiconazole (1.1 EC)	0.25 oz (7.4 ml)	0.035 oz (0.99 g)
+ Chlorothalonil (4.17 F)	1.5 oz (44.4 ml)	0.78 oz (22.17 g)
Propiconazole (1.1 EC)	0.25 oz (7.4 ml)	0.035 oz (0.99 g)
+ Vinclozolin (50 WP)	0.5 oz (14.2 g)	0.25 oz (7.09 g)
Propiconazole (1.1 EC)	0.25 oz (7.4 ml)	0.035 oz (0.99 g)
+ Anilazine (4 F)	1.0 oz (28.4 g)	0.50 oz (14.2 g)

[a]For a listing of trade names for each of these fungicides, refer to Appendix Table I.
[b]The information given in parenthesis after each fungicide indicates formulation type and amount of active ingredient. For an explanation of this terminology, refer to the section Types of Fungicide Formulations in Chapter 17—Selection and Use of Fungicides.

Hosts

1. **Turfgrasses**—velvet bentgrass (*Agrostis canina*), creeping bentgrass (*Agrostis palustris*), Colonial bentgrass (*Agrostis stolonifera*), and bermudagrass (*Cynodon dactylon*).
2. **All Known Gramineous Hosts**—A listing of common names for the following species is given in Appendix Table IV. *Agrostis canina* L., *A. palustris* Huds., *A. stolonifera* L., *Cynodon dactylon* (L.) Pers., *Pennisetum glaucum* (L.) R. Br., *P. purpureum* Schumach., *Saccharum officinarum* L., *Sorghum halepense* (L.) Pers., *Sorghum sudanense* (Piper) Stapf, *Sorghum vulgare* Pers., *Zea mays* L. (Bain and Edgerton, 1942; Wallace and Wallace, 1949; Howard et al., 1951; Sprague, 1950).

Disease Profile

Gloeocerspora sorghi overwinters as sclerotia and thick-walled mycelium in the debris of the previous season's growth. Resumption of growth of the fungus occurs when the soil temperature at a depth of 1 inch (2.5 cm) remains at 63 °F (17 °C) or above for seven days (Howard et al., 1951). Initial infections occur when the air temperatures reach 68 °F (20 °C). The germinating sclerotia produce hyphae that may in themselves penetrate the leaves, or they may aggregate and form sporodochia bearing large numbers of spores. The spores are disseminated to leaf surfaces by splashing water (Dean, 1966).

The fungus is able to gain access to the underlying leaf tissue by (a) direct penetration of the epidermis, (b) penetration of leaf hairs, and (c) by hyphal growth through open stomatal apertures. In instances of direct penetration of the epidermis, the spores germinate and form appresoria. Each appressorium develops an infection peg, the cuticle is punctured, and subcuticular hyphal growth takes place. The subcuticular hyphae then penetrate the walls of the underlying epidermal cells, infection is affected, and the colonization process begins (Figure 3-3) (Myers and Fry, 1978).

At all sites of host-parasite interaction, there is a disruption of chloroplasts and cell collapse prior to colonization of the tissue by the fungus. Pathogenic responses are manifested macroscopically as water soaking, chlorosis, or necrosis of affected tissue. These symptoms develop well ahead of the advancing mycelium (Myers and Fry, 1978).

The severity of copper spot has been shown to be greater on velvet bentgrass (*Agrostis canina*) grown under high nitrogen fertilization. This is thought to be caused by an increase in the total nitrogen content of plant exudates on the surface of the leaves which in turn enhance the capacity of the spores of *Gloeocerspora sorghi* to germinate and infect the underlying epidermal leaf tissue (Marion, 1974).

Severe outbreaks of copper spot are favored by air temperatures in the 79°–86°F (26–30°C) range in conjunction with extended periods of leaf wetness. Since the frequency of penetration of epidermal cells by germinating spores is heightened by the accumulation of plant exudates on the leaf surfaces, the most favorable atmospheric moisture conditions for infection are those that facilitate the accumulation of free water on the leaves with a minimum of leaf washing—such as frequent, light showers, or the extended periods of heavy fog or the mists that are common to coastal areas. Under these air temperature-leaf wetness conditions, infection and colonization proceeds very rapidly. Leaf lesions are formed within 24 hours from the time of infection, and abundant sporulation takes place 24–48 hours later (Howard et al., 1951; Marion, 1974).

Control

Copper spot may be controlled by applications of benomyl, thiophanate methyl, triadimefon, cyproconazole, chlorothalonil, anilazine, or iprodione. Preventive fungicidal applications should be made at 10–14 day intervals, beginning when the daytime air temperatures stabilize at 70–75 °F (31°–24 °C). Applications at curative dosage levels should be made at 4–7 day intervals until total recovery has been achieved, after which 10 days may usually be allowed to elapse between applications.

For a profile of these fungicides and the names of representative manufacturers, see Appendix Table I.

Sclerotium Blight

The Sclerotium blight pathogen (*Sclerotium rolfsii*) is known to parasitize over 500 species of plants in the tropics and the warmer areas of the temperate zones throughout the world. It has long been recognized to be an important pathogen of tree fruits, peanuts, sugar beets, forages, vegetables, and ornamentals in the southern and warmer western sections of the United States (Aycock, 1966; West, 1961).

Sclerotium blight was first described on bentgrass (*Agrostis palustris*) golf greens in North Carolina in 1975 (Lucas, 1976). The disease has since been identified on annual bluegrass, bentgrasses, and ryegrass in California, on bentgrass in Maryland, and on Kentucky bluegrass in North Carolina (Lucas, 1982; O'Neill, 1980; Punja and Grogan, 1982a).

Symptoms

Sclerotium blight is first seen on Kentucky bluegrass (*Poa pratensis*), as small, circular dead areas. Some green, apparently unaffected grass plants usually remain in the centers, thereby producing a frogeye appearance. These circular patches may enlarge up to 3 feet (0.9 meter) in diameter. Some of the affected areas may develop into partial circles of arcs, rather than distinctive, circular patches. An unusual characteristic of the patches formed by Sclerotium blight is that weeds, such as clover, are also killed in the affected areas (Plate 16-C, D).

On bentgrass and/or annual bluegrass golf greens, Sclerotium blight first appears as yellowish crescent-shaped patches or circular rings with apparently healthy-looking grass in the center. The diameter of these areas will vary from 8 to 36 inches (0.2–0.9 m) (Plate 16-A, B). Although these patches may continue to enlarge at a somewhat steady rate throughout the growing season, the center portions of apparently healthy grass expands, but at a slower rate. Patches that are initiated during late summer usually show a uniform death of plants throughout. If turf does remain in the centers, it is usually chlorotic and sparsely populated.

During humid weather, masses of coarse white mycelium may grow on debris on the soil surface and on the dying grass at the edge of the patches. Also, small, white to brown-colored, hard round bodies (sclerotia) 1/25 to 1/15 inch (1–2 mm) in diameter can frequently be seen on the dead grass or on the soil surface (Plate 16-E, F). The mycelium is not visible in dry weather, and sclerotia are difficult to find following periods of dry weather and later in the fall.

The Fungus

Sclerotium rolfsii Sacc.; telemorph *Athelia rolfsii* (Curzi) Tuu and Kimbrough

Description

Mycelium white, coarse, cells $150–250 \times 2–9$ μm, side branches smaller (2 μm), producing small, nearly spherical sclerotia about 1 mm diam., (0.5–1.5) tan colored on potato-dextrose agar; basidial hymenium very coarsely aerolate at first, consisting of clusters of basidia arranged in lines on a very tenuous subiculum; as basidia increase in number hymenium becomes denser but never forms a continuous or fleshy layer; when fully developed usually 30–40 μm thick, putty colored, becoming gray; basidia obovoid, $7–9 \times 4–5$ μm wide, bearing 2 or 4 parallel or divergent sterigmata, 2.5–4 μm or less often up to 6 μm long. Spores elliptical to obovate, rounded above, rounded or pointed at the base, apiculate, $3.5–5 \times 6–7$ μm, hyaline and smooth. Cystidia or incrusted hyphae not seen.

Procedures for Isolation and Culture

Sclerotium rolfsii grows well on potato dextrose agar (pH 6.8) and incubated at 24–26 °C with a 14 hour photoperiod under cool white fluorescent lights emitting approximately 1,500 lux. Sclerotial germination *in vitro* is highest at a media pH of 2.0–5.0 (Punja and Grogan, 1981a; 1982b).

Hosts

1. **Turfgrasses**—annual bluegrass (*Poa annua*), bermudagrass (*Cynodon dactylon*), creeping bentgrass (*Agrostis palustris*), Kentukcy bluegrass (*Poa pratensis*), annual ryegrass (*Lolium multiflorum*), and perennial ryegrass (*Lolium perenne*).
2. **All Known Gramineous Hosts**—A listing of common names for the following species is given in Appendix Table IV. *Agrostis palustris* Huds., *Arrhenatherum elatius* (L.) Presl, *Avena sativa* L., *Cynodon dactylon* (L.) Pers., *Hordeum vulgare* L., *Lolium multiflorum* Lam., *L. perenne* L., *Oryza sativa* L., *Poa annua* L., *P. pratensis* L., *Saccharum officinarum* L., *Sorghum vulgare* Pers., *Triticum aestivum* L., *Zea mays* L. (Lucas, 1976; Orr *et al.*, 1977; Sprague, 1950; Wells, 1959; Punja *et al.*, 1982a).

Disease Profile

In the eastern United States, Sclerotium blight usually appears in mid-summer. In California, the disease becomes apparent in the early spring (usually the second or third week in May) and continues throughout the summer.

Sclerotium rolfsii survives adverse climatic conditions in the form of sclerotia in the debris of the previous season's growth or in the soil. Air temperatures above 75 °F (24 °C) and regularly occurring periods of thatch wetness followed by short drying periods of 1–2 hours are the conditions most conducive to sclerotial germination. Once the sclerotia have germinated, rapid and abundant growth of the mycelium is favored by continually moist thatch (Boyle, 1961).

The sclerotia may undergo either "hyphal germination" or "eruptive germination." Hyphal germination is characterized by individual hyphal strands growing from the surface of the sclerotium. This process can be repeated several times from the same sclerotium. In the instances of hyphal germination, the hyphae do not use the sclerotium as an energy base;

therefore, they must grow saprophytically in the thatch and soil before they can infect living host tissue.

When eruptive sclerotial germination occurs, the nutrient reserves within the sclerotium serve as the energy base for the growth of the hyphae. These hyphae can infect living host tissue without receiving additional nutrients from an outside source. However, with this form of germination there is no succession of hyphal growths, each sclerotium produces only one hyphal mass (Punja and Grogan, 1981a, 1981b).

The climatic conditions most favorable for infection and rapid colonization of roots and crowns by *Sclerotium rolfsii* are air temperatures in the 85–95 °F (30–35 °C) range, and either extended time periods in which the relative humidity remains at 90–100 percent or rain showers at frequent enough intervals to maintain a moist, but not excessively wet, thatch. These are also the prerequisites for the formation of the sclerotia (Boyle, 1961; Lucas, 1976; Punja and Grogan, 1981a).

Control

Control of Sclerotium blight can be accomplished with applications of triadimefon, cyproconazole, or flutolanil. In the eastern United States, treatments should begin in late June. In California, the first fungicide application should usualy be made during the second or third week of May. Succeeding applications should continue at two week intervals for the remainder of the spring and summer months.

For a profile of these fungicides and the names of representative manufacturers, See Appendix Table I.

Melanotus White Patch

Melanotus white patch has been reported from Alabama, Georgia, Kentucky, North Carolina, Tennessee, Virginia, and the District of Columbia. The disease was reported initially on fescue (*Festuca* spp.), but more recently has been diagnosed on creeping bentgrass (*Agrostis palustris*) under golf green management.

Symptoms

On fescue, Melanotus white patch is first seen as circular, white to off-white patches of blighted turfgrass ranging from 3–14 inches (8–36 cm) in diameter. Individual patches may be surrounded by a salmon-pink border. Also, the grass leaves within the affected areas may mat together and eventually become closely pressed to the soil surface. Under conditions favorable for disease development, the patches may coalesce to involve large areas of turfgrass (Plate 5-B, C).

Individual turfgrass blades are bleached to a light tan color, starting at the tip and progressing toward the leaf sheath. The disease is restricted to the leaf blades, with the crowns of the plants remaining unaffected. Both the mycelium and the fruiting bodies of the causal fungus occur commonly on the surfaces of the affected leaves. The mycelium develops as a grayish-white cobwebby growth on the leaves. The fruiting structures are very distinctive, and, therefore, serve as a valuable aid to diagnosis. These are small grayish-white mushroom-like bodies, 1/16 to 5/16 inch (2–8 mm) in diameter. They develop initially as small round balls. Eventually, they open and the familiar gills found on mushrooms are apparent on their lower sides (Plate 5-E).

On bentgrass golf greens Melanotus white patch is seen as irregularly shaped off-white patches of blighted turfgrass ranging from 2–3 inches (5–8 cm) in diameter (Plate 5-D).

The Fungus

Melanotus phillipsii (Berk. and Br.) Singer

Description

Pileus brown to brown-red, often almost whitish when dry. Lamellae adnate. Spores smooth, 5.7–6.3 × 2.7–3.3 μm, pale melleous in color, comparatively thin but undoubtedly double walled and inconstant, small to faint germ pore. Basidia remarkably short and broadly clavate, hyaline, 4-spored, about 6 μm broad. The cheilocystidia are clavate, most of them with a filiform elongation. Pleurocystidia absent.

Procedures for Isolation and Culture

Melanotus phillipsii grows well on malt extract agar at 24 °C. Sporocarps are also produced on this medium (Wick, 1982).

Turfgrass Hosts

Creeping bentgrass (*Agrostis palustris* Huds.), tall fescue (*Festuca arundinacea* Schreb.), red fescue (*Festuca rubra* L.), and Chewings fescue (*Festuca rubra* var. *commutata* Gaud.)

Disease Profile

Melanotus white patch is more severe on tall fescue stands during their first year of establishment. Also, heavily seeded grass is usually more severely affected by the disease than grass seeded at an appropriate rate.

The development of the disease is favored by hot, humid weather. Damage is greatest when the daytime air temperatures exceed 85 °F (30 °C) and the night temperatures do not fall below 70 °F (21 °C). In a given stand of grass, the most severe level of disease development occurs in the areas exposed to full sunlight rather than shaded areas. Also, outbreaks of Melanotus white patch are heaviest under conditions of low soil moisture content.

Control

Tests with currently available turfgrass fungicides have failed to control this disease. Certain cultural practices, however, are helpful in reducing disease severity. Since Melanotus white patch is favored by hot, dry weather conditions, watering at frequent enough intervals to maintain the soil close to field capacity (-0.033 MPa) during these times will alleviate the problem to some extent. Also, although this information is usually of little solace to the owner of the fescue turf that is severely affected by this disease, since development of Melanotus white patch is highly dependent on high air temperatures, and the causal fungus does not colonize crown tissue, with the return of cooler growing temperatures, total recovery of the affected plants often occurs.

WINTER PATCH DISEASES

Fusarium Patch

Formerly known as "pink snow mold," Fusarium patch is the most commonly occurring low temperature disease of cool season turfgrasses in North America, the British Isles, Western Europe, Norway, Sweden, Iceland, Japan, New Zealand, and Australia. The development of Fusarium patch is favored by cold, humid conditions; therefore, severe outbreaks can occur either under snow cover or in the absence of snow. In many areas of the world this disease develops most commonly during the months of late fall through early spring; however, in the cool, humid sea climates of coastal regions of the United States, Canada, the British Isles, and New Zealand, outbreaks can occur at any time of the year during cool, wet weather (Smith, 1987; McBeath, 1985).

Symptoms

When outbreaks occur during cold, wet weather, Fusarium patch is first seen as roughly circular, water-soaked appearing spots 2–3 inches (5–7.5 cm) in diameter. The color of the center portions of the developing patches changes to reddish-brown and then to tan. The leaves of the affected plants tend to mat together. Also, a faint growth of white or dull pink mycelium may develop at the margins of the patches. The pink coloration is highly transitory and is usually noticeable only during early daylight hours. On turf with a high population of annual bluegrass (*Poa annua*), the patches often develop distinctive reddish-brown borders.

The size of the patches may expand to 12 inches (30 cm) or more in diameter within 48–72 hours from the onset of symptoms. Sometimes the plants in the center of a patch will begin recovering from the disease while the pathogen is still active at the periphery, producing a frogeye pattern. Under conditions of extended leaf wetness and low air temperatures, adjacent patches often coalesce, resulting in a uniform blighting of large areas of turf.

When Fusarium patch develops under a snow cover, as the snow melts, the prevailing overall symptoms are roughly circular, dull white patches from 3–12 inches (7.5–30 cm) in diameter. When the predominant species of the turf is annual bluegrass (*Poa annua*), these patches may also have reddish-brown borders 0.5–2 inches (1–5 cm) wide. The most recently revealed patches near the edges of the receding snow line are often covered with an abundant growth of white to light pink mycelium. Also, the leaf blades are usually matted together. Under conditions of extended leaf wetness, numerous, very small, pink-colored clusters of spores (sporodochia) may also develop on the surfaces of the leaves. A photographic display of the range of symptoms of Fusarium patch is given in Plate 19.

The Fungus

Microdochium nivale (Fr.) Samuels and Hallett; telemorph *Monographella nivalis* (Schaf.) E. Muller; syn. *Fusarium nivale* (Fr.) Ces.

Description

Mycelium somewhat cobwebby or stringy when young, faintly pale salmon or flesh color to pale rose, producing conidia loosely in the mycelium or in orange to paler colored spore masses; most of the spores in younger cultures are nonseptate to 3-septate, often without an evident heel, 0-septate spores measure 2.0–2.8 μm × 8–12 μm (average 2.4 μm × 9.6 μm); 1-septate spores measure 2.4–3 μm × 13–18 μm; 3-septate spores measure 2.8–3 μm × 19–27 μm; and 4–7 septate spores measure 2.5–4.0 μm × 19–30 μm (Figure 4-22).

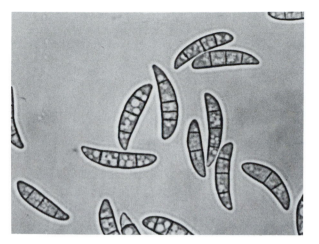

Figure 4-22. Conidia of *Microdochium nivale. Courtesy Paul E. Nelson.*

Perithecia attached to a wrinkled stromatic substrate, biscuit-shaped or oval in outline, 125–200 × 300–800 μm; plectenchymatous. Spores in one or sometimes 2 rows, 8 in each elongate ascus, spindle-form, straight or curved, smooth, 1–3 septate, 3.2 μm × 15.2 μm, mostly 3.0–3.4 μm × 13–18 μm (2–4 μm × 10–20 μm).

Procedures for Isolation and Culture

In culture, the fungus grows at temperatures from 0–32 °C, with an optimum of 20 °C. Abundant mycelial growth, and sporulation is produced on potato-dextrose agar at 20 °C. in diffuse light (Dahl, 1934).

Hosts

1. **Turfgrasses**—Colonial bentgrass (*Agrostis tenuis*), creeping bentgrass (*Agrostis palustris*), velvet bentgrass (*Agrostis canina*), bermudagrass (*Cynodon dactylon*), annual bluegrass (*Poa annua*), Kentucky bluegrass (*Poa pratensis*), annual ryegrass (*Lolium multiflorum*), perennial ryegrass (*Lolium perenne*), Chewings fescue (*Festuca rubra* var. *commutata*), sheep fescue (*Festuca ovina*), tall fescue (*Festuca arundinacea*), and red fescue (*Festuca rubra*).

2. **All Known Gramineous Hosts**—A listing of common names for the following species is given in Appendix Table IV. *Agropyron cristatum* (L.) Gaertn., *A. dasytachyum* (Hook.) Scribn., *A. desertorum* (Fisch.) Schult., *A. inerme* (Scribn. and Smith) Rydb., *A. intermedium* (Host) Beauv., *A. repens* (L.) Beauv., *A. rigidum* Beauv., *A. riparium* Scribn. and Smith, *A. semicostatum* (Steud.) Nees,

A. sibiricum (Willd.) Beauv., *A. smithii* Rydb., *A. spicatum* (Pursh) Scribn. and Smith, *A. subsecundum* (Link) Hitchc., *A. trachycaulum* (Link) Malte, *A. trichophorum* (Link) Richt., *Agrostis alba* L., *A. canina* L., *A. exarata* Trin., *A. palustris* Huds., *A. tenuis* Sibth., *Avena byzantina* C. Koch, *A. sativa* L., *Bromus carinatus* Hook. and Arn., *B. commutatus* Schrad., *B. erectus* Huds., *B. inermis* Leyss., *B. japonicus* Thunb., *B. mollis* L., *B. purgans* L., *B. racemosus* L., *B. rigidus* Roth, *B. secalinus* L., *B. tectorum* L., *Calamagrostis breweri* Thurb., *C. canadensis* (Michx) Beauv., *Cynodon dactylon* (L.) Pers., *Dactylis glomerata* L., *Elymus canadensis* L., *E. excelsus* Turcz., *E. glaucus* Buckl., *E. macounii* Vasey, *E. sibiricus* L., *Festuca arundinacea* Schreb., *F. dertonensis* (All.) Aschers. and Graebn., *F. idahoensis* Elmer, *F. megalura* Nutt., *F. myuros* L., *F. ovina* L., *F. rubra* L., *F. rubra* var. *commutata* Gaud., *Holcus lanatus* L., *Hordeum brachyantherum* Nevski, *H. bulbosum* L., *H. jubatum* L., *H. murinum* L., *H. secalinum* Guss., *H. vulgare* L., *Hystrix patula* Moench, *Koeleria cristata* (L.) Pers., *Lolium multiflorum* Lam., *L. perenne* L., *Oryzopsis bloomeri* (Boland) Ricker, *O. hymenoides* (Roem. and Schult.) Ricker, *Phleum phleoides* (L.) Karst., *P. pratense* L., *Poa ampla* Merr., *P. annua* L., *P. arctica* R. Br., *P. bulbosa* L., *P. cusickii* Vasey, *P. leptocoma* Trin., *P. palustris* L., *P. pratensis* L., *P. secunda* Presl, *P. trivialis* L., *Secale cereale* L., *Sitanion hystrix* (Nutt.) J. G. Smith, *S. jubatum* J. G. Smith, *Stipa columbiana* Macoun., *S. columbiana* var. *nelsoni* (Scribn.) Hitchc., *S. comata* Trin. and Rupr., *S. lemmoni* (Vasey) Scribn., *Triticum aestivum* L. (Dahl, 1934; Index Plant Dis., 1960; Sprague, 1950).

Disease Profile

Snow cover is not a requirement for the development of Fusarium patch. Also, although it is commonly thought of as a disease of late fall, winter, and early spring, in certain regions of the world, outbreaks of Fusarium patch can occur during any month of the year. The optimum conditions for development of Fusarium patch are high atmospheric humidity and air temperatures ranging from 32–45 °F (0–7 °C). However, under the conditions of extended leaf wetness brought on by ground fogs, mists, or frequent, light rain showers, severe outbreaks of Fusarium patch can also occur at air temperatures up to 65 ° F (18 ° C). When the air temperatures reach 70 °F (21 °C), the fungus ceases to be pathogenic (Dahl, 1934; Smith, 1987).

A deep, persistent snow that has been deposited

on unfrozen ground also establishes optimum conditions for development of Fusarium patch. The reason for this is that the humid atmosphere and microclimate temperatures created by the snow cover are ideal for the growth of *Microdochium nivale*. Furthermore, during these times, respiration continues but the plants do not have sufficient light for photosynthesis. As the result, the carbohydrate reserves in the leaves are lowered, which in turn increases their vulnerability to infection and colonization by the fungus (Smith, 1987).

Microdochium nivale survives adverse climatic conditions as dormant mycelium in the host or in debris of previously diseased leaves. Abundant conidial production occurs soon after the onset of optimum temperatures. Conidia are carried to the leaves by splashing water, where primary infections are accomplished by penetration through stomata and cut leaf tips. Direct penetration of healthy epidermal cells has not been observed, however, when the leaves have been injured either by a heavy frost or intermittent exposures to freezing temperatures, penetration through these cells takes place in great abundance. Growth of the organism through the tissues of the leaf is at first intercellular, with abundant hyphal branching and growth in all directions. When the cells collapse, the fungus almost fills the spaces they occupied. When a leaf is severely diseased, pink clusters of spores (sporodochia) develop through the stomata in rows (Dahl, 1934; Tyson, 1936).

The severity of Fusarium patch is much greater when the pH of the top 1 inch (2.5 cm) of soil is 6.5 and above (Smith, 1958) (Table 4-13). Also, applications of fertilizer high in water soluble nitrogen late in the growing season, or during the winter months, is particularly conducive to the development of the disease (Brauen *et al.*, 1975; Dahl, 1934; Lebeau, 1968; Smith, 1953; Tyson, 1936). It is not known whether

this change in the pattern of Fusarium patch is due to (a) increased susceptibility of the plants to infection and colonization, or (b) the development of longer grass in the late fall and early winter months and thus creating a more extensive microclimate favorable for development of the disease. Most likely, both sets of conditions contribute to the situation.

Control

Cultural Practices

In stands of turfgrass with a history of Fusarium patch, applications of fertilizers comprised of readily available forms of nitrogen late in the growing season should be avoided. If such fertilization practices are deemed necessary, then the turf in question should be treated simultaneously with a fungicide.

Regulation of soil pH is important to the successful control of Fusarium patch. In regions characterized by alkaline soils, every effort should be made to maintain the pH of the soil in the acid range. Where acidic soils are the order of the day, applications of lime should be made in the spring rather than late in the growing season.

The grass must not be left uncut in the fall. Raise the cutting height approximately 20 percent at the end of the growing season to allow for better cold temperature survival, and continue to mow until top growth is stopped.

Management practices that hold thatch at 0.5 inch (1.3 cm) or less will subsequently aid in reducing the severity of Fusarium patch. Also, either the use of snow fences or the planting of shrub or tree wind breaks to minimize snow accumulation in areas highly prone to drifts will help reduce the severity of the disease. In early spring, rapid draining and drying of surface moisture by removal of the mycelial crust from the surface of affected turf, along with fertilization with 4 ounces (114 g) readily available nitrogen per 1,000 square feet (93 m²), will favor recovery of the grass.

Use of Resistant Grasses

Annual bluegrass (*Poa annua*) is extremely susceptible to Fusarium patch. Under heavy pressure from the disease, it is not uncommon for the entire population of plants within the affected area to be killed.

The bentgrasses rank next in order of susceptibility, with creeping bentgrass (*Agrostis palustris*) and velvet bentgrass (*Agrostis canina*) being more resistant to the disease than Colonial bentgrass (*Agrostis tenuis*). Colonization of roots and crowns of

Table 4-13. The effect of different rates of calcium carbonate on the pH of the top 1 inch (2.5 cm) of soil and the occurrence of Fusarium patch. *After Smith, 1958.*

Calcium carbonate per square yard	Trial A		Trial B	
	pH	Disease Incidence*	pH	Disease Incidence[a]
0	4.6	0.4	4.3	1.3
2 oz	6.5	5.5	4.6	5.6
4 oz	6.8	7.1	5.2	17.9
8 oz	7.1	11.1	6.4	31.6
16 oz	7.2	15.9	7.0	44.0

[a]Disease incidence is based on percent of turfgrass surface blighted. The percentage given for each treatment is the average of readings taken over a 4 month period.

bentgrass plants by the fungus is common and under heavy disease pressure, death of a high population of plants within the affected area can occur.

Kentucky bluegrass (*Poa pratensis*), perennial ryegrass (*Lolium perenne*), and red fescue (*Festuca rubra*) rank third in order of susceptibility. Under heavy disease pressure, foliar blighting may be complete, but extensive crown and root colonization by the fungus is rare, and when the air temperatures move into the 60–75 °F (15–24 °C) range, the affected plants usually recover.

Use of Fungicides

Fusarium patch may be controlled by single component applications of either mercury chlorides, triadimefon, cyproconazole, propiconazole, thiophanate methyl, benomyl, or fenarimol, or by the use of two or three component combinations of quintozene, iprodione, chlorothalonil, or vinclozolin (Table 4-14), or a commercial mixture of oxycarboxin, carbathlin and thiram (Arrest 75 W™) (Fushtey, 1980; Gould et al., 1961, 1965; Burpee, 1988; Smith and Mortensen, 1981; Worf, 1988).

Control failures have been reported after repeated use of certain of these materials. In the United States, tolerance of *Microdochium nivale* to iprodione and vinclozolin has been reported from the Pacific Northwest (Chastagner and Vassey, 1979), and benomyl tolerance on the part of the fungus is thought to occur commonly in the Canadian prairies (Smith and Mortensen, 1981).

In climates in which winter snows are common, the treatment should be made within two weeks of the first predicted snowfall of the season, with midwinter and early spring applications when weather conditions permit. In regions with snow-free climates, fungicide treatments should begin just prior to the advent of cold, wet weather, and if the turf in question has a history of severe outbreaks of Fusarium patch, and either triadimefon, iprodione, propiconazole, thiophanate methyl, benomyl, fenarimol, or vinclozolin is being used, the succeeding applications should be made at 2–3 week intervals as long as the cold, wet weather persists.

For a profile of each of these fungicides and a listing of representative trade names and manufacturers, see Appendix Table I.

Typhula Blight

Typhula blight is a major disease of cool season turfgrasses in the United States, Canada, Switzerland, Austria, Germany, the Netherlands, the British Isles, Norway, Sweden, and Japan (Smith, 1987). The disease can develop during cold, wet weather, however, it is usually most severe when the turf is covered with snow for an extended period of time.

Symptoms

Typhula blight is first seen in overall view as light yellow discolored areas of 1–2 inches (2.5–7 cm) in diameter. The leaves of the plants in these infection centers soon progress from a scalded, discolored appearance to a grayish white—finally becoming matted together in the latter stages of decomposition. As these areas enlarge, a characteristic halo of grayish-while mycelial growth up to 1 inch in diameter develops at their advancing margin. Affected areas may measure up to 1–2 feet (30–60 cm) in diameter, but under optimum conditions for disease development, due to a coalescence of infection centers, zones of blighted turfgrass may be much larger (Plate 20-A, B, C, D, E).

A primary diagnostic feature of Typhula blight is the presence of characteristic sclerotia embedded in the leaves and crowns of diseased plants. These hardened fungus bodies range in size from an ordinary pinhead to 3/16 inch (5 mm) in diameter. Early in the season, they are yellow or light brown. Eventually, they turn dark brown, are ovoid to spherical, and of irregular, rough contour (Plate 20-F, Plate 21-F).

The Fungi

A. *Typhula incarnata* Lasch ex. Fr. [*Typhula itoana* Imai (?)]

Table 4-14. Fungicide combinations for the control of Fusarium patch

Fungicide Combinations[a,b]	Rate Formulated Product per 1,000 ft² (93 m²)
Iprodione (50 WP) +	8 oz (226.8 g)
Chlorothalonil (4.17 FLO)	8 oz (226.8 g)
Chlorothalonil (75 WP) +	6 oz (170.1 g)
Quintozene (75 WP)	6 oz (170.1 g)
Iprodione (50 WP) +	2 oz (56.7 g)
Chlorothalonil (75 WP) +	4 oz (113.2 g)
Quintozene (75 WP)	4 oz (113.2 g)
Vinclozolin (50 WP) +	2 oz (56.7 g)
Chlorothalonil (75 WP) +	4 oz (113.2 g)
Quintozene (75 WP)	4 oz (113.2 g)

[a]Fungicides are listed by coined names, see Appendix Table I for representative trade names of each.
[b]The information in parenthesis after each fungicide name indicates formulation type and concentration of active ingredient.

Description

Plants 3.4–30 mm high, solitary or in small groups form the sclerotium, simple, rarely with a branch. Head 1–20 × 0.4–2 mm, filiform, cylindric, ellipsoid-oblong, when short becoming hollow, acute then blunt, often subarcuate, whitish then flesh color or rose-pink. Stem 5–20 × 0.5–1 mm, translucent white or whitish cream, then greyish or dingy brownish, puberulous. Spores mostly 7–10 × 3–5 μm, white, smooth, ellipsoid or ovoid, flattened adaxially. Basidia mostly 20–30 × 4–6 um. Hyphae 3.5–6 μm wide, thin walled, clamped, with a few gloeocystidium-like hyphae, more or less agglutinated throughout the hymenium; incrusted with crystals in the subhymenium and sparsely in the stem. Sclerotia 0.5–4.5 × 0.5–2 mm, subglobose, more or less flattened, smooth, drying or ageing rough, sometimes irregular, pinkish orange when immature, then tawny to reddish brown or dark brown, erumpent, often falling off, singly or (in culture) coalescent. Medulla wholly agglutinated, often filamentous in the center, hollow in large sclerotia. Cuticle 8 μm thick, golden to reddish brown.

Procedures for Isolation and Culture

In culture, the organism grows well on potato-dextrose agar. Growth occurs between 0–18 °C, with an optimum of 9–12 °C. Sclerotia are produced in 5–10 days at 9–12 °C (Remsberg, 1940).

Hosts

1. **Turfgrasses**—Colonial bentgrass (*Agrostis tenuis*), creeping bentgrass (*Agrostis palustris*), velvet bentgrass (*Agrostis canina*), tall fescue (*Festuca arundinacea*), red fescue (*Festuca rubra*), perennial ryegrass (*Lolium perenne*), annual bluegrass (*Poa annua*), and Kentucky bluegrass (*Poa pratensis*).
2. **All Known Gramineous Hosts**—A listing of common names for the following species is given in Appendix Table IV. *Agropyron spicatum* (Pursh) Scribn., *A. subsecundum* (Link) Hitchc., *Agrostis canina* L., *A. palustris* Huds., *A. tenuis* Sibth., *Avena sativa* L., *Bromus tectorum* L., *Dactylis glomerata* L., *Elymus glaucus* Buckl., *Festuca arundinacea* Schreb., *F. rubra* L., *Holcus lanatus* L., *Hordeum vulgare* L., *Lolium perenne* L., *Phleum pratense* L., *Poa annua* L., *P. palustris* L., *P. pratensis* L. *P. secunda* Presl, *P. trivialis* L., *Secale cereale* L., *Stipa columbiana* var. *nelsoni* (Scribn.) Hitchc., *Triticum aestivum* L., (Howard *et al.*, 1951; Sprague, 1940; Wernham and Chilton, 1943; Wernham and Kirby, 1940).

The Fungi

B. *Typhula ishikariensis* Imai

Description

The designation *Typhula ishikariensis* has been redefined by Arsvoll and Smith (1978) as three subspecies. This was accomplished by (a) erecting *Typhula ishikariensis* Imai var. *ishikariensis* Arsvoll and Smith, (b) combining *Typhula ishikariensis* with *Typhula idahoensis* Remsberg to form *Typhula ishikariensis* Imai var. *idahoensis* Arsvoll and Smith, and (c) combining *Typhula ishikariensis* with *Typhula hyperborea* Extstrand to form *Typhula ishikariensis* Imai var. *canadensis* Arsvoll and Smith. All three varieties are pathogenic to turfgrasses. For a discussion of the basis for these recombinations and subspecies descriptions, see Arsvoll and Smith (1978) and Smith (1987).

Hosts

1. **Turfgrasses**—Colonial bentgrass (*Agrostis tenuis*), creeping bentgrass (*Agrostis palustris*), velvet bentgrass (*Agrostis canina*), tall fescue (*Festuca arundinacea*), red fescue (*Festuca rubra*), Chewings fescue (*Festuca rubra* var. *commutata*), sheep fescue (*Festuca ovina*), perennial ryegrass (*Lolium perenne*), annual bluegrass (*Poa annua*), and Kentucky bluegrass (*Poa pratensis*).
2. **All Known Gramineous Hosts**—A listing of common names for the following species is given in Appendix Table IV. *Agropyron cristatum* (L.) Gaertn., *A. inerme* (Scribn. and Sm.) Rydb., *A. intermedium* (Host.) Beauv., *A. smithii* Rydb., *Agrostis canina* L., *A. palustris* Huds., *A. tenuis* Sibth., *Bromus carinatus* Hook. and Arn., *B. inermis* Leyss, *B. tectorum* L., *Deschampsia elongata* (Hook.) Munro, *Festuca arundinacea* Schreb., *F. ovina* L., *F. rubra* L., *F. rubra* var. *commutata* Guad., *Hordeum nodosum* L., *Lolium perenne* L., *Poa annua* L., *P. pratensis* L., *Phleum pratense* L., *Stipa columbiana* var. *nelsoni* (Scribn.) Hitchc., *S. comata* Trin. and Rupr., *Triticum aestivum* L. (Smith, 1987; Sprague, 1950; Vaartnou and Elliott, 1969).

Disease Profile

The optimum conditions for development of Typhula blight are prolonged periods of high atmospheric humidity and air temperatures ranging from 36–40 °F (2–5 °C). Although mild cases of the disease are known to occur in regions where there is usually little or no snow cover, severe outbreaks normally develop only in areas in which the winter weather is characterized by persistent snow covers.

Typhula ishikariensis is usually associated with the development of Typhula blight where winters are longer and more severe than is the case with *Typhula incarnata* (Smith, 1980). Also, *Typhula ishikariensis*-incited outbreaks of Typhula blight are usually more severe than those incited by *Typhula incarnata*. There is no evidence that *Typhula ishikariensis* is the more pathogenic of the two species (Wernham and Chilton, 1943). Rather, since it is found primarily in regions where snow cover persists for a longer period of time, the greater disease severity is probably due to the fact that the energy reserves of the turfgrasses become more depleted, thus increasing their vulnerability to colonization by the fungus (Smith, 1987).

Both fungi survive the warm summer months in the form of sclerotia. In late fall, under the stimulus of cold weather, high humidity, and exposure to light rays of short wave length (2700 Å–3200 Å), the sclerotia produce basidiocarps (Remsberg, 1940). Basidiospores are discharged during periods of rainfall or persistent fog and are dispersed by wind and splashing water. During cold, wet weather or under a snow cover, sclerotia also germinate to produce mycelia. Light is not necessary for mycelial production. Although basidiospores are capable of producing infections, the vast majority of primary infections are initiated by mycelium produced by the direct germination of sclerotia (Smith, 1987; Sprague and Rainey, 1950).

Control

Cultural Practices

Late summer or early fall applications of nitrogenous fertilizers should be avoided. However, in the event of low soil fertility, moderate applications of balanced fertilizer may be made in late fall when the plants are entering into dormancy in order to facilitate rapid plant regrowth in the spring. Also, the installation of snow fences or the establishment of shrub or tree wind breaks to minimize snow accumulation in areas highly prone to drifts will help reduce the severity of Typhula blight.

Management practices that hold thatch at 0.5 inch (1.3 cm) or less will subsequently aid in reducing the severity of Typhula blight.

Breaking up the matted turfgrass in the affected areas by brushing or raking before applying fungicides will facilitate faster plant recovery.

Use of Fungicides

Typhula blight may be controlled by single component applications of either mercury chlorides, flutolanil, propiconazole, cyproconazole, or triadimefon, or the use of two or three component combinations of quintozene, flutolanil, vinclozolin, or iprodione (Table 4-15), or a commercial mixture of oxycarboxin, carbathlin and thiram (Arrest 75 W™). The first application should be made within two weeks of the first predicted snowfall of the season. When feasible, fungicide applications should also be made at midwinter and early spring (Burpee *et al.*, 1990; Fushtey, 1980; Stienstra, 1980; Vargas and Beard, 1970).

For a profile of each of these fungicides and a listing of representative trade names and manufacturers, see Appendix Table I.

Sclerotinia Patch

Sclerotinia patch has been reported to occur in Sweden, Norway, Finland, Canada, Alaska, Minnesota, and Colorado.

Symptoms

In overall view, the disease is first seen as small yellowish-green areas 2–4 inches (5–10 cm) in diameter. The leaves of the affected plants soon turn grayish white and become matted together. As these areas enlarge, a dark gray mycelial growth may be seen near the advancing margins. Individual patches

Table 4-15. Fungicide combinations for the control of Typhula blight

Fungicide Combinations[a,b]	Rate Formulated Product per 1,000 ft² (93 m²)
Iprodione (50 WP) +	8.0 oz (226.8 g)
Chlorothalonil (4.17 FLO)	8.0 oz (226.8 g)
Chlorothalonil (75 WP) +	6.0 oz (170.1 g)
Quintozene (75 WP)	6.0 oz (170.1 g)
Iprodione (50 WP) +	2.0 oz (56.7 g)
Chlorothalonil (75 WP) +	4.0 oz (113.2 g)
Quintozene (75 WP)	4.0 oz (113.2 g)
Vinclozolin (50 WP) +	2.0 oz (56.7 g)
Chlorothalonil (75 WP) +	4.0 oz (113.2 g)
Quintozene (75 WP)	4.0 oz (113.2 g)
Flutolanil (50 WP) +	4.3 oz (121.7 g)
Quintozene (75 WP)	4.0 oz (113.2 g)

[a]Fungicides are listed by coined names, see Appendix Table I for representative trade names of each.
[b]The information in parenthesis after each fungicide name indicates formulation type and concentration of active ingredient.

may measure up to 24–36 inches (60–90 cm) in diameter. Under optimum conditions these often coalesce to create large areas of uniformly blighted turfgrass (Plate 21-A, B, C). Under severe disease conditions, crown and crown bud tissues become extensively rotted.

A key diagnostic feature of Sclerotinia patch is the presence of small dull black sclerotia embedded in and on the surface of diseased leaves. These are in contrast to the light yellow to reddish-brown sclerotia characteristic of Typhula blight (Plate 21-D, E, F).

The Fungus

Myrioclerotinia borealis (Bubak and Vleugel) Kohn; syn. *Sclerotinia borealis* Bubak and Vleugel

Description

Sclerotia tuberoid, variously shaped, usually more or less elongated, oblong to nearly circular, sometimes curved or lobed, mostly 3–8 × 2–4 mm, black, easily detached from the substrate. Spermatia known only in culture, hyaline, globose, 2.5–3.5 μm, produced endogenously in flask-shaped phialides borne in clusters on the mycelium. Conidia lacking. Apothecia arising from the sclerotia singly or in groups, stipitate, cyathiform, expanding to shallow cup-shaped, 2.5–5.5 mm diam., bister to Natal brown, hymenium even or umbilicate-depressed, fleshy, margin even or sometimes irregular; stipe 2–6 mm long, about 1 mm diam. at the apex, tapering slightly toward the base, paler than the hymenium, finely pubescent above to subtomentose at the base; tissue of the hypothecium and stipe prosenchymatous, composed of ascending, more or less parallel to interwoven, hyaline to faintly yellowish hyphae 6–8 μm diam., curving toward the outside and forming a more compact excipular zone, appearing pseudoparenchymatous, with short, hyaline hairs arising from the outer cells; subhymenium a narrow, compact zone of closely interwoven, slender, yellowish hyphae about 3 μm diam.; asci cylindric, tapering below to a long, slender stalk, eight spored, 175–200 × 11–14 μm; ascospores curved or unequal sided, uniserate, 17–21 × 6–8 μm; paraphyses hyaline, filiform, septate, simple, 2–3 μm diam., tips sometimes slightly enlarged.

Procedures for Isolation and Culture

The fungus grows well on potato dextrose agar at 5–10 °C. Apothecia may be produced in culture by the following incubation technique: The fungus should be grown on sterilized wheat grains in the dark at 5 °C. for three months. The sclerotia are then removed and placed on moist, sterilized, quartz sand in the dark at 0 °C for two months. They should be placed in the dark at 5 °C for one month and then transferred to growing conditions of alternating daylight–darkness, and maintained at a temperature of 10 °C with intermittent fluctuations of ±5 °C. Mature apothecia usually develop in two months from the intiation of the final incubation period (Groves and Bowerman, 1955).

Hosts

1. **Turfgrasses**—creeping bentgrass (*Agrostis palustris*), Colonial bentgrass (*Agrostis tenuis*), velvet bentgrass (*Agrostis canina*), red fescue (*Festuca rubra*), tall fescue (*Festuca arundinacea*), Kentucky bluegrass (*Poa pratensis*), and perennial ryegrass (*Lolium perenne*).

2. **All Known Gramineous Hosts**—A listing of common names for the following species is given in Appendix Table V. *Agropyron dasystachyum* (Hook.) Scribn., *A. desertorum* (Fisch.) Schult., *A. intermedium* (Host) Beauv., *Agrostis canina* L., *A. palustris* Huds., *A. tenuis* Sibth., *Alopecurus pratensis* L., *Arrhenatherum elatius* (L.) Presl, *Bromus erectus* Huds., *B. inermis* Leyss., *Dactylis glomerata* L., *Elymus canadensis* L., *E. giganteus* (L.) Vahl., *E. sibiricus* L., *Festuca arundinacea* Schreb., *F. rubra* L., *Lolium perenne* L., *Phleum pratense* L., *Poa ampla* Merr., *P. compressa* L., *P. pratensis* L., *P. trivialis* L., *Secale cereale* L. (Groves and Bowerman, 1955; Kallio, 1966; Lebeau and Logsdon, 1958).

Disease Profile

The primary infection and the elevated colonization stages of Sclerotinia patch develop under different weather conditions. Ascospores serve as the principal means of infection and these are only produced and dispersed in the fall. The colonizations that result from these infections, however, remain in the incipient stage until the turf has been covered with snow for an extended period of time. The impact of the fall weather on spore production, and the depth and longevity of snow cover during the winter and early spring months, then, are critical factors in determining the ultimate incidence and severity of this disease.

The optimum weather conditions for the development of Sclerotinia patch are extended periods of frequent rainfalls and daily air temperatures ranging between 49–59 °F (6–15 °C), culminated by a deep, persistent snow cover that has been deposited on unfrozen ground. If the fall weather is dry and the air temperatures stabilize rapidly in the low 40s F, and/or the winter months are marked by light, infrequent snowfalls, the incidence and severity of the disease will be minimal.

Myriosclerotinia borealis survives the warm summer months in the form of sclerotia. Under the stimulus of a moisture-saturated soil and daily air temperatures that range between 49–59 °C (6–15 °C), the sclerotia germinate to produce apothecia. Spread of the fungus is accomplished by wind-borne ascospores. Infection is accomplished by entry of hyphae through wounds and stomates and direct penetration at the junctures of epidermal cells (Arsvoll, 1976; Smith, 1987; Tomiyama, 1955).

The fungus does not sporulate at air temperatures less than 45 °F (6 °C). Also, it does not have a strong competitive saprophytic ability. Therefore, the majority of the patches that occur after the onset of winter weather evolve from the incipient colonizations that developed during the fall months. Spread of the fungus from plant to plant under snow cover is accomplished through contact of colonized leaves with healthy ones (Sakuma and Narita, 1963; Smith, 1987).

The optimum temperature range for patch formation is 32–35 °F (0–2 °C). The reason for the heightened severity of Sclerotinia patch under deep, persistent snow cover is that the humid atmosphere and microclimate temperatures are ideal for the growth of *Myriosclerotinia borealis*. Also, under these conditions, respiration continues, but the plants do not have sufficient light for photosynthesis. As the result, the carbohydrate reserves in the leaves become depleted, which in turn increases their susceptibility to infection and colonization by the fungus (Bruehl and Cunfer, 1971; Smith, 1987).

Applications of fertilizer high in water soluble nitrogen late in the growing season or immediately after snow melt in the spring will increase the severity of Sclerotinia patch (Tomiyama, 1955). Development of the disease is also greater when the grass is grown at low levels of phosphorus or on highly acid soils (Arsvoll and Larsen, 1977).

Control

Cultural Practices

High rates of nitrogenous fertilizers in the late summer and fall should be avoided and soil phosphorous maintained at an adequate level. The soil pH should be maintained in the pH 5.6–6.0 range. However, in areas where Fusarium patch and take-all patch are also a major problem, fall applications of lime should be avoided, and care should be taken not to adjust the pH into the alkaline range.

Use of Resistant Grasses

Red fescue (*Festuca rubra*) is extremely susceptible to Sclerotinia patch. The bentgrasses rank next in order of susceptibility, with creeping bentgrass (*Agrostis palustris*) being more resistant to the disease than Colonial bentgrass (*Agrostis tenuis*). Kentucky bluegrass (*Poa pratensis*) is the most resistant species. Except for very severe outbreaks of the disease, affected stands of Kentucky bluegrass will usually show good recovery during the following growing season (Smith, 1987).

Use of Fungicides

Sclerotinia patch may be controlled with two applications of quintozene, benomyl, chlorothalonil, a mixture of thiram, carboxin, and oxycarboxon, or a mixture of quintozene and thiophanate methyl. The first application should be made in September and the second in October (Smith, 1976).

For a profile of each of these fungicides and a listing of representative trade names and manufacturers, see Appendix Table I.

Cottony Snow Mold

Cottony snow mold is known to occur in Alaska, the lower snowfall regions of western Canada, and the higher snowfall regions of the Canadian prairies. In addition to the commonly cultivated cool season turfgrasses, the incitant (*Coprinus psychromorbidus*) is capable of causing severe damage to a diverse list of other crop species (Broadfoot, 1941; Cormack, 1948).

Symptoms

The overall symptom pattern for cottony snow mold is similar to that for Fusarium patch. With the resumption of plant growth at the first spring thaw, there appear irregularly shaped areas of grass which are pale yellow at first and then become bleached in appearance. Ranging generally up to one foot in diameter, these areas may coalesce and involve large sections of turfgrass. Death of the entire plant usually results (Plate 22-A, B).

Cottony snow mold may be distinguished from Fusarium patch by the production of a mat of light gray hyphal growth over the affected areas, as opposed to the pinkish mycelial growth characteristic of the latter disease. The absence of light brown sclerotia embedded in the leaves, the chief diagnostic feature of Typhula blight, serves to distinguish this disease from cottony snow mold.

The Fungus

Coprinus psychromorbidus Redhead and Traquair

Description

Pileus 7–12 mm wide, conic to polane when fully mature, narrowly umbonate; margin finely plicate-striate, uplifted with age and splitting; pileus surface dry, ornamented with scattered, felt-like and recurved scales that are remnants of a universal veil, scale color light orange yellow to yellowish brown especially on the disc where scales are concentrated; pileus color pure white when young, changing to light gray or light grayish yellowish brown to grayish yellowish brown when mature; flesh very thin, up to 1.5 mm thick on the disc, watery white to pale gray; odor fungoid. **Lamellae** narrow, moderately close, free or attached at a ring around apex of stipe, gray to brownish black or black with age, deliquescent. **Stipe** 40–70 mm long and 2–3 mm wide at maturity, equal or slightly enlarged at the base, central hollow; flesh white and watery, fibrous; surface smooth to fibrous-silky, finely prunose near apex, furfuraceous at the base; color white to creamy white. **Primordia** (young buttons) pure white with brownish scales developing during expansion; mature basidiocarps deliquescent with evolution of HCN.

Spore deposit chocolate brown to brownish black. **Basidiospores** (6.4–) 7.2–8.8(9.6) × 4.5–5.6(–6.4) μm, pale brown or yellow brown to blackish brown in KOH and H$_2$O, elliptical to broadly elliptical and obscurely inequilateral in profile, elliptical, ovate or rarely subcordate in face view, smooth, thick-walled with apical pore present, pore slightly excentric, narrow to broad, spore apex consipicuously truncate. **Basidia** 12.0–22.0 × 8.8–10.0 μm, short clavate to subsaccate, thin-walled, four-spored, hyaline. **Brachybasidioles** (see Van de Bogart, 1976) 20.0–25.0 × 12.0–20.0 μm, saccate to broadly elliptical, thin-walled, hyaline, surrounding the basidia in a rosette pattern. **Pleurocystidia** 65.0–100.0 × 15.0–20.0 μm, fusiform to fusoid-ventricose, apex obtuse, thin-walled, hyaline, bridging lamellae. **Cheilocystidia** 20.0–25.0 × 10.0–18.0 μm saccate, thin-walled, hyaline, similar to brachybasidioles.

Lamellar trama compactly interwoven, hyphae branched, cylindrical to inflated, 2.4–8.8 μm wide, thin-walled, hyaline. **Subhymennium** subcellubar, interwoven, cells elliptical to irregularly inflated, 4.0–6.4(–8.8) μm wide, thin-walled, hyaline. **Pileus trama** interwoven, hyphae cylindrical to inflated, branched, 3.2–12.0 μm wide, thin-walled, hyaline. **Pileus cuticle** filamentous to subcellular, hyphae more or less radially arranged, 3.2–8.0 μm wide, thin-walled, hyaline. **Universal veil** loosely interwoven, hyphae branched, 2.4–9.6 μm wide, conspicuously gnarled to diverticulate, projections sharp to blunt, thin-walled near cuticle to thick-walled and refractile when mature, hyaline to yellowish brown in KOH. **Stipe hyphae** parallel, cylindrical, to slightly inflated, 3.2–6.4 μm wide, thin-walled, hyaline. Clamps regularly present throughout the basidiocarp, inconspicuous on inflated hyphae (Traquair, 1980; Redhead and Traquair, 1981).

Procedures for Isolation and Culture

Coprinus psycromorbidus grows slowly in culture. On potato dextrose agar (Difco) at 22 °C the plates are covered in 6–7 weeks (0.5–1.2 mm/day). The rate is faster at 13 °C (1.6–4.4 mm/day), with optimal temperatures in the 13–15 °C range.

The fungus may be isolated directly from leaves, crowns, and shoots by plating unwashed, colonized tissue fragments on potato dextrose agar and incubating at 1 °C. When recovery from plant specimens is difficult, isolation can be facilitated by incubating turf plugs in either a glass or plastic moist chamber at 4 °C under fluorescent light, and then examining the material for the presence of a nonsporulating, white basidiomycete with abundant clamp connections and cottony growth (Smith, 1981).

The advancing zone of cultures on potato dextrose agar (Difco) is even to uneven, and closely appressed to the agar surface. After 6 weeks at 13 °C, the aerial mycelium is white and appressed to cottony-wooly or felt-like in appearance. The hyphae are hyaline, thin-walled, with clamp connections and measuring 1.6–4.0 μm in width. In 2–3 weeks, small (1.0–3.0 mm in diameter), globose to irregular and coalescing hyphal knots are produced on the surface and within the agar. Not all strains of the fungus produce sclerotia. When sclerotia are formed in culture, they are at first white to yellowish and then dark brown to black and develop at random or in concentric rings.

On potato dextrose agar, the reverse side of the colonies remain unchanged in color, or may become slightly yellowish to pinkish or lilac in some isolates when they are exposed to light. The odor of the cultures is fungoid and there is no evidence of fruiting on potato dextrose agar or malt extract agar.

Tests on the cultures for extracellular oxidase shows gallic acid positive, growth negative; tannic acid negative, growth negative; and gum guaiacum positive within five minutes. Tests for HCN give positive production by some isolates on potato dextrose agar (Traquair, 1980).

Hosts

1. **Turfgrasses**—creeping bentgrass (*Agrostis palustris*), Colonial bentgrass (*Agrostis tenuis*), velvet bentgrass (*Agrostis canina*), annual bluegrass (*Poa annua*), Kentucky bluegrass (*Poa pratensis*), tall fescue (*Festuca arundinacea*), red fescue (*Festuca rubra*), Chewings fescue (*Festuca rubra* var. *commutata*), and sheep fescue (*Festuca ovina*).
2. **All Known Gramineous Hosts**—A listing of common names for the following species is given in Appendix Table V. *Agropyron cristatum* (L.) Gaertn., *A. repens* (L.) Beauv., *A. trachycaulum* (Link) Malte., *Agrostis alba* L., *A. canina* L., *A. palustris* Huds., *A. tenuis* Sibth., *Bromus inermis* Leyss., *Festuca arundinacea* Schreb., *F. ovina* L., *F. rubra*, L., *F. rubra* var. *commutata* Gaud., *Phleum pratense* L., *Poa annua* L., *P. pratensis* L., *P. trivialis* L. (Cormack, 1948; Smith, 1975).

Disease Profile

When the turf has been established from seed, the plants are usually not affected by the disease during the first two years of growth (Cormack, 1952; Smith, 1969).

Cottony snow mold is a disease of dormant plants. After winter dormancy has been established, a prolonged period of association, 45–60 days, is required before the plants are sufficiently predisposed to invasion by the fungus. During this period, the organism grows saprophytically on plant debris. As the soil temperatures lower, the permeability of the turfgrass root cell membranes to the outward flow of a cyanogenic glycoside increases. This substrate is acted upon by B-glucosidase produced by the fungus. This reaction leads to the production of hydrogen cyanide (HCN), which is lethal to the root tissue. The damaged root tissue probably releases additional enzyme, thereby accelerating pathogenesis (Lebeau, 1966). Invasion of the host plant does not occur until after the tissues have absorbed lethal quantities of HCN. Once infection and initial colonization of the host has been accomplished, migration of the mycelium through the tissues is both intercellular and intracellular. Movement of the mycelium through cell walls is accomplished without the apparent formation of special structures of penetration.

The incidence and severity of cottony snow mold is greater in turf that has received late season applications of high rates of nitrogenous fertilizers.

Deep, persistent snow covers are not a requisite for the development of cottony snow mold. The optimum conditions for disease development are soil surface temperatures less than 32 °F (0 °C). The frozen soil surface prevents rapid dissipation of HCN being produced by the saprophytic growth of the fungus and thus brings about an increase in the rate and total amount of the toxicant being absorbed by the plants. Extended thaws at temperatures near freezing also favor the development of the disease. With the resumption of plant growth in the spring, the activity of the cottony snow mold pathogen ceases (Cormack, 1948; Lebeau, 1964; Lebeau and Dickson, 1955).

Spread of the pathogen is accomplished by the movement of infested soil and plant debris. Biotypes of the pathogen are known to exist that vary in degrees of pathogenicity and their ability to produce sclerotia (Smith, 1987). The means by which the nonsclerotial strains of the fungus survive the summer months is not known. It has been suggested that these types may be capable of persisting during adverse conditions as dormant mycelium in the thatch (Lebeau and Cormack, 1961).

Control

Cultural Practices

If it is deemed necessary to apply an inorganic nitrogenous fertilizer after the end of July, the rate should not exceed 4 ounces actual nitrogen per 1,000 square feet (0.1 kg N/92 m²). However, a slow release organic nitrogen fertilizer can be put down in September in conjunction with mercury chloride or chloroneb fungicides. This practice will bring about a good spring color and provide for the control of cottony blight (Lebeau, 1976).

The use of polyethylene sheeting to cover the turf during the winter months has been shown to increase the effectiveness of fungicides in the control of cottony snow mold. Also, the installation of snow fences to minimize snow accumulation in areas highly prone to drifts will help reduce the severity of the disease (Smith, 1987).

Use of Resistant Grasses

Annual bluegrass (*Poa annua*) is highly susceptible to cottony snow mold. Red fescue (*Festuca rubra*) and the bentgrasses (*Agrostis* spp.) rank next in order of susceptibility, and Kentucky bluegrass (*Poa pratensis*) shows the highest degree of resistance.

Where varietal resistance to cottony snow mold is concerned, the creeping bentgrass cultivars Penncross and Seaside are equal. Among Kentucky bluegrass cultivars, Dormie, Sydsport, and Park are most resistant to the disease, and Fylking, Barkenta, Golf, Sydsport, Cougar and Merion are the most susceptible (Lebeau, 1976; Smith, 1975; Smith, 1987; Smith and Cooke, 1978).

Use of Fungicides

Cottony snow mold may be controled with one late fall application of mercurous or mercuric chlorides used singly or as mixtures in the proportion of 2:1 mercurous:mercuric chloride. Quintozene, benomyl, chloroneb, or a mixture of thiram, carboxin and oxycarbon are effective substitutes for inorganic mercury. With highly susceptible species or cultivars, an application after the first killing frost and a second treatment just prior to the first snowfall is advisable (Smith, 1987).

For a profile of each of these fungicides and a listing of representative trade names and manufacturers, see Appendix Table I.

Frost Scorch

Symptoms

Beginning at the tips and progressing toward the sheaths, diseased leaves fade to a light yellow, and finally, a bleached white color—a pattern somewhat similar to that produced by cold injury. In the final stages of disease development, affected leaves are curled up, dry, and ridged. In addition to the rolled appearance, the leaves frequently terminate in long tendrils, formed by the failure of these portions to unfold. As these terminal areas of the leaves die and fail to unroll, the tip of the leaf next in order is often caught and held in the roll, and it in turn may hold the next leaf in order. Meanwhile, the growth of the basal portion of the leaves, together with the elongation of the internodes, tends to separate the lower halves of the leaves, producing a distinctive, looped pattern.

As the basal portions of the developing young leaves unfold, their surfaces are usually covered with a light gray weft of mycelium, which eventually forms small, bean-shaped sclerotia. White when young, and changing to almost black when mature, the sclerotia tend to form in rows. This feature has given rise to the earlier name used for the disease, "string of pearls" (Figure 4-23).

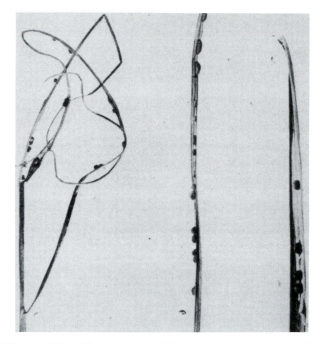

Figure 4-23.   Frost scorch of bluejoint reedgrass, showing rows of sclerotia of pathogen, and distinctive looped pattern of affected leaves. *After Stout, 1911.*

The Fungus

Sclerotium rhizodes Auers

Description

Sclerotia form in rows, bead-like, superficial on leaves, white when young, later brownish, becoming dark gray to black, oval to spherical, 1–5 mm in diameter. May be abundant (borne in rows) on leaf surfaces or solitary on leaf surfaces and in axils. Mycelium white in mass, septate, branched, no clamp connections, chiefly intercellular in leaf, stem, and rhizome.

Procedures for Isolation and Culture

In culture, the organism grows well on lima bean agar at 16 °C; however, some isolates are not psychrophylic (Stout, 1911; Smith, 1987).

Hosts

1. **Turfgrasses**—Kentucky bluegrass (*Poa pratensis*).
2. **All Known Gramineous Hosts**—A listing of common names for the following species is given in Appendix Table V. *Agropyron caninum* (L.) Beauv., *A. subsecundum* (Link) Hitchc., *Agrostis alba* L., *A. hiemalis* (Walt.) B. S. P., *A. scabra*

Willd., *Bromus ciliatus* L., *Calamagrostis canadensis* (Michx.) Beauv., *C. neglecta* (Ehrh.) Gaertn., Mey. and Schreb., *Glyceria grandis* S. Wats., *G. striata* (Lam.) Hitchc., *Holcus lanatus* L., *Hordeum jubatum* L., *Phleum pratense* L., *Poa pratensis* L., *Sphenopholis nitida* (Bieler) Scribn., *S. obtusata* (Michx.) Scribn., *S. pallens* (Bieler) Scribn., *Triticum aestivum* L. (Hungerford, 1923; Krietlow, 1942; Samson and Western, 1954; Sprague, 1950; Stout, 1911).

Disease Profile

Basically a cold, wet weather disease, frost scorch is usually most prevalent during the very early part of the growing season. Under conditions optimum for disease development, however, it has been shown that the disease can persist through the early part of the summer.

The pathogen survives its adverse seasons in the form of sclerotia, dormant mycelium within the host, and possibly as a soil saprophyte. Infection of new plants is initiated for the most part in the basal portions, i.e., crowns, roots, and rhizomes. Penetration of plant organs is direct. In the plant, the mycelium is systemic, being indiscriminate in its movement, as it progresses both intercellularly and intracellularly, involving all tissue groups. Primary colonization of newly formed leaves generally occurs from systemic mycelium (Stout, 1911). After formation, the sclerotia undergo a dormancy period of 2–24 months. They are very long lived, remaining viable up to 9 years (Davis, 1933).

Frost scorch is more severe when the soil fertility is low and the pH is in the highly acid range (Stirrup, 1932).

Control

There is no known chemical control for frost scorch. The impact of the disease on the turf can be diminished to some extent by (a) removing clippings from heavily diseased areas in order to reduce inoculum levels, (b) maintaining adequate soil fertility for maximum plant growth in the early spring, (c) and holding the soil pH in the upper level of the acid range.

Spring Dead Spot of Bermudagrass

Spring dead spot is known to occur in New South Wales, Australia, and the regions of the United States where temperatures are cold enough to induce winter dormancy of bermudagrass (*Cynodon dacty-*

lon). In the United States, spring dead spot was first observed in Oklahoma in 1936. It is now known to also occur in Alabama, Arkansas, California, North Carolina, South Carolina, Georgia, Kansas, Maryland, Mississippi, Missouri, Nebraska, Tennessee, Texas, and Virginia.

Depending on geographic location, one of four species of fungi functions as the incitant of this disease. *Leptosphaeria narmari* has been shown to be the principal incitant of spring dead spot of bermudagrass in Australia. In the United States, *Leptosphaeria korrae* has been identified as the incitant of spring dead spot in California and Maryland, *Gaeumannomyces graminis* var. *graminis* is regularly associated with the disease throughout the southeastern United States, and *Ophiosphaerella herpotricha* has been identified as the incitant of spring dead spot in Kansas (Crahay, Dernoden and O'Neill, 1988; Endo, Ohr and Krausman, 1985; McCarty and Lucas, 1989; Tisserat and Pair, 1989; Walker and Smith, 1972).

Symptoms

The major foliar symptoms of spring dead spot are first apparent when bermudagrass breaks winter dormancy and begins regrowth in the spring. In pure stands of bermudagrass, the disease is seen in overall view as very distinctive, depressed, well defined circular patches of straw-colored turf ranging from 6 inches (15 cm) to 3 feet (1 meter) or more in diameter. In some instances, small patches will have coalesced and formed arcs (Plate 23).

The patches are not as easily detected in the early spring on overseeded bermudagrass golf greens or in bermudagrass turf with high populations of winter weeds. They become more clearly defined as the winter annual plants die in late spring or early summer, but in comparison with the early spring symptoms of the disease in pure stands of bermudagrass, these patches are usually lighter in color and less clearly outlined.

Small elliptically shaped black to dark brown lesions form on culm bases, crown buds, roots, and stolons during the early stages of disease development. At the time of patch formation, the culm bases and crown buds develop a black to brown dry rot. The roots and stolons also become blackened and rotted and may be easily pulled loose from the parent plants. Strands of dark brown to black runner hyphae are often found on the surfaces of diseased roots and stolons.

Small, dark brown, flattened, irregularly shaped sclerotia develop on basal leaf sheaths, on the basal portions of the culms beneath the leaf sheaths, and on the stolons and roots. The sclerotia often have a network of brown, septate hyphae associated with them. Both sclerotia and the associated hyphae are easily detached from the plant surface.

The disease usually does not appear until the stand of bermudagrass is two years or older. In the central region of the United States, bermudagrass usually does not grow over the spring dead spot areas for several years and weeds often become established in the affected areas (Wadsworth and Young, 1960).

In southeastern United States, bermudagrass grows slowly into the affected areas. If the invasion of summer weeds is prevented by the use of selective herbicides, these areas will usually be covered with bermudagrass by the end of summer. On closely mowed, intensively managed bermudagrass turf, such as golf greens, the affected areas usually cannot be detected later in the summer. However, in stands of bermudagrass cut to 1 inch (2.54 cm) or more, the newly established plants in the patches grow more slowly than those in the healthy turf. As the result, up to the onset of dormancy in the fall, the turf in the recovering areas is usually shorter between mowings than the adjacent turf. Also, the bermudagrass that has grown into the affected areas remains green later into the fall than nearby apparently healthy turf.

When summer recovery does occur, outbreaks of spring dead spot often recur in many of the former patches during each successive winter. The diameter of these colonization sites will continue to enlarge for several years. In these instances, the plants in the center of the patches sometimes survive, giving them a distinctive frogeye appearance (Lucas, 1980b) (Plate 23 and Figure 4-24).

The Fungi

A. *Leptosphaeria korrae* Walker and Smith

Description

Pseudothecia erumpent, usually closely packed, 400–600 μm (including the neck), 300–500 μm wide, flask-shaped, with a globose body and a thick neck 50–150 μm long and 200 μm wide, often with thickened ridges around it. Pseudothecial wall 80–120 μm thick at the base, 40–80 μm at the sides, and 60–80 μm at the junction with the neck, composed of several layers of flattened brown cells 10–18 μm × 4–7 μm. Neck canal up to 80–100 μm wide, lined with hyaline upwardly pointing periphyses, and, in young pseudothecia, often colored reddish brown by some material between the periphyses (Plate 1-F).

Asci cylindrical to clavate, narrowed towards the foot-like base, 150–185 μm × 10–13 μm, bitunicate, eight-spored. **Ascospores** filiform, slightly twisted in a bundle and parallel to one another, pale brown, septate, 140–170 μm × 4–5 μm, an occasional very long spore to 210 μm, widest in the middle and tapering more towards the base than the apex, rounded at the ends. **Pseudoparaphyses** hyaline, septate, numerous, 1.5–2.0 μm wide. **Hyphae** on the host brown, septate, branched, 2.5–5.0 μm wide, often in strands of three or four and forming flattened dark sclerotia 50–400 μm in diameter (Walker and Smith, 1972).

Procedures for Isolation and Culture

Leptosphaeria korrae grows on a variety of supplemented agar-based media. Isolation attempts should be made only from crown and root tissue. Surface sterilization should be accomplished by soaking the specimens in sterile distilled water for one hour, then transferring them to a 1% NaOCl-95% ethanol solution (1:1) for 30 seconds, and then soaking them in sterile distilled water for one hour before plating. Supplementing the culture medium with 100 mg of streptomycin per liter aids in the reduction of secondary organisms.

The optimum growth temperature range for the fungus is 20–25 °C. A small amount of growth is usually evident about seven days after plating and becomes easily identifiable after another 10 days. On potato dextrose agar, the colonies are at first colorless, then off-white to light gray and somewhat floccose. As growth continues, both the media and older mycelium become almost black. The aerial growth of the fungus maintains some gray color. The reverse side of the culture is always black. The advancing hyphal margin sometimes shows a trace of curling back toward the center (Worf, Stewart and Avenius, 1986; Crahay, Dernoeden and O'Neill, 1988).

The production of pseudothecia of the fungus can be induced by either (i) growing the fungus on sterile oat grains (Jackson, 1984), (ii) incubating it in tubes containing wheat leaf agar medium (irradiated wheat leaf sections embedded in slants of water agar) (Smiley and Craven-Fowler, 1984), or (iii) inducing their formation on already colonized plant tissue. This latter procedure consists of immersing crowns or roots showing the characteristic dark brown runner hyphae on their surfaces in running tap water for 30 minutes. They should then be placed on plugs of moistened, gauze-covered, cotton, in sterile test tubes and incubated at 22 °C in an alternating 12 hour day-night light cycle. Care should be taken throughout

Figure 4-24. Spring dead spot of bermudagrass (*Cynodon dactylon*). *Courtesy W. A. Small.*

the incubation period to keep the cotton and gauze moistened. Under these conditions, ascocarps will be produced in approximately 6 weeks (Crahay, Dernoeden and O'Neill, 1988).

Hosts

1. **Turfgrasses**—annual bluegrass (*Poa annua*), creeping bentgrass (*Agrostis palustris*), bermudagrass (*Cynodon dactylon*), Chewings fescue (*Festuca rubra* var. *commutata*), red fescue (*Festuca rubra*), Kentucky bluegrass (*Poa pratensis*), perennial ryegrass (*Lolium perenne*).
2. **All Known Gramineous Hosts**—A listing of common names for the following species is given in Appendix Table IV. *Agrostis palustris* Huds., *Avena sativa* L., *Axonopus compressus* (Swartz) Beauv., *Cynodon dactylon* (L.) Pers., *Eremochloa ophiuroides* (Munro) Hack., *Festuca rubra* L., *F. rubra* var. *commutata* Gaud., *Lolium perenne* L., *Oryza sativa* L., *Poa annua* L., *P. pratensis* L., *Triticum aestivum* L. (Walker and Smith, 1972; Worf, Stewart and Avenius, 1986).

The Fungi

B. *Leptosphaeria narmari* Walker and Smith

Description

Pseudothecia erumpent, occurring in clusters or singly, up to 800 μm high (including the neck) and 650 μm wide, black, flask-shaped to widely obpyriform, with a more or less globose body and a thick neck 100–300 μm long and 300–450 μm wide, often with one or two thickened ridges around it. Pseudothecial wall 60–75 μm thick in body, to 100 μm thick in neck, composed of several layers of flattened brown cells 7–12 × 4–7 μm. Neck canal up to 150 μm wide, lined with hyaline upwardly pointing periphyses 45–70 × 2 μm, often colored by a reddish brown material between the periphyses. Asci clavate, narrowed toward the foot-like base, (100) 110–145 (155) × 11–13 μm, bitunicate, eight-spored. Ascospores biserate, pale brown, narrowly elliptical to slightly constricted at the central septum and sometimes very slightly at other septa. Pseudoparaphyses numerous, hyaline, septate, 1.5–3.0 μm wide. Hyphae on the host brown, septate, branched, 2.5–5.0 μm wide, often in strands of three or four and forming flattened dark sclerotia 40–400 μm in diameter (Walker and Smith, 1972).

Procedures for Isolation and Culture

The affected plant tissue should be surface sterilized in a 10 percent sodium hypochlorite solution for approximately one minute. Sections of tissue should then be transferred to nonacidified potato dextrose agar and incubated at 25 °C. The fungus grows out of the tissue within two days and should be subcultured as soon as possible to reduce the possibility of it being overrun by bacteria and other fungi.

On potato dextrose agar *Leptosphaeria narmari* first produces a hyaline mycelium. The center of the colony develops abundant aerial growth while the margin grows along the agar surface without many aerial hyphae. After about five days at 25 °C aerial mycelium spreads over the entire colony which then begins to develop a darker color. The color change begins in the center of the colony on both the aerial mycelium and the agar surface. Eventually, the whole aerial mycelium becomes dark gray while the agar surface takes on a greenish black color. This aerial mycelium has a strong tendency to form runner hyphae. These runners are composed of from a few to 50 or more hyphae. They are darker than the normal mycelium—becoming very dark brown to almost black in color. The fungus takes from two to three weeks to cover the surface of a 10 cm diameter petri dish. After 2–3 weeks growth, there are two types of hyphae present. A thick, light brown, strongly septate type averaging 3 μm to 4 μm wide, and a narrower hyaline type averaging 2 μm in thickness (A. M. Smith, 1965).

Hosts

1. **Turfgrasses**—Bermudagrass (*Cynodon dactylon*), African bermudagrass (*Cynodon transvaalensis*), St. Augustinegrass (*Stenotaphrum secundatum*), and kikuyugrass *Pennisetum clandestinum*).
2. **All Known Gramineous Hosts**—A listing of common names for the following species is given in Appendix Table IV. *Axonopus compressus* (Swartz) Beauv., *Cynodon dactylon* (L.) Pers., *C. transvaalensis* Burtt-Davy, *Hordeum vulgare* L., *Oryza sativa* L., *Pennisetum clandestinum* Hochst. ex Small, *Stenotaphrum secundatum* (Walt.) Kuntze, *Triticum aestivum* L. (Smith, 1965; Smith and Walker, 1972).

The Fungi

C. *Gaeumannomyces graminis* (Sacc.) von Arx and Oliver var. *graminis*; syn. *Ophiobolus graminis* Sacc.

Description

Mycelium comprising a limited growth of fine, grayish hyphae, and an abundant development of coarse, thick-walled, brown to black, irregular hyphae. Perithecia round to oblong, black, about 400 μm in diameter, formed in or beneath the leaf sheath with strands of mycelium associated with the base and the cylindrical curved beaks extending through the sheath tissues (Plate 2-F). Asci 10–15 μm × 100–165 μm, numerous, elongate, clavate, straight or curved, with numerous thread-like paraphyses in the young perithecia. Mature asci ejected from perithecia during periods of abundant moisture. Ascospores 8, hyaline, slender, tapering toward the ends, 3 μm × 75–138 μm; 5–7 septate at maturity. Under some conditions, minute falcate conidia are produced upon the germination of ascospores.

Procedures for Isolation and Culture

In standard laboratory procedures for maintaining cultures, the organism grows well on potato dextrose agar at 21 °C (Smith, 1956). However, where direct isolation from diseased roots and crowns is concerned, *Gaeumannomyces graminis* develops slowly in culture; therefore, it is often overgrown by other, faster growing, plant tissue and soil-inhabiting microorganisms. This problem can be alleviated to some extent by use of the modified Juhnke selective medium (Elliott, 1991a). This medium contains 39 g Difco dehydrated potato dextrose agar, 100 mg of streptomycin, 10 mg of dichloran, 10 mg of metalaxyl, 50 mg of vinclozolin, 500 mg a.i. of L-DOPA (L-B-3,4-dihydroxyphenylalanine), and 1 mg of CGA-173506 (a phenylpyrolle available from CIBA-GEIGY Corp, Agricultural Div., Greensboro, NC 27419). Add dehydrated potato dextrose agar to distilled water and autoclave at 15 psi (120 °C) for 20 minutes, and then cool to 50 °C. The remaining compounds should first be placed in 10 ml sterile distilled water and this suspension added to the molten potato dextrose agar just prior to pouring the plates. On Juhnke medium, isolates of *Gaeumannomyces*-type fungi are distinguished by the diffusion of a dark brown pigment (melanin) into the agar (Juhnke, Mathre and Sands, 1983).

Hosts

1. **Turfgrasses**—annual bluegrass (*Poa annua*), Colonial bentgrass (*Agrostis tenuis*), velvet bent-

grass (*Agrostis canina*), creeping bentgrasses (*Agrostis palustris*), bermudagrass (*Cynodon dactylon* and *Cynodon dactylon* × *Cynodon transvaalensis*), Kentucky bluegrass (*Poa pratensis*), red fescue (*Festuca rubra*), tall fescue (*Festuca arundinacea*), St. Augustinegrass (*Stenotaphrum secundatum*), and perennial ryegrass (*Lolium perenne*).

2. **All Known Gramineous Hosts**—A listing of common names for the following species is given in Appendix Table IV. *Agropyron caninum* (L.) Beauv., *A. cristatum* (L.) Gaertn., *A. intermedium* (Host) Beauv., *A. repens* (L.) Beauv., *A. smithii* Rydb., *A. trachycaulum* (Link) Malte, *Agrostis alba* L., *A. canina* L., *A. palustris* Huds., *A. stolonifera* L., *A. tenuis* Sibth., *Anthoxanthum odoratum* L., *Arrhenatherum elatius* (L.) Presl, *Avena byzantina* C. Koch, *A. sativa* L., *A. sterilis* L., *Bromus arvensis* L., *B. carinatus* Hook. and Arn., *B. ciliatus* L., *B. erectus* Huds., *B. inermis* Leyss., *B. japonicus* Thunb., *B. madritensis* L., *B. orcuttianus* Vasey, *B. racemosus* L., *B. secalinus* L., *B. sterilis* L., *B. tectorum* L., *B. vulgaris* (Hook.) Shear, *Cynodon dactylon* (L.) Pers., *Cynodon dactylon* (L.) Pers. × *Cynodon transvaalensis* Burtt-Davy, *Deschampsia caespitosa* (L.) Beauv., *D. danthonioides* (Trin.) Munro, *Elymus canadensis* L., *E. glaucus* Buckl., *E. villosus* Muhl., *E. virginicus* L., *E. virginicus* var. *australis* (Scribn. and Ball) Hitchc., *Festuca arundinacea* Schreb., *F. dertonensis* (All.) Aeschers. and Graebn., *F. megalura* Nutt., *F. myuros* L., *F. octoflora* Walt., *F. rubra* L., *Holcus lanatus* L., *Hordeum distichon* L., *H. jubatum* L., *H. murinum* L., *H. pusillum* Nutt., *H. vulgare* L., *Hystrix patula* Moensh, *Lolium multiflorum* Lam., *L. perenne* L., *Phalaris arundinacea* L., *Phleum pratense* L., *Poa annua* L., *P. canbyi* (Scribn.) Piper, *P. compressa* L., *P. pratensis* L., *P. trivialis* L., *Secale cereale* L., *Setaria geniculata* (Lam.) Beauv., *Stenotaphrum secundatum* (Walter) Kuntze, *Triticum aestivum* L. (Elliott, 1991b; Elliott, Hagan and Mullen, 1991; Kirby, 1922; Smith, 1956; Index Plant Dis., 1960).

The Fungi

D. *Ophiosphaerella herpotricha* (Fr.) Walker; syn. *Ophiobolus herpotrichus* (Fr.) Sacc.

Description

Pseudothecia on leaf sheaths, dark brown, body globose to subglobose 300–400 μm in diameter seated on the stem surface with a short conical neck to 100 μm long, 80 μm wide near the base but nar-rower above, erumpent through the covering leaf sheaths, joined to and surrounded by an abundant dark brown mycelium. Wall of the body of ascocarp 25–35 μm thick, of 6–8 layers of radially flattened cells 6–12 × 4–6 μm with brown unthickened or very slightly unthickened walls, outer layers dark brown, inner paler to almost hyaline, outer layer in surface view forming a textura angularis of cells 6–12 μm in diameter; wall of neck to 30 μm thick, ostiolar canal 20 (25) μm diam, periphyses not seen but globose hyaline cells present in canal in young ascocarps. Asci bitunicate, long, narrowly elongated clatate, apex to 3–4 μm thick, base foot-shaped, 150–190 × 7–9 μm, widest about 20–30 μm below apex. Ascospores eight per ascus, long, filiform, pale brown to brown in mass, pale brown singly, lying parallel or loosely twisted for part of their length, 12–16 septate with septa 10–14 μm apart, 140–180 × 2–2.5 (3) μm, apex rounded, base rounded and narrower, widest about 20 μm below apex, straight to curved or slightly sinuous. Pseudoparaphyses abundant, hyaline, septate, 2–3 μm wide, longer than the asci. Mycelium dark brown, attached to pseudothecia and giving them a hairy appearance and running over the surface of stems between leaf sheaths, little mycelium seen on outer surface of leaf sheaths, composed of dark brown branching septate hyphae 3–7 μm wide, some with nodular swellings, both smooth and rough-walled hyphae present, roughening from fine echinulations to coarse tubercules, some hyphae with intercalary hyphopodia present, abundant penetration points on stem surface associated with mycelium (Walker, 1980).

Procedures for Isolation and Culture

Ophiosphaerella herpotricha grows well on either nonacidified potato dextrose agar or malt agar. Isolation attempts should be made only from crown and root tissue. Surface sterilization should be accomplished by first rinsing the specimens in running tap water for one hour, then transferring them to a 1 percent NaOCl-95 percent ethanol solution (1:1) for 30 seconds, and soaking them in sterile distilled water for one hour before plating. Supplementing the culture medium with 100 mg of streptomycin per liter aids in the reduction of secondary organisms (Worf, Stewart and Avenius, 1986).

The fungus produces a white, septate, cottony mycelium on potato dextrose agar and malt agar. The colonies turn light tan to brown after 3–7 days. Some isolates produce a greenish tint in the center of the colony. The mycelium that is submerged in the agar eventually turns tan to dark brown. The optimal growth rates for *Ophiosphaerella herpotricha* on potato dextrose agar are 3.5–4.1 mm per day at temperatures between 20 and 25 °C (Tisseret and Pair, 1989).

Hosts

1. **Turfgrasses**—bermudagrass (*Cynodon dactylon*).
2. **All Known Gramineous Hosts**—A listing of common names for the following species is given in Appendix Table IV. *Bromus inermis* Leyss., *Chloris gayana* Kunth, *Cynodon dactylon* (L.) Pers., *Echinochloa crusgalli* (L.) Beauv., *Oryza sativa* L., *Vetiveria zizanioides* (L.) Nash, *Zea mays* L. (Tisserat and Pair, 1989; Walker, 1980).

Disease Profile

The fungi that incite spring dead spot infect and colonize the roots and stolons of bermudagrass in late summer or early fall when the prevailing daytime air temperatures are in the low to mid 70s F (21–24 °C). However, at this time of the year the regenerative capacity of bermudagrass is still very high; therefore, the effects of the disease on the growth and development of the plants is minimal. With the advent of colder fall and winter weather, the capacity of the bermudagrass to resist infections and compensate for the pathogenic effects of the fungus by producing new roots decreases. When the plants reach full dormancy, and the range of the daily air temperatures is 50 to 60 °F (10–15 °C) or less, extensive colonization of roots, crowns, and stolons by the fungus occurs, and death of the plants results (Crahay, Dernoden and O'Neill, 1988; Endo, Ohr and Krausmann, 1985; McCarty and Lucas, 1989; A. M. Smith, 1965; Smith, 1971).

Primary infections originate from mycelium growing on the surfaces of the roots and stolons. Penetration of the epidermal cells is direct and is facilitated by infection pegs originating from single lateral and intercalary cells on the diffuse mycelium, and from infection cushions. Mycelial movement through the underlying tissues is both intercellular and intracellular. In the later stages of disease development the hyphae penetrate the endodermis and colonize the vascular tissues. A brown occluding substance commonly develops in the vessel elements of the primary and secondary xylem. Brown to black fusiform sclerotia consisting of parallel hyphae develop in the cortex and vascular tissue of the primary roots. Also, lignitubers may form in the parenchymatous cells of any tissue group that is being colonized (Endo, Ohr and Krausman, 1985; Smith, 1965; Walker and Smith, 1972).

The primary roots are shorter than normal, but functional. As climatic conditions become more favorable for disease development, necrosis becomes more extensive in the primary roots and the secondary roots are destroyed before they become functional. Sometimes the secondary roots are colonized and killed before they emerge from the primary roots. If they have already emerged, the infection and initial colonization usually occurs where they are joined to the primary root.

Heavy thatch [thickness greater than ½ to ¾ inch (1.3–2.0 cm)] is conducive to the development of spring dead spot. The severity of the disease is also greater in turf maintained at low cutting heights.

Where plant nutrition is concerned, spring dead spot is more severe on bermudagrass grown at low potassium. Also, the use of nitrogenous fertilizers at high rates or the application of nitrogen late in the growing season will bring about an increase in the severity of the disease. The nitrogen effect is thought to be due to the fact that (a) high nitrogen nutrition stimulates the growth of leaves at the expense of the roots, thus lowering the plants capacity to compensate for the disease by establishing new roots, and (b) late applications of nitrogen delay dormancy, decreasing the low temperature hardiness of the plants and making them more vulnerable to the pathogenic effects of the spring dead spot fungi (Lucas and Gilbert, 1979; McCarty and Lucas, 1989; Lucas, 1980a; McCarty, Lucas and DiPaola, 1990).

Control

Cultural Practices

The following management practices will reduce the severity of spring dead spot: The fertilization program should (a) use minimum rates of nitrogen for spring and summer growth, (b) avoid late growing season applications of nitrogen, and (c) maintain adequate soil potassium levels. Thatch should be kept between ½ and ¾ inch (1.3–2.0 cm) in thickness, the turf mowed at the maximum height the use requirements will permit, and coring performed in the diseased areas to improve soil aeration and foster the production of new roots.

Use of Resistant Grasses

Although field observations indicate that there may some degree of resistance among various cultivars of bermudagrass, efforts to date have not yet led to the development of varieties resistant to either of the species of fungi that incite spring dead spot.

Use of Fungicides

Fenarimol is registered in the United States for control of spring dead spot. Single applications may be made from September through November, however, the earlier the application, the better the results. The rates of application vary according to the month the treatment is made. The manufacturer's schedule should be consulted for specific rates and dates of applications.

For a profile of fenarimol and a listing of its trade name and manufacturer, see Appendix Table I.

Pythium Patch

Pythium patch is caused by a yet unidentified low-temperature tolerant *Pythium* species. The disease has been diagnosed on creeping bentgrass (*Agrostis palustris*) and annual bluegrass (*Poa pratensis*) in Virginia, West Virginia, Kentucky, Connecticut, Massachusetts, and Maine. Development of Pythium patch is fostered by cold, humid weather. The ideal conditions for major outbreaks are extended periods of rainfall and air temperatures ranging from 38–45 °F (3–7 °C), or a deep, persistent snow cover that has fallen on unfrozen ground (Couch, unpublished data).

The disease is first seen in overall view as a distinctive brown discoloration of individual leaves. The necrosis usually begins at the tips and progresses downward to the sheaths. Initially, the affected areas of turf range in size from 2 inches (5 cm) to 3 feet (0.9 meter) in diameter and have a ragged appearance due to an irregular blending of diseased and healthy leaves. When environmental conditions are highly favorable for disease development, strands of white mycelial growth of the pathogen often develop among the leaves. Also, the affected areas rapidly evolve into irregular, patches of tan to light brown turf 2 to 6 feet (0.6–1.8 meters) in diameter with dark brown borders 1 to 2 inches (2.5–5 cm) wide. At this stage of disease development, a cursory examination of the turf may result in a misdiagnosis of the problem as Fusarium patch. A definitive diagnosis of Pythium patch requires a laboratory-based examination of the affected tissue for the presence of the pathogen (Plate 22-C, D, E, F).

Systematic field research has not been conducted on the use of chemicals for control of Pythium patch. However, applications of either metalaxyl or combinations of metalaxyl and mancozeb to creeping bentgrass/annual bluegrass golf greens at the rates used for control of Pythium blight have been observed to check the development of the disease. A profile of these two fungicides and names of representative manufacturers are given in Appendix Table I.

§ § §

Leaf Spots

HELMINTHOSPORIUM-INCITED DISEASES

The Helminthosporium-incited diseases are among the most important fungus disorders of turfgrasses. Their syndromes include leaf lesioning, leaf abscission, and root, rhizome, stolon, and crown rots.

Melting-Out of Kentucky Bluegrass

Melting-out of Kentucky bluegrass was reported in Czechoslovakia in 1916 and Madison, Wisconsin in the United States in 1922 (Drechsler, 1922). At first, the disease was considered to be a minor problem, however, melting-out has since been recognized as an important spring and fall disease of Kentucky bluegrass in Great Britain and the temperate climate regions of North America and continental Europe.

Symptoms

The disease occurs on all plant parts. On the leaves, it is first seen as minute, water-soaked lesions. These soon enlarge into dark, purplish-red, ovular areas ¼ to ⅜ inch (6–9 mm) long and ¹⁄₁₆ to ⅛ inch (2–3 mm) wide; the width being limited primarily by size of the leaf. As the lesions enlarge, the color of the centers changes to brown, and finally a dull white (Plate 24-A).

Although any area of the leaf may be parasitized, the incidence of infection is usually higher on the sheath. Lesions on the leaf sheath are generally not as regular in outline as those on the leaf blades, and the lighter colored center is usually missing. Colonization of the sheath tissue is often so extensive that the leaf is girdled at this point and drops from the plant. It is this leaf-dropping phase of the disease that has given rise to the name "melting-out." During severe outbreaks of the disease, bluegrass stands are commonly found with less than six leaves per square foot (0.3 m²) of turfgrass area.

Occurring in conjunction with the leaf lesioning phase of the disease is infection and colonization of the crowns, and ultimately, the roots and rhizomes. The disease in these plant parts is a rot, appearing at first as a reddish brown decay and finally turning dark brown to black as bacteria and other fungi begin to colonize the tissues. It is not unusual for diseased plants to wilt under soil moisture conditions that would normally seem adequate for growth.

The Fungus

Drechslera poae (Baudys) Shoemaker; syn. *Helminthosporium vagans* Drechs.

Description

Conidia emerging from stomata or between epidermal cells of tissues sometime after death, usually singly or less frequently in pairs; typically simple although occasionally branching; dark olivaceous; usually measuring 8–10 μm × 50–280 μm, 1–10 septate, the septa occurring at intervals of 15–40 μm; approximately straight up to point of attachment of first spore 40–150 μm from base; successive spores produced at apices of moderate, often pronounced geniculations.

Conidia dark olivaceous when mature; cylindrical or slightly tapering toward the hemispherical ends; measuring usually 17–23 μm × 25–130 μm; 1–10 (usually 5–8) septate; the septa are not associated with constrictions in the peripheral wall; the latter always thick and including the dark hilum within its contour. Germinating by the production of 3–11 germ tubes indiscriminately from end and middle segments, a single germ tube is usually produced from several or all segments (Drechsler, 1923) (Figure 5-1).

Procedures for Isolation and Culture

In culture, optimum temperature for growth of the fungus is 18 °C, with a minimum somewhat below 3 °C and a maximum between 30 °C and 35 °C. Sporu-

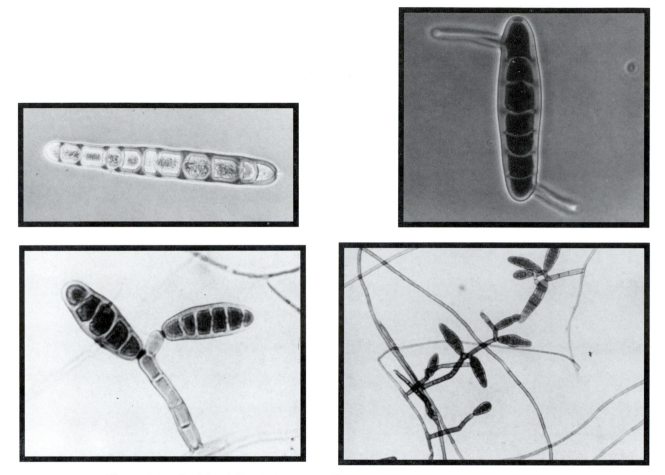

Figure 5-1.   Conidia of *Drechslera poae*. (Courtesy Austin Hagan and Philip Larsen).

lation is sparse on potato dextrose agar. However, sporulation does occur at fairly high levels in after 21 days growth on V-8 juice agar at 18 °C with alternating 12 hours fluorescent illumination (4K lux) (Hagan, 1980). High sporulation of *Drechslera poae* on malt extract agar can be obtained by the use of a water soak technique. This procedure consists of soaking 2–3 week old cultures growing on 1.5% malt extract agar in running tap water for 24–36 hours. After washing, the plates are kept open by slanting them without lids in an inverted position for 2–3 days and then the spores are harvested (Halisky and Funk, 1966).

Hosts

1. **Turfgrasses**—annual bluegrass (*Poa annua*), Canada bluegrass (*Poa compressa*), Kentucky bluegrass (*Poa pratensis*), rough bluegrass (*Poa trivialis*). Also a minor leaf spot pathogen of buffalograss (*Buchloe dactyloides*), tall fescue (*Fes-*

tuca arundinacea), annual ryegrass (*Lolium multiflorum*) and perennial ryegrass (*Lolium perenne*).

2. **All Known Gramineous Hosts**—A listing of common names for the following species is given in Appendix Table IV. *Agropyron desertorum* (Fisch.) Schult., *A. inerme* (Scribn. and Smith) Rydb., *A. intermedium* (Host) Beauv., *A. rigidum* Beauv., *Andropogon nodosus* (Willem.) Nash, *A. scoparius* Michx., *Buchloe dactyloides* (Nutt.) Engelm., *Chloris gayana* Kunth, *Echinochloa crusgalli* var. *frumantacea* (Roxb.) W. F. Wight, *Elymus giganteus* Vahl, *E. junceus* Fisch., *Festuca arundinacea* Schreb., *Lolium multiflorum* Lam., *L. perenne* L., *Muhlenbergia wrightii* Vasey, *Panicum antidotale* Retz., *P. virgatum* L., *Pennisetum glaucum* (L.) R. Br., *Poa ampla* Merr., *P. annua* L., *P. arida* Vasey, *P. bulbosa* L., *P. compressa* L., *P. pratensis* L., *P. secunda* Presl, *P. trivialis* L., *Secale montanum* Guss., *Sorghastrum nutans* (L.) Nash, *Sorghum almum* L., *S. halepense* (L.) Pers., *S. vulgare* Pers., *Sporobolus airoides* (Torr.) Torr.,

Stipa viridula Trin., *Trichachne californica* (Benth.) Chase (Drechsler, 1922; Horsfall, 1930; Moore and Couch, 1961; Sprague, 1946; Sprague, 1950).

Disease Profile

Spores of *Drechslera poae* are transmitted on seed harvested from diseased plants. Leaf fragments colonized by the melting-out pathogen are the principal source of inoculum for both the initial outbreaks of the disease and the continuation of its develoment throughout the spring season. The rate of production of *Drechslera poae* spores in the leaf litter is closely linked with thatch temperature. Sporulation begins when the thatch reaches 43 °F (6 °C) and the frequency increases simultaneously with the seasonal rise in daily air temperatures. Peak populations occur when the thatch temperatures range between 55–65 °F (13–18 °C). Finally, when the daily mean temperatures reach 68 °F (20 °C), spore production in the leaf litter ceases (Hagan and Larsen, 1985).

The release of spores into the atmosphere is greatest when either the leaf surfaces or the underlying leaf litter is dry. Discharge of spores from leaf lesions usually begins one to two hours after sudden drops in the ambient relative humidity. The release of conidia from the leaf litter increases substantially following periods of irrigation that are performed during times of extended low relative humidity. However, when the climatic conditions are characterized by extended periods of high relative humidity and continuously moist leaf litter, the release of spores does not increase following individual rain showers (Hagan, 1980).

The number of airborne spores is much higher during daylight hours than at night. Under dry climatic conditions, the incidence of *Drechslera poae* spores in the atmosphere of a Kentucky bluegrass turf begins to increase at about 8:00 a.m. (0800 GMT). The rate of spore release from lesions and colonized leaf litter peaks between noon and 2:00 p.m. (1200 and 1400 GMT), but the total airborne spore count continues to increase until approximately 8:00 p.m. (2000 GMT). The overall population of *Drechslera poae* spores in the atmosphere is its lowest when the duration of leaf wetness in the turf exceeds 20 hours per day (Hagan, 1980).

Mowing plays a major role in the dispersal of *Drechslera poae* conidia. Spore dispersal begins with leaf elongation (first mowing) in the spring and peak distribution occurs about mid-May. The distance of movement of conidia into the atmosphere appears to be limited to heights of 8 inches (20 cm) above the surface of the turf. This suggests relatively short dispersal distances (Nutter, Cole and Schein, 1982).

The optimum climatic conditions for the development of leaf lesions are air temperatures in the 65–75 °F (18–24 °C) range, high atmospheric humidity and overcast weather. Conidia serve as the principal form of inoculum. At 65 °F (18 °C) spore germination and penetration of the epidermal cell walls occurs within 4 hours of inoculation. At either 54 °F (12 °C) or 75 °F (24 °C), 8 hours are required for penetration, while at 43 °F (6 °C) or 85 °F (30 °C), 12 hours must elapse before leaf penetration occurs. The total number of successful epidermal cell penetrations is greater at 65–75 °F (18–24 °C). The bulk of spore germination occurs within 24 hours from the onset of favorable environmental conditions (Lukens, 1968; Hagan, 1980).

Penetration of the leaf surface is direct and occurs most commonly at the juncture of the walls of two adjacent epidermal cells (Figure 3-3). The epidermal cells are usually colonized before the mycelium begins to move between the cells of the underlying palisade parenchyma (Hagan, 1980).

There is a relationship between mowing height and the severity of melting-out. Plants cut at a height of 1 inch (2.5 cm) are more susceptible to the leaf lesion phase of the disease than those mowed at 2 inches (5 cm) (Lukens, 1970).

As a general rule, the severity of melting-out is greater when Kentucky bluegrass (*Poa pratensis*) turf is grown under high nitrogen fertilization (Halisky, Funk and Engel, 1966); however, this phenomenon does not hold true for all cultivars. The severity of melting-out is highest on 'Merion,' 'Windsor,' 'South Dakota,' and 'Belturf' when these cultivars are grown at high nitrogen nutrition and lowest when the nitrogen nutrition is low. With 'Pennstar,' however, the severity of melting-out is lowest when the plants are under high nitrogen nutrition and highest at low nitrogen levels (Table 5-1) (Couch, 1980).

As the result of experiments utilizing varied clipping heights and different degrees of light intensity to induce altered plant carbohydrate content, it has been postulated that the susceptibility of Kentucky bluegrass to *Drechslera poae* increases when the sugar content of the leaves is reduced (Lukens, 1970). For a further review of this hypothesis, see Helminthosporium leaf spot.

Under conditions favorable for the development of melting-out, infection and colonization of developing florets occurs. In these cases, the primary infections are brought about by direct growth of mycelium from overlying lesions on the unfolding leaves (Lukens, 1967b).

Infection and colonization of crowns and roots of new plants also occurs in the spring. Severe root and

Table 5-1. Influence of three nutritional levels on the susceptibility of five cultivars of Kentucky bluegrass to melting-out. *After Couch, 1980.*

Nutrition	Level of Disease Resistance[a]				
	Merion	Windsor	South Dakota	Belturf	Pennstar
Normal nitrogen, phosphorous and potassium	I	I	I	I	R
High nitrogen, normal phosphorus and potassium	S	S	S	S	I
Low nitrogen, normal phosphorus and potassium	R	R	R	R	S

[a]I = intermediate resistance, S = highly susceptible, R = highly resistant. The numerical values for each of the ranking groups shown were subjected to analysis of variance and were statistically significant at p = 0.01.

crown rot will develop if climatic conditions continue to be favorable for disease development for an extended period of time. With the advent of warm summer months, colonization of the plants is limited to crown and root tissue. However, if cool, wet weather occurs during this time, lesions can develop on the leaves.

Control

Cultural Practices

In turf with a known history of melting-out, the total amount of fertilizer used annually should be divided between fall and spring applications. Applications of high rates of readily available nitrogen fertilizers to the turf in the spring should be avoided. If spring fertilization is practiced, the nitrogen component of the mixture should be a slow release formulation.

When feasible, clippings should be removed. Also, since cutting heights of less than 1.5 inches (3.8 cm) will result in an increase in the severity of both the foliar and crown rot phases of the disease, if the use pattern of the area permits, the turf should always be mowed at cutting heights in the 1.5–2.0 inch (3.8–5.0 cm) range. If the management program for a stand of Kentucky bluegrass with a known history of melting-out does call for a cutting height lower than 1.5 inches (3.8 cm), the area in question should be monitored closely and a fungicide program initiated immediately at the first indication of an outbreak of the disease.

Use of Resistant Grasses

The 'Merion' cultivar is highly resistant to both the leaf spot and crown rot phases of melting-out. Since the release of 'Merion' in the early 1950s, several varieties of Kentucky bluegrass have been developed that are reported to have good resistance to the disease. Included in this list are 'Adelphi,' 'Baron,' 'Bonnieblue,' 'Fylking,' 'Nugget,' 'Pennstar,' 'Sodco,'

and 'Victa.' In selecting a particular cultivar, the spectrum of resistance to other diseases in the region in question should also be taken into consideration.

Use of Fungicides

The leaf lesion phase of melting-out can be controlled by the use of anilazine, chlorothalonil, iprodione, mancozeb, or vinclozolin. Preventive fungicidal applications should be made at 10–14 day intervals, beginning with leaf elongation (first mowing) in the spring and continuing at 10–14 day intervals as long as weather is conducive to disease development.

For a profile of these fungicides and a listing of representative trade names and manufacturers, see Appendix Table I.

Helminthosporium Leaf Spot of Cool Season Turfgrasses

Helminthosporium leaf spot is one of the most important summer diseases of Kentucky bluegrass, creeping bentgrass, and creeping red fescue in the United States and southern Canada. The disease is also known to occur on turfgrasses in northern and western regions of continental Europe and in Great Britain.

Symptoms

Kentucky bluegrass

On Kentucky bluegrass, the leaf lesions characteristic of this disease are very similar to those of the leaf spot phase of melting-out. They are first seen as small purplish spots, and as they increase in size, the centers turn brown, and then finally fade to a light tan with purplish brown borders (Plate 24-B). However, colonization of leaf sheaths is not as common as with melting-out.

The symptom pattern of Helminthosporium leaf spot is also characterized by a necrosis of the entire leaf blade. This blighting is manifested by a sudden collapse and drying of the leaf blades, after which the leaves blanch to a light straw color. During warm, humid weather of mid-summer, leaf blighting may occur within a period of 4–5 days from the time of initial infection. In overall view during this period, the disease pattern is seen as a brownish fading out of irregularly shaped turfgrass areas of various sizes.

A severe crown and root rot frequently develops in conjunction with the leaf-lesion phase of the disease which appreciably reduces both the vigor and drought tolerance of the plants.

Bentgrasses

The disease is first noticed on bentgrass bowling greens and golf course putting greens as a smoky blue cast of irregularly shaped areas of turf, varying in size from 1–4 feet (0.3–1.3 m) in diameter. This symptom is soon followed by yellowing and then complete blighting of the leaves within the affected areas. In the final stages of disease development, these areas show semi-definite margins, the leaves appear water-soaked and are matted down. At this point, if the diagnostic procedure is limited to a superficial field examination of the affected turf, Helminthosporium leaf spot can be mistakenly diagnosed as Pythium blight.

When bentgrass turf is managed at a ½ inch (13 mm) cutting height, the earliest symptoms are minute yellow flecks on the leaves. These enlarge into small ovular lesions, and then develop into irregularly shaped, water-soaked blotches (Klomparens, 1953).

The Fungus

Bipolaris sorokiniana (Sacc. in Sorok.) Shoemaker; telemorph *Cochliobolus sativus* (Ito and Kurib.) Drechsl. ex Dast.; syn. *Helminthosporium sorokinianum* Sacc. ex Sorok.

Description

Conidiophores brown, emerging from the stomata or between epidermal cells after death of the host tissue, singly or in fascicles of 2 or 3, 6–8 μm × 110–150 μm, up to 8-septate. Genticulations well defined, 5 or 6; spores curved, tapering eventually toward each rounded end, or spores irregularly, thickly boomerang-shaped, bent elliptical ovate to pip-shaped, rarely bilobed or triangular in outline, 3–10 septate, 15–20 μm × 60–120 μm, dark olive brown with a thick, brittle epispore, hilum conspicuous but situated within the contour of rounded basal end (Figure 5-2).

Abundant conidia without superfluous mycelial growth are produced on S.A.Y. agar (8.0 g sucrose, 1.2 g 1-asparagine, 0.6 g dipotassium hydrogen phosphate, 1.0 g yeast extract, 20 g flake agar, 1000 ml tap water). Optimum growth is obtained at pH 6.0 at 27 °C. (Bean and Wilcoxson, 1964a).

Hosts

1. **Turfgrasses**—Colonial bentgrass (*Agrostis tenuis*), creeping bentgrass (*Agrostis palustris*), velvet bentgrass (*Agrostis canina*), bermudagrass (*Cynodon dactylon*), annual bluegrass (*Poa annua*), Canada bluegrass (*Poa compressa*), Ken-

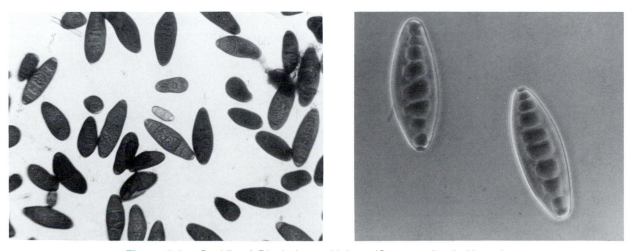

Figure 5-2. Conidia of *Bipolaris sorokiniana*. (Courtesy Austin Hagan).

tucky bluegrass (*Poa pratensis*), tall fescue (*Festuca arundinacea*), red fescue (*Festuca rubra*), annual ryegrass (*Lolium multiflorum*), and perennial ryegrass (*Lolium perenne*).

2. **All Known Gramineous Hosts**—A listing of the common names for the following species is given in Appendix Table IV. *Agropyron buonapartis* Th. Dur. and Schinz., *A. cristatum* (L.) Gaertn., *A. dasystachyum* (Hook.) Scribn., *A. desertorum* (Fisch.) Schult., *A. intermedium* (Host) Beauv., *A. inerme* (Scribn. and Smith) *A. mongolicum* Keng, Rydb., *A. repens* (L.) Beauv., *A. rigidum* Beauv., *A. riparium* Scribn. and Smith, *A. semicostatum* (Steud.) Nees, *A. sibiricum* (Willd.) Beauv., *A. smithii* Rydb., *A. subsecundum* (Link) Hitchc., *A. trachycaulum* (Link) Malte., *A. trichophorum* (Link) Richt., *Agrostis alba* L., *A. canina* L., *A. palustris* Huds., *A. tenuis* Sibth., *Ammophila arenaria* (L.) Link, *Andropogon furcatus* Muhl., *A. hallii* Hack., *Arthraxon hispidus* (Thunb.) Makino, *Avena byzantina* C. Koch., *A. fatua* L., *A. sativa* L., *A. sterilis* L., *Bouteloua curtipendula* (Michx.) Torr., *B. gracilis* (H. B. K.) Lag., *Bromus arvensis* L., *B. carinatus* Hook. and Arn., *B. catharticus* Vahl, *B. erectus* Huds., *B. inermis* Leyss., *B. japonicus* Thunb., *B. madritensis* L., *B. tectorum* L., *Calamovilfa longifolia* (Hook.) Scribn., *Cenchrus pauciflorus* Benth., *Chloris verticillata* Nutt., *Cynodon dactylon* (L.) Pers., *Dactylis glomerata* L., *Digitaria sanguinalis* (L.) Scop., *Echinochloa crusgalli* (L.) Beauv., *Elymus canadensis* L., *E. canadensis* var. *robustus* (Scribn. and Smith) Mackenz. and Bush, *E. dahuricus* Turcz., *E. dasystachys* Trin., *E. excelsus* Turcz., *E. glaucus* Buckl., *E. interruptus* Buckl., *E. junceus* Fisch., *E. macounii* Vasey, *E. sibiricus* L., *E. virginicus* L., *Eragrostis cilianensis* (All.) Lutati, *E. curvula* (Schrad.) Nees, *E. pilosa* (L.) Beauv., *Festuca arundinacea* Schreb., *F. octoflora* Walt., *F. rubra* L., *Hordeum bulbosum* L., *H. distichon* L., *H. jubatum* L., *H. murinum* L., *H. secalinum* Guss., *H. vulgare* L., *Hystrix patula* Moench, *Koeleria cristata* (L.) Pers., *Lolium multiflorum* Lam, *Muhlenbergia mexicana* (L.) Trin., *M. racemosa* (Michx.) B. S. P., *M. texana* Buckl., *Oryzopsis hymenoides* (Roem. and Schult.) Ricker, *Panicum capillare* L., *P. implicatum* Scribn., *P. miliaceum* L., *P. perlongum* Nash, *P. virgatum* L., *Phalaris arundinacea* L., *P. tuberosa* L., *Phleum pratense* L., *Poa annua* L., *Poa bulbosa* L., *P. compressa* L., *P. juncifolia* Scribn., *P. palustris* L., *P. pratensis* L., *P. secunda* Presl, *Secale cereale* L., *S. montanum* Guss., *Setaria italica* (L.) Beauv., *S. lutescens* (Weigel) Hubb., *S. viridis* (L.) Beauv., *Sorghum sudanense* (Piper) Stapf, *S. vulgare* Pers., *Stipa baicalensis* Roshev., *S. comata* Trin. and Rupr., *S. pulchra* Hitchc., *S. sibirica* Lam., *S. spartea* Trin., *S. viridula* Trin., *Triticum aestivum* L., *T. dicoccum* Schrank, *T. durum* Desf., *T. monococcum* L., *T. polonicum* L., *T. spelta* L., *T. timopheevi* (Zhukov.) Zhukov., *T. turgidum* L., *Zea mays* L. (Index Plant Dis., 1960; Klomparens, 1953; Sprague, 1950).

Disease Profile

Spores of *Bipolaris sorokiniana* are transmitted on seed harvested from diseased plants. Turfgrass leaf litter colonized by the pathogen serves as the principal source of inoculum both for the initial outbreaks of Helminthosporium leaf spot and the continued development of the disease during the growing season. The rate of saprophytic growth of the fungus, including the production of spores, is favored by cyclical patterns of drying and remoistening of the litter. This phenomenon is thought to be due to the dissipation of an inhibitory property during the dry period which normally keeps the fungus in a state of fungistasis, then when the leaf litter is remoistened, an abundant release of carbohydrates and proteins occurs which favors growth of the fungus. After the leaf litter has been moist for a period of time, the inhibitory property is reestablished, and the saprophytic growth of the fungus is once again inhibited (Colbaugh and Endo, 1974).

Helminthosporium leaf spot is a warm weather disease. The first leaf lesions usually appear in late spring, with disease severity increasing with the onset of warm, wet weather, and decreasing with the advent of cooler, fall weather. *Bipolaris sorokiniana* spores germinate on Kentucky bluegrass leaves 30–40 minutes from the onset of optimum environmental conditions. Leaf penetration by the germ tube may be either direct or through stomata (Figures 5-3 and 3-3). At 78 °F (26 °C), a minimum period of 8–10 hours of continuous leaf wetness is required for a high level of infections to occur.

There is a direct relationship between air temperatures and length of leaf wetness required to produce maximum infections. When the leaf surface temperature is 70 °F (21 °C), the leaves must be continually wet for 48 hours in order for a high incidence of infection to develop. However, when leaf surface temperatures are in the 80–90 °F (26–32 °C) range, the same amplitude of infection occurs within 24 hours (Couch and Smith, 1987).

Helminthosporium leaf spot is more severe on Kentucky bluegrass (*Poa pratensis*) that is mowed

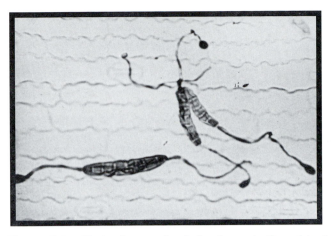

Figure 5-3. Photomicrograph of direct penetration of leaf surface by means of appressoria by germinating *Bipolaris* spores. *Courtesy Philip Larsen.*

to a height to 2 inches (5 cm) rather than 1½ inches (3.8 cm). Also, the disease is more severe when the grass is growing under high soil moisture stress or at high nitrogen fertilization (Couch, Moore and Shoulders, 1974; Couch and Smith, 1987b).

Penetration and colonization of leaves is facilitated by the production of certain extracellular enzymes by the pathogen. The foliage of Merion and Kenblue Kentucky bluegrass colonized by *Bipolaris sorokiniana* has been found to contain pectin methylesterase, polygalacturonase, polymethylgalacturonase, pectin methyl-*trans*-eliminase, polgalacturonate-*trans*-eliminase, cellulase C_x, and macerating enzyme activity. The levels of macerating enzyme activity, polygalacturonate-*trans*-eliminase, pectin methyl-*trans*-eliminase, and cellulase C_x are greater in diseased leaves of the variety Merion. This explains, in part at least, why Helminthosporium leaf spot is more destructive on Merion than Kenblue Kentucky bluegrass (Muse, Couch, Moore and Muse, 1972).

It has been reported that a correlation exists between the sugar content of foliage and the susceptibility of Kentucky bluegrass to the melting-out pathogen, *Drechslera poae* (Lukens, 1970) (see melting-out). In testing this hypothesis with Helminthosporium leaf spot, it has been found that the carbohydrate content of leaves of Kentucky bluegrass varieties is influenced by nutrition of the plants. A correlation between foliage sugar content and susceptibility to infection by *Bipolaris sorokiniana*, however, could not be established (Couch and Moore, 1971). Carbohydrate levels, then, are apparently not an important factor in determining the proneness of Kentucky bluegrass to Helminthosporium leaf spot.

The types of symptoms and the degree of severity of the foliar phase of Helminthosporium leaf spot has been shown to be directly related to atmospheric temperatures. At 68 °F (20 °C), leaf spotting occurs, but there is no leaf blighting; at 75 °F (24 °C), leaf spotting predominates, with a low order of blighting occurring; at 85 °F (30 °C), some leaf spotting occurs, but leaf blighting is the predominant symptom; and at 95 °F (35 °C), leaf spotting is completely absent, but leaf blighting is extensive (Weihing, Jenson and Hamilton, 1957).

Applications of either of the chlorophenoxy herbicides 2,4-D, 2,4,5-T, 2,4,5-TP, MCPP, or the benzoic acid herbicide dicamba will increase the susceptibility of Kentucky bluegrass (*Poa pratensis*) to the disease (Hodges, 1978, 1980). As a general rule, the susceptibility of Kentucky bluegrass to Helminthosporium leaf spot increases with increasing rates of nitrogen fertilization (Cheesman, Roberts and Tiffany, 1965; Couch and Moore, 1971, Roberts and Cheesman, 1964). However, it has also been reported that the potential for nutrition-induced changes in susceptibility is much greater in some cultivars than others (Couch, 1980).

Control

Cultural Practices

In turf with a known history of Helminthosporium leaf spot, applications of high rates of nitrogen fertilizers from June through early September should be avoided. If water soluble nitrogen fertilizers are used during this time, they should be applied on a split rate schedule in amounts just sufficient to support an adequate plant growth rate. The thatch layer should not be allowed to accumulate to a thickness greater than 0.5 inch (1.3 cm).

When the use pattern of the turf permits, Kentucky bluegrass (*Poa pratensis*) should be mowed at cutting heights in the 1.5–2.0 inch (3.8–5.0 cm) range, and if feasible, all clippings should be removed. However, if the management program for a stand with a known history of Helminthosporium leaf spot does call for a cutting height lower than 1.5 inches (3.8 cm), the area in question should be monitored closely and a fungicide program initiated immediately at the first indication of an outbreak of the disease.

Use of Resistant Grasses

Ranked in order of susceptibility to Helminthosporium leaf spot, annual bluegrass (*Poa annua*), Kentucky bluegrass (*Poa pratensis*), and creeping bentgrass (*Agrostis palustris*) are most prone to the disease. Perennial ryegrass (*Lolium perenne*) is next in susceptibility, and tall fescue (*Festuca arundinacea*) and creeping red fescue (*Festuca rubra*) are the most resistant.

The degrees of resistance of Kentucky bluegrass (*Poa pratensis*) cultivars to Helminthosporium leaf spot often vary from one geographic region to the next. This is probably due in part to the fact that the breeding material was not screened against the full range of the pathogenic biotypes of *Bipolaris sorokiniana* that exist in the regions where the cultivars are being grown (Kline and Nelson, 1963). Also, in the development of new cultivars the relative degrees of resistance of the various candidates to *Bipolaris sorokiniana* under different nutritional regimens are not usually taken into consideration. Consequently, when the cultivar is released and grown under nutritional regimens different from those in which it was screened, it may show a greater degree of vulnerability to the disease than had been expected. For example, in a comparison among twelve Kentucky bluegrass cultivars for resistance to Helminthosporium leaf spot, under low nitrogen nutrition, 'Park' was the most resistant in the group. At high nitrogen nutrition, however, it fell among the most susceptible. The variety 'Merion' was moderately resistant at low nitrogen nutrition and highly susceptible at high nitrogen nutrition. The cultivars 'Anheuser,' 'Belturf,' and 'Pennstar,' on the other hand, were highly resistant to the disease and this resistance was stable at all nutritional levels (Table 5-2) (Couch, 1980). Regional listings from the local agricultural advisory service should be consulted before selecting a Kentucky bluegrass cultivar. In reviewing

the information, particular attention should be paid to how thoroughly each of the cultivars has been tested in the region in question for resistance to Helminthosporium leaf spot.

Use of Fungicides

The leaf lesion phase of Helminthosporium leaf spot can be controlled by the use of anilazine, chlorothalonil, iprodione, mancozeb, or vinclozolin. A preventive fungicide program is essential for the most effective control of Helminthosporium leaf spot. In stands of turfgrass with a history of this disease, the first treatment should be made immediately after the first occurrence of night temperatures that do not drop below 70 °F (21 °C) and the relative humidity during the nighttime period under consideration is 85 percent or higher, and continued at 10–14 day intervals as long as weather is conducive to disease development.

For a profile of these fungicides and a listing of representative trade names and manufacturers, see Appendix Table I.

Red Leaf Spot of Bentgrass

Red leaf spot occurs in the United States, Australia, and Great Britain. The disease was first reported in the United States in 1920 on redtop (*Agrostis alba*) and autumn bentgrass (*Agrostis perennans*) growing in the Stamford-Norwalk area of Connecticut and on Long Island near Brooklyn, New York. The following year, it was diagnosed on bentgrass turf in the District of Columbia and in adjacent sections of Maryland and Virginia. By 1935, red leaf spot was known to occur on velvet bentgrass (*Agrostis canina*), creeping bentgrass (*Agrostis palustris*), and Colonial bentgrass (*Agrostis tenuis*) throughout the eastern and midwestern states (Drechsler, 1923; Drechsler, 1935).

In Australia, red leaf spot is of common occurrence on Colonial bentgrass in Victoria province (Paul, 1972). The disease has also been diagnosed on Colonial bentgrass in Great Britain (A. M. Smith, 1965).

Symptoms

Individual leaf lesions are circular to ovular, straw colored, and surrounded by reddish brown borders of variable width. On occasion, the characteristic lighter colored centers may be either extremely minute, or entirely absent. During periods of prolonged, wet weather, many of the lesions may be further surrounded by a belt of water-soaked tissue. Under conditions favorable for disease development,

Table 5-2. Comparative stability of twelve cultivars of Kentucky bluegrass to nutritionally induced changes in susceptibility to Helminthosporium leaf spot. *After Couch, 1980.*

	Stability Ranking[a]	Cultivar
Highly Stable	1	Anheuser
	2	Belturf, Pennstar
	3	Geary
	4	Delta, Fylking
	5	Newport
	6	Merion
	7	Windsor
	8	Cougar
	9	Kenblue
Highly Unstable	10	Park

[a]The numerical values for each ranking were subjected to analysis of variance, and the differences for each of these groups were statistically significant at $p = 0.05$.

lesions may overlap, producing pseudozonate patterns and giving the affected areas a reddish cast (Plate 24-D).

Severe colonization is often accompanied by withering of the leaves beginning at the tip and progressing toward the sheath. As the result, an overall view of a diseased stand of bentgrass may give a drought-stricken appearance, even though soil moisture may be adequate for plant growth.

The Fungus

Drechslera erythrospila (Drechs.) Shoemaker; telemorph *Pyrenophora erythrospila* Paul; syn. *Helminthosporium erythrospilum* Drechsler

Description

Conidiophores erect, brown or fuliginous, simple or occasionally somewhat branched, emerging singly or less often in pairs or larger groups mostly from between epidermal cells but sometimes from stomata, measuring mostly 6–9 μm × 75–275 μm, producing the first conidium usually 75–135 μm from the base and later conidia at variable successive intervals marked by genticulations containing 1–10 septa that delimit segments mostly 15–35 μm long.

Conidia, when mature, usually distinctly yellowish, sometimes light olivaceous; typically straight, rarely somewhat curved, mostly nearly cylindrical, the ends rather abruptly rounded off, containing 2–10 septa that are usually not marked by constrictions, but at times may be associated with perceptible constrictions; measuring usually 8–16 μm × 25–105 μm (average = 12.3 μm × 65 μm); individually including the nonprotruding hilum within the basal contour; germinating rather indiscriminately from any or all cells, but usually more abundantly from the thin-walled basal and apical cells than from the intermediate cells (Figure 5-4).

Procedures for Isolation and Culture

In culture, abundant sporulation of *Drechslera erythrospila* occurs on corn-meal agar when incubated for 6–8 weeks at 18 °C.

Hosts

1. **Turfgrasses**—Colonial bentgrass (*Agrostis tenuis*), creeping bentgrass (*Agrostis palustris*), and velvet bentgrass (*Agrostis canina*).
2. **All Known Gramineous Hosts**—A listing of the common names for the following species is given in Appendix Table IV. *Agrostis alba* L., *A. canina* L., *A. palustris* Huds., *A. perennans* (Walt.) Tuckerm., *A. stolonifera* L., *A. tenuis* Sibth. (Sprague, 1950).

Disease Profile

Diseased bentgrass crowns and tillers and leaf litter colonized by *Derechslera erythrospila* serve as the principal source of inoculum both for the initial outbreaks of red leaf spot and the continued development of the disease during the growing season.

Red leaf spot is a warm, wet weather disease. Primary infections of crown and leaf tissue usually occur in late spring. Infection and extensive colonization of crowns, roots and tillers often occur before the leaf lesion phase of the disease is evident. Disease incidence and severity increases as the air temperatures rise in June and July and peaks in late July and August. During periods of prolonged warm, wet

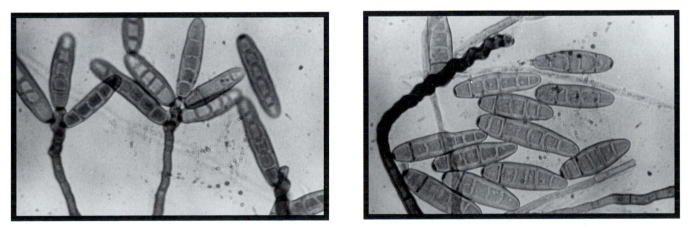

Figure 5-4. Conidia of *Drechslera erythrospila. Courtesy Austin Hagan.*

weather, the leaf blighting and crown and root rot phases of the disease may become severe, leading to the death of the plants.

The severity of red leaf spot is greater in turf under high nitrogen fertilization. Also, the development of the disease is more severe when the soil is deficient in either phosphorous, potassium, or calcium (Muse, 1974).

Control

Cultural Practices

Care should be taken to assure that the fertilization program is maintaining a proper balance of phosphorous, potassium and calcium. If it is deemed necessary to apply a water soluble nitrogenous fertilizer to the bentgrass turf during either late spring or summer, the product should be used in amounts just sufficient to support an adequate plant growth rate. Also, the thatch layer should not be allowed to accumulate to a thickness greater than 0.5 inch (1.3 cm).

Use of Fungicides

The leaf lesion phase of red leaf spot can be controlled by the use anilazine, chlorothalonil, iprodione, mancozeb, or vinclozolin. A preventive fungicide program is essential for effective control of this disease. In bentgrass turf with a known history of red leaf spot, a fungicide application should be made at the time of spring fertilization (Meyer and Turgeon, 1975). Successive applications should begin with the advent of warm humid weather in late spring and continued on a 7–10 day schedule as long as the climatic conditions are favorable for disease development.

For a profile of these fungicides and a listing of representative trade names and manufacturers, see Appendix Table I.

Helminthosporium Blight of Fescue, Ryegrass, and Bluegrass

Helminthosporium blight is one of the more common foliar diseases of fescues (*Festuca* spp.) and ryegrasses (*Lolium* spp.) in the United States, Canada, Finland, Sweden, Germany, Great Britain, New Zealand, and Australia (Drechsler, 1923; Luttrell, 1951a; Smith, Jackson and Woolhouse, 1989). In certain sections of the United States, the disease is also known to cause moderate to severe damage to Kentucky bluegrass (*Poa pratensis*) (Bean and Wilcoxson, 1964b).

Symptoms

On tall fescue and ryegrass the disease appears first as short, irregular, dark brown, transverse bars,

which resemble strands of dark thread drawn across the leaf. These bars eventually combine with short longitudinal streaks of brown tissue, producing a very finely developed network. Under optimum conditions for disease development, these net-like patterns aggregate; fusing into dark-brown, solid lesions, measuring ¼ to 1 inch (0.6–2.5 cm) long and ¹⁄₁₆ to ⅛ inch (2–3 mm) wide. Heavily colonized leaves ultimately turn yellow and die back from the tips (Plate 24-C) (Luttrell, 1951).

The characteristic net pattern of the disease on tall fescue is absent on the finer-leaved red fescue. On the leaves of the latter species, the typical lesions are small, reddish brown, irregularly shaped blotches. Leaf girdling by lesions occurs frequently, causing a yellowing and die-back from the tip.

In the warmer part of the summer, heavily diseased stands of red fescue go off color. At first they become yellow, and then finally fade to a light brown. At this time, characteristic "pockets" of dead turfgrass, ranging from 1–3 feet (0.3–0.9 m) in diameter, may develop.

The Fungus

Drechslera dictyoides (Drechs.) Shoemaker; telemorph *Pyrenophora dictyoides* Paul and Parberry; syn. *Helminthosporium dictyoides* Drechs.

Description

Sporophores dark brown or olivaceous; emerging singly or in groups of 2–6 from stomata or between epidermal cells; measuring usually 6–8 μm × 70–150 μm; 3–6 septate, the septa generally occurring at intervals of 1–30 μm; producing first spore usually at a distance of 50–100 μm from base; points of attachment of successive spores marked by moderately or strongly pronounced geniculations.

Conidia subhyaline and nearly colorless when newly proliferated, to yellow when fully matured; typically straight; maximum diameter usually at basal segment, 14–17 μm; tapering uniformly and very perceptibly to apical segment, the latter, in long spores, frequently not exceeding 8–9 μm in diameter, in short spores, it is usually of greater diameter; more rarely approximately cylindrical, or short ellipsoidal. Length, 23–115 μm, usually 50–70 μm, 1–7 septate, typically 3–5 septate, the septa not associated with perceptible constrictions except occasionally, and then constrictions most frequently present only at the basal septum; length of segments 7–24 μm, typically 12–15 μm. Contour of basal end, hemispherical; of apical end, hemispherical or hemiellipsoidal; peripheral wall or exospore uniformly thin,

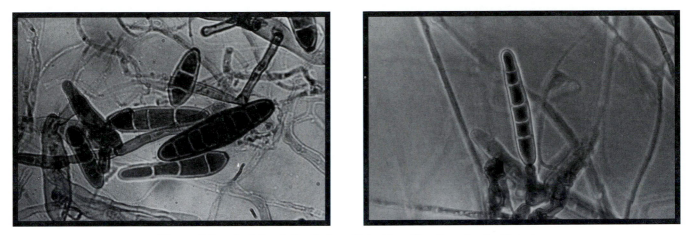

Figure 5-5. Conidia of *Drechslera dictyoides. Courtesy Austin Hagan.*

and entirely including the hilum within its contour. Germinating typically by two germ tubes, one from each end segment and produced usually at right or oblique angle to axis of spore; rarely by one or more germ tubes from intermediate segments (Figure 5-5).

Procedures for Isolation and Culture

In culture, conidia are produced on glucose-asparagine agar (3.8 g glucose, 0.5 g magnesium sulfate, 2.0 g potassium phosphate, 0.01 g ferric sulfate, 1.0 g DL-asparagine, 20 g agar, 1000 ml distilled water).

Hosts

1. **Turfgrasses**—Kentucky bluegrass (*Poa pratensis*), tall fescue (*Festuca arundinacea*), Chewings fescue (*Festuca rubra* var. *commutata*), red fescue (*Festuca rubra*), annual ryegrass (*Lolium multiflorum*), and perennial ryegrass (*Lolium perenne*).
2. **All Known Gramineous Hosts**—A listing of the common names for the following species is given in Appendix Table IV. *Festuca arundinacea* Schreb., *F. occidentalis* Hook., *F. pacifica* Piper, *F. rubra* L., *F. rubra* var. *commutata* Gaud., *Lolium multiflorum* Lam., *L. perenne* L., *Poa pratensis* L. (Bean and Wilcoxson, 1964b; Couch, 1957; Sampson and Western, 1940; Sprague, 1950).

Disease Profile

Spores of *Drechslera dictyoides* are transmitted on seed harvested from diseased plants. The pathogen also survives the winter months in diseased crowns and roots and in colonized leaf litter. During periods of extended rainfall in the early spring, leaves of the current season's growth are infected by conidia produced in these zones of overwintering. The dissemination of spores is accomplished both by wind and by splashing water.

Infection of crowns and roots of new plants also occurs in the spring. With the advent of warmer, drier weather in late spring and early summer, the leaf lesion phase of the disease decreases and severity of the crown and root rot phase increases. During late July and August, it is not uncommon for entire stands to be rendered useless due to the crown and root rot phase of this disease. The crown and root rot phase of Helminthosporium blight is one of the primary causes of summer "browning-up" of red fescues.

Control

Cultural Practices

In turf with a known history of Helminthosporium blight, the total amount of fertilizer used annually should be divided between fall and spring applications. Applications of high rates of readily available nitrogen fertilizers to the turf in the spring should be avoided. If spring fertilization is practiced, the nitrogen component of the mixture should be a slow release formulation.

Use of Fungicides

The leaf lesion phase of Helminthosporium blight can be controlled by the use of anilazine, chlorothalonil, iprodione, mancozeb, or vinclozolin. Preventive fungicidal applications should be made at 10–14 day intervals, beginning with leaf elongation (first mowing) in the spring and continuing at 10–14 day intervals as long as weather is conducive to disease development.

For a profile of these fungicides and a listing of

representative trade names and manufacturers, see Appendix Table I.

Brown Blight of Ryegrass

Brown blight of ryegrass is known to occur in the United States, Canada, the northern and western regions of continental Europe, Great Britain, New Zealand, and Australia.

Symptoms

Leaf lesions are of two types. The first are seen as small, ovular, chocolate brown spots, which eventually develop white centers. These may be very numerous, at times numbering as high as 100 per leaf. This large population of lesions gives an appearance similar to the net blotch effect on tall and meadow fescues caused by *Drechslera dictyoides*; however, the characteristic transverse markings of the latter disease are absent. The second lesion type takes the form of dark brown streaks ⅜ inch (6–9 mm) or more in length. Both lesion types may appear simultaneously on the same leaf blade. A high incidence of lesions usually causes the entire leaf to become blighted. This withering process begins at the tips of the leaves as a yellow discoloration and then progresses toward the sheath (Plate 24-F).

The Fungus

Drechslera siccans (Drechs.) Shoemaker; telemorph *Pryenophora lolii* Dovaston; syn. *Helminthosporium siccans* Drechs.

Description

Conidiophores olivaceous, emerging usually singly, less frequently in pairs, and rarely in groups of three from stomata or more especially from between epidermal cells on the vascular ridges; measuring 7–9 μm × 50–300 μm; 1–9 septate, the septa inserted at intervals of 15–90 μm; producing first conidium at a distance 50–250 μm from base; points of attachments of successive conidia at angles of geniculate irregularities occurring at intervals of 5–30 μm.

Conidia subhyaline or light fuliginous when newly proliferated, later becoming yellow, brownish, or brownish olivaceous, never dark olivaceous; when fully mature, provided with a moderately thick peripheral wall; typically straight or slightly curved; measuring usually 14–20 μm × 35–130 μm; usually subcylindrical, or tapering slightly more markedly toward the apex, the distal segment often not ex-

ceeding 10 μm in diameter, or rarely greater in diameter at the distal end than at the base. Apical and basal ends abruptly rounded off, the contours at the ends being approximately hemispherical. Hilum moderately conspicuous included within contours of peripheral wall. Germinating by the production of germ tubes from the intermediate as well as end segments, the basal and distal segments both usually participating in the process by the proliferation of 1 or 2 lateral or oblique germ tubes. Of the intermediate segments, one, several, or all may produce one or rarely two lateral germ tubes. Under natural conditions, germination by the production of one, or less frequently sporophoric processes, each bearing usually a single conidium, is not uncommon (Figure 5-6).

Procedures for Isolation and Culture

Isolates of *Drechslera siccans* vary in ability to sporulate on artificial media. Optimum results are obtained on glucose-asparagine agar (3.8 g glucose, 0.5 g magnesium sulfate, 2.0 g potassium phosphate, 0.01 g ferric sulfate, 1.0 g DL-asparagine, 20 g agar, 1000 ml distilled water).

Hosts

1. **Turfgrasses**—tall fescue (*Festuca arundinacea*), annual ryegrass (*Lolium multiflorum*), and perennial ryegrass (*Lolium perenne*).
2. **All Known Gramineous Hosts**—A listing of the common names for the following species is given

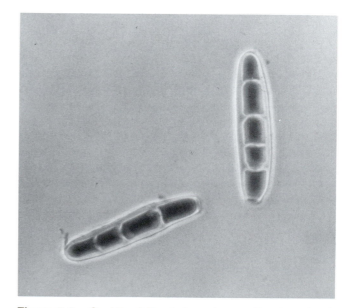

Figure 5-6. Conidia of *Drechslera siccans. Courtesy Austin Hagan.*

in Appendix Table IV. *Festuca arundinacea* Schreb., *Lolium multiflorum* Lam., *L. perenne* L. (Sampson and Western, 1940).

Disease Profile

Spores of *Drechslera siccans* are transmitted on seed harvested from diseased plants. The pathogen also survives its adverse season as dormant mycelium in diseased crowns and in leaf litter from the previous season's growth.

The leaf lesion phase of the disease develops first during the cool, wet weather of early spring. At this time, infection of crowns and roots of new plants also occurs. Secondary spread of the spores of the pathogen from plant to plant is accomplished by wind and by splashing water. During the warm summer months, the incidence of leaf lesions subsides and the severity of crown and root rot increases. However, with the advent of the cool, wet weather of fall, lesions can again develop on the leaves.

Control

There is no information on the degree of resistance of various cultivars to brown blight or the effectiveness of fungicides for the control of the leaf lesion phase of the disease.

Drechslera Leaf Blight of Bentgrass

Drechslera leaf blight occurs in humid, temperate regions of North America and Europe. Although the disease affects all commonly cultivated cool season turfgrass species, to date, it has only been reported to be a major problem on creeping bentgrass (*Agrostis palustris*) and Colonial bentgrass (*Agrostis tenuis*) (Spilker and Larsen, 1985).

Symptoms

On bentgrass, symptoms appear in early spring as red leaf lesions on the leaf blades and as tip dieback. At this stage of development, the disease can be misdiagnosed as red leaf spot. As the weather becomes warmer, entire leaves become necrotic, and eventually the whole plant is blighted down to the crown. Several small groups of adjacent plants will often be colonized, forming reddish brown, sunken areas approximately 1 inch (2.5 cm) in diameter composed of blighted plants. Under conditions favorable for development of the disease, these areas will coalesce, often involving several square yards (meters) of turf. In overall view, the affected turf assumes a reddish brown color. Disease symptoms continue to develop throughout the summer (Larsen *et al.*, 1981).

On tall fescue (*Festuca arundinacea*) and perennial ryegrass (*Lolium perenne*), the foliar symptoms first develop as short, irregular, dark brown, transverse bars, which resemble strands of dark thread drawn across the leaf. These eventually combine with short longitudinal streaks of brown tissue, producing a very finely developed network with much the same appearance as the lesions of Helminthosporium blight. The leaves also develop chlorotic streaks. Eventually, the entire blade turns yellow and withers at the tip and margins.

The Fungus

Drechslera catenaria (Drechs.) Ito; syn. *Helminthosporium catenarium* Drechs.

Description

Sporophores brown or olivaceous; emerging usually from the stomata, singly or in groups of two; measuring 5–8 × 60–200 μm; producing the first spore at a distance of 25–60 μm from base, and successive spores at intervals of 15–30, the point of attachment marked by scars at the apices of pronounced geniculations.

Spores 1–10 septate, the septa sometimes associated with slight constrictions or irregularities in the contour of the thin peripheral wall; subhyaline to light yellowish 14–18 × 30–200 μm, measured at their maximum diameter; the shorter ones usually straight, widest at the basal or second segment, tapering uniformly to approximately half the maximum diameter at tip; the longer ones often perceptibly crooked, irregular in diameter, frequently showing both a basal hilum and an apical scar, the apical scar marking the attachment of a secondary spore, and usually associated with a perculiar modification of the distal portion of the terminal segment, consisting in the prolongation of the later at a uniform diameter representing the minimum width of the spore. Secondary spores or spores of a higher order of the same diameter but usually considerably shorter less frequently septate, or continuous. Both types germinating normally by production of one or two lateral germ tubes from basal segment, and single lateral or oblique tube from terminal segment. Contour of basal end hemi-ellipsoidal, of distal end hemispherical; hilum and apical scar not protruding (Figure 5-7)

On potato glucose agar, aerial mycelium white or dirty yellowish, present as dense erect tufts 2–5 mm, high at point of plating and as small flecks scattered

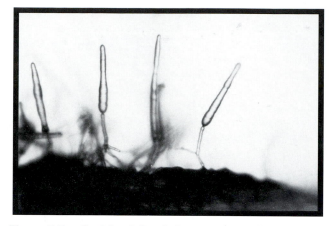

Figure 5-7. Conidia of *Drechslera catenaria. Courtesy Philip Larsen.*

sparsely over the surface; in either case consisting of sterile hyphae and an increasing number of conidial fructifications; the latter arising on the expanded terminations of hyphae not otherwise much modified, and consisting of a series of successively proliferated spores that may be either sessile or separated by intercalary, narrower sporophoric segments. The fructification frequently branching, as a result of the proliferation of lateral or oblique sporophoric processes from the basal or terminal segment of individual spores; and, less typically, sometimes consisting of miscellaneous processes of segments varying from 6–18 μm in thickness, and disarticulating at constricted septa marked by presence of scars or hyla (Drechsler, 1923).

Procedures for Isolation and Culture

The diseased plant specimens should be washed for one hour in running tap water and then surface-disinfested by soaking them in 0.5 percent sodium hypochlorite for 3 minutes. Sections of tissue should be plated aseptically on lactose casein hydrolysate agar (37.5 g lactose, 3.0 g casein hydrolysate, 1.0 g KH_2PO_4, 0.5 g $MgSO_4$, 2 ml microelement solution; 10 g agar per 1,000 ml deionized water). The microelement solution is prepared by dissolving 723.5 mg $Fe(NO_3)_3$, 439.8 mg $ZnSO_4·7H_2O$, and 203.0 mg $MnSO_4·4H_2O$ in deionized water to make 1,000 ml of solution (Malca and Ulstrup, 1962). Sporulation is enhanced when the cultures are incubated at 21 °C under continuous fluorescent light at 5500 lux for two weeks (Larsen *et al.*, 1981).

Hosts

1. **Turfgrasses**—Kentucky bluegrass (*Poa pratensis*), creeping bentgrass (*Agrostis palustris*), Colonial

bentgrass (*Agrostis tenuis*), creeping red fescue (*Festuca rubra*), tall fescue (*Festuca arundinacea*), and perennial ryegrass (*Lolium perenne*).

2. **All Known Gramineous Hosts**—A listing of the common names for the following species is given in Appendix Table IV. *Agrostis palustris* Huds., *A. tenuis* Sibth., *Cinna arundinacea* L., *Festuca arundinacea* Schreb., *F. pratensis* Huds., *F. rubra* L., *Hordeum vulgare* L., *Lolium perenne* L., *Phalaris arundinacea* L., *Phleum pratense* L., *Poa pratensis* L., *P. trivialis* L., *Sorghum sudanense* (Piper) Stapf, *Triticum aestivum* L. (Drechsler, 1923; Lefebvre and Johnson, 1941; Misra, Prakash and Singh, 1972; Misra and Singh, 1972; Spilker and Larsen, 1985; Zeiders, 1976).

Disease Profile

Spores of *Drechslera catenaria* are transmitted on seed harvested from diseased plants. In established turf, diseased crowns and leaf litter colonized by the pathogen serve as the principal source of inoculum for the initial outbreaks of the disease. Severe outbreaks of Drechslera leaf blight are favored by extended periods of leaf wetness. Primary infections of crown and leaf tissue occur in early spring. Severity of both the leaf blighting and the crown rot phases of the disease increase into early summer.

Drechslera catenaria is highly pathogenic to the creeping bentgrass (*Agrostis palustris*) cultivars 'Toronto,' 'Seaside,' 'Cohansey,' 'Emerald,' and 'Penncross,' and to 'Highland' Colonial bentgrass (*Agrostis tenuis*) (Spilker and Larsen, 1985).

Control

Control of Drechslera leaf blight throughout the growing season can be obtained with two applications at ten day intervals of iprodione at 2 oz a.i. per 1,000 square feet (61 g a.i./100 m²) of turf in April (Larsen, Hagan, Joyner and Spilker, 1981).

For a profile of iprodione and a listing of representative trade names and manufacturers, see Appendix Table I.

Zonate Eyespot of Bentgrass, Bluegrass, and Bermudagrass

Zonate eyespot was first diagnosed on bermudagrass (*Cynodon dactylon*) in Texas in 1911 (Heald and Wolf, 1911). The pathogen has since been found to be capable of causing severe damage to bentgrasses (*Agrostis* spp.) and Kentucky bluegrass (*Poa pratensis*), as well as the species of crabgrass (*Digitaria* spp.) and quackgrass (*Agropyron* spp.) that commonly infest established landscape and recreation turf (Drechsler, 1923; Howard, Rowell and Keil, 1951).

Symptoms

On turfgrass mowed at 1 inch (2.5 cm) and higher, zonate eyespot is first seen as minute, brown spots on the leaves. These lesions increase in length and width, finally becoming elongate, with the centers fading to dull white or light straw color. At this stage of development, the lesions are surrounded by narrow, brown borders. This difference in coloration, coupled with the elongate shape of the older lesions produces the eyespot feature that is characteristic of this disease.

Under conditions favorable for disease development, the lesions sometime occupy the entire width of the leaf blade. When this happens, these areas usually develop a number of irregularly concentric brown markings, giving them a distinctly zonate appearance (Plate 24-E). The complete blighting and total browning of leaves due to coalescence of lesions is not uncommon.

On bentgrass managed at bowling green and golf green mowing height, zonate eyespot is seen in overall view as irregularly shaped patches of blighted turfgrass varying in size from 2 to 9 inches (5–23 cm) in diameter. Individual leaf symptoms first develop as small yellow lesions. These individual lesions enlarge rapidly and soon coalesce, causing the entire leaf to turn yellow, wither, and then turn brown (Jackson and Fenstermacher, 1973).

The Fungus

Drechslera gigantea (Heald and Wolf) Ito; syn. *Helminthosporium giganteum* Heald and Wolf

Description

Conidiophores dark brown, many-septate, 9–12 μm × 200–400 μm, with a slightly bulbous base. Conidia elongated, cylindrical, with slightly tapering ends; 5-septate; hyaline when living, pale brown when dead; extremely large 15–21 μm × 300–315 μm (Figure 5-8).

Hosts

1. **Turfgrasses**—bermudagrass (*Cynodon dactylon*), creeping bentgrass (*Agrostis palustris*), velvet bentgrass (*Agrostis canina*), and Kentucky bluegrass (*Poa pratensis*).
2. **All Known Gramineous Hosts**—A listing of the common names for the following species is given

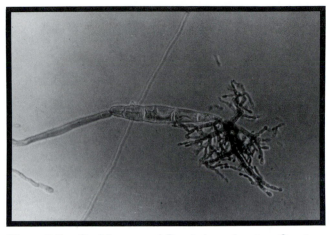

Figure 5-8.   Conidiospore of *Drechslera gigantea. Courtesy Austin Hagan.*

in Appendix Table IV. *Agropyron intermedium* (Host) Beauv., *A. repens* (L.) Beauv., *A. rigidum* Beauv., *Agrostis canina* L., *A. palustris* Huds. *A. stolonifera* L., *Andropogon pertusus* (L.) Willd., *Bromus inermis* Leyss., *Cenchrus brownii* R. S., *C. echinatus* L., *Cocos nucifera* L., *Commelina elegans* H. B. K., *Cynodon dactylon* (L.) Pers., *Digitaria ischaemum* (Schreb.) Schreb., *D. sanguinalis* (L.) Scop., *Echinochloa crusgalli* (L.) Beauv., *Eleusine indica* (L.) Gaertn., *Elymus virginicus* L., *Eragrostis cilianensis* (All.) Lutati, *E. pectinacea* (Michx.) Nees, *Festuca hookeriana* F. Meull., *Leersia virginica* Willd., *Muhlenbergia mexicana* (L.) Trin., *M. schreberi* Gmel., *Panicum anceps* Michx., *P. clandestinum* L., *P. dichotomiflorum* Michx., *P. maximum* Jacq., *Pennisetum alopecuroides* (L.) Spreng., *P. ciliare* (L.) Link, *Phalaris arundinacea* L., *P. arundinacea* var. *picta* L., *P. tuberosa* var. *stenoptera* (Hack.) Hitchc., *Phleum pratense* L., *Poa compressa* L., *P. pratensis* L., *Saccharum officinarum* L., *Setaria uniseta* Fourn., *Spodipogon sibericus* Trin., *Trichachne insularis* (L.) Nees, *Tripsacum dactyloides* (L.) L. (Drechsler, 1923; Drechsler, 1929b; Heald and Wolf, 1911; Howard, Rowell and Keil, 1951; Meredith, 1963; Muchovej, 1987; Monteith and Dahl, 1932).

Disease Profile

Zonate eyespot is a warm, wet weather disease. Outbreaks usually first occur in mid to late June. Development of the disease usually reaches its peak in late August.

Overwintering of *Drechslera gigantea* is accomplished as dormant mycelium in leaf litter and the crown tissue of turfgrass plants colonized during the previous growing season. The principal source of primary inoculum is decomposing leaf litter. Spores are carried to the leaves by air currents and splashing water.

Highly localized outbreaks of zonate eyespot within a stand of turfgrass are of common occurrence. *Drechslera gigantea* spores usually do not survive for more than 14 days after maturity. This restricted pattern of disease development, then, is probably caused by abrupt changes in the microclimate which (a) prevents leaf infections in new turf areas by spores that have already been produced, and (b) limits the further production of spores. As the result, the disease does not spread—it is confined to the original colonization site (Drechsler, 1923).

Control

There is no information on the degree of resistance of various cultivars to zonate eyespot or the effectiveness of fungicides for the control of the leaf lesion phase of the disease.

Leaf Blotch of Bermudagrass

Symptoms

In overall view, affected areas are straw colored, irregular in outline, and range from 2 inches to several feet (5 cm–2 m) in diameter. Leaf lesions are first seen as small, olive-green spots. As these enlarge, they form irregularly-shaped blotches, which are, in turn, brownish green to black in appearance (Plate 25-A). When lesions are numerous, the leaves wither and gradually fade to a light tan.

The Fungus

Bipolaris cynodontis (Marig.) Shoemaker; telemorph *Cochliobolus cynodontis* Nelson; syn. *Helminthosporium cynodontis* Marig.

Description

Conidiophores single or in pairs, dark brown, 4–6 μm × 50–150 μm; conidia 11–14 μm × 27–80 μm, elongate, curved, at times straight, tapering slightly towards abruptly rounded ends; subhyaline to fuliginous, never brown or dark olivaceous, 3–9 septate, septa not associated with constrictions in the relatively thin peripheral wall, germination by production of 2 bipolar germ tubes (Figure 5-9).

Hosts

1. **Turfgrass**—bermudagrass (*Cynodon dactylon*).

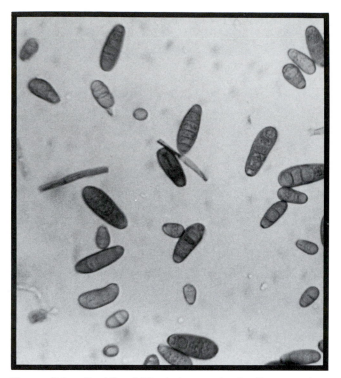

Figure 5-9. Conidia of *Bipolaris cynodontis*. Courtesy Austin Hagan.

2. **All Known Gramineous Hosts**—A list of the common names for the following species is in Appendix Table IV. *Cynodon dactylon* (L.) Pers., *Eleusine indica* (L.) Gaertn., *Muhlenbergia mexicana* (L.) Trin. (Drechsler, 1923).

Disease Profile

Bipolaris cynodontis survives adverse weather as mycelium in the crowns and roots of diseased plants. Development of the leaf lesion phase of the disease is favored by cool, wet weather; consequently, leaf blighting is most common during the months of late winter and early spring. With the advent of warm, relatively dry summer months, the incidence of leaf lesions decreases and the severity of crown and root rot incited by the pathogen increases. The severity of both the leaf lesion and root and crown rot phases of the disease is greater on bermudagrass growing under low potassium nutrition (Matocha and Smith, 1980).

Control

The bermudagrass (*Cynodon dactylon*) cultivars 'Tifgreen,' 'Turftex,' and 'Ormond' are highly resistant to leaf blotch (Slana, 1977). The severity of both the leaf lesion and crown rot phases of the disease can be lessened by employing a fertilization program that provides the proper balance of nitrogen, phosphorous and potassium (Matocha and Smith, 1980).

There is no information on the effectiveness of fungicides for the control of the leaf lesion phase of leaf blotch.

Stem and Crown Necrosis of Bermudagrass

Symptoms

Diseased plants are stunted and spindly in appearance. Leaves borne close to stem lesions become chlorotic and eventually turn brown. Individual lesions on the stem and crown are dark purple to black in color. Externally, these lesions are usually very small, but the underlying tissue may be extensively rotted. This diseased stem tissue is a dark brown to black, moist rot, and is usually confined to the pith between nodes. Occasionally, however, necrotic brown vascular streaks may extend internodally beyond the main zone of necrosis. In advanced stages of disease development, the crowns may become completely rotted (Gudauskas, 1962).

The Fungus

Bipolaris spicifera (Bain) Subram.; telemorph *Cochliobolus spicifer* Nelson); syn. *Helminthosporium spiciferum* (Bain.) Nicot.

Description

Conidiophores dark olivaceous to brown, simple or compound, with septa 5 to 50 μm apart and with the conidia produced at irregular intervals. Conidia chiefly 4-celled, borne in clusters of 2 to 3 to 50 or more, dark olivaceous to brown, usually rather symmetrical in shape, tapering toward the rounded ends, 20–41 × 10.2–20.4 μm, frequently 30–34 × 10.2–13.6 μm (Figure 5-10).

Hosts

1. **Turfgrass**—bermudagrass (*Cynodon dactylon*).
2. **All Known Gramineous Hosts**—A listing of common names for the following species is given in Appendix Table IV. *Avena sativa* L., *Bromus inermis* Leyss., *Cynodon dactylon* (L.) Pers., *Oryza sativa* L., *Pennisetum glaucum* (L.) R. Br., *Sorghum sudanense* (Piper) Stapg, *S. vulgare* Pers. (Freeman, 1978; Gudauskas, 1962).

Disease Profile

Bipolaris spicifera is transmitted on the surface of bermudagrass seeds (Freeman, 1970). The fungus is capable of killing emerging seedlings, but does not penetrate uninjured surfaces of mature plants. In Alabama, the meadow spittlebug (*Philaenus leucophthalmus*) has been associated with the initiation of Helminthosporium stem and crown rot of Coastal bermudagrass (Gudauskas, 1962). (See also Seedling Diseases).

Additional Helminthosporial Pathogens of Bermudagrass

In addition to the two species listed above, *Bipolaris stenospila* (Drechs.) Shoemaker, *Setosphaeria rostrata* Leonard [syn. *Drechslera rostrata* (Drechs.)

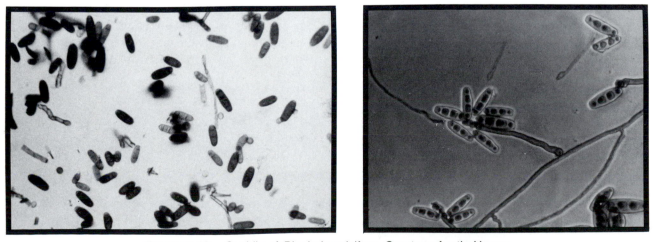

Figure 5-10. Conidia of *Bipolaris spicifera. Courtesy Austin Hagan.*

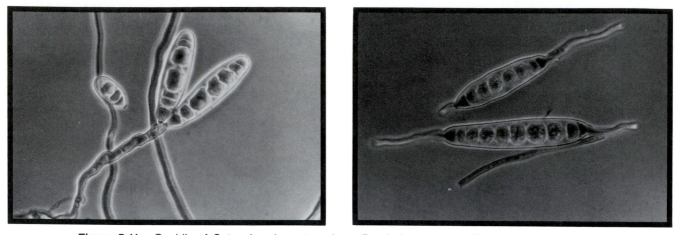

Figure 5-11. Conidia of *Setosphaeria rostrata* (syn. *Drechslera rostrata*). Courtesy Austin Hagan.

Shoemaker], and *Drechslera triseptata* (Drechs.) Subramanian and Jain have been reported to be pathogenic to bermudagrass (Drechsler, 1923; Freeman, 1964a). Among these, *Bipolaris stenospila* is apparently the most destructive, with *Drechslera triseptata* and *Setosphaeria rostrata* ranking second in pathogenic potential (Figure 5-11).

Simultaneous infections by varying combinations of these species occurs commonly. The plant parts affected include leaves, stems and/or crowns and roots. Apparently infections may occur at any time the grass is not in dormancy.

The total damage to a stand of bermudagrass by these fungi can be extensive. Fungus colonization of the plants is often confined to crowns and roots. As the result, thinning out of the stand of grass may develop to an advanced state in the complete absence of leaf lesions.

Additional research is needed on this particular group of pathogens to more clearly identify epidemiological patterns and delineate and characterize the specific diseases incited by each species.

Helminthosporium Crown and Root Rot of Zoysiagrass

Symptoms

In overall view, diseased stands of grass show a general thinning out and regrowth is slow after mowing or wear. Stems may show small dark brown to purplish lesions. The more pronounced symptom pattern, however, is a dry, dark brown to black rot of stems, crowns, and roots. In advanced stages of disease development, the root systems may become completely rotted.

The Fungus

Bipolaris tetramera (McKinney) Shoemaker; syn. *Helminthosporium tetramera* McKinney

Description

Conidiophores dark olivaceous to brown, simple or compound, with septa 5 to 50 μm apart and with the conidia produced at irregular intervals. Conidia chiefly 4-celled, borne in clusters of 2 to 3 to 50 or more, dark olivaceous to brown, usually rather symmetrical in shape, tapering toward the rounded ends, 20–41 × 10.2–20.4 μm, frequently 30–34 × 10.2–13.6 μm.

Procedures for Isolation and Culture

In culture, the fungus grows rapidly at temperatures as high as 30 °C; however, conidia lose viability in less than 2 weeks at these temperatures. On the other hand, conidial viability is retained as long as 6 months at 5 °C. Pathogenicity of isolates is generally lost after 2 to 4 subcultures on potato dextrose agar. The fungus is generally more stable when cultured on sterilized zoysiagrass (Bell, 1967).

Hosts

1. **Turfgrass**—zoysiagrass (*Zoysia japonica*).
2. **All Known Gramineous Hosts**—A listing of the common names for the following species is given in Appendix Table IV. *Triticum aestivum* L., *Zoysia japonica* Steud. (Bell, 1967; Sprague, 1950).

Disease Profile

The crown and root rot phases of the disease are most severe in May and September. The pathogen shows a wide range of variability for pathogenicity. Injury to individual stands of zoysia may vary from slight to severe. The epidemic patterns in the latter case may in turn vary from tardive to explosive.

Control

There is no information on the effectiveness of fungicides for the control of Helminthosporium crown and root rot of zoysiagrass. The impact of the disease on the turf can be lessened by maintaining the thatch layer at a thickness no greater than 0.5 inch (1.3 cm). Care should be taken to assure that the fertilization program is supplying the proper balance of nitrogen, phosphorous and potassium. Also, shallow irrigations of the turf should be avoided. Rather, the duration of each watering should provide for penetration of the soil to a depth of 6 inches (15 cm).

GRAY LEAF SPOT

Gray leaf spot affects a wide range of warm season and cool season turfgrasses. It is a major disease of St. Augustinegrass (*Stenotaphrum secundatum*) and ryegrasses (*Lolium* spp.) in the south central and southeastern regions of the United States. Severe outbreaks have also been reported on perennial ryegrass (*Lolium perenne*) in the northeastern and north central states (Bain, Patel and Patel, 1972; Freeman, 1967; Landschoot and Hoyland, 1992). Gray leaf spot is also known to occur on turfgrasses in the Caribbean, South America, Africa, Asia, Australasia, and the warm temperate regions of Europe (Smith, Jackson and Woolhouse, 1989).

Symptoms

Leaf lesions begin as olive green to brown water-soaked dots smaller than a pin head. These enlarge rapidly to form spots that are at first round to oval, and then elongate. The maximum size of individual lesions varies with turfgrass species. On ryegrasses (*Lolium* spp.), centipedegrass (*Eremochloa ophiuroides*), and bermudagrass (*Cynodon dactylon*), older lesions usually measure ⅟₁₆ inch (1.5 mm) wide by ⅛ inch (3 mm) long, while on St. Augustinegrass, mature lesions may range up to ½ inch (13 mm) in length (Plate 25-E).

As the lesions enlarge, they develop depressed, blue gray centers with slightly irregular purple to brown margins that are in turn bordered by a ring of yellow tissue. During extended periods of leaf wetness, the pathogen sporulates abundantly in the centers of the spots giving them a velvety gray appearance. Leaves with high numbers of lesions become yellow, then they wither and turn brown. In overall view, a severely affected turf may appear scorched as though drought stricken.

Symptoms on the spike and sheath closely resemble those on the blade, while spots on the culm are brown to black. Culm and spike infection is common only during periods of high disease incidence.

The Fungus

Pyricularia grisea (Cke.) Sacc.; telemorph *Magnaporthe grisea* (Hebert) Barr

Description

Conidiophores gray or tinted, septate, basal cell somewhat swollen, simple or sparingly branched, penetrating through the stomates in clusters of 2–5, geniculate, 4–5 μm × 60–120 μm; conidia single, fuscous, terminal in scorpiod cymes, ovate, 2-septate with the apical cell cone-shaped or slightly rostrate, conidia broadest at lower septum, base with slight hilum-like terminal where it breaks from the stalk, 9–12 μm × 18–22 μm.

Procedures for Isolation and Culture

In culture, the organism sporulates well on a 2 percent rice polish agar, or V-8 Juice agar (15 g agar, 200 ml V-8 Juice, 2 g $CaCO_3$, and 800 ml distilled water) (Malca and Owen, 1957). On potato dextrose agar, isolates that are gray to white in coloration are generally highly pathogenic, whereas black isolates tend to be weakly pathogenic. Mycelial production among individual isolates varies from abundant aerial growth to vary sparse and appressed (Trevathan, 1982). The pathogenicity of isolates can be maintained by periodic transfers to ryegrass agar (10 g finely ground ryegrass leaves, 3 g $CaCO_3$, and 15 g agar per 1,000 ml distilled water) (Moss and Trevathan, 1987).

Hosts

1. **Turfgrasses**—Colonial bentgrass (*Agrostis tenuis*), creeping bentgrass (*Agrostis palustris*), annual bluegrass (*Poa annua*), Kentucky bluegrass (*Poa pratensis*), bermudagrass (*Cynodon dactylon*), centipedegrass (*Eremochloa ophiuroides*), red fescue (*Festuca rubra*), tall fescue (*Festuca arundinacea*), annual ryegrass (*Lolium multiflorum*), perennial ryegrass (*Lolium perenne*), and St. Augustinegrass (*Stenotaphrum secundatum*).
2. **All Known Gramineous Hosts**—A listing of common names for the following species is given

in Appendix Table IV. *Agrostis palustris* Huds., *A. tenuis* Sibth., *Alopecurus pratensis* L, *Anthoxanthum odoratum* L., *Arundo donax* L., *Avena byzantina* C. Koch, *A. sativa* L., *A. sterilis* L., *Brachiaria mutica* (Forssk.) Stapf, *Bromus catharticus* Vahl, *B. inermis* Leyss., *B. sitchensis* Trin., *Cladium jamaicense* Crantz, *Commelina erecta* L., *Cynodon dactylon* (L.) Pers., *Dactylis glomerata* L., *Digitaria cillaris* (Rentz.) Koeler, *D. decumbens* Stent, *D. horizontalis* Willd., *D. ischaemum* (Schreb.) Schreb. ex Muhl., *D. sanguinalis* (L.) Scop., *D. serotina* (Walt.) Michx., *Echinochloa colonum* (L.) Link, *E. crusgalli* (L.) Beauv., *E. crusgalli* var. *frumentacea* (Roxb.) W. F. Wright, *Eleusine coracana* (L.) Gaertn., *E. indica* (L.) Gaertn., *Eragrostis curvula* (Schrad.) Nees, *E. lugens* Nees, *Eremochloa ophiuroides* (Munro) Hack., *Eriochloa villosa* (Thunb.) Kunth, *Euphorbia preslii* Guss., *Festuca altaica* St. Yves, *F. arundinacea* Schreb., *F. rubra* L., *Hedychium coronarium* J. Koenig, *Hierochloe odorata* (L.) Beauv., *Holcus lanatus* L., *Hordeum vulgare* L., *Hystrix patula* Moench, *Leersia chinensis* , *L. hexandra* Swartz, *L. japonica* , *L. oryzoides* (L.) Swartz, *L. virginica* Willd., *Lolium multiflorum* Lam., *L. perenne* L., *Muhlenbergia racemosa* (Michx.) B. S. P., *Oryza sativa* L., *Panicum dichotomiflorum* Michx., *P. miliaceum* L., *P. texanum* Buckl., *Paspalum plicatulum* Michx., *P. stramineum* Nash, *P. undulatum* Poir., *Pennisetum clandestinum* Hochst. ex Chiov., *P. purpureum* Schumach., *P. typhoides* (N. L. Burnm.) Stapf and Hubb., *Poa annua* L., *P. pratensis* L., *P. trivialis* L., *Polygonium pennsylvanicum* L., *Rhynchelytrum roseum* (Nees) Stapf and Hubb., *Scolochloa festucacea* (Willd.) Link, *Setaria faberii* Herrm., *S. glauca* Beauv., *S. italica* (L.) Beauv., *S. lutescens* (Weigel) Hubb., *S. pumila*, *S. viridis* (L.) Beauv., *Sorghum sudanense* (Piper) Stapf, *Stenotaphrum glabrum* Trin., *S. secundatum* (Walt.) Kuntze, *Triticum aestivum* L., *Zea mays* L. (Hardison, 1942; Index Plant Dis., 1960; Purchio and Muchovej, 1991; Trevathan, 1982; Sprague, 1950).

Disease Profile

Gray leaf spot occurs during moderate to warm weather accompanied by periods of prolonged leaf wetness. The pathogen overwinters as free conidia and as dormant mycelium in lesions on the lower leaves of earlier diseased plants and in plant residue from the previous season's growth. Spores are disseminated by wind and splashing water. Primary infection of newly developing leaves occurs with the advent of spring rains. As the mean daily air temperatures increase, and with prolonged periods of high atmospheric humidity, there is a progressive buildup in disease incidence. Development of the disease in epidemic proportions requires a succession of continual leaf wetness periods of 24 hours or longer and air temperatures in the 70–85 °F (21–29 °C) range (Landachoot and Hoyland, 1992; Malca and Owen, 1957; Moss and Trevathan, 1987; Trevathan, 1982).

Free water on the leaf surface is required for spore germination. Under proper environmental conditions the spores germinate and form appressoria within 16 hours (Figure 3-3). Eight hours after germination, penetration of the epidermal cells has been accomplished and active parasitism begun. Incipient lesions appear 5–6 days after this, and, within 24 hours, these enlarge to form the characteristic dull gray, mature lesions.

Leaf penetration by the germ tubes is both direct and through stomates. Direct penetration is apparently the more common mode of entry. Movement of the mycelium through the leaf tissue proceeds both intercellularly and intracellularly. The mesophyll cells are actively parasitized by the pathogen, but vascular tissue is rarely invaded (Malca and Owen, 1957).

With perennial ryegrass (*Lolium perenne*), gray leaf spot is more severe on newly seeded turf than older, tillered plants (Table 5-3) (Landschoot and Hoyland, 1992). Incidence of the disease on St. Augustinegrass (*Stenotaphrum secundatum*) is greater when the plants are grown under high nitrogen fertilization. Rates from 1 to 8 pounds of actual nitrogen per 1,000 square feet of turf (0.5–4 kg/100 m^2) have been shown to increase the numbers of leaf lesions from 65 to 125 percent over the amount in plants that had not been fertilized since the previous growing season (Freeman, 1964b).

Control

Cultural Practices

Applications of high rates of nitrogen fertilizers during wet summer months should be avoided. If water soluble nitrogen fertilizers are used during this time, they should be applied on a split rate schedule in amounts just sufficient to support an adequate plant growth rate.

Decreasing the length of time the leaves are wet will aid in reducing the incidence of gray leaf spot. The duration of the period of daily leaf wetness can be reduced by two to four hours by following a nighttime watering schedule in which the irrigation is performed after sunset and completed before sunrise (see Chapter 16, Figure 16-2).

Table 5-3. Relationship between age of plant and air temperature and the development of gray leaf spot lesions on perennial ryegrass (*Lolium perenne*). After Landschoot and Hoyland, 1992

	Length of Foliar Lesions (mm)							
	72 °F (22 °C)				85 °F (29 °FC)			
Age of Plant	10 days[a]	14 days	18 days	Mean[b]	10 days	14 days	18 days	Mean
4 weeks	10.7	14.8	25.4	17.0	14.6	18.8	51.7	28.4
20 weeks	5.1	5.3	12.8	7.7	6.4	7.7	35.3	16.5

[a]Days after inoculation.
[b]Length of foliar lesions averaged over three rating dates.

Use of Resistant Grasses

St. Augustinegrass cultivars that are not blue green ('Roselawn' and 'Florida Common') and the blue green cultivar 'Florotam' are resistant to gray leaf spot. The blue green cultivars 'Bitterblue' and 'Floratine' are highly susceptible to the disease (Atilano, 1983).

Annual ryegrass (*Lolium multiflorum*) is more susceptible to gray leaf spot than perennial ryegrass (*Lolium perenne*) (Trevathan, 1982).

Use of Fungicides

Effective control of gray leaf spot can be realized with applications of chlorothalonil. Repeated applications may be necessary to maintain control during prolonged periods of high disease pressure (Elliott and Cisar, 1989).

For a profile of chlorothalonil and a listing of representative trade names and manufacturers, see Appendix Table I.

BLACK LEAF SPOT

Black leaf spot affects numerous species of cool season and warm season turfgrassses throughout the world. Occurrences of the disease have been observed in West Africa, South Africa, Argentina, Australia, Austria, Germany, Brazil, Canada, China, Egypt, France, Ghana, Germany, Great Britain, Italy, India, Japan, Java, Nepal, New Guinea, New Zealand, Papua, Philippines, Portugal, Sri Lanka, Sweden, Switzerland, Tanganyika, Taiwan, the United States, and the West Indies (Parbery, 1967).

Symptoms

In overall view, affected turfgrass areas are yellow green mottled or bright yellow. The leaf lesions develop as conspicuous, glossy, crust-covered, black spots in linear rows on both the upper and lower surfaces. Light halos of chlorotic tissue may surround the lesions, but, even with a very high incidence of lesioning, the leaves may remain green for a long period of time. Ultimately, however, affected leaves turn yellow and wither. As the older leaves move into advanced senescence, the areas immediately surrounding the black spots often remain green longer than the adjacent leaf tissue, thus creating a "green island" effect.

The Fungi

A. *Phyllachora bulbosa* Parbery

Description

Asci ellipsoid, briefly stipitate, 96–112 × 11–16 µm; paraphyses twice as long as asci; ascospores monostichous, moderately to narrowly ovoid or ellipsoid, occasionally oval, 13–17 × 6.5–7.5 µm; spermatiophores cylindric, apices moderately acuminate often bent, bases slightly swollen to noticeably bulbose, body 10–13 × 1.5 µm; base 1.5–2.5 µm in diameter; spermatia filiform, taper gradually to apex, abruptly acuminate at base, 14–14 × 0.5 µm (Parbery, 1967).

Hosts

1. **Turfgrasses**—zoysiagrass (*Zoysia matrella*).
2. **All Known Gramineous Hosts**—A listing of common names for the following species is given in Appendix Table IV. *Zoysia macrantha* Desv., *Z. matrella* (L.) Merr. (Parbery, 1967; Parbery, 1971).

The Fungi

B. *Phyllachora cynodontis* (Sacc.) Niessl.

Description

Asci clavate, with a stipe 20–25 µm long, sometimes shorter, spore-bearing part 45–50 µm × 12–15 µm; ascospores monostichous, distichous, or inordinate in arrangement, hyaline to pale yellow, predominantly ovoid, sometimes oval, with turgid appearance, 8–15 × 5–6 μm. Spermatia filiform, hyaline, guttulate, 8–14 × 0.5 μm. Spermatiophores cylindric with rounded to slightly swollen apices, 7–10 × 1.5 μm. Appressioria sessile, 4 obclavate, brown (Parbery, 1967).

Hosts

1. **Turfgrass**—bermudagrass (*Cynodon dactylon*).
2. **All Known Gramineous Hosts**—A listing of common names for the following species is given in Appendix Table IV. *Bouteloua curtipendula* (Michx.) Torr., *Chloris castillpoama* Lillo and Par., *C. radiata* (L.) Swartz, *Cynodon dactylon* (L.) Pers. (Parbery, 1967; Parbery 1971).

The Fungi

C. *Phyllachora fuscens* Speg.

Description

Asci cylindric-clavate, 60–65 × 10–12 μm; paraphyses filiform with swollen apices; ascospores distichous, ellipsoid, full and symmetrical, 12–16 × 5–7 μm (Parbery, 1967)

Hosts

1. **Turfgrass**—Colonial bentgrass (*Agrostis tenuis*).
2. **All Known Gramineous Hosts**—A listing of common names for the folowing species is given in Appendix Table IV. *Agrostis tenuis* Sibth., *Poa anceps* Forst (Parbery, 1967).

The Fungi

D. *Phyllachora graminis* (Pers.) Fckl.

Description

Cylpei dark brown to black, developed in the epidermal cells overlying and sometimes beneath perithecia; perithecia with pseudoparenchymatous walls, ostiolate, ostiole extending through the clypeus. Asci ellipsoid to cylindric, each possessing an ascus crown at apex, with short basal pedicel 60–70 × 8–10 μm; ascospores one-celled, oval to ovoid or ovoid with obtuse end flattened or blunted (ovoid-truncate), hyaline, 7–14 μm long by 4–7 μm wide, monostichous, appressoria brown, oval to clavate sessile or on short germ tubes; spermagonia infrequently found; spermatia filiform 9–14 μm × 0.5–1 μm; spermatiophores simple, tapered to a rounded apex 12–15 × 1.5–2.5 μm (Parbery, 1967).

Hosts

1. **Turfgrasses**—Colonial bentgrass (*Agrostis tenuis*), annual bluegrass (*Poa annua*), red fescue (*Festuca rubra*), and tall fescue (*Festuca arundinacea*).
2. **All Known Gramineous Hosts**—A listing of common names for the following species is given in Appendix Table IV. *Agropyron caninum* (L.) Beauv., *A. cristatum* (L.) Gaertn., *A. repens* (L.) Beauv., *A. smithii* Rydb., *A. subsecundum* (Link) Hitchc., *A. trachycaulum* (Link) Malte, *A. triticeum* Gaertn., *Agrostis alba* L., *A. tenuis* Sibth., *Asprella hystrix* Willd., *Brachyelytrum erectum* (Schreb.) Beauv., *B. sylvaticum* Hack., *Brachypodium flexum* Nees, *B. sylvatiacum* (Huds.) Beauv., *Bromus anomalus* Rupr., *B. asper* Murray, *B. ciliatus* L., *B. erectus* Huds, *B. inermis* Leyss., *B. purgans* L., *B. syriaci*, *B. trinii* Desv., *Calamagrostis canadensis* (Michx.) Beauv., *C. inexpansa* A. Gray, *Cinna arundinacea* L., *Elymus canadensis* L., *E. canadensis* var. *brachystachys* (Scribn. and Ball) Farwell, *E. canadensis* var. *robustus* Scribn. and Smith, *E. condensatus* Presl, *E. eurpoaeus* L., *E. glaucus* Buckl., *E. mollis* Trin., *E. riparius* Wiegand, *E. triticoides* Buckl., *E. villosus* Muhl., *E. virginicus* L., *Festuca arundinacea* Schreb., *F. rubra* L., *Hordeum jubatum* L., *Lasiacis divaricata* (L.) Hitchc., *L. sorghoidea* (Desv.) Hitchc. and Chase, *Panicum virgatum* L., *Pappophorum mucronultatum* Nees, *Phleum pratense* L., *Poa annua* L., *P. nemoralis* L., *P. sudetica*, *Schizachne purpurascens* (Torr.) Swallen, *Triticum aestivum* L., *Uniola laxa* (L.) B. S. P. (Index Plant Dis., 1960; Orton, 1944; Parbery, 1967, Sprague, 1950).

The Fungi

E. *Phyllachora silvatica* Sacc. and Speg.

Description

Asci cylindrical to narrowly ellipsoid, 75–100 × 10–15 μm, briefly stipitate, ascospores variable in size and shape, most commonly narrowly oval, ovoid, or ellipsoid and often slightly curved to areniform, sometimes semi-ellipsoid, 12–22 × 4.5–0.8 μm; appressoria oval, brown and sessile; spermatia filiform, 14–21 0.8 μm; spermatiophore single or bibranched, each branch bottle-shaped and 10–12 × 1.5–3 μm (Parbery, 1967).

Hosts

1. **Turfgrasses**—red fescue (*Festuca rubra*), hard fescue (*Festuca ovina* var. *duriuscula*), and sheep fescue (*Festuca ovina*).

2. **All Known Gramineous Hosts**—A listing of common names for the following species is given in Appendix Table IV. *Distichlis maritima* Raf., *Festuca dertonensis* (All.) Aschers. and Graebn., *F. dumentorum* L., *F. idahoensis* Elmer., *F. megalura* Nutt., *F. occidentalis* Hook., *F. ovina* L., *F. ovina* var. *duriuscula* (L.) Koch., *F. rubra* L., *Sporobolus caroli* Mez., *S. cryptandrus* (Torr.) A. Gray, *S. elongatus* R. Br. (Index Plant Dis., 1960; Orton, 1944, Parbery, 1967).

Disease Profile

Development of the disease is favored by cool, wet weather. The black leaf spot fungi are obligate biotrophs, consequently, they cannot be grown on artificial media. The invading mycelium is confined to the intercellular spaces of the leaf mesophyll. Invagination of cells has not been observed. During the later stages of colonization, yellow zones of host tissue often surround the colonization sites. As the fungus begins to sporulate, however, these zones usually disappear.

In senescing leaves, a green-island effect commonly develops. Any necrosis that may occur in conjunction with *Phyllachora* colonization sites in the mesophyll is brought on by the invasion of the affected tissue by secondary leaf surface inhabiting microorganisms.

The dark colored effect in the colonization sites that gives rise to the 'black spot' phenomenon is caused by the development of crust-like structures (clypei) produced by the black leaf spot fungus. These usually develop in both upper and lower epidermal cells (Parbery, 1967).

Control

Generally speaking, black leaf spot does not cause severe damage; therefore, there are no published reports of attempts to control the disease.

CHAR SPOT

Char spot occurs on cool season turfgrasses in the United States, Canada, Scandinavia, Western Europe, and New Zealand.

Symptoms

At first, reddish brown, elliptical lesions with white spore-bearing centers develop mostly on the upper surfaces of the leaves. Later, these lesions are covered with conspicuous, dull black stromatic tissue of the pathogen similar to the 'tar spot' symptom caused by species of *Phyllachora*. Also, small black dots (pycnidia) are sometimes conspicuous in the margins of the lesions.

The Fungus

Cheilaria agrostis Lib.; syn. *Septogloeum oxysporum* Sacc., Bomm., and Rousa.

Description

Spores borne in obscure acervuli or in pycnidia usually in the center of the lesion or about its periphery, 80–160 μm in diameter, ostiolate; conidiophores hyaline, subcuspidate, or nearly globular in some cases; spores yellow to subhyaline, fusoid, often flattened slightly on one side, subtruncate at the base, tapering to an obliquely pointed apex, 0–3 septate, but mostly 2-septate, 2.5–6 μm × 20–38 μm.

Hosts

1. **Turfgrasses**—velvet bentgrass (*Agrostis canina*), creeping bentgrass (*Agrostis palustris*), Colonial bentgrass (*Agrostis tenuis*), perennial ryegrass (*Lolium perenne*), and Kentucky bluegrass (*Poa pratensis*).

2. **All Known Gramineous Hosts**—A listing of the common names for the following species is given in Appendix Table IV. *Agropyron repens* (L.) Beauv., *A. spicatum* (Pursh) Scribn. and Smith, *A. trachycaulum* (Link) Malte, *Agrostis alba* L., *A. canina* L., *A. exarata* Trin., *A. hallii* Vasey, *A. hiemalis* (Walt.) B. S. P., *A. scabra* Willd., *A. palustris* Huds., *A. tenuis* Sibth., *Alopecurus pratensis* L., *Arrhenatherum elatius* (L.) Presl, *Bromus carinatus* Hook. and Arn., *B. ciliatus* L., *Calamagrostis canadensis* (Michx.) Beauv., *C. inexpansa* A. Gray, *C. rubescens* Buckl., *Elymus condensatus* Presl, *E. triticoides* Buckl., *Glyceria elata* (Nash) Hitchc., *Lolium perenne* L., *Muhlenbergia asperifolia* (Nees and Mey.) Parodi, *Poa pratensis* L. (Index Plant Dis., 1960; Latch, 1966; Sprague, 1950).

Disease Profile

Char spot is a cool wet weather disease. Outbreaks normally occur during the months of late winter and early spring and in mid to late fall.

Control

There are no published reports of attempts to control char spot.

SEPTORIA LEAF SPOTS

Septoria Leaf Spot of Bluegrasses
(*Poa* spp.)

Symptoms

Minute, dark gray to brown lesions occur on the leaves. Fading to a light straw color with age, these individual spots may reach ⅛ inch (3 mm) or more in length. The developing lesions may be bordered by red or yellow bands of necrotic tissue. Frequently, the lesions coalesce to form light tan to straw-colored spots with reddish brown borders up to ⅜ inch (9 mm) long and involving the entire width of the leaf. When this happens, the entire leaf turns yellow from the tip downward. This latter symptom pattern is very similar to that of Sclerotinia dollar spot. In contrast with Sclerotinia dollar spot, however, the locations that comprised the centers of the initial Septoria leaf spot lesions usually contain the small black fruiting bodies (pycnidia) of the pathogen.

The Fungi

A. *Septoria macropoda* Pass.

Description

Pycnidia subepidermal, slightly erumpent, mostly flattened and appressed to the upper leaf epidermis, sometimes subglobose, walls thin (5–11 μm), 60–135 μm × 66–160 μm in diameter, 50–80 μm high; conidiophores subulate to subcylindric, 1.5–2.5 μm × 4–7 μm; conidia filiform, 1.0–1.5 μm × 30–40 μm.

Hosts

1. **Turfgrass**—annual bluegrass (*Poa annua*).
2. **All Known Gramineous Hosts**—A listing of common names for the following species is given in Appendix Table IV. *Poa annua* L., *P. kelloggii* Vasey (Index Plant Dis., 1960).

The Fungi

B. *Septoria macropoda* var. *grandis* Sprague

Description

Pycnidia often large but averaging 65–190 μm in diameter, 40–90 μm tall, pycnidia subepidermal, brown, somewhat flattened at the apex, wall 7–14 μm thick, mostly 9–11 μm; pycnophores ampulliform, rubulate, or subcylindric, 1.3–2.3 μm × 3–6 μm; conidia filiform to very narrowly filiform clavate, 1–3

septate, 1.4–2.4 μm × 50–70 μm in winter, 1.4–1.9 μm × 40–60 μm in spring.

Hosts

1. **Turfgrass**—Kentucky bluegrass (*Poa pratensis*).
2. **All Known Gramineous Hosts**—A listing of the common names for the following species is given in Appendix Table IV. *Poa ampla* Merr., *P. arida* Vasey, *P. canbyi* (Scribn.) Piper, *P. compressa* L., *P. cusickii* Vasey, *P. gracillima* Vasey, *P. nervosa* (Hook.) Vasey, *P. nevadensis* Vasey, *P. pratensis* L., *P. scabrella* (Thurb.) Benth., *P. secunda* Presl, *P. vaseyochloa* Scribn. (Index Plant Dis., 1960; Sprague, 1950).

The Fungi

C. *Septoria macropoda* var. *septulata* (Gonz. and Frag.) Sprague

Description

Pycnidia obscure, at least until the lesions fade to straw color; pycnidia subepidermal, slightly erumpent, variable, from somewhat flattened globose to true globose, compact, wall 5–9 μm thick, dark brown, 60–180 μm × 70–240 μm, commonly about 160 μm in diameter, 50–95 μm tall, pycnophores elongate, flask-shaped to nearly filiform, 1.5–2.0 μm × 3–6 μm, conidia filiform, sharp pointed (needlelike), cross walls obscure, 1.3–1.7 μm × 40–60 μm.

Hosts

1. **Turfgrass**—Kentucky bluegrass (*Poa pratensis*).
2. **All Known Gramineous Hosts**—A listing of the common names for each of the following species is given in Appendix Table IV. *Poa compressa* L., *P. nervosa* (Hook.) Vasey, *P. pratensis* L.

The Fungi

D. *Septoria oudemansii* Sacc.

Description

Pycnidia yellow brown, subglobose, somewhat erumpent, outer wall composed of a yellow brown layer 6–7 μm thick, surrounding a hyaline layer 4–4.5 μm thick, all cells of wall with solid contents; conidiophores bulbous, 1.8–2.2 μm × 4–5 μm; macrospores cylindrical but slightly thicker at the usual central septum, other spores tapered to nearly lanceolate, contents bright hyaline with small uniform oil drops adjacent to the septum, 1-septate macrospores 1.7–2.8 μm × 12–24 μm; microspores sometimes present, ranging in size from 2 μm × 4 μm to nearly as large as the macrospores.

Hosts

1. **Turfgrass**—Kentucky bluegrass (*Poa pratensis*).
2. **All Known Gramineous Hosts**—A listing of common names for the following species is given in Appendix Table IV. *Eragrostis refracta* (Muhl.) Scribn., *Poa ampla* Merr., *P. arachnifera* Torr., *P. canbyi* (Scribn.) Piper, *P. compressa* L., *P. juncifolia* Scribn., *P. nevadensis* Vasey, *P. palustris* L., *P. pratensis* L., *P. secunda* Presl (Index Plant Dis., 1960).

Septoria Leaf Spot of Bentgrasses (*Agrostis* spp.)

Symptoms

Leaf lesions are scattered over the tips of the blade. Gray to gray-green at first, these spots gradually fade to a pale straw-color. In contrast with some of the other Septoria leaf spots, the minute, black fruiting bodies (pycnidia) of the pathogens are rather obscure.

The Fungi

A. *Septoria calamagrostidis* (Lib.) Sacc.

Description

Pycnidia obscure, scattered, strongly flattened, subepidermal, dark brown, appearing black in spots, 50–140 μm × 50–180 μm in diameter, 50–85 μm deep, walls thin, of overlapped hyphae; pycnophores small, blunt, bottle-shaped, seldom more than 1.5–3.5 μm wide, pycnospores filiform, distinctly 0–5, mostly 3, septate, curved and often sinuous, 1.0–2.0 μm × 25–73 (40–65) μm.

Hosts

1. **Turfgrass**—creeping bentgrass (*Agrostis palustris*).
2. **All Known Gramineous Hosts**—A listing of common names for the following species is given in Appendix Table IV. *Agrostis diegoensis* Vasey, *A. exarata* Trin., *A. hiemalis* (Walt.) B. S. P., *A. palustris* Huds., *A. rossae* Vasey, *A. scabra* Willd., *Trisetum canescens* Buckl., *T. cernuum* Trin., *T. spicatum* (L.) Richt. (185).

The Fungi

B. *Septoria triseti* Speg. em. Sprague

Description

Pycnidia not prominent, black-brown, ostiolate, sub-stomatal, globose to flattened at the ostiolar end where it is appressed against the leaf epidermis, 40–100 μm (mostly 40–80 μm) in diameter, formed of irregular, oblong-polyhedral, parenchymatous cells, in strands, which converge in radii toward the ostiole, brown outer cells two layers thick (3 μm) with 2 or 3 inner hyaline layers (3–5 μm thick), giving rise to narrowly bulbous-cylindric conidiophores, 2.5–3.5 μm. Condia filiform to subbacillar or sometimes narrowly fusiform, straight, bent or less often moderately curved, 0–1 septate, 0.8–2.0 μm × 16–43 μm.

Hosts

1. **Turfgrasses**—Colonial bentgrass (*Agrostis tenuis*) and creeping bentgrass (*Agrostis palustris*).
2. **All Known Gramineous Hosts**—A listing of common names for the following species is given in Appendix Table IV. *Agrostis alba* L., *A. ampla* Hitchc., *A. castellana* Boiss. and Reut., *A. palustris* L., *A. tenuis* Sibth. (Index Plant Dis., 1960).

Septoria Leaf Spot of Tall Fescue (*Festuca arundinacea*)

Symptoms

Leaf lesions appear as numerous, small, irregularly-shaped blotches. "Greasy" brown at first, they gradually fade to a light straw color. At this stage, the lesions appear speckled due to the presence of the numerous, minute black fruiting bodies (pycnidia) of the fungus.

The Fungus

Septoria tenella Cke. and Ell.

Description

Pycnidia creosote brown, 60–120 μm × 95–130 μm, more or less elliptical in cross section, composed of tightly crushed, oblong to polyhedral cells averaging 0.5–3 μm wide; conidiophores small, cylindrical to very narrowly subulate, averaging 1 μm × 4 μm; conidia extremely variable, filiform to short bacillar, 0.8–2.1 μm × 5–70 μm, commonly 1.0–1.5 μm × 25–45 μm.

Hosts

1. **Turfgrasses**—tall fescue (*Festuca arundinacea*), Chewings fescue (*Festuca rubra* var. *commutata*), and sheep fescue (*Festuca ovina*).

2. **All Known Gramineous Hosts**—A listing of common names for the following species is given in Appendix Table IV. *Festuca arundinacea* Schreb., *F. dertonensis* (All.) Aschers. and Graebn., *F. idahoensis* Elmer., *F. mairei* St. Yves, *F. octoflora* Walt., *F. ovina* L., *F. rubra* var. *commutata* Guad. (Index Plant Dis., 1960; Sprague, 1950).

Septoria Leaf Spot of Ryegrasses (*Lolium* spp.)

Symptoms

Small blotches develop on the leaves. These lesions are at first yellowish green but later turn to a dark chocolate brown. In the case of infections by *S. loligena*, the older spots may be slightly paler in the centers and have lighter brown borders. Due to the dark color of the lesions, the small, brown fruiting bodies (pycnidia) of the pathogen are usually not readily apparent.

The Fungi

A. *Septoria loligena* Sprague

Description

Pycnidia light golden brown to brown, walls thin, subglobose, not prominent, 80–120 μm in diameter; conidia bacillar, clear hyaline, 0–3 septate, 2.7–4.2 μm × 25–50 μm.

Host

Annual ryegrass (*Lolium multiflorum* Lam.) (Index Plant Dis., 1960).

The Fungi

B. *Septoria tritici* f. sp. *lolicola* Sprague and A. J. Johnson; telemorph *Mycospharella graminicola* (Fuckel) Sand.

Description

Pycnidia globose to subglobose, sometimes ellipsoid, 80–150 μm × 90–180 μm, mostly 120–150 μm × 120–150 μm, ostiole 10–25 μm × 10–30 μm in diameter, peridia up to 15 μm thick, pale to deeper amber brown, smooth, outer cells subcubical to oblong, inner cells interwoven, polyhedral, giving rise to conidiophores 1.5–2.3 μm × 3–6 μm, slightly pyriform to subcylindric, ends acute with blunt terminal; conidia numerous, hyaline, acute with small oil drops, 0–5 septate, slightly enlarged at the base, and tapering to a rounded base, distal cells tapering to subwhip-like slightly strongly curved, 1.3–2.8 μm × 31–85 μm.

Procedures for Isolation and Culture

Septoria tritici var. *lolicola* grows slowly on potato dextrose agar. Maximum growth occurs between 20–25 °C, but colonies average only 11 mm in diameter after 21 days growth at these temperatures. Colonies are circular, flattened, have little mycelium, and are colored creamy brown from the mass of spores. These spores are variable in shape and size, and frequently bud. At 25 °C, colonies are black and convoluted, and although sporulation is not profuse as at other temperatures, the spores more closely resemble those on ryegrass leaves (Latch, 1966).

Turfgrass Hosts

Annual ryegrass (*Lolium multiflorum* Lam.) and perennial ryegrass (*Lolium perenne* L.) (Index Plant Dis., 1960).

Disease Profile

The Septoria leaf spots are cool, wet weather diseases. Turf growing in the shaded areas of trees, shrubs or buildings is most commonly affected. The pathogens survive the winter months as pycnidia in debris from the previous season's growth. With the advent of spring rains, the conidia are carried by splashing water to the leaves, where they germinate and initiate the primary infections. These diseases decrease in incidence during the warm summer months, but may once again appear in epidemic proportions during periods of extended leaf wetness in the fall.

Control

Use of Resistant Grasses

Certain varieties of Kentucky bluegrass have been reported to vary in their susceptibility to *Septoria macropoda* var. *septulata*. This range of susceptibility has been ranked as follows: (a) *high resistance*, 'Windsor'; (b) *intermediate resistance*, 'Newport'; 'Park'; (c) *low resistance*, 'Kenblue'; 'Delta'; and (d) *high susceptibility*, 'Merion' (Gaskin, 1965b).

Use of Fungicides

Successful fungicidal control of Septoria leaf spots has not been reported.

STAGONOSPORA LEAF SPOTS

Stagonospora Leaf Spot of Kentucky Bluegerass (*Poa pratensis*)

Symptoms

Small brown dot-like lesions develop on the leaves. Mature lesions may reach ⅛ inch (3 mm) or more in length. Fading to a light straw color with age, the developing lesions are often bordered by red or yellow bands of necrotic tissue. Individual lesions frequently coalesce to form light tan to straw-colored, irregularly-shaped blotches with reddish brown borders up to ⅜ inch (9 mm) long. In the final stages of disease development, small black fruiting bodies (pycnidia) of the pathogen develop in the centers of the lesions. When the incidence of lesions is high, the entire leaf often turns yellow from the tip downward.

The Fungus

Stagonospora nodorum (Berk.) Cast. and Germano; telemorph *Leptosphaeria nodorum* Muller; syn. *Septoria nodorum* (Berk.) Berk.

Description

Pycnidia scattered, sometimes seriately arranged, spherical, flattened, or elongate, subepidermal, 160–210 μm in diameter, wall thin, soft, parenchymatous, at first light brown, later becoming dark brown or black, ostiolate; conidia short, cylindrical, 0–3 septate, 2–4 μm × 15–32 μm.

Hosts

1. **Turfgrass**—Kentucky bluegrass (*Poa pratensis*).
2. **All Known Gramineous Hosts**—A listing of common names for the following species is given in Appendix Table IV. *Agropyron repens* (L.) Beauv., *A. smithii* Rydb., *A. spicatum* (Pursh) Scribn. and Smith, *A. trachycaulum* (Link) Malte, *Cinna latifolia* (Trevir.) Griseb., *Deschampsia atropurpurea* (Wahl.) Scheele, *D. caespitosa* (L.) Beauv., *D. danthonioides* (Trin.) Munro ex Benth., *D. elongata* (Hook.) Munro, *Elymus canadensis* L., *E. excelsus* Turcz., *E. giganteus* Vahl, *E. glaucus* Buckl., *E. junceus* Fisch., *E. sibiricus* L., *Festuca obtusa* Bieler, *F. subulata* Trin., *Glyceria striata* (Lam.) Hitchc., *Hordeum brachyantherum* Nevski, *H. jubatum* L., *H. pusillum* Nutt., *H. vulgare* L., *Hystrix patula* Moench, *Melica bulbosa* Geyer, *M. californica* Scribn., *Poa nervosa* (Hook.) Vasey, *P. palustris* L., *P. pratensis* L., *Secale cereale* L., *Stipa viridula* Trin., *Triticum aestivum* L., *T.*

dicoccum Schrank, *T. spelta* L. (Index Plant Dis., 1960; Sprague, 1950).

Stagonospora Leaf Spot of Fescues (*Festuca spp.*)

Symptoms

Leaf lesions develop as numerous, small, irregularly shaped brown necrotic areas that eventually fade to a light straw color. In the later stages of disease development, the lesions become speckled in appearance due to the presence of the numerous, minute black fruiting bodies (pycnidia) of the fungus. On red fescue, when the incidence of lesions per leaf is high, the individual lesions coalesce causing the entire leaf to turn light brown and then tan.

The Fungus

Stagonospora avenae (Frank) Bissett; telemorph *Leptosphaeria avenaria* G. F. Weber; syn. *Septoria avenae* Frank

Description

Pycnidia more or less scattered in rows, subepidermal, globose to subglobose, 90–150 μm in diameter (average 120 μm), wall smooth, brown to black, ostiole round to oval, 20–30 μm in diameter; conidia bacillar, 3-septate, hyaline 3–4 μm × 24–45 μm. Perithecia globose to subglobose, 60–130 μm in diameter, walls smooth, black, thin, ostiole 12–20 μm in diameter; asci narrowly clavate with rounded tips, hyaline, thin-walled, 10–18 μm × 30–100 μm; ascospores fusoid, straight or slightly curved, ends obtuse, rounded, 3-septate, constricted at the septa, especially the central septum, second cell from the top usually swollen, light yellow to slightly olivaceous, 4.5–6.0 μm × 23–38 μm.

Hosts

1. **Turfgrasses**—red fescue (*Festuca rubra*) and tall fescue (*Festuca arundinacea*).
2. **All Known Gramineous Hosts**—A listing of common names for the following species is given in Appeneix Table IV. *Agropyron cristatum* (L.) Gaertn., *Agrostis exarata* Trin., *Arrhenatherum elatius* (L.) Presl, *Avena sativa* L., *Calamagrostis canadensis* (Michx.) Beauv., *Elymus glaucus* Buckl., *Festuca arundinacea* Schreb., *F. rubra* L., *Glyceria elata* (Nash) Hitchc., *G. grandis* S. Wats., *G. occidentalis* (Piper) J. C. Nels., *G. pauciflora* Presl, *G. striata* (Lam.) Hitchc., *Oryzopsis hymenoides* (Roem. and Schult.) Ricker, *Schizachne purpura-*

scens (Torr) Swallen, *Scolochloa festucacea* (Willd.) Link (Index Plant Dis., 1960; Sprague, 1950).

Disease Profile

The epidemiology of Stagonospora leaf spots is similar to the Septoria leaf spots. They are cool, wet weather diseases. Turf growing in the shaded areas of trees, shrubs or buildings is most commonly affected.

The pathogens survive the winter months as pycnidia in debris from the previous season's growth. With the advent of spring rains, the conidia are carried by splashing water to the leaves, where they germinate and initiate the primary infections. These diseases decrease in incidence during the warm summer months, but may once again appear in epidemic proportions during periods of extended leaf wetness in the fall.

Control

There is no information on the degree of resistance of various turfgrass cultivars to Stagonospora leaf spots or the effectiveness of fungicides for the control of these diseases.

CERCOSPORA LEAF SPOTS

Cercospora Leaf Spot of St. Augustinegrass (*Stenotaphrum secundatum*)

Symptoms

Dark brown to purple oblong spots develop on the sheath and leaf blades. Newly formed spots are uniformly colored but tend to develop a tan center as the disease develops. Lesions are usually distinct, but some coalescence does occur when disease incidence is high. Individual lesions measure 1/16 to 1/8 inch (1–3 mm) wide by 1/8–1/4 inch (3–6 mm) long. Severely affected leaves turn yellow and eventually die, causing the turf to have a thinned-out appearance. Sporulation of the pathogen during moist weather causes the spots to develop a whitish sheen (Plate 25-F and Figure 5-12A).

At certain stages of disease development, Cercospora leaf spots closely resemble those incited by the gray leaf spot pathogen (*Pyricularia grisea*). However, when the total syndromes for the two diseases

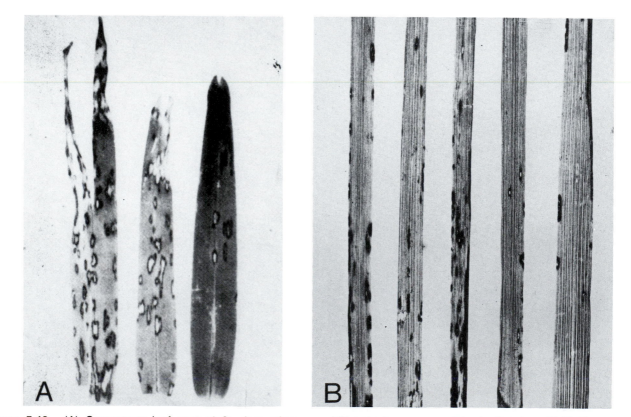

Figure 5-12. (A) Cercospora leaf spot of St. Augustinegrass (*Stenotaphrum secundatum*). *Courtesy T. E. Freeman.* (B) Cercospora leaf spot of tall fescue (*Festuca arundinacea*). *Courtesy John Hardison.*

are taken into consideration, the lesions caused by *Pyricularia grisea* are usually larger, more oval, and lighter brown than those incited by the Cercospora leaf spot fungus (Freeman, 1959).

The Fungus

Cercospora fusimaculans Atk.

Description

Sporulation amphigenous but more profuse on the upper leaf surface; stroma small, usually filling the stomatal opening; fasicles rarely dense; conidiophores brown, slightly clavate, irregular near the conic tip, spore scar distinct, 0–2 septate, 20–43 × 3–4 μm; conidia hyaline to subhyaline, cylindric to slightly obclavate, straight to variously curved, sometimes catenulate, indistinctly 2–7 septate, base obconically truncate, tip usually blunt, 33–60 × 1.8–3 μm (Freeman, 1959).

Procedures for Isolation and Culture

The fungus grows slowly but sporulates on Difco potato dextrose agar fortified with 0.5 percent yeast extract. The rate of sporulation in culture varies among isolates (Freeman, 1959).

Hosts

1. **Turfgrass**—St. Augustinegrass (*Stenotaphrum secundatum*).
2. **All Known Gramineous Hosts**—A listing of common names for the following species is given in Appendix Table IV. *Echinochloa crusgalli* (L.) Beauv., *Leptoloma cognatum* (Schult.) Chase, *Panicum dichotomiflorum* Michx., *P. dichotomum* L., *P. latifolium* L., *P. leibergii* (Vasey) Scribn., *P. maximum* Jacq., *P. pacificum* Hitchc. and Chase, *P. perlongum* Nash, *P. praecocius* Hitchc. and Chase, *P. scribnerianum* Nash, *P. virgatum* L., *P. xalapense* H. B. K. (Sprague, 1950).

Disease Profile

The development of Cercospora leaf spot is favored by warm humid weather. Outbreaks of the disease in epidemic proportions require prolonged periods of continual leaf wetness and air temperatures in the 70–80 °F (21–27 °C) range. Also, the severity of Cercospora leaf spot is greater when the plants are grown under low nitrogen fertilization (Freeman, 1967; McCoy, 1973).

Control

Cultural Practices

A significant reduction in disease severity can be achieved by increasing the levels of nitrogen fertilization. However, high nitrogen fertilization brings about an increase in gray leaf spot of St. Augustinegrass. Therefore, if both diseases are occurring concurrently in the same turf, then an increase in the rate of nitrogen fertilization to reduce the severity of Cercospora leaf spot will need to be balanced by a schedule of fungicide applications to compensate for the increase in severity of gray leaf spot.

Decreasing the length of time the leaves are wet will aid in reducing the incidence of Cercospora leaf spot. The duration of the period of daily leaf wetness can be reduced by two to four hours by following a nighttime watering schedule in which the irrigation is performed after sunset and completed before sunrise (see Chapter 16, Figure 16-2).

Use of Resistant Grasses

The yellow green types of St. Augustinegrass are more susceptible to Cercospora leaf spot than the blue-green ones (Freeman, 1967).

Use of Fungicides

Effective control of Cercospora leaf spot has been achieved with applications of either anilazine or chlorothalonil (McCoy, 1973).

For a profile of each of these fungicides and a list of representative manufacturers, see Appendix Table I.

Cercospora Leaf Spot of Tall Fescue (*Festuca arundinacea*)

Symptoms

Oval to elongate lesions ⅛ to ¼ inch (3–6 mm) long develop initially on the tips and then spread over the remainder of the leaves. Purple brown at first, older spots have dull gray centers with purple to purple brown borders (Figure 5-12 B). When lesions are in high incidence, tip die-back of the leaves is common.

The Fungus

Cercospora festucae Hardison

Description

Stromata none or only a few brown cells; conidiophores in spreading fascicles of 2–8, or rarely in dense fascicles, near base pale to medium olivaceous brown, paler and sometimes more narrow toward the tip, sparingly septate, rarely geniculate, not branched, almost straight, rounded or subtruncate tip, 3.5–5 μm × 30–800 μm; conidia hyaline, acicular, curved or undulate, indistinctly multiseptate, base truncate, tip acute, 2–4 μm × 40–300 μm.

Hosts

1. **Turfgrass**—tall fescue (*Festuca arundinacea*).
2. **All Known Gramineous Hosts**—A listing of common names for the following species is given in Appendix Table IV. *Bromus inermis* Leyss., *Festuca arundinacea* Schreb. (Index Plant Dis., 1960, Sprague, 1950).

SPERMOSPORA LEAF SPOTS

Spermospora leaf spots have been reported on cool season turfgrasses in temperate, humid regions of North America, western continental Europe, Finland, Great Britain, Ireland, Greenland, and New Zealand (Smith, Jackson and Woolhouse, 1989).

Spermospora Eyespot of Kentucky Bluegrass (*Poa pratensis*)

Symptoms

The leaf lesions are at first small, circular light brown spots. They enlarge to the width of the leaf and develop distinctive straw-colored centers and surrounding borders of yellow. Finally, the spots become dull brown overall and then fade to a straw color.

The Fungus

Spermospora poagena (Sprague) MacGarvie and O'Rourke; syn. *Cercosporella poagena* Sprague

Description

Conidiophores hyaline, obscure, arising from hyaline, thinly-formed aggregating hyphae; conidia hyaline, elongate, broadly filiform to obclavate, bases blunt, tapering gradually, apices either abruptly acuminate or attenuate at tips, 4–7 septate, 3.6–4.6 μm × 45–90 μm.

Host

Kentucky bluegrass (*Poa pratensis* L.) (Index Plant Dis., 1960).

Spermospora Leaf Spot of Red Fescue (*Festuca rubra*)

Symptoms

The leaf lesions are elongate, dull straw color to olive brown, and bordered by conspicuous lighter brown halos. In cases of high lesion incidence, leaf girdling occurs, causing a yellowing and die-back from the tip. Heavily diseased stands of red fescue may go off color. At first, the turf becomes yellow and then finally fades to a light brown.

The Fungus

Spermospora ciliata (Sprague) Deighton; syn. *Spermospora subulata* f. *ciliata* Sprague

Description

Vegetative mycelium hyaline to strongly chlorine, septate, branched, 1–2 μm in diameter, stromatic mycelia olivaceous to dull black, aggregated at or near the surface of the leaf from which are produced short, hyaline to strongly chlorinous conidiospores 1.5–2.0 μm × 5–20 μm. Conidia hyaline, borne blunt, broad base down, subulate to subulate-filiform, tapering to a whip-like distal portion which is sometimes straight, usually curved or flexuous, rarely reflexed. Conidia 2-septate, sometimes 1-septate, basal septum at broadest portion of subulate base, sometimes lightly constricted at second septum from base, which usually is at basal end of which-like distal portion, occasionally with an oblique basal cilium, 3.3–4.3 μm × 33–55 μm.

Procedures for Isolation and Culture

The fungus makes good growth on potato dextrose agar. At 20 °C colonies are flattened with a dark brown periphery and a radially convoluted light brown center. Growth occurs from 5–28 °C, and sporulation is good, although at 5–15 °C the macroconidia are atypical when compared with those in leaf lesions (Latch, 1966).

Hosts

1. **Turfgrass**—Chewings fescue (*Festuca rubra* var. *commutata*), red fescue (*Festuca rubra*).
2. **All Known Gramineous Hosts**—A listing of common names for each of the following species is given in Appendix Table IV. *Agrostis alba* L., *A. tenuis* Sibth., *Bromus vulgaris* (Hook.) Shear, *Calamagrostis rubescens* Buckl., *C. scribneri* Beal, *Deschampsia caespitosa* (L.) Beauv., *Festuca rubra*

L., *F. rubra* var. *commutata* Gaud., *Melica bulbosa* Geyer, *M. smithii* (Porter) Vasey, *M. spectabilis* Scribn., *Stipa lettermani* Vasey, *Trisetum spicatum* (L.) Richt. (Index Plant Dis., 1960; Sprague, 1950).

Spermospora Leaf Spot of Tall Fescue (*Festuca arundinacea*) and Ryegrasses (*Lolium* spp.)

Symptoms

On tall fescue, the foliar lesions are at first chocolate brown. They then turn reddish brown and often become surrounded by halos of chlorotic leaf tissue. Sporulation usually occurs on the ridged upper side of the leaves.

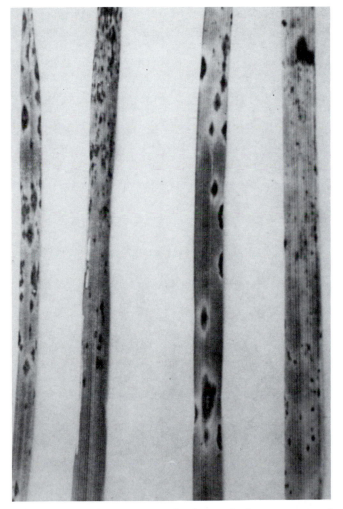

Figure 5-13. Spermospora leaf spot lesions on annual ryegrass (*Lolium multiflorum*). *After MacGarvie and O'Rourke, 1969.*

On ryegrasses, the lesions develop as brown oval spots up to ⅛ inch (3 mm) long with gray brown to reddish brown borders. During prolonged periods of high atmospheric humidity, the centers of the lesions commonly develop white centers made up of spores of the pathogen. Also, although the lesions are usually scattered over the entire leaf blade, sometimes they become concentrated near the edges—giving rise to a "burning" effect to the leaf margins (Figure 5-13).

The Fungus

Spermospora lolii MacGarvie and O'Rourke

Description

In epidermis and cuticle of the host, the mycelium is inter- and intracellular, hyaline, branched, septate and 1.5–2.5 μm wide. The fungal cells in the cuticle of the host are swollen and irregular in shape, 3.5 to 8 μm × 5 to 12 μm, sometimes aggregated to form a thin stromatic plate. From each of these swollen cells arise one or more narrow (1 μm wide) conidiophores which penetrate the cuticle and become swollen above (4.5–7 μm wide), each bearing a blastic terminal conidium. Occasionally the first conidium is pushed to one side by the continued growth of the conidiophore which then produces a second terminal conidium.

Conidia are hyaline, fusiform or narrowly obclavate-fusiform, often slightly curved, tapering gradually from the basal septum to the hilum and tapering into a narrow, straight of curved, apical rostrum, 2–6 septate, rarely constricted, 40.0–70.0 μm × 3.5–4.75 μm. A narrow lateral appendage 3.5 μm long and 0.25 μm wide is occasionally borne near the base of the conidium. Microconidia are sometimes borne on the normal conidiophores, 1 septate, cylindric, 3.5–8.75 μm × 1–1.5 μm (Figure 5-14) (MacGarvie and O'Rourke, 1969).

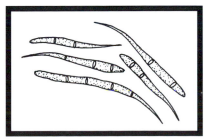

Figure 5-14. Conidia of *Spermospora lolii*. *After MacGarvie and O'Rourke, 1969.*

Hosts

1. **Turfgrasses**—annual ryegrass (*Lolium multiflorum*), perennial ryegrass (*Lolium perenne*), and tall fescue (*Festuca arundinacea*).
2. **All Known Gramineous Hosts**—A listing of common names for the following species is given in Appendix Table IV. *Dactylis glomerata* L., *Festuca arundinacea* Schreb., *F. patensis* Huds., *Lolium multiflorum* Lam., *L. perenne* L. (MacGarvie and O'Rourke, 1969).

Disease Profile

Spermospora leaf spots can occur at any time during the plant growing seasons. However, the incidence and severity of these diseases is highest during the cool, humid months of late winter, spring and fall and lowest during the warm summer months.

Control

There is no information on the degree of resistance of various turfgrass cultivars to Spermospora leaf spots or the effectiveness of fungicides for the control of these diseases.

PSEUDOSEPTORIA LEAF SPOT

Symptoms

Leaf lesions are first seen as slightly elongate, purple blotches. As the lesions mature, the centers turn light yellow and rows of black dots (pycnidia) are conspicuous in the faded areas. Under conditions of high incidence of lesions, the entire plant may assume a purple cast.

The Fungi

A. *Pseudoseptoria donacis* (Pass.) Sutton; syn. *Selenophoma donacis* (Pass.) Sprague and A. G. Johnson

Description

Pycnidia erumpent, small to subprominent, brown, globose, ostiolate, 40–150 μm in diameter, peridia or pycnidia composed of coarse compacted polygonal cells which produce cuspidate conidiophores, from the inner pycnidial wall, composed of hyaline bulbous initials, walls 5–12.5 μm thick, conidiophores 2–3 μm × 2.5–5 μm; conidia stoutly falcate to boomerang-shaped, 2.0–4.5 μm × 18–35 μm.

Hosts

1. **Turfgrasses**—Kentucky bluegrass (*Poa pratensis*), red fescue (*Festuca rubra*), sheep fescue (*Festuca ovina*), and tall fescue (*Festuca arundinacea*).
2. **All Known Gramineous Hosts**—A listing of common names for the following species is given in Appendix Table IV. *Agropyron albicans* Scribn. and Smith, *A. cristatum* (L.) Gaertn., *A. dasystachyum* (Hook.) Scribn., *A. inerme* (Scribn. and Smith) Rydb., *A. latiglume* (Scribn. and Sm.) Rydb., *A. repens* (L.) Beauv., *A. riparium* Scribn. and Smith, *A. smithii* Rydb., *A. spicatum* (Pursh) Scribn. and Smith, *A. subsecundum* (Link) Hitchc., *A. trachycaulum* (Link) Malte, *Arrhenatherum elatius* (L.) Presl, *Arundo donax* L., *Avena sativa* L., *Calamovilfa longifolia* (Hook.) Scribn., *Dactylis glomerata* L.,. *Danthonia californica* Boland, *D. spicata* (L.) Beauv., *Daschampsia danthonioides* (Trin.) Munro ex Benth., *Elymus aristatus* Merr., *E. canadensis* L., *E. condensatus* Presl, *E. flavescens* Scribn. and Smith, *E. giganteus* Vahl, *E. glaucus* Buckl., *E. junceus* Fisch., *E. macounii* Vasey, *E. mollis* Trin., *E. villosus* Muhl., *E. virginicus* L., *Festuca arundinacea* Schreb., *F. idahoensis* Elmer, *F. octoflora* Walt., *F. ovina* L., *F. rubra* L., *Hesperochloa kingii* (S. Wats.) Rydb., *Hordeum secalinum* Guss., *H. vulgare* L., *Hystrix patula* Moench, *Koeleria cristata* (L.) Pers., *Melica harfordii* Boland, *Oryzopsis hymenoides* (Roem. and Schult.) Ricker, *Panicum virgatum* L., *P. wilcoxianum* Vasey, *Phalaris arundinacea* L., *Phleum pratense* L., *Phragmites communis* Trin., *Poa alpina* L., *P. ampla* Merr., *P. arctica* R. Br., *P. arida* Vasey, *P. compressa* L., *P. cusickii* Vasey, *P. epilis* Scribn., *P. fendleriana* (Steud.) Vasey, *P. glauca* Vahl, *P. gracillima* Vasey, *P. juncifolia* Scribn., *P. nemoralis* L., *P. nervosa* (Hook.) Vasey, *P. nevadensis* Vasey, *P. palustris* L., *P. pratensis* L., *P. secunda* Presl, *P. stenantha* Trin., *P. trivialis* L., *Puccinellia airoides* (Nutt.) Wats. and Coult., *Secale cereale* L., *Sitanion hystrix* (Nutt.) J. G. Smith, *Sporobolus asper* (Michx.) Kunth., *S. clandestinus* (Bieler) Hitchc., *S. cryptandrus* (Torr.) A. Gray, *S. giganteus* Nash, *S. heterolepis* (A. Gray) A. Gray, *Stipa columbiana* Macoun., *S. comata* Trin. and Rupr., *S. lemmoni* (Vasey) Scribn., *S. richardsoni* Link, *S. spartea* Trin., *S. viridula* Trin., *Triticum aestivum* L. (Index Plant Dis., 1960; Samson and Western, 1954; Sprague, 1950; Sprague, 1962).

The Fungi

B. *Pesudoseptoria everhartii* (Sacc. and Syd.) Sutton; syn. *Selonophoma everhartii* Sprague and A. G. Johnson

Description

Pycnidia small, black to creosote brown, ostiolate, globose, 50–80 µm, sometimes 100 µm in diameter; conidiophores few, cuspidate, arising from hyaline initial cells; conidia short, sharply arcuate, 1.0–1.5 µm × 10–15 µm.

Hosts

1. **Turfgrass**—red fescue (*Festuca rubra*).
2. **All Known Gramineous Hosts**—A listing of common names for the following species is given in Appendix Table IV. *Agrostis diegoensis* Vasey, *A. hiemalis* (Walt.) B. S. P., *A. scabra* Willd., *Aristida adscensionis* L., *A. longiseta* Steud., *A. oligantha* Michx., *Bouteloua curtipendula* (Michx.) Torr., *Calamagrostis canadensis* (Michx.) Beauv., *C. inexpansa* A. Gray, *C. koelerioides* Vasey, *C. montanensis* Scribn., *C. rubescens* Buckl., *C. scribneri* Beal, *Deschampsia atropurpurea* (Wahl.) Scheele, *D. caespitosa* (L.) Beauv., *D. danthonioides* (Trin.) Munro ex Benth., *D. elongata* (Hook.) Munro ex Benth., *Festuca octoflora* Walt., *F. ovina* L., *F. ovina* var. *brachyphylla* (Schult.) Piper, *F. rubra* L., *Muhlenbergia cuspidata* (Torr.) Rydb., *M. racemosa* (Michx.) B. S. P., *Phalaris arundinacea* L., *Phleum pratense* L., *Phragmites communis* Trin., *Puccinellia airoides* (Nutt.) Wats. and Coult., *Sphenopholis obtusata* (Michx.) Scribn., *Trisetum spicatum* (L.) Richt., *T. wolfii* Vasey (Index Plant Dis., 1960; Sprague, 1950).

Disease Profile

Pseudoseptoria leaf spot is a cool, wet weather disease. The pathogens survive the winter months as pycnidia in debris from the previous season's growth. With the beginning of spring rains, the conidia are carried by splashing water to the leaves, where they germinate and initiate the primary infections. Incidence of the disease decreases significantly during the summer, but outbreaks usually reoccur during periods of extended leaf wetness in the fall.

Control

There is no information on the degree of resistance of various Kentucky bluegrass and fescue cultivars to Pseudoseptoria leaf spot or the effectiveness of fungicides for the control of the disease.

ASCOCHYTA LEAF SPOTS

Ascochyta Leaf Spot of Ryegrasses (*Lolium* spp.)

Symptoms

Leaf lesions first develop as small, purplish to chocolate brown, punctate spots. With time, these enlarge and the centers fade to fawn, and, finally, straw color. The minute brown fruiting bodies (pycnidia) of the pathogen are usually conspicuous in the centers of older lesions.

The Fungus

Ascochyta desmazieresii Cav.

Description

Pycnidia immersed, yellow brown, subglobose, ostiolate, 140–220 µm diam. Ostiole circular, 10 µm wide, bordered with dark brown pseudoparenchymatic, 2–4 layers of cells thick, outermost layer yellow brown, innermost layers hyaline. Conidiogenous cells (permanent) shortly cylindrical, hyaline, phialidic. Conidia bylindrical, base truncate or uniseptate, 2–4 percent 2–3 septate, 14–20 µm × 2–2.5 µm (Punithalingam, 1979).

Turfgrass Hosts.

annual ryegrass (*Lolium multiflorum* Lam.) and perennial ryegrass *Lolium perenne* L. (Sprague, 1950).

Ascochyta Leaf Spot of Tall Fescue (*Festuca arundinacea*)

The Fungus

Ascochyta hordei Hara.

Description

Pycnidia immersed, becoming erumpent, pale luteous to ocharaceous, subglobose, up to 160 µm diam., ostiolate; ostiole nearly rounded up to 30 µm wide, surrounded by cells slightly darker than the outer pycnidial wall. Pycnidial wall pseudoparenchymatic, composed of 2–3 layers of thin walled isodiametric cells, the outermost layer luteous to ochraceous, the innermost layer hyaline. Conidiogenous cells (permanent) hyaline, somewhat doliiform, phialidic. Conidia pale luteous, cylindrical to somewhat narrowly ellipsoid, slightly narrowed near base and apex, base flat or rounded, apex rounded, medianly uniseptate, rarely 2-septate, not usually constricted at the septum, usually not guttulate, 17–20 μm × 3.5–4 μm; wall smooth to finely roughened (Punithalingam, 1979).

Hosts

1. **Turfgrass**—tall fescue (*Festuca arundinacea*).
2. **All Known Gramineous Hosts**—A listing of the common names for each of the following species is given in Appendix Table IV. *Agropyron cristatum* (L.) Gaertn., *Bromus carinatus* Hook. and Arn., *Festuca arundinacea* Schreb., *Holcus lanatus* L., *Hordeum brachyantherum* Nevski, *H. murinum* L., *H. vulgare* L., *Phleum phleoides* Karst., *Stipa robusta* (Vasey) Scribn. (Index Plant Dis., 1960; Punithalingam, 1979; Sprague, 1950).

Ascochyta Leaf Spot of Kentucky Bluegrass (*Poa pratensis*), Fescues (*Festuca* spp.), and Perennial Ryegrass (*Lolium perenne*)

Symptoms

Leaf lesions are circular to eliptical, brown or fawn colored, and usually develop either red borders or thin brown discolored ones.

The Fungus

Ascochyta sorghi Sacc.; syn. *Ascochyta graminicola* Sacc.

Description

Pycnidia abundant prominently on the upper surface in groups, occasionally on the lower surface, in severely infected plants also found on the leaf sheaths intermixed with sclerotia, subcuticular to immersed, eventually breaking through the epidermis and appearing to be superficial to the unaided eye, rust to sepia, up to 200 μm diam. Pycnidial wall stromatic, many layers of cells thick, outer most layer rust sepia colored, the inner layers hyaline. Conidiogenous cells (permanent) cylindrical to doliiform or somewhat lageniform, hyaline, phialidic. Conidia hyaline, broadly ellipsoid, straight or somewhat oblong, sometimes reniform, rounded at base and apex, medially uniseptate 16–20 μm × 6–8 μm; conidial wall approximately 0.5 μm thick (Punithalingam, 1979).

Procedures for Isolation and Culture

On potato dextrose agar the colonies are grayish white in color, raised up slightly from the agar sur-face and covered by a compact weft of mycelium. Maximum growth is at 20 °C. Colonies grown for 14 days on potato dextrose agar at 20 °C average 68 mm in diameter. Sporulation is poor on potato dextrose agar but abundant on sterile straw-water agar (Latch, 1966).

Hosts

1. **Turfgrasses**—Kentucky bluegrass (*Poa pratensis*), red fescue (*Festuca rubra*), sheep fescue (*Festuca ovina*), tall fescue (*Festuca arundinacea*) and perennial ryegrass (*Lolium perenne*).
2. **All Known Gramineous Hosts**—A listing of common names for the following species is given in Appendix Table IV. *Agropyron desertorum* (Fisch.) Schult., *A. repens* (L.) Beauv., *A. smithii* Rydb., *A. spicatum* (Pursh) Scribn. and Smith, *A. trachycaulum* (Link) Malte, *Agrostis alba* L., *A. canina* L., *Andropogon furcatus* Muhl., *A. scoparius* Michx., *Arrhenatherum elatius* (L.) Presl, *Avena sativa* L., *Beckmannia syzigachne* (Steud.) Fernald, *Bromus carinatus* Hook. and Arn., *B. commutatus* Schrad., *B. inermis* Leyss., *B. japonicus* Thunb., *B. tectorum* L., *Calamagrostis canadensis* (Michx.) Beauv., *Dactylis glomerata* L., *Deschampsia elongata* (Hook.) Munro ex Benth., *Elymus canadensis* L., *E. condensatus* Presl, *E. glaucus* Buckl., *E. macounii* Vasey, *E. virginicus* L., *Festuca arundinacea* Schreb., *F. ovina* L., *F. rubra* L., *Hierochloe odorata* (L.) Beauv., *Holcus lanatus* L., *Hordeum brachyantherum* Nevski, *H. jubatum* L., *H. murinum* L., *H. vulgare* L., *Hystrix patula* Moench, *Lolium perenne* L., *Melica bulbosa* Geyer, *Muhlenbergia mexicana* (L.) Trin., *Panicum capillare* L., *Phalaris arundinacea* L., *Poa bulbosa* L., *P. gracillima* Vasey, *P. pratensis* L., *P. secunda* Presl, *Schizachne purpurascens* (Torr.) Swallen, *Schlerochloa dura* (L.) Beauv., *Secale cereale* L., *Setaria lutescens* (Weigel) Hubb., *Sitanion hystrix* (Nutt.) J. G. Smith, *S. jubatum* J. G. Smith, *Sorghum halepense* (L.) Pers., *S. sudanense* (Piper) Stapf, *S. vulgare* Pers., *Sphenopholis intermedia* (Rydb.) Rydb., *Stipa comata* Trin. and Rupr., *S. occidentialis* Thurb., *S. viridula* Trin., *Trisetum canescens* Buckl, *Triticum aestivum* L. (Index Plant Dis., 1960; Sprague, 1950).

Control

There is no information on the degree of resistance of various cultivars to Ascochyta leaf spot or the effectiveness of fungicides for the control of the disease.

RHYNCHOSPORIUM LEAF BLOTCH

Symptoms

Lesions develop on leaves and sheaths as irregular-shaped scald-like blotches variable in size up to ⅛ inch (3 mm) wide and ⅜ inch (10 mm) long. They first appear on the under surface of the leaves as dark green, water-soaked patches, later turning gray, and finally light brown with dark brown borders. Lesions that develop near the leaf tip are not well defined, and the general browning that results in this portion of the leaf may be confused with either frost or wind damage (Latch, 1966).

The Fungi

A. *Rhynchosporium orthosporum* Caldwell

Description

Conidia hypophyllous, borne directly on mycelium, cylindrical rarely beaked, one-septate, hyaline, 12.0–22.5 μm × 1.5–3.0 μm.

Procedures for Isolation and Culture

Surface sterilize by immersing leaves with young lesions in 75 percent ethanol for 30 seconds and then in a 10 percent sodium hypochlorite for 75 seconds. Then plate on either yeast-malt extract agar or potato dextrose agar and incubate at 20 °C (Latch, 1966; Wilkins, 1973).

Hosts

1. **Turfgrasses**—annual ryegrass (*Lolium multiflorum*) and perennial ryegrass (*Lolium perenne*).
2. **All Known Gramineous Hosts**—A listing of common names for the following species is given in Appendix Table IV. *Agropyron subsecundum* (Lk.) Hitchc., *Agrostis alba* L., *Alopecurus pratensis* L., *Calamagrostis canadensis* (Michx.) Beauv., *Dactylis glomerata* L., *Elymus glaucus* Buckl., *Lolium multiflorum* Lam., *L. perenne* L. (Sprague, 1950).

The Fungi

B. *Rhynchosporium secalis* (Oud.) J. J. Davis

Description

Mycelium 0.6–3.0 μm in diameter; conidia sessile, hyaline, 1-septate, allantoid, 2.3–5.4 μm × 11–22 μm.

Procedures for isolation and culture

In culture, the organism grows well, and produces abundant spores, on lima bean agar (Difco™) at 17 °C (Schein, 1960).

Hosts

1. **Turfgrasses**—annual ryegrass (*Lolium multiflorum*) and perennial ryegrass (*Lolium perenne*).
2. **All Known Gramineous Hosts**—A listing of common names for the following species is given in Appendix Table IV. *Agropyron dasystachyum* (Hook.) Scribn., *A. elmeri* Scribn., *A. intermedium* (Host) Beauv., *A. pungens* (Pers.) Roem., *A. repens* (L.) Beauv., *A. riparium* Schribn. and Smith, *A. semicostatum* (Steud.) Nees, *A. smithii* Rydb., *A. subsecundum* (Link) Hitchc., *A. trachycaulum* (Link) Malte, *A. trichophorum* (Lk.) Richt., *Agrostis alba* L., *Bouteloua curtipendula* (Michx.) Torr., *B. gracilis* (H. B. K.) Lag., *Bromus arvensis* L., *B. carinatus* Hook. and Arn., *B. frondosus* (Shear) Woot. and Standl., *B. inermis* Leyss., *B. pumpellianus* Scribn., *B. secalinus* L., *Danthonia spicata* (L.) Beauv., *Elymus canadensis* L., *E. condensatus* Presl, *E. glaucus* Buckl., *E. innovatus* Beal, *E. junceus* Fisch., *E. triticoides* Buckl., *E. virginicus* L., *Festuca idahoensis* Elmer, *Hordeum distichon* L., *H. jubatum* L., *H. murinum* L., *H. vulgare* L., *Lolium multiflorum* Lam., *L. perenne* L., *Phalaris arundinacea* L., *Secale cereale* L., *S. montanum* Guss. (Index Plant Dis., 1960; Schein, 1958; Sprague, 1950).

Disease Profile

The pathogens overwinter as dormant mycelium on both dead and living leaf tissue. Rhynchosporium leaf blotch is a cool, humid weather disease. In early spring, conidia are produced, carried to newly developing leaves by splashing water, and primary infections are accomplished (Stedman, 1980). Secondary conidia are produced in great numbers as long as cool, wet weather persists. With the onset of the warm, less humid summer months, the incidence and severity of the disease decreases. However, it can break out in epiphytotic proportions if wet weather persists during the weeks of late autumn.

Infection of the leaves is accomplished by direct penetration of the cuticle and walls of the epidermal cells. Mycelial growth in the host is scant prior to the degeneration of the epidermal cells at the sites of penetration. After these cells collapse, however, an extensive mycelial pad develops, on which is borne the conidia.

Isolates of *Rhynchosporium orthosporum* and *Rhychosporium secalis* have been shown to vary as to host specificity and degree of pathogenicity among cultivars within a species (Schein, 1958; Wilkins, 1973).

Control

A wide range of variability in susceptibility to *Rhynchosporium orthosporum* exists among cultivars of both annual and perennial ryegrass (Latch, 1966; Wilkins, 1973). Successful fungicidal control of Rhynchosporium leaf blotch has not been reported.

BROWN STRIPE

Symptoms

Expression of brown stripe symptoms varies somewhat with host species and age of the plant. Leaf lesions occur most commonly, however, as small, circular, water-soaked spots which are olive gray when wet and fade to a dull gray when dry. As the lesions mature, they increase in size—developing eventually into pronounced, elongate streaks. With the increase in size of lesions, the color changes to dark brown or purplish brown with dull gray centers. High incidence of lesions on the leaves and sheaths causes the leaves to wither progressively from the tips downward.

The Fungus

Cercosporidium graminis (Fuckel) Deighton; syn. *Scolecotrichum graminis* Fuckel

Description

Conidiophores fasiculate on the upper surface, arranged as a series of black dots; olive-brown, unbranched, irregular or slightly geniculate, 4–5 µm × 30–50 µm; conidia 8–10 µm × 35–45 µm, elongate, bottle-shaped, base broadly rounded with prominent hilum, 1-(sometimes 2) septate.

Procedures for Isolation and Culture

In culture, the organism grows well on either potato dextrose agar or oatmeal agar at 25–28 °C. The fungus does not sporulate well in culture. Maximum spore production is obtained on V-8 juice agar (15 g agar, 200 ml V-8 Juice, 2 g $CaCO_3$, and 800 ml distilled water) and under ultraviolet irradiation (Braverman, 1954).

Hosts

1. **Turfgrasses**—creeping bentgrass (*Agrostis palustris*), Colonial bentgrass (*Agrostis tenuis*), Kentucky bluegrass (*Poa pratensis*), tall fescue (*Festuca arundinacea*), red fescue (*Festuca rubra*), annual ryegrass (*Lolium multiflorum*), and perennial ryegrass (*Lolium perenne*).

2. **All Known Gramineous Hosts**—A listing of common names for the following species is given in Appendix Table IV. *Agropyron caninum* (L.) Beauv., *A. cristatum* (L.) Gaertn., *A. dasystachyum* (Hook.) Scribn., *A. griffithsi* Scribn and Smith, *A. inerme* (Scribn. and Smith) Rydb., *A. repens* (L.) Beauv., *A. riparium* Scribn. and Smith, *A. smithii* Rydb., *A. spicatum* (Pursh) Scribn. and Smith, *A. subsecundum* (Link) Hitchc., *A. trachycaulum* (Link) Malte, *Agrostis alba* L., *A. castellana* Boiss. and Reut., *A. exarata* Trin., *A. hallii* Vasey, *A. hiemalis* (Walt.) B. S. P., *A. oregonesis* Vasey, *A. palustris* Huds., *A. rossae* Vasey, *A. scabra* Willd., *A. scabra* var. *geminata* (Trin.) Swallen, *A. tenuis* Sibth., *Alopecurus aequalis* Sobol., *A. carolinianus* Walt., *A. geniculatus* L., *A. pratensis* L. *Arrhenatherum elatius* (L.) Presl, *A. elatius* var. *bulbosum* (Willd.) Spenner, *Arundinaria gigantea* (Walt.) Muhl., *A. tecta* (Walt.) Muhl., *Avena sativa* L., *Beckmannia syzigachne* (Steud.) Fernald, *Bromus arenarius* Labill., *B. carinatus* Hook. and Arn., *B. catharticus* Vahl, *B. ciliatus* L., *B. frondosus* (Shear) Woot. and Standl., *B. inermis* Leyss., *B. laevipes* Shear, *B. mollis* L., *B. orcuttianus* Vasey, *B. pacificus* Shear, *B. purgans* L., *B. secalinus* L., *B. sitchensis* Trin., *B. vulgaris* (Hook.) Shear, *Calamagrostis canadensis* (Michx.) Beauv., *C. canadensis* var. *scabra* (Presl) Hitchc., *C. inexpansa* A. Gray, *Cinna arundinacea* L., *C. latifolia* (Trevir.) Griseb., *Cynosorus cristatus* L., *Dactylis glomerata* L., *Danthonia californica* Boland, *Deschampsia atropurpurea* (Wahl.) Scheele, *D. caespitosa* (L.) Beauv., *D. danthonioides* (Trin.) Munro ex Benth., *D. elongata* (Hook.) Munro ex Benth., *Digitaria sanguinalis* (L.) Scop., *Elymus antarcticus* Hook., *E. aristatus* Merr., *E. canadensis* L., *E. condensatus* Presl, *E. flavescens* Scribn. and Smith, *E. giganteus* Vahl, *E. glaucus* Buckl., *E. innovatus* Beal, *E. mollis* Trin., *E. sibiricus* L., *E. triticoides* Buckl., *E. virginicus* L., *Eragrostis secundiflora* Presl, *Festuca arundinacea* Schreb., *F. rubra* L., *Glyceria borealis* (Nash) Batchelder, *G. elata* (Nash) Hitchc., *G. fluitans* (L.) R. Br., *G. grandis* S. Wats., *G. leptostachya* Buckl., *G. pauciflora* Presl, *G. septentrionalis* Hitchc., *G. striata* (Lam.) Hitchc., *Hordeum brachyantherum*

Nevski, *H. jubatum* L., *H. jubatum* var. *caespitosum* (Scribn.) Hitchc., *H. pusillum* Nutt., *H. vulgare* L., *Hystrix patula* Moench, *Koeleria cristata* (L.) Pers., *Leersia oryzoides* (L.) Swartz, *Lolium multiflorum* Lam., *L. perenne* L., *Melica bulbosa* Geyer, *M. geyeri* Munro, *M. smithii* (Porter) Vasey, *M. spectabilis* Scribn., *M. subulata* (Griseb.) Scribn., *Milium effusum* L., *Muhlenbergia filiformis* (Thurb.) Rydb., *M. mexicana* (L.) Trin., *M. racemosa* (Michx.) B. S. P., *M. sylvatica* (Torr.) Torr., *Oryzopsis hymenoides* (Roem. and Schult.) Ricker, *Phleum alpinum* L., *P. pratense* L., *Phragmites communis* Trin., *Poa alpina* L., *P. ampla* Merr., *P. arachnifera* Torr., *P. arida* Vasey, *P. canbyi* (Scribn.) Piper, *P. compressa* L., *P. gracillima* Vasey, *P. interior* Rydb., *P. juncifolia* Scribn., *P. longiligula* Scribn. and Will., *P. nemoralis* L., *P. nervosa* (Hook.) Vasey, *P. nevadensis* Vasey, *P. pratensis* L., *P. secunda* Presl, *P., stenantha* Trin, *P. trivialis* L., *Secale cereale* L., *S. montanum* Guss., *Sitanion hanseni* (Scribn.) J. G. Smith, *S. hystrix* (Nutt.) J. G. Smith, *Spartina gracilis* Trin., *Stipa columbiana* Macoun, *S. columbiana* var. *nelsoni* (Scribn.) Hitchc., *S. comata* Trin. and Rupr., *S. coronata* Thurb., *S. elmeri* Piper and Brodie, *S. lemmoni* (Vasey) Scribn. *S. lettermani* Vasey, *S. occidentalis* Thurb., *S. speciosa* Trin. and Rupr., *S. thurberiana* Piper, *S. viridula* Trin., *S. williamsii* Scribn., *Trisetum canescens* Buckl., *T. flavescens* (L.) Beauv., *T. montanum* Vasey, *T. spicatum* (L.) Richt. (Index Plant Dis., 1960; Sprague, 1950).

Disease Profile

The pathogen survives the winter months as stromata in living leaves and in debris from the previous season's growth. With early spring rains, and a rise in air temperature, the stromata swell and rupture the epidermal cells of the affected leaves. Conidiophores emerge through the ruptured epidermis and conidia are formed. Spore dissemination from plant to plant is accomplished primarily by means of splashing and wind-driven water.

During the relatively warmer and drier summer months, the incidence and severity of brown stripe decreases. However, the return of cool, wet autumn weather again provides optimum conditions for disease development.

Control

There is no information on the degree of resistance of various cultivars to brown stripe or the effectiveness of fungicides for the control of the disease.

PHLEOSPORA LEAF SPOT

Symptoms

Leaf lesions range in size and shape from small, circular brown spots, to elongate eyespots with dark brown or purple brown margins and white or gray white centers ½ inch (1.2 cm) long. Older lesions sometimes develop yellow or buff-colored margins (Figure 5-15). The minute brown fruiting bodies (pycnidia) of the pathogen are usually conspicuous in the centers of older lesions. Leaves with a high incidence of lesions turn yellow from the tips downward and then fade to a light brown.

The Fungus

Phleospora graminearum Sprague and Hardison

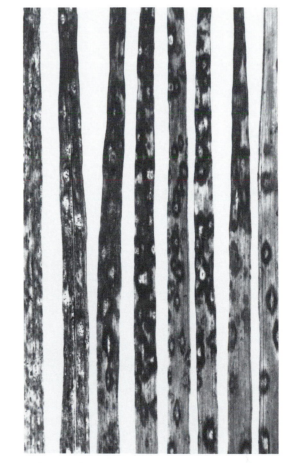

Figure 5-15. Phleospora leaf spot of tall fescue (*Festuca arundinacea*). *Courtesy Natsuki Nishihara.*

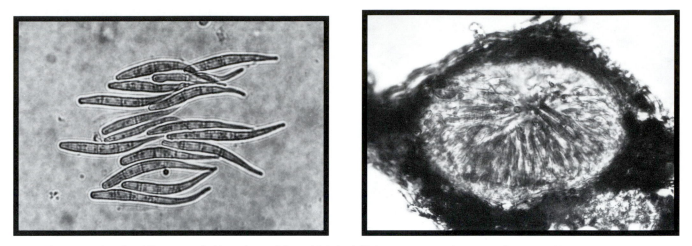

Figure 5-16.   Conidiospores (left) and pycnidium (right) of *Phleospora graminearum. Courtesy Natsuki Nishihara.*

Description

Pycnidia subgregarious, at first immersed, nonostiolate, brown, later erumpent, prominent, with small ostiole, subglobose, 90–160 µm. Pale brown, upper layer finally breaking away, context translucent and golden colored; pycnophores blunt, short, 3–5 µm wide, hyaline, pycnospores yellow-hyaline obclavate, tapering to a blunt point, base totunded or blunt, variable, 30–55 µm × 3.3–5.6 µm, 1 to 6 septate (Figure 5-16) (Hardison and Sprague, 1943).

Hosts

1. **Turfgrass**—tall fescue (*Festuca arundinacea*).
2. **All Known Gramineous Hosts**—A listing of common names for the following species is given in Appendix Table IV. *Agropyron repens* (L.) Beauv., *Elymus canadensis* L., *Festuca arundinacea* Schreb. (Sprague, 1950; Nishihara, 1972).

Disease Profile

Phleospora leaf is primarily a cool, wet weather disease. Its incidence is highest during the months of late winter, spring and fall and lowest during the warm summer months.

Control

There are no published reports of attempts to control Phleospora leaf spot.

MASTIGOSPORIUM LEAF SPOT

Mastigosporim leaf spot occurs on Colonial bentgrass (*Agrostis tenuis*), creeping bentgrass (*Agrostis palus-*

tris), and perennial ryegrass (*Lolium perenne*). Outbreaks of the disease have been reported from the United States, Canada, Great Britian, France, Germany, Norway, and Sweden.

Symptoms

Numerous brown or black necrotic spots with purplish-brown margins and off-white centers develop on the leaf blades, and, less frequently on the leaf sheaths. The individual lesions are elliptical and measure ⅛ to ¼ inch (3–6 mm) long when mature. When the incidence of lesions per leaf is high, tip dieback, and ultimately, death of the entire leaf may occur (Figure 5-17).

The Fungi

A. *Mastigosporium rubricosum* (Dearn. and Barth.) Sprague; syn. *Mastogosporium rubricosum* var. *agrostidis* Bollard

Description

Mycelia in host epidermal and subepidermal, endophytic, or somewhat ectophytic, septate, coarse, branched, hyaline; conidiophores brief, single or in small groups, short, stipitate, continuous; conidia clear hyaline, elliptical-navicular, constricted at the 3 septa, 29–60 µm × 9–17 µm (Sprague, 1950) (Figure 5-18).

Hosts

1. **Turfgrasses**—creeping bentgrass (*Agrostis palustris*) and Colonial bentgrass (*Agrostis tenuis*).
2. **All Known Gramineous Hosts**—A listing of common names for the following species is given

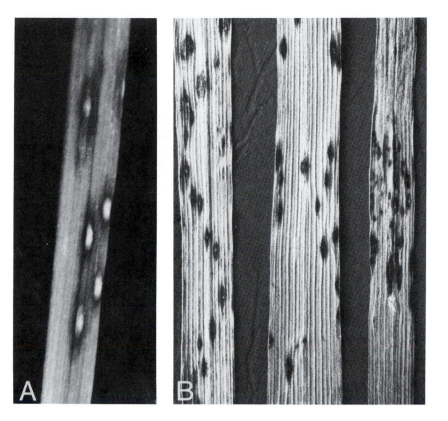

Figure 5-17. Mastigosporium leaf spot of (A) Colonial bentgrass (*Agrostis tenuis*) and (B) tall fescue (*Festuca arundinacea*).

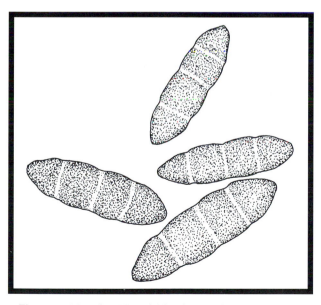

Figure 5-18. Conidia of *Mastigosporium rubricosum*.

in Appendix Table IV. *Agrostis alba* L., *A. canina* L., *A. exarata* Trin., *A. palustris* Huds., *A. tenuis* Sibth., *A. verticillata* Vill., *Calamagrostis canadensis* (Michx.) Beauv., *C. canadensis* var. *scabra* (Presl) Hitchc., *Dactylis glomerata* L., *Trisetum cernuum* Trin. (Sprague, 1950).

The Fungi

B. *Mastigosporium album* Riess.

Description

Conidia elliptical, 4–5 septate, with 1–3 filiform appendages from apical or subapical cells at the distal end, 33–85 μm × 8–16 μm with a mean value of 52 μm × 12 μm (Lacey, 1967).

Hosts

1. **Turfgrass**—perennial ryegrass (*Lolium multiflorum*).
2. **All Known Gramineous Hosts**—A listing of the common names for the following species is given in Appendix Table IV. *Alopecurus pratensis* L., *A. nigricans, Cynosurus cristatus* L., *C. pratensis, Deschampsia caespitosa* (L.) Beauv., *Lolium perenne* L. (Bollard, 1950a; Lacey, 1967).

Isolation and Culture of the Pathogens

Mastigosporium album and *Mastigosporium rubricosum* grow very slowly and sporulate poorly on artificial media. When cultured on either Dox, 2 percent malt agar, or potato dextrose agar, the average colony reaches 16 mm in diameter after four weeks incubation at 18 °C. Optimum growth rate and sporulation for both species is obtained on grass leaf decoction agar (100 g fresh grass leaves chopped and steamed in 1,000 ml distilled water for three hours; chopped leaves then removed by filtration through cheese cloth and agar added to the filtrate).

On grass leaf decoction agar, the colonies are brown with scarcely any aerial hyphae. When incubated at 12–18 °C, conidia are produced in a moist slimy pile in the center of each colony. Very few spores are produced at incubation temperatures of 20 °C or above. Also, spore germination is very low between 20–25 °C and ceases above 25 °C. The pathogenicity of isolates of either species does not diminish after extended periods of storage in culture (Bollard, 1950a).

Disease Profile

Mastigosporium leaf spot is a cool wet weather disease. Plant tissue colonized during a previous outbreak serves as the principal source of inoculum for renewed occurrences of the disease. Spores are the primary form of inoculum.

Entry into the leaves is accomplished by direct penetration of intact epidermal cells. Once inside the epidermal cell, the germ tube rapidly develops an extensive mycelium. The colonized epidermal cells become dark yellow or brown in color within 4–5 days from the moment of infection. Necrosis of mesophyll cells occurs in advance of infection and colonization by the invading hyphae. First, the cells immediately adjacent to the affected epidermal cells become yellow. Their protoplasmic contents then degenerate, become darker in color and adhere to the cell walls. It is the aggregation of these dark-colored walls that gives the lesion its dark appearance. In a step sequence, the contents of cells removed from the sites of immediate fungal colonization become disorganized. Once cell death occurs, hyphal growth then takes place within the affected area. There is no sign of zonation; tissues showing one condition blend imperceptibly with tissues showing another. However, some lateral delimitation of lesions is affected by the longitudinal veins of the leaves. These strands of vascular tissue, with their accompanying layers of sclerenchyma, form a barrier which the fungal hyphae does not penetrate. Sometimes a slight browning develops in the mesophyll cells beyond the vein but hyphal penetration of this area does not occur (Bollard, 1950b).

Control

There is no information on the degree of resistance of various cultivars of either perennial ryegrass or bentgrasses to Mastigosporium leaf spot or the effectiveness of fungicides for the control of the disease.

RAMULARIA LEAF SPOT

Ramularia leaf spot occurs on cool season turfgrasses in the humid, temperate climates of the United States, Canada, Europe, Scandinavia, Finland, Asia, and New Zealand.

Symptoms

Leaf spot lesions are usually of the "eyespot" type but vary according to the grass species being affected, the number of lesions per leaf, and the time of year.

On bentgrasses (*Agrostis* spp.) lesions are oval, measuring up to ⅛ inch (3 mm) by ¼ inch (4 mm) but generally ¹⁄₁₆ inch (1 mm) by ⅛ inch (3 mm), with off-white centers surrounded by a thick reddish brown border which is in turn surrounded by a wide orange or yellow halo. The lesions tend to remain small when there are many per leaf. In these instances, the halos coalesce and the leaf dies prematurely (Figure 5-19 B).

On annual bluegrass (*Poa annua*), the lesions are similar to those on ryegrasses and fescues but lighter in color and their yellow halos do not stand out so sharply (Latch, 1964).

On ryegrasses (*Lolium* spp.) and fescues (*Festuca* spp.), the lesions are nearly circular, up to ⁵⁄₁₆ inch (6 mm) in diameter, deep brown, and only rarely is the center lighter in color; usually the center is the darkest region of the spot (Figure 5-19 A).

The Fungus

Ramularia pusilla Unger [*Ramulaspera holcilanati* (Cav.) Lindroth. (?); *Ovularia pusilla* (Ung.) Sacc.]

Description

The conidiophores are hyaline, rarely branched, 1–3 septate, emerging from stomata on both leaf surfaces and arising from a small mycelial stroma. They are indeterminate in growth so that when a conidium is formed terminally it is pushed to one side as the conidiophore continues to elongate. A maximum of six conidial scars may be seen on a single conidiophore and it is the formation of these scars and slight bending of the conidiophore which gives the appearance of twisting. As the result, the older

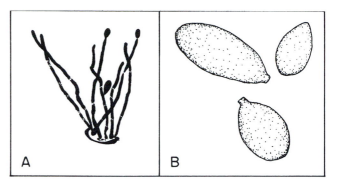

Figure 5-20. Conidia and conidiophores of *Ramularia pusilla*. *After Latch, 1964.*

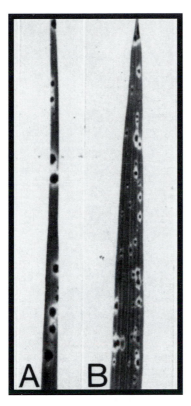

Figure 5-19. Ramularia leaf spot of (A) perennial ryegrass (*Lolium perenne*) and (B) bentgrass (*Agrostis stolonifera*). *After Latch, 1964.*

conidiophores are slightly tortuous. Conidiophore length varies with weather conditions, being longer after prolonged wet periods. Lengths vary from 32–119 μm × 1.5–3.5 μm, with the average in the range 50–60 μm × 2.5–3.0 μm.

The conidia are ellipsoidal to ovate, non septate, hyaline, and the outer wall is minutely echinulate. At the point of attachment to the conidiophore there is a well-defined scar. Collections of conidia from different grass species can vary greatly in their measurements. However, although spore measurements differ between hosts, they are constant on any given host. On Colonial bentgrass, the conidial sizes range from 10.5–18.0 μm × 6.9–9.8 μm (Latch, 1964) (Figure 5-20)

Procedures for Isolation and Culture

Colonies on potato dextrose agar grow slowly. Growth occurs at temperatures of 1–30 °C, with maximum growth at 20–25 °C. Colonies at 20 °C are raised up from the agar surface, colored white and dark brown, mildly convoluted, and after 21 days growth, average 26 mm in diameter. Sporulation in culture is sparse (Latch, 1966).

Hosts

1. **Turfgrasses**—annual bluegrass (*Poa annua*), annual ryegrass (*Lolium multiflorum*), perennial ryegrass (*Lolium perenne*), Colonial bentgrass (*Agrostis tenuis*), creeping bentgrass (*Agrostis palustris*), and Chewings fescue (*Festuca rubra* var. *commutata*).
2. **All Known Gramineous Hosts**—A listing of common names for the following species is given in AppendixTable IV. *Agropyron cristatum* (L.) Gaertn., *A. repens* (L.) Beauv., *A. trachycaulum* (Lk.) Malte, *Agrostis alba* L., *A. humilis* Vasey, *A. oregonensis* Vassey, *A. palustris* Huds., *A. tenuis* Sibth., *Alopecurus alpinus* J. E. Smith, *Anthoxanthum odoratum* L., *Arrhenatherum elatius* (L.) Presl, *Bromus carinatus* Hook. and Arn., *B. catharticus* Vahl., *B. inermis* Leyss., *Calamagrostis canadensis* (Michx.) Beauv., *Elymus glaucus* Buckl., *Festuca idahoensis* Elmer, *F. megalura* Nutt., *F. myuros* L., *F. rubra* var. *commutata* Gaud., *Holcus lanatus* L., *Lolium marschallii* Stev., *L. multiflorum* Lam., *L. perenne* L., *Poa ampla* Merr., *P. longiligula* Scribn. and Will., *Trisetum spicatum* (L.) Richt. (Latch, 1964; Sprague, 1950).

Disease Profile

Ramularia leaf spot can occur at any time during the plant growing seasons. However, the incidence and severity of the disease is highest during the cool, humid months of late winter, spring and fall and lowest during the warm summer months.

Control

There are no reports of fungicidal control of Ramularia leaf spot.

Molds, Mildews, Rusts, and Smuts

SLIME MOLDS

Slime molds are commonly found on partially submerged logs and stones in streams and lakes and along stream banks. At least two species are known to colonize the surfaces of turfgrass leaves.

Symptoms

All above-ground plant parts as well as the surface of the thatch or soil may be covered with a creamy white to translucent, slimy growth. With time, this slimy overgrowth changes to distinctive, ash gray fruiting structures. The affected areas of turfgrass assume a dull gray appearance due to the high population of fruiting bodies on the leaves (Plate 28-F). Varying in size from a few inches to several feet, the shape of the overall areas ranges from circular to serpentine streaks (Plate 28-E).

The Fungi

A. *Mucilago spongiosa* (Leyss.) Morg.
Aethalium white or cream-colored, of variable size and shape, 1–7 cm long and half as broad, component tubes resting on a common hypothallus and protected by a more or less deciduous calcareous porous cortex; peridial walls thin, and where exposed iridescent, generally whitened by a thin coating of lime crystals; capillitium scanty, of simple, mostly dark-colored, slightly anastanosing threads; columella indefinite or none; hypothallus white, spongy; spore mass black; spores violaceous, exceedingly rough, large 12–15 μm. Plasmodium creamy white.

The Fungi

B. *Physarum cinereum* (Batsch) Pers.
Sporangia sessile, closely gregarious or heaped, subglobose, elongate or plasmodiocarpous, more or less densely coated with lime; capillitium strongly developed, the internodes more or less richly calcareous and badhamioid, the lime-knots rounded and angular; spore mass purplish brown, spores clear violaceous, distinctly warted, 7–11 μm. Plasmodium watery white or colorless.

Of these two species, *Physarum cinereum* is more commonly found in the United States.

Hosts

All commonly cultivated turfgrasses, as well as the grass weed species found in association with them, are colonized by these two species of slime molds.

Disease Profile

The pathogens survive adverse weather conditions as spores. Under cool, humid weather condition, these spores absorb water, the cell walls crack open, and a single, naked, uninucleate, motile swarm spore emerges from each. These motile swarm spores ingest microorganisms and decaying organic matter, and leave behind the undigested debris. With time, these swarm spores may divide by fission several times and then change their form by retracting their flagella and becoming more rounded. Ultimately, they unite in pairs, nuclear fusion results, and the zygotes are formed. The zygotes are nonflagellate, and continue their existence as naked, ameboid cells which ingest food, increase in size, and become multinucleate due to a series of mitotic nuclear divisions. This growth form of the organism is called the plasmodium, and is the stage of growth that creates the slimy effect on the leaves of turfgrass plants. Eventually, the plasmodium undergoes changes that lead to the production of the fructifications. The process by which the fruiting structures are formed is a complex one, and varies among species. Spread of the pathogens is accomplished primarily by wind-borne spores (Figure 6-1).

With the accumulation of the plasmodium on the surface of the leaves, due to exclusion of light and

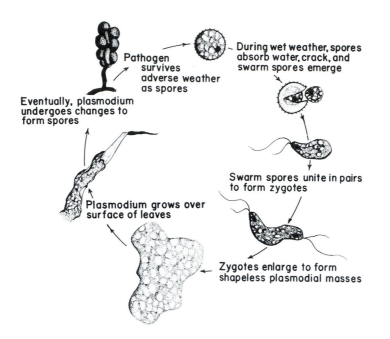

Figure 6-1. Cycle of development of slime mold on turfgrasses.

interference with respiration and transpiration processes, there is a disturbance of the metabolic activity of the underlying leaf cells. As the fruiting structures of the slime molds are formed, even more light is excluded form the leaves. In time, the thus altered physiological activity of the leaf cells results in overall leaf chlorosis. In this condition, the leaves are predisposed to invasion, and, in many cases, complete destruction by secondary bacteria, yeasts, and fungi.

Control

Cultural Practices

Removal of the spore masses by washing the leaves with a stream of water has been a standard recommendation for control of slime molds for many years. This method, however, should not be used during times of prolonged wet weather.

Slime mold development is favored by wet weather. If the leaves are washed during periods marked by frequent rain showers, this will only serve to spread the pathogens to previously unaffected areas, and, thus promote a buildup in disease incidence. Leaf washing for slime mold control, then, should be performed only in cases of forecasts of prevailing dry weather.

When prevailing weather conditions do not permit leaf washing, mechanical removal of spore masses

by raking, brushing, or poling, the affected areas will aid materially in the reduction of disease severity.

Use of Fungicides

Slime molds may be effectively controlled by the application of any turfgrass fungicide. For a listing of fungicides for turfgrass use, see Appendix Table I.

DOWNY MILDEW (Yellow Tuft)

Outbreaks of downy mildew of St. Agustinegrass (*Stenotaphrum secundatum*) incited by *Sclerophthora macrospora* were first reported in the spring of 1969 in Florida and Texas (Jones and Amador, 1969). A disease of bentgrasses (*Agrostis* spp.) commonly known as "yellow tuft" has been observed in northeastern United States, southeastern Canada and northern Europe since the early 1920s. Over the years, attempts to determine the cause of yellow tuft met with failure. The connection between yellow tuft of cool season turfgrasses and downy mildew of St. Augustinegrass was made during the 1970s when research at the University of Rhode Island demonstrated that the downy mildew pathogen is also the incitant of yellow tuft (Jackson and Dernoeden, 1980). The term "downy mildew" has been retained as the standard name for the disease on both warm season and cool season grasses.

Downy mildew is now known to be an important disease of St. Augustinegrass in the southern region of the United States and several species of cool season turfgrasses in northern United States, southern Canada, Australasia, and Europe.

Symptoms

With the cool season grasses, during the early stages of disease development the affected leaf blades are slightly broader and thicker than those of healthy plants. There is also a reduction in the rate of plant growth, but the magnitude is so slight that it is difficult to detect in mown turf.

As the disease progresses, dense, yellow clusters of plants develop. In bentgrass (*Agrostis* spp.) and red fescue (*Festuca rubra*) the width of these patches is ⅜ to 1 inch (1–3 cm), while in stands of Kentucky bluegrass (*Poa pratensis*) or perennial ryegrass (*Lolium perenne*) they are usually 1 to 3 inches (3–10 cm) in diameter. These patches develop during cool wet weather in late winter and early spring and again in early fall. They usually first occur in low lying areas in which the turf is frequently covered with water (Plate 27-C, D, E).

Each patch is made up of a dense cluster of yellow shoots that have developed from buds in the crowns and on stolons. Adventitious root development on the shoots within these clusters is very sparse, therefore the individual tufts can be easily pulled loose from the adjacent turf. During periods of high air temperature and drought stress, the entire cluster may wither and turn brown. However, many of the basal tillers at the periphery of the tufts survive these conditions and the disease will continue to be manifested in the same locations each year.

The symptoms of downy mildew on St. Augustinegrass (*Stenotaphrum secundatum*) are characterized by white, raised linear streaks that develop parallel to the midvein of the leaves. In addition to the streaking, leaves become yellow and then die back from the tips. Under conditions of high humidity, a "down" of fungal growth develops on the surface of the leaves. When drying of the leaf surfaces occurs, the down takes on the appearance of a dirty-white residue. The white-streak leaf symptom seen in the early stages of downy mildew can be confused with the leaf-streaking symptom associate with the virus-incited disease, St. Augustine decline. However, the St. Augustine decline symptoms are more yellow in color, and striping symptom is not as pronounced (Plates 27-A, B and 28-C, D).

When conditions continue to be favorable for disease development for an extended period of time, there is often a distortion of leaves and stunting of plant growth; however, the yellow tuft symptom that characterizes downy mildew on cool season grasses does not develop on St. Augustinegrass.

The Fungus

Sclerophthora macrospora (Sacc.) Thirum., Shaw and Naras; syn. *Sclerospora macrospora* Sacc.

Description

Mycelium intercellular, coenocytic, aggregating near the vascular bundles, diameter variable (3–60 μm). Sporangia limonoform, apically poroid (Plate 27-F), 37.8–60.8 × 70–100 μm, borne on sporangiophores emerging from stomata from lobed pads. Zoospores ovoid to pyriform, 14–20 × 5–10 μm, laterally biflagellate with anterior whiplash and posterior tinsel flagella; encysted zoospores spherical, 11.2–15.3 μm in diameter; germination by single hypha 5–60 μm long with protoplasm concentrated in swollen tip. Oogonia globose to roughly spherical, 60–90 μm in diameter with irregularly pitted walls about 7 μm thick; antheridia are amphigynous. Oospores globose to roughly spherical, 50–75 μm in diameter with a smooth wall 5–8 μm thick; germinating to produce a single sporangium.

Detection in Host Tissue

Sclerophthora macrospora is an obligate parasite; consequently, it does not grow on synthetic media. Detection of mycelium in host tissue can be accomplished as follows: Clear the host cells of chlorophyll by immersing the specimen in a warm solution of 5 percent potassium hydroxide. Then place the tissue in an solution of zinc chloroiodide (50 g zinc chloride, 16 g potassium iodide, 17 ml water). Add an excess of iodine and allow to stand for several days. The mycelium of *Sclerophthora macrospora* will stain deep bluish purple while the host tissue remains nearly colorless. Slides prepared by this procedure cannot be stored for future reference for the stain in the mycelial walls of the fungus will fade within 1 to 2 hours from the time of removal of the tissue from the zinc chloroiodide solution (Tuite, 1969; Ulstrup, 1952).

Hosts

1. **Turfgrasses**—Colonial bentgrass (*Agrostis tenuis*), creeping bentgrass (*Agrostis palustris*), velvet bentgrass (*Agrostis canina*), annual bluegrass (*Poa annua*), Kentucky bluegrass (*Poa pratensis*),

red fescue (*Festuca rubra*), tall fescue (*Festuca arundinacea*), perennial ryegrass (*Lolium perenne*), and St. Augustinegrass (*Stenotaphrum secundatum*).

2. **All Known Gramineous Hosts**—A listing of common names for the following species is given in Appendix Table IV. *Agropyron cristatum* (L.) Gaertn., *A. repens* (L.) Beauv., *A. smithii* Rydb., *A. trachycaulum* (Link) Mattei, *Agrostis canina* L., *A. palustris* Huds., *A. tenuis* Sibth., *Avena fatua* L., *A. sativa* L., *Bromus commutatus* Schrad., *B. inermis* Leyss., *B. japonicus* Thunb., *Dactylis glomerata* L., *Digitaria ischaemum* (Schreb.) Schreb., *D. sanguinalis* (L.) Scop., *Eleusine coracana* (L.) Gaertn., *E. indica* (L.) Gaertn., *Elymus macounii* Vasey, *Eragrostis cilianensis* (All.) Link., *E. pectinacea* (Michx.) Nees, *Festuca arundinacea* Schreb., *F. rubra* L., *Holcus lanatus* L., *Hordeum jubatum* L., *H. vulgare* L., *Lolium perenne* L., *Muhlenbergia asperifolia* (Nees and Mey.) Parodi, *Oryza sativa* L., *Panicum capillare* L., *P. miliaceum* L., *P. virgatum* L., *Pennisetum glaucum* (L.) R. Br., *Phalaris arundinacea* L., *Phleum pratense* L., *Poa annua* L., *P. pratensis* L., *P. trivialis* L., *Saccharum officinarum* L., *Schedonnardus paniculatus* (Nutt.) Trel., *Secale cereale* L., *Setaria lutescens* (Weigel) Hubb., *S. viridis* (L.) Beauv., *Sorghum vulgare* Pers., *S. vulgare* var. *sudanense* (Piper) Hitch., *Sporobolus neglectus* Nash., *Stenotaphrum secundatum* (Walt.) Kuntze, *Triticum aestivum* L., *Zea mays* L. (Jackson, 1980a; Roth, 1967; Semeniuk and Mankin, 1964; Semenuik and Mankin, 1966; Ulstrup, 1955).

Disease Profile

Downy mildew is a cool, wet weather disease. Outbreaks are most likely to occur when the air temperatures are in the 60 to 70 °F (16–21 °C) range during periods of frequent rainfall. Turf is particularly vulnerable to severe outbreaks of downy mildew when it is growing in low-lying areas that are subjected to frequent flooding, or in locations in which water-saturated soil exists for extended periods of time.

The downy mildew fungus survives adverse climatic conditions as dormant oospores in diseased plant tissue, thatch and leaf litter, and as mycelium in the tissue of crowns of currently diseased plants. Mycelium in diseased plants serves as the major source of inoculum for rapid buildup of the disease within a stand of grass or its spread to an adjacent turf. The fungus sporulates more abundantly on diseased crabgrasses (*Digitaria* spp.) than on cultivated

turfgrass hosts; therefore, these species can serve as an important source of both current and long-term inoculum.

Under cool air temperatures, a water-saturated soil and high atmospheric humidity, large numbers of spore-bearing structures (sporangia) are produced. When free water is present on the plant surfaces, the sporangia release motile zoospores. The zoospores encyst and then germinate to produce a hyphal strand that infects the underlying plant tissue. Diseased Kentucky bluegrass leaves covered with water at 59 to 70 °F (15–21 °C) can generate sporangia and liberate zoospores in 4 to 6 hours. Young seedlings submerged in water can be infected by zoospores within 6 hours (Dernoden and Jackson, 1980).

Sporangial development on diseased St. Augustinegrass leaves takes place over a temperature range of 41–75 °F (5–24 °C), with the greatest production occurring at 59 °F (15 °C). The optimum temperatures for the liberation of zoospores from sporangia and for zoospore encystment and germination are 59–68 °F (15–20 °C). Infection of leaves by zoospores occurs between 50–77 °F (10–25 °C), with an optimum at 59 °F (15 °C) (Bruton and Toler, 1980). At the time of zoospore encystment, the flagella are retracted and the spores round up. A single germ tube is then produced, with the protoplasm of the spore concentrated near the advancing tip. The germ tubes of individual spores vary in length from 5 to 500 microns. They develop appressoria at the tips and become aligned with the cell walls of the host (Figure 3-3) (Bruton, 1979).

Where primary infections in young seedlings are concerned, infection occurs in the mesocotyl region. The ruptured coleoptile at the point of emergence of the first leaf is also a major infection site. With older plants, the shoot apices, axillary buds, and the non-cutinized meristem in the basal portion of leaves are the principal sites of infection. The mycelium grows intercellularly in the meristematic tissues of the shoots and axillary buds. When infection of the developing leaf primordia occurs, the fungus keeps pace with leaf growth, expanding into new tissues as they develop (Jackson and Dernoden, 1980).

With regard to the dynamics of infection and colonization of new tillers that are forming on currently diseased plants, the mycelium first establishes a complex intercellular network within the existing crown tissue, then it extends into the newly developing leaf and shoot meristems. In instances where leaf formation has already occurred, the mycelium grows along the vascular bundles of the stems and through the leaf sheaths. As it moves into the upper portion of the sheath, there is an increase in the incidence of branching of hyphae into adjacent parenchymatous tissue. When the mycelium reaches the leaf lamina, there is first a massive development of hyphae along the vascular bundles, then the hyphae branch out into the mesophyll tissue and move to new bundles. The advancing hyphae fill the schizogenous intercellular spaces, and from these locations, narrow hyphae grow between the cells. The parasitic process is facilitated by penetration of the cell wall and invagination of the protoplast without rupturing the plasma membrane (Bruton, 1979).

When the hyphae enter the substomatal cavities on the leaves and the upper portions of the sheaths, they form distinctive, lobed, irregularly thickened pads. Under favorable atmospheric conditions, sporangiophores develop on these pads and then protrude through the open stomates. Each sporangiophore produces six or more lemon-shaped sporangia. These are the fungal structures that give the characteristic down appearance to the leaf surface (Plate 27-E, F) (Bruton, 1979; Jackson, 1980a).

The susceptibility of turfgrasses to the downy mildew fungus is not affected by soil pH or levels of fertilization. Symptoms of the disease on cool season grasses are less noticeable when either iron sulfate or nitrogenous fertilizers are applied but the effect is one of masking the symptoms rather than increasing the plants' resistance to the disease (Jackson, 1982).

Control

Cultural Practices

Since soil saturation is a necessary requirement for the development of downy mildew, good drainage of the turf area and the maintenance of adequate water infiltration rates in the soil through various coring procedures is an important aspect to the successful control of the disease. Iron sulfate at 10 to 20 pounds per acre (11–22 kg/ha) will mask downy mildew symptoms in sod fields (Jackson, 1980b).

Use of Resistant Grasses

There are no reported differences in resistance to downy mildew between and among species of cool season turfgrasses. In an evaluation of twelve cultivars of St. Augustinegrass (*Stenotaphrum secundatum*) none demonstrated superior resistance to the disease. However, among the cultivars tested, the most resistant was 'Florantine,' the most susceptible was 'New Zealand Red Leaf,' and two common Texas cultivars, 'Texas Common' and 'Floratam' were intermediate in resistance (Toler, 1983; Toler, Bruton and Grisham, 1983).

Use of Fungicides

Control of downy mildew can be accomplished with applications of metalaxyl or propamocarb. Histological examination of St. Augustinegrass (*Stenotaphrum secundatum*) leaf blades seven days after the application of metalaxyl showed that the treatment had eradicated the fungus (Bruton, Toler and Grisham, 1986).

For a profile of these fungicides and a listing of representative trade names and manufacturers, see Appendix Table I.

POWDERY MILDEW

Generally speaking, the damage to turf by powdery mildew is usually minimal. However, the disease can be a major problem when susceptible cultivars are grown in areas with poor air circulation or in shaded locations.

Symptoms

The signs of the fungus are usually evident before the appearance of macroscopic symptoms of powdery mildew. The fungus is usually first seen as isolated wefts of fine, gray white, cobwebby growth that is confined for the most part to the upper surface of the leaves. This growth rapidly becomes more dense, and may involve the entire leaf surface. After this, the individual leaves assume a gray white appearance (Plate 25-B). In cases of high disease incidence, sections, or entire turfgrass stands, may be dull white, rather than the characteristic green color.

As colonization of the leaves by the pathogen becomes more intense, chlorotic lesions develop. These gradually enlarge, turning to pale yellow as they do so. In the final stages of disease development, the entire leaf may be pale yellow in color.

The Fungus

Erysiphe graminis D. C.

Description

Mycelium more or less persistent, effused or forming scattered patches, at first white, frequently becoming buff, pale brown or weathering to gray; cleistothecia large, 135–280 μm, mostly 200 μm in diameter, scattered or gregarious, globose-depressed, becoming concave, usually more or less immersed in mycelium. Cells of cleistothecium obscure; appendages rudimentary, few or numerous, very short, simple or sparingly branched, pale brown; asci numerous, 9–30, usually from 15–20, varying from cylindrical to ovate-oblong, more or less longly pedicellate, 25–40 μm × 70–108 μm; spores 8 (rarely 4), 10–13 μm × 20–23 μm. Conidia formed in chains on short upright conidiophores; spore hyaline, oval, 14–17 μm × 25–33 μm.

Hosts

1. **Turfgrasses**—bermudagrass (*Cynodon dactylon*), Kentucky bluegrass (*Poa pratensis*), Chewings fescue (*Festuca rubra* var. *commutata*), red fescue (*Festuca rubra*), and sheep fescue (*Festuca ovina*).
2. **All Known Gramineous Hosts**—A listing of common names for the following species is given in Appendix Table IV. *Aegilops cylindrica* Host, *Agropyron cristatum* (L.) Gaertn., *A. dasystachyum* (Hook.) Scribn., *A. desertorum* (Fisch.) Schult., *A. inerme* (Scribn. and Smith) Rydb., *A. repens* (L.) Beauv., *A. riparium* Scribn. and Smith, *A. sibiricum* (Willd.) Beauv., *A. smithii* Rydb., *A. spicatum* (Pursh) Scribn. and Smith, *A. striatum* Nees, *A. subsecundum* (Link) Hitchc., *A. trachycaulum* (Link) Malte, *A. trichophorum* (Link) Richt., *Agrostis alba* L., *A. diegoensis* Vasey, *A. exarata* Trin., *A. semiverticillata* (Forsk.) C. Christ., *Avena byzantina* C. Koch, *A. fatua* L., *A. sativa* L., *Beckmannia syzigachne* (Steud.) Fernald, *Bromus breviaristatus* Buckl., *B. carinatus* Hook. and Arn., *B. catharticus* Vahl, *B. commutatus* Schrad., *B. erectus* Huds., *B. inermis* Leyss., *B. mollis* L., *B. racemosus* L., *B. rigidus* Roth, *B. secalinus* L., *B. vulgaris* (Hook.) Shear, *Buchloe dactyloides* (Nutt.) Engelm., *Calamagrostis canadensis* (Michx.) Beauv., *C. rubescens* Buckl., *Catabrosa aquatica* (L.) Beauv., *Cinna arundinacea* L., *Cynodon dactylon* (L.) Pers., *Dactylis glomerata* L., *Deschampsia danthonioides* (Trin.) Munro ex Benth., *Digitaria sanguinalis* (L.) Scop., *Elymus canadensis* L., *E. condensatus* Presl, *E. dahuricus* Turcz., *E. glaucus* Buckl., *E. junceus* Fisch., *E. sibiricus* L., *E. triticoides* Buckl., *E. villosus* Muhl., *E. virginicus* L., *Festuca idahoensis* Elmer, *F. ovina* L., *F. rubra* L., *F. rubra* var. *commutata* Gaud., *F. rubra* var. *heterophylla* Mutel., *Glyceria striata* (Lam.) Hitchc., *Hordeum brachyantherum* Nevski, *H. distichon* L., *H. jubatum* L., *H. murinum* L., *H. pusillum* Nutt., *H. secalinum* Guss., *H. vulgare* L., *Hystrix patula* Moench, *Koeleria cristata* (L.) Pers., *Melica californica* Scribn., *Milium effusum* L., *Phalaris arundinacea* L., *Phleum pratense* L., *Poa alpina* L., *P. ampla* L., *P. arachnifera* Torr., *P. arida* Vasey, *P. canbyi* (Scribn.) Piper, *P. cusickii* Vasey, *P. epilis* Scribn., *P. glau-*cifolia Scribn. and Will., *P. gracillima* Vasey, *P. interior* Rydb., *P. juncifolia* Scribn., *P. leptocoma* Trin., *P. longifolia* Trin., *P. nemoralis* L., *P. nervosa* (Hook.) Vasey, *P. nevadensis* Vasey, *P. palustris* L., *P. pratensis* L., *P. scabrella* (Thurb.) Benth., *P. secunda* Presl, *P. sylvestris* A. Gray, *P. vaseyochloa* Scribn., *Polypogon monspeliensis* (L.) Desf., *Puccinellia distans* (L.) Parl., *Secale cereale* L., *Sitanion hanseni* (Scribn.) J. G. Smith, *S. hystrix* (Nutt.) J. G. Smith, *S. jubatum* J. G. Smith, *Sphenopholis obtusata* (Michx.) Scribn., *Sporobolus giganteus* Nash, *Stipa californica* Merr. and Davy., *Triticum aestivum* L. (Hardison, 1943; Hardison, 1945a; Index Plant Dis., 1960; Sprague, 1950).

Disease Profile

The powdery mildew fungus survives the winter months as cleistethecia on debris from the previous season's growth, and as dormant mycelium in host tissue, consequently, conidia, ascospores, or both spore forms, may serve as primary inoculum.

The spores are disseminated by wind and, under favorable environmental conditions, germinate within 2 hours from the time they come in contact with the leaf surface, and the infection process begins. Penetration of the leaf surface is direct. The comparatively short germ tubes develop appressoria. From the appressorium, a penetration-peg is produced—which grows through the cuticle and epidermal wall. When the cell wall has been penetrated, a specialized absorption structure (haustorium) is produced which invaginates the protoplast without rupturing the plasma membrane, thereby forming a delicately balanced contact with the host (Figure 3-3). At this point, active parasitism of the cytoplasm begins.

Since the mycelium is not systemic in the host, distribution of the fungus over the leaf surface occurs as the result of a high population of spores in the primary inoculation, and/or by the production and spread of secondary conidia. These secondary conidia are usually produced 3–4 days from the time of primary leaf infection.

After the death of diseased leaves in late fall and early winter, cleistothecia are produced on their surface, and the cycle of fungus development is complete.

Optimum environmental conditions for the development of powdery mildew include (a) reduced air circulation; (b) high atmospheric humidity, but not visibly free water on the surfaces of the leaves, (c) low light intensity; and (d) an air temperature of 65 °F (18 °C).

The importance of reduced light intensity in the development of powdery mildew is illustrated by the fact that the disease is usually more severe on turf-grass growing in shaded areas than in full natural light. This is probably due to reduced air temperatures from shading. It could, however, be the result of altered metabolism of the host, the powdery mildew fungus, or both.

Control

Cultural Practices

Where powdery mildew is of frequent recurrence, if possible, the employment of management practices to improve air drainage and reduce shading will aid in the reduction of disease severity. It is not suggested, however, that the axe be applied to the spreading chestnut tree to control the powdery mildew on the grass below. In this case, a fungicidal program is definitely to be preferred as the most desirable approach.

Use of Resistant Cultivars

Erysiphe graminis is highly specialized as to the grass species it will colonize. This phenomenon has been well established for the cereals as well as many related grasses. The form of the fungus appearing on barley, for example, will not parasitize wheat, while the form that is pathogenic to oats will not colonize barley, etc. This degree of host specificity also exists for *E. graminis* on the various turfgrass species (Hardison, 1943; Hardison, 1945a; Hardison, 1945b).

Differences in degree of susceptibility of various varieties and clones of turfgrasses to powdery mildew is known. 'Merion' Kentucky bluegrass (*Poa pratensis*), for example, is more susceptible to *Erysiphe graminis* than 'Kenblue' Kentucky bluegrass. Selection of the latter variety, however, solely because of its higher degree of resistance to powdery mildew cannot be justified (see Melting Out of Kentucky Bluegrass).

Use of Fungicides

Effective control of powdery mildew can be accomplished by applications of either cyproconazole, propiconazole or triadimefon. For a profile of these fungicides and a listing of representative manufacturers, see Appendix Table I.

RUSTS

Although the various rust diseases of turfgrasses have been recognized for many years, they have generally been considered to be one of the minor disease problems of this plant group. However, with the more widespread use of zoysiagrass (*Zoysia japonica*), the development of the fine-leafed perennial ryegrasses (*Lolium perenne*), and the introduction of the highly rust-susceptible 'Merion' variety of Kentucky bluegrass (*Poa pratensis*) and certain cultivars of bermudagrass (*Cynodon dactylon*), rusts now rank among the major diseases of both cool season and warm season turfgrasses.

Symptoms

Early leaf lesion development is seen as light yellow flecks. As these lesions enlarge, they may become somewhat elongate, and, in cases of high incidence, show definite orientation in rows parallel with the veins of the leaves. Finally, with the rupture of the cuticle and epidermis, the lesions develop into reddish brown pustules (Plate 25-C, D). As the pustules enlarge, the cuticle and epidermis that formerly covered each is pushed back to produce a characteristic collar-effect.

In cases of high disease incidence, the leaves of the affected plants turn yellow—beginning at the tips and progressing toward the sheaths. At this stage of disease development, the entire stand of turfgrass may appear yellow in color.

The Fungi

A. *Puccinia coronata* Corda f. sp. *agropyri* Erikss., f. sp. *agrostidis* Erikss., f. sp. *alopecuri* Erikss., f. sp. *avenae* Erikss., f. sp. *bromi* F. and L., f. sp. *calamagrostis* Erikss., f. sp. *elaegni* F. and L., f. sp. *festucae* Erikss., f. sp. *glyceriae* Erikss., f. sp. *holci* Kleb., f. sp. *lolii* Erikss., f. sp. *phalaridia* Kleb.

Description

Uredia amphigenous, brownish yellow, sometimes with few colorless paraphyses; urediospores globoid or broadly ellipsoid, 16–20 μm × 18–24 μm; wall pale yellow, 1–1.5 μm thick, finely echinulate, the pores 6–8, scattered, indistinct. Telia amphigenous, long covered by the epidermis, occasionally with few subepidermal paraphyses; teliospores clavate-oblong, 13–19 μm × 30–67 μm, with 3–10 digitate projections above, narrowed below, slightly or not constricted at septum; wall chestnut brown above, paler below, 1–1.5 μm thick at sides, 7–15 μm above, including projections; pedicel tinted, very short.

Hosts

1. **Turfgrasses**—Colonial bentgrass (*Agrostis tenuis*), creeping bentgrass (*Agrostis palustris*), tall

fescue (*Festuca arundinacea*), annual ryegrass (*Lolium multiflorum*), and perennial ryegrass (*Lolium perenne*).

2. **All Known Gramineous Hosts**—A listing of common names for the following species is given in Appendix Table IV. *Agropyron repens* (L.) Beauv., *A. smithii* Rydb., *A. trachycaulum* (Link) Malte, *Agrostis alba* L., *A. diegoensis* Vasey, *A. exarata* Trin., *A. longiligula* Hitchc., *A. palustris* Huds., *A. tenuis* Sibth., *A. thurberiana* Hitchc., *Alopecurus aequalis* Sobol., *Ammophila arenaria* (L.) Link, *A. breviligulata* Fernald, *Arundo donax* L., *Arrhenatherum elatius* (L.) Presl., *Avena barbata* Brot., *A. fatua* L., *A. hookeri* Scribn., *A. sativa* L., *Beckmannia erucaeformis* (L.) Host, *B. syzigachne* (Steud.) Fernald, *Bromus anomalus* Rupr., *B. ciliatus* L., *B. inermis* Leyss., *B. polyanthus* Scribn., *B. pumpellianus* Scribn., *Calamagrostis canadensis* (Michx.) Beauv., *C. hyperborea* Lange, *C. inexpansa* A. Gray, *C. koeleriodes* Vasey, *C. montanensis* Scribn., *C. neglecta* (Ehrh.) Gaertn. Mey. and Schreb., *C. nutkaensis* (Presl) Steud., *C. purpurascens* R. Br., *C. rubescens* Buckl., *C. scopulorum* Jones, *Cinna arundinacea* L., *C. latifolia* (Trevir) Griseb., *Deschampsia caespitosa* (L.) Beauv., *Elymus canadensis* L., *E. dahuricus* Turcz., *E. innovatus* Beal, *E. triticoides* Buckl., *E. virginicus* L., *Festuca arundinacea* Schreb., *F. ovina* L., *F. subulata* Trin., *Glyceria elata* (Nash) Hitchc., *G. grandis* S. Wats., *G. pauciflora* Presl, *G. striata* (Lam.) Hitchc., *Hierochloe odorata* (L.) Beauv., *Holcus lanatus* L., *Lagurus ovatus* L., *Lamarckia aurea* (L.) Moench, *Lolium multiflorum* Lam., *L. perenne* L., *Paspalum setaceum* Michx., *Phalaris arundinacea* L., *P. canariensis* L., *P. caroliniana* Walt., *Poa arachnifera* Torr., *P. compressa* L., *Polypogon monspeliensis* (L.) Desf., *Schizachne purpurascens* (Torr.) Swallen, *Scolochloa festucacea* (Willd.) Link, *Trisetum canescens* Buckl., *T. cernuum* Trin., *T. spicatum* (L.) Richt. (Arthur, 1929; Eshed and Dinoor, 1981; Index Plant Dis., 1960; Lancashire and Latch, 1966).

3. **Alternate Hosts**—*Rhamnus cathartica* L. and *Rhamnus frangula* L.

The Fungi

   B. *Puccinia crandallii* Pam. and Hume.

Description

   Uredia hypophyllous, light chestnut brown; urediospores ellipsoid or obovoid, 23–27 μm × 29–35 μm; wall light yellow, 2–2.5 μm thick, finely echinulate, the pores 6–8, scattered. Telia hypophyllous,

oblong, dark brown; teliospores ollipsoid, 15–24 μm × 35–50 μm, rounded or obtuse at both ends or truncate above, somewhat constricted at septum; wall cinnamon brown, 1.5–2.5 μm thick at sides, 5–12 μm and darker above; pedicel pale cinnamon brown, 1–1-1/2 the length of the spore.

Hosts

1. **Turfgrass**—red fescue (*Festuca rubra*) and sheep fescue (*Festuca ovina*).
2. **All Known Gramineous Hosts**—A listing of common names for the following species is given in Appendix Table IV. *Festuca elmeri* Scribn. and Merr., *F. idahoensis* Elmer, *F. occidentalis* Hook., *F. ovina* L., *F. rubra* L., *F. subulata* Trin., *F. viridula* Vasey, *Hesperochloa kingii* (S. Wats.) Rydb., *Poa fendleriana* (Steud.)Vasey, *P. longiligula* Scribn. and Will. (Arthur, 1929; Index Plant Dis., 1960).
3. **Alternate Hosts**—*Symphoricarpos albus* (L.) Blake, *S. mollis* Nutt., *S. occidentalis* Hook., *S. orbiculatus* Moench, *S. oreophilus* Gray, *S. vaccinioides* Rydb. (Arthur, 1929).

The Fungi

   C. *Puccinia cynodontis* Lacroix.

Description

   Uredia chiefly hypophyllous, cinnamon brown; uredisopores globoid, 19–23 μm × 20–26 μm; wall cinnamon brown, 1.5–3 μm thick, very finely verrucose, the pores 2, sometimes 3, equatorial. Telia chiefly hypophyllous, blackish brown; teliospores ellipsoid or oblong, 16–22 μm × 28–42 μm, obtuse or attenuate at each end, slightly constricted at septum; wall dark chestnut brown, paler at each end, 1.5–2.5 μm thick at sides, 6–12 μm above; pedicel nearly colorless, 1-1/2 the length of the spore or less.

Host

1. **Turfgrass**—bermudagrass (*Cynodon dactylon*).
2. **Alternate Host**—*Plantago* spp. Reported in Europe and Japan only (Arthur, 1929).

The Fungi

   D. *Puccinia festucae* (D C.) Plowr.

Description.

   Uredia hypophyllous, yellow; urediospores broadly ellipsoid, 19–23 μm × 20–26 μm; wall pale yellow, 1–1.5 μm thick, finely echinulate, the spores

5–7, scattered, distinct. Telia hypophyllous, soon naked, chestnut brown; teliospores narrowly oblong or cylindric, 13–19 μm × 45–58 μm, with 2–5 erect projections above, 10–25 μm long, narrowed below, slightly constricted at septum; wall chestnut brown above, paler below, 1 μm thick at sides, much thicker above; pedicel pale chestnut brown, short.

Host

1. **Turfgrass**—sheep fescue (*Festuca ovina* L.) (Index Plant Dis., 1960).
2. **Alternate Hosts**—*Lonicera coerulea* L., *L. prolifera* (Kirchner) Rehder (Arthur, 1929).

The Fungi

E. *Puccinia graminis* Pers. f. sp. *agrostidis* Erikss., f. sp. *airae* Erikss. and Henn., f. sp. *avanae* Erikss. and Henn., f. sp. *bromi* Erikss., f. sp. *graminicola*, f. sp. *phlei-pratensis* (Erikss. and Henn.) Stak. and Piem., f. sp. *poae* Erikss. and Henn., f. sp. *secalis* Erikss, and Henn., f. sp. *tritici* Erikss. and Henn.

Description.

Uredia caulicolous and epiphyllous, reddish brown; urediospores oblong or ellipsoid, 13–24 μm × 31–42 μm; wall golden brown at maturity, 1.5–2 μm thick, strongly echinulate, the pores 4, rarely 5, equatorial. Telia chiefly caulicolous, blackish brown; teliospores ellipsoid or oblong clavate, 16–23 μm × 35–58 μm, rounded or narrowed both above and below, moderately constricted at septum; wall darker chestnut brown, paler below, 1–1.5 μm thick at sides, 5–10 μm above; pedicel colored next to spore, as long as spore or longer.

Hosts

1. **Turfgrasses**—annual bluegrass (*Poa annua*), colonial bentgrass (*Agrostis tenuis*), creeping bentgrass (*Agrostis palustris*), bermudagrass (*Cynodon dactylon*), tall fescue (*Festuca arundinacea*), red fescue (*Festuca rubra*), and Kentucky bluegrass (*Poa pratensis*).
2. **All Known Gramineous Hosts**—A listing of common names for the following species is given in Appendix Table IV. *Agropyron caninum* (L.) Beauv., *A. dasystachyum* (Hook.) Scribn., *A. pseudorepens* Scribn. and Smith, *A. repens* (L.) Beauv., *A. smithii* Rydb., *A. subsecundum* (Link) Hitchc., *A. trachycaulum* (Link) Malte, *Agrostis alba* L., *A. canina* L., *A. palustris* Huds., *A. perennans* (Walt.) Tuckerm., *A. tenuis* Sibth., *Alopecurus aequalis* Sobol., *A. geniculatus* L., *A. howellii* Vasey,

A. pratensis L., *Ammophila breviligulata* Fernald, *Anthoxanthum aristatum* Boiss., *A. odoratum* L., *Arrhenatherum elatius* (L.) Presl, *Avena barbata* Brot., *A. fatua* L., *A. sativa* L., *Beckmannia erucaeformis* (L.) Host, *B. syzigachne* (Steud.) Fernald, *Bouteloua curtipendula* (Michx.) Torr., *B. gracilis* (H.B.K.) Lag., *Briza maxima* L., *B. minor* L., *Bromus anomalus* Rupr., *B. ciliatus* L., *B. hordeaceus* L., *B. japonicus* Thunb., *B. polyanthus* Scribn., *B. pumpellianus* Scribn. *B. purgans* L., *B. rigidus* Roth, *B. secalinus* L., *B. tectorum* L., *B. tectorum* var. *nudum* Mert. and Koch, *Buchloe dactyloides* (Nutt.) Engelm., *Calamagrostis canadensis* (Michx.) Beauv., *C. hyperborea* Lange, *C. inexpansa* A. Gray, *Catabrosa aquatica* (L.) Beauv., *Calamovilfa longifolia* (Hook.) Scribn., *Cinna arundinacea* L., *C. latifolia* (Trevir.) Griseb., *Cynodon dactylon* (L.) Pers., *Dactylis glomerata* L., *Danthonia spicata* (L.) Beauv., *Deschampsia caespitosa* (L.) Beauv., *D. danthonioides* (Trin.) Munro ex Benth., *D. elongata* (Hook.) Munro, *D. holciformis* Presl, *Echinochloa crusgalli* (L.) Beauv., *Elymus canadensis* L., *E. condensatus* Presl, *E. dahuricus* Turcz., *E. flavescens* Scribn. and Smith, *E. glaucus* Buckl., *E. macounii* Vasey, *E. sibiricus* L., *E. triticoides* Buckl., *E. virginicus* L., *E. virginicus* var. *australis* (Scribn. and Ball) Hitchc., *E. virginicus* var. *glabriflorus* (Vasey) Bush, *E. virginicus* var. *submuticus* Hook., *Festuca arizonica* Vasey, *F. arundinacea* Schreb., *F. californica* Vasey, *F. eastwoodae* Piper, *F. elmeri* Scribn. and Merr., *F. idahoensis* Elmer, *F. megalura* Nutt., *F. myuros* L., *F. octoflora* Walt., *F. pacifica* Piper, *F. rubra* L., *Gastridium ventricosum* (Gouan) Shinz and Thell., *Glyceria elata* (Nash) Hitchc., *G. grandis* S. Wats., *G. pauciflora* Presl, *G. striata* (Lam.) Hitchc., *Hordeum brachyantherum* Nevski, *H. distichon* L., *H. hystrix* Roth., *H. jubatum* L., *H. jubatum* var. *caespitosum* (Scribn.) Hitchc., *H. vulgare* L., *Hystrix patula* Moench, *Koleria cristata* (L.) Pers., *Lagurus ovatus* L., *Lamarckia aurea* (L.) Moench, *Limnodea arkansana* (Nutt.) L. H. Dewey, *Milium effusum* L., *Molinia caerulea* (L.) Moench, *Muhlenbergia asperifolia* (Nees and Mey.) Parodi, *M. cuspidata* (Torr.) Rydb., *M. mexicana* (L.) Trin., *Panicum virgatum* L., *Phalaris angusta* Nees, *P. arundinacea* L., *P. californica* Hook. and Arn., *P. caroliniana* Walt., *Phleum graecum* Boiss. and Neldr., *P. paniculatum* Huds., *P. phleoides* Karst., *P. pratense* L., *Poa annua* L., *P. arachnifera* Torr., *P. arida* Vasey, *P. bulbosa* L., *P. chapmaniana* Scribn., *P. compressa* L., *P. howellii* Vasey and Scribn., *P. interior* Rydb., *P. juncifolia* Scribn., *P. nevadensis* Vasey, *P. palustris* L., *P. pratensis* L., *P. scabrella* (Thurb.) Benth., *P. se-*

cunda Presl, *P. trivialis* L., *Polypogon monspeliensis* (L.) Desf. *Puccinellia airoides* (Nutt.) Wats. and Coult., *P. distans* (L.) Parl., *P. nuttalliana* (Schult.) Hitchc., *P. nutkaensis* (Presl) Lam and Weath., *Secale cereale* L., *Sitanion hystrix* (Nutt.) J. G. Smith, *S. jubatum* J. G. Smith, *Sphenopholis obtusata* (Michx.) Scribn., *Sporobolus asper* (Michx.) Kunth., *S. cryptandrus* (Torr.) A. Gray, *Stipa comata* Trin. and Rupr., *S. viridula* Trin., *Tridens flavus* (L.) Hitchc., *Trisetum canescens* Buckl., *Triticum aestivum* L., *T. compactum* Host, *T. dicoccoides* Koern, *T. dicoccum* Schrank, *T. durum* Desf., *T. freycenetii* Host, *T. monococcum* L., *T. polonicum* L., *T. spelta* L., *T. turgidum* L. (Arthur, 1929; Index Plant Dis., 1960; Welty and Mellbye, 1989).

3. **Alternate Hosts**—*Berberis canadensis* Mill., *B. vulgaris* L., *Mahonia* spp. (Arthur, 1929).

The Fungi

F. *Puccinia montanensis* Ellis

Description

Uredia chiefly epiphyllous, elliptic, forming long lines, cinnamon brown, with numerous clavate paraphyses; urediospores ellipsoid, 19–26 μm × 21–32 μm; wall pale cinnamon brown, 1.5–2 μm thick, finely echinulate, the pores, 8–10, scattered. Telia chiefly hypophyllous, oblong or linear, often forming long lines, long covered by the epidermis, with dark subepidermal paraphyses; teliospores irregularly oblong, 18–34 μm × 35–64 μm, truncate or angularly rounded above, narrowed below, slightly constricted at septum; wall cinnamon or chestnut brown, 1.5–2.5 μm thick at sides, 3–7 μm and darker above; pedicel colored, very short.

Hosts

1. **Turfgrass**—velvet bentgrass (*Agrostis caninum*).
2. **All Known Gramineous Hosts**—A listing of common names for the following species is given in Appendix Table IV. *Agropyron albicans* Scribn. and Smith, *A. caninum* (L.) Beauv., *A. dasystachyum* (Hook.) Scribn., *A. inerme* (Scribn. and Smith) Rydb., *A. pseudorepens* Scribn. and Smith, *A. repens* (L.) Beauv., *A. smithii* Rydb., *A. smithii* var. *palmeri* Heller, *A. subsecundum* (Link) Hitchc., *A. trachycaulum* (Link) Malte, *Elymus canadensis* L., *E. glaucus* Buckl., *E. macounii* Vasey, *E. sibiricus* L., *E. triticoides* Buckl., *E. virginicus* L., *E. virginicus* var. *submuticus* Hook., *Hordeum jubatum* L., *Hystrix patula* Moench,

Lolium multiflorum Lam., *Melica imperfecta* Trin., *Sitanion hystrix* (Nutt.) J. G. Smith (Arthur, 1929; Index Plant Dis., 1960).
3. **Alternate Host**—*Berberis fendelor* Gray (Arthur, 1929).

The Fungi

G. *Puccinia pattersoniana* Arth.

Description

Uredia epiphyllous, brownish yellow; urediospores ellipsoid or obovoid, 19–30 μm × 29–39 μm; wall golden yellow, 2–3 μm thick, echinulate, the pores 8–10, scattered. Telia chiefly epiphyllous, chestnut-brown; teliospores ellipsoid or oblong, 16–23 μm × 29–37 μm, usually rounded at both ends, somewhat constricted at septum; wall cinnamon brown, uniformly 1–1.5 μm thick, minutely striate; pedicel colorless, about length of spore.

Hosts

1. **Turfgrasses**—annual ryegrass (*Lolium multiflorum*).
2. **All Known Gramineous Hosts**—A listing of common names for the following species is given in Appendix Table IV. *Agropyron inerme* (Scribn. and Smith) Rydb., *A. spicatum* (Pursh) Scribn. and Smith, *A. subsecundum* (Link) Hitchc., *A. trachycaulum* (Link) Malte, *Elymus condensatus* Presl, *E. triticoides* Buckl., *Lolium multiflorum* Lam., *Sitanion jubatum* J. G. Smith (Arthur, 1929; Index Plant Dis., 1960).
3. **Alternate Host**—*Brodiaea douglasii* Wats. (Arthur, 1929).

The Fungi

H. *Puccinia piperi* Ricker

Description

Uredia amphigenous, cinnamon brown; urediospores globoid or ellipsoid, 15–18 μm × 21–26 μm; wall pale- or brownish yellow, 1.5–2 μm thick, finely echinulate, the pores 8–10, scattered. Telia hypophyllous, long covered by epidermis, surrounded by thin layer of brown subepidermal paraphyses; teliospores oblong or oblong-clavate, 19–26 μm × 42–62 μm, rounded or tuncate above, usually narrowed below, slightly constricted at septum; wall dark chestnut brown, 1.5–2.5 μm thick at sides, twice as thick above, frequently with a few longitudinal angles, giving a striate appearance; pedicel colorless, 1–1½ the length of the spore. Monospores common. Pycnia and aecia unknown.

Hosts

1. **Turfgrasses**—tall fescue (*Festuca arundinacea*).
2. **All Known Gramineous Hosts**—A listing of common names for the following species is given in Appendix Table IV. *Festuca arundinacea* Schreb., *F. megalura* Nutt., *F. octoflora* Walt., *F. pacifica* Piper, *F. reflexa* Buckl. (Arthur, 1929, Index Plant Dis., 1960).

The Fungi

I. *Puccinia poae-sudeticae* (Westend.) Jorstad

Description

Uredia chiefly epiphyllous, orange yellow, with numerous peripheral paraphyses, variously bent and incurved, mostly capitate with narrow neck and linear-clavate pedicel; urediospores globoid or ellipsoid, 18–24 μm × 21–29 μm; wall nearly colorless, 1.5–2 μm thick, finely verrucochinulate, the pores about 8, scattered, often obscure. Telia hypophyllous, long covered by the epidermis, with subepidermal paraphyses; teliospores oblong or clavate, 18–25 μm × 39–55 μm, obtuse or rounded above, somewhat narrowed below, slightly or not constricted at septum; wall chestnut brown, 1.5 μm thick at sides, 3–6 μm above; pedicel tinted, short. Pycnia and aecia unknown.

Hosts

1. **Turfgrasses**—annual bluegrass (*Poa annua*) and Kentucky bluegrass (*Poa pratensis*).
2. **All Known Gramineous Hosts**—A listing of common names for the following species is given in Appendix Table IV. *Alopecurus aequalis* Sobol., *A. alpinus* J. G. Smith, *Anthoxanthum odoratum* L., Catabrosa aquatica (L.) Beauv., *Deschampsia caespitosa* (L.) Beauv., *Eragrostis refracta* (Muhl.) Scribn., *Festuca arundinacea* Schreb., *Phleum alpinum* L., *Poa alpina* L., *P. ampla* Merr., *P. annua* L., *P. arachnifera* Torr., *P. arida* Vasey, *P. bigelovii* Vasey and Scribn., *P. canbyi* (Scribn.) Piper, *P. compressa*, L., *P. fendleriana* (Steud.) Vasey, *P. interior* Rydb., *P. macrantha* Vasey, *P. nemoralis* L., *P. nervosa* (Hook.) Vasey, *P. palustris* L., *P. pratensis* L., *P. trivialis* L., *P. vaseyochloa* Scribn., *Trisetum spicatum* (L.) Richt. (Arthur, 1929; Index Plant Dis., 1960).

The Fungi

J. *Puccinia rubigo-vera* (DC.) Wint. f. sp. *agropyri* Erikss.

Description

Uredia usually amphigenous, cinnamon brown, with few or no colorless paraphyses; urediospores globoid or broadly ellipsoid, 13–24 μm × 16–32 μm; wall pale cinnamon or yellowish, 1–2 μm thick, finely echinulate, the pores 6–8, sometimes 4–6, scattered, usually distinct. Telia chiefly hypophyllous, oblong, scattered, long covered by epidermis, with thin layers of dark brown subepidermal paraphyses; teliospores oblong, clavate or cylindric 13–24 μm × 32–65 μm, or on some hosts 10–18 μm × 26–45 μm, rounded or truncate above, narrowed below, usually not constricted at septum; wall chestnut brown paler below, 1 μm or less thick at sides, 3–7 μm above; pedicel colored, very short.

Hosts

1. **Turfgrasses**—Kentucky bluegrass (*Poa pratensis*), red fescue (*Festuca rubra*) and tall fescue (*Festuca arundinacea*).
2. **All Known Gramineous Hosts**—A listing of common names for the following species is given in Appendix Table IV. *Aegilops cylindrica* Host, Agropyron *caninum* (L.) Beauv., *A. dasystachyum* (Hook.) Scribn., *A. saxicola* (Scribn. and Smith) Piper, *A. smithii* Rydb., *A. spicatum* (Pursh) Scribn. and Smith, *A. trachycaulum* (Link) Malte, *Agrostis alba* L., *A. hiemalis* (Walt.) B. S. P., *A. perennans* (Walt.) Tuckerm., *Alopecurus aequalis* Sobol., *A. geniculatus* L., *Avena barbata* Brot., *A. fatua* L., *A. sativa* L., *Bromus anomalus* Rupr., *B. anomalus* var. *lanatipes* (Shear) Hitchc., *B. breviaristatus* Buckl., *B. carinatus* Hook. and Arn., *B. catharticus* Vahl, *B. ciliatus* L., *B. commutatus* Schrad., *B. grandis* (Shear) Hitchc., *B. japonicus* Thunb., *B. madritensis* L., *B. marginatus* Nees, *B. mollis* L., *B. polyanthus* Scribn., *B. pumpellianus* Scribn., *B. purgans* L., *B. racemosus* L., *B. rigidus* Roth, *B. rigidus* var. *gussonei* (Parl.) Coss. and Dur., *B. rubens* L., *B. scoparius* L., *B. secalinus* L., *B. sitchensis* Trin., *B. sterilis* L., *B. tectorum* L., *B. trinii* Desv., *Cinna arundinacea* L., *C. latifolia* (Trevir.) Griseb., *Dactylis glomerata* L., *Elymus ambiguus* Vasey and Scribn., *E. arenarius* L., *E. arenicola* Scribn. and Smith, *E. canadensis* L., *E. canadensis* var. *brachystachys* (Scribn. and Ball) Farwell, *E. condensatus* Presl, *E. excelsus* Turcz., *E. glaucus* Buckl., *E. mollis* Trin., *E. triticoides* Buckl., *E. vancouverensis* Vasey, *E. virescens* Piper,

E. virginicus L., *Festuca arundinacea* Schreb., *F. rubra* L., *F. scabrella* Torr., *Fluminea festucacea* (Willd.) Hitchc., *Glyceria grandis* S. Wats., *Holcus lanatus* L., *Melica geyeri* Munro, *Poa ampla* Merr., *P. annua* L., *P. arida* Vasey, *P. bigelovii* Vasey and Scribn., *P. canbyi* (Scribn.) Piper, *P. fendleriana* (Steud.) Vasey, *P. interior* Rydb., *P. juncifolia* Scribn., *P. nervosa* (Hook.) Vasey, *P. nevadensis* Vasey, *P. palustris* L., *P. pratensis* L., *P. scabrella* (Thurb.) Benth., *P. secunda* Presl, *Puccinellia airoides* (Nutt.) Wats. and Coult., *P. nuttalliana* (Schult.) Hitchc., *Secale cereale* L., *S. montanum* Guss., *Sitanion hystrix* (Nutt.) J. G. Smith, *S. jubatum* J. G. Smith, *Trisetum montanum* Vasey, *T. spicatum* (L.) Richt., *Triticum aestivum* L., *T. dicoccoides* Koern., *T. dicoccum* Schrank, *T. monococcum* L., *T. polonicum* L., *T. spelta* L., *T. turgidum* L. (Arthur, 1929; Index Plant Dis., 1960).

3. **Alternate Hosts**—*Aconitum delphinifolium* D.C., *Actea alga* (L.) Mill., *A. arguta* Nutt., *Anemone piperi* Britt., *Aquilegia coerulea* James, *A. elegantula* Greene, *A. flavescens* Wats., *A. formosa* Fisch., *A. laramiensia* Nels., *A. truncata* Fisch. and Mey., *Clematis lasiantha* Nutt., *C. ligusticifolia* Nutt., *C. pauciflora* Nutt., *Delphinium bicolor* Nutt., *D. cucullatum* Nels., *D. depauperatum* Nutt., *D. geraniifolium* Rydb., *D. geveri* Greene, *D. glaucescens* Rydb., *D. nelsoni* Greene, *D. occidentale* Wats., *D. reticulatum* Nells., *D. robustum* Rydb., *Rannunculus aleophilus* Nels., *R. californicus* Benth., *R. cymbalaris* Pursch., *R. glaberrimus* Hook., *R. occidentalis* Nutt., *Thalictrum alpinum* L., *T. fendleri* Engelm., *T. occidnetale* Gray, *T. sparsiflorum* Turcz., *Virona hirsutissima* (Pursh.) Heller, *V. jonseii* (Ktze.) Rydb., *V. scotii* (Porter) Rydb. (Arthur, 1929).

The Fungi

K. *Puccinia zoysiae* Diet.

Description

Uredia without paraphyses. Urediospores verrucose; 15 to 17 μm; wall hyaline to yellowish, 2 to 2.5 μm thick; pores equatorial, 5 to 7. Telia exposed; teliospores chestnut brown; side walls 2 to 3 μm thick; apical wall 4 to 6 μm thick; pedicel 100 μm long; 16–21 μm × 28 to 42 μm.

Hosts

1. **Turfgrass**—manilagrass (*Zoysia matrella*), zoysiagrass (*Zoysia japonica*) and emerald zoysia (*Zoysia tenuifolia* × *Zoysia japonica*).

2. **All Known Gramineous Hosts**—A listing of common names for the following species is given in Appendix Table IV. *Zoysia japonica* Steud., *Z. matrella* (L.) Merr., *Z. pungens* Willd., *Z. tenuifolia* Willd., *Z. tenuifolia* × *Z. japonica* (Freeman, 1965; Gough and McDaniel, 1969; Gudauskas and McCarter, 1966; Holcomb and Motsinger, 1967; Kozelnicky and Garrett, 1966; Kreitlow, Juska and Haard, 1965; Tucker and Dale, 1967).

3. **Alternate Host**—*Paederia chinensis*.

The Fungi

L. *Uromyces dactylidis* Otth.

Description

Uredia and telia as in *P. rubigo-vera*, except the teliospores are one-celled, obovate, 15–19 μm × 24–29 μm, usually surrounded by abundant subepidermal paraphyses; wall 1.5 μm thick at sides, 3–4 μm above.

Hosts

1. **Turfgrass**—Kentucky bluegrass (*Poa pratensis*).

2. **All Known Gramineous Hosts**—A listing of common names for the following species is given in Appendix Table IV. *Dactylis glomerata* L., *Poa palustris* L., *P. pratensis* L., *P. scabrella* (Thurb.) Benth., *P. secunda* Presl, *P. trivialis* L. (Arthur, 1929).

3. **Alternate Host**—*Rannunculus repens* L. (Arthur, 1929).

The Fungi

M. *Uromyces jacksonii* A. and F.

Description

Uredia amphigneous, tardily dehiscent by slit in the epidermis, yellow, without paraphyses; urediospores globoid or broadly ellipsoid, 21–27 μm × 24–30 μm; wall pale yellow, 1.5–2 μm thick, finely echinulate, the pores 6–8, scattered. Telia amphigenous, long covered by the epidermis, blackish; teliospores angularly globoid or ellipsoid, 19–25 μm × 20–30 μm; wall light chestnut brown, uniformly 1.5 μm thick; pedicel colorless, about half the length of the spore. Pycnia and aecia unknown.

Hosts

1. **Turfgrass**—creeping bentgrass (*Agrostis palustris*).

2. **All Known Gramineous Hosts**—A listing of common names for each of the following species is given in Appendix Table IV. *Agrostis alba* L., *A. hallii* Vasey, *A. pallens* Trin., *A. palustris* Huds., *Deschampsia caespitosa* (L.) Beauv., *D. danthonioides* (Trin.) Munro ex benth., *D. elongata* (Hook.) Munro ex benth., *Hordeum brachyantherum* Nevski, *H. jubatum* L., *Scribneria bolanderi* (Thurb.) Hack. (Arthur, 1929; Index Plant Dis. 1960).

Disease Profile

The pattern of development for this group of diseases is highly complex due to the fact that of the 13 species of rust fungi reported parasitizing turfgrasses, all but 3 (*Puccinia piperi*, *Puccinnia poae-sudeticae*, and *Uromyces jacksonii*) go through 5 morphologically distinct spore stages. The matter is further complicated in that for the same rust species, host specificity of the various spore types may involve both grasses and woody shrubs, or grasses and herbaceous ornamental plants.

Since the development cycle of all the 5-spore-stage, alternate-host rusts on turfgrasses is for general illustrative purposes practically the same, and since the rust species (*Puccinia graminis* f. sp. *agrostis*) parasitizing the Merion variety of Kentucky bluegrass (*Poa pratensis*) incites the most important disease of the group (Britton and Cummins, 1959), the cycle for this species will be used in the following description.

The pathogen overwinters as dormant mycelium in diseased turfgrass plants and as teliospores (Figure 6-2, 1). Survival as dormant mycelium in the crowns of infected plants is more common in regions characterized by mild winters of short duration. In the more northern areas, however, during years of less severe winter months, dormant mycelium may serve as the primary source of inoculum the following growing season.

In the case of survival as teliospores, in early spring these spores germinate and produce the next spore stage—basidiospores (Figure 6-2, 2). The basidiospores are carried by wind to the alternate host

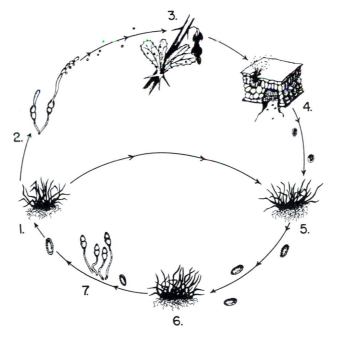

Figure 6-2.   Cycle of development of rust (*Puccinia graminis* f. sp. *agrostis*) on 'Merion' Kentucky bluegrass (*Poa pratensis*). (1) The pathogen overwinters as dormant mycelium in colonized plant tissue as teliospores. (2) In the spring, the teliospores germinate to produce basidiospores. (3) The basidiospores are carried by wind to barberry plants, where they germinate and infect and colcnize the tissue of the upper portions of the leaves. (4) From these primary infections, pycnia, bearing pycniospores, are produced. After fusion of pycnial strains of opposite sex, aecia, bearing aeciospores, are produced on the lower surfaces of the barberry leaves. (5) The aeciospores are carried by wind to bluegrass plants, where they germinate and infect the leaves. From these primary points of infection and colonization, or from overwintering mycelium in plants that had been infected and colonized earlier, uredinia, bearing urediospores, are produced. (6) The urediospores are wind-disseminated to other grass plants, and thus serve to increase the incidence of the disease. (7) In late fall and early winter, teliospores are produced on the leaves of rust-colonized bluegrass plants.

(*Berberis* spp.), where, under favorable environmental conditions, they germinate and infect the upper surfaces of the leaves (Figure 6-2, 3). From these primary infections, pycnia, bearing the next spore stage—pycniospores, are produced (Figure 6-2, 4). The pycnia serve as the "male" and "female" components of the developmental stages of the fungus. When the nucleus of one sex type migrates into the cell of an opposite sex type, a more vigorous growing, binucleate, mycelium is produced. At this stage of development, new genic material may be introduced that will increase, or decrease, the pathogenic capabilities of the pathogen. Since the seed of Merion Kentucky bluegrass is produced asexually (by apogamy), the rust disease on this variety is rather unique in that the pathogen may be hybridized, but not the host.

This more vigorous-growing mycelium masses on the lower side of the barberry leaf and produces aecia ("cluster cups"), bearing the next spore stage—aeciospores (Figure 6-2, 4). These spores are not able to infect barberry. Disseminated by wind, they are usually spread only for very short distances. When they come in contact with the leaves of a suitable grass host species, infections occur, and the uredinia, bearing urediospores, the next spore stage, are produced (Figure 6-2, 5). The urediospores ("repeating spores") infect only the grass host, and serve to increase the incidence of the disease (Figure 6-2, 6). Wind disseminated, they may be carried for great distances from the point of origin. In late fall and early winter, teliospores are produced on the leaves of the turfgrass host, and the cycle is complete (Figure 6-2, 7).

Urediospore penetration of the leaves of the grass host is by growth of the germ tubes through open stomates. After entry into the substomatal chamber, the hyphae form a mass of mycelium. From this mass, hyphal growth is initiated. When the tip of the hypha comes in contact with the cell wall, it swells and is separated from the rest of the hypha by a newly formed cell wall. Thus is formed the haustorial mother cell. Penetration of the cell wall of the host is accomplished by a combination of mechanical pressure and enzymatic activity. After penetration of the host cell wall, the specialized absorption structure (haustorium) forms. As the haustorium enlarges, it invaginates the protoplast without rupturing the plasma membrane; thereby, forming a delicately balanced contact with the host (Figure 3-3, C).

After the successful establishment of the fungus, uredinial mycelial growth continues throughout the immediate infection site, and, with the massing of this mycelium, the fruiting bodies (uredinia) begin forming. Simultaneously, hyphal growth proceeds intercellularly to unaffected areas distant from the zone of primary infection. These cells are then parasitized in the manner described above, and new centers of sporulation are produced.

Successful establishment of *Puccinia graminis* in epiphytotic proportions requires two sets of environmental conditions. The optimum prepenetration environment is a 4 to 8 hour period of (a) low light intensity, (b) air temperatures in the 70–75 °F (21–24 °C) range, and (c) high atmospheric humidity. With entry into the stomatal chamber accomplished, the optimum environmental combination for successful penetration of the host cell wall is a 8 to 16 hour period of (a) high light intensity, (b) air temperatures in the 85–95 °F (30–35 °C) range, and (c) a slow drying of the leaf surfaces (Rowell, Olien and Wilcoxson, 1958; Sharp *et al.*, 1958).

The incidence and severity of colonization of Kentucky bluegrass (*Poa pratensis*) by *Puccinia graminis* is higher when the plants are grown at low nitrogen fertilization combined with high soil moisture stress (Cheeseman, Roberts and Tifany, 1965). Also, crown rust (*Puccinia coronata*) colonization of perennial ryegrass (*Lolium perenne*) has been found to be more severe when the plants are grown at low nitrogen levels (Couch and Joyner, 1976; Lancashire and Latch, 1966).

Control

Cultural Practices

A management program that brings about a reduction in the incidence and severity of rust is one that includes collection and removal of leaf clippings (Kozelnicky and Garrett, 1966; Paris, 1971), provides irrigations with short enough intervening time intervals to hold the soil in the root zone near field capacity levels, and maintains an adequate level of nitrogen fertilization.

Management practices that decrease the length of time the leaves are wet will also aid in decreasing the incidence of rust. The duration of the periods of daily leaf wetness can also be reduced by two to four hours by following a nighttime watering schedule in which the irrigation system is set to begin at least three hours after sunset and programmed to be completed before sunrise (see Chapter 16, Figure 16-2).

Use of Resistant Grasses

The comparative susceptibility of cultivars of Kentucky bluegrass (*Poa pratensis*) to *Puccinia graminis* is given in Table 6-1.

Table 6-1. Comparative susceptibility of cultivars of Kentucky bluegrass to *Puccinia graminis. After Watkins et al., 1981.*

Most Resistant		Intermediate	Most Susceptible
Park	Galaxy	Fanfare	Plus
Baniff	Bonnieblue	Newport	Bono
NuDwarf	Nugget	Fylking	Bensun
Delta	Sydsport	Bristol	Enprima
Baron	Glade	Emmundi	Entopper
South Dakota	Majestic	Cougar	Merion
Adelphi		Enoble	Vantage
Aquila		Victa	
Parade		Pennstar	
Geary		Touchdown	
Enita		Birka	
Rugby		Cheri	

The fine-leafed perennial ryegrasses are highly susceptible to *Puccinia coronata.* With bermudagrass, the variety Sunturf is highly susceptible to *Puccinia graminis.* In Florida, Meyer zoysia (*Zoysia japonica*) and Emerald zoysia (*Zoysia japonica* × *Zoysia tenuifolia*) have been reported to be more susceptible to *Puccinai zoysiae* than manillagrass (*Zoysia matrella*) (Freeman, 1965). In Alabama, however, these 3 species were reported to be equally susceptible to the pathogen (Gudauskas and McCarter, 1966).

Use of Fungicides

Control of rust can be accomplished by applications of either propiconazole, triadimefon, or mancozeb. For a profile of these fungicides and a listing of representative manufacturers, see Appendix Table I.

LEAF SMUTS

The leaf smuts are world-wide in distribution. They are destructive to both cool season and warm season turfgrasses. Their effect on the plant includes overall growth retardation and the shredding and death of leaves. Plants colonized by the leaf smut fungi recover more slowly from mowing and wear, are less capable of responding to high adverse environmental conditions, and are predisposed to infection and colonization by other microorganisms.

Stripe Smut

Symptoms

Turfgrass plants colonized by the stripe smut fungus usually make slow vegetative growth. In ad-

dition, the inflorescences may be stunted or entirely absent. Long, yellow-green streaks develop on the leaves of the affected plants, and as the disease progresses, these streaks become gray in color. In the final stages of disease development, the cuticle and epidermal cells covering these streaks are ruptured—exposing the underlying, black spore masses of the pathogen. With this, the leaves split into ribbons and curl from the tips downward. The leaf blades then turn light brown, wither, and die (Plate 26-B, C, D, E). In field diagnoses, the disease may be confused with flag smut. Because of the close similarity of the field signs and symptoms of stripe smut and flag smut, positive differentiation between the two requires a microscope-aided examination of the chlamydospores (Halisky, Bachelder and Funk, 1966).

Symptom expression is more readily apparent in late spring and early fall. Plants that have been growing at 90 °F (32 °C) for prolonged periods usually do not show symptoms. On the other hand, extended periods of air temperatures in the 50–60 °F (10–15 °C) range are very conducive to symptom expression (Kozelnicky, 1969; Kreitlow, 1943).

The Fungus

Ustilago striiformis (Westend.) Niessl.

Description

Chlamydospores mostly globose to subglobose or ellipsoid, dark olive brown, more or less prominently echinulate, 9–11 μm in diameter (Figure 6-3).

Procedures for Isolation and Culture

In culture, the organism grows well on oat meal agar at 21–24 °C. On this medium, viable chlamydospores are produced in great abundance (Leach, Lowther and Ryan, 1946).

Hosts

1. **Turfgrasses**—Colonial bentgrass (*Agrostis tenuis*), creeping bentgrass (*Agrostis palustris*), annual bluegrass (*Poa annua*), Kentucky bluegrass (*Poa pratensis*), sheep fescue (*Festuca ovina*), hard fescue (*Festuca ovina* var. *brachyphylla*), perennial ryegrass (*Lolium perenne*),
2. **All Known Gramineous Hosts**—A listing of common names for the following species is given in Appendix Table IV. *Agropyron caninum* (L.) Beauv., *A. cristatum* (L.) Gaertn., *A. dasystachyum* (Hook.) Scribn., *A. inerme* (Scribn. and Smith) Rydb., *A. repens* (L.) Beauv., *A. sibiricum* (Willd.) Beauv., *A. smithii* Rydb., *A. spicatum*

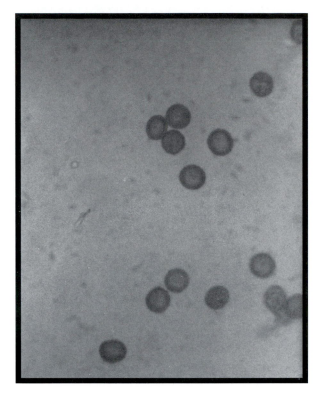

Figure 6-3. Chlamydospores of *Ustilago striiformis.*

(Pursh) Scribn. and Smith, *A. striatum* Nees, *A. subsecundum* (Link) Hitchc., *A. trachycaulum* (Link) Malte, *Agrostis alba* L., *A. castellana* Boiss. and Reut., *A. exarata* Trin., *A. humilis* Vasey, *A. microphylla* Steud., *A. palustris* Huds., *A. perennans* (Walt.) Tuckerm., *A. rossae* Vasey, *A. scabra* Willd., *A. stolonifera* L., *A. tenuis* Sibth., *Ammophila arenaria* (L.) Link, *A. breviligulata* Fernald, *Andropogon virginicus* L., *Beckmannia syzigachne* (Steud.) Fernald, *Bromus ciliatus* L., *B. inermis* Leyss., *Calamagrostis canadensis* (Michx.) Beauv., *C. montanensis* Scribn., *C. pickeringii* A. Gray, *C. scribneri* Beal, *Dactylis glomerata* L., *Danthonia intermedia* Vasey, *Deschampsia atropurpurea* (Wahl.) Scheele, *D. caespitosa* (L.) Beauv., *Elymus canadensis* L., *E. condensatus* Presl, *E. glaucus* Buckl., *E. macounii* Vasey, *E. sibiricus* L., *E. triticoides* Buckl., *E. virginicus* L., *Eragrostis refracta* (Muhl.) Scribn., *Festuca arundinacea* Schreb., *F. idahoensis* Elmer, *F. obtusa* Bieler, *F. occidentalis* Hook., *F. ovina* L., *F. ovina* var. *brachyphylla* (Schult.) Piper, *F. thurberi* Vasey, *Holcus lanatus* L., *Hordeum jubatum* L., *Hystrix patula* Moench, *Koeleria cristata* (L.) Pers., *Lolium perenne* L., *Melica spectabilis* Scribn., *Phalaris arundinacea* L., *Phleum alpinum* L., *P. pratense* L., *Poa alpina* L., *P. annua* L., *P. arctica* R. Br., *P.*

canbyi (Scribn.) Piper, *P. compressa* L., *P. curtifolia* Scribn., *P. juncifolia* Scribn., *P. longifolia* Trin., *P. palustris* L., *P. pratensis* L., *P. secunda* Presl., *P. trivialis* L., *Puccinellia airoides* (Nutt.) Wats. and Coult, *P. nuttalliana* (Schult.) Hitchc., *Sitanion hystrix* (Nutt.) J. G. Smith, *S. jubatum* J. G. Smith, *Trisetum spicatum* (L.) Richt. (Fischer, 1953; Index Plant Dis., 1960).

Disease Profile

The stripe smut fungus survives winter months as dormant mycelium in diseased plants and as chlamydospores in the thatch or on seed. After production, the chlamydospores of some races of *Ustilago striiformis* undergo an after ripening dormancy for a period up to 265 days—others are able to germinate immediately (Fischer, 1940; Krietlow, 1947; Kreitlow, Juska and Haard, 1965).

The chlamydospores resume growth under soil conditions favorable for the development of turfgrass seedlings. The chlamydospores germinate to produce promycelia. On the promycelia are borne sporidia, which, in turn, germinate to produce germ tubes. When the individual germ tubes come in contact with germ tubes of opposite sex strains, they fuse, and following nuclear migration to produce a dicaryotic condition, an infection thread develops which is then capable of penetrating the host.

Infection of young turfgrass seedlings occurs through coleoptiles, while with older plants, tillers probably serve as the chief avenues of entry of the pathogen (Hodges and Britton, 1969; Leach, Lowther and Ryan, 1946). After penetration has been accomplished, the mycelium grows systemically throughout the host.

The pattern of colonization within Kentucky bluegrass (*Poa pratensis*) is dependent on the site at which infection occurs. Infection of the coleoptile will lead to a colonization of the primary crown. In highly susceptible hosts, all new growth from this crown will be colonized by the fungus. When infection of axillary buds on rhizomes or stolons occurs, the crowns that develop from these sites will be permeated by the mycelium. However, if infection of an axillary bud on an existing crown occurs, then the mycelium does not enter the crown tissue. Instead, it only invades the organs that develop from that bud (Hodges and Britton, 1970; Hodges, 1976b).

The production of the various growth forms of the pathogen and the degree of mycelial movement from colonized creeping bentgrass (*Agrostis palustris*) stolons into axillary buds and then into the developing leaves is directly related to air temperature. When the day-night air temperatures are in the 45–55 °F (7–13 °C) range, the fungus will continue to grow in the developing stolons, but very few chlamydospores are formed. At temperatures of 60–70 °F (15–21 °C), the growth rate of the fungus in the stolons and the developing tillers is rapid. When day-night temperatures fall in the 75–78 °F (24–29 °C) range, the leaves and stems are colonized to the extent that the massing chlamydospores force a rupture of the cuticle and epidermal cells—producing the leaf striping effect that is the chief field diagnostic feature of the disease. Finally, when the day-night temperatures reach 90–100 °F (32–38 °C), the tissues remain colonized, but the growth of the fungus is inhibited and the visible symptoms of the disease diminish (Hodges, 1970).

Although spring applications of high rates of nitrogenous fertilizers can bring about a remission of stripe smut symptoms (Lukens, 1966), it has been shown that in the long run this practice actually causes an increase in the intensity of the disease (Halisky, Funk and Bachelder, 1966). The incidence and severity of stripe smut will be lowest in turf receiving adequate rates of balanced fertilizer, and highest in turf that is growing under an imbalance of either nitrogen, phosphorous or potassium (Hull, Jackson and Skogley, 1979).

A very high degree of host specificity has been reported for *Ustilago striiformis*. The form appearing on Kentucky bluegrass (*Poa pratensis*) will not necessarily parasitize creeping bentgrass (*Agrostis palustris*), etc. (Fischer, 1940).

Control

Cultural Practices

Some of the damage caused by stripe smut can be offset by fertilization practices that promote good growth of the affected turf. Applications of high rates of nitrogenous fertilizers should be avoided. Instead, the fertilizer should be a balanced formulation and applied at intervals that provide a uniform rate of growth throughout the season. Stripe smut diseased turf is highly vulnerable to damage from heat and drought stress, therefore, during hot dry weather it is important that particular attention be given to addressing the heightened irrigation needs of the affected area.

Use of Resistant Grasses

The stripe smut organism shows a high degree of pathogenic specialization to both host species and to cultivars within a species. Six distinct subspecies

have been designated within *Ustilago striiformis* based on the grass genera they will parasitize. Only two of these affect turfgrasses—the subspecies *poae*, which only colonizes bluegrasses (*Poa* spp.), and the subspecies *agrostidis*, which only parasitizes bentgrasses, (*Agrostis* spp.) (Thirumalachar and Dickson, 1953; Halisky, Funk and Bachelder, 1966).

The creeping bentgrass (*Agrostis palustris*) varieties, 'Evansville,' 'Seaside,' 'Pennlu,' 'Toronto,' and 'Washington,' have been reported to be highly susceptible to stripe smut (Gaskin, 1965a; Healy, Britton and Butler, 1965).

The comparative susceptibility of nineteen cultivars of Kentucky bluegrass (*Poa pratensis*) to stripe smut is given in Table 6-2. When considering varietal susceptibility to *Ustilago striiformis*, it is important to bear in mind that due to the distribution and predominance of pathogenic strains of the stripe smut organism, the relative susceptibility of cultivars may vary with location (Gaskin, 1965a; Hodges, 1976a; Halisky, Funk and Bachelder, 1966; Kreitlow and Juska, 1959). When establishing Kentucky bluegrass on a site with a known history of stripe smut, then, the use of a seed blend of three to four cultivars will reduce the likelihood of major reduction in overall turf quality by the disease.

Table 6-2. Comparative susceptibility of 19 cultivars of Kentucky bluegrass (*Poa pratensis*) to stripe smut and flag smut. *After Hodges, 1976a.*

Cultivar	Percentage of Smutted Shoots	
	Stripe Smut	Flag Smut
Adelphi	0.2	1.8
Arboretum	3.3	17.2
Arista	1.5	0
Baron	0.9	6.6
Bonnieblue	0.1	9.4
Cougar	0	0.1
Delta	0.1	13.8
Fylking	0.8	52.1
Kenblue	0.1	32.6
Merion	2.6	76.5
Newport	4.4	4.7
Nugget	0	0.7
Olymprisp	49.4	0.3
Park	0.1	22.4
Pennstar	0.2	10.1
Prato	0	49.5
Sodco	0.2	15.8
Sydsport	10.6	2.4
Windsor	2.6	11.4

Use of Fungicides

Control of stripe smut can be accomplished by applications of either cyproconazole, propiconazole, triadimefon, fenarimol, or benomyl (Cole *et al.*, 1978; Halisky, Funk and Babinski, 1969; Jackson and Dernoeden, 1979). A profile of each of these fungicides and a listing of representative manufacturers is given in Appendix Table I.

For optimum results, the fungicide should be applied in either October or in the early spring before grass growth begins. A single application during dormancy of the turf will usually contain the disease during the growing season. However, if fungicidal treatment is initiated during the growing season, then repeated applications may be required in order to maintain a satisfactory level of stripe smut control.

Flag Smut

Symptoms

Turfgrass plants affected with flag smut may be noticeably retarded in rate of vegetative growth. In addition to being stunted, diseased plants are sometimes distorted due to the malformation of leaves. Early leaf lesion symptoms are evident as gray to grayish black streaks in the leaf blades and leaf sheaths. In field diagnoses, the disease may be confused with stripe smut. As with stripe smut, the sori are covered by the cuticle and epidermal cells in early stages of disease development, but ultimately the epidermis ruptures, releasing the dark brown to black spore masses and causing the leaves to become shredded (Niehaus, 1968). Because of the close similarity of the field signs and symptoms of flag smut and stripe smut, positive differentiation between the two requires a microscope-aided examination of the chlamydospores (Halisky, Funk and Bachelder, 1966).

The Fungus

Urocystis agropyri (Preuss) Schrot.; syn. *Ustilago festucae* Ule, *Ustilago poae* (Liro) Padw., *Ustilago tritici* Korn.

Description

Spore balls globose to elongate, mostly 18–35 μm × 35–40 μm, composed of 1–16 spores and a completely investing cortex of hyaline to brownish, smaller, sterile cells. Spores globose to subglobose, dark reddish-brown to olivaceous brown, smooth, 12–18 μm in diameter (Figure 6-4).

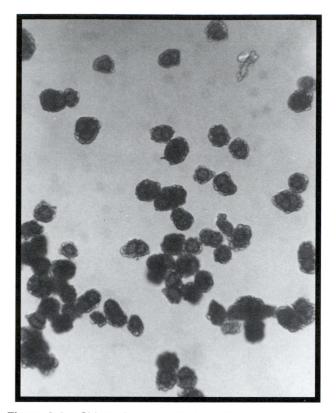

Figure 6-4. Chlamydospores of *Urocystis agropyri.*

Procedures for Isolation and Culture

In culture, the organism grows on either potato dextrose agar or malt extract agar at 21–24 °C (Thirumalachar and Dickson, 1949).

Hosts

1. **Turfgrasses**—Colonial bentgrass (*Agrostis tenuis*), creeping bentgrass (*Agrostis palustris*), Kentucky bluegrass (*Poa pratensis*), red fescue (*Festuca rubra*).
2. **All Known Gramineous Hosts**—A listing of common names for the following species is given in Appendix Table IV. *Agropyron inerme* (Scribn. and Smith) Rydb., *A. repens* (L.) Beauv., *A. smithii* Rydb., *A. spicatum* (Pursh) Scribn. and Smith, *A. subsecundum* var. *andunum* (Scribn. and Smith) Hitchc., *A. trachycaulum* (Link) Malte, *Agrostis alba* L., *A. palustris* Huds., *A. tenuis* Sibth., *Bromus carinatus* Hook. and Arn., *B. ciliatus* L., *B. marginatus* Nees, *Calamagrostis canadensis* (Michx.) Beauv., *Dactylis glomerata* L., *Elymus aristatus* Merr., *E. canadensis* L., *E. canadensis* var. *robustus* (Scribn. and Smith) Mackenz. and Bush, *E. cinereus* Scribn. and Merr., *E. condensatus* Presl, *E. glaucus* Buckl., *E. virginicus* L.,

Festuca rubra L., *Glyceria striata* (Lam.) Hitchc., *Hesperochloa kingii* (S. Wats.) Rydb., *Hordeum brachyantherum* Nevski, *H. jubatum* L., *H. nodosum* L., *Koeleria cristata* (L.) Pers., *Melica imperfecta* Trin., *Phleum alpinum* L., *P. pratense* L., *Poa ampla* Merr., *P. canbyi* (Scribn.) Piper, *P. nervosa* (Hook.) Vasey, *P. pratensis* L., *P. secunda* Presl, *Sitanion jubatum* J. G. Smith, *Trisetum spicatum* (L.) Richt., *Triticum aestivum* L., (Fischer, 1953; Index Plant Dis., 1960).

Disease Profile

Urocystis agropyri survives the adverse winter season as dormant mycelium in diseased plants and as chlamydospores in the soil or on seed. The chlamydospores germinate concurrently with the seed to produce promycelia. Sporidia are borne on the promycelia, which in turn, germinate to produce germ tubes. When the individual germ tubes of one sexual strain contact those of opposite sex factors, they fuse and dicaryotic infection threads are formed. These infection threads are capable of penetrating the coleoptiles of developing seedlings or underground lateral buds of mature turfgrass plants. In the host, the pathogen is systemic. Eventually, the leaves and stems are colonized, and the sori are produced that ultimately erupt to produce the chief field diagnostic feature of the disease (Griffiths, 1924, Noble, 1923).

Soil moisture and soil temperatures have a pronounced effect on the development of flag smut. With low soil moisture levels, infection occurs from 50–68 °F (10–15 °C) range, while at points near saturation capacity, the optimum temperature for infection is 50 °F (10 °C) (Faris, 1933).

Control

Cultural Practices

The impact of cultural practices on the development of flag smut has not been documented. However, as is the case with stripe smut some of the damage caused by this disease can be offset by fertilization practices that promote good growth of the affected turf. Applications of high rates of nitrogenous fertilizers should be avoided. Instead, the fertilizer should be a balanced formulation and applied at intervals that provide a uniform rate of growth throughout the season. Flag smut diseased turf is also highly vulnerable to damage from heat and drought stress; therefore, during hot dry weather it is important that particular attention be given to addressing the heightened irrigation needs of the affected area.

Use of Resistant Grasses

Urocystis agropyri shows a high degree of pathogenic specialization (Fischer and Holton, 1957). A wide range in susceptibility to the organism is known to exist among clones and cultivars of Kentucky bluegrass (*Poa pratensis*) (Gaskin, 1965c; Hodges 1976a). The relative susceptibility of nineteen cultivars to flag smut is given in Table 6-2.

Use of Fungicides

Control of flag smut can be accomplished by applications of either propiconazole, triadimefon, fenarimol, or benomyl (Cole *et al.*, 1978; Halisky, Funk and Babinski, 1969; Jackson and Dernoeden, 1979). A profile of each of these fungicides and a listing of representative manufacturers is given in Appendix Table I.

For optimum results, the fungicide should be applied in either October or in the early spring before grass growth begins. A single application during dormancy of the turf will usually contain the disease during the growing season. However, if fungicidal treatment is initiated during the growing season, then repeated applications may be required in order to maintain a satisfactory level of flag smut control.

Blister Smut

Symptoms

Lesions first appear as numerous spots of water-soaked tissue on lower surface of the leaves. These areas develop into gray black, angular to oblong blister-like spots. The individual lesions may be surrounded with a halo of chlorotic tissue, which in turn gives the turf an overall yellowish cast. Blister smut is most common on leaf blades but may also occur on the sheaths, and still less frequently, on the floral bracts of affected turfgrass plants. Unlike stripe smut and flag smut, the epidermis of the host remains intact over the developing masses of chlamydospores, thus creating the characteristic "blister" effect.

The Fungus

Entyloma dactylidis (Pass.) Cif.; syn. *Entyloma crastophylum* Sacc., *Entyloma irregulare* Johans., *Entyloma oryzae* Syd.

Description

Spores subglobose, oblong, polyhedral, to irregular, tending to adhere in irregular groups and diffi-

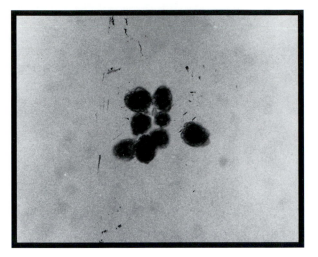

Figure 6-5. Chlamydospores of *Entyloma dactylidis*.

cult to separate, light olivaceous brown to dark smoky brown, 7–11 μm × 8–17 μm; exospore smooth, without a sheath (Figure 6-5).

Hosts

1. **Turfgrasses**—annual bluegrass (*Poa annua*), Kentucky bluegrass (*Poa pratensis*).

2. **All Known Gramenious Hosts**—A listing of common names for the following species is given in Appendix Table IV. *Agrostis alba* L., *A. semiverticillata* (Forsk.) C. Christ., *Glyceria pallida* (Torr.) Trin., *Holcus lanatus* L., *Leptoloma cognatum* (Schult.) Chase, *Muhlenbergia mexicana* (L.) Trin., *Oryza sativa* L., *Panicum dichotomiflorum* Michx., *Phleum pratense* L., *Poa annua* L., *P. canbyi* (Scribn.) Piper, *P. compressa* L., *P. juncifolia* Scribn., *P. nevadensis* Vasey, *P. pratensis* L., *P. secunda* Presl, *P. vaseyochloa* Scribn., *Zizania aquatica* L. (Fischer, 1953).

Control

Use of Resistant Grasses

In field tests involving twelve Kentucky bluegrass (*Poa pratensis*) cultivars, 'Adorno,' 'Cougar,' 'Delft,' 'Enporo,' 'Fylking,' 'Majestic,' 'Merion,' and 'Nugget' were found to be most resistant to blister smut, and 'Baron,' 'Galaxy,' 'Parade,' and 'Victa' most susceptible (Fushtey and Taylor, 1977; Gould, Brauen and Goss, 1977).

Use of Fungicides

There are no reports of fungicidal control of blister smut.

§ § §

7

Senectopathic Disorders

The tissues of the various organs of turfgrass plants follow set patterns of growth and development as they progress from juvenility to maturity, and finally into senescence.[1] Leaves undergo rapid and massive cell replication during their juvenile growth stage. As they emerge from the whorls, cuticles are formed and waxes are deposited on their surface. When the expansion process slows, the mesophyll cells begin to produce nutrients for use by other plant parts. This is the mature state of the leaf.

With increasing age, the processes of senescence begin. As senescence progresses, there is a decline in the chlorophyll content of the leaf. Also, the respiratory rate decreases, there is a drop in fresh and dry weights, the leaf becomes smaller, the amount of free fatty acids increases, and there is general decline in the quality of protein. Where physical characteristics of the leaf are concerned, in their green and yellow green stages, the cells are turgid, yellow leaves are flaccid, and brown leaves are parchment-like. The basic semipermeability of plasma membranes is maintained until late senescence, at which point it decreases. The cuticles of older leaves are thinner and frequently have a high number of rifts or cracks that extend to the underlying epidermal cell wall. Once the shift to senescence has been initiated in the leaf mesophyll the changes that are set in motion are irreversible and the death of these cells is imminent (Figure 7-1) (Anderson and Rowen, 1965; Muchovej, 1986; Osborne, 1959).

When set within the normal growth cycle of the turfgrass plant, senescence of leaves does not have a strong impact on the quality of the turf. This is due to the fact that during the time the metabolism of the older leaves is changing, new leaves are being formed. As the result, any negative effect the death of earlier formed leaves might have had on either the total well being of the plant or the overall appearance of the turf is counteracted. However, if a high percentage of

leaves in a dense stand of turfgrass shifts into senescence simultaneously, a significant deterioration in turf quality will result.

There are certain biotic and abiotic factors which can induce premature senescence in the leaves and crowns of turfgrass plants. These include (a) the pathogenic effects of parasitic fungi, insects, and root feeding nematodes, (b) high air temperatures, (c) high soil temperatures, (d) low light intensity, (e) high soil moisture stress, (f) anaerobic soil conditions, (g) nutrient excesses, (h) nutrient deficiencies, (i) certain mowing and thatch management practices, and (j) the toxic side effects of pesticides.

The majority of microorganisms that are pathogenic to turfgrasses are capable of infecting and colonizing both juvenile and mature plant tissue; however, there are species that are only pathogenic to senescent tissue. Those that can only incite disease in senescent tissue are referred to as **senectophytes**. Biotically incited diseases that can only develop after plant tissue is in advanced senescence are known as **senectopathic disorders**.

The determination of whether the condition at hand is a senectopathic disorder is essential to the development of an effective control program. If the diagnostic work-up has revealed the presence of a microorganism that is a known pathogen of juvenile and mature plant tissue, and the climatic conditions favor development of the disease it incites, then the application of pesticides for its control is clearly in order. However, since senescence is an irreversible condition that in itself leads to death of the affected tissue, if the disease in question is diagnosed as senectopathic, attempts to control the problem with pesticides will at best be only marginally successful. In order for effective management of the disorder to be realized, the factors that are causing a large percentage of the leaves to become senescent simultaneously must be dealt with.

At present, three senectopathic disorders of turfgrasses have been defined: anthracnose, Curvularia blight, and Leptosphaerulina leaf blight.

---

[1]Senescence from *senescens* (L) meaning to grow old; aging.

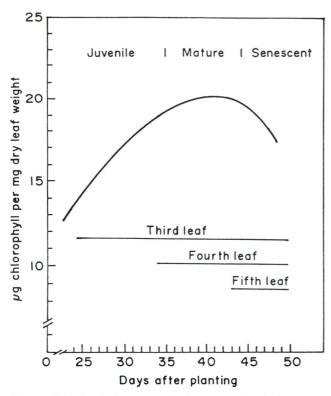

Figure 7-1. Leaf vigor curve for the second leaf of creeping bentgrass (*Agrostis palustris*) plants showing the three stages of vigor: juvenile, mature and senescent. *After Muchovej, 1986.*

Anthracnose

Anthracnose occurs on a wide range of cool season and warm season turfgrasses; however, severe cases of the disorder are limited primarily to annual bluegrass (*Poa annua*), bentgrasses (*Agrostis* spp.), perennial ryegrass (*Lolium perenne*), and red fescue (*Festuca rubra*).

Symptoms

During warm, wet weather the older leaves of annual bluegrass (*Poa annua*) turn yellow and then become tan to brown. Leaf discoloration usually starts at the tip and progresses downward to the sheath; however, under conditions of acute high air temperature stress, the entire leaf yellows uniformly. Numerous, small, raised, black fruiting bodies (acervuli) with spines (setae) protruding from them can be seen on the surfaces of dead leaves with the aid of a magnifying lens (Figure 7-2).

In overall view, the annual bluegrass component of stands comprised of mixtures of turfgrass species develops a yellow green cast which soon fades to

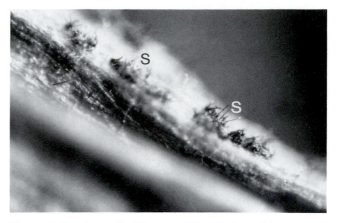

Figure 7-2. Acervuli with setae (S) of *Colletotrichum graminicola* on the surface of a dead annual bluegrass (*Poa annua*) leaf.

yellow, and then becomes brown, giving the turf a blotchy appearance. In dense stands of annual bluegrass, the discoloration and dying out of the turf is more uniform.

During cool wet weather in late spring and early summer, plants affected with anthracnose may develop a basal rot. On annual bluegrass, a dark brown discoloration develops on the bases of leaf sheaths and stems. The leaves then turn yellow, beginning at the tips and progressing down the blades to the sheaths. The older leaves are the first to be affected. The sheath and stem bases eventually turn black and the stems can be easily pulled loose from the crowns. Irregular patches ranging from ½ to 6 inches (1–15 cm) in diameter may develop in dense stands of annual bluegrass. These areas are at first yellow, then brick red, and finally brown.

On bentgrasses, there is a blackening of the sheath and crown tissues that at times extends into the adventitious roots. The older leaves are affected first. Scattered patches may form that are irregular in outline, and range in diameter from ½ to 18 inches (1–45 cm) or more. Their color is first gray green to tan and finally a dull brown (Smith, Jackson and Woolhouse, 1989).

The Fungus

Colletotrichum graminicola (Ces.) Wils.; telemorph *Glomerella graminicola* Politis

Description

Acervuli dark brown or black, elongate; setae few or many, dark brown or black, 1 to 2 septate, 60–120 μm long and 6–8 μm thick at the base; conidio-

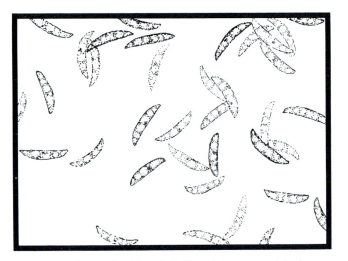

Figure 7-3. Conidia of *Colletotrichum graminicola.*

phores very short, 6–12 × 1–2 μm; conidia falcate, spindle or boat shaped, 2 to several-guttulate, 18–26 × 3–4 μm (Figure 7-3).

Procedures for Isolation and Culture

Colletotrichum graminicola grows well on potato dextrose agar (Difco) at 25 °C. The fungus may be isolated from diseased tissue by surface sterilization in 2 percent sodium hypochlorite and then plating small segments directly onto acidified potato dextrose agar (Jackson and Herting, 1985). Isolates vary in their capacity to sporulate in culture. Optimum sporulation is usually obtained on cornmeal agar (Difco).

Cultivated Turfgrass Hosts

bermudagrass (*Cynodon dactylon* L.), annual bluegrass (*Poa annua* L.), Kentucky bluegrass (*Poa pratensis* L.), Colonial bentgrass (*Agrostis tenuis* Sibth.), creeping bentgrass (*Agrostis palustris* Huds.), velvet bentgrass (*Agrostis canina* L.), centipedegrass (*Echinichloa crusgalli* (L.) Beauv.), red fescue (*Festuca rubra* L.), sheep fescue (*Festuca ovina* L.), tall fescue (*Festuca arundinacea* Schreb.), annual ryegrass (*Lolium multiflorum* Lam.), perennial ryegrass (*Lolium perenne* L.), and zoysiagrass (*Zoysia japonica* Steud.) (Index Plant Dis., 1960; Sprague, 1950).

Disease Profile

The basal rot phase of anthracnose on annual bluegrass (*Poa annua*) and bentgrasses (*Agrostis* spp.) develops when the air temperatures range between 60–75 °F (15–24 °C) and subsides with the

advent of warmer weather. The leaf blight stage of the disease occurs on annual bluegrass, bentgrasses (*Agrostis* spp.), red fescue (*Festuca rubra*), and perennial ryegrass (*Lolium perenne*) after there has been a succession of daytime air temperatures between 85–95 °F (29–35 °C) combined with extended periods of leaf wetness.

Colletotrichum graminicola is capable of surviving during mild winters as hyphae and conidia in plant tissue (Wolff, 1947). The fungus is an active colonizer of thatch and leaf litter which serve as the principal sources of inoculum for initial leaf and crown tissue infections.

Infection and colonization of mature turfgrass plants by *Colletotrichum graminicola* occurs only when the tissue in question has been weakened by biotic and abiotic stress factors such as (a) high populations of root, crown or leaf feeding insects, (b) high populations of root feeding nematodes, (c) parasitism of the crown and leaf tissues during their juvenile and mature stages of growth by pathogenic fungi, (d) extremes in soil fertility levels, (e) high air temperatures, (f) cold injury, (g) anaerobiosis, (h) soil moisture stress, and (i) soil compaction.

Smith (1959b) has observed anthracnose to be "very common . . . on weak *Poa annua.*" In studies on the pathogenic potential of *Colletotrichum graminicola* on creeping bentgrass (*Agrostis palustris*), Kentucky bluegrass (*Poa pratensis*), and tall fescue (*Festuca arundinacea*), Wolff (1947) found that although several cultivars of seedling bentgrass were susceptible to infection by the fungus, mature grasses inoculated in a variety of ways, never developed symptoms of anthracnose. She also reported that "the fungus has been conspicuous in dead or injured turf, which harbored other fungi known to be pathogenic [however] the author has never found a clear-cut case of turf disease that could be attributed to *C. graminicola* alone." As the result of this research, Wolff concluded that "*Colletotrichum graminicola* is a saprophyte, growing in soil and on dead and diseased grass tissue. It is not pathogenic to mature turf."

Smith (1954) planted annual bluegrass (*Poa annua*) seed in an agar medium on which a culture of *Colletotrichum graminicola* was growing and found that the fungus infected the seminal roots and actively colonized the root and stem tissues of the developing seedlings. However, when Jackson and Hertig (1985) conducted pathogenicity tests with *Colletotrichum graminicola* on annual bluegrass and creeping bentgrass (*Agrostis palustris* cv. 'Penncross') seedlings growing in a sterile inorganic plant nutrient solution instead of agar, they found that "none of the five isolates under any of the imposed [temperature] regimes [50 °F (10 °C) and 77 °F (25 °C)] generated severe symptoms on the host grasses. Despite the abundance of vegetative, propagative and penetrative structures produced by the fungus on the plant surfaces, the two hosts species remained almost disease-free after four weeks exposure. Indeed, the plants were still remarkably healthy after a further six weeks incubation. The inference from this axenic trial that *C. graminicola* is not an aggressive turfgrass pathogen supports earlier observations by Wolff (1947)."

Where development of the basal rot phase of the disease is concerned, Jackson and Herting (1985) have concluded that "*C. graminicola* is associated with basal rot of turfgrasses under cool weather conditions but other factors allow or assist this fungus in the expression of severe outbreaks."

Pathogenicity tests conducted by the author using isolates of *Colletotrichum graminicola* recovered from annual bluegrass (*Poa annua*) collected from North Carolina, Virginia, New Jersey, Ohio, Michigan, Illinois, Wisconsin, and California have shown that infection and colonization of annual bluegrass leaves in the juvenile and mature stages of growth will not occur unless the leaves have been predisposed by exposure to air temperatures in the 86–95 °F (30–35 °C) range (unpublished data). This finding is in agreement with the report of Bolton and Cordukes (1981) that the optimum temperature for infection of four week old seedlings of annual bluegrass, red fescue (*Festuca rubra*), and Kentucky bluegrass to *Colletotricum graminicola* was 86–92 °F (30–33 °C).

In addition to the abiotic stresses, occurrences of anthracnose are commonly associated with high populations of root feeding nematodes and/or the development of one or more of the Helminthosporium-incited diseases. Using a 10-year-old velvet bentgrass (*Agrostis canina* cv. 'Kingstown') test site with a high population of parasitic nematodes (predominantly *Hoplolaimus* spp.), the presence of Helminthosporium leaf spot (incited by *Bipolaris sorokiniana*), and a history of anthracnose, Jackson and Herting (1985) found that applications of fungicides and nematicides were required to prevent the occurrence of anthracnose.

Control

Cultural Practices

Employment of various cultural practices to minimize the occurrence of factors that accelerate leaf senescence will reduce the incidence and severity of anthracnose.

- The thatch layer should not be allowed to accumulate to a thickness greater than 0.5 inch (1.3 cm).
- Syringing or light watering of the turf during the hottest time of the day will aid in the reduction of the length of time the leaves are subjected to acute heat stress.
- The reduction of soil compaction by coring and the employment of the most appropriate procedure to improve water infiltration rates are requisites to the reduction of the incidence and severity of anthracnose.
- Frequent, shallow waterings should be avoided. Rather, irrigations should be of sufficient duration to wet the soil throughout the rooting zone and often enough to maintain the soil near field capacity (−0.033 MPa).
- In the development of the fertilization program, care should be taken to prevent the development of phosphorous and potassium deficiencies. With the warm season grasses, late summer fertilizations that may increase the plants vulnerability to winter damage should be avoided.

Use of Resistant Grasses

Turfgrass species that are highly vulnerable to heat stress or cold injury are most severely affected by anthracnose. Of the cool season turfgrasses, severe cases occur most often on annual bluegrass (*Poa annua*). Major outbreaks of anthracnose can also develop on the bentgrasses (*Agrostis* spp.), red fescue (*Festuca rubra*) and perennial ryegrass (*Lolium perenne*), but the frequency is sporadic.

Use of Fungicides

Since infection and colonization of leaves and crowns by *Colletotrichum graminicola* takes place only in tissue that is in advanced senescence, there is little or no benefit to be gained from the application of fungicides for the expressed purpose of controlling anthracnose. Instead, a complete diagnostic work-up should be performed on the turf in question and a preventive pesticide program implemented to control the primary pathogens (fungi, nematodes, insects) that have been identified. Control of the diseases these organisms incite will lower the possibility of the simultaneous shift of large numbers of leaves and crowns into advanced senescence and thus reduce the opportunity for anthracnose to develop (Couch, 1979a).

Curvularia Blight

Symptoms

Turf exposed to full sun and growing near sidewalks and paved areas is most severely affected by Curvularia blight. The disease is first seen in overall view as irregularly shaped, mottled patches that fade to yellow, and then become brown. Individual leaf symptoms develop as a dappled, yellow green discoloration beginning at the tips. As the discoloration extends downward toward the leaf sheath, it progressively turns yellow and then brown. In the advanced stages of disease development, the affected leaves shrivel and die.

When conditions are particularly favorable for the development of Curvularia blight, colonization of the leaf sheaths and crowns can also occur. When the disease goes into the crown rot phase on bentgrass (*Agrostis* spp.) being managed at golf green mowing heights, discrete tan to brown patches of blighted grass 2 to 4 inches (5–10 cm) in diameter often develop. With Kentucky bluegrass (*Poa pratensis*) and red fescue (*Festuca rubra*), the crown rot phase of the disease gives the turf a ragged or thinned-out appearance.

The Fungi

Six species of Curvularia are known to be capable of inciting disease in leaves and crowns of various cool season and warm season turfgrasses growing under high air temperature stress.

A. *Curvularia geniculata* (Tracy and Earle) Boedijn; telemorph *Cochliobolus geniculatus* Nelson

Description

Conidiophores brown, septate, simple, geniculate at the tips, variable in length, 4–5 μm in diameter, spores brown, unequally ventricose-fusiform, mostly 4-septate, the third cell from the base slightly larger and darker, and the end cells nearly hyaline, more or less curved to nearly straight, mostly not curved, 28–36 × 11–14 μm. Spores produced in culture on malt extract agar 28–40 × 11–15 μm (Figure 7-4 A) (Sprague, 1950).

Cultivated Turfgrass Hosts

bermudagrass (*Cynodon dactylon* L.), annual bluegrass (*Poa pratensis* L.) creeping bentgrass (*Agrostis palustris* Huds.), red fescue (*Festuca rubra* L.), tall fescue (*Festuca arundinacea* Schreb.), Kentucky bluegrass (*Poa pratensis* L.), and zoysiagrass (*Zoysia japonica* Steud.) (Bell, 1967; Bugnicourt, 1950; Hodges, 1972; Howard, Rowell and Keil, 1951; Lutrell, 1954b).

B. *Curvularia inaequalis* (Shaer) Boedijn

Description

Conidiophores brown, septate, simple or sometimes branched, geniculate at the tip, variable in length, 4–6 μm in diameter. Spores 3 to 5 celled, ventricose fusiform, mostly 4-septate, the third cell especially enlarged, 27–35 × 11–16 μm. Spores produced in culture on malt extract agar 28–40 × 11–16 μm, sometimes 5-septate. Differs from *Curvularia geniculata* in being slightly broader in proportion to length with the ends more obtusely rounded, this difference being mostly confined to the third cell and, as a result, the spores are more strongly curved than in *Curvularia geniculata* (Figure 7-4 B) (Sprague, 1950).

Cultivated Turfgrass Hosts

annual bluegrass (*Poa annua* L.), red fescue (*Festuca rubra* L.) tall fescue (*Festuca arundinacea* Schreb.), and zoysiagrass (*Zoysia japonica* Steud.) (Bell, 1967; Howard, Rowell and Keil, 1951).

C. *Curvularia intermedia* Boedijn; telemorph *Cochliobolus intermedius* Nelson

Description

Mycelium composed of branched, septate, subhyaline to pale brown, smooth or verruculose, 2–5 μm thick hyphae. Conidiophores arising singly or in groups terminally and laterally on the hyphae, simple or loosely branched, straight or flexuous, often with a series of slightly thickened nodes, pale to dark brown, smooth-walled, septate, often 1 mm and sometimes more than 1 mm long, 5–9 μm thick. Conidia borne in clusters at the apex of the conidiophore and roughly in vertices at the nodes, straight or slightly curved, approximately ellipsoidal or broadly fusiform but always somewhat unequal-sided, 3-septate, the middle septum usually truly median and traversing the conidium at its widest point, the basal cell often the narrowest, the cell at each end usually subhyaline or pale brown, intermediate cells brown or dark brown, smooth-walled, 27–40 (32) μm long, 13–20 (15.6) μm thick in the broadest part. Colonies on potato dextrose agar effused, grayish brown, cottony.

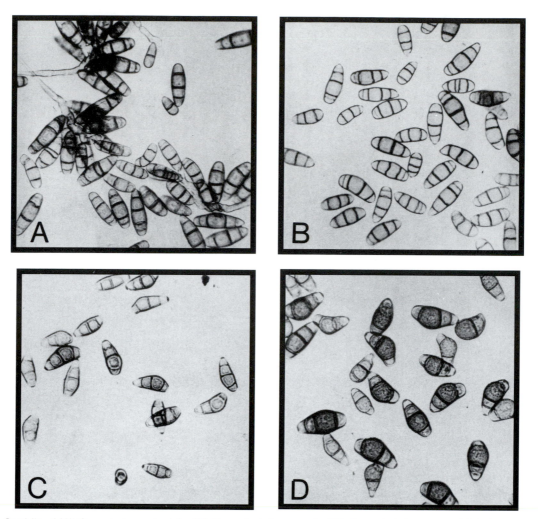

Figure 7-4.   Conidia of (A) *Curvularia geniculata*, (B) *Curvularia inaequalis*, (C) *Curvularia lunata*, and (D) *Curvularia trifolii. After Groves and Skolko, 1945.*

Cultivated Turfgrass Hosts

bermudagrass (*Cynodon dactylon* L.), creeping bentgrass (*Agrostis palustris* Huds.), Kentucky bluegrass (*Poa pratensis* L.), and red fescue (*Festuca rubra* L.) (Brown, Cole and Nelson, 1972).

D. *Curvularia lunata* (Wakker) Boedijn; telemorph *Cochliobolus lunatus* Nelson and Haasis

Description

Conidiophores are pale brown, septate, simple or branched, geniculate at the tip, variable in length, 3–5 μm in diameter; conidia pale brown, 3-septate, the third cell from the base is larger and darker colored than the others, unequally ventricose-fusiform, more or less curved to nearly straight, 19–30 × 8–12 μm. Spores produced in culture on malt extract agar are

19–32 × 9–15.5 μm, commonly 22–28 × 10–13 μm (Figure 7-4 C) (Sprague, 1950).

Cultivated Turfgrass Hosts

annual bluegrass (*Poa annua* L.), Kentucky bluegrass (*Poa pratensis* L.), creeping bentgrass (*Agrostis palustris* Huds.), velvet bentgrass (*Agrostis canina* L), red fescue (*Festuca rubra* L.), tall fescue (*Festuca arundinacea* Schreb.), and zoysiagrass (*Zoysia japonica* Steud.) (Bell, 1967; Brown, Cole and Nelson, 1972; Muchovej and Couch, 1987; Luttrell, 1954a).

E. *Curvularia protuberata* Nelson and Hodges

Description

Mycelium composed of branched, septate, subhyaline to pale brown, smooth-walled, 2–5 μm thick hyphae. Conidiophores arising singly or in groups, terminally and laterally on the hyphae, also on stromata, simple or branched, straight or flexuous, sometimes geniculate, septate, rather pale brown, smooth-walled, up to 500 μm long, 3–5 μm thick. Conidia acropleurogenous, straight or slightly curved, cylindrical to ellipsoidal, sometimes ventricose, with a markedly protuberant hilum at the base, almost always 4-septate, the central cell the largest, the cell at each end usually subhyaline or pale brown, intermediate cells brown or dark brown, smooth-walled, 27–38 (32.8) μm long, 10–14 (12.6) μm thick in the broadest part. Colonies on potato dextrose agar effused, dark gray or very dark grayish brown, velvety.

Cultivated Turfgrass Hosts

creeping bentgrass (*Agrostis palustris* Huds.), Kentucky bluegrass (*Poa pratensis* L.), and red fescue (*Festuca rubra* L.) (Brown, Cole and Nelson, 1972).

F. *Curvularia trifolii* (Kaufmann) Boedijn

Description

Conidiophores brown, septate, simple, geniculate at the tip, 5–6 μm in diameter; spores brown to olive brown, 3-septate, the third cell much larger and darker than the others, unequally ventricose, fusiform, mostly strongly curved, sometimes forked or triangular lobed, 25–35 × 11–15 μm. Spores produced in culture on malt extract agar are 25–35 × 12–16 μm (Figure 7-4 D) (Sprague, 1950).

Cultivated Turfgrass Hosts

bermudagrass (*Cynodon dactylon* L.), annual bluegrass (*Poa annua* L.) Colonial bentgrass (*Agrostis tenuis* Sibth.), creeping bentgrass (*Agrostis palustrus* Huds.), and Chewings fescue (*Agrostis rubra* var. *commutata* Gaud.) (Faloon, 1976).

Procedures for Isolation and Culture

The various Curvularia species that colonize turfgrasses grow well at 21–24 °C on various amended agar media, including potato dextrose agar and malt extract agar (Difco).

Disease Profile

The optimum conditions for outbreaks of Curvularia blight on cool season grasses are several days in succession of daytime air temperatures between 85–95 °F (30–35 °C) combined with extended periods of leaf wetness (Brown, Cole and Nelson, 1972; Faloon, 1976). With the warm season grasses, Curvularia blight develops during early spring on plants that have received winter damage and during summer and early fall on turf that has been stressed by high populations of root feeding nematodes, insects, fertility imbalances, or drought (Bell, 1967; Freeman and Simone, 1988).

The various species that incite Curvularia blight are active colonizers of thatch and leaf litter which serve as the principal sources of inoculum for the initial outbreaks of the disease. Penetration of the plant is accomplished by growth of mycelium and spore germ tubes through (a) cut leaf tips, (b) leaf and crown surface wounds, and (c) Helminthosporium-incited lesions.

On creeping bentgrass (*Agrostis palustris*), mycelial growth through cut tips or surface wounds into underlying tissue can occur at any stage of growth, but if the leaf is either in a juvenile or mature stage of growth, the fungus will only grow between the cells. The actual penetration and colonization of cells does not occur until prolonged high temperature stress has caused the tissue to shift into advanced senescence (Muchovej and Couch, 1987). When entry of leaf or crown tissue takes place through lesions incited by the Helminthosporium leaf spot pathogen (*Bipolaris sorokiniana*), regardless of air temperature, tissue colonization by the Curvularia blight fungus begins immediately (Mower, 1962; Muchovej and Couch, 1987). When air temperatures are in the 85–95 °F (30–35 °C) range, there is a synergistic effect between *Bipolaris sorokiniana* and the invading Curvularia species that results in greater disease severity than that brought on by either pathogen individually (Hodges and Madsen, 1978).

Spring applications of the herbicides 2,4-D (dichlorophenoxyacetic acid), MSMA (monosodium acid methanearsonate), or dicamba (3,6-dichloro-o-anisic acid) at high rates will increase the severity of Curvularia blight on creeping bentgrass (*Agrostis palustris*) during the months of high temperature stress (Smith and Couch, 1987).

Control

Cultural Practices

Employment of various cultural practices to minimize the occurrence of factors that accelerate leaf senescence will reduce the incidence and severity of Curvularia blight. The thatch layer should not be allowed to accumulate to a thickness greater than 0.5 inch (1.3 cm). In the development of the fertilization program, care should be taken to avoid the development of phosphorous and potassium deficiencies. Also, high rates of nitrogen should not be applied during drought or periods of high air temperatures. With the warm season grasses, late summer fertilizations that may increase the plants vulnerability to winter damage should be avoided. Frequent, shallow waterings should also be avoided. The irrigations should be of sufficient duration to thoroughly wet the soil throughout the rooting zone and frequent enough to maintain the soil near field capacity (-0.033 MPa).

Use of Resistant Grasses

Annual bluegrass (*Poa annua*) and bentgrasses (*Agrostis* spp.) are more vulnerable to outbreaks of Curvularia blight than other turfgrasses.

Use of Fungicides

Since colonization of leaves and crowns by the Curvularia blight fungi takes place only after their tissues are in advanced senescence, there is little to be gained from the application of fungicides for the expressed purpose of controlling this disease. On the other hand, the reduction of biotically induced stress on the turfgrass plants through the use of pesticides to control primary turfgrass pathogens will lessen the possibility of the premature shift of large numbers of leaves and crowns into advanced senescence and thus diminish the likelihood of the development of Curvularia blight.

Leptosphaerulina Leaf Blight

Symptoms

Individual leaf symptoms develop as a yellow discoloration beginning at the tips. As the discoloration extends downward toward the leaf sheath, the leaf progressively turns yellow and then brown. Necrosis may extend into the sheath. In the advanced stages of disease development, the affected leaves shrivel and die. Small brown fruiting structures of the fungus often develop on the upper and lower surfaces of dead leaves.

The Fungi

A. *Leptosphaerulina australis* Mc Alpine; syn. *Pleospora gaumannii* Muller, *Pseudoplea gaumannii* (Muller) Wehmeyer

Description

Ascocarps immersed, globose, membranous, parenchymatous, pale brown, opening by a broad pore, averaging 150 μm in diameter; asci saccate 75–80 × 28–50 μm with 8 ascospores; ascospores oblong, bluntly conical at base and rounded at tip, 30–32 × 11 μm, at first hyaline but ultimately brown, 5 septate, muriform when mature, usually with 2 longitudinal septa (Figure 7-5 A).

Procedure for Isolation and Culture

When incubated at 20–25 °C, the fungus develops mature ascocarps in less than a week on 20 percent V-8 juice agar (Graham and Luttrell, 1961).

Cultivated Turfgrass Hosts

annual bluegrass (*Poa annua* L.), Kentucky bluegrass (*Poa pratensis* L.), Colonial bentgrass (*Agrostis tenuis* Sibth.), creeping bentgrass (*Agrostis palustris* Huds.), red fescue (*Festuca rubra* L.), tall fescue (*Festuca arundinacea* Schreb.), annual ryegrass (*Lolium multiflorum* Lam.), and perennial ryegrass (*Lolium perenne* L.) (Dunlap, 1944; Graham and Luttrell, 1961; Muller, 1951; Ormund, Hughes and Shoemaker, 1970; Wehmeyer, 1955).

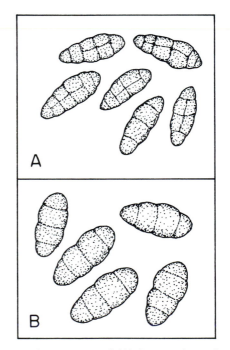

Figure 7-5. Ascospores of (A) *Leptosphaerulina australis* and (B) *Leptosphaerulina trifolii. After Graham and Luttrell, 1961.*

B. *Leptosphaerulina trifolii* (Rost.) Petr.; syn. *Sphaerulina trifolii* Rost

Description

Ascocarps 124–207 μm in diameter; asci 62–95 × 42–59 μm; ascospores 25–49 × 11–21 μm, means 29.2–43.3 × 13.4–18.5 μm, 3–4 × 0–2 septate, means 3.0–3.1 × 0–1 septa, 0–80 percent muriform (Figure 7-5 B).

Procedure for Isolation and Culture

When incubated at 20–25 °C, the fungus develops mature ascocarps in less than a week on 20 percent V-8 juice agar. Colonies in culture become covered with a dense black crust of large, often compound ascocarps (Graham and Luttrell, 1961).

Cultivated Turfgrass Hosts

Leptosphaerulina trifolii has been identified on senescent leaves of annual bluegrass (*Poa annua* L.) and Kentucky bluegrass (*Poa pratensis* L.) in the United States.

Disease Profile

Both species of *Leptosphaerulina* grow saprophytically on thatch and leaf litter and probably survive adverse climatic conditions as mycelium and ascocarps. Infection and colonization of leaves takes place only after the tissue has become senescent through natural growth processes or as the result of environmental stresses.

Other Incitants of Senectopathic Disorders

Nigrospora sphaerica (Sacc.) Mason, *Fusarium accuminatum* Ellis and Everh., *Fusarium crookwellense* Burgess, Nelson and Toussoun, *Fusarium graminearum* Schwabe, and *Fusarium heterosporium* Nees:Fr. have been implicated in the development of senectopathic disorders of the leaves and crowns of cool season turfgrasses (Smiley, Dernoden and Clarke, 1992; Thompson, Fowler and Smiley, 1982). However, the capacity of these species to function as primary invaders in the infection and colonization of senescent tissue has not yet been defined.

§ § §

8

Root Dysfunctions, Declines, and Rots

ANAEROBIOSIS (Black Layer)

Anaerobiosis is a dynamic series of events taking place in an oxygen depleted (anaerobic) environment. When the soil becomes anaerobic, there are significant changes in both the form and solubility of nutrient elements. In their reduced state, certain of these elements are taken up by the plant more rapidly than they can be metabolized, thereby becoming toxic. Others become limited in availability. Water saturated soils promote the growth of anaerobic microorganisms which produce metabolites that are detrimental to plant growth. Ultimately, root systems become dysfunctional in anaerobic soils. As the result, their ability to absorb water and nutrients is reduced significantly, causing the plants to develop symptoms of nutrient deficiency even though adequate levels exist in the soil.

Anaerobiosis is a widespread and important problem in sports turf management. The condition is commonly referred to as "black layer" when observed in sandy media. Anaerobiosis also occurs on greens constructed with soil/sand/organic matter mixtures and on fairways; however, the classic black layer is less visible.

Diagnostic Features

The early indication of anaerobiosis is a progressive decline in the rate of water infiltration. Also, there is a gradual reduction in the vigor of the turf. The plants develop a pale green to yellow color. There is a thinning, and finally bronzing and death in patches and strips in lower areas of a green or where there is a high frequency of foot and machinery traffic. Root development is restricted or completely prevented. Reseedings fail to develop in the affected areas except where aeration holes filled with permeable topdressing penetrate the underlying anaerobic layer.

In the advanced stages of anaerobiosis, black layers may develop in the soil profile (Plate 29-D, E).

These layers can form in soil supporting turf or in media free of turf (*e.g.*, sand bunkers) (Plate 29-F). Their thickness is variable. They may be confined to the top 1–2 inches (2.5–5.0 cm) of the soil, but can occur at depths of 4–6 inches (10–15 cm) or more. There is sometimes more than one black layer in the overall soil profile and the layers may form on an even plane or be wavy. Quite often, algal growth develops on the surface of the turf or soil surface. When the soil is water soaked, hydrogen sulfide is often produced in large quantities, giving the plugs a distinctive, "rotten egg" smell. This odor is almost unnoticeable when the black layer is dry. Plugs pulled from a black layer zone may be slimy to the touch when wet, and may display a fine crystalline appearance. Infiltration of water through the layer is progressively restricted.

The impact of anaerobiosis on plant growth can be either chronic or acute. It can exist in growing media long before there is strong evidence of affected plant growth.

Disease Profile

Anaerobiosis is the consequence of a water-saturated soil that has been brought on by frequent flooding, extended periods of high rainfall, excessive irrigation, or inadequate drainage due either to compaction, the construction of rooting zones on inadequately drained bases, or the formation of impermeable layers within established seedbed mixes.

How Water Impermeable Layers Are Formed

Water-impermeable layers within seedbed mixes of sand-based golf greens can develop as the consequence of improper particle size distribution, and/or the formation of a gelatinous substance (biofilm) that plugs both the capillary and non capillary pores.

Improper particle size distribution. When an incompatible top dressing is not adequately integrated into the existing greens mixture, subsurface layers with different textures will develop. Failure to properly blend even small amounts of incompatible top dressing with the existing material can eventually lead to layering. The reason for this is that the downward flow of water is restricted when it must cross an interface between two textural classes. This is most evident when the finer texture is above coarser material. Soil water carries solutes and suspended particles of clay, sand, and organic matter. When the velocity of its downward movement is slowed by even a low order textural barrier, particulate matter is deposited. As these particles accumulate, the total porosity of the soil in the location in question is reduced. This means that the next water moving into that zone will be slowed even further, again depositing suspended solids. By this process, distinct layers are produced that impede the downward movement of water. This gives rise to what are commonly referred to as "perched" water tables in the rooting zone (Figure 8-1).

Decomposing grass roots can also facilitate the development of water-impermeable layers within the greens mixture. During the warm months of late spring and early summer, a large portion of the root mass of bentgrasses (*Agrostis* spp.) and annual bluegrass (*Poa annnua*) die. This establishes a spongy, organic mat which serves as a textural barrier that slows water movement and retains a high percentage of its organic and mineral solids at that level. If procedures are not implemented to correct this condition, water retention will increase. Also, when sod grown on a fine textured mixture is laid over a coarser root zone mix, a perched water table, accom-

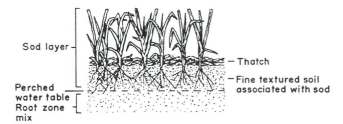

Figure 8-2. Development of a perched water table when sod grown on a fine-textured soil is placed over a coarse-textured root zone mix.

panied by anaerobiosis, may develop at the interface between the two mixture types (Figure 8-2).

The formation of biofilm. Under conditions of prolonged water saturation, layers of biofilm often develop that further impede the flow of water through the root zone and foster the development of anaerobiosis. A soil biofilm is an assemblage of bacterial cells that is both enclosed by and attached to the wetted surfaces of particles of clay, sand and organic matter by means of a polysaccharide-containing slime known as a "glycocalyx" (Eighmy, Maratea and Bishop, 1983). The slime component of the biofilm contains a large number of chain-like organic molecules (polymers) which forms a sponge-like water-absorbing matrix within which the bacteria are able to survive and nutrients become concentrated. These polymers eventually extend beyond the areas of immediate microbial growth and thus create a much larger biomass than that which have been formed by the bacterial cells alone (Lindenbach and Cullimore, 1989).

Initially, bacteria attach to the soil and sand particles and to the roots and form a coherent, colorless biofilm. At this stage, the biofilm contains an assortment of several species of bacteria that are competing for nutrients, water and oxygen. The species that are not mutually competitive eventually dominate and then proceed freely to increase in numbers. The enlarging biofilms then extend over the sand and soil particles and merge with neighboring slimes, forming a much larger biomass. The developing biomass plugs the capillary pores and "strings out" into the water in the larger pore spaces, reducing the flow of water, oxygen and nutrients through the root zone.

As the biomass continues to enlarge, oxygen is no longer able to penetrate it uniformly and an internal stratification of bacterial species begins to develop. The bacteria near the surfaces of the mass are those that require available oxygen (aerobic), while

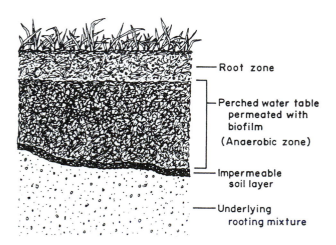

Figure 8-1. Cross section of rooting mixture of a sand-based golf green showing impermeable soil layer and perched water table permeated with biofilm.

the innermost portions are occupied by anaerobic species, including the sulfur reducing forms which not only do not require oxygen, but may be inhibited by it. During this time, there is a constant interchange of organic materials and nutrients between the aerobic and anaerobic zones within the biomass. Also, metallic elements (particularly iron and manganese) become entrapped within the slime matrix and in the cell walls of the bacteria.

The primary nutrients necessary for the development of the biomass are carbon, nitrogen, and sulfur. Root exudates, decomposing turfgrass roots, and organic matter that has been added to the rooting mixture are principal sources of carbon nutrition for biofilm-forming bacteria. Also, blue-green algae produce organic carbon, and in some cases organic nitrogen, from inorganic sources which also can promote biofilm formation.

Where nitrogen fertilization is concerned, biofilm formation is more extensive in areas fertilized with urea than those in which either ammonium sulfate or ammonium nitrate is used (Table 8-1). This is probably due to the fact that the nitrogen in the urea is more readily available to the sulfur reducing bacteria in the biomass (Smith, 1988).

Sulfur is a major nutrient for certain biofilm-forming bacteria. The reason biomasses turn black is the development of metallic sulfides (particularly iron and manganese sulfides). These sulfides are produced as the end product of a reaction in which bacterially generated hydrogen sulfide reacts with the reduced form of these elements (i.e., ferrous and manganous ions) to produce insoluble sulfides.

Table 8-1. Relationship between nitrogen fertilizer source, sulfur and iron on the development of the black layer phase of anaerobiosis. *After Smith, 1988.*

Treatment	Rate 1000 ft^2	Rate 93 m^2	Severity of Black Layer[a]
Ammonium nitrate	0.5 lb N	0.23 kg N	2.0
Ammonium nitrate	0.5 lb N	0.23 kg N	1.5
+ colloidal sulfur	2.0 lb	0.90 kg	
+ ferrous sulfate	2.0 lb	0.90 kg	
Urea	0.5 lb N	0.23 kg N	3.0
Urea	0.5 lb N	0.23 kg N	3.2
+ colloidal sulfur	2.0 lb	0.90 kg	
+ ferrous sulfate	2.0 lb	0.90 kg	
Ammonium sulfate	0.5 lb N	0.23 kg N	1.7
Ammonium sulfate	0.5 lb N	0.23 kg N	2.5
+ colloidal sulfur	2.0 lb	0.90 kg	
+ ferrous sulfate	2.0 lb	0.90 kg	

[a]Rating based on 0 to 5 scale where 0 = no symptoms and 5 = death of all plants.

There are two major groups of bacteria able to generate sulfides. The first group includes many species which will degrade the sulfur containing amino acids in proteins to release hydrogen sulfide. In the low organic matter environment of sand-based greens, hydrogen sulfide can be produced by the reduction of either sulfur or sulfate. This only occurs in the absence of oxygen by a group of specialized bacteria known as the dissimilatory sulfur- or sulfate-reducing bacteria. Since there is a shortage of organic nitrogenous sources within the biofilm during its blackened stage of development, it is more likely that the hydrogen sulfide would be produced by these species.

Only one genus of sulfur-reducing bacteria (*Desulfuromonas*) is able to reduce elemental sulfur to hydrogen sulfide. All of the remaining species utilize sulfate. Where the irrigation water is high in sulfate and no elemental sulfur has been applied to the greens, the dominant sulfur-reducing species likely to be associated with the formation of the blackened stage of biofilm development would be from the larger group of sulfate-reducing species. Where elemental sulfur has been added to the green, *Desulfuromonas* may become a major bacterial component of the blackened biofilm. In any event, **it is important to bear in mind that the addition of elemental sulfur to a sand-based green is not necessary in order for the slime layers to become blackened**.

There is a direct relationship between rate of water infiltration and biofilm formation. The acceptable infiltration rate for sand-based golf greens is 6 to 12 inches (15–31 cm) per hour. Sand-based greens become vulnerable to the development of biofilm when the infiltration rate ranges between 2.8 and 7 inches (7.0–17.8 cm) per hour. At an infiltration rate of 1.5 to 2.7 inches (3.8–7.0 cm) per hour, blackened biofilm may become visible, and when the rate diminishes to 0.7 to 1.3 inches (1.8–3.3 cm) per hour, layers of blackened biofilm-impregnated sand can develop (Table 8-2) (Cullimore, 1990).

The overall biomass layers are made up of individual slime formations ranging in shape and size from globular masses 0.08 inch (2 mm) in diameter to complex, planar arrangements measuring as large as 25 × 18 × 4.8 inches (98 × 71 × 19 mm). Occasionally, very small (0.2–1.0 mm) intensely black globular masses are dispersed within the rooting mixture outside the main layering area and sometimes they will be attached directly to the roots. The larger, planar masses consist of a series of horizontally layered, somewhat wavy strata which extend outward in plate-like fashion. The outermost (peninsulate) plates are joined to the main unit by columnar processes which are in turn joined together by interconnective

Table 8-2. Relationship between infiltration rate and extent of anaerobiosis in creeping bentgrass green— gauged by the development of black layers. *After Cullimore, 1990.*

Infiltration Rate per Hour		Black Layer Status
Inches	Centimeters	
>7.0	>17.8	Excellent permeability, no black layer
2.8–7.0	7.0–17.8	Good permeability, occasional traces of black layer
1.5–2.7	3.8–7.0	Poor permeability, black layer present
0.7–1.3	1.8–3.3	Very poor permeability, black layer serious
0.2–0.6	0.5–1.5	Almost impervious to water, black layer dominant
<0.2	<0.5	Impervious to water, black layer very aggressive

lateral plates (Figure 8-3) (Cullimore, Nilson, Taylor and Nelson, 1990).

Sealing of the soil surface by either dust, and/or the growth of blue-green algae also fosters the development of anaerobiosis. In areas subject to dust storms such as the prairie provinces of Canada and the midwestern section of the United States surface sealing in established turf by wind-borne clay and silt is of common occurrence (Smith, 1988). Blue-green algae produce mucilage, slime and or other organic products that fill the pore spaces in the top 1 inch (2.54 cm) of the sand. These substances bind

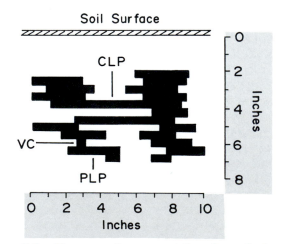

Figure 8-3. Diagrammatic representation of a vertical profile of a section of a soil biomass at the blackened stage of development showing peninsulate lateral plates (PLP), interconnective lateral plates (CLP), and vertical columns (VC). *Adapted from Cullimore, Nilson, Taylor, and Nelson, 1990.*

sand particles together and are extremely hydrophilic. As the result, air space is reduced, the rate of gas exchange between the root zone and the air is decreased, and there is a significant drop in water penetration rates. Also, once these conditions are established, the surface inch (2.54 cm) of the green remains wet even when it is watered judiciously (Hodges, 1989).

High nitrate content and high soluble salt content also contribute to anaerobic conditions by lowering the vapor pressure of soil water, thereby reducing evapotranspiration rates and slowing the plant's ability to cool itself (Hall, 1989). Also, when irrigation water is drawn directly from rivers or ponds that contain fine particles, these particles will migrate in a sandy profile and accumulate to form blockage of water flow.

Once anaerobic conditions have been established, denitrification (the conversion of nitrate to unusable nitrogen gas) increases, and manganese, iron and sulfur are reduced to plant nonutilizable forms. Also, toxic byproducts of anaerobic decomposition accumulate, such as ferrous sulfide, acetic, butyric and phenolic acids, ethylene, methane and hydrogen sulfide. In addition, the anaerobic microorganisms produce metabolites that are detrimental to plant growth.

When ethylene, methane and hydrogen sulfide are trapped in an oxygen depleted soil, death of the roots occurs within a short period of time. For example, based on the biologic assumptions that (a) there are 7.4 grams (0.38 oz) fresh weight bentgrass roots in an 8 inch (20.3 cm) depth under a 4 inch (10 cm) diameter plug, (b) aeration porosity in the mixture is 30 percent, (c) that 0.2 ml oxygen is being utilized per hour per gram fresh weight of root tissue, (d) that air contains 210 ml of oxygen per liter and the evapotranspiration is occurring at a rate of 0.295 inch (75 mm) per day, (e) the lateral diffusion of gases is being significantly hampered by the excessive moisture in the soil profile; and the agronomic assumptions that, (f) algae or dust has sealed the surface, (g) a perched water table exists at the 4 inch (10 cm) depth, (h) the capillary water has become anaerobic, and (i) 70 percent of the root system is in the surface 4 inches (10 cm), **in 9.7 days, all of the oxygen in the root zone will be depleted and death of root tissue will begin.** Furthermore, under the added conditions of high atmospheric humidity, high amounts of readily available nitrogen, a high level of soluble salts, and no evapotranspiration, **in about 70 hours, all of the oxygen in the root zone will be depleted and death of root tissue will begin** (Hall, 1989).

Control

A key element in the effective management of anaerobiosis is frequent monitoring of water infiltration rates. Measurement of the rate of water penetration of the thatch and the velocity of its movement through the underlying root zone mixture can be accomplished with a field infiltrometer (Figure 8-4). The base-line (initial) infiltration rates for pre-selected locations on each green should be recorded. Measurements should then made at these sites at two week intervals throughout the growing season. At

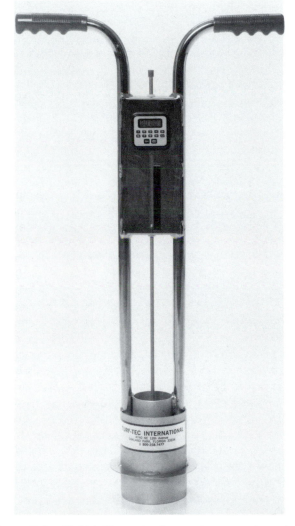

Figure 8-4. Field infiltrometer for use in measuring rate of water movement through thatch and underlying seedbed mixture. *Courtesy Turf Tec International, Oakland Park, Florida.* An evaluation of the effectiveness of the corrective procedure should be made by performing a follow-up measurement of the infiltration rate of the treated area.

the first indication of a decrease, even though it may not appear to be significant, the cause should be identified and appropriate remedial measures taken immediately.

Prevention of the development of anaerobiosis requires that steps be taken to avert the formation of texturally altered layers within the rooting mixture. Although the potential for layering is greater when there is a conversion of the rooting mixture to a finer material, any change in the texture of topdressing materials can eventually result in layer formation. Therefore, regardless of the change in composition, a gradual transition between old and new textural types is most desirable (Gockel, 1987). The simplest method for obtaining a gradual transition is to begin with intensive aeration in early fall when the cores can be shredded and blended with a relatively heavy topdressing with the new material. This procedure should be repeated each fall. The intervening topdressings should be made during the times in which there is a need for regular mowing. They should be light and frequent, and the application amounts should be equivalent to the rate of grass growth (Latham, 1987).

Either coring with very narrow, hollow-tines or pin-spiking should be performed on greens in which it has been determined that the death of large masses of grass roots in late spring and early summer is impeding the downward movement of water. If each operation is followed by a light application of topdressing, some of the material will be dragged into the holes and thus maintain their integrity. Also, the use of topdressing will reduce the potential for development of high concentrations of organic matter near the surface, which, in turn produces soft, water-retaining playing surfaces. This procedure will improve water infiltration rates and provide an opportunity for new root growth for the remainder of the summer season. The fall cultivation of these greens should be performed in such a manner that the decomposing roots and fine-textured mineral solids that accumulated in the root zone during the previous months will be thoroughly mixed with the existing base.

Another important aspect of effective management of anaerobiosis is the control of surface algae. An important factor in both the rate and extent of development of blue-green algae on sand or soil surfaces is pH. Greens constructed with calcareous sands (pH 7.5 or above) are more prone to colonization by blue-green algae than sands with a lower pH. Irrigation water in the alkaline range stimulates the growth of blue-green algae. Watering practices (or excessive rainfall) that keep greens excessively wet will promote algal growth, especially on calcareous sands. The use of hydrated lime as a desiccant for control of surface algae can be self defeating. The short-term benefit of reduction in algal growth due to the absence of free water on the soil and plant surfaces will be offset in the long term by an increase in population levels of algae brought on by the increase in alkalinity. The very close mowing practices associated with modern golf also contributes to the development of blue-green algae. These reduced mowing heights allow additional light penetration to the surface of the sand, and since blue-green algae are photosynthetic plants, the increase in light intensifies their development (Hodges, 1989).

Mancozeb and chlorothalonil are registered in the United States for control of algae on established turf. These materials are most effective when used in a preventive program. Since they also control certain fungus-incited diseases of turfgrasses, their inclusion in the spray schedule can serve more than one purpose. For a profile of each of these compounds and a list of representative manufacturers, see Appendix Table I.

When it has been determined that anaerobiosis has developed, the first priority is to increase the oxygen levels in the root zone. This can be accomplished by the use of coring procedures and closely monitoring the irrigation program. Because the coring process physically removes soil from the profile, it enables a great volume of air to enter the anaerobic areas. If maximum benefits are to be realized from this procedure, the coring must be deep enough to penetrate the underlying textural barriers (see Plate 29-E). When coring is accomplished by use of very narrow hollow-tines, it causes a minimal disturbance to the smoothness of the playing surface and can be performed throughout the year. Large tines should be limited to fall or spring use.

Where water management during anaerobic conditions is concerned, the soil moisture level should be allowed to be extracted by the plants to a point well below field capacity between irrigations. In order to achieve this, it will be necessary to use a combination of frequent, light syringings and manually controlled irrigation of the affected greens while the underlying physical conditions are being corrected. During periods of prolonged rainfall, it is important to make certain that surface drainage is possible on all parts of the green. Also, any reduction in numbers of rounds per day until the weather conditions normalize will be helpful in reducing the severity of the problem.

High nitrogen fertilization during this time should be avoided. Urea in particular should not be used. If fertilization is considered necessary, it should be balanced applications of nitrogen, phosphorous and potassium made in minimal amounts.

Once procedures are in place to deal with the immediacy of the situation, the next priority is to determine the nature and extent of the drainage barriers and implement procedures to correct the problem. It is important to compile all available information on construction and cultivation practices used on the green in question—the texture of the original seed bed and rooting zone mixtures, uniformity of seed bed depth, types and frequency of cultivation, and topdressing history. Detailed inspection will help to determine if the problem is due to compaction, the formation of water-impermeable layers in the seed bed and rooting zone, or inadequately drained bases. With this information, a plan for correcting the problem can then be developed.

Deep cultivation will alleviate problems with anaerobiosis that has developed as the result of water-impermeable layers within the rooting zone. Several commercially manufactured units are currently available that can penetrate to depths ranging from 2 to 16 inches (5–41 cm), including deep drills, straight-line slicers, and hollow tine aerifiers. The appropriate choices concerning the type of equipment to be used, the timing of cultivation, procedure frequency, and correct soil moisture conditions at the time of treatment requires a good knowledge of each technique and the exact nature of the underlying physical problems (Carrow, 1992).

PYTHIUM-INCITED ROOT AND CROWN DISEASES

A large number of *Pythium* species are known to cause diseases of turfgrasses throughout the world. There is a wide range of variability among the various Pythiums in their virulence on various turfgrass species and in their ability to infect and colonize various host organs on the same grass species. Although most *Pythium* species can infect and colonize all plant parts, some are primarily leaf colonizers while others are principally root and crown invaders.

Individual isolates within species are known to vary in form of tissue colonization. For example, isolates of some species infect and colonize root tissue of creeping bentgrass (*Agrostis palustris*). The roots become dysfunctional where their ability to absorb water from the soil is concerned, but they do not become necrotic. Other isolates of the same species, however, will cause a distinctive root and crown rot that brings about a thinning of plant population and an overall decline in the quality of the turf.

The species that incite foliar diseases of turfgrasses are listed in the coverage of Pythium blight in Chapter 4. *Pythium dissimile* Vaartaja, *Pythium irregulare* Buisman, *Pythium violae* Chesters and Hickman, and *Pythium splendens* Braun are known to cause root and crown rot of perennial ryegrass (*Lolium perenne*) in Australia (Dewan and Sivasithamparam, 1988). *Pythium graminicola* Subramanium and *Pythium periplocum* Drechs. are reported to be root and crown pathogens of manilagrass (*Zoysia matrella* (L.) Merr. in Japan (Ichitani, Tani and Umakoshi, 1986). The species of *Pythium* that infect and colonize root and crown tissue of creeping bentgrass (*Agrostis palustris*) are listed in Table 8-3.

Pythium Root Dysfunction of Creeping Bentgrass

Root dysfunction is the inability of what would appear to be a healthy root system to adequately absorb water and mineral nutrient elements from the soil. The fungus thoroughly colonizes the roots but fails to produce root rot. Under optimum growing conditions, there is no evidence of adverse effects on the plants. However, when the plants are placed under stress, death of large areas of turf can occur within a relatively short period of time.

Pythium-induced root dysfunction is a disease of creeping bentgrass (*Agrostis palustris*) growing in sand and sand/loam media. The disease occurs most commonly on old golf courses where the greens have been rebuilt with high sand content mixes; however, it can also develop on sand greens on newly constructed courses.

Symptoms

The above ground symptoms of Pythium root dysfunction are first seen as small, irregularly-shaped pale green to light yellow areas ranging from 1–4 inches (2.5–10 cm) in diameter. Pale green to light yellow strips may also develop at the interface of the high sand content mix of the green and the collar apron of soil. Within a few days from the first appearance of symptoms, the color of the affected areas changes to light brown. As the disease progresses, individual patches of affected grass frequently coalesce to envelop sections of turf ranging from 1–10 feet (0.3–3 m) in diameter. During hot, humid weather, entire greens may die within 7–14 days from the onset of symptoms. Certain aspects of the above ground symptom pattern for Pythium root dysfunction are similar to Pythium foliar blight (see Chapter 4), however, with Pythium root dysfunction, the leaves of the affected plants are free of colonization by Pythium species.

Examination of the root systems of diseased plants reveals white, normal appearing roots. Although there is no necrosis, when affected roots are incubated in the laboratory using tissue culture chambers, the pathogen grows from the tissues within 6–12 hours. In the advanced stages of disease development, affected roots may become slightly buff-colored and develop bulbous root tips. Also, the root tips eventually become disorganized and devitalized (Figure 8-5 B, C) (Hodges, 1985a).

The Fungi

A. *Pythium arrhenomanes* Drechs.
Description

Mycelium intra- and intercellular, hyphae measuring 2.0–5.5 µm in diameter. Sporangia inflated, filamentous, lobulate, forming complexes of elements up to 20 µm or more in diameter, zoospores 20–50 or more in a vesicle borne on an evacuation tube usually 3–4 µm in diameter and of variable length, up to 75 µm, biciliate, measuring approximately 12 µm in diameter upon encystment. Oogonia subspherical to spherical, acrobenous, occasionally intercalary, walls smooth and thin, measuring 17.3–56.3 µm, mean 30.1 µm, in diameter. Antheridia of dielinous origin, numerous, 15–25 often visible, usually borne terminally though occasionally laterally on 4–8 branches

Table 8-3. Species of Pythium pathogenic to roots and crowns of creeping bentgrass (*Agrostis palustris*).

Pythium aphanidermatum	(Abad *et al.*, 1992; Nelson and Craft, 1991; Saladini, 1980)
Pythium aristosporum	(Abad *et al.*, 1992; Nelson and Craft, 1991)
Pythium arrhenomanes	(Abad *et al.*, 1992)
Pythium graminicola	(Abad *et al.*, 1992; Nelson and Craft, 1991; Saladini, 1980)
Pythium irregulare	(Abad *et al.*, 1992)
Pythium myriotylum	(Abad *et al.*, 1992; Saladini, 1980)
Pythium tardecrescens	(Abad *et al.*, 1992)
Pythium torulosum	(Abad *et al.*, 1992; Nelson and Craft, 1991)
Pythium ultimum var. *sporangiiferum*	(Abad *et al.*, 1992)
Pythium ultimum var. *ultimum*	(Abad *et al.*, 1972)
Pythium vanterpoolii	(Nelson and Craft, 1991)

each usually contributing up to 4 antheridia, antheridial cells are crook-necked, 6–9 μm wide and 12–25 μm long, making narrow contact with the oogonium. Oospores plerotic, 15.5–54.2 μm, mean 28.2 μm in diameter, wall 1.2–2.0 μm, (usually 1.6 um) thick, containing a single reserve globule.

Hosts

1. **Turfgrasses**—creeping bentgrass (*Agrostis palustris*), Kentucky bluegrass (*Poa pratensis*), tall fescue (*Festuca arundinacea*), red fescue (*Festuca rubra*), St. Augustinegrass (*Stenotaphrum secundatum*) (Hodges, 1985a; Sprague, 1950).
2. **All Known Gramineous Hosts**—A complete listing of Gramineous hosts is given for *Pythium arrhenomanes* in the section on Pythium blight.

The Fungi

B. *Pythium aristosporum* Vanterpool

Description

Hyphae measuring 2.5 to 6.5 μm in diameter, producing numerous appressoria. Sporangia inflated filamentous, digitate, lobulate, simple or complex, usually germinating by production of germ tubes, though rarely producing reniform, biciliate zoospores, about 10 to 12 μm in diameter when encysted. Oogonia subspherical, both smooth and thin walled, usually acrogenous on short lateral branches, intercalary, measuring 21 to 36 μm, average 28.8 μm, in diameter. Antheridia diclinous and monoclinous, usually 3 to 6, though as many as 8 or more, clavate, crook necked, 6.8 μm wide and 17.4 μm long, making narrow to moderate apical contact with the oogonial wall; a single antheridial branch may supply as many as 4 antheridial cells, the whole forming entanglements about the oogonium, though vegetative prolongations are rare. Oospores aplerotic, single with a smooth, dark wall 1.5 to 2.0 μm thick, containing a single reserve globule and refringent body, oospore measuring 13 to 30 μm, average 24.2 μm in diameter.

1. **Turfgrass Hosts**—creeping bentgrass (*Agrostis palustris*), annual bluegrass (*Poa annua*), and perennial ryegrass (*Lolium perenne*).
2. **All Known Gramineous Hosts**—A listing of the common names for the following species is given in Appendix Table IV. *Agropyron trachycaulum* (Link) Malte, *Agrostis palustris* Huds., *Dactylis glomerata* L., *Echinochloa crusgalli* (L.) Beauv., *Hordeum vulgare* L., *Lolium perenne* L., *Poa an-*

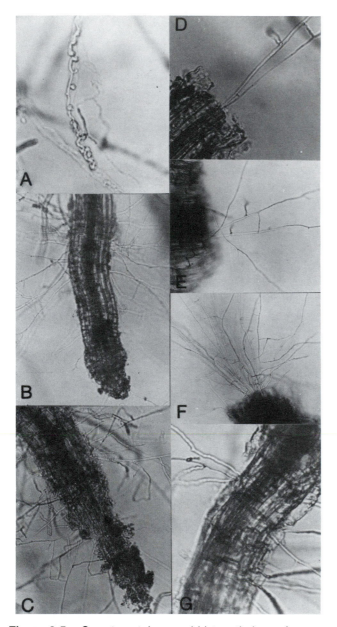

Figure 8-5. Symptomatology and histopathology of creeping bentgrass colonized by *Pythium aristosporum* or *Pythium arrhenomanes*. (A) Mycelium in root hair. (B) Bulbous root tip and growth of mycelium from region of elongation. (C) Devitalized root tip. (D) Growth of mycelium from vascular cylinder within six hours after incubation. (E) Growth of mycelium from the interface of the cortex and vascular cylinder. (F) Massive growth of mycelium from all root tissue after twelve hours of incubation. (G) Direct growth of mycelium from cortical tissue of root. Note absence of rotted tissue or lesions. *Courtesy C. F. Hodges. Reprinted by permission from Plant Disease 69:336–340.*

nua L., *Secale cereale* L., *Triticum aestivum* L. (Hodges, 1985a; Fischer *et al.*, 1942; Nelson and Craft, 1991a; Vanterpool and Sprague, 1942).

Procedures for Isolation and Culture

For a description of procedures for isolation and culture of Pythium species pathogenic to turfgrasses, refer to Pythium Blight (Chapter 4).

Disease Profile

The foliar death phase of Pythium root dysfunction occurs during hot, humid weather the first or second growing season after the green has been established. Severe damage may persist for up to three successive years. After this, the disease usually decreases in severity, and within five years it either ceases to be a problem or occurs at a much reduced level of activity.

The source of the pathogens in renovated or newly constructed greens is not known. They may be introduced with the sand or peat, or they may be present in the collar-apron soil that is commonly left during installation of the sand medium. Although Pythium root dysfunction occurs most commonly in sand greens, pathogenicity tests have failed to note any significant difference in severity of the disease between plants grown in either sand or sand-loam media. The heightened severity of the disease in bentgrass greens established in new sand media is probably due to the lack of other microorganisms which would normally serve as competitors and antagonists to the pathogens. Conversely, the decrease in disease severity that takes place over a three to five year period is probably brought on by more competitive microflora becoming established in the sand.

Pythium arrhenomanes and *Pythium aristosporum* can infect and thoroughly colonize bentgrass roots during the optimal growing conditions of spring and early summer and the fungus and host co-exist during this time without any evidence of root necrosis or foliar decline. However, with the advent of hot weather, although the roots continue to remain free of necrosis the foliage dies very rapidly. This rapid death of the leaves, even though they are not being colonized by the fungus, implies that under high temperature stress the colonized roots are dysfunctional where uptake and translocation of water is concerned. Although the fungus colonizes the vascular cylinder (Figure 8-5 D, E) and the root tip (Figure 8-5 B, C), there is no evidence of physical blockage of the movement of water through the vessels. Recent studies indicate that colonization of the vascular cylinder by the fungus does not occur until the root is dead or dying as a result of the disease and/or aging of the root (personal communication, C. F. Hodges). This means that the dysfunction is probably due to the production of a metabolite by the invading fungus that impairs root uptake of water (Hodges, 1985a).

Control

Attempts to control Pythium root dysfunction with either contact or penetrant fungicides that are active against Pythium species have not been successful. In certain situations, coring and filling the holes with sand topdressing in order to stimulate root growth may provide some degree of recovery from the problem. However, since damage cannot be curtailed by chemical means, when severe outbreaks have occurred, it will be necessary to reestablish the turf once the period of high temperature stress has ended (Hodges, 1985b).

Pythium Decline of Creeping Bentgrass

Pythium decline of bentgrass (*Agrostis palustris*) is prevalent on greens constructed with soil or sand/loam media; however, severe outbreaks of the disease occur most frequently on greens that have been built with high sand content mixes.

Symptoms

The roots and crowns of affected plants develop a root and crown decay. In overall view, small, irregularly shaped, pale green to light brown patches 2 to 4 inches (5–10 cm) in diameter may develop after periods of extended rainfall. The more common above ground symptom pattern for this disease, however, is a general decline in plant vigor and a thinning out of the turf that begins in mid-spring and worsens during the summer months.

In addition to the thinning-out pattern, the leaves of the plants in these areas become pale green to light yellow and then light brown. In contrast with Pythium blight, the leaves of the plants afflicted with Pythium decline are free of colonization by Pythium species. During extended periods of hot weather, Pythium-induced decline can lead to a total loss of bentgrass greens.

Because of the vague nature of its above ground symptoms, positive diagnosis of this disease always requires that a determination be made as to whether the causal fungus is present in the root and crown tissues. Typically, diagnosis for a Pythium-incited disease hinges on the observation of oospores or sporangia in the affected tissues. However, several of the species that incite Pythium decline in turfgrasses do not commonly form reproductive structures in the diseased tissue. Furthermore, nonpathogenic species of Pythium are also known to colonize decomposing turfgrass roots and crowns (Hodges, 1985a; Nelson and Craft, 1991). This means that if the diagnosis of Pythium decline is to be accurate, the affected root and crown tissue should be placed on plated culture media and the taxonomic position of all Pythium isolates determined. For a description of procedures for isolation and culture of Pythium species, see Pythium Blight (Chapter 4).

The Fungi

A listing of Pythium species known to be pathogenic to roots and crowns of creeping bentgrass (*Agrostis palustris*) is given in Table 8-3.

Disease Profile

The species that incite Pythium decline of creeping bentgrass (*Agrostis palustris*) are common inhabitants of golf green rooting media; however, they usually do not cause significant damage unless the plants are weakened by environmental and/or management stresses.

The decline of creeping bentgrass (*Agrostis palustris*) greens is greatest during extended periods of high day-night air temperatures. Also, since surface temperatures are higher on turf with restricted wind movement, outbreaks of the disease on any given golf course will usually be more severe on greens constructed in low lying areas bordered by trees.

High salt concentration in the soil and thatch is a major factor in the development of Pythium decline. In the past, arid and semi-arid regions were the chief areas where salinity was considered to be a problem in turfgrass management. Now, however, with the degradation of many ground and surface water supplies and the widespread use of high sand content greens in golf course construction, salinity problems develop where these difficulties have not been encountered before.

The use of irrigation water containing large amounts of dissolved salts can cause an accumulation of salt in the rooting media. Sand mixtures used in greens construction often have low cation exchange capacities which facilitates the rapid leaching of nutrients. This requires the use of unusually large amounts of fertilizer. Some greens may need as much as 20 pounds (9 kg) of nitrogen per 1,000 square feet (93 m^2) during the first year. These heavy applications of fertilizer can result in the rapid accumulation of salts in the thatch and root zone. When the salt levels become high, the root systems are impaired, thus increasing their susceptibility to infection and colonization by pathogenic Pythium species (Lucas, 1990; Rasmussen and Stanghellini, 1988).

The development of Pythium decline is also favored by high soil moisture levels. Severity of the disease increases during periods of wet weather or when the rooting media are chronically water saturated due to either poor surface drainage, the formation of water-impermeable layers within seedbed mixes, or inadequately drained bases.

Control

Cultural Practices

Irrigation water quality, irrigation and fertilization practices, and infiltration rates and internal drainage are important factors in the control of Pythium decline of bentgrass greens. Both the irrigation water and samples taken from the rooting zones of the greens should be tested frequently throughout the year for salt content. If infiltration and percolation rates are adequate and internal drainage for the green is not impaired, excess salts may be leached out of turfgrass root zones by periodic heavy irrigation.

Good quality irrigation water should have a sodium absorption ratio (SAR) no greater than 4. Water with a high electrical conductivity value (EC) can be used safely if the rooting media has a high infiltration rate, adequate internal drainage, and the irrigation system can always supply excess water. Frequent, shallow irrigations of sand-based greens will result in an increase in accumulation of salts in the thatch layer and root zone (Horst, 1991).

Because of the high leaching rates of high sand content greens, tests should be conducted frequently on the rooting media to determine current fertility levels. Smaller amounts of fertilizer should be applied each time to these greens than would normally be used on ones with higher cation exchange capacities. Even small amounts of slow release fertilizers should be used. In addition to avoiding extremes in the nutritional level of the rooting media, this method also helps maintain the soluble salt content in the root zone at less than phytotoxic levels (Lucas, 1990).

Maintaining high infiltration rates and good subsurface drainage is essential to the control of Pythium decline. Refer to the section entitled Anaerobiosis for a description of procedures for monitoring the infiltration rates of greens and correcting problems due to the formation of water impermeable layers in the root zone.

Use of Fungicides

The use of fungicides for control of Pythium decline has been marked by mixed degrees of success. The most suitable procedure is to treat preventively with a mixture of mancozeb and fosetyl Al at full label rates in 5 gallons of water per 1,000 square feet (19 liters per 93 m^2). For a profile of these fungicides and a listing of representative trade names and manufacturers, see Appendix Table I.

GAEUMANNOMYCES DECLINE OF BERMUDAGRASS

Gaeumannomyces decline of bermudagrass is a destructive disease of hybrid bermudagrass (*Cynodon dactylon* × *Cynodon transvaalensis*) managed as golf course putting greens in the portion of the southeastern region of the United States characterized by warm, humid summers and mild winters. The pathogen has also been identified as the incitant of spring dead spot of bermudagrass in sections of southeastern United States where winter dormancy is induced by cold temperatures.

Symptoms

In overall view, the disease is first seen as irregularly shaped light yellow patches measuring from 8 inches to 3 feet (0.2–1.0 m) in diameter. Yellowing and necrosis is first observed on the lower leaves. Foliar lesions are absent. The root systems of affected plants are short and discolored, with dark-colored lesions on the roots. The surfaces of affected roots and stolons may bear dark strands of mycelium mostly running parallel to the main axes. Eventually, the roots and associated stolons become completely rotted. Entire plants may die, resulting in a thinning of the turf. In the advanced stages of disease development, bare patches may develop and coalesce. New bermudagrass tillers may develop in the patch areas, but they soon become colonized by the pathogen and also decline. The outer margins of a golf green often exhibit the disease symptoms first; eventually, how-

ever, the symptoms may be expressed across the entire green (Elliott and Landschoot, 1991).

The Fungus

Gaeumannomyces graminis (Sacc.) Arx and D. Olivier var. *graminis*; syn. *Ophiobolus graminis* Sacc.

Description

Refer to Spring Dead Spot of Bermudagrass (Chapter 4).

Hosts

1. **Turfgrasses**—annual bluegrass (*Poa annua*), Colonial bentgrass (*Agrostis tenuis*), velvet bentgrass (*Agrostis canina*), creeping bentgrasses (*Agrostis palustris*), bermudagrass (*Cynodon dactylon* and *Cynodon dactylon* × *Cynodon transvaalensis*), Kentucky bluegrass (*Poa pratensis*), red fescue (*Festuca rubra*), tall fescue (*Festuca arundinacea*), St. Augustinegrass (*Stenotaphrum secundatum*), and perennial ryegrass (*Lolium perenne*).

2. **All Known Gramineous Hosts**—For a listing of all known Gramineous hosts of *Gaeumannomyces graminis* var. *graminis*, refer to Spring Dead Spot of Bermudagrass (Chapter 4).

Procedures for Isolation and Culture

For a description of procedures for isolation and culture of *Gaeumannomyces* species pathogenic to turfgrasses, refer to Spring Dead Spot of Bermudagrass (Chapter 4).

Disease Profile

Gaeumannomyces decline of bermudagrass occurs when the continuing daily air temperature average is greater than 80 °F (27 °C), the ongoing relative humidity is higher than 75 percent, and precipitation occurs almost daily. The severity of the disease is also greater in turf maintained at low cutting heights or growing in soil low in potassium.

The fungus spreads from plant to plant by growing along the surfaces of roots, stolons and rhizomes. Local distribution from one site to the next is by transport of infested soil and diseased plant tissue on coring and dethatching equipment. Long range transport of the pathogen and its introduction into new locations can be accomplished by the use of sprigs already colonized by the pathogen. Since sprigs are normally planted into fumigated soil, populations of suppressive soil-borne organisms are low, which enables the pathogen to spread rapidly on the new root systems. This is probably the reason that bermudagrass golf greens often show decline symptoms within two to three years of their establishment (Elliott, 1991b; Elliott, 1993b).

Control

Cultural Practices

Thatch should be kept at ½ inch (1.3 cm) in thickness, the turf mowed at the maximum height the use requirements will permit, and coring performed in the diseased areas to improve soil aeration and foster the production of new roots. The aerification process should be accomplished with large tines and the procedure should be performed every three to four weeks during the late spring, summer and early fall months. Aerification should be accomplished to a depth of 6 inches (15 cm). Cores should be removed and topdressing accomplished with pathogen-free material. The topdressing should be accomplished with a topsoil mix containing up to 30 percent organic matter. Also, a light topdressing each week may be useful on the areas that are already showing symptoms.

The nitrogen component of the fertilization program should be based on the use of acidifying fertilizers such as ammonium sulfate. Avoid nitrate nitrogen sources. Also, attention should be given to maintaining adequate potassium levels. Nitrogen and potassium should be applied in a 1:1 ratio at ½ to 1 pound (227–453 g) per 1000 square feet (93 m²) per week.

Do not use hydrated lime to control algae. In the long term, the lime may exacerbate the algal problem (see Anaerobiosis). In the short term it will cause the pH to increase quickly, thus increasing the severity of the decline (Elliott and Freeman, 1992).

Use of Resistant Grasses

Both 'Tifdwarf' and 'Tifgreen' cultivars of hybrid bermudagrass (*Cynodon dactylon × Cynodon transvaalensis*), the most widely grown cultivars on golf greens, are susceptible to Gaeumannomyces decline (Elliott and Landschoot, 1991).

Use of Fungicides

Propicinazole, triadimefon, and fenarimol are labeled for use on bermudagrass. Although none of them has bermudagrass decline specifically listed on its label, they show promise in controlling the disease. Control seems to be best achieved when the fungicide is applied after aerifying or spiking the green. The fungicide should be lightly watered into the root zone immediately after application. The labels for these products should be read carefully before using. Fenarimol is not recommended for fall applications if the green will be overseeded with a fenarimol sensitive, cool season grass. Propiconazole should not be applied to bermudagrass golf greens when the air temperatures exceed 90 °F (32 °C). Also, propiconazole applications to bermudagrass greens should not exceed 4 fluid ounces (118 ml) per 1,000 square feet (93 m²) every 30 days (Elliott and Freeman, 1992). For a profile of each of these fungicides and a list of representative manufacturers, see Appendix Table I.

TAKE-ALL ROOT ROT OF ST. AUGUSTINEGRASS

Take-all root rot is a destructive disease of St. Augustinegrass used in lawns in residential landscapes in Florida, Alabama, Texas, and California.

Symptoms

Above ground symptoms consist of chlorotic, thinning turf in circular to irregular patches 2 to over 15 feet (0.6–5.0 m) in diameter. Death of plants in the affected areas is common (Figure 8-6). The overall appearance is similar at times to those of Rhizoctonia blight (incited by *Rhizoctonia solani*). However, unlike Rhizoctonia blight, there is no basal leaf and sheath rot, therefore, the leaves do not separate easily from the plant. The roots of plants in these patches are short and rotted. The stolons can be readily lifted from the ground. Sod producers are unable to harvest sod, because the sod strength is severely weakened by the root rot. Nodes are usually rotted also and black lesions develop on stolons (Elliott, 1993a).

The Fungus

Gaeumannomyces graminis (Sacc.) Arx and D. Olivier var. *graminis*; syn. *Ophiobolus graminis* Sacc.

Description

Refer to Spring Dead Spot of Bermudagrass (Chapter 4).

Figure 8-6.   Severe patch symptoms associated with take-all root rot of St. Augustinegrass. Note the bare ground and rotting stolons. *Courtesy Monica Elliott.*

Hosts

1. **Turfgrasses**—annual bluegrass (*Poa annua*), Colonial bentgrass (*Agrostis tenuis*), velvet bentgrass (*Agrostis canina*), creeping bentgrasses (*Agrostis palustris*), bermudagrass (*Cynodon dactylon* and *Cynodon dactylon* × *Cynodon transvaalensis*), Kentucky bluegrass (*Poa pratensis*), red fescue (*Festuca rubra*), tall fescue (*Festuca arundinacea*), St. Augustinegrass (*Stenotaphrum secundatum*), and perennial ryegrass (*Lolium perenne*).
2. **All Known Gramineous Hosts**—For a listing of all known Gramineous hosts of *Gaeumannomyces graminis* var. *graminis*, refer to Spring Dead Spot of Bermudagrass (Chapter 4).

Procedures for Isolation and Culture

For a description of procedures for isolation and culture of *Gaeumannomyces* species pathogenic to turfgrasses, refer to Spring Dead Spot of Bermudagrass (Chapter 4).

Disease Profile

There does not appear to be a relationship between take-all root rot incidence and severity and soil type, cultivar or age of St. Augustinegrass. Development of the disease is favored by warm, humid weather, with major symptom expressions occurring during the summer and fall months and the frequency of daily precipitation is high. The pathogen colonizes underground plant parts, and since St. Augustinegrass is vegetatively propagated, it is likely that the disease can be spread to new locations with sprigs or sod (Elliott, 1993a).

Control

There is no indication of varietal resistance to take-all root rot. The disease has been observed on 'Floratam,' 'Jade,' 'Raleigh' in Florida, and on common St. Augustinegrass in Alabama. Also, the pathogen has been isolated from 'DelMar,' 'Jade,' 'Dalsa 8401,' 'Mercedes,' 'Bitterblue,' 'Standard,' California common, Scott's '138,' '770' and '2090,' 'Sunclipse' 'Raliegh,' 'Milberger M1,' 'Seville,' and 'Floratam' in California (Elliott, 1993a; Wilkinson and Pedersen, 1993).

There are no fungicides registered for control of this disease. The use of acidifying fertilizers such as ammonium sulfate and maintaining adequate soil potassium levels offer the best possibility for reducing disease severity.

POLYMYXA ROOT ROT

Symptoms

Plants affected with Polymyxa root rot are characterized by a general loss of intensity of green coloration and slowness of regrowth after mowing or heavy wear. The feeder root systems are restricted in growth and show a brown, dry rot. Since the pathogen is an obligate parasite, detection of its presence must be accomplished by clearing and staining the roots. Warm lacto-phenol serves as a satisfactory clearing and staining solution (Britton and Rogers, 1963).

The Fungus

Polymyxa graminis Ledingham

Description

Resting spores spherical or polyhedral, 5 to 7 μm in diameter, smooth, with yellow brown outer walls. Zoosporangia large with persistent smooth thin walls; zoosporangia formed by septation of the mature thallus. Discharge tube segmented. Zoospores numerous, 4 to 5 μm in diameter, diflagellate and heterokont, discharged without vesicle formation. Non-hypertrophing, obligate parasite.

Hosts

1. **Turfgrasses**—creeping bentgrass (*Agrostis palustris*) and hybrid bermudagrass (*Cynodon dactylon* × *Cynodon transvaalensis*).
2. **All Known Gramineous Hosts**—A listing of the common names for each of the following species is given in Appendix Table IV. *Agropyron repens* (L.) Beauv., *Agrostis palustris* Huds., *Cynodon dactylon* (L.) Pers. × *Cynodon transvaalensis* Burtt-Davy 'Tifgreen,' *Hordeum vulgare* L., *Secale cereale* L., *Triticum aestivum* L. (Brittan and Rogers, 1963; Dale and Murdoch, 1969; Sprague, 1950).

Disease Profile

The pathogen colonizes primarily the feeder root system causing necrosis of epidermal and cortical cells. Root hairs are also colonized extensively. The highest incidence of primary root infections occurs in late fall and early spring. The formation of zoosporangia of the pathogen is greatest during conditions ideal for maximum root growth of bentgrasses. Optimum conditions for root infection are high soil moisture and air temperatures between 60–65 °F (15–18 °C). Frequent and close mowing enhances the development of the disease.

PYRENOCHAETA ROOT ROT

Pryenochaeta root rot is normally regarded as a minor disease of bentgrass, bermudagrass, creeping red fescue and Kentucky bluegrass. Under conditions of plant stress, however, it may contribute materially to the degeneration of a stand of turfgrass.

Symptoms

The disease is characterized by a red discoloration of the root system. Younger roots are a distinct pink color, while older roots tend to be reddish brown (Meyer and Sinclair, 1970).

The Fungus

Pyrenochaeta terrestris (Hans.) Gorenz, Walker and Larson

Description

Pycnidia subglobose, ostiolate, papillate, dark brown to black, with scattered setae about the ostiole, setae light to dark brown, 1 to 5 septate, 8 to 120 μm, pycnidia carbonaceous, 170 to 350 μm, sometimes gregarious. Pycnospores continuous, hyaline, oblong-ovoid, 3.7 to 5.8 μm × 1.8 to 2.3 μm, bioguttulate, sessile in the pycnidium, escaping as a gelatinous mass through ruptures, rarely as a gelatinous cirrus through the ostiole. Mycelium septate, hyaline, guttulate, 1.0 to 4.5 μm, frequently anastamosing.

Procedures for Isolation and Culture

The fungus grows slowly in culture. Isolation can be facilitated on potato dextrose agar by adding a surfactant to the medium to slow the rate of growth of associated fungi (Meyer and Sinclair, 1970).

Hosts

1. **Turfgrasses**—creeping bentgrass (*Agrostis palustris*), bermudagrass (*Cynodon dactylon*), red fescue (*Festuca rubra*), and Kentucky bluegrass (*Poa pratensis*).
2. **All Known Gramineous Hosts**—A listing of common names for each of the following species is given in Appendix Table IV. *Agropyron ciliare* (Trin.) Franch, *A. cristatum* (L.) Gaertn., *A. desertorum* (Fisch.) Schult., *A. elongatum* (Host) Beauv., *A. intermedium* (Host) Beauv., *A. michnoi* Roschev., *A. mongolicum* Keng, *A. pendulinum* (Nevski) Ined. (fide Swallen), *A. repens* (L.) Beauv., *A. semicostatum* (Steud.) Nees, *A. sibiricum* (Willd.) Beauv., *A. smithii* Rydb., *A. trachycaulum* (Link) Malte, *Agrostis palustris* Huds., *Andropogon furcatus* Muhl., *A. hallii* Hack., *Arthraxon hispidus* var. *cryptatherus* (Hack.) Honda, *Avena sativa* L., *Bouteloua curtipendula* (Michx.) Torr., *B. gracilis* (H. B. K.) Lag., *Bromus arvensis* L., *B. carinatus* Hook. and Arn., *B. erectus* Huds., *B. inermis* Leyss, *Calamovilfa longifolia* (Hook.) Scribn. *Cenchrus pauciflorus* Benth., *Cynodon dactylon* (L.) Pers., *Dactylis glomerata* L., *Distichlis stricta* (Torr.) Rydb., *Echinochloa crusgalli* (L.) Beauv., *E. crusgalli* var. *frumentacea* (Roxb.) Wright, *Elymus canadensis* L., *E. dahuricus* Turcz., *E. interruptus* Buckl., *E. junceus* Fisch., *E. sibiricus* L., *Festuca octoflora* Walt., *F. rubra* L., *Hordeum brevisubu-*

latum (Trin.) Lk., *H. distichon* L., *H. vulgare* L., *Koeleria cristata* (L.) Pers., *Muhlenbergia squarrosa* (Trin.) Rydb., *Oryzopsis hymenoides* (Roem. and Schult.) Rick., *Panicum capillare* L., *P. miliaceum* L., *P. virgatum* L., *Phleum alpinum* L., *P. pratense* L., *Poa compressa* L., *P. pratensis* L., *P. secunda* Presl, *Saccharum officinarum* L., *Schedonnardus paniculatus* (Nutt.) Trel., *Setaria italica* (L.) Beauv., *S. lutescens* (Weigel) F. T. Hubb., *S. viridis* (L.) Beauv., *Sorghum vulgare* Pers., *S. vulgare* var. *sudanense* (Piper) Hitchc., *Stipa comata* Trin. and Rupr., *S. viridula* Trin., *S. williamsii* Scribn., *Triticum aestivum* L., *T. dicoccum* Schrank, *T. durum* Desf., *T. spelta* L., *T. timopheevi* Zhukov., *Zea mays* L. (Index Plant Dis. 1960; Meyer and Sinclair, 1970; Sprague, 1950).

PSEUDOCERCOSPORELLA BASAL ROT

Symptoms

Affected plants are usually retarded in growth and the leaves are pale green. Lesioning usually conspicuous on the bases of the leaf sheaths. These spots are sometimes circular but more often elongate, up to ⅛ inch (3 mm) long, and light tan to white with brown borders. Later in development of the disease, these necrotic areas extend inward, and eventually, involve the larger portion of the crown and root tissue. The necrosis is at first light in color. Later, it progresses to a brown, dry rot at the ground level. At this stage of development, the surfaces of the lesions assume a black, charred appearance, with still darker brown borders. Eventually, the entire plant may be easily broken loose at this point.

The Fungus

Pseudocercosporella herpotrichoides (Fron) Deighton; syn. *Cercosporella herpotrichoides* Fron.

Description

Vegetative mycelium yellow to dark brown, linear celled; stromatic mycelium medium to very heavy walled, frequently consisting of polygonal cells forming charred masses on the outside of the stems and sheaths or occurring in cells in the interior of diseased culms. Conidiophores simple or slightly branched, sometimes swollen at the base and elongated, produced from subicula. Conidia somewhat curved, obclavate, 2 to many celled (usually 5–7), 1.5–3.5 μm × 30–80 μm (usually 40–60 μm long).

Hosts

1. **Turfgrasses**—creeping bentgrass (*Agrostis palustris*) and Kentucky bluegrass (*Poa pratensis*).
2. **All Known Gramineous Hosts**—A listing of the common names for each of the following species is given in Appendix Table IV. *Aegilops cylindrica* Host, *A. ovata* L., *A. triuncialis* L., *Agropyron cristatum* (L.) Gaertn., *A. dasystachyum* (Hook.) Scribn., *A. inerme* (Scribn. and Smith) Rydb., *A. riparium* Scribn. and Smith, *Agrostis palustris* Huds., *Avena sativa* L., *Bromus carinatus* Hook. and Arn., *B. inermis* Leyss., *B. japonicus* Thunb., *B. sterilis* L., *B. tectorum* L., *Festuca idahoensis* Elmer, *Hordeum vulgare* L., *Koeleria cristata* (L.) Pers., *Poa pratensis* L., *Poa secunda* Presl, *Secale cereale* L., *Sitanion hystrix* (Nutt.) J. G. Smith, *Triticum aestivum* L., *T. dicoccum* Schrank, *T. durum* Desf., *T. monococcum* L., *T. spelta* L. (Cunningham, 1965; Index Plant Dis., 1960; Sprague, 1950).

Disease Profile

Pseudocercosporella basal rot is a cold, wet weather disease. The fungus survives on colonized leaf litter. Spores are produced during wet weather in late fall, winter and early spring. Germination of spores occurs at temperatures as low as 32 °F (0 °C). Soil temperatures of 40–50 °F (5–10 °C) and frequent daily precipitation is highly conducive to disease development. Spore dispersal is accomplished primarily by splashing and wind-driven rain (Pitt and Bainbridge, 1983; Rowe and Powelson, 1973).

9

Fairy Rings

Fairy rings is the name commonly used for the circles of mushrooms or circular bands of rapidly growing grass that develop in established turf. The term "fairy rings" has its origin in the myths and superstitions associated with their occurrence in the Middle Ages. The circles were thought by some to be the dancing sites of fairies. An essay published in 1563 suggested that they were caused by strikes of lightning, and although the author declared that only "ignorant people affirm [these] to be the rings of the Fairies dances," accounts of supernatural activities associated with the occurrence of the rings persisted. In Holland, for example, the dead grass in the center of the ring was supposed to mark the place where the devil churned his butter. In France, intentional entrance into one of the rings would result in an encounter with large toads with bulging eyes. If a Scottish farmer tilled an area containing fairy rings, then "weirdless days and weary nights are his to his deein' day." A more optimistic view of fairy rings was taken in England, where it was considered a good omen to build a house on land supporting them (Ramsbottom, 1953; Shantz and Piemeisel, 1917).

There are two basic types of fairy rings: (1) **edaphic**[1]—rings that are produced by fungi that colonize primarily the soil, and (2) **lectophilic**[2]—rings that are produced by fungi that colonize primarily leaf litter and thatch.

EDAPHIC FAIRY RINGS

Edaphic fairy rings are produced by fungi that colonize primarily the soil. Depending on the nature of the soil profile and the presence or absence of organic matter, these fungi may go to a depth of 2–3 feet (0.6–1 m).

---

[1]Edaphic from *edaphos* (Gr) referring to the soil or earth as a foothold for higher plants.
[2]Lectophilic from *lectus* (L) meaning bed, litter or thatch, and *philos* (Gr) meaning love of, or favorably disposed toward.

Symptoms

In overall view, the zones of stimulated grass are seen as more or less continuous, circular bands of turfgrass that are darker green and faster growing than the adjacent plants of the same species. These belts of greener plants may range from 4–12 inches (10–30 cm) wide, and the diameter of the circles they form will usually vary from 3–12 feet (0.9–3.7 m). Several distinct rings frequently occur in the same area. In these cases, as the rings converge on each other, fungus activity ceases in the zones of contact. As the result, the concentric shape of the original rings gives way to a scalloped effect.

A characteristic feature of fairy rings is the presence of the fruiting bodies of the associated fungi (sporophores) in the band of stimulated turfgrass. Commonly referred to as "mushrooms," "toadstools," and "puffballs," from time to time these structures may be abundant throughout the circumference of the rings (Plate 29-A).

The symptomotology for edaphic fairy rings may range from the simplest form of appearance of orderly rings of mushrooms or puffballs, causing no apparent damage to the plants, to complex inner and outer ring systems of stimulated grass, which are in turn separated by zones of dead turfgrass. Accordingly, a classification system has been developed that recognizes three basic types of edaphic fairy rings (Shantz and Piemeisel, 1917).

Type I: Those in which the grass is ultimately killed or badly damaged.
Type II: Those in which the grass is only stimulated.
Type III: Those which apparently do not influence the growth of the turfgrass.

The makeup of a Type I fairy ring in its more complex form is shown in Figure 9-1. Note that this type of ring has two stimulated zones. There is an outer zone of stimulation in which the fruiting structures of the causal fungus are present. This is de-

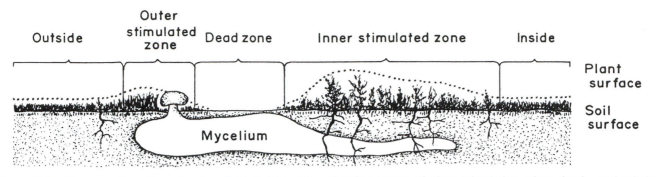

Figure 9-1. Cross section of a complex, Type I, fairy ring—showing zones of plant stimulation, plant death, and relative distribution of fungus mycelium in the soil.

limited on the inner side by a zone of dead plants, which in itself is bordered by another ring of stimulated turfgrass. Symptoms of a Type I fairy ring are shown in Plate 29-B, C.

The Fungi

Fifty-four species of basidiomycetous fungi have been reported to be capable of developing edaphic fairy rings. The size of the fruiting bodies among the various species range from ⅜ inch (1 cm) to 12 inches (30 cm) in diameter. For a full listing of the individual species that form edaphic fairy rings, see Table 9-1.

Hosts

All cultivated turfgrasses are affected by the fungi that develop edpahic fairy rings. In addition, the small grains, i.e., wheat (*Triticum* spp.), oats (*Avena sativa*), barley (*Hordeum* spp.), and rye (*Secale cereals*), respond to the presence of edaphic fairy ring fungi in the manner characteristic of the turfgrasses.

Disease Profile

Edaphic fairy rings begin from transported bits of mycelium, or less frequently from germination of basidiospores. The rudimentary fairy ring is generally first seen as a cluster of fruiting bodies. As the mycelium progresses outward from the point of origin, formation of the circular pattern of darker green, faster growing grass becomes apparent. Two to three years from the beginning of active colonization of the soil are usually required for zonations characteristic of Type I and Type II rings to develop.

The rate of outward movement, as well as overall diameter of the ring, is determined by prevailing weather conditions and the fungus species in question. Variations in rate of enlargement of fairy rings

have been recorded from 3 inches (7.6 cm) to 2 feet (0.6 m) per year. Areas void of vegetation, or currently supporting active fairy rings, serve as barriers to the outward progress of the rings.

Although the diameters of typical fairy rings range from 3 feet (1 m) to 12 feet (3.7 m), rings have been found in Southern Alberta that measure up to 2,600 feet (800 m) across (Lebeau and Hawn, 1961). Two hundred foot (61 m) wide fairy rings have been found in Colorado, and a ring 2,000 feet (600 m) in diameter has been reported occurring near Belfort in Eastern France (Shantz and Piemeisel, 1917; Becker, 1953). A conservative estimate of the age of the rings in Alberta would be 1,000–1,200 years. The rings in Colorado rings are at least 300 years old, while the age of the fairy ring near Belfort has been estimated at about 700 years.

The factors that bring about enlargement in the diameter of fairy rings, and the reasons for growth stimulation, and ultimate death of grass in Type I and Type II rings are interrelated. Through the saprophytic action of the fungus mycelium, the protein portion of nonliving organic matter in the soil is reduced to ammonia. This unites with other compounds or is changed by bacteria to nitrites, and ultimately by other bacteria into nitrates. The resulting accumulation of nitrogen in the soil in a form that is readily available to higher plants is what brings about the typical growth pattern of conspicuous bands of taller, darker green plants (Mathur, 1970; Shantz and Piemeisel, 1917; Smith, 1957a).

In friable, sandy-loam soils, the mycelium of the fairy ring fungus may penetrate to depths of 12–20 inches (30–50 cm). In high clay-content soils, however, mycelial growth may be limited to the upper 1–2 inches (2.5–3.0 cm) (Smith, Jackson and Woolhouse, 1989). When the soil mass supporting the stimulated band of grass becomes fully permeated with mycelium, it becomes almost impervious to the

Table 9-1. Species of basidiomycetous fungi that form edaphic fairy rings

Agaricus arvensis Schaeff:Fr	(Schantz and Piemeisel, 1917; Smith, 1957a; Smith, Jackson and Woolhouse, 1989)
Agaricus campestris Fr.	(Smith, 1957a)
Calocybe carnea (Bull:Fr) Kuhner	(Smith, Jackson and Woolhouse, 1989)
Calocybe gambosa (Fr.) Singer	(Bayliss-Elliot, 1926; Ramsbottom, 1953)
Calvatia cyathiformis f. sp. *fragilis* (Vitt.) Smith	(Shantz and Piemeisel, 1917)
Calvatia cyanthiformis (Bosc.) Morgan	(Shantz and Piemeisel, 1917; Smith, 1957a)
Camarophyllus pratensis (Pers:Fr) Kummer	(Smith, Jackson and Woolhouse, 1989)
Camarophyllus niveus (Fr.) Karst	(Smith, Jackson and Woolhouse, 1989)
Camarophyllus virgeneus (Wulf:Fr) Kummer	(Lees, 1869; Smith, Jackson and Woolhouse, 1989)
Clarulinopsis corniculata (Fr.) Corner	(Smith, Jackson and Woolhouse, 1989)
Clitocybe rivulosa (Pers: Fr) Kummer	(Smith, Jackson and Woolhouse, 1989)
Clitocybe nebularis (Batsch:Fr) Kummer	(Stahl, 1900)
Clitocybe maxima (Fl. Wett. Fr.) Kummer	(Ramsbottom, 1953; Rea, 1922)
Clitocybe infundibuliformis (Schaeff:Fr) Quel	(Lees, 1869)
Chlorophyllum molybites (Meyer:Fr) Mass.	(Schantz and Piemeisel, 1917)
Collybia butryacea (Bull:Fr) Quel	(Smith, 1957a; Smith, Jackson and Woolhouse, 1989)
Collybia confluens (Pers:Fr.) Kummer	(Lees, 1869)
Coprinus comatus (Muller:Fr) Gray	(Smith, Jackson and Woolhouse, 1989)
Coprinus atramentarius (Bull:Fr) Fr.	(Smith, Jackson and Woolhouse, 1989)
Dintinum repandum (L:Fr) Gray	(Ballion, 1906; Lees, 1869)
Disciseda borista (Kl.) P. Henn	(Schantz and Piemeisel, 1917)
Hebeloma crustuliniforme (Bull:St. Am) Quel	(Lees, 1869)
Hydnellum suaveolens (Scop.) Karst.	(Thomas, 1905)
Hydnum compactum (Pers.) Fr.	(Ludwig, 1906)
Hygrocybe coccinea (Schaeff:Fr) Kummer	(Smith, Jackson and Woolhouse, 1989)
Hygrocybe psittacina (Schaeff:Fr) Karst	(Smith, 1957a)
Hygrocybe reai (R. Maire) Lange	(Smith, Jackson and Woolhouse, 1989)
Hygrophoropsis aurantiaca (Wulfen:Fr) Maire	(Smith, Jackson and Woolhouse, 1989)
Lactarius insulsus Fr.	(Ludwig, 1906)
Lactarius piperatus (Fr.) S. F. Gray	(Lees, 1869)
Lactarius torminosus (Schaeff:Fr) Gray	(Ludwig, 1906)
Lepista nudua (Bull:Fr) Cooke	(Bayliss-Elliot, 1926)
Lepista personata (Fr) Cooke	(Bayliss-Elliot, 1926; Smith, 1957a; Smith, Jackson and Woolhouse, 1989)
Leucoagaricus naucinus (Fr.) Sing.	(Howard, Rowell and Keil, 1951)
Leucopaxillus giganteus (Fr.) Sing	(Ballion, 1906)
Lycoperdon curtisii Berkeley	(Coker and Couch, 1928; Shantz and Piemeisel, 1917)
Lycoperdon hiemale Bull	(Smith, Jackson and Woolhouse, 1989)
Lycoperdon perlatum Pers.	(Gregory, 1982; Smith, Jackson and Woolhouse, 1989)
Macrolepiota procera (Scop:Fr) Sing.	(Howard, Rowell and Keil, 1951)
Marasmius oreades (Bolt:Fr) Fr.	(Bayliss-Elliot, 1926; Smith, 1957a; Smith, Jackson and Woolhouse, 1989)
Marasmius urens (Bull) Fr.	(Lees, 1869)
Melanoleuca grarmopodia (Bull:Fr) Pat.	(Lees, 1869)
Melanoleuca melaleuca (Pers:Fr) Murr.	(Shantz and Piemeisel, 1917)
Nolanea staurospora Bres.	(Smith, Jackson and Woolhouse, 1989)
Panaeolus campanulatus (L.) Quel	(Smith, Jackson and Woolhouse, 1989)
Panaeolina foenisecii (Pers:Fr) Maire	(Smith, Jackson and Woolhouse, 1989)
Paxillus involutus (Butsch:Fr) Fr.	(Ludwig, 1906)
Psilocybe semilanceata (Fr.) Kummer	(Smith, Jackson and Woolhouse, 1989)
Scleroderma verrucosum (Vaill.) Pers.	(Smith, 1957a; Smith Jackson and Woolhouse, 1989)
Suillus grevillei (Klotzsch) Singer	(Ludwig, 1906)
Tricholoma columbetta (Fr.) Kummer	(Massart, 1910)
Tricholoma panoeolum (Fr.) Quell	(Bayliss-Elliot, 1926)
Tricholoma sordidum Fr.	(Beard, Vargas and Rieke, 1973)
Tricholoma terreum (Schaeff:Fr) Kummer	(Wollaston, 1807)

penetration of surface water. Because of the accelerated rate of plant growth brought on by the increased availability of soil nitrogen, the moisture in the fungus-permeated soil is depleted more rapidly than in adjacent areas, and since the moisture in this zone cannot be replaced in quantities sufficient to sustain growth, death of plants results. In temperate climates, the soil in these bands usually remains hydrophobic for 6–8 weeks, while with irrigated turf in arid to semi-arid regions, these hydrophobic zones may persist for 12–18 months.

The depletion of organic matter needed for growth of the fairy ring fungus, and the development of ammonia and various staling products in the rhizosphere causes the fungus to die out in the center of the ring. The hyphae at the periphery of the stimulated zone, however, grow outward into new soil. This eventually results in the development of a new band of stimulated plant growth, and thus the enlargement of the diameter of the ring.

Studies on the pathology of fairy rings formed by *Marasmius oreades* of has shown that this organism can infect and colonize the roots of Kentucky bluegrass (*Poa pratensis*), creeping red fescue (*Festuca rubra*) and Colonial bentgrass (*Agrostis tenuis*) (Filer, 1965a). Also, hydrogen cyanide, a compound toxic to the roots of these grass species has been found in *Marasmius oreades* infested soil (Filer, 1965b; Filer 1966a; Lebeau and Hawn, 1963a). With *Marasmius oreades*-based fairy rings, then, the nature of pathogenesis is probably a complex combination of (1) depletion of available nitrogen for plant growth, (2) development of a hydrophobic soil, and (3) direct pathogenic activities of the fungus on the root system.

Fertilization of turf with natural organic fertilizers has been associated with heavy mushroom infestations (Gould, Miller and Polley, 1955). An increase in nitrogen fertility has been shown to bring about an increase in the intensity of development of Type I *Tricholoma sordidum* fairy rings (Beard, Vargas and Rieke, 1973) (Table 9-2).

Control

Fairy ring fungi have been shown to be vulnerable to the toxic effects of certain fungicides, and some fungicides are presently registered for fairy ring control in Europe. Nevertheless, success in the control of fairy ring with fungicidal applications is marginal at best. The hydrophobic condition of the soil makes it difficult to reach and permeate the mycelial mass with aqueous solutions or suspensions of fungicides—even when penetration is aided by coring and the use of wetting agents. Also, large

Table 9-2. The effect of five nitrogen rates on *Tricholoma* fairy ring development in Merion Kentucky bluegrass. *After Beard, Vargas and Rieke, 1973.*

Annual nitrogen application rate, kg/are	Ave. number *Tricholoma* fairy rings present[a]	Soil pH tests	
		1968	1970
0	0 a	7.3	7.3
2.0	0 a	7.2	7.1
3.9	3 b	7.2	7.1
5.9	5 c	6.9	6.9
7.8	6 c	6.5	6.5

[a]Rings per 0.9 × 9 m plot. Treatments with the same letter are not significantly different at p = .05.

quantities of fungicide are required, and if control is achieved, it is often short lived.

The most reliable techniques for control of fairy ring are (1) replacement of the fungus infested soil, (2) fumigation with methyl bromide, or (3) prolonged soaking of the soil with water.

Replacement of Infested Soil

Eradication by removing the mycelium-infested soil is the oldest known means of controlling fairy rings. Although less labor intensive procedures for eliminating the fairy ring fungi can now be used, this method still finds ready application in areas with low populations of small rings.

A trench 12 inches (31 cm) deep and extending 18 inches (46 cm) on either side of the stimulated zone should be dug and the soil discarded. In removing the infested soil, it is very important not to spill it on the adjacent, healthy turfgrass. The trench should then be filled with fresh soil from a source free of fairy rings, and the area sodded or reseeded.

Fumigation with Methyl Bromide

Methyl bromide is an effective fairy ring control fumigant, however, proper use of the material requires a maximum of skill and precaution. It cannot be over emphasized that methyl bromide in its final form is a poisonous gas, therefore, when the material is being used, extreme caution should be exercised to keep all children and pets away from the area.

In order for maximum control to be realized, the following procedures should be conformed to:

1. Treatment should not be made until the soil is 60°F (16°C) or warmer.
2. Mark off an area 18 inches (46 cm) from the outer and inner edges of the stimulated zone.

3. Immediately before treating, mow the grass short in the marked off area and core or punch holes in the sod 2 inches (5 cm) apart and 2–4 inches (5–10 cm) deep with a spading fork.
4. Place evaporating pans at regular intervals in the area to be treated in such a fashion that they may be reached easily after the covering plastic sheeting is in place.
5. Cover the marked off area with the plastic sheeting. The sheeting should be supported above the soil by the use of stakes, sacks filled with straw, or polyethylene pillows.
6. The edges of the plastic sheeting should be placed in shallow trenches, covered with soil, and this, in turn, wetted to further aid in the sealing process.
7. Release the methyl bromide at 2 pounds per 100 square feet (0.9 kg/9 m²) through tubes into the evaporating pans under the plastic sheeting. The odorized type of methyl bromide, containing 2 percent chloropicrin, is to be preferred because of the safety factor.
8. Leave the plastic sheeting for 36–48 hours. After this remove the covering, and allow the treated areas to aerate for 7–14 days before reseeding or resodding.

Prolonged Water Soaking of Soil

This system consists of water soaking the soil for a distance of 18 inches on either side of the stimulated zone and to a depth of 12 inches (30 cm), and maintaining this condition for a period of 4–6 weeks. A hydrogun or a tree root feeder are ideal for establishing the water soaked condition. If these are not available, and surface irrigation is to be employed, then the area to be treated should be uniformly perforated with a hand aerifier or garden fork to a depth of 4–6 inches (10–15 cm) prior to the first application of water. It is important that the soil remain saturated throughout the entire treatment period; therefore, water should be applied to the affected area every second day (Lebeau and Hawn, 1963b).

LECTOPHILIC FAIRY RINGS

The primary activity of lectophilic fairy ring fungi takes place in the leaf litter and thatch. Lectophilic fairy rings can occur on turf under any type of management, but are best known for their development on bowling greens and golf greens. Their impact on the turf ranges from little or no damage to the production of unsightly rings to the development of circular patches of dead grass.

Symptoms

The symptom patterns for lectophilic fairy rings range from the development of either (1) arcs or complete circles of mushrooms with no apparent effect on the plants, (2) circular bands of darker green grass, (3) circular bands of yellow grass, or (4) circular bands of dead turfgrass. Occasionally, white mycelial growth can be observed on the lower leaves of affected plants, permeating the thatch layer to a depth of 0.25 inch (7 mm). The belts of affected grass may range from 2–4 inches (6–10 cm) wide, and the diameter of the circles they form will usually vary from 1–6 feet (0.3–1.8 m). Several rings often develop simultaneously in the same area. In these cases, if they converge, fungus activity ceases at the areas of contact. As the result, the concentric shape of the original rings changes to a scalloped effect. The infested thatch often develops a strong "mushroom odor." Also, the growth rate of young roots developing at the nodes may temporarily slowed down.

A system of classification has been developed that recognizes three basic types of lectophilic fairy rings (Smith, Jackson and Woolhouse, 1989).

Type A: Produces sparse to abundant mycelium, with or without mushrooms, which develops on shoot bases and in the thatch with little or no apparent effect on grass growth.
Type B: Produces stimulated grass growth and/or turfgrass discoloration. Thatch degradation is apparent but the plants are not severely injured and will eventually recover.
Type C: Produces severe injury to the grass. During the initial stages of formation, the growth of the turf may or may not be stimulated.

The Fungi

Coprinus kubickae Pilat and Svrcek, *Marasmius siccus* (Schwein) Fr., and *Trechispora alnicola* (Bourd. and Galz.) Liberta. Certain sterile (nonsporophore forming) Basidiomycetes have also been found to be capable of forming lectophilic fairy rings (Dale, 1972; Redhead and Smith, 1981; Smith, Stynes and Moore, 1970; Jackson, 1972; Wilkinson, 1987).

Hosts

All turfgrasses are affected by the fungi that form lectophilic fairy rings.

Disease Profile

The lectophilic fairy ring species *Trechispora alnicola* has been shown to be mildly pathogenic to the roots of Kentucky bluegrass (*Poa pratensis*). Hyphal penetration of the root epidermal cells by direct means, and mycelial movement through the underlying cortical tissue is intracellular. Distinct lesioning or general necrosis of the colonized roots does not develop; rather, during the advanced stages of colonization, the affected roots become tan to light brown and may be slightly stunted. Complete remission of root systems is common (Wilkinson, 1987).

A sterile, lectophilic fairy ring Basidiomycete has also been shown to be capable of infecting and colonizing the lower stems, crowns and roots of annual bluegrass (*Poa annua*) and Kentucky bluegrass (*Poa pratensis*). The hyphae of this species enter the crowns through breaks in the epidermis associated with emerging leaves. Mycelial movement through the underlying tissue is both intercellular and intracellular. Penetration of the cell walls is accomplished through pit pairs. Some hyphal swelling occurs adjacent to these points of entry. Colonization is confined primarily to the cortical tissue; however, penetration and colonization of the vessel elements and tracheids of the xylem can occur. Histological examination of crown tissue from wilting turfgrass plants colonized by this fungus has revealed colonization of the vascular tissue and the plugging of vessel elements with a chromophilic material that stains strongly with safranin (Pennypacker, Sanders and Cole, 1982).

In some instances, the thatch and underlying soil within the zones of activity of lectophilic fairy rings becomes hydrophobic (Plate 30-B, C). This condition appears to be brought on by the coating of large, individual soil particles by fungus-engendered, hydrophobic material (Miller and Wilkinson, 1977; Wilkinson and Miller, 1978). Although these "localized dry spots" are usually thought of as problems unique to sand-based golf greens, they can also develop on greens that have been constructed with soil mixtures and in fairway and landscape turf.

Not all lectophilic fairy rings lead to the development of localized dry spots, nor are these water repellant zones always preceded by visible ring formation. Therefore, although certain lectophilic fairy ring species appear to be involved in the formation of localized dry spots, it is highly possible that this phenomenon can be brought on by a much wider range of thatch-inhabiting microflora.

Since the species that form lectophilic fairy rings are thatch and litter colonizers, factors that affect the thickness and general condition of the thatch will have a direct bearing on their development. Also, soil sterilization procedures, and/or the use of certain fungicides that lower the populations of either competitors or antagonistic soil and thatch-inhabiting microorganisms on established turf may bring about an increase in the formation of lectophilic rings (Dale, 1972; Kackley, Dernoeden and Grybauskas, 1989).

Control

Cultural Practices

Prevention of the accumulation of heavy thatch layers through the use of vertical cutting and coring equipment will reduce the incidence of lectophilic fairy rings. The hydrophobic condition created by the presence of the fairy ring fungi can be alleviated by a combination of coring and the use of wetting agents. Once wetting of the thatch and underlying soil has been accomplished, it is very important that measures be taken to maintain this profile in a continuously moist condition (Wilkinson and Miller, 1978).

Chemical Control

Drench applications of flutolanil have been reported to be effective in controlling the development of lectophilic fairy rings. For a profile of flutolanil and a listing of representative manufacturers, see Appendix Table I.

§ § §

10

Seedling Diseases

The various seedling diseases can create many problems in a turfgrass management program. This is particularly true in overseeding of bermudagrass (*Cynodon dactylon*) golf greens for winter use or in attempts to reestablish grass in an existing turf that has been damaged by a root and crown pathogen.

The term "damping-off" is commonly used to refer to seedling diseases. It is an appropriate designation in that it describes a common symptom pattern. However, the expression can be misleading because it creates the impression of a single disease, when in reality, "damping-off" is a general term applied to either one, or a combination of seedling diseases. These diseases may be incited by pathogenic fungi or be entirely physiogenic in makeup (caused by excessive or inadequate soil moisture, extremely cool soil temperatures, highly saline soils, etc.). In addition, it is possible for a given seedling disease to be entirely physiogenic at the outset and then the problem be compounded by the colonization of the weakened plants by saprophytes and secondary parasites.

Stage of seedling development at the time of disease occurrence has been used to classify types of damping-off. Under this system, the expressions preemergence damping-off and postemergence damping-off are used to denote the major groups and the various incitants are cataloged accordingly. Although applicable in a broad sense, use of this system often requires qualification in that the physical environment and the strain of the inciting fungus often determine whether the pathogenic condition is to be preemergence or postemergence in its occurrence. A more workable system for classification of seedling diseases is one based on the association of the incitant rather than stage of plant growth (e.g., Fusarium damping-off).

PYTHIUM DAMPING-OFF

Seedling diseases incited by *Pythium* spp. are a problem wherever turfgrasses are established from seed. They are especially common in the warm-humid regions of the southern United States where dormant warm-season grasses are overseeded with a cool-season species in order to maintain the aesthetic and usable quality of the turf during winter months. Pythium damping off can also be a problem in more temperate climates when attempts are made to repair areas that are severely damaged by Pythium blight by seeding.

Symptoms

In overall view, the stand appears "patchy." Areas of dense, vigorous-growing seedlings are spotted with patches of either dead plants or devoid of plants. These patches may range from 1 inch to a foot (2.5–31 cm) or more in diameter.

A characteristic feature of Pythium damping-off is a high order of preemergence killing of seedlings. In these cases, the deterioration process begins soon after the seed coat is broken. When the disease develops after emergence, the plants first become necrotic at the soil surface. As the stems progressively deteriorate upward, the seedlings appear water soaked, eventually collapsing due to the weakened stems. In humid weather, affected plants collapse into a matted mass and may soon be covered with the white mycelial growth of the fungus, whereas, when the atmospheric humidity is relatively low, the plants shrivel and then turn brown.

The Fungi

Both pathogenic and nonpathogenic *Pythium* spp. are commonly associated with soil under turf. A listing of species known to be pathogenic to turfgrass seedlings is given in Table 10-1. For a description of procedures for isolation and culture of Pythium species, see Pythium Blight (Chapter 4).

Disease Profile

The Pythium species that incite damping off are common inhabitors of turf rooting media. They pro-

Table 10-1. Species of Pythium pathogenic to turfgrass seedlings.

Pythium aphanidermatum	(Abad *et al.*, 1992; Nelson and Craft, 1991; Saladini, 1980)
Pythium aristosporum	(Abad *et al.*, 1992; Nelson and Craft, 1991)
Pythium arrhenomanes	(Abad *et al.*, 1992)
Pythium graminicola	(Abad *et al.*, 1992; Nelson and Craft, 1991; Saladini, 1980)
Pythium irregulare	(Abad *et al.*, 1992)
Pythium myriotylum	(Abad *et al.*, 1992; Saladini, 1980)
Pythium tardecrescens	(Abad *et al.*, 1992)
Pythium torulosum	(Abad *et al.*, 1992; Nelson and Craft, 1991)
Pythium ultimum var. *sporangiiferum*	(Abad *et al.*, 1992)
Pythium ultimum var. *ultimum*	(Abad *et al.*, 1972)
Pythium vanterpoolii	(Nelson and Craft, 1991)

duce thick walled resting spores (oospores) which enables them to survive for extended periods of time. Generally speaking, the incidence and severity of Pythium-incited seedling death is favored by water-saturated soil; however, the resting structures of some species are capable of germinating by production of mycelium and can infect and colonize developing seedlings when the soil moisture level is below saturation. It is doubtful that the incidence and severity of Pythium damping-off is affected significantly by soil fertility (Freeman, 1980). Where air temperatures are concerned, *Pythium aphanidermatum*, *Pythium graminicola*, *Pythium aristosporum*, *Pythium torulosum*, and *Pythium vanterpoolii* have been shown to be equally pathogenic to creeping bentgrass (*Agrostis palustris*) seedlings at 55 °F (13 °C) and 83 °F (28 °C). Also, there is no significant difference among cool season grasses in their resistance to Pythium damping off (Freeman, 1980; Freeman and Horn, 1963).

FUSARIUM DAMPING-OFF

Symptoms

In overall view, the affected areas characteristically appear as small, light yellow patches. Fusarium damping-off is typically a postemergence disease problem, the seedlings are most often affected in the time period between emergence and development of the first 2–3 leaves. The individual seedlings are light yellow at first. Eventually they take on a bronze

hue and collapse. Withering of the stems may or may not be evident.

The Fungi

A. *Fusarium culmorum* (W. G. Smith) Sacc.; syn. *Fusarium roseum* (LK) emend Snyder and Hanson f. sp. *cerealis* (Cke.) "Culmorum." For a description of this species and procedures for isolation and culture, see Fusarium Blight (Chapter 4).

The Fungi

B. *Microdochium nivale* (Fr.) Samuels and Hallett; telemorph *Monographella nivalis* (Schaf.) E. Muller; syn. *Fusarium nivale* (Fr.) Ces. For a description of this species and procedures for isolation and culture, see Fusarium Patch (Chapter 4).

Disease Profile

Fusarium culmorum is the incitant of the warm weather patch disease, Fusarium blight. The fungus can be transmitted on turfgrass seed (Cole, Braverman and Duich, 1968). It is also an active colonizer of soil and thatch. The incidence of *Fusarium culmorum*-incited damping-off can be very high when attempts are made to restore a turf that has been severely damaged by Fusarium blight by seeding, or when post-seeding covers are used to aid in the uniform establishment of a newly seeded area. The fungus is most active as a damping-off organism in the temperature range of 50–70 °F (10–20 °C) (Slykhuis, 1947).

Microdochium nivale incites the winter patch disease, Fusarium patch. The fungus is an active colonizer of thatch and soil. The fungus can infect and actively colonize turfgrass seedlings until the prevailing air temperatures reach 70 °F (20 °C). Therefore, the incidence of damping off caused by *Microdochium nivale* can be very high in the spring months on overseed areas that have been severely damaged by Fusarium patch during the preceding winter season.

RHIZOCTONIA DAMPING-OFF

Symptoms

Rhizoctonia damping-off is predominantly a postemergence seedling disease; however, certain strains of the pathogen are also capable of causing a high incidence of preemergence seedling death. Individual plants first show necrosis at the ground level. The deterioration of the stems then progresses rapidly upward as a dry rot—resulting in a pronounced withering, and, subsequently, a distinctive "wire stem" effect. Finally, the affected plants collapse, shrivel and fade to a light brown color.

The Fungus

Rhizoctonia solani Kuhn. For a description of this species and procedures for isolation and culture, see Rhizoctonia Blight (Chapter 4).

Disease Profile

Survival of the fungus for extended periods of time in the absence of a suitable host is by means of sclerotia in the soil and embedded in plant refuse. Sclerotia are known to be transmitted in the seed of ryegrass (*Lolium* spp.) and Colonial bentgrass (*Agrostis tenuis*) (Leach and Pierpoint, 1948; Richardson,

1979). Primary infection of seedlings can come from mycelium from germinating seed-borne sclerotia or from the thatch and soil. The optimum temperatures for infection and colonization of seedlings by *Rhizoctonia solani* range between 60–75 °F (16–24 °C).

Control of Seedling Diseases

Cultural Practices

Rate of seedling development is an important factor in the incidence and severity of damping off. Slow growth causes the seedlings to remain in a highly vulnerable state for a longer period of time. It is important, then, to use fresh seed with a high germination rate and strong emergence force. Also, do not attempt to compensate for the possibility of plant loss due to damping off by seeding at excessively high rates. Postemergence damping off will proceed much more rapidly in a dense stand of seedlings.

Table 10-2. Turfgrass foliar, root and seedling pathogens known to be transmitted by seed. *After Richardson, 1979.*

Turfgrass	Pathogen	Disease Incited
Bermudagrass (*Cynodon dactylon*)	*Bipolaris sorokiniana*	Helminthosporium leaf spot
	Bipolaris stenospila	Helminthosporium leaf blight and stem rot
	Setosphaeria rostrata	Damping-off
Bentgrasses (*Agrostis* spp.)	*Drechslera catenaria*	Drechslera leaf blight
	Drechslera erythrospila	Red leaf spot
	Fusarium culmorum	Fusarium blight
	Fusarium poae	Fusarium blight
	Rhizoctonia solani	Rhizoctonia blight Damping-off
Kentucky Bluegrass (*Poa pratensis*)	*Bipolaris sorokiniana*	Helminthosporium leaf spot
	Drechslera catenaria	Drechslera leaf blight
	Drechslera dictyoides	Helminthosporium blight
	Drechslera gigantea	Zonate eyespot
	Drechslera poae	Melting-out
	Fusarium culmorum	Fusarium blight
	Fusarium poae	Fusarium blight
	Ustilago striiformis	Stripe Smut
Fescues (*Festuca* spp.)	*Bipolaris sorokiniana*	Helminthosporium leaf spot
	Cercospora festucae	Cercospora leaf spot
	Drechslera catenaria	Drechslera leaf blight
	Drechslera dictyoides	Helminthosporium blight
	Drechslera siccans	Brown blight
	Fusarium culmorum	Fusarium blight
	Sclerophthora macrospora	Downy mildew
	Pseudoseptoria donacis	Pseudoseptoria leaf spot
Ryegrasses (*Lolium* spp.)	*Bipolaris sorokiniana*	Helminthosporium leaf spot
	Drechslera dictyoides	Helminthosporium blight
	Drechslera siccans	Brown blight
	Microdochium nivalis	Fusarium patch
	Rhizoctonia solani	Rhizoctonia blight Damping-off

Avoid deep seeding depths. When seed is planted too deeply, the nutrient reserves of the developing seedlings are used up before they are able to synthesize new materials, making them more vulnerable to infection and colonization by pathogenic fungi. In preparing the seedbed for planting, do not use high rates of nitrogenous fertilizers. Excessive applications of nitrogen can bring about an increase in incidence and severity of damping off. The fertilization program should provide a balance in levels of nitrogen, phosphorous and potassium.

Chemical Control

Several species of fungi that are pathogenic to turfgrasses are known to be transmitted by seed (Table 10-2). The treatment of turfgrass seed with fungicides prior to planting can serve two purposes: reduce the incidence of preemergence damping off caused by fungi already present in the seedbed, and decrease the possibility of the introduction of root and/or foliar pathogens into a newly seeded area.

Treatment of seed with thiram will reduce the potential for introduction of either stripe smut, Fusarium blight, Fusarium patch, or "Helminthosporium" leaf and crown disease fungi into newly seeded areas and reduce damping-off caused by the later three organisms (Smith, 1957b). Seed treated with metalaxyl will provide a high degree of control of Pythium-incited damping-off.

When overseeding dormant bermudagrass (*Cynodon dactylon*) golf greens with a cool season grass for use during winter months, or reseeding areas that have been heavily damaged by one of the patch diseases, maximum control of damping-off is achieved by a program that includes both a fungicidal treatment of the seed and preplanting application of a fungicide to the seedbed. The seed bed should be sprayed with a fungicide that is effective in control of the target fungus just prior to seeding. Application of the fungicide should again be made to the area at the time of seedling emergence (when a green cast is visible). After this, a protective fungicide spray schedule should be followed (Shoulders, Couch and Schmidt, 1984).

For a profile of the above-listed fungicides and a listing of representative manufacturers, see Appendix Table I.

§ § §

11

Diseases of the Inflorescence

COVERED SMUT

Symptoms

Both the foliar and root growth of infected plants is often noticeably retarded. The chief field diagnostic feature of the disease, however, is seen at the time of floral formation and seed set. Frequently, the spikes and floral parts of diseased plants are abnormal in shape and color. Diseased seed retain their greenish cast longer than healthy. At maturity, they are off-color, appearing somewhat darker than healthy seed. Ultimately, only the pericarps of the diseased seed remain, with the interiors being completely replaced with the brown, powdery spore masses of the pathogen.

The Fungi

A. *Tilletia pallida* G. W. Fischer

Description

Spores pale yellowish brown to hyaline, globose, 18–25 μm in diameter, with hyaline, irregular to conical spines 3 μm high, enveloped in a hyaline sheath usually extending slightly beyond the spines. Sterile cells few, usually much smaller than the spores, hyaline, thin-walled, smooth.

Hosts

1. **Turfgrasses**—velvet bentgrass (*Agrostis canina*) and creeping bentgrass (*Agrostis palustris*).
2. **All Known Gramineous Hosts**—A listing of the common names for the following species is given in Appendix Table IV. *Agrostis altissima* (Walt.) Tuckerm., *A. canina* L., *A. palustris* Huds. (Index Plant Dis., 1960).

The Fungi

B. *Tilletia decipiens* (Pers.) Korn.

Description

Spores globose, subglobose, to ovoid, pale violaceous yellow to yellowish brown with a violaceous tinge, 23–29 μm in diameter; exospore reticulate, with reticulations 1.5–3.5 μm wide and 2.5–3.5 μm deep, embedded in a hyaline, gelatinous sheath that extends up to 2.5 μm beyond their periphery. Sterile cells few, mostly globose to subglobose, hyaline, 12–17 μm in diameter, often enclosed in a thin, hyaline sheath.

Host

Colonial bentgrass (*Agrostis tenuis* Sibth.)

Disease Profile

Both pathogens survive the winter months, and are disseminated, as chlamydospores on seed. Germinating concurrently with the seed, the chlamydospores produce promycelia. At the apexes of the promycelia are borne primary sporidia. The primary sporidia fuse in place in pairs to form characteristic H-shaped structures. These fused primary sporidia germinate to produce dicaryotic, secondary sporidia. The secondary sporidia then germinate, forming infection threads which are then capable of penetrating the host.

The infection threads produced by the secondary sporidia penetrate the developing turfgrass seedlings and proceed intercellularly until the culm primordia are reached. After this, the pathogen grows with the host tissue until floral formation. At the time of flower development, and subsequent seed formation, these tissue groups are colonized, and, eventually, all but the pericarps of the seed are replaced by the spores of the pathogen.

Control

When seed is known to be infested with chlamydospores, it should be treated before planting with thiram according to the manufacturer's recommended rate. For a profile of thiram and a listing of representative manufacturers, see Appendix Table I.

LOOSE SMUTS

Kentucky Bluegrass (*Poa pratensis*)

Symptoms

Inflorescences of diseased plants are distorted. The seed are soon replaced with powdery, brown spore masses, which, unlike covered smut are not covered with a persistent seed pericarp. Consequently, the spores are easily dislodged, and, in the later stages of disease development, only the naked rachis may remain.

The upper leaves and leaf sheaths of affected plants are also colonized by the pathogen, thus causing the development of elongate, pale green, progressing to brown, streaks similar to those of stripe smut.

The Fungus

Ustilago trebouxii H. and P. Syd.

Description

Spores globose to ovoid, light olive brown, very minutely echinulate (appearing smooth in some collections) tending to be lighter and more granular-echinulate on one side, 3.5–5 μm × 3.5–7 μm or mostly 4–5 μm in diameter.

Hosts

1. **Turfgrass**—Kentucky bluegrass (*Poa pratensis*).
2. **All Known Gramineous Hosts**—A listing of the common names for each of the following species is given in Appendix Table IV. *Distichlis stricta* (Torr.) Rydb., *Elymus canadensis* L., *E. triticoides* Buckl. *Hordeum brachyantherum* Nevski, *H. jubatum* L., *H. jubatum* var. *caespitosum* (Scribn.) Hitchc., *Poa pratensis* L., *P. secunda* Presl, *Puccinellia airoides* (Nutt.) Wats. and Coult., *P. distans* (L.) Parl., *Sitanion hanseni* (Scribn.) J. G. Smith, *S. hystrix* (Nutt.) J. G. Smith, *S. jubatum* J. G. Smith, *Stipa coronata* Thurb. (Fischer, 1953).

Bermudagrass (*Cynodon dactylon*)

Symptoms

The branches of the inflorescence are turned into linear, dusty, brown spore masses. With complete colonization by the pathogen, all of the floral parts, with the exception of the rachis, are destroyed.

The Fungus

Ustilago cynodontis (Pass.) Henn.

Description

Spores mostly globose to subglobose, light yellowish brown, 5–8 μm in diameter; exospore smooth.

Host

bermudagrass (*Cynodon dactylon* (L.) Pers.) (Index Plant Dis.. 1960).

St. Augustinegrass

Symptoms

Inflorescences of diseased plants are usually very distorted. The seed are soon replaced with masses of dark brown spores which are at first covered with a thin, grayish peridium. This peridial layer ruptures easily, thus exposing the very dusty spore masses to the elements. After this, the spores are easily dislodged, and the naked rachis is soon exposed.

The Fungus

Ustilago affinis Ell. and Ev.

Description

Spores clear yellowish brown, globose or irregularly globose to ovoid, or somewhat angular, 4–7 μm in diameter, or 4–5 μm × 7–8 μm; exospore smooth, very thin.

Host

St. Augustinegrass (*Stenotaphrum secundatum* (Walt.) Kuntze) (Index Plant Dis., 1960).

SILVER TOP (White Heads, White Top)

One of the most serious diseases of turfgrasses grown for seed, outbreaks of silver top have been known to cause from 80–85 percent reduction in yield. With stands past their third year of production, complete loss of seed crops due to the disease have been reported.

Symptoms

The disease is usually first noticed at the time of seed formation. In sharp contrast with their healthy neighbors the seed heads of affected plants wither

Figure 11-1. Silver top of Chewings fescue (*Festuca rubra* var. *commutata*). (1) Diseased culms, showing decayed and shriveled areas above the first node. (2) Healthy panicle (a, b) and two unexpanded, blanched, diseased panicles. *After Keil, 1946.*

before they become fully mature. Silvery in appearance at first, with time, the heads of diseased plants assume a characteristic blanched, white color. Distinct lesions, ranging from ⅛–½ inch (3–13 mm) in length, usually form just above the uppermost node of the culm. Complete degeneration of the tissue at this point is not uncommon, thereby causing the culm to weaken and break (Figure 11-1).

The Fungus

Fusarium poae (Peck.) Wollenweber; syn. *Fusarium tricinctum* f. sp. *poae* (Peck) Snyder and Hansen

Description

Fusarium poae grows well on potato dextrose agar at 21 °C. Microconidia begin forming after about 3 days from the time of single sporing. On potato dextrose agar, the mycelium is cobwebby, carmine rose or buff—becoming powdery with the formation of microconidia. Microconidia are citron shaped, 0–1 septate, 8–12 μm × 7–10 μm. Macroconidia are 3–5 septate, 3.0–4.2 μm × 18–36 μm, narrowly sickle-shaped, and pointed at both ends; the foot cell is not prominent (Sprague, 1950; Booth, 1971).

Hosts

1. **Turfgrasses**—creeping bentgrass (*Agrostis palustris*), Colonial bentgrass (*Agrostis tenuis*), annual bluegrass (*Poa annua*), Kentucky bluegrass (*Poa pratensis*), Chewings fescue(*Festuca rubra* var. *commutata*), hard fescue (*Festuca ovina* var. *duriuscula*), red fescue (*Festuca rubra*), tall fescue (*Festuca arundinacea*), annual ryegrass (*Lolium multiflorum*), and perennial ryegrass (*Lolium perenne*).

2. **All Known Gramineous Hosts**—A listing of the common names for each of the following species is given in Appendix Table IV. *Agrostis palustris* Huds., *A. stolonifera* L., *A. tenuis* Sibth., *Avena byzantina* K. Koch., *A. sativa* L., *Bouteloua curtipendula* (Michx.) Torr., *B. gracilis* (H. B. K.) Lag., *Bromus inermis* Leyss., *Dactylis glomerata* L., *Elymus junceus* Fisch., *Festuca arundinacea* Schreb., *F. octoflora* Walt., *F. ovina* L., *F. ovina* var. *duriuscula* (L.) Koch, *F. rubra* L., *F. rubra* var. *commutata* Gaud., *Hordeum jubatum* L., *H. vulgare* L., *Lolium multiflorum* Lam., *L. perenne* L., *Muhlenbergia racemosa* (Michx.) B. S. P., *Panicum capillare* L., *P. miliaceum* L., *Phleum pratense* L., *Poa annua* L., *Poa nemoralis* L., *P. palustris* L., *P. pratensis* L., *P. trivialis* L., *Setaria lutescens* (Wei-

gel) Hubb, *S. viridis* (L.) Beauv., *Triticum aestivum* L., *T. durum* Desf., *Zea mays* L. (Couch and Bedford, 1966; Keil, 1946; Sprague, 1950).

Disease Profile

Cool, damp weather conditions apparently favor development of the disease. The pathogen survives adverse seasons as dormant mycelium on and in diseased plants, and as a saprophyte in the soil and on turfgrass debris. Spread of the fungus is accomplished by a species of mite (*Pediculopsis graminum* Reuter). In addition, this vector also provides the infection courts for the entry of the pathogen into the host plant. As they move through the fungus mycelium growing over the surface of diseased plants, the bodies of the mites become contaminated with spores. The mites migrate to the succulent tissue in the region just above the uppermost node of the culm and begin feeding. After the culm has been injured by this feeding process, the spores of the pathogen germinate and invade the plant tissue. The route of movement of the fungus mycelium through the tissue is both intercellular and intracellular. Parenchymatous cells are the first to degenerate. These are followed in turn by the collenchyma and sclerenchyma, and finally the vessel elements are colonized (Keil, 1946).

Control

Where local laws permit, burning the turfgrass in areas affected by the disease will appreciably reduce loss in the seed crop. For best results, the raking and burning should be done either as early as possible in the spring before the flower primordia have started to develop, or at some time during the winter when the weather permits. Under most conditions, it should only be necessary to burn over an area one time every 3–5 years (Keil, 1946).

CHOKE

Choke occurs in North America, Europe, the former USSR, and New Zealand. Under climatic conditions favorable for the development of the disease seed yield may be reduced as much as 70 percent.

Symptoms

In the early stage of the disease, young leaves of developing tillers are covered with a fine weft of white mycelial growth (Figure 11-2, b). Under favor-

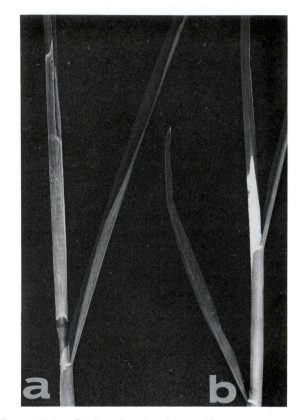

Figure 11-2. Choke of orchardgrass (*Dactylis glomerata*). Early ascigerous (A) and (B) conidial stages of pathogen. *Courtesy J. H. Western.*

able environmental conditions, this mycelium develops into a dense stromatic sheath, completely enveloping the young inflorescence and causing it to degenerate. With the red fescues in particular, as the panicle emerges, all, or a portion, of the spikelets may be covered with the white stromatic growth of the pathogen. The fungus growth increases in thickness on the floral parts, as well as on the sheaths of the upper leaves, becoming first yellow, then orange. Ultimately, characteristic dull orange, spongy collars are formed around the sheaths or culms (Figure 11-2 a).

The Fungus

Epichloe typhina (Fr.) Tul.; anamorph *Acremonium typhinum* Morgan-Jones and Gams

Description

Stomata cream colored, later dark orange, surrounding sheaths or culms of living grasses, 2–5 cm long, conidia 1–3 μm × 3–9 μn, ovoid, hyaline; followed by perithecia, soft carnose-membranaceous, yellow, 300–600 μm high, 250 μm in diameter, ostiole prominent, immersed, somewhat elongate; asci cylindrical 6–9 μm × 150–230 μm; 8 spores per ascus, filiform, yellowish, nearly as long as the asci, 1.5–2 μm in diameter, septate at intervals of 8–12 μm.

Hosts

1. **Turfgrasses**—creeping bentgrass (*Agrostis palustris*), Colonial bentgrass (*Agrostis tenuis*), red fescue (*Festuca rubra*), sheep fescue (*Festuca ovina*), and Kentucky bluegrass (*Poa pratensis*).
2. **All Known Gramineous Hosts**—A listing of the common names for each of the following species is given in Appendix Table IV. *Agropyron inerme* (Scribn. and Smith) Rydb., *A. smithii* Rydb., *A. spicatum* (Pursh) Scribn. and Smith, *A. trachycaulum* (Link) Malte, *Agrostis alba* L., *A. scabra* Willd., *A. perennans* (Walt.) Tuckerm., *A. palustris* Huds., *A. tenuis* Sibth., *Alopecurus aequalis* Sobol., *Andropogon gerardi* Vitman, *A. scoparius* Michx., *Bouteloua gracilis* (H. B. K.) Lag., *Calamagrostis canadensis* (Michx.) Beauv., *Calamovilfa gigantea* (Nutt.) Scribn. and Merr., *Cinna arundinacea* L., *Dactylis glomerata* L., *Danthonia spicata* (L.) Beauv., *Elymus canadensis* L., *E. dahuricus* Turcz., *E. virginicus* L., *Festuca ovina* L., *F. rubra* L., *Glyceria canadensis* (Michx.) Trin., *G. fluitans* (L.) R. Br., *G. septentrionalis* Hitchc., *G. striata* (Lam.) Hitchc., *Hystrix patula* Moench, *Koeleria cristata* (L.) Pers., *Leersia oryzoides* (L.) Swartz, *Melica bulbosa* Geyer, *Phleum pratense* L., *Poa bulbosa* L., *P. compressa* L., *P. pratensis* L., *P. secunda* Presl, *P. stenantha* Trin., *P. trivialis* L., *Sphenopholis nitida* (Bieler) Scribn., *S. obtusata* (Michx.) Scribn., *S. pallens* (Bieler) Scribn. (Index Plant Dis., 1960; Sampson and Western, 1954; Sprague, 1950).

Disease Profile

The fungus survives from year to year as systemic, perennial mycelium in the host. It is also seed transmitted. The extent of the "choking" effect (formation of stroma on the inflorescence) is determined by the rate and stage of growth of the floral apex. Extensive growth of the fungus within the stem tissues occurs only when the floral apex area is between the double-ridge and spiklet-primordium states of growth. If the rate of apical elongation is rapid between these stages of development, colonization of the floral tissue does not occur. The invading fungus is literally outpaced and is confined to the panicle branches and spiklets (Kirby, 1961). With grasses such as red fescue (*Festuca rubra*), which usually does not flower the year of seeding, even though colonized internally with *Epichloe typhina*, development of the fungus on the surface of the inflorescence usually does not occur until the second or third year of growth.

Conidiospores and ascospores are able to germinate on the cut surfaces of orchardgrass (*Dactylis glomerata*) stubble and penetrate and colonize the stems (Western and Cavett, 1959). Although viable conidia can be transmitted from plant to plant by the fly *Phorbia phrenione* Seguy, (Kohlmeyer and Kohlmeyer, 1974), a species common to North America, Europe, Mexico and East Asia, the capacity of *Epichloe typhina* spores to initiate infections on turfgrass species under seed production management conditions has not yet been demonstrated. The primary means of spread within a stand is accomplished by the infection of newly formed tillers by mycelial growth from the diseased parent plant. Spread of the fungus to new locations is by the use of vegetative propagative material from diseased plants and infested seed.

ERGOT

Ergot is one of the oldest recognized plant diseases. The malady affects only the flowering parts of the plants, where the seed are replaced by the sclerotial bodies of the pathogen. In addition to the disease causing large reduction in seed yield, when the sclerotial bodies of the pathogen are eaten in sufficient quantities, they can cause an alkaloid poisoning of animals. Small quantities of the poison act on the nervous system, causing lethargy and paralysis. Large doses bring about a degeneration of the small terminal arteries, which results in mummification of the extremities and subsequent dropping off of ears, tails, and feet. Abortion in pregnant livestock is another effect of consumption of ergot sclerotia.

Symptoms

The first indication of the disease is seen as an exudation of sticky liquid from the young florets. This is the so-called honeydew stage of disease development. Insects feed on this exudate, and, consequently, are usually in high populations around the diseased spikes. Examination of the internal structure of the developing florets reveals that the ovaries are permeated with this whitish, slimy mass.

These slimy masses gradually change into horn-shaped, purple-black sclerotia with white interiors. These sclerotia replace the seed in the infected

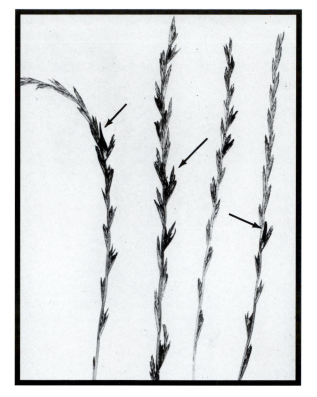

Figure 11-3. Ergot of perennial ryegrass (*Lolium perenne*), showing sclerotia of pathogen. *After Sampson and Western, 1954.*

flowers. As they develop, the floral bracts spread apart and the sclerotial bodies, when fully mature, are usually very prominent as they protrude beyond the floral bracts (Figure 11-3).

When the hosts floral tissue matures before the ergot sclerotia, such as with some bluegrasses (*Poa* spp.) and red fescue (*Festuca rubra*), the disease does not progress beyond the honeydew stage. Loss of the seed crop in this case is just as great as though sclerotia had formed—positive disease diagnosis, however, is sometimes more difficult.

The Fungus

Claviceps purpurea (Fr.) Tul.

Description

Sclerotia 2–25 mm long, horn-shaped, pseudo-parenchymatous, purple black on surface, white in the interior, replacing ovaries; 1–60 flesh colored, stalked stromata develop from each sclerotium, stromata 5–25 mm long; perithecia flask shaped, embedded in the knob-like apex of the stromata, slightly protruding at ostiolar end, 150–175 μm × 200–250 μm; asci hyaline, slightly curved, club shaped with

somewhat tapering ends, 4 μm × 100–125 μm, paraphyses present; ascospores 8 per ascus, filiform, finally septate, 0.6–0.7 μm × 50–76 μm. Spores sometimes forcibly discharged, sometimes exuded in a mucilaginous material. Conidia nonseptate, 2–3 μm × 4–6 μm, produced in honeydew mass.

Hosts

1. **Turfgrasses**—Colonial bentgrass (*Agrostis tenuis*), creeping bentgrass (*Agrostis palustris*), velvet bentgrass (*Agrostis canina*), annual bluegrass (*Poa annua*), Kentucky bluegrass (*Poa pratensis*), tall fescue (*Festuca arundinacea*), meadow fescue (*Festuca elatior*), sheep fescue (*Festuca ovina*, red fescue (*Festuca rubra*), Chewings fescue (*Festuca rubra* var. *commutata*), annual ryegrass (*Lolium multiflorum*), and perennial ryegrass (*Lolium perenne*).

2. **All Known Gramineous Hosts**—A listing of the common names for each of the following species is given in Appendix Table IV. *Agropyron albicans* Scribn. and Smith, *A. caninum* (L.) Beauv., *A. cristatum* (L.) Gaertn., *A. dasystachyum* (Hook.) Scribn., *A. desertorum* (Fisch.) Schult., *A. griffithsi* Scribn. and Smith, *A. inerme* (Scribn. and Smith) Rydb., *A. intermedium* (Host) Beauv., *A. repens* (L.) Beauv., *A. riparium* Scribn. and Smith, *A. semicostatum* (Steud.) Ness, *A. sibiricum* (Willd.) Beauv., *A. smithii* Rydb., *A. spicatum* (Pursh) Scribn. and Smith, *A. subsecundum* (Link) Hitchc., *A. trachycaulum* (Link) Malte, *A. trichophorum* (Link) Richt., *Agrostis alba* L., *A. canina* L., *A. exarata* Trin., *A. hiemalis* (Walt.) B. S. P., *A. palustris* Huds., *A. scabra* Willd., *A. stolonifera* L., *A. tenuis* Sibth., *Alopecurus aequalis* Sobol., *A. geniculatus* L., *A. pratensis* L., *Ammophila arenaria* (L.) Link, *A. breviligulata* Fernald, *Andropogon gerardi* Vitman, *A. hallii* Hack., *A. saccharoides* Swartz, *A. scorparius* Michx., *A. virginicus* L., *Arrhenatherum elatius* (L.) Presl, *Avena sativa* L., *Bouteloua curtipendula* (Michx.) Torr., *B. gracilis* (H. B. K.) Lag., *Brachiaria platyphylla* (Griseb.) Nash, *Bromus carinatus* Hook. and Arn., *B. ciliatus* L., *B. erectus* Huds., *B. inermis* Leyss., *B. pumpellianus* Scribn., *B. secalinus* L., *Calamagrostis canadensis* (Michx.) Beauv., *C. inexpansa* A. Gray, *C. neglecta* (Ehrh.) Gaertn. Mey. and Schreb., *C. nutkaensis* (Presl.) Steud., *Cinna arundinacea* L., *Dactylis glomerata* L., *Danthonia parryi* Scribn., *D. spicata* (L.) Beauv., *Deschampsia caespitosa* (L.) Beauv., *Distichlis spicata* (L.) Greene, *Elymus ambiguus* Vasey and Scribn., *E. canadensis* L., *E. canadensis* var. *robustus* (Scribn. and Smith) Mackenz. and

Bush, *E. condensatus* Presl, *E. dahuricus* Turcz., *E. giganteus* Vahl, *E. glaucus* Buckl., *E. innovatus* Beal, *E. junceus* Fisch., *E. mollis* Trin., *E. salsuginosus* Turcz., *E. triticoides* Buckl., *E. virginicus* L., *E. virginicus* var. *submuticus* Hook., *Erianthus alopecuroides* (L.) Ell., *Festuca arundinacea* Schreb., *F. elatior* L., *F. idahoensis* Elmer, *F. octoflora* Walt., *F. ovina* L., *F. rubra* L., *F. rubra* var. *commutata* Gaud., *Glyceria borealis* (Nash) Batchelder, *G. canadensis* (Michx.) Trin., *G. fluitans* (L.) R. Br., *G. grandis* S. Wats., *G. pauciflora* Presl, *G. septentrionalis* Hitchc., *G. striata* (Lam.) Hitchc., *Helictotrichon hookeri* (Scribn.) Henr., *Hesperochloa kingii* (S. Wats.) Rydb., *Hierochloe odorata* (L.) Beauv., *Holcus lanatus* L., *Hordeum brachyantherum* Nevski, *H. jubatum* L., *H. murinum* L., *H. vulgare* L., *Hystrix patula* Moench, *Koeleria cristata* (L.) Pers., *Lolium multiflorum* Lam., *L. perenne* L., *L. subulatum* Vis., *Panicum maximum* Jacq., *Phalaris arundinacea* L., *P. arundinacea* var. *picta* L., *P. canariensis* L., *Phleum pratense* L., *Phragmites communis* Trin., *Poa ampla* Merr., *P. annua* L., *P. arida* Vasey, *P. canbyi* (Scribn.) Piper, *P. compressa* L., *P. fendleriana* (Steud.) Vasey, *P. fulva* Trin., *P. glaucifolia* Scribn. and Will., *P. juncifolia* Scribn., *P. longifolia* Trin., *P. nemoralis* L., *P. nervosa* (Hook.) Vasey, *P. nevadensis* Vasey, *P. palustris* L., *P. pratensis* L., *P. scabrella* (Thurb.) Benth., *P. secunda* Presl, *P. stenantha* Trin., *Puccinellia distans* (L.) Parl., *Secale cereale* L., *S. montanum* Guss., *Setaria macrostachya* H. B. K., *S. viridis* (L.) Beauv., *Sitanion hystrix* (Nutt.) J. G. Smith, *Sorghastrum nutans* (L.) Nash, *Spartina alterniflora* Loisel, *S. cynosuroides* (L.) Roth, *S. gracilis* Trin., *S. patens* (Ait.) Muhl., *S. pectinata* Link, *Stipa columbiana* Macoun., *S. columbiana* var. *nelsoni* (Scribn.) Hitchc., *S. comata* Trin. and Rupr., *S. lettermani* Vasey, *S. robusta* (Vasey) Scribn., *S. spartea* Trin., *S. viridula* Trin., *Tripsacum dactyloides* (L.) L., *Trisetum canescens* Buckl., *Triticum aestivum* L., *T. dicoccum* Schrank, *Zizania aquatica* L., *Z. aquatica* var. *angustifolia* Hitchc. (Index Plant Dis., 1960; Sprague, 1950).

Disease Profile

The pathogen survives the winter months as sclerotia. In the spring, the sclerotia that are buried in the soil germinate to produce stromata and perithecia. Ascospores are forcibly discharged from the perithecia and carried by wind to the developing flowers. Penetration of the young ovary tissue occurs and absorptive hyphae are established in the vascular system of the rachilla. After this, the rapidly developing hyphal (honeydew) mass develops in the ovary. Conidial production then occurs, and secondary infection of flowers on the same plant or primary infection of a new plant may follow. Dissemination of conidia is accomplished primarily by the movement of insects attracted to the honeydew ooze of diseased flowers. With time, sclerotia form in the diseased flower heads, and the cycle is completed.

Spread of *Claviceps purpurea* over great distances is accomplished by seed-borne sclerotia. The fungus is known to possess a high degree of physiologic specialization. Races of the organism have been found that are restricted to a very few grass hosts, while other forms are known that parasitize large numbers of grass species.

Control

Control of ergot in Kentucky bluegrass (*Poa pratensis*) has been reported with single applications of either propiconazole and tebuconazole combined with a wetting agent. Timing of applications is important. When the fungicide is applied at the pre-anthesis growth stage, 100 percent control of the production of sclerotia or panicle exudate (honeydew) is achieved and seed germination is not affected. Treatments made at mid-anthesis or late-anthesis are less effective in control and may reduce seed viability (Schultz *et al.*, 1993).

BLIND SEED

Blind seed affects a wide range of cool season turfgrasses but is particularly severe on ryegrasses (*Lolium* spp). With ryegrasses, the disease is known to be capable of causing a reduction in percent germination to the extent that the seed is not only unfit for certification, but is also not saleable under any market classification.

Symptoms

Diagnosis of the disease in the field requires the removal of the glumes. With this, affected seed are seen to be covered with a pale pink slimy exudate. At seed maturity, this exudate dries to waxy masses which cause the kernels to be rusty brown in color. Fully developed seed may or may not be shrunken, depending on the time of floral infection.

When examined under the diaphanoscope, severely diseased seed are opaque. This method is not satisfactory for accurate determination of percentage infection, however, for opacity decreases with corresponding decrease in disease severity. In addition, opacity due to weathering is frequently confused with that caused by blind seed. Another rapid, and more positive, laboratory technique for diagnosis of blind seed consists of placing each seed in a drop of water on a microscope slide, and, after one or both glumes have been removed, examining the water around the seed with a microscope at approximately 100 ×. In the cases of diseased seed, the characteristic spores of the pathogen will be present in the water in large numbers.

The Fungus

Gloeotinia granigena (Quel.) Schum.; syn. *Phialea temulenta* Prill. and Del.; anamorph *Endoconidium temulentum* Pril. and Del.

Description

Apothecia small, fleshy, arising singly or in small numbers from colorless, septate, intertwining hyphae, 3–4 μm wide, ramifying throughout the pericarp, tests, and endosperm; discs pale pinkish cinnamon, darkening to cinnamon when old, 1–3.5 mm (usually 2.5 mm) in diameter, at first almost closed, opening into a cup-shape, and finally becoming flat or slightly recurved, with a smooth margin; stalks cylindrical, 0.4 mm × 1–8 mm, smooth; structure fairly uniform throughout, consisting of hyaline, parallel hyphae, occasionally intertwining and seldom branched; hypothecium 22–27 μm deep, composed of fine interlacing hyphae, 2 μm in diameter; asci cylindrical-clavate, very little thickened at the apex, pore not staining blue with iodine, 3.3–7 μm × 66–116 μm (usually 6 μm × 73 μm), 8-spored; ascospores smooth, unicellular, ellipsoidal, with pointed ends, biguttulate, hyaline, 3–6 μm × 7.6–12 μm (usually 4.5 μm × 9.5 μm), obliquely uniserate in the upper half to 3/4 of the ascus; paraphyses simple, filiform, hyaline, not swollen at the apex, 2–4 μm in diameter.

Macroconidia unicellular, uninucleate, cylindrical to slightly crescentic, with rounded ends, usually biguttulate, hyaline, 3.3–6.0 μm × 11–21 μm (usually 4 μm × 16 μm), developed in large numbers in summer in succession from the apexes of short outgrowths from the hyphae on the pericarp.

Microconidia in pink pulvinate sporodochia, 0.5 mm × 1–1.5 mm on the surface of caryopses; conidiophores septate, guttulate, hyaline, 2 or 3 times branched; microconidia unicellular, uninucleate, ovoid, guttulate, hyaline, 2.7–3.2 μm × 3.4–4.8 μm (usually 3 μm × 4 μm), the first formed by a constriction below the apex of the conidiophore, the rest developed in succession inside a tube, 3–5 μm, formed by the terminal portion of the conidiophore.

In culture, the organism grows well, and sporu-

lates on either 2 percent oat meal agar or potato-dextrose agar at 20–24 °C (Calvert and Muskett, 1945).

Hosts

1. **Turfgrasses**—creeping bentgrass (*Agrostis palustris*), velvet bentgrass (*Agrostis canina*), red fescue (*Festuca rubra*), tall fescue (*Festuca arundinacea*), sheep fescue (*Festuca ovina*), annual ryegrass (*Lolium multiflorum*), and perennial ryegrass (*Lolium perenne*).
2. **All Known Gramineous Hosts**—A listing of the common names for each of the following species is given in Appendix Table IV. *Agrostis canina* L., *A. palustris* Huds., *Aira caryophyllea* L., *Alopecurus geniculatus* L., *Bromus racemosus* L., *Cynosurus cristatus* L., *C. echinatus* L., *Danthonia californica* Boland, *Deschampsia caespitosa* (L.) Beauv., *Festuca arundinacea* Schreb., *F. elatior* L.,. *F. myuros* L., *F. ovina* L., *F. rubra* L., *Glyceria borealis* (Nash) Batchelder, *Holcus lanatus* L., *Hordeum hystrix* Roth, *Lolium multiflorum* Lam., *L. perenne* L., *L. temulentum* L., *Poa pratensis* L., *P. trivialis* L., *Secale cereale* L. (Calvert and Muskett, 1945; Sampson and Western, 1954; Index Plant Dis., 1960).

Disease Profile

The pathogen overwinters in colonized seeds. When the diseased seeds are planted, they do not decay as do other nonviable seeds, but, instead, remain intact until early summer when ryegrass is flowering. At this time, these fungus-permeated seeds give rise to apothecia. These fruiting structures (1–3 per seed) grow to the surface of the soil, where they ultimately mature to produce asci and ascospores.

The ascopores are discharged into the air streams and carried to the flowers of the grass host. Infection of the flowers is accomplished by the ascospores that land at a point just below the stigma. The first macroscopic indication of the disease is usually evident 9–14 days from the time of infection, when the immature green color of the developing seeds is replaced by a dull brown hue.

Secondary infection is accomplished by the spread of macroconidia from colonized seeds to flowers or lately fertilized ovaries on the same spikes or spikes of adjoining plants. Further secondary spread is by means of microconidia. Spore dissemination in these cases is accomplished by splashing and wind-driven water (Figure 11-4).

If infection occurs early in floral development, the embryo will be destroyed and seed development stopped. Mature, nonviable seeds are the result of infections after the embryonic tissues and the endosperm have been differentiated. If infection is later

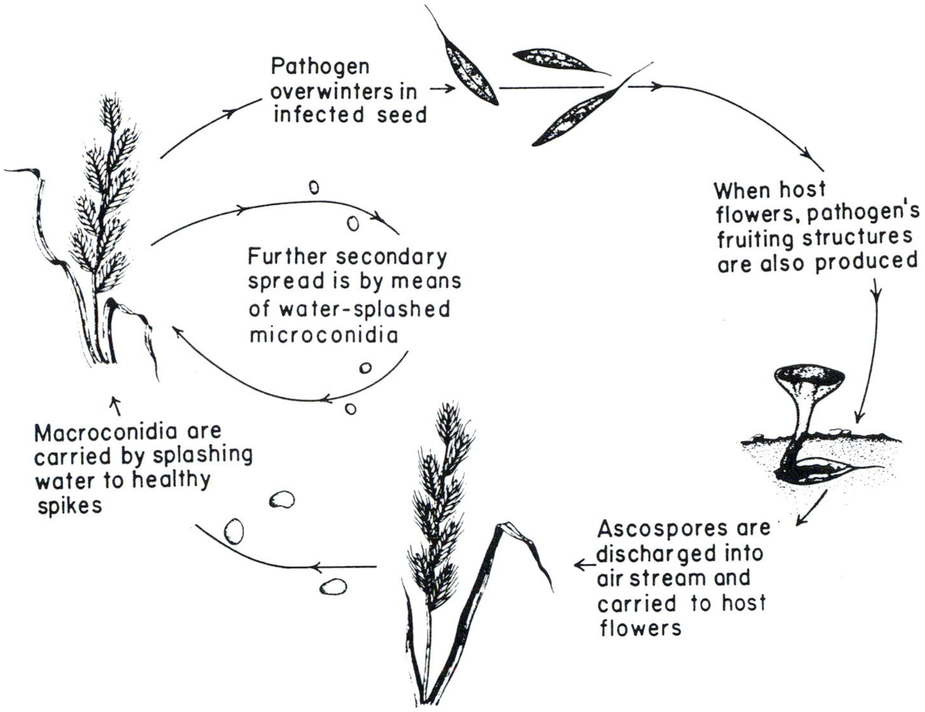
Pathogen
overwinters in
infected seed
When host
flowers, pathogen's
fruiting structures
are also produced
Ascospores are
discharged into
air stream and
carried to host
flowers
Macroconidia are
carried by splashing
water to healthy
spikes
Further secondary
spread is by means
of water-splashed
microconidia

Figure 11-4. Cycle of development of blind seed of turfgrass.

than this, the embryo may escape colonization, although conidia are produced on the surface of the seeds. These seeds are viable.

The probability of successful infection decreases rapidly after flowering has ceased. Conditions that are conducive to an extension of the period during which the glumes are open, thus exposing the stigmas in a receptive state, will extend the period of successful infection. Cool, wet weather favors this type of plant response as well as the spread of the pathogen (Hardison, 1949). The pathogen does not survive in ryegrass seeds kept under standard storage conditions for a 2-year period.

Control

Cultural Practices

Effective control of blind seed in ryegrass grown for seed production has been obtained by using seed that has been stored for a period of 22–24 months. In addition, it has been shown that planting seed to a depth of at least ½ inch (13 mm) with complete soil coverage will materially reduce the incidence of the disease.

Where local laws permit, burning over a stand of ryegrass after seed harvest will bring about a reduction in disease incidence the following season. This practice is generally recommended only for fields with marginal infestation after the first or second years' crops. Burning of older fields usually results in an increasing of the weed population and causes a decrease in seed yield. In these cases, it is best to take the fields out of production (Hardison, 1948; Hardison, 1949).

Seed Treatment

Complete eradication of the pathogen from infected and infested seed can be obtained by use of a vapor heat combination of an approach period of 20 minutes at 130 °F (129 °C) followed by 30 minutes at 145 °F (63 °C) (Miller and McWhorter, 1948).

Since the disease can be effectively controlled through the use of 2-year-old seed and/or planting depths of ½ inch (13 mm) or more, seed treatment has its greatest value when aged seed is in short supply, or it is necessary to free valuable seed stock of the pathogen.

PART THREE

Diseases of Turfgrasses Caused by Viruses and Prokaryotes

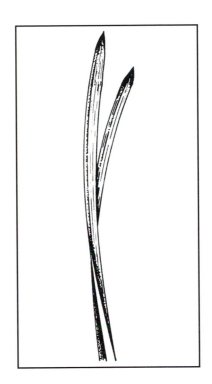

Piper, *P. pratensis* L., *P. trivialis* L., *Secale cereale* L., *Setaria lutescens* (Weigel) Hubb., *S. viridis* (L.) Beauv., *Sitanion hystrix* (Nutt.) J. G. Smith, *S. jubatum* J. G. Smith, *Sorghum sudanense* (Piper) Stapf, *S. halepense* (L.) Pers., *Triticum aestivum* L., and *Zea mays* L. (Bruehl and Toko, 1957; Grafton, Poehlman and Sechler, 1982).

Disease Profile

Spread of the virus in the field is by means of aphids. The English grain aphid, *Macrosiphum avenae* Fab., is a principal vector. Four other aphids, the apple grain aphid, *Rhopalosiphum prunifoliae* Fitch, the corn leaf aphid, *Rhopalosiphum maidis* Fitch, the rose grass aphid, *Macrosiphum dirhodum* Walker, and the greenbug, *Toxoptera graminum* Rondani, also can serve as vectors (Bruehl and Toko, 1957). A wide range of variability exists among annual ryegrass (*Lolium multiflorum*) genotypes for reductions in growth rate caused by the barley yellow dwarf virus (Wilkins and Catherall, 1977). Also, yellow dwarf reduces growth rate in annual ryegrass but it increases tillering, which makes these plants successful competitors with healthy plants for available space (Carr, 1975).

LEAF MOSAICS

In contrast with leaf mottling, which is an irregular formation of defined light and dark green patches on the leaf blade, the "mosaic" symptom pattern is characterized by intermingled shades of normal and light green or yellowish colorations. It is most clearly seen by using one's hand to screen full light from the surface of the leaf.

Western Ryegrass Mosaic of Tall Fescue and Ryegrasses

Symptoms

The leaves of affected plants develop a distinctive light green mottle.

The Virus

Western ryegrass mosaic virus. The western ryegrass mosaic virus has only been characterized in a limited fashion. Attempts to transmit the virus by three species of aphids have failed; consequently, the means of spread in the field is not known (Bruehl, Toko and McKinney, 1957).

Hosts

1. **Turfgrasses**—tall fescue (*Festuca arundinacea*), annual ryegrass (*Lolium multiflorum*), and perennial ryegrass (*Lolium perenne*).
2. **All Known Gramineous Hosts**—A listing of the common names for each of the following species is given in Appendix Table IV. *Avena fatua* L., *A. sativa* L., *Bromus commutatus* Schrad., *B. mollis* L., *B. racemosus* L., *B. secalinus* L., *B. tectorum* L., *Dactylis glomerata* L., *Festuca arundinacea* Schreb., *Hordeum leporinum* Link, *Lolium multiflorum* Lam., *L. perenne* L., *L. remotum* Schrank, *L. temulentum* L., *Triticum aestivum* L. (Bruehl, Toko and McKinney, 1957).

Ryegrass Mosaic of Cool Season Turfgrasses

Symptoms

Foliar symptoms are first seen as a light green mottle. From this, the disease progresses to a distinctive chlorotic and then necrotic streaking.

The Virus

Ryegrass mosaic virus. For details concerning the characterization of ryegrass mosaic virus refer to Slykhuis and Paliwal (1972).

Hosts

1. **Turfgrasses**—Colonial bentgrass (*Agrostis tenuis*), Kentucky bluegrass (*Poa pratensis*), tall fescue (*Festuca arundinacea*), annual ryegrass (*Lolium multiflorum*), and perennial ryegrass (*Lolium perenne*).
2. **All Known Gramineous Hosts**—For a listing of the common names for each of the following species, see Appendix Table IV. *Agrostis tenuis* Sibth., *Alopecurus agrestis* L., *Avena fatua* L., *A. sativa* L., *Bromus arvensis* L., *B. inermis* Leyss., *B. sterilis* L., *Cynosurus cristatus* L., *Dactylis glomerata* L., *Festuca arundinacea* Schreb., *Lolium multiflorum* Lam., *L. perenne* L., *Oryza sativa* L., *Poa annua* L., *P. pratensis* L., *P. trivialis* L. (Mulligan, 1960).

Disease Profile

Ryegrass mosaic has been shown to be capable of causing severe damage to stands of annual ryegrass (*Lolium multiflorum*) (Heard and Roberts, 1975). Spread of the virus in the field is by means of the eriophyid mite, *Abacarus hystrix* Nalepa. Minimum feeding time for acquisition of the virus by the vector is two hours. Retention time is 12 hours (Mulligan, 1960). Mowing does not spread ryegrass mosaic virus from diseased turf to a stand of plants free of the virus; however, mowing will bring about an increase in the number of diseased plants within a turf in which the virus is already present (Gibson and Plumb, 1976).

Bromegrass Mosaic of Cool Season Turfgrasses

Symptoms

A mottling of the leaves develops that varies from a faint green to a light yellow mosaic. Affected plants are also stunted and slow in regrowth after mowing.

The Virus

Bromegrass mosaic virus. For details concerning the characterization of brome mosaic virus refer to Lane (1977).

Hosts

1. **Turfgrasses**—creeping bentgrass (*Agrostis palustris*), Colonial bentgrass (*Agrostis tenuis*), velvet bentgrass (*Agrostis canina*), Kentucky bluegrass (*Poa pratensis*), annual ryegrass (*Lolium multiflorum*), rough bluegrass (*Poa trivialis*), and perennial ryegrass (*Lolium perenne*).

2. **All Known Gramineous Hosts**—A listing of the common names for each of the following species is given in Appendix Table IV. *Agropyron cristatum* (L.) Gaertn., *A. elongatum* (Host) Beauv., *A. intermedium* (Host) Beauv., *A. repens* (L.) Beauv., *A. trachycaulum* (Link) Malte, *Agrostis canina* L., *A. scabra* Willd., *A. palustris* Huds., L., *A. tenuis* Sibth., *Andropogon gerardi* Vitman, *A. scoparius* Michx., *Aristida oligantha* Michx., *Avena byzantina* C. Koch., *A. sativa* L., *Bromus inermis* Leyss., *B. purgans* L., *Dactylis glomerata* L., *Elymus canadensis* L., *E. villosus* Muhl., *E. virginicus* L., *Euchlaena mexicana* Scrad., *E. perennis* Hitchc., *Hordeum jubatum* L., *H. vulgare* L., *Hystrix patula* Moench, *Lolium multiflorum* Lam., *L. perenne* L., *Muhlenbergia frondosa* (Poir.) Fernald, *M. mexicana* (L.) Trin., *M. racemosa* (Michx.) B.S.P., *Panicum capillare* L., *Phleum alpinum* L., *P. pratense* L., *Phragmites communis* Trin., *Poa bulbosa* L., *P. interior* Rydb., *P. nemoralis* L., *P. palustris* L., *P. pratensis* L., *P. subcaerulea* Sm., *P. trivialis* L., *Secale cereale* L., *Sporobolus asper* (Michx.) Kunth., *Stipa spartea* Trin., *Triticum aestivum* L., *Zea mays* L. (Slykhuis, 1967; Ford, Fagbenle and Stoner, 1970).

Disease Profile

Spread of the virus in the field is thought to be accomplished by the feeding of flea beetles.

§ § §

Diseases of Turfgrasses Caused by Prokaryotes

Prokaryotes are single-celled organisms that have an envelope surrounding the cytoplasm. Unlike fungi, the genetic material of prokaryotes is not organized into a membrane-bound nucleus and mitosis does not take place along with cell divisions. The cells contain one chromosome which is usually attached to the cell membrane and folded several times to form a compact mass. Two forms of prokaryotes are known to cause disease in turfgrasses, **bacteria** and **mollicutes**.

The cell envelope of the majority of species of plant pathogenic bacteria is made up of a rigid wall with outer and inner membranes. The major functions of the outer membrane include (a) providing channels for passage of nutrients into the cell, (b) protection of the cell from antibiotics and other toxic substances, (c) facilitating adhesion to other cells during the reproductive process, and (e) prevention of cell desiccation. The basic component of the cell wall is a macromolecule called **peptidoglycan**, however the specific composition of bacterial cell walls varies among species. This feature is used as an aid in diagnostic procedures (Figure 13-1).

Mollicutes are the smallest known free-living organisms. The term "mollicute" is derived from the Latin expressions *mollescens* (softening) and *cutis* (skin). In contrast with bacteria, mollicute cells lack a rigid wall. Instead, the cell envelope is comprised of a highly pliable, lipid-based plasma membrane. Members of two genera of Mollicutes are known to be pathogenic to turfgrasses, *Mycoplasma* and *Spiroplasma*.

Mycoplasmas possess both ribonucleic acid (RNA) and deoxyribonucleic acid (DNA) and apparently reproduce by budding. They are usually spherical or ovoid in shape and range in size from 0.3 to 2 μm in diameter. Mycoplasmas are resistant to penicillin but are sensitive to the antibiotic tetracycline (Razin, 1969).

Spiroplasmas are distinguished from mycoplasmas by their shape. They form as helically coiled filaments that measure 0.12 μm wide and 2 to 4 μm long. The number of turns in the helix varies from two to four depending on the age of the cell. Spiroplasmas are also resistant to penicillin and sensitive to tetracycline (Goto, 1990).

BACTERIAL WILT

Bacterial wilt has been reported occurring on ryegrasses (*Lolium* spp.), bluegrasses (*Poa* spp.), fescues (*Festuca* spp.) and Colonial bentgrass (*Agrostis tenuis*) in Switzerland, Belgium, France, Germany, Great Britain, Norway, and the Netherlands. In the United States outbreaks of the disease to date have been limited to the 'Toronto C-15' cultivar of creeping bentgrass (*Agrostis palustris*).

Symptoms

In overall view, affected creeping bentgrass (*Agrostis palustris*) golf greens develop an uneven, mottled appearance with irregularly shaped green areas interspersed throughout large sections of reddish brown turf (Plate 26-A). The leaves wilt from the tip downward toward the sheath. Within 24–48 hours from the onset of wilting, the leaves turn blue green and become shriveled and twisted, after which they become a reddish brown. During the early wilting stage, root and crown tissues are white and healthy appearing. However, soon after the death of the leaves, brown necrotic streaks develop in their vascular tissue. Ultimately, death and decomposition of the entire plant occurs.

On ryegrasses (*Lolium* spp.), tall fescue (*Festuca arundinacea*), and Kentucky bluegrass (*Poa pratensis*), leaves develop chlorotic and then necrotic stripes along the veins and leaf margins. The striping usually extends from the sheaths upward throughout the entire length of the blades. At high air temperatures, young leaves curl and wither without discoloration or lesions. During warm weather, plants disappear rather quickly, and the phenomenon is often attributed to summer drought.

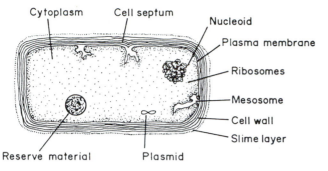

Cytoplasm   Cell septum   Nucleoid   Plasma membrane   Ribosomes   Mesosome   Cell wall   Slime layer   Reserve material   Plasmid

Figure 13-1.   A diagrammatic illustration of a bacterial cell.

The "ooze test" can be used as a aid in diagnosing bacterial wilt. This procedure consists of placing a small piece of stem or leaf on a microscope slide. The tissue should them be cut transversely with a sharp instrument, immersed in a drop of water, and examined immediately under a light microscope. If the disease is bacterial wilt, masses of bacteria will be observed streaming from the vascular tissue (Figure 13-2).

The Pathogen

Bacterial wilt is incited by the bacterium *Xanthomonas campestris* pv. *graminis* (Egli, Goto and Schmidt) Dye

Procedures for Isolation and Culture

The bacterium grows well on glucose, yeast extract agar (5 g glucose, 5 g yeast extract, 4 g $CaCO_3$, 20 g agar, 1,000 ml water). Isolation from diseased plant tissue may be accomplished by crushing the tissue in sterile water, streaking the suspension out on glucose, yeast extract agar and incubating 28 °C. *Xanthomonas campestris* will appear as slimy, yellow colonies within 48–72 hours. The bacterial cells stain as gram negative rods measuring 0.3 μm wide by 2.5 μm long (Van Den Mooter *et al.*, 1981).

Hosts

1. **Turfgrasses**—Colonial bentgrass (*Agrostis tenuis*), creeping bentgrass (*Agrostis palustris*), annual bluegrass (*Poa annua*), Kentucky bluegrass (*Poa pratensis*), red fescue (*Festuca rubra*), tall fescue (*Festuca arundinacea*), hard fescue (*Festuca ovina* var. *duriuscula*), annual ryegrass (*Lolium multiflorum*), and perennial ryegrass (*Lolium perenne*).
2. **All Known Gramineous Hosts**—A listing of the common names for the following species is given in Appendix Table IV. *Agropyron repens* (L.) Beauv.,

Agrostis alba L., *A. palustris* Huds., *A. tenuis* Sibth., *Alopecurus pratensis* L., *Arrhenatherum elatius* (L.) Presl, *Avena sativa* L., *Bromus tectorum* L., *Cynosurus cristatus* L., *Dactylis glomerata* L., *Festuca arundinacea* Schreb., *F. ovina* var. *duriuscula* (L.) Koch, *F. rubra* L., *Hordeum vulgare* L., *Lolium multiflorum* Lam., *L. perenne* L., *Oryza sativa* L., *Phleum alpinum* L., *P. arenarium* L., *P. phleoides* Karst., *P. pratense* L., *Poa annua* L., *P. compressa* L., *P. nemoralis* L., *P. pratensis* L., *P. trivialis* L., *Secale cereale* L., *Triticum aestivum* L., *Zea mays* L. (De Cleene *et al.*, 1981; Egli and Schmidt, 1982; Egli, Goto and Schmidt, 1975; Roberts and Vargas, 1984; Wilkins and Exley, 1977).

Disease Profile

The bacterium overwinters in diseased plants. Although primary infections occur through wounds, cultural practices such as mowing and coring do not

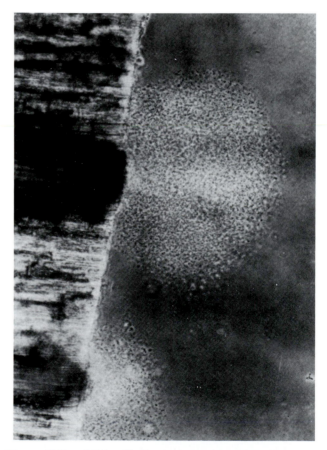

Figure 13-2.   A "cloud" of bacteria emerging from the vascular tissue of a grass leaf that has been cut transversely and immersed in a drop of water. Courtesy Thomas Egli.

appear to be a major factor in the spread of the disease within creeping bentgrass (*Agrostis palustris*) golf greens (see Plate 26-F). Uniform distribution of bacterial wilt on bentgrass greens occurs only when the turf has been established from diseased stolons (Couch, 1981).

Xanthomonas campestris colonizes vascular tissue in the leaves, stems, roots and crowns. Large masses of bacterial cells develop in the vessels thus preventing the normal movement of water through the plants. This leads to wilting and necrosis of meristematic tissue at the margins of the leaves and in the leaf ribs (Egli, Goto and Schmidt, 1975; Schmidt and Neusch, 1980).

There is a relationship between the height of cut of creeping bentgrass (*Agrostis palustris*) golf greens and the severity of bacterial wilt. The disease is less severe in the collars than on the putting surface. Also, greens cut at $^2/_{16}$ inch (2 mm) are more severely affected by the disease than when the putting surface is maintained at higher cuts. Rainfall, air temperature, moisture saturated soil, and radiant energy levels also impact on the development of bacterial wilt. The disease is most severe on bentgrass golf greens following periods of cool air temperatures and continuing rainfall, particularly where soils drain slowly. Also, occurrences of bacterial wilt are usually more severe when these periods of rainfall are followed by two or three bright days (Couch, 1981).

Control

Cultural Practices

Golf or bowling greens afflicted with bacterial wilt should be maintained at a cutting height of $^3/_{16}$ to $^1/_4$ inch (3–4 mm). When creeping bentgrass is propagated vegetatively, the stolons, or sod that has been produced from stolons, should be checked prior to use for the presence of the bacterial wilt pathogen.

Use of Resistant Varieties

Differences in susceptibility to bacterial wilt have been identified for cultivars of annual ryegrass (Schmidt and Neusch, 1980). Also the strain of *Xanthomonas campestris* that is pathogenic to 'Toronto C-15' creeping bentgrass (*Agrostis palustris*) apparently does not infect and colonize other creeping bentgrass cultivars.

Use of Bactericides

High rates of the antibiotic oxytetracycline (Mycoshield™, Pfizer Corporation) has been found to bring about a remission of the symptoms of bacterial wilt (Couch, 1981; Roberts *et al.*, 1982). However, since the effects are only temporary and the individual treatments are very expensive, use of the material on a field scale for control of the disease is not feasible. The only satisfactory long term solution is replacement of the affected turf with sod or stolons that have been certified to be free of the causal bacterium.

RYEGRASS YELLOWS

Symptoms

Leaves of annual ryegrass (*Lolium multiflorum*) first develop a yellow to reddish mottle. As the mottling enlarges, the intensity of the yellowing increases. Stunting of diseased plants is not apparent and the frequency of tillering is not reduced. Perennial ryegrasss (*Lolium perenne*) colonized by the pathogen does not show visible symptoms (Banttari, 1966).

The Pathogen

Ryegrass yellows is incited by the aster yellows mycoplasma. This organism has a thermal inactivation point of 40°C, and withstands a dilution of 1:1000 in neutral 0.85 percent sodium chloride for periods of 5 minutes or less.

Hosts

1. **Turfgrasses**—annual ryegrass (*Lolium multiflorum*) and perennial ryegrass (*Lolium perenne*).
2. **All Known Gramineous Hosts**—A listing of common names for the following species is given in Appendix Table IV. *Agropyron subsecundum* (Link) Hitchc., *Bromus arvensis* L., *Hordeum vulgare* L., *Lolium multiflorum* Lam., *L. perenne* L., *Phalaris canariensis* L., *Triticum durum* Desf. (Banttari, 1966).

Disease Profile

The mycoplasma that incites ryegrass yellows is spread in the field by leafhoppers. The chief vector is *Macrosteles fascifrons* Stal. In general, a latent period of 10 days is required from the time of initial feeding before the vector can transmit the pathogen. Strains with differences in pathogenic potential have been reported for the aster yellows mycoplasma (Banttari, 1966).

WHITE LEAF OF BERMUDAGRASS

White leaf of bermudagrass (*Cynodon dactylon*) has been reported from the Republic of Taiwan, Thailand, and Israel (Chen, Lee and Chen, 1972; Zelcer *et al.*, 1972; Stem, 1992).

Symptoms

In overall view, white leaf is seen as isolated patches of light yellow to off-white turf measuring 0.5 to 2 inches (1.3–5 cm) in diameter. The internodes of the upper portions of the stems of affected plants are shortened, causing the leaves to be massed at the terminal ends of the stems, creating a "witches' broom" effect. The leaves of affected plants are at first pale yellow. They then turn a distinctive dull white. Also, the leaves of diseased plants are slightly broader and flatter than normal.

The Pathogen

Chen, Lee and Chen (1972) and Zelcer *et al.* (1972) reported that white leaf of bermudagrass is probably caused by an unidentified mollicute they found in association with diseased tissue. In a later study, Chen *et al.* (1977) characterized the organism as a spiroplasma. By means of serological tests they determined that the relationships between the bermudagrass white leaf spiroplasma, the corn stunt spiroplasma, and *Spiroplasma citri* was more distinct than that between the sproplasmas from corn and citrus. Additional studies will be necessary, however, before a decision can be made concerning the appropriate species designation for the white leaf spiroplasma.

Procedure for Isolation and Culture

The white leaf spiroplasma has been cultivated at 30 °C on liquid and solid cell-free media consisting of mycoplasma broth components, sucrose and horse serum (Chen *et al.*, 1977).

Hosts

1. **Turfgrass**—bermudagrass (*Cynodon dactylon* (L.) Pers.
2. **All Known Gramineous Hosts**—A listing of common names for the following species is given in Appendix Table IV. *Brachiaria distachya* A. Camus, *Cynodon dactylon* (L.) Pers., (Chen, Lee and Chen, 1972).

Disease Profile

Apparently the disease does not cause a severe thinning or loss of turf. Its primary impact is aesthetic. The pathogen is thought to be transmitted by leafhoppers.

§   §   §

PART FOUR

Diseases of Turfgrasses Caused by Nematodes

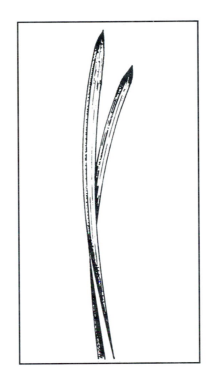

Diseases of Turfgrasses Caused by Nematodes

CHARACTERISTICS OF PLANT PARASITIC NEMATODES

Nematodes constitute one of the more abundant forms of animal life. In addition to the numerous, free-living, saprophagous species that participate in the decomposition of dead organic matter, pathogenic species are known for practically all forms of plant and animal life. Among the species that parasitize turfgrasses, there are forms that infect and colonize only leaf and floral tissue and species that feed only on roots.

The word "nematode" is of Greek origin and means thread-like. Species parasitizing humans and animals are commonly called threadworms or roundworms, and may be quite large. As a group, the plant pathogenic forms are generally smaller in size, averaging approximately 1/25 inch (0.1 mm) long as adults, and are usually referred to simply as nematodes, or by the highly descriptive term, eelworms.

The first report in the United States of the adverse effects of root-feeding nematodes on turf quality came from Florida in 1953. Large populations of four genera of ectoparasitic nematodes were found to be parasitizing the root systems of declining St. Augustinegrass (*Stenotaphrum secundatum*) lawns in the Tampa Bay area (Kelsheimer and Overman, 1953). The first experiment designed to test a nematicide for control of nematodes in established turf was performed in 1953. A bermudagrass (*Cynodon dactylon*) golf green in Sanford, Florida, with high population levels of sting, stubby-root, and lance nematodes was injected with a mixture of dichloropropane and ethylene dibromide. The treatment gave excellent control of the nematodes and resulted in an outstanding growth response of the bermudagrsss (Perry and Horn, 1969). Root-infecting nematodes are known to be capable of causing major damage to stands of turfgrass in all climatic zones of the world.

Life Cycles

In general, the life cycles of plant pathogenic nematodes are comparatively simple. They are bisexual as a group; however, many are parthenogenetic. The females lay eggs which hatch into juveniles. The eggs of some species can survive without hatching for years, but hatch within a relatively short period of time when the roots of host plants grow near them. The juveniles may be similar to adults in overall appearance and undergo a series of four molts before adulthood is reached. With some exceptions, the cuticles are shed with each molt. The periods of growth between molts are called juvenile stages—the first juvenile stage occurring before the first molt, etc. (Figure 14-1). The rate of nematode activity, growth and reproduction increases as the soil temperature rises from 50°F (10°C) to about 90°F (32°C). The minimum life span of a single generation of root-feeding nematodes is about four weeks.

With the exception of the reproductive system, the organs of the juveniles are highly developed at the time of hatching. For most nematode species, development of the reproductive system and increase in size are the principal changes that occur during the various juvenile stages. Exceptions to this rule are found with the cyst and root-knot nematodes. These will be discussed in the descriptions of the life cycles of these two groups.

Methods of Feeding

Plant-parasitic nematodes are obligate parasites. They feed only on living host cells. Penetration of the host cell is accomplished by a stylet (Figure 14-2). The stylet serves first to inject digestive enzymes into the host cell and then to withdraw the partially digested cell contents. In addition to making cell contents more easily ingested and utilized as food, with many nematode species such as the root-

Figure 14-1. Photomicrograph of developmental stages of the spiral nematode, *Rotylenchus boxopholus* Golden. From left to right: egg, newly hatched juvenile, first, second, and third stage juveniles, and mature female (approximately 180×). *Courtesy A. H. Golden.*

knot group, this secretion causes an alteration of cell growth, which in turn brings about a pronounced modification of certain host tissues. As the result, special nurse tissues are formed on which the nematodes can feed (Christie, 1959).

Feeding time per cell may vary widely among species. With some species, a total period of only 5–10 seconds is required from the time of puncture of the cell wall to the complete withdrawal of the cell contents, whereas other species may feed for several days on one site. Orientation of the various nematodes pathogenic to turfgrasses with relation to feeding positions varies from ectoparasitic to endoparasitic. **Ectoparasitic** nematodes spend their entire life cycle outside of roots and feed only on tissues they can reach from their location on the root's surface. These species are usually migratory. **Endoparasitic** nematodes spend at least part of their life cycle inside the roots. They may either be **migratory** (all stages move freely in, through, and out of root tissues), or **sedentary** (most of the life cycle being spent in a permanent feeding position within the root, and only one or two juvenile stages free to move to new feeding sites) (Figures 14-3 and 14-4).

Requirements for Pathogenicity

In order for root-feeding nematodes to have an adverse effect on turf quality they must be able to produce population levels in sufficient numbers to initiate a high incidence of feeding sites within a relatively short period of time. The actual number of root-feeding nematodes required to impair the overall growth and development of turfgrass varies among species. Certain nematode species are more pathogenic than others and, therefore, will cause damage at lower population levels. For example, the damage threshold level for the ring nematode (*Criconemella* spp.) on bentgrass (*Agrostis* spp.) has been estimated at 2,000 nemas per 100 cm^3 of soil (Todd and Tisserat, 1990), whereas the damage threshold for the needle nematode (*Longidorus breviannulatus*) is 20 nemas per 100 cm^3 of soil (Forer, 1977). Also, within any given nematode species, the population levels required to produce various degrees of injury to the plants will vary according to the degree of stress to which the plants are being subjected. As plant vigor decreases due to such factors as lowered cutting heights or high air temperatures, the number of nemas needed to bring about major damage also decreases.

Symptoms

With the root-feeding nematodes, above-ground symptoms vary somewhat with the turfgrass and nematode species involved. In general, however, foliar symptoms result from an improperly functioning root system. Affected plants may show various shades of light green to yellow. Nematodes have a non-uniform or clustered distribution in the soil, therefore, the areas showing damage vary in shape and size and also, in contrast with the patch diseases, the boundaries between good turf and poor turf are not

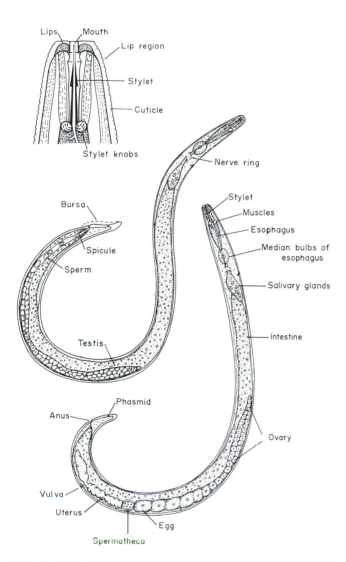

Lips   Mouth
Lip region
Stylet
Cuticle
Stylet knobs
Nerve ring
Bursa
Stylet
Muscles
Esophagus
Spicule
Median bulbs of esophagus
Sperm
Salivary glands
Testis
Intestine
Phasmid
Anus
Ovary
Vulva
Uterus
Egg
Spermatheca

Figure 14-2. Diagrammatic representation of adult female and male plant parasitic nematodes showing body parts and an enlarged view of anterior section showing pre-feeding position of the stylet.

sharply defined (Plate 30-D, E, F). Since the affected plants lack vigor, they have a reduced ability to withstand dry soil conditions, low fertility, extremely high air temperatures, and other adverse growing conditions. Under these stresses, active colonization of the leaves, crowns and roots by otherwise weakly pathogenic fungi such as *Colletotrichum graminicola* and *Curvularia* spp. is common (see Chapter 7, Senectopathic Disorders).

FLORAL AND FOLIAR NEMATODES

Grass Seed Nematode

In certain areas of the Pacific Northwest, this nematode incites a major disease problem in bentgrasses grown for seed production. Affecting the floral regions of the plants, the disease has been known to cause up to 75 percent loss of seed crops (Apt, Austenson and Courtney, 1960).

Symptoms

The primary response of diseased plants is the production of galls in the inflorescences. These modifications of infected flowers are very striking. The glumes are 2–3 times larger, and the outer paleae are 5–8 times normal size. Also, contrasted with normal seed, the nematode galls are 5–8 times longer and have a characteristic purplish color. These elongated, purplish galls, enclosed by their malformed glumes and paleae, create a spiked appearance to the panicle (Apt, Austenson and Courtney, 1960; Goodey, 1930) (Figure 14-5).

The Nematode

Anguina agrostis (Steinbuch) Filipjev.

Hosts

1. **Turfgrasses**—creeping bentgrass (*Agrostis palustris*), Colonial bentgrass (*Agrostis tenuis*), annual bluegrass (*Poa annua*), and Kentucky bluegrass (*Poa pratensis*).
2. **All Known Gramineous Hosts**—A listing of common names for the following species is given in Appendix Table IV. *Agrostis alba* L., *A. canina* L., *A. capillaris* L., *A. exarata* Trin., *A. palustris* Huds., *A. tenuis* Sibth., *Festuca ovina* , *Poa alpina* L., *P. annua*, *P. pratensis* L. (Courtney and Howell, 1952; Marcinowski, 1909; Steinbuch, 1799).

Disease Profile

During seed harvest, debris containing mature galls is scattered over the soil surface. The nematodes in these galls remain in a quiescent state until the surrounding plant tissue becomes softened by fall and winter rains. After this, the encased, second stage juveniles escape, and moving about in films of water, migrate to living plants. Entering the sheaths of these plants, the juveniles remain thus enclosed near the apical meristems ("growing points") until the boot stage of growth in early spring.

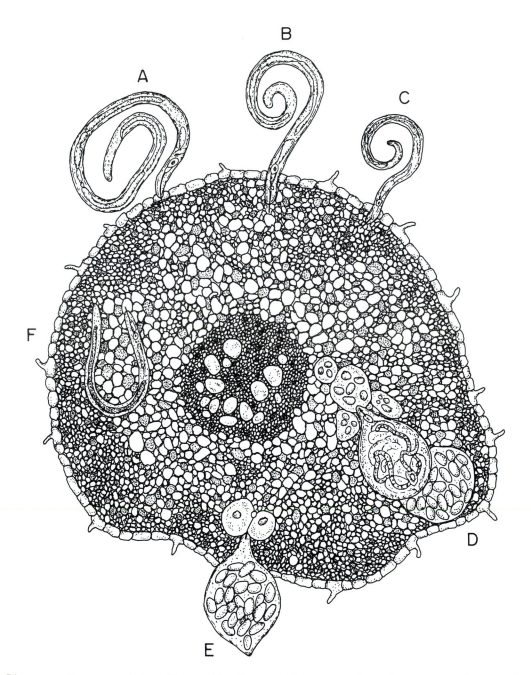

Figure 14-3.   Diagrammatic representation of types of feeding on turfgrass roots by various genera of nematodes. (A) *Belono-laimus* (sting nematode), (B) *Hoplolaimus* (lance nematode), (C) *Helicotylenchus* (spiral nematode), (D) *Meloidogyne* (root knot nematode), (E) *Heterodera* (cyst nematode), and (F) *Pratylenchus* (root lesion nematode).

When the florets start to develop, actual plant penetration is then accomplished as the juveniles enter the young ovaries and begin feeding. With this, they pass through the third juvenile stage and then to adults in a very short period of time. During this time, the parasitized florets, through a combination of abortion and/or complete suppression of the growth of their various parts, are transformed into the characteristic, purplish, malformed galls.

Usually, 1–3 each of male and female nematodes are found per gall (Figure 14-6). Egg laying lasts about two weeks, and in this time span each female will produce up to 1,000 eggs. The life cycle is completed in about three to four weeks.

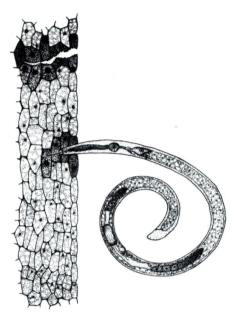

Figure 14-4. Diagrammatic representation of an ectoparasitic nematode feeding on cortical tissue of a grass root. Note position of head and stylet. (180×)

Shortly after egg laying is completed, the adult nematodes die and their bodies soon degenerate. Also, during this period, egg hatching begins. Growth of the juveniles through the first molt into the second juvenile stage occurs in very short order. About 3–4 weeks are required from the third molt of the parent generation to the second juvenile stage of the offspring. After the second juvenile stage is reached, however, the nemas remain in this state until the penetration of the young floral ovaries the following spring. As the result, only one generation of grass seed nematodes is produced each year (Courtney and Howell, 1952; Goodey, 1930; Jensen, Howell and Courtney, 1958) (Figure 14-7).

In a migratory state, the grass seed nematode cannot survive for more than one season in the soil. When encased in dried galls, however, the nemas can exist in a quiescent state up to six years (Courtney and Howell, 1952). Spread of the nematode over long distances is accomplished by infested debris mixed with seed or on harvest machinery.

Control

Prevention of seed formation, and thus breaking the cycle of development of the nematode, is at present the most satisfactory means of control. This can be accomplished best by either clipping, or the use of

maleic hydrazide to prevent floral formation (Courtney, Peabody and Austenson, 1962). Pasturing may be effective if it is thorough enough to prevent floral formation over the entire area.

Either a one year fallow, or rotation with a nonsusceptible crop species will provide effective control if in either case the management program completely prevents floral formation from volunteer plants remaining from the previous grass crop. Stubble burning after harvest is a satisfactory control measure if conditions permit a thorough burning of all crop refuse.

Sanitation is very important in the prevention of the spread of the nematodes from one planting to the next. Before moving into a noninfested stand, all machinery, seed bags, and miscellaneous equipment should be freed of surplus trash and then cleaned by steaming. In addition, workers should remove accu-

Figure 14-5. Response of bentgrass florets to infection and colonization by the grass seed nematode (*Anguina agrostis*). Left, healthy; Right, diseased. *After Jensen, Howell and Courtney, 1958.*

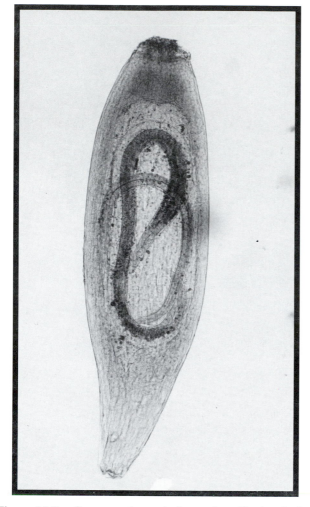

Figure 14-6. Grass seed nematodes enclosed in developing bentgrass gall (approximately 100×). *Photograph by F. P. McWhorter.*

mulated crop debris from pockets, cuffs of trousers, shoes, etc.

Leaf Gall Nematodes

Symptoms

Although severely diseased leaves appear to be shorter than healthy ones, colonization by leaf gall nematodes does not appreciably reduce plant vigor. The galls occur most commonly at the base of the leaves, but at times they may be found near the tips. Occasionally, two or more galls may fuse, but more frequently they occur singly. As single galls, they are more or less spindle shaped, and, on broader leafed turfgrasses, vary in size from 1/16–1/8 inch (1.5–3 mm) wide and 1/8–5/8 inch (3–16 mm) long. Greenish-

yellow in color at first, they gradually change to reddish purple, and finally purplish black.

The Nematodes

A. *Anguina graminis* (Hardy) Filipjev.

Hosts

1. **Turfgrasses**—hard fescue (*Festuca ovina* var. *duriuscula*).
2. **All Known Gramineous Hosts**—A listing of common names for the following species is given in Appendix Table IV. *Festuca capillata* Lam., *F. ovina* L., *F. ovina* var. *duriuscula* (L.) Koch (Goodey, 1927; Goodey, 1934).

The Nematodes

B. *Ditylenchus graminophila* (Goodey) Filipjev

Turfgrass Host. creeping bentgrass (*Agrostis tenuis*) (Goodey, 1933).

Disease Profile

The cycle of development for *Ditylenchus graminophila* has been studied in detail (Goodey, 1933; Goodey, 1934). During the fourth juvenile stage, the nematodes emerge from the old galls and migrate to young, developing leaves. Penetration is accomplished while the leaves are still enclosed by the leaf sheaths. After entry, the nematodes go through their fourth molt, and during this time the surrounding host tissue is stimulated to produce galls.

In the case of a simple gall, only the leaf tissue between, and on either side, of two parallel veins is involved. Increase in size of the gall is accomplished by both increase in number and size of cells. The mesophyll cells in particular are much enlarged, becoming oblong in the process. Their cytoplasm is granular in appearance and their nuclei are distinctly round and much larger than those of healthy cells. Many of the abortive mesophyll cells eventually degenerate to give rise to cavities within the gall. The developing nematodes may lie free in these cavities. The red color of the galls is caused by discoloration of the cytoplasm of the epidermal cells and those mesophyll cells immediately beneath.

When adulthood is reached, pairing of the nematodes occurs, after which the egg laying process begins. After eggs hatch, the nemas pass through three molts to the fourth juvenile stage. They then migrate from the parent gall to new zones of infection and the cycle of development is completed.

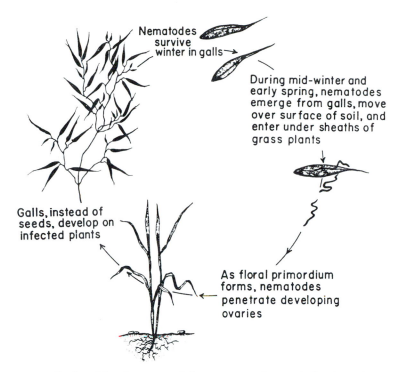

Nematodes survive winter in galls

During mid-winter and early spring, nematodes emerge from galls, move over surface of soil, and enter under sheaths of grass plants

Galls, instead of seeds, develop on infected plants

As floral primordium forms, nematodes penetrate developing ovaries

Figure 14-7. Cycle of development of the grass seed nematode, *Anguina agrostis.*

ROOT-FEEDING NEMATODES

The root-feeding nematode species pathogenic to turfgrasses may be placed in one of four major classes based on a combination of nematode morphology, feeding positions, and host symptoms: Cyst Nematodes, Cystoid Nematodes, Endoparasitic Nematodes, and Ectoparasitic Nematodes. Since this is a natural classification, exceptions do occur. The justification for its use lies not only in its orderly grouping of several genera of pathogenic nematodes, but also in the fact that it is extremely useful in teaching concepts of control.

Cyst Nematodes

Root Symptoms

Although some necrosis develops, signs of the actual nematode constitute the primary diagnostic feature of the disease. Small, but conspicuous, pearly white female bodies (cysts) of the nematode are attached to the fibrous roots of diseased plants. Ranging from 1/25–1/10 inch (0.1–0.3 mm) in diameter, these cysts gradually turn tan or light brown with age.

The Nematodes

A. *Heterodera leuceilyma* Eduardo and Perry

Turfgrass Host. St. Augustinegrass (*Stenotaphrum secundatum*) (Dunn and Noling, 1993).

The Nematodes

B. *Heterodera major* (O. Schmidt) Franklin; syn. *Heterodera avenae* Filipjev

Hosts

1. **Turfgrasses**—tall fescue (*Festuca arundinacea*), red fescue (*Festuca rubra*), annual ryegrass (*Lolium multiflorum*), and perennial ryegrass (*Lolium perenne*).

2. **All Known Gramenious Hosts**—A listing of the common names for the following species is given in Appendix Table IV. *Arrhenatherum elatius* (L.) Presl, *Avena sativa* L., *A. sterilis* L., *A. strigosa* Schreb., *Brachypodium ponticum* Velen., *B. sylvaticum* (Huds.) Beauv., *Bromus arvensis* L., *B. sterilis* L., *Dactylis glomerata* L., *Festuca ampla* Hack., *F. clavata* Moench, Meth., *F. arundinacea* Schreb., *F. rubra* L., *F. rubra* var. *heterophylla* Mutel., *Hordeum jubatum* L. *H. murinum* L., *H. spontaneum* Koch, *H. vulgare* L., *Koeleria cristata* (L.) Pers., *K. phleoides* (Vill.) Pers., *Lolium multiflorum* Lam., *L. perenne* L., *L. temulentum* L., *Phalaris minor* Retz., *Phleum pratense* L., *Poa nemoralis* L., *P. trivialis* L., *Secale cereale* L., *Sor-*

ghum vulgare Pers., *Triticum aestivum* L., *T. monococcum* L., *T. polonicum* L., *T. spelta* L. (Hesling, 1958; Winslow, 1954).

The Nematodes

C. *Heterodera punctata* Thorne

Turfgrass Hosts. Colonial bentgrass (*Agrostis tenuis*), creeping bentgrass (*Agrostis palustris*), and St. Augustinegrass (*Stenotaphrum secundatum*) (Chitwood, 1955; Franklin, 1951).

The Nematodes

D. *Heterodera iri* Matthews

Turfgrass Hosts. annual bluegrass (*Poa annua*), creeping bentgrass (*Agrostis palustris* Huds.), and velvet bentgrass (*Agrostis canina* L.) (LaMonde and Wick, 1991).

Disease Profile

The eggs and juveniles overwinter in soil-borne cysts. The juveniles undergo the first molt in the eggs (Hagemeyer, 1951). During the second larval stage, the nemas emerge from the cysts and enter the roots of the hosts. Both the males and females undergo their successive molts to adulthood in the cortical tissues of the roots. While undergoing the third and fourth molts, the females increase in diameter, becoming lemon-shaped in the process. After feeding begins by the juveniles, they break through the cortical and epidermal tissues and as adults lie with only their heads embedded in the root tissues.

After production, some eggs are extruded from the uterus, but most remain within the female bodies. The eggs are protected by the cysts, and hatch over a long period of time. Soil moisture levels do not influence egg hatch, but low moisture retards the emergence of hatched nemas from the cysts (Wallace, 1955; Wallace, 1956). Soil temperatures of 65–75 °F (18–24 °C) appear to be optimum for egg hatch, host penetration, and growth of the cyst nematodes on turfgrasses.

Cystoid Nematodes

Cystoid nematodes are distinguished from true cyst nematodes by the difference in the location of the vulva in relation to the anus and the failure of the female bodies to turn tan or light brown with age. They are distinguished from root-knot nematodes by their thicker cuticles and the absence of egg sacs.

To date, one species of cystoid nematode has been reported parasitic to turfgrass (Heald and Golden, 1969).

The Nematode

Meloidodera charis Hopper

Turfgrass Host. St. Augustinegrass (*Stenotaphrum secundatum*) (Heald and Golden, 1969).

Endoparasitic Nematodes

Rootknot Nematodes

Rootknot is one of the older known nematode-incited diseases. The problem was first described on greenhouse grown cucumbers in England in 1855 (Berkeley, 1855). Rootknot nematodes are a very important group of pathogens of agricultural crops in general. They rank with cyst nematodes as being the best known of plant parasitic forms. Eight species are known to parasitize turfgrasses.

Symptoms

The rootknot nematodes consistently produce the most distinctive symptom pattern of any of the root-feeding turfgrass nematodes. Both fibrous and lateral roots develop characteristic swellings which vary in shape from spherical to elongate spindles. The color of these swellings is the same as that of adjacent noncolonized root tissue.

The Nematodes

A. *Meloidogyne arenaria* (Neal) Chitwood

Turfgrass Hosts. bermudagrass (*Cynodon dactylon*), african bermudagrass (*Cynodon transvaalensis*), and hybrid bermudagrass *Cynodon transvaalensis* × *Cynodon dactylon*) (Riffle, 1964).

The Nematodes

B. *Meloidogyne graminicola* Golden and Birchfield

Hosts

1. **Turfgrasses**—annual bluegrass (*Poa annua*), bermudagrass (*Cynodon dactylon*) and zoysiagrass (*Zoysia japonica*).
2. **All Known Gramineous Hosts**—A listing of common names for the following species is given in Appendix Table IV. *Alopecrus carolinianus*

Walt., *Avena sativa* L., *Cynodon dactylon* (L.) Pers., *Dactyloctenium aegyptiacum* Willd., *Echinochloa colonum* (L.) Link, *E. crusgali* (L.) Beauv., *Eleusine indica* (L.) Gaertn., *Eragrostis plumosa* L., *Hordeum vulgare* L., *Ischaemum rugosum* Trin., *Oryza sativa* L., *Paspalum sanguinola* Lam., *Pennisetum typhoides* Stapf and Hubbard, *Poa annua* L., *Sorghum bicolor* Moench, *Sorghum vulgare* Pers., *Triticum aestivum* L., *Zea mays* L. (Griffin, 1984; Jepson, 1987).

The Nematodes

C. *Meloidogyne graminis* (Sledge and Golden) Whitehead; syn. *Hypsoperine graminis* Sledge and Golden

Hosts

1. **Turfgrasses**—bahiagrass (*Paspalum notatum*), bermudagrass (*Cynodon dactylon*), Kentucky bluegrass (*Poa pratensis*), tall fescue (*Festuca arundinacea*), St. Augustinegrass (*Stenotaphrum secundatum*), and zoysiagrass (*Zoysia japonica*).
2. **All Known Gramineous Hosts**—A listing of common names for the following species is given in Appendix Table IV. *Cynodon dactylon* (L.) Pers., *C. transvaalensis* Burtt-Davy, *Festuca arundinacea* Schreb., *Paspalum notatum* Flugge, *Poa pratensis* L., *Sorghum vulgare* Pers., *Stenotaphrum secundatum* (Walt.) Kuntze, *Triticum aestivum* L., *Zea mays* L., *Zoysia japonica* Steud. (Dickerson, 1966; Minton and Ivey, 1967; Perry and Maur, 1969; Sledge, 1960; Southards, 1967).

The Nematodes

D. *Meloidogyne hapla* Chitwood

Turfgrass Hosts. bermudagrass (*Cynodon dactylon*), Kentucky bluegrass (*Poa pratensis*), and St. Augustinegrass (*Stenotaphrum secundatum*) (Dist., 1960; Perry, Darling and Thorne, 1959).

The Nematodes

E. *Meloidogyne incognita* Chitwood

Turfgrass Hosts. creeping bentgrass (*Agrostis palustris*), bermudagrass (*Cynodon dactylon*, 'Sunturf' bermudagrass (*Cynodon magennisii*), african bermudagrass (*Cynodon transvaalensis*), Kentucky bluegrass (*Poa pratensis*), and rough stalk bluegrass (*Poa trivialis*) (Gaskin, 1965d; Hodges and Taylor, 1966).

The Nematodes

F. *Meloidogyne marylandi* Jepson and Golden

Turfgrass Hosts. bermudagrass (*Cynodon dactylon*) and zoysiagrass (*Zoysia japonica*) (Jepson, 1987).

The Nematodes

G. *Meloidogyne microtyla* Mulvey, Townshend and Potter

Hosts

1. **Turfgrasses**—Kentucky bluegrass (*Poa pratensis*), Colonial bentgrass (*Agrostis tenuis*), red fescue (*Festuca rubra*), and annual ryegrass (*Lolium multiflorum*).
2. **All Known Gramineous Hosts**—A listing of common names for the following species is given in Appendix Table IV. *Agropyron repens* (L.) Beauv., *Agrostis alba* L., *A. tenuis* Sibth., *Arrhenatherum elatius* (L.) Presl, *Avena fatua* L., *A. sativa* L., *Bromus inermis* Leyss., *B. secalinus* L., *B. tectorum* L., *Dactylis glomerata* L., *Digitaria sanguinalis* (L.) Scop., *Echinochloa crusgalli* (L.) Beauv., *E. pungens* (Poir) Rydb., *Elymus virginicus* L., *Eragrostis pectinacea* (Michx) Nees, *Hordeum jubatum* L., *H. vulgare* L., *Hystrix patula* Moench, *Leersia oryzoides* (L.) Swartz, *Lolium multiflorum* Lam., *Panicum capillare* L., *Phlaris arundinacea* L., *Phleum pratense* L., *Poa pratensis* L., *Secale cereale* L., *Setaria viridis* (L.) Beauv., *Triticum vulgare* L. (Jepson, 1987).

The Nematodes

H. *Meloidogyne naasi* Franklin

Hosts

1. **Turfgrasses**—Colonial bentgrass (*Agrostis tenuis*), creeping bentgrass (*Agrostis palustris*), annual bluegrass (*Poa annua*), Kentucky bluegrass (*Poa pratensis*), Chewings fescue (*Festuca rubra* var. *commutata*), tall fescue (*Festuca arundinacea*), red fescue (*Festuca rubra*), annual ryegrass (*Lolium multiflorum*), and perennial ryegrass (*Lolium perenne*).
2. **All Known Gramineous Hosts**—A listing of common names for the following species is given in Appendix Table IV. *Agropyron repens* (L.) Beauv., *Agrostis alba* L., *A. palustris* Huds., *A. tenuis* Sibth., *Avena sativa* L., *Dactylis glomerata* L., *Digitaria sanguinalis* (L.) Scop., *Festuca arun-*

dinacea Schreb., *F. rubra* L., *F. rubra* var. *commutata* Gaud., *Hordeum vulgare* L., *Lolium multiflorum* Lam., *L. perenne* L., *Oryza sativa* L., *Poa annua* L., *P. pratensis* L., *P. trivialis* L., *Secale cereale* L., *Triticum aestivum* L. (Griffin, 1984; Radewald *et al.*, 1970).

Disease Profile

Eggs of the root-knot nematodes overwinter in the soil and in roots of infected plants. The juveniles undergo the first molt in the eggs. In the second juvenile stage, the nemas escape into the soil and move to new root zones, or develop in the root in which they were produced. Most penetration occurs at root tips. After becoming embedded in the root tissue, the juvenile head situates in an intercellular space close to the proxylem. The feeding process is restricted to the cells in the immediate areas of the head. With the successive molts, secretions from the nematodes stimulates nearby cells to form giant cells which serve to nurse the developing parasite. In addition, cells more distant from the embedded nematode are stimulated to abnormal size and number, thus producing the characteristic galls (Christie, 1936).

At maturity, the majority of the male nematodes migrate from the roots to move freely in the soil. During their parasitic phase of development, however, like the females, they stimulate the production of root knots.

The female root-knot nematode remains in the same position in the root tissue throughout her entire life. When mature, she is semispherical to pear shaped, with a distinctive, protruding neck region. Under optimum environmental conditions, *i.e.*, a suitable host and soil temperature of 70 °F (21 °C) for *Meloidogyne hapla* and 80 °F (27 °C) for *Meloidogyne naasi*, females begin laying eggs within one month from the time of root penetration as larvae. The egg laying process is preceded by the extrusion of a gelatinous mass through the anus, then the eggs are deposited through the vulva into this protective material.

When the posterior end of the female protrudes from the root, or is near the root surface, the egg masses accumulate in the soil at the root surface. If the female is more deeply embedded in the root tissue, however, the egg masses accumulate within the plant tissue.

Soil moisture in the readily available range, field capacity (−0.033 MPa) to permanent wilting percentage (−1.5 MPa), does not influence the hatchability of eggs of the Northern root-knot nematode (*Meloidogyne hapla*). Migration of the hatched juve-

niles, however, is reduced considerably at the lower soil moisture levels (Couch and Bloom, 1960).

Meloidogyne naasi is highly pathogenic on creeping bentgrass (*Agrostis palustris*) in combination with *Pratylenchus penetrans* and *Tylenchorhynchus agri* (Sikora *et al.*, 1972). *Meloidogyne incognita* is more pathogenic on bermudagrass (*Cynodon* spp.) than *Meloidogyne hapla* or *Meloidogyne arenaria* (Riggs, Dale and Hamblen, 1962). Annual ryegrass (*Lolium multiflorum*), Kentucky bluegrass (*Poa pratensis*) are moderate to extremely susceptible to *Meloidogyne incognita*, *Meloidogyne incognita*, and *Meloidogyne arenaria* (McGlohon, Sasser and Sherwood, 1961).

Root Lesion Nematodes (Meadow Nematodes)

Symptoms

In early stages of disease development, minute, brown lesions are present on the roots. Due to continued nematode feeding at the margins, these lesions gradually enlarge. With the colonization of the affected areas by secondary invaders, the lesions may girdle the root, thus causing root pruning. In this manner, with high populations of root lesion nematodes, the entire root systems of affected plants may be destroyed.

The Nematodes

A. *Pratylenchus brachyurus* (Godfrey) Goodey

Turfgrass Hosts. bermudagrass (*Cynodon dactylon*), Kentucky bluegrass (*Poa pratensis*), centipedegrass (*Eremochloa ophiuroides*, St. Augustinegrass (*Stenotaphrum secundatum*, and zoysiagrass (*Zoysia japonica*) (Dist., 1960; Good, Steele and Ratcliffe, 1959; Mai, Crittenden and Jenkins, 1960).

The Nematodes

B. *Pratylenchus hexincisus* Taylor and Jenkins

Hosts

1. **Turfgrass**—bermudagrass (*Cynodon dactylon*).
2. **All Known Gramineous Hosts**—A listing of common names for the following species is given in Appendix Table IV. *Andropogon ischaemum* L., *A. saccharoides* Swartz, *A. scoparius* Michx., *Aristida purpurea* Nutt., *Avena sativa* L., *Bromus catharticus* Vahl, *Cynodon dactylon* (L.) Pers., *Digitaria* spp., *Elymus canadensis* L., *Panicum ramosum*

L., *Secale cereale* L., *Sorghum halepense* (L.) Pers., *S. vulgare* Pers., *Triticum aestivum* L. (Dist., 1960).

The Nematodes

C. *Pratylenchus neglectus* Rensch

Turfgrass Hosts. Colonial bentgrass (*Agrostis tenuis*), creeping bentgrass (*Agrostis palustris*), red fescue (*Festuca rubra*), tall fescue (*Festuca arundinacea*), sheep fescue (*Festuca ovina*), Canada bluegrass (*Poa compressa*), Kentucky bluegrass (*Poa pratensis*), rough stalk bluegrass (*Poa trivialis*) and perennial ryegrass (*Lolium perenne*) (Townshend, Eggens and McCollom, 1973).

The Nematodes

D. *Pratylenchus penetrans* (Cobb) Chitwood and Oteifa

Hosts

1. **Turfgrasses**—Kentucky bluegrass (*Poa pratensis*) and zoysiagrass (*Zoysia japonica*).
2. **All Known Gramineous Hosts**—A listing of common names for the following species is given in Appendix Table IV. *Agropryon cristatum* (L.) Gaertn., *A. intermedium* (Host) Beauv., *A. trachycaulum* (Link) Malte, *A. trichophorum* (Link) Richt., *Alopecurus pratensis* L., *Arrhenatherum elatius* (L.) Presl, *Avena sativa* L., *Bromus inermis* Leyss., *Dactylis glomerata* L., *Elymus canadensis* L., *Festuca arundinacea* Schreb., *Hordeum vulgare* L., *Phleum pratense* L., *Poa pratensis* L. *Secale cereale* L., *Triticum aestivum* L., *Zoysia japonica* Steud. (Dist, 1960; Goodey and Franklin, 1956; Jensen, 1953; Mai, Crittenden and Jenkins, 1960; Perry, Darling and Thorne, 1959).

The Nematodes

E. *Pratylenchus pratensis* (de Man) Filipjev

Hosts

1. **Turfgrasses**—Kentucky bluegrass (*Poa pratensis*), and bentgrasses (*Agrostis* spp.).
2. **All Known Gramineous Hosts**—A listing of common names for the following species is given in Appendix Table IV. *Agrostis* spp., *Dactylis glomerata* L., *Echinochloa colonum* (L.) Link, *Eleusine indica* (L.) Gaertn., *Oryza sativa* L., *Poa pratensis* L., *Sorghum sudanense* (Piper) Stapf,

(Index Plant Dis., 1960; Mai, Crittenden and Jenkins, 1960; Troll and Tarjan, 1954).

The Nematodes

F. *Pratylenchus zeae* Graham

Hosts

1. **Turfgrass**—bermudagrass (*Cynodon dactylon*).
2. **All Known Gramineous Hosts**—A listing of common names for the following species is given in Appendix Table IV. *Avena sativa* L., *Brachiaria mutica* (Forsk) Stapf., *Cynodon dactylon* (L.) Pers., *Dactylis glomerata* L., *Oryza sativa* L., *Panicum maximum* Jacq., *P. purpurascens* Raddi, *Saccharum officinarum* L., *Secale cereale* L., *Sorghum vulgare* Pers., *Zoysia* spp. (Dist., 1960; Lordello and Filho, 1969).

Disease Profile

Penetration of roots is accomplished by both juveniles and adults. Root lesion nematodes may feed as ectoparasites. As a rule, however, they invade the more mature areas behind the root tips (Godfery, 1929; Linford, 1939). Within the roots, the nematodes feed freely on the parenchymatous cells of the cortex. The various *Pratylenchus* species are highly migratory, they move freely in and out of the root tissue. Both juveniles and adults disrupt root tissue by forcing their way either through or between the cells. This leads to a progressive breakdown of the root. Through the initiation of necrotic areas on the roots, lesion nematodes create an environment that is favorable for secondary invaders. Troll and Rohde (1966) found *Pratylenchus penetrans* in all root tissues except the root cap of annual ryegrass (*Lolium multiflorum*), red fescue (*Festuca rubra*), and Kentucky bluegrass (*Poa pratensis*). *Pratylenchus brachyurus* is more active at soil temperatures in the 80–90 °F (27–32 °C) range, while *Pratylenchus penetrans* is more active at 70 °F (21 °C) (Graham, 1951). At the optimum temperatures for these two species, the time required to complete the life cycles is 40–60 days.

Burrowing Nematodes

Symptoms

The necrotic areas on the roots are similar to those produced by root lesion nematodes. The lesions are at first small, brown spots. Through coalescence, those gradually enlarge to become distinct cavities on the larger roots. Root girdling, and subsequent pruning as the result of lesion formation is common. Colonization of the fibrous roots may result in a general root rot, and, therefore, complete destruction of a major portion of the root system.

The Nematode

Radopholus similus (Cobb) Thorne

Hosts

1. **Turfgrass**—bahiagrass (*Paspalum notatum*), bermudagrass (*Cynodon dactylon*).
2. **All Known Gramineous Hosts**—A listing of common names for the following species is given in Appendix Table IV. *Axonopus* sp., *Cynodon dactylon* (L.) Pers., *Digitaria sanguinalis* (L.) Scop., *Panicum hemitomon* Schult., *P. maximum* Jacq., *Paspalum notatum* Flugge, *Rhynchelytrum roseum* (Nees) Stapf and Hubb., *Saccharum officinarum* L., *Stenotaphrum secundatum* (Walt.) Kuntze (Christie, 1936; Feder and Feldmesser, 1957; Kelsheimer and Overman, 1953).

Ectoparasitic Nematodes

The life cycles of the ectoparasitic nematodes are relatively simple and closely parallel the generalized description given in the introduction to this chapter. In the following, the ectoparasitic groups will be outlined, the grass hosts of the various species listed, and where distinctive, symptoms and cycles of disease development described. Since the control measures are essentially the same for all the root-feeding species, they are given in a separate, concluding section.

Spiral Nematodes

Spiral nematodes are among the most frequent species found associated with turfgrass roots. It is not uncommon for two or more species of spiral nematodes to be occurring together in the same turf.

Symptoms

The stand of turfgrass supporting high populations of spiral nematodes is sparse and difficult to maintain because of sharp reduction in plant vigor. Individual plants are pale and chlorotic, and have relatively long, narrow leaf blades. The roots of these plants are poorly developed, discolored brown, and their cortexes slough prematurely (Figure 14-8).

The Nematodes

A. *Helicotylenchus cornurus* Anderson

Figure 14-8.   Impact of spiral nematode (*Helicotylenchus digonicus*) on growth of Kentucky bluegrass (*Poa pratensis*). Plants at left are from an area treated with a nematicide, plants at right are from an adjacent area not treated with a nematicide. *Courtesy V. G. Perry.*

Turfgrass Hosts. annual bluegrass (*Poa annua*) and creeping bentgrass (*Agrostis palustris*) (Davis, Wilkinson and Kane, 1993).

The Nematodes

B. *Helicotylenchus digonicus* Perry

Turfgrass Hosts. Colonial bentgrass (*Agrostis tenuis*), creeping bentgrass (*Agrostis palustris*), Canada bluegrass (*Poa compressa*), Kentucky bluegrass (*Poa pratensis*), rough stalk bluegrass (*Poa trivialis*), tall fescue (*Festuca arundinacea*), red fescue (*Festuca rubra*), and perennial ryegrass (*Lolium perenne*) (Perry, Darling and Thorne, 1959; Townshend, Eggens and McCollum, 1973).

The Nematodes

C. *Helicotylenchus erythrinae* (Zimmermann) Golden; syn. *Rotylenchus erythrinae* (Zimmermann) Goodey

Hosts

1. **Turfgrasses**—Colonial bentgrass (*Agrostis tenuis*), creeping bentgrass (*Agrostis palustris*), bermudagrass (*Cynodon dactylon*), Kentucky bluegrass (*Poa pratensis*), perennial ryegrass (*Lolium perenne*), St. Augustinegrass (*Stenotaphrum secundatum*), and zoysiagrass (*Zoysia japonica*).
2. **All Known Gramineous Hosts**—A listing of common names for the following species is given in Appendix Table IV. *Agrostis palustris* Huds., *A. tenuis* Sibth., *Cynodon dactylon* (L.) Pers., *Dactylis glomerata* L., *Lolium perenne* L., *Poa pratensis* L., *Stenotaphrum secundatum* (Walt.) Kuntze, *Zoysia japonica* Steud. (Dist., 1960; Goodey and Franklin, 1956; Mai, Crittenden and Jenkins, 1960; Troll and Tarjan, 1954).

The Nematodes

D. *Helicotylenchus melancholicus* (Lordell) Andrassy

Turfgrass Host. bermudagrass (*Cynodon dactylon*) (Mai, Crittenden and Jenkins, 1960).

The Nematodes

E. *Helicotylenchus microlobus* Perry

Turfgrass Host. Kentucky bluegrass (*Poa pratensis*) (Perry, Darling and Thorne, 1959).

The Nematodes

F. *Helicotylenchus nannus* (Steiner) Andrassy

Hosts

1. **Turfgrasses**—bermudagrass (*Cynodon dactylon*), annual ryegrass (*Lolium multiflorum*), perennial ryegrass (*Lolium perenne*), and zoysiagrass (*Zoysia japonica*).
2. **All Known Gramineous Hosts**—A listing of common names for each of the following species is given in Appendix Table IV. *Andropogon ischaemum* L., *A. saccharoides* Swartz, *Bouteloua hirsuta* Lag., *Cynodon dactylon* (L.) Pers., *Dactylis glomerata* L., *Elymus canadensis* L., *Festuca* spp., *Lolium multiflorum* Lam., *L. perenne* L., *Panicum ramosum* L., *Paspalum dilatatum* Poir., *Tridens albescens* (Vasey) Woot. and Standl., *Zoysia japonica* Steud. (Dist., 1960; Mai, Crittenden and Jenkins, 1960).

The Nematodes

F. *Helicotylenchus platyurus* Perry

Turfgrass Host. Kentucky bluegrass (*Poa pratensis*) (Perry, Darling and Thorne, 1959).

The Nematodes

G. *Helicotylenchus pseudorobustus* (Steiner) Golden

Turfgrass Host. creeping bentgrass (*Agrostis palustris*) (Todd and Tisserat, 1990).

The Nematodes

H. *Helicotylenchus pumilus* Perry

Turfgrass Host. Kentucky bluegrass (*Poa pratensis*) (Perry, Darling and Thorne, 1959).

The Nematodes

H. In addition to the above-mentioned species, unidentified *Helicotylenchus* spp. have also been reported on centipedegrass (*Eremochloa ophiuroides*), manilagrass (*Zoysia matrella*), and Emerald zoysia (*Zoysia tenuifolia* × *Zoysia japonica*) (Good, Steele and Ratcliffe, 1959).

Disease Profile

When active growth of the roots resumes after the spring thaw, the nematodes become active and begin feeding. Because the host plant produces a flush of root and top growth during the cool, moist months of spring and early summer, damage is not evident in the growth rate of the plants even though nematode populations are high. During this period, however, root growth is limited to the top few inches of soil by the activity of the nematodes. As the result, with the advent of higher temperatures and decreased available soil moisture, the plants begin to decline. It is at this time that the populations of spiral nematodes reach their peak. With the resultant summer dormancy of the turfgrass, there is a decline in nematode numbers. In the cooler weeks of early fall, plant growth resumes. This is accompanied by an increase in nematode population (Perry, Darling and Thorne, 1959).

Sting Nematodes

Symptoms

Lesions may be distributed throughout the roots, but, more characteristically, due to active parasitism of the root tips, the root system is sharply restricted in overall development, and, also may be quite malformed. Also, under conditions of very high nematode populations, severe chlorosis and death of the leaves occurs (Plate 30-D, E) (Rhoades, 1962; Winchester and Burt, 1964).

The Nematodes

A. *Belonolaimus gracilis* Steiner

Turfgrass Host. St. Augustinegrass (*Stenotaphrum secundatum* (Kelsheimer and Overman, 1953).

The Nematodes

B. *Belonolaimus longicaudatus* Rau

Hosts

1. **Turfgrasses**—bermudagrass (*Cynodon dactylon*), centipedegrass (*Eremochloa ophiuroides*), manilagrass (*Zoysia matrella*), annual ryegrass (*Lolium multiflorum*), and St. Augustinegrass (*Stenotaphrum secundatum*).
2. **All Known Gramineous Hosts**—A listing of the common names for each of the following species is given in Appendix Table IV. *Avena sativa* L., *Cynodon dactylon* (L.) Pers., *Eremochloa ophiuroides* (Munro) Hack., *Hordeum vulgare* L., *Lolium multiflorum* Lam., *Stenotaphrum secundatum*

(Walt.) Kuntze, *Uniola paniculata* L., *Zea mays* L., *Zoysia matrella* (L.) Merr. (Good, Minton and Jaworski, 1965; Nutter and Christie, 1959; Rau, 1958).

The Nematodes

C. Unidentified *Belonolaimus* spp. have also been reported on zoysiagrass (*Zoysia japonica*), and *Emerald zoysia* (*Zoysia tenuifolia* × *Zoysia japonica*) (Good, Steele and Ratcliffe, 1959).

Disease Profile

For the most part, sting nematodes feed at root tips. They feed primarily from the outside, with only the stylets penetrating the roots.

Stunt Nematodes

Symptoms

The root disorders incited by the members of this group are distinctive in that definite lesions are absent. Rather, affected roots are shriveled, sparsely developed, and conspicuously shortened.

The Nematodes

A. *Tylenchorhynchus acutus* Allen

Hosts

1. **Turfgrass**—bermudagrass (*Cynodon dactylon*).
2. **All Known Gramineous Hosts**—A listing of the common names for each of the following species is given in Appendix Table IV. *Andropogon gerardi* Vitman, *A. saccharoides* Swartz, *A. scoparius* Michx., *Aristida purpurea* Nutt., *Avena sativa* L., *Bouteloua curtipendula* (Michx.) Torr., *Bromus catharticus* Vahl, *Cynodon dactylon* (L.) Pers., *Digitaria* spp., *Elymus canadensis* L., *E. virginicus* L., *Hordeum vulgare* L., *Panicum ramosum* L., *Paspalum dilatatum* Poir., *Secale cereale* L., *Sorghum halepense* (L.) Pers., *S. vulgare* Pers., *Zea mays* L. (Dist., 1960).

The Nematodes

B. *Tylenchorhynchus claytoni* Steiner

Hosts

1. **Turfgrasses**—Colonial bentgrass (*Agostis tenuis*), creeping bentgrass (*Agrostis palustris*), annual bluegrass (*Poa annua*), Kentucky bluegrass (*Poa pratensis*), and zoysiagrass (*Zoysia japonica*).

2. **All Known Gramineous Hosts**—A listing of the common names for each of the following species is given in Appendix Table IV. *Agrostis palustris* Huds., *A. tenuis* Sibth., *Avena sativa* L., *Dactylis glomerata* L., *Paspalum dilatatum* Poir., *Poa annua* L., *P. pratensis* L., *Triticum aestivum* L., *Zea mays* L., *Zoysia japonica* Steud., *Z. matrella* (L.) Merr. (Dist., 1960; Krusberg, 1956; Lucas, Blake and Barker, 1974; Mai, Crittenden and Jenkins, 1960).

The Nematodes

C. *Tylenchorhynchus dubius* (Butschli) Filipjev

Hosts

1. **Turfgrasses**—Colonial bentgrass (*Agrostis tenuis*), creeping bentgrasses (*Agrostis palustris*), and Kentucky bluegrass (*Poa pratensis*).
2. **All Known Gramineous Hosts**—A listing of the common names for each of the following species is given in Appendix Table IV. *Agrostis palustris* Huds., *Agrostis tenuis* Sibth., *Avena sativa* L., *Poa pratensis* L., (Dist., 1960; Mai, Crittenden and Jenkins, 1960; Troll and Tarjan, 1954).

The Nematodes

D. *Tylenchorhynchus lamelliferus* (de Man) Filipjev

Turfgrass Host. perennial ryegrass (*Lolium multiflorum*) (Bridge and Hague, 1974).

The Nematodes

E. *Tylenchorhynchus martini* Fielding

Hosts

1. **Turfgrass**—zoysiagrass (*Zoysia japonica*).
2. **All Known Gramineous Hosts**—A listing of the common names for each of the following species is given in Appendix Table IV. *Oryza sativa* L., *Saccharum officinarum* L., *Sorghum vulgare* Pers., *Zea mays* L., *Zoysia japonica* Steud. (Dist, 1960).

The Nematodes

F. *Tylenchorhynchus maximus* Allen

Turfgrass Host. Kentucky bluegrass (*Poa pratensis*) (Perry, Darling and Thorne, 1959).

The Nematodes

G. *Tylenchorhynchus nudus* Allen

Turfgrass Host. Kentucky bluegrass (*Poa pratensis*) (Perry, Darling and Thorne, 1959).

The Nematodes

H. In addition to the above-mentioned species, unidentified *Tylenchorhynchus* spp. have been reported on bermudagrass (*Cynodon dactylon*) centipedegrass (*Eremochloa ophiuroides*), St. Augustinegrass (*Stenotaphrum secundatum*) and Emerald zoysia (*Zoysia tenuifolia* × *Zoysia japonica*) (Good, Steele and Ratcliffe, 1959).

Disease Profile

High populations of *Tylenchorhynchus dubius* cause a significant reduction in growth of Colonial bentgrass (*Agrostis tenuis*), creeping bentgrass (*Agrostis palustris*), and Kentucky bluegrass (*Poa pratensis*) (Jakobsen, 1975; Laughlin and Vargas, 1972; Smolik and Malek, 1973).

On bentgrasses (*Agrostis* spp.), *Tylenchorhynchus dubius* feeds primarily on the root hairs and epidermal cells immediately behind the root tips. Only the stylet penetrates the cells and there is no readily visible necrosis at the feeding sites (Laughlin and Vargas, 1972). On perennial ryegrass (*Lolium perenne*), however, *Tylenchorhynchus dubius, Tylenchorhynchus maximus*, and *Tylenchorhynchus lamelliferus* feed as browsing ectoparasites, with *Tylenchorhynchus maximus* grouping in clusters or aggregations on epidermal root cells, causing a mechanical breakdown of epidermal, cortical and vascular tissue (Bridge and Hague, 1974).

Increase in nematode populations is favored by soil temperatures in the 85–90 °F (30–32 °C) range. Under moist soil conditions, stunt nematodes can survive for several months in the absence of suitable host plants (Krusberg, 1956).

Ring Nematodes

Symptoms

Necrotic lesions are present at the root tips as well as along the sides of the roots. In cases of high nematode population, extensive root rotting may occur. Ring nematodes have been associated with severe chlorosis of St. Augustinegrass (*Stenotaphrum secundatum*) (Good, Christie and Nutter, 1956; Kelsheimer and Overman, 1953; Parris, 1957).

The Nematodes

A. *Criconemella cylindricum* (Kir'ianova) Raski

Turfgrass Hosts. Kentucky bluegrass (*Poa pratensis*), St. Augustinegrass (*Stenotaphrum secundatum*) and manilagrass (*Zoysia matrella*) (Mai, Crittenden and Jenkins, 1960; Todd and Tisserat, 1993).

The Nematodes

B. *Criconemella ornata* (Raski) Luc and Raski; syn. *Criconemoides cylindricus* Raski

Turfgrass Hosts. bermudagrass (*Cynodon dactylon*), creeping bentgrass (*Agrostis palustris*), and Kentucky bluegrass (*Poa pratensis*) (Feldmesser and Golden, 1972; Johnson, 1970; Todd and Tisserat, 1990).

The Nematodes

C. *Criconemella rustica* (Micoletzker) Luc and Raski (= *Criconemella lobatum* (?))

Turfgrass Hosts. centipedegrass (*Eremochloa ophiuroides*), St. Augustinegrass (*Stenotaphrum secundatum*), and Emerald zoysiagrass (*Zoysia tenuifolia* × *Zoysia japonica*) (Johnson and Powell, 1968).

The Nematodes

D. *Criconemella curvata* Raski; syn. *Criconemoides curvatus* Raski

Turfgrass Hosts. annual bluegrass (*Poa annua*) and creeping bentgrass (*Agrostis palustris*) (Davis, Wilkinson and Kane, 1993).

The Nematodes

E. *Hemicycliophora typica* deMan

Turfgrass Host. St. Augustinegrass (*Stenotaphrum secundatum*) (Dist., 1960).

The Nematodes

F. In addition to the above-mentioned species, unidentified *Criconemella* spp. have also been reported on bermudagrass (*Cynodon dactylon*), centipedegrass (*Eremochloa ophiuroides*), St. Augustinegrass (*Stenotaphrum secundatum*), zoysiagrass (*Zoysia japonica*), and Emerald zoysia (*Zoysia tenuifolia* ×

Zoysia japonica (Good, Steel and Ratcliffe, 1959; Kelsheimer and Overman, 1953; Nutter and Christie, 1959).

Pin Nematodes

Symptoms

Affected plants are noticeably stunted. Shortening of internodes is quite conspicuous. Distinct lesions are present on the roots. There is a marked increase in overall size of root systems, but the lateral roots are not as well developed in proportion. Tillering is much greater in diseased plants.

The Nematodes

A. *Paratylenchus hamatus* Thorne and Allen

Turfgrass Hosts. bermudagrass (*Dactylis glomerata*), and Kentucky bluegrass (*Poa pratensis*) (Mai, Crittenden and Jenkins, 1960).

The Nematodes

B. *Paratylenchus nanus* Cobb

Turfgrass Hosts. annual ryegrass (*Lolium multiflorum*) and perennial ryegrass (*Lolium perenne*) (Mai, Crittenden and Jenkins, 1960).

The Nematodes

C. *Paratylenchus projectus* Jenkins

Hosts

1. **Turfgrasses**—Colonial bentgrass (*Agrostis tenuis*), creeping bentgrass (*Agrostis palustris*), Canada bluegrass (*Poa compressa*), Kentucky bluegrass (*Poa pratensis*), rough stalk bluegrass (*Poa trivialis*), tall fescue (*Festuca arundinacea*), and red fescue (*Festuca rubra*), and perennial ryegrass (*Lolium perenne*).
2. **All Known Gramineous Hosts**—A listing of common names for each of the following species is given in Appendix Table IV. *Agrostis palustris* Huds., *A. tenuis* Sibth., *Andropogon saccharoides* Swartz, *Avena sativa* L., *Bouteloua curtipendula* (Michx.) Torr., *Bromus inermis* Leyss., *Dactylis glomerata* L., *Festuca arundinacea* Schreb., *F. rubra* L., *Festuca ovina* L., *Hordeum vulgare* L., *Lolium perenne* L., *Pennisetum glaucum* (L.) R. Br., *Phleum pratense* L., *Poa pratensis* L., *Secale cereale* L., *Sorghum sudanense* (Piper) Stapf, *Tri-*

ticum aestivum L., *Zea mays* L. (*Z. mays* var. *saccharata* Bailey) (Coursen and Jenkins, 1958; Coursen, Rhode and Jenkins, 1958; Mai, Crittenden and Jenkins, 1960; Norton, 1959; Townshend, Eggens and McCollom, 1973).

Stubby Root Nematodes

Symptoms

Affected plants develop a pronounced chlorotic condition and display a reduction in rate of growth. Their roots are characterized by large, brownish lesions that are irregular in shape and often extend deep into the tissue. Lesion incidence is greater near the root tips, but necrotic areas may usually be found along the entire length of the root system. Affected root tips are usually slightly swollen and then decompose.

The Nematodes

A. *Paratrichodorus christiei* Allen

Hosts

1. **Turfgrasses**—Kentucky bluegrass (*Poa pratensis*), tall fescue (*Festuca arundinacea*), red fescue (*Festuca rubra*), and St. Augustinegrass (*Stenotaphrum secundatum*).
2. **All Known Gramineous Hosts**—A listing of common names for each of the following species is given in Appendix Table IV. *Avena sativa* L., *Bromus inermis* Leyss., *Cynodon dactylon* (L.) Pers., *Dactylis glomerata* L., *Festuca arundinacea* Schreb., *F. rubra* L., *Hordeum vulgare* L., *Lolium perenne* L., *Penniseteum glaucum* (L.) R. Br., *Phleum pratense* L., *Poa pratensis* L., *Secale cereale* L., *Sorghum halepense* (L.) Pers., *S. sudanense* (Piper) Stapf, *Stenotaphrum secundatum* (Walt.) Kuntze, *Triticum aestivum* L., *Zea mays* L., (*Z. mays* var. *saccharata* Bailey) (Coursen, Rhode and Jenkins, 1958; Dist., 1960; Good, Christie and Nutter, 1956; Good, Minton and Jaworski, 1965).

The Nematodes

B. *Paratrichodorus primitivus* de Man; syn. *Trichodorus obtusus* Chitwood and Hannon

Hosts

1. **Turfgrass**—bermudagrass (*Cynodon dactylon*).
2. **All Known Gramineous Hosts**—A listing of the common names for each of the following species is

given in Appendix Table IV. *Avena sativa* L., *Cynodon dactylon* (L.) Pers. *Triticum aestivum* L., *Zea mays* L. (Chitwood, 1955; Dist. 1960).

The Nematodes

C. *Paratrichidorus proximus* Allen

Turfgrass Host. St. Augustinegrass (*Stenotaphrum secundatum*) (Rhoades, 1965).

The Nematodes

E. In addition to the above-mentioned species, unidentified *Trichodorus* spp. have also been reported on centipedegrass (*Eremochloa ophiuroides*), zoysiagrass (*Zoysia japonica*), manilagrass (*Zoysia matrella*), and Emerald zoysia (*Zoysia tenuifolia* × *Zoysia japonica*) (Good, Steele and Ratcliffe, 1959).

Disease Profile

Only actively growing roots are parasitized. Just prior to feeding, the nematode becomes oriented parallel to the surface of the root, with its anterior portion bent at a right angle so that the stylet is pointed directly at an epidermal cell and is in contact with it. After this, the stylet moves in a sideways direction, thus, apparently puncturing the cell wall by a rasping action rather than a direct thrust. Feeding time per cell is usually 5–10 seconds. As a rule, only the epidermal cells, root hairs, and outer cortical cells are parasitized.

Root damage is caused by decreased cell multiplication in the root tips rather than outright destruction of cells. On heavily parasitized roots, there are no definite root caps or regions of elongation.

Populations of stubby root nematodes build up rapidly. At soil temperatures of 86°F (30°C), the nematodes complete their life cycles in 16–17 days. At 72°F (22°C), 21–22 days are required to complete the cycle (Rhoades, 1965).

Dagger Nematode

Symptoms

Affected plants are chlorotic and stunted. Slightly sunken, reddish-brown to black lesions are present on the roots. The overall root system is restricted in its development, and, in cases of extensive feeding, severe root rot may develop.

Table 14-1. Relative susceptibility of cool season turfgrass cultivars to three species of plant parasitic nematodes. *After Townshend, Eggens and McCollum, 1973.*

Turfgrass Species and Cultivar	Nematode Species and Host Rating[a]		
	Root Lesion Nematode (*Paratylenchus neglectus*)	Pin Nematode (*Paratylenchus projectus*)	Spiral Nematode (*Helicotylenchus digonicus*)
Colonial Bentgrass (*Agrostis tenuis*)			
Exeter	Non-host	Poor host	Non-host
Highland	Non-host	Poor host	Poor host
Creeping Bentgrass (*Agrostis palustris*)			
Penncross	Moderate host	Moderate host	Non-host
Smarged	Non-host	Non-host	Poor host
Tall Fescue (*Festuca arundinacea*)			
Backafall	Non-host	Non-host	Poor host
Kentucky 31	Moderate host	Poor host	Moderate host
Manade	Moderate host	Moderate host	Poor host
Red Fescue (*Festuca rubra*)			
Arctared	Non-host	Good host	Good host
Barfalla	Moderate host	Poor host	Moderate host
Boreal	Non-host	Poor host	Good host
Dawson	Moderate host	Moderate host	Good host
Duraturf	Non-host	Non-host	Moderate host
Echo	Non-host	Moderate host	Moderate host
Elco	Moderate host	Moderate host	Moderate host
Erika	Moderate host	Non-host	Good host
Golfrood	Moderate host	Moderate host	Good host
Highlight	Non-host	Good host	Good host
Illahee	Non-host	Moderate host	Moderate host
Oasis	Non-host	Moderate host	Good host
Olds	Non-host	Non-host	Good host
Oregon	Poor host	Moderate host	Good host
Pennlawn	Poor host	Moderate host	Moderate host
Polar	Poor host	Good host	Good host
Polo	Non-host	Moderate host	Moderate host
Ruby	Non-host	Poor host	Moderate host
Sceempter	Non-host	Poor host	Moderate host
Turf	Moderate host	Moderate host	Moderate host
Perennial Ryegrass (*Lolium perenne*)			
Brabantia	Poor host	Non-host	Moderate host
Kent	Moderate host	Good host	Moderate host
Norlea	Moderate host	Moderate host	Good host
Viris	Poor host	Good host	Non-host
Canada Bluegrass (*Poa compressa*)			
Commercial Ont.	Good host	Poor host	Moderate host
Commercial U.S.	Non-host	Non-host	Poor host
Kentucky Bluegrass (*Poa pratensis*)			
Aristida	Good host	Moderate host	Moderate host
Atlas	Good host	Poor host	Good host
Baron	Good host	Moderate host	Moderate host
Captan	Good host	Non-host	Good host
Couger	Non-host	Moderate host	Moderate host
Delft	Moderate host	Moderate host	Poor host
Delta	Good host	Non-host	Good host
Fusa	Non-host	Non-host	Good host
Fylking 0217	Good host	Moderate host	Good host
Geary	Moderate host	Moderate host	Moderate host
Golf	Moderate host	Poor host	Moderate host
Hundbella Soma S-644	Moderate host	Non-host	Moderate host
Merion	Moderate host	Moderate host	Poor host
Merion Dutch	Moderate host	Moderate host	Good host
Nike	Moderate host	Poor host	Good host
Nuggett	Good host	Non-host	Good host

Table 14-1. Relative susceptibility of cool season turfgrass cultivars to three species of plant parasitic nematodes. *After Townshend, Eggens and McCollum, 1973.* (continued)

Turfgrass Species and Cultivar	Nematode Species and Host Rating[a]		
	Root Lesion Nematode (*Paratylenchus neglectus*)	Pin Nematode (*Paratylenchus projectus*)	Spiral Nematode (*Helicotylenchus digonicus*)
Park	Poor host	Poor host	Good host
Primo	Moderate host	Poor host	Goodhost
Prato	Moderate host	Poor host	Good host
Skandia II	Moderate host	Moderate host	Good host
Skreszowice SK-46	Moderate host	Moderate host	Good host
Spaths	Moderate host	Moderate host	Good host
Steinacher	Non-host	Moderate host	Good host
Sydsport	Good host	Non-host	Moderate host
Windsor	Moderate host	Non-host	Moderate host
Rough Stalk Bluegrass (*Poa trivialis*)			
Dasas S-64	Moderate host	Good host	Good host
Ino	Moderate host	Poor host	Moderate host

[a]non-host, 0–50; poor host, >50; moderate host, >500; good host, >5,000 nematodes per 0.5 lb. (0.45 kg) moist soil.

graphic locations and the degree of stress to which the plants are being subjected. Also, damage thresholds are difficult to interpret for mixed populations of nematode species. From a practical standpoint, then, damage threshold levels should not be taken as absolutes, but used as reference points by an experienced diagnostician to determine whether application of a nematicide is warranted. A listing of currently referenced damage threshold levels for certain species of root-feeding nematodes on warm season and cool season turfgrasses is given in Table 14-2.

The following procedure for collecting samples from established turf for population takes into consideration the fact that nematode numbers are often inversely related to the degree of soundness of the root system, and therefore the density of parasitic nematodes may be lower in poor turf than in adjacent sod that is growing vigorously (Johnson and Powell, 1968; Ratanaworabhan and Smart, 1969). (The discernible damage during the summer months is often related to a nematode population level at an earlier date). It also addresses the likelihood that within a given location, such as a golf green, certain sections of turf will have higher population levels than others, and that within these sections the numbers for certain species may vary according to sampling depth (Wick, 1982).

- Begin the sampling process in early spring at the time the soil temperature at the 2 inch (5 cm) depth reaches 50°F (10°C) and continue at 3–4 week intervals throughout the growing season.
- Using a standard 1 inch (2.5 cm) soil tube, take a composite sample of 15 to 30 cores per 500 to 1,000 square feet (46–93 m²). It is important that the

individual composite samples represent turf of similar health and/or site characteristics. For example, if a portion of a golf green is showing severe stress, cores should be gathered throughout that immediate area. For comparison, however, a separate set of cores should be taken from an adjacent, apparently healthy area.

- Samples should be taken to a depth of 4 inches (10 cm), not including the thatch. This depth will help compensate for the vertical zoning of species.
- The total volume of the composite sample for each location should be at least 0.5 pint (250 cm³). At the time of collection, the sample should be placed in an airtight container such as a plastic bag to prevent desiccation.
- Clearly identify the sample number on the outside of each container. Also, provide the nematode assay laboratory with the following information: (1) the species of grass predominant in the area sampled, (2) a description of the primary symptoms of the problem at hand, (3) the depth to which the sample was taken, (4) nematicides, fungicides, herbicides and plant growth regulators used in the area over the past two years, (5) a description of environmental and management stress factors that may have affected the growth and development of the plants, and (6) a list of the primary fungus-incited diseases common to the area in question.
- The period of time between the collection of the samples and their delivery to the nematode assay laboratory should be minimal. In the event the laboratory performing the assay is not in the immediate locality in which the samples were taken, they should be forwarded by express delivery service.

Table 14-2. Damage threshold levels of certain nematodes pathogenic to turfgrasses.[a]

Nematode Species	Turfgrass Affected	Damage Threshold (nematodes/100 cm³ soil)
Awl (*Dolichodorus* spp.)	Bentgrass	150
	Bermudagrass	80
	Centipedegrass	80
	St. Augustinegrass	80
	Tall Fescue	50
Dagger (*Xiphinema americanum*)	Bentgrass	200
	Bermudagrass	300
	Centipedegrass	200
	St. Augustinegrass	200
	Tall Fescue	150
Lance (*Hoplolaimus galeatus*)	Bentgrass	150
	Bermudagrass	50
	Centipedegrass	50
	St. Augustinegrass	50
	Tall Fescue	100
Needle (*Longidorus breviannulatus*)	Bentgrass	20
Pin *Paratylenchus projectus*	Tall Fescue	130
Ring (*Criconemella* spp.)	Bentgrass (warm climates)	500
	Bentgrass (cool climates)	1,500
	Bermudagrass	1,000
	Centipedegrass	300
	St. Augustinegrass	500
	Tall Fescue	150
Root Knot (*Meloidogyne* spp.)	Bentgrass	100
	Bermudagrass	300
	Tall Fescue	200
	St. Augustinegrass	80
Root Lesion (*Pratylenchus* spp.)	Bentgrass	150
	Bermudagrass	150
	Centipedegrass	150
	Tall Fescue	150
	St. Augustinegrass	150
Sheath (*Hemicycliophora* spp.)	Bentgrass	200
	Bermudagrass	200
	Centipedegrass	200
	Tall Fescue	80
	St. Augustinegrass	80
Spiral (*Helicotylenchus* spp.)	Bentgrass	600
	Bermuagrass	1,000
	Centipedegrass	1,000
	Tall Fescue	1,000
	St. Augustinegrass	1,000
Sting (*Belonolaimus longicatus*)	Bentgrass	20
	Bermudagrass	20
	Centipedegrass	20
	Tall Fescue	12
	Zoysiagrass	20
Stubby Root (*Trichodorus christiei*)	Bentgrass	100
	Bermudagrass	100
	Centipedegrass	100
	Tall Fescue	150
	St. Augustinegrass	50
Stunt (*Tylenchorhynchus* spp.)	Bentgrass	300
	Bentgrass	350
	Kentucky Bluegrass	400
	Centipedegrass	100
	Tall Fescue	100
	St. Augustinegrass	200

[a]Compiled from Dunn and Noling (1993), Todd and Tisserat (1993), Vittum, Wick and Sweir (1987), and data supplied by Bruce Martin, Clemson University.

The laboratory methods used will determine the numbers and types of nematodes recovered from soil samples (Riedel, 1979). For this reason, it is important to avoid switching back and forth from one laboratory to another. Either use one nematode assay laboratory consistently or send split samples to several laboratories.

Use of a preplanting soil fumigant.   The soil fumigant metam-sodium (Vapam™) may be used prior to seeding or the placement of sod to reduce the population of root-feeding nematodes. Optimum results are obtained with this material when the old sod is completely stripped from the area and the soil is tilled thoroughly two weeks or more before treatment to break up clods and facilitate the decomposition of old stems and roots. A week before treatment, the soil should be cultivated again and then irrigated to insure wetting to a depth of 4 inches (10 cm) or greater. At the time the metam-sodium is applied, the soil should be moist and the temperature at 4 inches (10 cm) deep 60 °F (16 °C) or greater. Cultivate lightly immediately before application if the soil is crusted. The effectiveness of metam-sodium is much greater if the area is covered by a plastic sheet for two days after treatment. Seeding or the placement of sod should not be accomplished until all odor of the chemical has escaped. Tillage or raking no deeper than treatment depth will help accelerate the escape of fumes from the soil.

Use of nonfumigant nematicides on established turf.   The organophosphate nematicides fenamiphos (Nemacur™) and ethoprop (Mocap™) are effective in the control of root-feeding nematodes in established turf (Giblin-Davis, Cisar and Bilz, 1988; Murdoch, Apt and Tashiro, 1977; Todd and Tisserat, 1990). These materials are usually applied to the turf surface in granular formulations. The active ingredients are dissolved from the granules by irrigation or rain water and carried into the soil.

1. *Fenamiphos*—Fenamiphos is absorbed through the roots and moves throughout the plant's tissues; therefore, it is effective against wide range of ectoparasitic and endoparasitic species (Table 14-3). Although death of the nematode is not instant, the material acts rapidly to halt its ability to feed. Fenamiphos interferes with motor activity in nematodes by blocking neuroenzymes. When first exposed, the nematode enters a prelethal phase in which it makes irregular movements (twitches) followed by paralysis. Initially, the paralysis may cease, but the respite is only temporary, and finally body crinkling and death occurs (Bunt, 1975).

Table 14-3.   Relative effectiveness of the nematicides fenamiphos (Nemacur™) and ethoprop (Mocap™) for the control of certain root-feeding nematodes pathogenic to turfgrass. *After Dunn and Nolling, 1987.*

| | Expected Effectiveness | |
Nematode	Fenamiphos (Nemacur™)	Ethoprop (Mocap™)
Awl (*Dolichodorus* spp.)	Good	Good
Lance (*Hoplolaimus* spp.)	Good	Poor
Ring (*Criconemella* spp.)	Good	Moderate
Root-knot (*Meloidogyne* spp.)	Moderate	Poor
Sheath (*Hemicycliphora* spp.)	Good	Moderate
Spiral (*Helicotylenchus* spp.)	Good	Good
Sting (*Belonolaimus* spp.)	Good	Good
Stubby root (*Trichodorus* spp.)	Good	Moderate

When exposed to very low concentrations of fenamiphos, nematodes may remain in the prelethal phase for a very long time, but they eventually die. The residual activity of fenamiphos lasts for up to 12 weeks. Surface applications of the material eventually become effective at depths of 10–12 inches (25–30 cm); however, downward dispersal through the soil is rather slow. The reason for the slow movement is that fenamiphos has a strong polar property which causes it to disperse in such a manner that all valences in the soil become saturated from the surface downward. When it reaches the 10–12 inch (25–30 cm) depth, all of the product is bound to soil particles and therefore downward movement ceases. Because of its slow dispersal, optimum results are obtained with fenamiphos when it is applied on a preventive schedule—*i.e.*, before the nematode population reaches a high level (Homeyer and Wagner, 1981).

2. *Ethoprop*—Ethoprop is not absorbed and translocated in nematicidal amounts within the plant, therefore, it does not provide good control of endoparasites such as lance and root knot nematodes. Its greatest effectiveness is against sting and spiral nematodes (Table 14-3). Ethoprop can be phytotoxic to certain species of ornamental plants, because of this it should not be used within the drip lines of trees and shrubs. Also, ethoprop should not be applied to wet leaves and it should not be used on newly seeded areas until the plants are well established.

Turfgrass mowed at ³⁄₈ inch (10 mm) and lower is prone to injury by ethoprop at rates higher than 2.3 pounds (1 kg) of 10 percent active ingredient granular formulation per 1,000 square feet (93 m²). Bentgrasses (*Agrostis* spp.) and ryegrasses (*Lolium* spp.) are more sensitive to ethoprop than other turfgrasses. Phytotoxicity is likely to occur when using the material on these two species at all cutting heights. The turf will normally outgrow this injury; however, if the risk of phytotoxicity is unacceptable, then ethoprop should not be used.

Maximizing nematicide effectiveness.   For maximum results, nematicides should not be applied to established turf until after the temperature at 4 inches (10 cm) deep reaches 60 °F (16 °C) or greater. This will insure that a high percentage of the nematode population is in the larval to adult stages of development, rather than the more resistant egg stage.

Cultivation practices that improve water infiltration into the soil such as coring, spiking, and vertical mowing should be performed just before the application of a nematicide. At the time of treatment, the soil should be moist, but not water saturated. Immediately after the application has been made the treated area should be irrigated with ½ inch (13 mm) of water. Since new roots must be generated, the response of turf to nematicidal treatment may not always be rapid. Close attention to cultivation and watering practices that maximize root growth and development after the application of a nematicide is very important.

Fenamiphos and ethoprop only reduce the population level of root-feeding nematodes, they do not completely eradicate them from the soil. Therefore, if a nematicide program is once advised, it is important to conduct nematode assays periodically to determine when the affected areas should be treated again.

The prolonged use of any nematicide may reduce its effectiveness. Since no nematicide is equally effective against all nematode species, prolonged and frequent use of the product enables resistant species to become dominant. Also, frequent applications of a nematicide can promote the build up of microorganisms which metabolize ("feed on") the material and thus significantly reduce its longevity in the soil (Dunn and Noling, 1993).

§   §   §

PART FIVE

Fundamentals of Turfgrass Disease Control

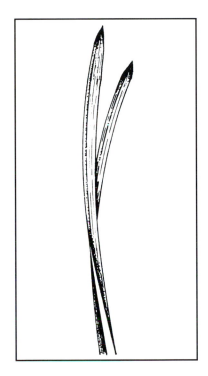

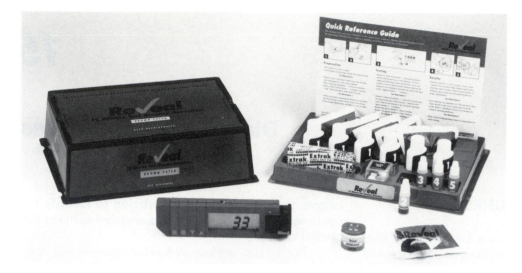

Figure 15-1. Immunoassay kit for use in field diagnosis of Rhizoctonia blight of turfgrasses. *Courtesy Ciba-Geigy Corporation, Greensboro, North Carolina.*

is based on the use of antibodies and is commonly referred to by the acronym ELISA (enzyme-linked immunosorbant assay). Antibodies are molecules that bind with unrelated molecules, normally proteins. Animals often synthesize antibodies in response to the invasion of cells by foreign proteinaceous substances. For example, when cells of the Rhizoctonia blight pathogen (*Rhizoctonia solani*) are injected into a rabbit or a mouse, their immune systems produce antibodies that attach only to the proteins of that particular organism. These antibodies can be produced in large quantities by fusing antibody-producing cells isolated from the spleen of an immunized animal with myeloma cells in tissue culture. (Myeloma cells are animal cells that have the capacity to grow for extended periods of time in culture). The hybrid cells (called "hybridomas") are transferred to a selective medium that will only support their growth and are allowed to divide and produce the antibody. The antibody is separated from the culture medium by chemical procedures and used for detecting the presence of *Rhizoctonia solani* in diseased plant tissue.

Immunoassay kits based on the ELISA system are commercially available for use as an aid in both laboratory and field diagnosis of certain turfgrass diseases (Figure 15-1). The procedure for the use of these diagnostic kits is simple. First, an antibody (called the "capture antibody") that has an affinity for the protein of a specific fungal pathogen is placed on the surface of a chemically treated solid support where it becomes immobilized. Cell sap that has been extracted from diseased tissue is then added to the

solid support. If protein of the pathogen for which the antibody has been produced is present in the sap it will adhere to the capture antibody. After this, a second antibody of similar origin to the capture antibody but has been linked with an enzyme is placed on the preparation. The enzyme-linked antibody will also stick to the protein of the pathogen. As the result, a sandwich is formed with the capture antibody on the lower side, the enzyme-linked antibody on the upper side and the protein from the pathogen in the middle. The preparation is then flooded with a colorless enzyme substrate that converts the upper, enzyme-linked antibody to a colored product. The intensity of the color that develops is proportional to the pathogen level in the diseased tissue (Figure 15-2). A digital read-out of the color intensity can then be taken with a battery-operated colorimeter that is made available by the manufacturer of the kit. The entire test can be completed in less than 30 minutes.

Immunoassay kits provide an excellent opportunity for the turfgrass management specialist to develop a systematic program of field monitoring for the development of specific diseases. The program should begin with monitoring areas with a history of the disease in question two to four weeks before fungicide applications would normally begin. This will establish baseline readings before the weather favors early outbreaks of the disease. Once a control program has been initiated, a test should be performed 3 to 4 days after fungicide application to determine the pathogen level. Tests should also be conducted regularly near the end of fungicide spray

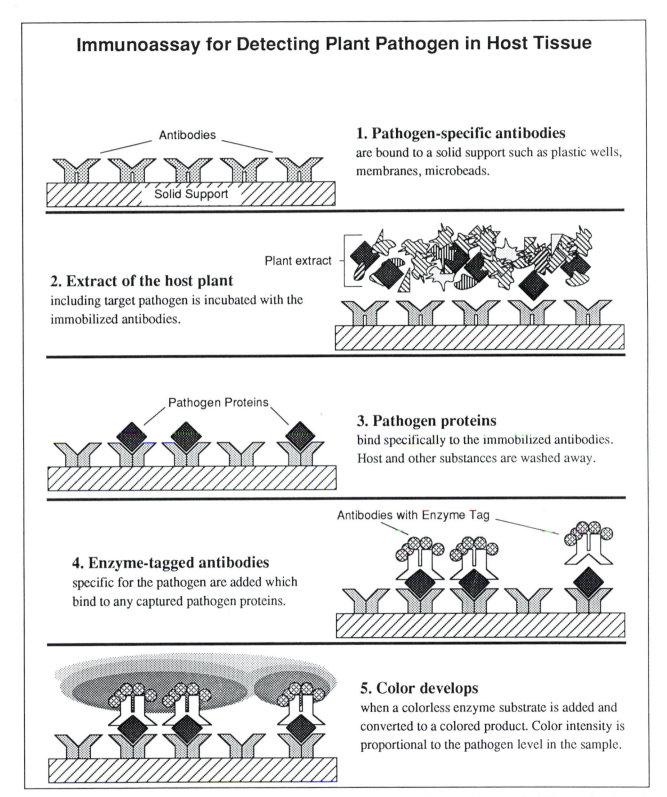

Immunoassay for Detecting Plant Pathogen in Host Tissue

Antibodies

Solid Support

1. Pathogen-specific antibodies
are bound to a solid support such as plastic wells, membranes, microbeads.

Plant extract

2. Extract of the host plant
including target pathogen is incubated with the immobilized antibodies.

Pathogen Proteins

3. Pathogen proteins
bind specifically to the immobilized antibodies. Host and other substances are washed away.

Antibodies with Enzyme Tag

4. Enzyme-tagged antibodies
specific for the pathogen are added which bind to any captured pathogen proteins.

5. Color develops
when a colorless enzyme substrate is added and converted to a colored product. Color intensity is proportional to the pathogen level in the sample.

Figure 15-2. Immunoassay procedure for detecting a pathogen in turfgrass tissue. *Courtesy Agri-Diagnostics Associates, Cinnaminson, New Jersey.*

intervals to help refine reapplication schedules. For example, if the schedule calls for additional fungicide applications at 10 to 20 days, the testing should begin 8 to 10 days following the most recent spray and continued every two to three days until the pathogen level rises. Monitoring of the area should be continued for two to three weeks into the early fall or "off-season" for the disease. This will detect late surges that may occur in the development of the pathogen. Also, these records of pathogen levels at the end of one season will provide a valuable reference point for interpreting the levels obtained during the weeks just before fungicide applications for control of the disease would normally begin the following season.

DETERMINING THE CAUSE OF ROOT DECLINES

Among the more common causes of root decline are (a) anaerobic soil conditions, (b) high soil salinity, (c) weakly pathogenic soil inhabiting fungi, and (d) root-feeding nematodes. Diagnostic workups for determining causality in root declines should take each of these factors into consideration.

Sooner or later, anaerobic layers develop within the root zones of all golf greens. One indication that oxygen deficiency has developed in the rooting mixture is a significant decrease in the rate of water infiltration. Where determination of the cause of a root decline is concerned, then, the diagnostic procedure should always include an evaluation of the rate of water movement through the root zone. For a description of the procedure for measuring of the rate of water penetration of the thatch and the velocity of its movement through the underlying root zone mixture, refer to the material on control of anaerobiosis in Chapter 8 - Root Dysfunctions, Declines and Rots.

The degradation of many ground and surface water supplies in recent years and the use of unusually large amounts of fertilizer to compensate for the rapid leaching of nutrients on high sand content golf greens has resulted in the development of problems with salt toxicity in geographic regions where these difficulties have not been encountered before. Salinity tests on the thatch and rooting mixture should be performed periodically throughout the growing season. Rather than conducting tests on bulk samples, the assessments should be made on samples drawn from thatch, from the surface 2 inches (5.0 cm), and from layers within the root zone in which the downward flow of water has been impeded.

The salinity readings should be entered in the permanent management record. In addition to identifying immediate episodes of acute salt toxicity, the long term record of these tests will provide the information needed by the diagnostician in determining whether chronic salt toxicity has been the principal predisposing agent where infection and colonization of the crowns and roots by senectopathic soil-inhabiting fungi is concerned.

In addition to causing severe injury to turfgrass roots within a relatively short period of time, under certain circumstances, parasitic nematodes can also bring about the gradual decline of root systems. Nematode-incited root decline of turfgrasses is common in both subtropical and temperate climatic zones. The problem occurs most frequently on bentgrass (*Agrostis* spp.) and bermudagrass (*Cynodon dactylon*) growing under the low mowing heights of golf green management. Assessment of the role of parasitic nematodes in root decline can be accomplished by a program of (a) assaying the site for nematode population levels, (b) applying a nematicide in a test location within the area under observation, (c) conducting a posttreatment assay of nematode populations in both the treated and nontreated areas, and then (d) determining the degree of correlation between reduction in nematode population levels and root development in the areas in question.

COLLECTION OF SAMPLES FOR LABORATORY WORKUPS

For a description of the procedure for conducting a nematode assay, refer to Control of Root-Feeding Nematodes in Chapter 14—Diseases Caused by Nematodes. Samples collected for laboratory workups for detection of fungus and bacterial pathogens should be taken from within the areas of most severe damage and from nearby locations with both healthy and diseased plants. A golf green cup cutter is an ideal instrument for pulling samples. If one is not available, then a knife or small shovel should be used to remove a section of sod 4 to 6 inches (10–15 cm) in diameter and to the depth of the root system.

In the event the samples are to be mailed or shipped to the diagnostic laboratory by express delivery service, they should be sealed in plastic bags and packaged very tightly to prevent their being broken up while en route. The information accompanying the samples should include (a) name, address and telephone number of the sender, (b) site location of each sample, (c) species and cultivar(s) of grass comprising the sample, (d) the size of the area affected and description of the symptoms, (e) weather conditions for one week preceding the outbreak of the disease, including both daytime and nighttime air temperatures (f) the management program for the area in question, including mowing height, coring and vertical mowing schedule, fertilization dates and rates, and (g) a listing of all pesticides and growth regulators used for the previous twelve months. If the problem at hand is one of root growth and development, the results of salinity tests for the present season and infiltration rates of both the affected and nearby apparently healthy areas should also be included.

MAINTAINING RECORDS OF DIAGNOSES AND CONTROL PROCEDURES

A record of disease outbreaks, diagnoses and the effectiveness of efforts at control is important part of a disease management program. Also, laws in many localities require that a record be maintained of outbreaks of diseases for which pesticides have been used. The information should include (a) the name of the disease and its incitant, (b) grasses affected, (c) description of symptoms (d) specific location, (e) date of occurrence, (f) weather conditions for one week prior to, and including, the outbreak, and (g) control measures applied and degree of success.

§ § §

Developing Integrated Disease Control Strategies

The most effective disease control strategy is a cohesive program that incorporates all the factors known to reduce the severity of the target disease. In determining which resources to use in the program, the turfgrass management specialist must take into consideration the effect each component will have on (a) the functional and aesthetic standards that have been defined for the turf, (b) environmental quality, and (c) public health.

The basic resources for diminishing outbreaks of turfgrass diseases may be placed in one of four categories: (a) cultural practices, (b) use of disease resistant genotypes, (c) biological control, and (d) use of pesticides. **Cultural practices** consist of utilizing management techniques that reduce the incidence of disease by either making the immediate environment less conducive to the growth and development of pathogenic microorganisms or altering the disease susceptibility of the plants. **Use of disease resistant genotypes** involves planting species or varieties of turfgrass that are genetically capable of warding off infection and colonization by pathogenic microorganisms. **Biological control** is a procedure that reduces the amount of viable inoculum present in the turf by fostering the development or introduction of microorganisms that are antagonistic to the pathogen. **Use of pesticides** consists of applying fungicides, nematicides or bactericides to suppress the development of disease by either killing outright or diminishing the pathogenic potential of disease-producing microorganisms.

CULTURAL PRACTICES

Plant Nutrition and Soil pH

Plant nutrition and soil pH can significantly alter the incidence and severity of certain turfgrass diseases. Where nutrition is concerned, calcium, nitrogen, potassium, and phosphorous appear to have the greatest impact on disease development. These ef-

fects are most noticeable in the management of high sand content golf greens due to their high leaching rates.

Calcium deficient plants are usually more vulnerable to infection and colonization by pathogenic fungi. It has been shown that red leaf spot, Fusarium blight, Pythium blight, and Corticium red thread are more severe when the plants are grown under low calcium nutrition (Couch and Bedford, 1966; Moore, Couch and Bloom, 1963; Muse, 1974; Muse and Couch, 1965).

The incidence and severity of leaf rust of perennial ryegrass (*Lolium perenne*) is significantly lower when the plants are grown under high nitrogen fertilization (Couch and Joyner, 1976). However, the severity of melting-out, Helminthosporium leaf spot, red leaf spot, Pythium blight, Fusarium blight, Rhizoctonia blight, Sclerotinia dollar spot, and Cercospora leaf spot is greater when the turf is grown under high nitrogen nutrition. With Rhizoctonia blight, Pythium blight, Corticium red thread, melting out, and Helminthosporium leaf spot, the increase in disease severity brought on by high nitrogen nutrition can be offset to some extent by concurrently increasing the phosphorous and potassium levels. However, the increase in susceptibility of turf grown at high nitrogen nutrition to Sclerotinia dollar spot and red leaf spot is not altered by additional applications of phosphorous and potassium (Bloom and Couch, 1960; Couch and Bloom, 1960; Freeman, 1967; McCoy, 1973, Moore, Couch and Bloom, 1963; Muse, 1974; Muse and Couch, 1974).

Both nitrogen source and the timing of fertilizer applications can be important factors in the development of winter patch diseases. Applications of nitrogenous fertilizers late in the growing season should be avoided in turf with a history of either Fusarium patch, Typhula blight, or Sclerotinia patch. If late growing season fertilization practices are deemed necessary, the turf in question should be treated simultaneously with a fungicide. In the event of low soil fertility, moderate applications of balanced fertilizer may be made in late fall when the plants are entering into dormancy in order to facilitate rapid plant regrowth in the spring. Where cottony snow mold control is concerned, if it is deemed necessary to apply an inorganic nitrogenous fertilizer after the end of July, the rate should not exceed 4 ounces actual nitrogen per 1,000 square feet (0.1 kg N/93 m²). However, a slow release organic nitrogen fertilizer can be put down in September in conjunction with mercury chloride or chloroneb fungicides. In bermudagrass (*Cynodon dactylon*) turf with a history of outbreaks of spring dead spot, potassium levels should be monitored frequently in order to identify immediate needs for correcting deficiencies. Also, minimum rates of nitrogen should be used for spring and summer growth, and late growing season applications of nitrogenous fertilizers should be avoided.

The severity of both the leaf lesion and root and crown rot phases of leaf blotch of bermudagrass is greater on plants growing under low potassium nutrition (Matocha and Smith, 1980). Gaeumannomyces decline of bermudagrass is also more severe under deficient potassium nutrition (Elliott and Freeman, 1992). Outbreaks of red leaf spot of creeping bentgrass (*Agrostis palustris*) and Helminthosporium crown and root rot of zoysiagrass (*Zoysia japonica*) are more severe when either potassium or phosphorous are deficient (Bell, 1967; Muse 1974).

Soil reaction is a significant factor in the development of Fusarium patch, take all patch, summer patch, and Gaeumannomyces decline of bermudagrass. All three diseases are more severe at high pH levels. The severity of take-all patch and Fusarium patch is much greater when the pH of the top 1 inch (2.5 cm) of soil is 6.5 and above (Table 4-13) (Smith, 1956; 1958). Summer patch is more severe when the soil pH is greater than 6.0 (Thompson *et al.*, 1993). Acidifying fertilizers such as ammonium sulfate and ammonium nitrate will lower soil pH and bring about a reduction in the incidence of these diseases. With the cool season grasses, however, the exclusive use of ammonium sulfate for a period of years will reduce plant vigor and increase the susceptibility of the turf to dying out during periods of drought, resulting in an increase in population levels of annual bluegrass (*Poa annua*). Ammonium nitrate fertilization, on the other hand, has been shown to bring about a reduction in the population levels of annual bluegrass. Therefore, when using inorganic nitrogenous fertilizers to lower soil pH in turf comprised of cool season grasses, the fertilization schedule should alternate between ammonium sulfate and ammonium nitrate (Eggens, Wright and Carey, 1989).

Thatch Management

Thatch is a tightly intermingled layer of living and dead grass stems, leaves, and roots that develops between the soil surface and the zone of green vegetation. When this layer consists of intermixed soil, stems, and roots, it is generally referred to as a **mat**. The entire thatch may be transformed into a mat as a result of topdressings or when turf growing on a flood plain becomes covered with silt as the consequence of flooding. Also, a mat layer of limited thickness may form in the section of thatch adjacent to the soil surface. A less-densely packed layer of partially undecomposed leaf clippings commonly forms on the surface of the thatch or mat body. This is termed a **pseudothatch** and is defined as the uppermost surface layer of the thatch or mat which consists primarily of relatively undecomposed leaf clippings (Figure 16-1).

The buildup of thatch results from an imbalance between accumulation and decomposition of organic surface debris. Any cultural or environmental factor that stimulates excessive plant growth or impairs decomposition of debris will contribute to the development of thatch. The presence of a shallow thatch layer is desirable for it adds to the surface resiliency and wear tolerance of the turf. Generally speaking, ½ inch (1.3 cm) is considered to be an appropriate thatch thickness where protection of the turf from wear injury is concerned. An excessive accumulation of thatch can result in turf that is more susceptible to stresses from the physical environment and the development of fungus-incited diseases. Thatching tends

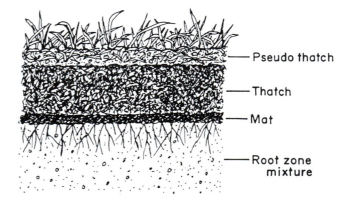

Figure 16-1. Cross section of sod showing the layers that develop between the soil surface and the zone of green vegetation. The pseudothatch is formed from partially decomposed leaf clippings, the thatch is made up of living and dead grass stems leaves and roots, and the mat is a mixture of soil, stems, and roots.

to raise the vital crowns, lateral stems, and roots out of the protective layer of soil and into the thatch or mat zone. As the result, under conditions of heavy thatch, the plants are more vulnerable to heat, cold, and drought injury. Also, chlorosis is of more common occurrence in heavily thatched turf.

Many of the fungi that are pathogenic to turfgrasses survive as saprophytes in the thatch and mat zones until the environmental conditions are conducive to infection and colonization of actively growing plant tissue. The incidence and severity of Pythium blight is greater in turf with a high thatch accumulation. This is probably due to the enhanced growth of the various species of Pythium. For example, it has been shown that the production of oospores by *Pythium aphanidermatum* is significantly greater in the thatch of bentgrass-annual bluegrass turf than in the underlying soil (Hall, Larsen and Schmitthenner, 1980). In order for the Sclerotium blight pathogen, *Sclerotium rolfsii*, to infect and colonize turfgrass plants, the fungus must first grow saprophytically in the thatch (Punja and Grogan, 1981a, 1981b). Pseudothatch has been shown to serve as the primary source of inoculum for the initial outbreaks of Helminthosporium leaf spot and melting out of Kentucky bluegrass and for the continued development of these diseases during the growing season (Colbaugh and Endo, 1974; Hagan and Larsen, 1985).

Excessive thatch accumulation is associated with the occurrence of severe outbreaks of Fusarium blight (Bean, 1966; Couch and Bedford, 1966; Partyka, 1976). Thatch thickness greater than ½ inch (1.3 cm) is conducive to the development of Rhizoctonia blight, Rhizoctonia yellow patch, Rhizoctonia sheath spot, and Sclerotinia dollar spot (Martin *et al.*, 1983; Burpee and Martin, 1992; Wagner and Halisky, 1981). With the winter patch diseases, management practices that hold thatch at ½ inch (1.3 cm) or less will aid in reducing the severity of Fusarium patch, Typhula blight, and cottony snow mold (Smith, 1987). The severity of spring dead spot of bermudagrass (*Cynodon dactylon*) is greater when the thatch accumulation is greater than ½ to ¾ inch (1.3–2.0 cm) (Lucas and Gilbert, 1979).

The fungus species that form lectophilic fairy rings are thatch and mat colonizers. Factors that affect the thickness and general condition of these layers will have a direct bearing on ring development (Dale, 1972; Kackley, Dernoeden and Grybaukuskas, 1989). Also, the hydrophobic condition of thatch and soil known as "localized dry spot" is generated by certain species of thatch inhabiting fungi; therefore, this condition is more likely to develop in heavily thatched turf (Miller and Wilkinson, 1977; Wilkinson and Miller, 1978).

Mowing Height

As a general rule, when the cutting height of sports and landscape turf is lowered the level of its susceptibility to disease increases. Gaeumannomyces decline of hybrid bermudagrass (*Cynodon dactylon* × *Cynodon transvaalensis*) managed as golf course putting greens is more severe on turf maintained at ultra low cutting heights (Elliott, 1991b). The incidence of take-all patch is higher on creeping red fescue (*Festuca rubra*) cut at ¾ inch (1.9 cm) than when mowed at 1½ inches (3.8 cm) (Goss and Gould, 1973) (Figure 4-3). Summer patch is more severe on Kentucky bluegrass (*Poa pratensis*) cut at 1½ inches (4 cm) than at 2¼ inches (6 cm) (Davis and Dernoeden, 1991). The severity of spring dead spot of bermudagrass (*Cynodon dactylon*) is also greater in turf maintained at low cutting heights. Kentucky bluegrass plants cut at a height of 1 inch (2.5 cm) are more susceptible to the leaf lesion phase of melting-out than those mowed at 2 inches (5 cm) (Lukens, 1970). Helminthosporium leaf spot of Kentucky bluegrass is more severe on plants cut at less than 1.5 inches (3.8 cm) (Couch, 1980). There is also a relationship between the height of cut of creeping bentgrass (*Agrostis palustris*) golf greens and the severity of bacterial wilt. The disease is always less severe in the taller cut collars than in the adjoining putting areas of golf greens. Furthermore, golf greens clipped at ²⁄₁₆ inch (3 mm) or less are more severely affected by the disease than when the putting surface is maintained at higher cuts (Couch, 1981).

Soil Moisture Stress

Soil moisture stress within the readily available range [field capacity to permanent wilting percentage (−0.033 MPa to −1.5 MPa)] can have a significant effect on the growth and development of the turfgrass plant. When the moisture content of the soil adjacent to the absorbing roots reaches the permanent wilting percentage, cell turgor is lost, stomata close, and transpiration and photosynthesis rates are lowered. Where metabolic activity is concerned, as the soil moisture content reaches stress levels near the permanent wilting percentage the plant undergoes certain metabolic changes. There is usually a stimulation of hydrolytic and a retardation of condensation reactions which results in an alteration in the relationships between sugars and starches and between amino acids and proteins. These various changes can in turn impact on the plant's vulnerability to infection and colonization by pathogenic microorganisms (Couch, Purdy and Henderson, 1967).

The severity of Rhizoctonia blight is not affected by soil moisture stresses between field capacity and the permanent wilting percentage (Bloom and Couch, 1960). However, outbreaks of Melanotus white patch are most severe under conditions of low soil moisture content. Also, the incidence and severity of Fusarium blight is greater when the soil moisture content is low (Koehane, 1967; Endo and Colbaugh, 1974). The severity of Fusarium blight at low soil moisture levels is increased even further when the plants are also growing under high nitrogen nutrition (Figure 4-5) (Cutright and Harrison; 1970). The susceptibility of bentgrass to Pythium blight is greater when the plants are growing at soil moisture stresses near the permanent wilting percentage (Moore, Couch and Bloom, 1963). Grass growing at soil moisture levels of 3/4 field capacity or less is more susceptible to Sclerotinia dollar spot than turf which is maintained at field capacity (Figure 4-7) (Couch and Bloom, 1960).

Leaf Wetness

The source of the free water on the surface of the leaves and the length of time leaves are wet are important factors in the development of fungus-incited foliar diseases of turfgrasses. Through leachates from underlying tissue and guttation fluids, leaf surfaces are subject to deposits of a wide range of types of chemical compounds including vitamins, amino acids, sugars, pectic substances, and sugar alcohols. When these materials become dissolved in the leaf surface water they then serve as a nutritional base for the growth and development of invading fungi. Leaf surface moisture that has accumulated as the result of light, intermittent rainfalls or condensation of fog or dew will contain a higher concentration of these compounds than free water that has developed from heavy, extended rainfalls.

The duration of leaf wetness has a direct bearing on the number of infections per leaf. When the air temperature is optimum for growth of a parasitic fungus, a much shorter wetting period is required for infection to occur than at sub- or extra-optimal temperatures. With most of the foliar diseases of turfgrasses that occur during growing seasons, when the initial level of inoculum is high and the day-night air temperatures are optimum for growth of the pathogen, a single leaf wetting period of 12–24 hours will trigger a major disease outbreak. However, if the initial inoculum level is low, then a close succession of two to three leaf wetting periods of 48–72 hours each is usually required before the disease reaches severe proportions.

When the climatic conditions are such that guttation fluids and the condensation of fog and dew is the principal source of free water on the leaf surfaces, practices should be employed that reduce the durations of continuous leaf wetness to less than 12 hours. One such procedure is the early morning removal of dew and guttation water from leaf surfaces by either whisking the surface of the turf with long, limber poles or by dragging a water hose across the area. Also, the duration of daily periods of leaf wetness can be shortened two to four hours by following a nighttime watering schedule in which the irrigation system is set to begin at least three hours after sunset and programmed to be completed before sunrise (Figure 16-2).

USE OF DISEASE RESISTANT GENOTYPES

The various species of grass used for sports and landscape turf show a wide range of variability in their susceptibility to certain diseases. For example, with the Helminthosporium-incited leaf and crown diseases, Kentucky bluegrass (*Poa pratensis*) and annual bluegrass (*Poa annua*) are highly susceptible to melting-out, but tall fescue and perennial ryegrass (*Lolium perenne*) are very resistant to the disease. Helminthosporium blight is a major disease of fescues (*Festuca* spp.) but a minor problem of Kentucky bluegrass and perennial ryegrass. Perennial ryegrass is very susceptible to brown blight but tall fescue is highly resistant to the disease.

Differences also exist in levels of susceptibility of individual turfgrass species to patch diseases. For example, annual bluegrass and Kentucky bluegrass are both very susceptible to summer patch, whereas species of fine fescue are only moderately susceptible, and creeping bentgrass (*Agrostis palustris*) and perennial ryegrass are highly resistant to the disease. Where resistance to Fusarium blight is concerned, annual bluegrass and the bentgrasses show the highest degree of susceptibility to the disease, Kentucky bluegrass is next in susceptibility, and perennial ryegrass and the fescues are the most resistant species. Pythium blight and Rhizoctonia blight are much more severe on annual bluegrass than other cool season grasses. Of the three species of bentgrass used for fine turf, colonial bentgrass (*Agrostis tenuis*)

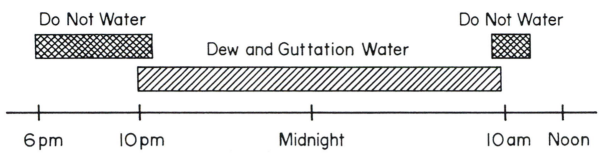

Figure 16-2.   Illustration of how watering schedules impact on the duration of daily periods of leaf wetness.

is the most susceptible to Rhizoctonia blight, velvet bentgrass (*Agrostis canina*) ranks second in vulnerability, and creeping bentgrass (*Agrostis palustris*) shows the highest degree of resistance to the disease.

Improving disease resistance within a species is a standard objective of turfgrass breeding programs. The research procedure for selecting and evaluating promising new turfgrass genotypes includes comparisons of the levels of disease resistance of the candidates to those of varieties currently in use. The results of these tests are used ultimately to prepare lists showing comparative levels of resistance of commercially available cultivars to specific diseases. These compilations may be obtained from turfgrass seed producers and turfgrass management advisory services.

The degree of resistance of the species and varieties under management to the major diseases in the immediate area will determine the level of intensity needed to carry out a successful disease control program. For example, Rhizoctonia blight and Pythium blight are much more difficult to control on perennial ryegrass (*Lolium perenne*) and creeping bentgrass (*Agrostis palustris*) in the extended hot and humid summer weather of subtropical climates than in relatively cool temperate zones. Therefore, when ryegrass and/or bentgrass are used as primary species for golf turf in subtropical climates, if high quality putting green, tee, and fairway turf is to be maintained, the disease control strategy must call for fungicide application schedules that have been designed to prevent initial outbreaks of these diseases. Also, annual bluegrass dependent situations will require a more intensive fungicide program for control of both warm season and cold season diseases than if the predominant species making up the turf were either bentgrass or Kentucky bluegrass.

In landscape turf such as lawns, cemeteries and parks, the use of blends and mixtures in turfgrass cultivars and/or species will provide some degree of buffering against major damage to the overall quality of the turf by any one disease. However, when selecting the components of the mixture, it is important to bear in mind that the inclusion of a large proportion of a highly susceptible genotype will dilute the overall population level of disease resistance and thereby nullify the advantage of using a blend (Ostergaard, 1983).

BIOLOGICAL CONTROL

Biological control of a plant disease is accomplished by the use of a biotic agent that either lowers the population density of the pathogen or reduces its disease producing activities. The more feasible approaches to biocontrol of turfgrass diseases fall into one of two groupings: (a) use of preparations containing known microbial species that are detrimental to the growth and development of specific pathogens, and (b) use of organic materials colonized by complex mixtures of unidentified microbial species that have the potential to restrict the growth and development of pathogenic fungi and nematodes.

Use of Preparations Containing Known Microbial Antagonists

Varying degrees of success have been reported from field and greenhouse-based tests for the control of turfgrass diseases by infesting the turf with known microbial antagonists. Reduction in the incidence and severity of Gaeumannomyces patch of bentgrass (*Agrostis* sp.) has been achieved by infesting the soil with the nonpathogenic fungus *Phialophora graminicola* (Wong and Siviour, 1979). Autoclaved grain preparations of the nonpathogenic thatch and soil inhabiting fungus *Typhula phacorrhiza* applied as a topdressing to creeping bentgrass (*Agrostis palustris*) turf have provided up to 74 percent control of Typhula blight (Burpee *et al.*, 1987; Lawton and Burpee, 1990). The incidence and severity of Rhizoctonia blight of creeping bentgrass golf greens has been reduced by the infestation of the turf with sterilized grain colonized with nonpathogenic isolates of a binucleate species of *Rhizoctonia* (Burpee and Goulty, 1984). Suppression of the development of Rhizoctonia blight on tall fescue (*Festuca arundinacea*) has been accomplished with nonpathogenic isolates of a binucleate species of *Rhizoctonia* and with a preparation of the fungus *Laetisaria arvalis* (Sutker and Lucas, 1987). A 63 percent reduction in the incidence of Sclerotinia dollar spot for a period of 32 days has been achieved by topdressing creeping bentgrass golf greens with a cornmeal-sand mixture colonized with the bacterium *Enterobacter cloacae* (Nelson and Craft, 1991b).

Once experimental evidence has shown that reduction of a turfgrass disease can be obtained through the use of a specific microbial antagonist, additional research must be carried out to determine its usefulness as a functional biocontrol agent before it can be placed into commercial use. Specifically, it must be shown that (a) the antagonist can readily establish itself in the turf and persist at high population levels for long periods of time, (b) the growth and development of the antagonist is not adversely affected by pesticides currently being used in the disease control program, (c) the antagonist is active against local strains of the target pathogen, (d) the reduction in disease provided by use of the antagonist is enough to permit a significant decrease in the amount of pesticide currently being used to control the target pathogen, and (e) the antagonist does not jeopardize the stability of the biological environment and is not injurious to the health of animals and humans.

(a) The antagonist must be readily established in the turf and persist at high population levels. In order for biocontrol to be effective, there must be a continuous balance between the population densities of the antagonist and the pathogen. This means that the antagonist must become quickly established in the turf and be able to maintain the population level needed to lower the disease producing potential of the target pathogen. Competition with other organisms that are already colonizing the soil and thatch, plus the constant replenishment of grass tissue which fosters the growth of the pathogen makes that difficult. Repeat applications of large quantities of preparations of the antagonistic species are usually required in order to achieve and maintain levels of disease suppression that approximate those provided by fungicides. For example, an application of 41 pounds of a grain preparation of *Typhula phacorrhiza*

per 1,000 square feet (18.6 kg/93 m²) of turf is needed to produce the same level of Typhula blight control provided by 6.85 ounces of active ingredient per 1,000 square feet (194 g/93 m²) of the fungicide quintozene (PCNB) (Burpee and Lawton, 1990). The decision of whether to use an antagonist, then, must take into consideration how much of the material is required to provide a significant reduction in disease development and how long the individual applications will last.

(b) Growth and development of the antagonist must not be adversely affected by currently used pesticides. It is generally recognized that biocontrol procedures in themselves will not provide satisfactory levels of disease reduction in high management turf, and, therefore, they will need to be used in conjunction with a pesticide program. There is always a likelihood that pesticides being used in the disease control program may be toxic to the antagonist or may be restricting the growth and development of indigenous microbes that are necessary for the biocontrol species to become established in the turf. Therefore, the impact of pesticides currently in use on the growth and development of the antagonist is an important consideration in the selection of biocontrol agents.

(c) The antagonist must be active against local strains of the target pathogen. Many of the species of fungi that are pathogenic to turfgrasses are known to have biotypes that differ in their vulnerability to fungicides, their degrees of pathogenicity to different turfgrass varieties, or in the environmental parameters needed for optimum infection and colonization of host tissue. This means that the mechanisms of action for biocontrol that are functional against one strain of a pathogenic fungus may not restrict the growth and development of a different biotype. For this reason, before being offered for use commercially, an antagonist must have been widely field tested within the prospective marketing regions to determine its level of effectiveness against the target pathogen in these localities.

(d) The level of disease reduction provided by the antagonist must permit a significant decrease in pesticide usage. A biocontrol system based on the use of a single microbial species is highly specific. Unlike many fungicides, it will not control a wide range of pathogenic fungi, it has only one target. Since the level of disease reduction provided by the antagonist is fractional rather than absolute, and since that fraction is a portion of only one disease, the level of

Table 16-1. Impact of inorganic and natural organic fertilizers on the incidence and severity of Sclerotinia dollar spot of creeping bentgrass (*Agrostis palustris*). *After Hsiang et al., 1991.*

Treatment[a]	NPK Analysis	Appllication Rate 1000 ft^2	93 m^2	Percent Disease Reduction[b] 7/24	8/7	8/21	9/3
Non-treated control	—	—	—	0 a	0 a	0 a	0 a
Ringer Turf	10-2-6	9.9 lbs	4.5 kg	*11 a	30 a	50 b	66 c
Ammonium nitrate	34-0-0	2.9 lbs	1.3 kg	35 b	57 d	51 c	98 d
Ringer Lawn Restore	9-4-4	10.8 lbs	4.9 kg	14 ab	40 d	52 b	67 c
Milorganite	6-0-0	16.3 lbs	7.4 kg	7 ab	22 bc	15 a	19 b
Sandaid	1-0-2	22.1 lbs	10.0 kg	5 ab	*5 ab	*4 a	13 ab
Bovamura	5-0-0	16.9 fl oz	0.5 L	15 ab	*19 a	*4 a	3 a

[a]All fertilizers and amendments applied every four weeks starting June 5.
The composition of each of the natural organic products listed in this table is given in Table 16-6.
[b]Numbers marked with an asterisk (*) indicate an increase in disease rather than a reduction. Comparisons based on Duncan's Multiple Range Test. Means with the same letter are not significantly different at p = 0.05.

control provided by the antagonist must at least offset fungicide consumption for control of the target disease to the extent that its cost to the disease management program is covered.

(e) The antagonist must not jeopardize the stability of the bio-environment or human and animal health. Protection of the integrity of the environment is one of the primary reasons that the concept of biological control has gained much support. Before a biocontrol agent is placed into general use, however, it must be clearly demonstrated that in itself it does not jeopardize the stability of the biological environment or the health of human and animal life. Ideally, the agents that have been selected should be microflora that are indigenous to the area so that the danger of introducing potentially damaging organisms is minimal.

Use of Natural Organic Products

Many natural organic products such as composts, sewage sludge, organic fertilizers, and manure-based preparations are colonized by complex mixtures of microorganisms. The possibility exists that when these materials are applied to turf, the microbial species they carry might become established in the thatch and soil and then restrict the growth and development of the resident pathogens.

Tests conducted at Cornell University have shown reductions in the incidence of Sclerotinia dollar spot of creeping bentgrass golf greens ranging from 9 to 74 percent respectively when treated with various manure products, sewage sludge from different sources, brewery and manure composts, and commercially available natural organic fertilizers consisting

Table 16-2. Inorganic, synthetic organic, and natural organic fertilizer effect on microbial populations in creeping bentgrass (*Agrostis palustris*) golf green eight weeks after application (propagules per gram dry weight). *After Hsiang et al., 1991.*

Treatment[a]	NPK Analysis	Application Rate 1000 ft^2	93 m^2	Fungi ($\times$ 10^4)[b] Thatch	Soil	Bacteria ($\times$ 10^6)[b] Thatch	Soil
Non-treated control	—	—	—	44 ab	11 b	120 ab	36 ab
Ringer Turf	10-2-6	9.9 lbs	4.5 kg	54 ab	13 ab	197 ab	59 ab
Ammonium nitrate	34-0-0	2.9 lbs	1.3 kg	81 a	27 a	197 ab	59 ab
Sulfur coated urea	35-0-0	3.3 lbs	1.5 kg	44 ab	13 ab	240 a	98 b
Sandaid	1-0-2	22.1 lbs	10.0 kg	44 ab	16 ab	197 ab	49 ab
Windsor, Ontario sewage sludge[c]		10.8 lbs	4.9 kg	30 b	13 ab	66 ab	36 ab
Milorganite	6-2-0	10.8 lbs	4.9 kg	54 ab	15 ab	49 b	22 b
Bovamura	5-0-0	47.3 fl oz	1.4 L	44 ab	12 b	161 ab	49 ab
Ringer Greens	10-2-6	11.9 lbs	4.5 kg	73 a	22 ab	217 ab	66 ab

[a]All fertilizers and amendments applied every four weeks starting June 5.
The composition of each of the natural organic products listed in this table is given in Table 16-6.
[b]Comparisons based on Duncan's Multiple Range Test. Means with the same letter are not significantly different at p = 0.05.
[c]Nitrogen, phosphorous and potassium analysis not given.

hydrolyzed poultry feather meal, wheat germ, soybean meal, brewers yeast, bone meal, blood meal, sulfate of potash, and supplemented with species of *Bacillus* and the fungus *Trichoderma viride* (Table 16-6) (Nelson and Craft, 1992). Inorganic and synthetic nitrogen fertilizers were not included in these trials.

Field trials at Guelph University compared the effects of ammonium nitrate and sulfur coated urea with a commercially available liquid manure product, a granular sea plant material, a Norwegian kelp meal, several commercially available natural organic fertilizers, and sewage sludge from different sources on (a) the severity of Sclerotinia dollar spot on a creeping bentgrass golf green and (b) microbial activity in the thatch and soil of a creeping bentgrass golf green and a Kentucky bluegrass lawn (Table 16-6). Disease reductions in the plots treated with ammonium nitrate ranged from 35 to 98 percent. The reduction levels for the plots treated with the natural organic products varied from 3 to 67 percent (Table 16-1). There were no quantitative differences in microbial activity between the plots treated with the various inorganic and natural organic products and the nontreated control plots (Tables 16-2 and 16-3) (Hsiang *et al.*, 1991).

Research at Virginia Tech has compared the effects of various formulations of synthetic organic and natural organic fertilizers on the development of Sclerotinia dollar spot of creeping bentgrass under golf green management and Rhizoctonia blight of turf-type tall fescue (Table 16-6). The various synthetic and natural organic formulations caused increases in the incidence and severity of Rhizoctonia blight ranging from 100 to 240 percent (Table 16-4). In the Sclerotinia dollar spot trial, a 65 percent reduction in

Table 16-4. Impact of synthetic organic and natural organic fertilizers on the incidence and severity of Rhizoctonia blight of 'Bonsai' turf-type tall fescue (*Festuca arundinacea*). After Couch, 1991.

Treatment[a]	NPK Analysis	Total N Applied per 1000 ft²	Total N Applied per 93 m²	Percent Disease Increase[b]
Non-treated control	—	—	—	0 a
Ringer Turf	10-2-6	3.00 lbs	1.4 kg	66 ab
Methylene urea	41-0-0	3.00 lbs	1.4 kg	81 abc
Urea	46-0-0	2.25 lbs	1.0 kg	87 abc
Ringer Dispatch 2	7-1-3	1.50 lbs	0.7 kg	96 abc
Sulfur coated urea	38-0-0	1.80 lbs	0.8 kg	111 bcd
IBDU (isobutylidene diurea)	31-0-0	3.00 lbs	1.4 kg	149 bcde
Sustane	5-2-4	3.00 lbs	1.4 kg	174 cde
Ringer Lawn Restore	9-4-4	2.70 lbs	1.2 kg	186 cde
Ringer FWY/ LCO	12-2-6	3.00 lbs	1.4 kg	213 de
Ringer Greens	6-1-3	1.80 lbs	0.8 kg	246 e

[a]Fertilizers applied June 3, June 27 and August 1.
The composition of each of the natural organic products listed in this table is given in Table 16-6.
[b]Disease incidence and severity ratings performed on August 28. Comparisons based on Duncan's Multiple Range Test. Means with the same letter are not significantly different at p = 0.05.

Table 16-3. Inorganic, synthetic organic, and natural organic fertilizer effect on microbial populations in Kentucky bluegrass (*Poa pratensis*) lawn eight weeks after application (propagules per gram dry weight). After Hsiang et al., 1991.

Treatment[a]	NPK Analysis	Application Rate 1000 ft²	Application Rate 93 m²	Fungi (× 10⁴)[b] Thatch	Fungi (× 10⁴)[b] Soil	Bacteria (× 10⁶)[b] Thatch	Bacteria (× 10⁶)[b] Soil
Non-treated control	—	—	—	60 a	20 ab	266 ab	59 b
Ringer Turf	10-2-6	9.9 lbs	4.5 kg	89 a	18 ab	294 ab	59 b
Ammonium nitrate	34-0-0	2.9 lbs	1.3 kg	120 a	20 ab	359 ab	59 b
Ringer Lawn Restore	9-4-4	10.8 lbs	4.9 kg	60 a	13 ab	884 a	89 ab
Milorganite	6-0-0	16.3 lbs	7.4 kg	98 a	27 a	294 ab	80 ab
Sulfur coated urea	35-0-0	3.3 lbs	1.5 kg	73 a	16 ab	397 ab	89 ab
Sandaid	1-0-2	22.1 lbs	10.0 kg	89 a	20 ab	325 ab	132 a
Alginate	1-0-2	22.1 lbs	10.0 kg	81 a	12 b	325 ab	89 ab
Windsor, Ontario sewage sludge[c]		10.8 lbs	4.9 kg	89 a	15 ab	266 ab	80 ab
Bovamura	5-0-0	16.9 fl oz	0.5 L	98 a	13 ab	197 b	66 ab

[a]All fertilizers and amendments applied every four weeks starting June 12. The composition of each of the natural organic products listed in this table is given in Table 16-6.
[b]Comparisons based on Duncan's Multiple Range Test. Means with the same letter are not significantly different at p = 0.05.
[c]Nitrogen, phosphorous and potassium analysis not given.

Table 16-5. Impact of synthetic organic and natural organic fertilizers on the incidence and severity of Sclerotinia dollar spot of 'Penneagle' creeping bentgrass (*Agrostis palustris*) under golf green management. *After Couch, 1991.*

Treatment[a]	NPK Analysis	Total N Applied per 1000 ft²	Total N Applied per 93 m²	Percent Disease Reduction[b]
Non-treated control	—	—	—	0 a
Ringer Lawn Restore	9-4-4	2.70 lbs	1.2 kg	7 ab
Sulfur coated urea	38-0-0	1.80 lbs	0.8 kg	15 abc
Urea	46-0-0	2.25 lbs	1.0 kg	26 abc
Methylene urea	41-0-0	3.00 lbs	1.4 kg	18 abc
Ringer Greens	6-1-3	1.80 lbs	0.8 kg	37 cde
Ringer DisPatch 2	7-1-3	1.50 lbs	0.7 kg	48 def
Ringer FWY/LCO	12-2-6	3.00 lbs	1.4 kg	53 ef
Sustane	5-2-4	3.00 lbs	1.4 kg	58 ef
Ringer Turf	10-2-6	3.00 lbs	1.4 kg	60 ef
IBDU (iso-butylidene diurea)	31-0-0	3.00 lbs	1.4 kg	65 f
Iprodione				100 g

[a]Fertilizers applied May 15, June 17 and July 15. Iprodione applied at 0.50 ounce a.i. per 1000 sq ft (14.2 g 93 m²) July 14 and August 21. The composition of each of the natural organic products listed in this table is given in Table 16-6.
[b]Disease incidence and severity ratings performed on August 27. Comparisons based on Duncan's Multiple Range Test. Means with the same letter are not significantly different at p = 0.05.

Table 16-6. Composition of the commercially available natural organic products listed in Tables 16-1, 16-2, 16-3, 16-4, and 16-5.

Product Name	Composition
Alginate	A 1-0-2 Norwegian kelp material.
Bovamura	A 5-0-0 fertilizer derived from cow manure.
Milorganite	A 6-0-0 fertilizer derived from sewage sludge.
Ringer Greens	A 6-1-3 fertilizer derived from hydrolyzed poultry feather meal, wheat germ, Soybean meal, bone meal, brewers yeast, and sulfate of potash, and supplemented with *Bacillus subtilis*, other *Bacillus* spp., and *Trichoderma viride*.
Ringer FWY/LCO	A 12-2-6 fertilizer derived from hydrolyzed poultry feather meal, wheat germ, blood meal, bone meal, and sulfate of potash, and supplemented with *Bacillus subtilis*, other *Bacillus* spp., and *Trichoderma viride*.
Ringer Turf	A 10-2-6 fertilizer derived from hydrolyzed poultry feather meal, blood meal, wheat germ, bone meal, sulfate of potash, and supplemented with *Bacillus subtilis*, other *Bacillus* spp., and *Trichoderma viride*.
Ringer DisPatch 2	A 7-1-3 fertilizer derived from hydrolyzed poultry feather meal, wheat germ, soybean meal, brewers yeast, bone meal, blood meal, sulfate of potash, and supplemented with unspecified microbial species.
Ringer Lawn Restore	A 9-4-4 fertilizer derived from hydrolyzed poultry feather meal, wheat germ, soybean meal, bone meal, blood meal, sulfate of potash, and supplemented with species of *Bacillus* and the fungus *Trichoderma viride*.
Sandaid	A 1-0-2 granular sea plant material.
Sustane	A 5-2-4 fertilizer derived from turkey manure combined with softwood shavings.

disease severity was obtained with one of the synthetic organic nitrogen formulations and 37 to 65 percent reductions with certain of the natural organic products (Table 16-5) (Couch, 1991).

In summation, where natural organic products colonized by complex mixtures of unidentified microbial species are concerned, research evidence to date indicates that these materials do not contribute in a unique manner to the control of turfgrass diseases, nor do they enhance quantitative microbial activity in the thatch or soil of established turf. In other words, inorganic, synthetic organic, and natural organic fertilizers used in accordance with the manufacturer's suggested rates and application schedules have the same impact on the incidence and severity of disease and the same effect on microbial activity in the thatch and soil.

USE OF PESTICIDES

Fungicidal and nematicidal protection is an essential component of the majority of turfgrass disease control strategies. An understanding of the nature of these two types of pesticides and appropriate procedures for their use is necessary for the development of meaningful disease control strategies. The nature of fungicides and procedures for maximizing their effectiveness in turfgrass disease control is reviewed in Chapter 17—Selection and Use of Fungicides. For a description of procedures for determining injury thresholds of root-feeding nematodes in established turf and the selection and use of fumigant and non-fumigant nematicides to reduce nematode population levels, refer to Control of Root-Feeding Nematodes in Chapter 14—Diseases Caused by Nematodes.

Selection and Use of Fungicides

FUNGICIDE NOMENCLATURE

There is a wide variety of chemicals available for the control of fungus-incited diseases of turfgrasses. The basic fungicides used in turfgrass disease control are sometimes grouped according to either their chemistry, such as "dicarboximides," or their biochemical modes of action, such as "demethylation inhibitors." The terms used for the individual fungicide groups may vary among publications depending on the degree of specificity chosen by the author. For example, iprodione (Chipco 26019™) may be listed as a dicarboximide in one publication and as an anilide in another, and propiconazole (Banner™) as either a demethylation inhibitor or a sterol biosynthesis inhibitor.

Three names are used in commerce and practice to designate a fungicide—a chemical name, a common (coined) name, and a proprietary or trade name. The chemical name is usually complex and has little meaning to the turfgrass management specialist; however, it is developed by an internationally accepted system of nomenclature for chemical compounds, and assures that the same name will always be used for the compound worldwide.

The common (coined) name is assigned to a fungicide as a means of avoiding the difficulties nonchemists sometimes have in either remembering, recognizing or pronouncing the chemical name. Common names are developed by designated national committees and are usually standardized on an international basis, occasionally, however, some names may vary among countries.

The trade name is the name registered by the manufacturer or marketing agency of a particular fungicide. There may be more than one trade name for the same fungicide. For example, iprodione is marketed for use in turfgrass disease control as Chipco 26019™ and Rovral™, vinclozolin as Vorlan™ and Curalan™, and thiram as Spotrete™ and Arrest 75W™.

The following is an example of the full nomenclature of a turfgrass fungicide:

Group:	Phenylamides
Chemical Name:	N-(2,6-dimethylphenuyl)-N-(methoxyacetyl) alanine methyl ester
Coined Name:	metalaxyl
Trade Names:	Subdue™, Apron™

The official label for a registered fungicide will bear all three names and the percentage of active ingredient(s) and inert materials. The label also carries the patent and federal registration numbers, directions for use, and information pertaining to product safety. The basic fungicides used for control of turfgrass diseases are listed by coined and representative trade names in Table 17-1.

FUNGICIDAL MODES OF ACTION

The term **fungicide** refers classically to a chemical that kills fungi within a very short period of time. In actual practice, however, some chemicals used to control fungus-incited diseases are fungistatic. Rather than killing the fungus immediately, they handicap its ability to infect and colonize the plant by either preventing spore germination or growth and development of the mycelium. This impairment immediately restricts the pathogenic capabilities of the organism and eventually brings about its death.

Fungicides are grouped according to their topical and biochemical modes of action.

Topical Mode of Action

Topical mode of action identifies the location in or on the plant in which the fungitoxic or fungistatic activities take place. The two basic topical modes of action are contact and penetrant.

Contact fungicides are only effective against fungi that are present on the external parts of the plant. Contact fungicides protect the plant from infection but have no impact on reducing the degree of colonization of tissue after invasion has occurred. Chlorothalonil (Daconil 2787™) and mancozeb (Fore™)

Table 17-1. Basic fungicides used for control of turfgrass diseases listed according to topical mode of action.

Topical Mode of Action	Common Name	Representative Registered Trade Names[a]
Contact	Anilazine	Dyrene
	Chloroneb	Teremec SP
	Chlorothalonil	Daconil 2787
	Ethazol	Koban
	Maneb	Dithane M-22
	Mancozeb	Fore, Manzate 200 DF
	Mercury Chlorides	Calo-Clor, Calo-Gran
	Thiram	Thiram Flowable Fungicide
	Quintozene (PCNB)	Turfcide, Terraclor,
Localized Penetrant	Iprodione	Chipco 26019, Rovral
	Propamocarb	Banol
	Vinclozolin	Vorlan, Curalan
Acropetal Penetrant	Benomyl	Tersan 1991 DF
		Benomyl Systemic Fungicide
	Cyproconazole	Sentinel
	Fenarimol	Rubigan
	Flutolanil	Prostar
	Metalaxyl	Subdue
	Propiconazole	Banner
	Thiophanate methyl	Fungo 50, Cleary 3336
	Triadimefon	Bayleton
Systemic Penetrant	Fosetyl Al	Aliette

[a]No discrimination is intended when the same chemical is marketed under other trade names, nor is endorsement by the author of the products bearing these names implied.

are examples of contact fungicides used for control of turfgrass diseases. **Penetrant** fungicides are chemicals that when applied to the surface of a plant penetrate into the underlying tissue in quantities that are toxic to the target organism. Penetrant fungicides have the capacity to function both as protectants on the plant surface and as eradicants of fungi from colonized tissue. There are three forms of penetrant fungicides: localized penetrants, acropetal penetrants, and systemic penetrants.

Localized penetrants pass into the underlying tissue in quantities that are toxic to the target organism and remain in the immediate vicinity of entry. Vinclozolin (Vorlan™, Curalan™), propamocarb (Banol™), and iprodione (Chipco 26019™, Rovral™) are localized penetrants.

Acropetal penetrants are translocated only in the xylem (water conducting tissue), therefore, after entering the plant they are moved only upward in fungitoxic quantities. With the exception of fosetyl Al (Aliette™), all presently marketed fungicides that are translocated within the plant are acropetal penetrants.

Systemic penetrants are translocated in both the xylem and phloem (water and food conducting tissue), thus they become uniformly distributed in

fungitoxic quantities throughout the plant. The Pythium blight control fungicide fosetyl Al (Aliette™) is the only systemic penetrant fungicide currently marketed for turfgrass disease control.

The topical mode of action of each of the basic fungicides used for control of turfgrass diseases is given in Table 17-1 and in Appendix Table I.

Biochemical Mode of Action

Metabolism is a collective term used to describe the sum of chemical reactions within a living cell that bring about the energy-releasing breakdown of molecules and the synthesis of new protoplasm. It is the life process of the cell. The workings of metabolism are a complex series of interlocking and mutually dependent biochemical pathways. Each pathway is in itself made up of a step-sequence of events. If a step in the pathway is disrupted, the pathway ceases to perform its function. If the pathway cannot perform its function, then the overall metabolic process is disrupted, and if the overall metabolic process is disrupted, the growth and development of the cell is impaired.

Biochemical mode of action refers to the effects of the fungicide on the metabolic processes of the fungal cell. Research on biochemical mode of action seeks to identify specific sites in the metabolic pathways that are disrupted by the fungicide in question. The general effects of many fungicides on the metabolism of fungi have been defined, but the specific sites of action in the respective pathways are not easy to determine, therefore, the precise function that has been interfered with has not always been clearly identified. Certain fungicides are known to be site specific, others have a nonspecific or general mode of action, affecting a wide range of metabolic pathways simultaneously. Site specific fungicides are more prone to the development of resistance on the part of the pathogen.

FUNGICIDE GROUPS

For the most part, fungicide grouping is usually based on chemical structures. Although the constituents of certain groups have similar topical or biochemical modes of action, there are many examples of compounds that are closely related chemically that function in completely dissimilar manners. The individual groups and the biochemical modes of action of their components are as follows:

Aromatic Hydrocarbons (Substituted Benzenes)

The aromatic hydrocarbons used for turfgrass disease control are chloroneb (Teremec SP™), ethazol (Koban™), and quintozene (Terraclor™). Aromatic hydrocarbons are thought to affect DNA synthesis and block the activity of certain respiratory enzymes. Also, chloroneb and ethazol prevent the development of cell wall membranes and quintozene restricts the formation of chitin, which is a primary component of the cell walls of many of the fungi that are pathogenic to turfgrasses. These compounds volatilize rapidly after application to foliage and are sensitive to ultraviolet light, which decreases their longevity.

Benzimidazoles

The two members of this group that are used for turfgrass disease control are benomyl (Tersan 1991™) and thiophanate methyl (Fungo 50™, Cleary 3336™). The benzimidazoles were the first acropetal penetrants to be used for control of turfgrass diseases. When either benomyl or thiophanate methyl are applied to the plant, they undergo a degradative cyclization to give the same fungitoxic compound. Their biochemical mode of action probably involves an inhibition of DNA synthesis and interference with nuclear division by binding to tubulin which is a protein component of spindle fibers in cells undergoing mitosis.

Carbamates

The carbamates most commonly used in turfgrass disease control are thiram (Spotrete™, Thiram Flowable Fungicide™), maneb (Dithane M-22™), mancozeb (Fore™, Manzate 200™), and propamocarb (Banol™). Thiram was the first organic fungicide to be marketed for use on turf. It has been in commercial use for the control of turfgrass diseases since the mid-1930s. The fungitoxicity of thiram stems from its ability to chelate certain metal ions, thus enabling them to pass through the lipid barriers of the fungal cell wall. Its biochemical mode of action is probably based on direct interference with the respiratory processes of the cell.

Propamocarb enters the plant tissue in the areas of deposit; however, once it has passed into the plant it is rapidly degraded, and therefore is not translocated in fungitoxic amounts to other tissues. The biochemical mode of action of propamocarb is thought to be based on alteration of fatty acid composition, which in turn alters the fluidity of the cell membranes.

Zineb, maneb and mancozeb are contact fungicides. They are metal-containing formulations of ethylenebisdithiocarbamate (EBDC). The fungitoxicity of these compounds is thought to be due to chemical inactivation of important thiol containing systems, thus inhibiting enzyme activity within the fungal cell. Maneb and mancozeb control a very broad spectrum of turfgrass diseases. Also, mancozeb functions synergistically with metalaxyl and propamocarb in the control of Pythium blight. The preplant soil fumigant meptam-sodium (Vapam™) commonly used for nematode and weed control in turfgrass management is also a dithiocarbamate.

Carboximides

Two carboximides are used in turfgrass disease control, flutolanil (Prostar™), and oxycarboxin (Arrest Systemic Fungicide™). These compounds interfere with respiration of the fungal cells by blocking the activity of certain respiratory enzymes.

Demethylation Inhibitors (DMIs)

The members of this group presently being marketed for use in turfgrass disease control are triadimefon

(Bayleton™), propiconazole (Banner™), cyproconazole (Sentinel™), and fenarimol (Rubigan™). These materials are also referred to as sterol biosynthesis inhibitors (SBIs). The DMIs inhibit sterol synthesis in sensitive fungi. With the exception of the Pythium blight fungi, ergosterol is an essential component of fungal turfgrass pathogens. Ergosterol is related to cholesterol and necessary for the formation of cell membranes. One of the vital functions of cell membranes is to protect cell contents from outside chemicals by selectively screening what flows into the cell.

Dicarboximides

The dicarboximides used in turfgrass disease control are iprodione (Chipco 26019™, Rovral™), and vinclozolin (Vorlan™, Curalan™). These fungicides interfere with respiration by blocking the activity of certain respiratory enzymes.

Nitriles

Chlorothalonil (Daconil 2787™) is the only member of the nitrile group marketed for use as a turfgrass fungicide. Chlorothalonil reacts with glutathione, an important regulator of normal cell metabolism, to disrupt the regulation of cell functions. It also inhibits sulfur-dependent enzymes in the cell which then brings about a disruption of cell functions. Chlorothalonil volatilizes rapidly after application to foliage and is sensitive to ultraviolet light, which decreases its longevity.

Phenylamides

Metalaxyl (Subdue™, Apron™) is the only phenylamide that is used for turfgrass disease control. Metalaxyl easily penetrates the plant surface or seed coat and is rapidly translocated in the water conducting tissue (xylem); therefore, it has both protective and curative properties. The biochemical mode of action of metalaxyl is based on interference with the ribonucleic acid (RNA) template complex of sensitive fungi, thus inhibiting ribosomal RNA synthesis. Metalaxyl is unique in that among the various fungi pathogenic to turfgrass it only restricts the formation of RNA in the species that incite Pythium blight and yellow tuft/downy mildew.

Phosphonates

One member of this group, fosetyl Al (Aliette™), is registered for use in the control of Pythium blight of turfgrasses. After fosetyl Al it enters the plant, it

quickly degrades to phosphonate (phosphonic acid) which then functions as a fungicide. The biochemical mode of action of fosetyl Al is complex, involving both direct and indirect mechanisms. The degree of involvement of each factor most likely depends on the sensitivity of the fungus in question to direct inhibition by phosphonate and the host plant's defense response to the tissue being colonized.

Triazines

Anilazine (Dyrene™) is the only triazine marketed as a turfgrass fungicide. The ultimate sites of action of anilazine are not known. However, the material reacts quickly with amino groups and to some extent with thiols. It is likely, then, that it brings about the inhibition of a variety of cell processes by non-specific combination with essential cell components.

TYPES OF FUNGICIDE FORMULATIONS

Fungicides are rarely marketed as pure active ingredients. Most often, the basic fungicidal chemicals are placed on granules or mixed with powders or solvents and wetting and sticking agents to make products that are easy to package, easy to apply, easy to mix with water, stable during storage, and more effective. The finished product is called a fungicide formulation and is ready to use as it is packaged or after it has been diluted in a water carrier. Fungicides are prepared in one or more of the following types of formulations:

Aqueous Suspension (AS)

A water suspension of microdroplets of a liquid pesticide that have been surrounded by oil.

Dry Flowable (DF) (WDG)

A dry pesticide formulated by preparing uniformly sized microgranules from an aqueous suspension of a wettable powder. The finished product is free of dust, can be measured volumetrically, and disperses readily when placed in water.

Emulsifiable Concentrate (E) (EC)

Produced by dissolving the toxicant and an emulsifying agent in a petroleum-based solvent. The strength of the formulation is usually stated in pounds of active ingredient per gallon of concentrate.

Flowable (F) (FL) (FLO)

A suspension of microfine particles of dry technical ingredient in a water base to which a thickener has been added. (Water base paint is formulated by this same procedure).

Granular (G)

A type of formulation for dry application with spreading equipment in which a pesticide is absorbed, mixed with, or impregnated into a generally inert carrier in such a way that the final product consists of small granular particles. The mesh size of the particles of individual formulations will vary from fine (10–14 mesh) to coarse (7–10 mesh) depending on the type of carrier, the nature of the pesticide and the type of area to be treated.

Water Dispersable Granules (WDG)

See Dry Flowables.

Wettable Powder (WP)

A powder formulation which, when added to water forms a suspension used for spraying.

SYNERGISTIC FUNGICIDE COMBINATIONS

When two or more pesticides with different biochemical modes of action but toxic to the same organism are combined into a single spray application, the efficacy level of the mixture will either be synergistic, antagonistic, or additive.

Synergism is the combined action of two or more pesticides in which the control provided by their joint application is greater than the control that has been predicted by an appropriate reference model. The dynamics of synergy are based on one component of the mixture (known as the potentiator) acting directly on the target organism to make it more vulnerable to the toxic effects of the other. The advantages of using synergistic fungicide combinations are threefold: (a) with certain turfgrass diseases, a synergistic interaction can mean a significant reduction in the amount of fungicide required to maintain acceptable levels of disease control, (b) the heightened effectiveness of a synergistic fungicide combination provides a greater measure of control under conditions of heavy disease pressure, and (c) synergistic combinations reduce the possibility of the development of resistance to the fungicide in question.

Antagonism is a level of control provided by the joint application of two or more pesticides which is less than that of the control predicted by an appropriate reference model. Antagonism is brought on by one of the components of the mixture making the target organism less sensitive to the toxic effects of the other. The possible mechanisms for antagonism among fungicides are biochemical, competitive, and physiological. **Biochemical antagonism** is a decrease in the amount of given pesticide at the site of action. This occurs when the antagonist reduces the rate of movement of the other material either into the fungus cell or to the site of action within the cell. **Competitive antagonism** occurs when the antagonist acts reversibly at the same site of action as the primary pesticide thereby preventing its binding to the receptor site and the formation of a fungicide-receptor complex that may be necessary to the development of toxicity. **Physiological antagonism** occurs when two pesticides act on different metabolic sites within the cells of the target organism to produce opposite effects on the same physiological process. Each material is able to act on its primary sites for toxicity, but the opposing actions of the two within the cell on other metabolic sites results in a net reduction in their fungicidal activities.

The **additive control** level of a reduced rate fungicide mixture is commonly used as the reference model for determining synergy or antagonism. Additive control is not the direct sum of the efficacy levels of the respective components of the mixture; instead, it is an adjusted value that has been arrived at by the use of a mathematical model. The degree of additivity of the mixture is determined by a two step process. First, a series of tests is conducted to assess the disease control potential of (a) the full rate of each component of the mixture when it is applied singly, (b) the reduced rate of each component when it is applied singly, and (c) a mixture of the components at their reduced rates. This data is then used in a mathematical model which takes into consideration the fact that when the individual components of a suboptimal dosage rate mixture are acting independently, the control potential of the mixture is always less than that of the full label rate of the most effective component used alone (Table 17-2). The reason for this is that in a reduced rate mixture, there will be a certain number of escapes from each component that are not acted upon the other. If the test results show that the actual level of disease control provided by the fungicide mixture is the same as its calculated control potential, then the combination is said to be additive. If the mixture gives a higher degree of control, then the combination is synergistic. How-

Table 17-2. Theoretical additive disease control values of two and three component tank mixes of turfgrass fungicides computed by the method of *Colby (1967)*.

Actual disease control provided by single component applications of:			
Fungicide "A"	Fungicide "B"	Fungicide "C"	Theoretical additive control of mixture
50%	50%	—	75.0%
75%	75%	—	93.8%
50%	25%	—	62.5%
25%	25%	—	43.3%
90%	90%	—	99.0%
50%	50%	50%	87.5%
33.3%	33.3%	33.3%	70.4%

ever, if the actual control level of the mixture is less than the calculated theoretical control potential, then the combination is antagonistic.

In studies at Virginia Tech, synergistic combinations of fungicides have been identified for the control of Pythium blight and Sclerotinia dollar spot. In the Pythium blight study, mancozeb, fosetyl Al, propamocarb, metalaxyl, ethazol, and chloroneb were tested at various fractional low label rates in varying combinations against metalaxyl-sensitive and metalaxyl-resistant isolates of *Pythium aphanidermatum* on perennial ryegrass (*Lolium perenne*). Four of the interactions were synergistic and one was antagonistic (Table 17-3). The combination of mancozeb and metalaxyl was also synergistic against the metalaxyl resistant strains of the fungus (Table 17-4) (Couch and Smith, 1991). The utilization of these findings in the development of programs for the control of Pythium blight is discussed in the Pythium blight section of Chapter 4—Patch Diseases.

In the Sclerotinia dollar spot study, nine fungicides at various fractional low label rates and in

Table 17-3. Interactions among fungicide combinations in the control of Pythium blight. *After Couch and Smith, 1991.*

Interaction	Fungicide combination[a]
Synergistic	Mancozeb + Metalaxyl
	Mancozeb + Propamocarb
	Fosetyl Al + Propamocarb
	Fosetyl Al + Metalaxyl
Antagonistic	Mancozeb + Chloroneb
Additive	Mancozeb + Fosetyl Al
	Metalaxyl + Propamocarb
	Mancozeb + Ethazol

[a]See Table 17-1 for a listing of representative trade names for each fungicide.

Table 17-4. Effectiveness of fractional low label rate combinations of mancozeb and metalaxyl in the control of Pythium blight of perennial ryegrass (*Lolium perenne*) incited by a metalaxyl-resistant strain of *Pythium aphanidermatum. After Couch and Smith, 1991.*

Fungicide and fractional label amount per 1,000 ft^2 (93 m^2)[a]	Percentage disease control	
	Expected[b]	Actual[c]
Check	—	0 a
Metalaxyl 1/5× (1.42 g a.i.)	—	0 a
Metalaxyl 1× (7.09 g a.i.)	—	0 a
Mancozeb 1/2× (68.04 g a.i.)	—	64.0 b
Mancozeb 1× (136.08 g a.i.)	—	77.0 c
Mancozeb 1/2× (68.04 g a.i.) + metalaxyl 1/5 × (1.42 g a.i.)	64	78.0[syn]

[a]See Table 17-1 for representative trade names
[b]computed according to method of Gowing (1960)
[c]protected l.s.d. (p = 0.05); confidence interval + − 8.8; means followed by the same letter are not significantly different from each other (syn = synergistic).

varying combinations were field tested over a four year period for control of this disease on 'Penncross' and 'Penneagle' creeping bentgrass (*Agrostis palustris*) under golf green and golf tee management. Five of the combinations were synergistic and the remainder were additive (Table 17-5). The degree of synergy in each of the fractional rate combinations provided control levels equal to or better than the best control given by either of the components of the mixture used at its full label rate (Tables 17-6, 17-7) (Couch and Smith, 1989). The utilization of these findings in the development of programs for the control of Sclerotinia dollar spot is discussed in the section on Sclerotinia dollar spot control in Chapter 4—Patch Diseases.

FUNGICIDAL RESISTANCE

Fungicidal resistance among turfgrass pathogens is a relatively recent phenomenon. The first reports of field resistance to a turfgrass fungicide came during the early to mid-1960s. Instances of the failure of anilazine (Dyrene™) to control Sclerotinia dollar spot (incited by *Sclerotinia homoeocarpa*) were observed in Ohio, Illinois, Pennsylvania, New York, and Virginia. In 1973, resistance of the Sclerotinia dollar spot fungus to the benzimidazoles (Tersan 1991™, Fungo 50™, Cleary 3336™) was reported in the north central and eastern regions of the United States. During the 1980s, resistance to benomyl (Tersan 1991™) was reported on the part of the Fusarium patch fungus, *Microdochium nivalis*, in Washington state, instances of metalaxyl (Subdue™) resistance in

Table 17-5. Interactions among fungicide combinations in the control of Sclerotinia dollar spot. *After Couch and Smith, 1989.*

Interaction	Fungicide combination[a]
Synergistic	Propiconazole + Triadimefon
	Propiconazole + Iprodione
	Propiconazole + Chlorothalinol
	Propiconazole + Anilazine
	Propiconazole + Vincolozolin
Additive	Propiconazole + Mancozeb
	Propiconazole + Thiophanate methyl
	Propiconazole + Fenarimol
	Anilazine + Mancozeb
	Anilazine + Thiophanate methyl
	Anilazine + Vinclozolin
	Chlorothalonil + Mancozeb
	Chlorothalonil + Anilazine
	Chlorothalonil + Vinclozolin
	Chlorothalonil + Thiophanate methyl
	Triadimefon + Chlorothalonil
	Triadimefon + Iprodione
	Triadimefon + Anilazine
	Triadimefon + Mancozeb
	Thiophante methyl + Vinclozolin
	Iprodione + Anilazine
	Iprodione + Mancozeb
	Iprodione + Chlorothalonil
	Chipco 26019 + Fenarimol
	Mancozeb + Vinclozolin
	Mancozeb + Thiophanate methyl

[a]See Table 17-1 for a listing of representative trade names for each fungicide.

the Pythium blight pathogen, *Pythium aphanidermatum*, were documented in Pennsylvania, Kentucky, and Ohio, and resistance to iprodione (Chipco 26019™, Rovral™) in the Sclerotinia dollar spot fungus was detected in Michigan. In the early 1990s, resistance to the demethylation inhibitors triadimefon (Bayleton™), propiconazole (Banner™), and fenarimol (Rubigan™) to the Sclerotinia dollar spot fungus was observed in Illinois, Michigan, Ohio, Kentucky and Pennsylvania.

Fungicidal resistance is a stable, inheritable adjustment by a fungus to the toxic effects of a fungicide. The primary mechanisms of resistance to fungicides are either alterations at the sites of action in the fungal cell that decrease its affinity to the fungicide, or a change in the uptake of the chemical so that less of it reaches the site of action. Neutralization of the toxic principle of the pesticide by metabolic activity of the target organism (detoxification) is common in insecticide resistance but rarely occurs with fungicides.

Certain of the changes in the fungus cell that bring about resistance to a fungicide are regulated by a single gene (monogenic) and others by multiple genes (polygenic). Monogenic resistance develops in a single step and is usually stable from one generation to the next. The resistance of the Sclerotinia dollar spot fungus to benzimidazoles is monogenic. Polygenic resistance usually develops in increments (i.e., the resistant segment of the fungus population progressively becomes more predominant). Polygenic resistance is less stable than monogenic resistance. The resistance of the Sclerotinia dollar spot fungus to demethylation inhibitors is polygenic.

Fungicides that are at highest risk for the development of resistance are those that affect a single

Table 17-6. Effectiveness of fractional low label rates of propiconazole and iprodione in the control of Sclerotinia dollar spot of creeping bentgrass (*Agrostis palustris*). *After Couch and Smith, 1989.*

Fungicide and fractional label amount per 1,000 ft² (93 m²)[a]	Percentage disease control	
	Expected[b]	Actual[c]
Check	—	0 a
Iprodione ¼ × (5.32 g a.i.)	—	0 a
Propiconazole ½ × (0.99 g a.i.)	—	11.4 a
Propiconazole 1 × (1.98 g a.i.)	—	29.5 a
Propiconazole ½ × (0.99 g a.i.) + iprodione ¼ × (5.32 g a.i.)	11.4	55.9 b[syn]
Iprodione 1 × (21.26 g a.i.)	—	63.5 b

[a]See Table 17-1 for representative trade names;
[b]computed according to method of Gowing (1960);
[c]protected l.s.d. (p = 0.05); confidence interval + − 28.8; means followed by the same letter are not significantly different from each other (syn = synergistic).

Table 17-7. Effectiveness of fractional low label rates of propiconazole and triadimefon in the control of Sclerotinia dollar spot of creeping bentgrass (*Agrostis palustris*). *After Couch and Smith, 1989.*

Fungicide and fractional label amount per 1,000 ft² (93 m²)[a]	Percentage disease control	
	Expected[b]	Actual[c]
Check	—	0 a
Propiconazole ½× (0.99 g a.i.)	—	2.9 a
Propiconazole 1× (1.98 g a.i.)	—	4.5 a
Triadimefon ¼× (1.77 g a.i.)	—	28.4 b
Propiconazole ½× (0.99 g a.i.) + triadimefon ¼× (1.77 g a.i.)	30.5	72.5 c[syn]
Triadimefon 1× (21.26 g a.i.)	—	84.8 c

[a]See Table 17-1 for representative trade names;
[b]computed according to method of Gowing (1960);
[c]protected l.s.d. (p = 0.05); confidence interval ±26.7; means followed by the same letter are not significantly different from each other (syn = synergistic).

metabolic site and in which the resistance factor is controlled by one gene. Fungicides that are at lowest risk for development of resistance are those that affect more than one metabolic site in the fungus cell and the factors for resistance are controlled by multiple genes (Table 17-8).

At times, resistance to two or more fungicides is governed by the same genetic factor. This phenomenon is referred to as **cross resistance**. Cross resistance often occurs among closely related compounds. The Sclerotinia dollar spot fungus develops cross resistance to the benzimidazoles [benomyl (Tersan 1991™), and thiophanate methyl (Fungo 50™, Cleary 3336™)], to the sterol inhibitors [propiconazole (Banner™), triadimefon (Bayleton™), fenarimol (Rubigan™)], and to the dicarboximides [iprodione (Chipco 26019™, Rovral™) and vinclolozin (Vorlan™, Curalan™)].

Major occurrences of fungicidal resistance generally do not develop spontaneously. Fungicide resistant biotypes are usually already present in low levels in the existing pathogen population of the turf. Increases in the population density of the resistant strains are brought on by the fungicide program. If the fungicide selection is limited to a material that targets only the sensitive forms, the resistant strains will eventually comprise the bulk of the population, and its disease control effectiveness will be lost. In other words, the use of either the same fungicide for an extended period of time or several fungicides with closely related biochemical modes of action in close

Table 17-8. Relationship between action sites, number of genes involved in the regulation of resistance factors, and potential for the development of resistance to certain turfgrass fungicides.

Fungicide Group	Number of Action Sites	Gene Regulation	Resistance Potential
Benzimidazoles benomyl thiophanate methyl	Single site	Monogenic	Very high
Phenylamides metalaxyl	Single site	Monogenic	Very high
Sterol Biosynthesis Inhibitors triadimefon propiconazole fenarimol	Single site	Polygenic	High
Dicarboximides iprodione vinclozolin	Multisite	Monogenic	Moderate
Phosphonates fosetyl Al	Multisite	Polygenic	Low

sequence with each other is highly conducive to the buildup of resistant strains of the target fungus. Also, the application of a fungicide at less than low label rates will eventually lead to disease control failures. The reason for this is that suboptimal rates permit the increase of a broader range of resistant biotypes than if the full label rate are being used.

Applications of either benomyl, thiophanate-methyl, or thiophanate-ethyl to a stand of turfgrass in which a strain of *Sclerotinia homoeocarpa* resistant to these fungicides is already at a high population level will bring about a significant increase in the incidence and severity of Sclerotinia dollar spot (Table 4-11) (Couch and Smith, 1991b).

The duration of the enhanced level of resistance to the fungicide in question depends on the biological fitness of the resistant strain of the fungus. In order to survive at population levels high enough to incite major outbreaks of disease, resistant strains must be able to compete successfully with the established microbes in the thatch and soil. If the resistant strains are not strong, aggressive competitors, the high population densities required to produce major outbreaks of the disease cannot be sustained. The benzimidazole resistant strains of the Sclerotinia dollar spot fungus (*Sclerotinia homoeocarpa*) are strong competitors with other microbes in the biosphere; therefore, once a high level of resistance to either benomyl or thiophanate methyl becomes established in a stand of turfgrass, it remains constant for several years. On the other hand, the strains of *Sclerotinia homoeocarpa* that are resistant to the sterol biosynthesis inhibitors (SBIs) are not strong competitors with the SBI-sensitive forms, consequently, after an absence of 12 months, propiconazole, triadimefon or fenarimol can usually be included in the Sclerotinia dollar spot control program again.

Tactics for Minimizing the Risk of Development of Fungicidal Resistance

The development of individual cases of fungicidal resistance, particularly with such diseases as Pythium blight and Fusarium patch, can result in extensive damage to a stand of grass before alternative fungicides can be placed into use. For this reason, turfgrass disease control programs should always include tactics for minimizing this risk.

An effective strategy for reducing the likelihood of fungicidal resistance developing is one that rotates among fungicides with different biochemical modes of action and utilizes the available resources to provide maximum disease control at all times. Specifically:

1. The same fungicide should not be used for more than three successive applications before switching to a fungicide with a different mode of action.
2. Fungicides should not be used as single component sprays at less than the manufacturers' low label rates.
3. When possible, use fungicide mixtures that have been shown to be synergistic in the control of the target disease.
4. Tank mixtures of fungicides should not be prepared at less than low label dosage levels unless the combinations have been shown to be synergistic in the control of the target disease.
5. If possible, always apply the fungicides on a preventive disease control schedule rather than relying on curative treatments.
6. The spray should be applied uniformly over the area being treated. Fringes of the spray swaths that do not receive a full dose of the fungicide are ideal locations for buildups in the population of fungicide resistant biotypes.

OPTIMUM FUNGICIDE DILUTION RATES

The optimum dilution level for a turfgrass fungicide is the one at which it gives the highest level of disease control. For the first 70 years of fungicide use on turfgrass, the primary factors in the determination of appropriate dilution levels per 1,000 square feet (93 m^2) of turfgrass were operational expediencies (size of area being sprayed, type of sprayer, time required to complete the operation) and the need to prevent phytotoxicity.

From 1920 through the early 1930s, cadmium and mercury-based fungicides were the mainstay in turfgrass disease control. These materials were highly phytotoxic. However, it was soon learned that they could be used safely at their most effective disease control dosage levels if they were applied in 5–10 gallons of water per 1,000 square feet (21–42 liters/93 m^2). The exact dilution point within this range was determined by the air temperatures at the time of application—the higher the temperature, the more dilute the spray. During these years, then, 5–10 gallons per 1,000 square feet came to be the standard range for fungicide application.

The introduction of the organic fungicide thiram into turfgrass disease control programs in the early 1930s enabled turfgrass management specialists to use more concentrated sprays. Also, users found that

not only was thiram a good fungicide in its own right, but in tank mixes, it served to reduce the phytotoxic potential of mercury fungicides. This meant that it was no longer necessary to compensate for the burning potential of mercuries by the use of extremely high gallonages; therefore, 4 gallons (16.8 liters) of water per 1,000 square feet (93 m^2) became the standard dilution level for applying fungicides to golf greens and tees.

During the 1950s, sprayers with tanks of 100 gallon (420 liters) capacity and less and equipped with broadcast booms came into widespread use. This equipment made high gallonage sprays impractical, so by the end of the decade, application rates of 1 to 2 gallons per 1,000 square feet (4.2–8.4 liters/93 m^2) had become the general dilution rate for fungicides. The advent of acropetal penetrant fungicides in the late 1960s, along with the increasing practice of spraying large acreages (golf course fairways, parks and recreation areas) for disease control, provided the impetus for even further reduction in dilution levels. The standard dilution level for golf greens and tees dropped to ½ to 1 gallon of spray per 1,000 square feet (2.1–4.2 liters/93 m^2). One-quarter gallon of water per 1,000 square feet (1 liter/93 m^2) became a common dilution rate for fungicide application to large acreages.

In recent years, research has been conducted to determine the extent various dilution levels affect the effectiveness of spray formulations of various turfgrass fungicides. In a series of experiments on golf green and fairway-managed grass, chlorothalonil (Daconil 2787™), anilazine (Dyrene™), triadimefon (Bayleton™), iprodione (Chipco 26019™), propiconazole (Banner™), and vinclozolin (Vorlan™, Curalan™) were applied at their low label rates in 0.25, 0.5, 1, 2, 4, 8, 16 and 32 gallons of water per 1,000 square feet of turf. The diseases in these trials included Sclerotinia dollar spot, Rhizoctonia blight, and melting-out of Kentucky bluegrass. Two criteria were used to determine comparative effectiveness of the fungicides at the different dilution levels: (a) the length of time required to establish control, and (b) how long this level of control lasted (Couch, 1985c).

This research has shown that (a) dilution levels can significantly effect the performance of turfgrass fungicides, (b) each turfgrass fungicide has a specific dilution level for optimum performance, (d) the magnitude of dilution determines the initial degree of disease control, and with certain fungicides, it also establishes how long the control will last (Figure 17-1), and (e) where individual fungicides are concerned, some formulations are highly dilution specific, while others are effective over a fairly wide

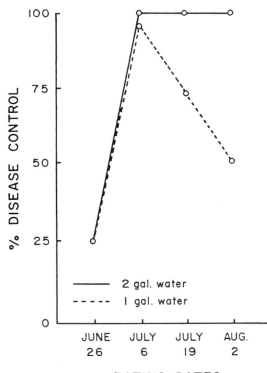

Figure 17-1.   Longevity of control of Sclerotinia dollar spot of creeping bentgrass (*Agrostis palustris*) by triadimefon (Bayleton™) applied in 1 gallon (4.2 liters) of water *vs.* 2 gallons (8.4 liters) of water per 1,000 square feet (93 m²). *After Couch, 1985c.*

Table 17-9.   Optimum dilution levels of certain fungicides used at label dosage rates for the control of turfgrass diseases. *After Couch, 1985c.*

Fungicide	Optimum Dilution per 1000 ft² (93 m²)
Chlorothalonil (Daconil 2787™)	1.0 gal (4.2 L)
Anilazine (Dyrene™)	1.0–2.0 gal (4.2–8.4 L)
Triadimefon (Bayleton™)	2.0 gal (8.4 L)
Iprodione (Chipco 26019™)	0.5–4.0 gal (2.1–8.4 L)
Propiconazole (Banner™)	2.0 gal (8.4 L)
Vinclozolin (Vorlan™, Curalan™)	1.0–2.0 gal (4.2–8.4 L)

range of dilutions. The optimum dilution levels for maximum disease control for the fungicides used in these tests are listed in Table 17-9.

RELATIONSHIP BETWEEN NOZZLE TYPE, PRESSURE AT THE NOZZLE, AND FUNGICIDE EFFECTIVENESS

In turfgrass management, flat fan, whirl chamber, and flooding are the most commonly used nozzle types for broadcast boom and semiboom spraying. Flat fan nozzles (Figure 17-2) produce a fan-like spray pattern. They are particularly well suited for use on broadcast booms. When spaced properly on a boom that is operating at the proper height above the turf, they will provide uniform application over a wide swath. At 40 psi (276 kPa), a Spraying Systems[1] Teejet™ flat fan nozzle using a T-8002 tip, or a Delavan[2] flat fan nozzle fitted with an LF 80-2 tip, will

[1]Spraying Systems Co., North Avenue at Schmale Road, Wheaton, Illinois 60189-7900 U.S.A.
[2]Delavan, Inc., 20 Delavan Drive, Lexington, Tennessee 38351 U.S.A.

deliver 0.2 gallon (0.76 liter) of spray per minute with 16.5 percent of the droplets aerosol size (smaller than 100 microns).

Whirl chamber nozzles contain a secondary chamber through which the spray material flows in a swirling motion. This action absorbs some of the energy in the liquid after it exits from the primary chamber. The spray leaves the secondary chamber at a lower velocity and produces a hollow-cone pattern made up of much larger drops than those emitted by flat fan nozzles. The Delavan Corporation markets two designs of whirl chamber nozzles: RD and RA. The RD Raindrop™ has been designed for spraying by aircraft. This nozzle consists basically of a conventional disc-core hollow-cone nozzle to which a special cap has been added.

The RA Raindrop™ nozzle (Figure 17-3) was developed for use on ground operated sprayers. It uses a right-angle whirl chamber and a Raindrop™ cap. At 40 psi (276 kPa), the Raindrop™ RA-15 nozzle delivers 1.5 gallons (5.7 liters) of spray per minute with only 0.4 percent of the droplets aerosol size This significantly reduces the potential for spray drift. The large orifice in the Raindrop™ nozzle reduces the possibility of plugging. Also with the Raindrop™ nozzle, there is less likelihood that a skip will occur when the boom is suddenly jolted due to the wheels of the sprayer striking small obstacles.

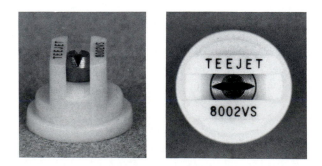

Figure 17-2.   Flat fan T-8002 nozzle tip.

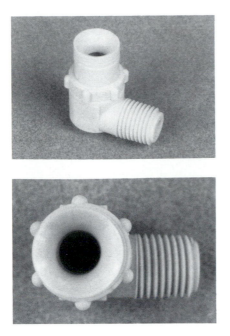

Figure 17-3. Whirl chamber (Raindrop™) RA-15 nozzle.

Flooding nozzles produce a fan-like spray pattern comprised of coarse droplets. They are commonly used to apply fertilizer solutions and preemergence and postemergence herbicides. Some turfgrass management specialists have adopted the practice of using these nozzles in a fan configuration to apply pesticides to large acreages. The Spraying Systems Floodjet™ TK-30 nozzle delivers 6 gallons (25.2 liters) of spray per minute at 40 psi (276 kPa), with 8.5 percent of the droplets aerosol size.

Field tests have compared the relative effectiveness of turfgrass fungicides when applied at different pressures with flat fan, whirl chamber, and flooding nozzles (Couch, 1985c; Couch and Smith, 1987a). The specific nozzle types included in these trials were (a) Spraying Systems TeeJet™ flat fans fitted with T-800050, T-8002, and T-8008 tips, (b) Delavan Raindrop™ RA-6, RA-10, and RA-15, and (c) Spraying Systems FloodJet™ TK-30. The individual pressures at the nozzles for the flat fan nozzles equipped with T-800050, T-8002 and T-8008 tips were 10, 30, 60 and 90 psi (69, 207, 414, 621 kPa). With the Raindrop™ RA-6, RA-10, RA-15 and FloodJet™ TK-30 nozzles, the pressures were 20, 30, 40 and 55 psi (138, 207, 276, 380 kPa). Each nozzle-type/nozzle-pressure combination was used to apply acropetal penetrants [triadimefon (Bayleton™) and fenarimol (Rubigan™)], a localized penetrant [iprodione (Chipco 26019™)], and contact fungicides [anilazine (Dyrene™) and chlorothalonil (Daconil 2787™)]. The diseases included in the experiments were Sclerotinia dollar spot of creeping bentgrass (*Agrostis palustris*) under golf green management, melting-out of Kentucky bluegrass (*Poa pratensis*) maintained at a height of 1.5 inches (3.8 cm), and Rhizoctonia blight of tall fescue (*Festuca arundinacea*) cut at 2.5 inches (6.4 cm).

Fungicides applied with the Spraying Systems TeeJet™ flat fan with a T-8002 tip and the Delavan Raindrop™ RA-10 and RA-15 gave the best levels of disease control. It was also found that in addition to nozzle type, pressure at the nozzle is a major factor in determining fungicide effectiveness. For example, when anilazine (Dyrene™) and iprodione (Chipco 26019™) were applied with flat fan nozzles at 10 psi (69 kPa), they were 50 percent less effective in the control of Sclerotinia dollar spot than when applied at either 30, 60 or 90 psi (207, 414, 621 kPa) (Figures 17-4, 17-5). Also, the longevity of control for anilazine (Dyrene™) applied at the higher nozzle pressure was much greater than the treatments made at 10 psi (69 kPa). For the flat fan nozzle, maximum disease control was obtained when fungicides are applied at 30–60 psi (207–414 kPa) (Figure 17-5). With the Delavan Raindrop™ nozzle, there was a significant drop in disease control when the pressure level drops below 30 psi (207 kPa). The pressure level for maximum disease control with the Raindrop™ RA-10 and RA-15 nozzles is 40 psi (276 kPa).

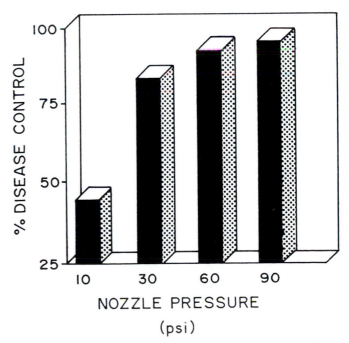

Figure 17-4. Relationship of nozzle pressure to the effectiveness of anilazine (Dyrene™) in the control of Sclerotinia dollar spot of creeping bentgrass (*Agrostis palustris*). *After Couch, 1985c.*

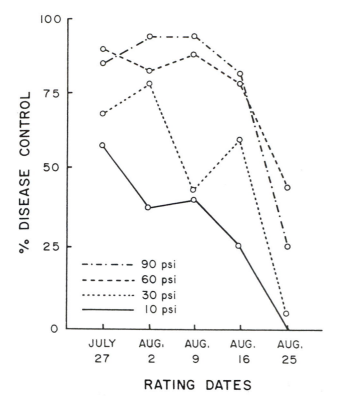

Figure 17-5. Comparative levels of initial control and longevity of control of Sclerotinia dollar spot of creeping bentgrass (*Agrostis palustris*) by anilazine (Dyrene™) as affected by nozzle pressure. (Note: The last day of fungicide application was July 27). *After Couch, 1985c.*

The disease control performance of individual fungicides applied with the FloodJet™ TK-30 was significantly inferior to treatments made with either flat fan or whirl chamber nozzles. For example, the effectiveness of iprodione (Chipco 26019™) was 50 percent less when it was applied with the FloodJet™ TK-30 than when applied with the flat fan nozzle (Figure 17-6).

In summary, the most efficient system for applying spray formulations of turfgrass fungicides is a broadcast boom properly configured with flat fan nozzles (either Spraying Systems T-8002 or T-8004 or Delavan LF 80-2 or LF 80-4 tips), and delivering 30–60 psi (207–414 kPa) at the nozzles, or with Delavan Raindrop™ RA-10 or RA-15 nozzles operating at 40 psi (276 kPa). **Flooding nozzles should not be used to apply fungicides to turfgrass.**

EFFECT OF pH OF THE PREPARATION AND IN-TANK STORAGE TIME ON FUNGICIDE STABILITY

The pH of the spray solution can have a significant effect on the performance of certain pesticides. With the benzimidazole fungicides (Tersan 1991™, Fungo 50™, Cleary 3336™), the parent compound is not toxic to fungi. It is after the spray has been applied to the plants that these materials break down into a fungicidal compound. The process of decomposition to the fungicidal breakdown product is more rapid when the spray preparation is in the acid range.

A pH range of 7.5 to 8.5 is common in untreated water throughout the North American continent. The pH of water treated for urban use is often highly alkaline—ranging between 9.0 and 9.5. The active ingredients of some pesticide formulations undergo hydrolysis to nontoxic compounds when the spray preparation is alkaline. Hydrolysis is an irreversible chemical reaction in which the hydroxyl ions in the water interact with the pesticide in such a manner as to break it down into a nontoxic compound. Even in instances where the active ingredient component of a fungicide formulation is stable under alkaline conditions, there is still the possibility that in this pH range, the character of the formulation may become altered.

Of the various types of pesticides, insecticides are more prone to alkaline hydrolysis than fungicides. Organophosphate, carbamate and synthetic pyrethroid insecticides are particularly sensitive to breakdown when the spray solution is alkaline.

Field research has been conducted to determine the effect of acid and alkaline pH levels and storage time of spray tank preparations on the ability of

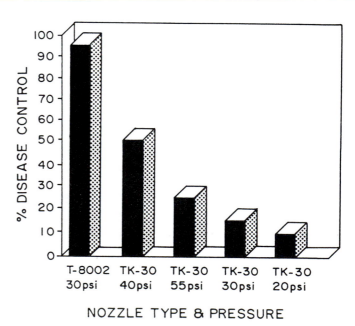

Figure 17-6. Comparative effectiveness of iprodione (Chipco 26019™) in the control of Sclerotinia dollar spot of creeping bentgrass (*Agrostis palustris*) when applied with FloodJet™ TK-30 nozzles vs. flat fan T-8002 tips. *After Couch, 1985c.*

seven standard turfgrass fungicides to control Sclerotinia dollar spot of creeping bentgrass (*Agrostis palustris*) (Couch and Smith, 1987a). In this series of tests, disease control among the various pH treatments was compared on the basis of initial reduction in the incidence of the disease, and how long the control lasted. The fungicides tested in these trials were vinclozolin (Vorlan™, Curalan™), anilazine (Dyrene™), chlorothalonil (Daconil 2787™), iprodione (Chipco 26019™, Rovral™), fenarimol (Rugbigan™), propiconazole (Banner™), and triadimefon (Bayleton™). Additives were used to adjust the individual tank preparations to pH 3.5, 6.5 and 9.5 respectively. A portion of each spray preparation was applied to the turf immediately, and the remainder stored for 20 hours at 71°F (22°C) and then used.

These studies showed the following:

1. The initial preparations of vinclozolin (Vorlan™, Curalan™), iprodione (Chipco 26019™, Rovral™), propiconazole (Banner™), and triadimefon (Bayleton™) are tank stable in the pH 3.5–9.5 range. Also, storage for a period of 24 hours at these pH levels apparently does not alter the disease control effectiveness of these fungicides.
2. Anilazine (Dyrene™) is alkaline sensitive. At pH 9.5, the effectiveness of the initial tank preparation drops rapidly. If the spray preparation is in the acid range (pH 3.5–6.5), and it is used at the time it is made up, there will not be a reduction in disease control potential. However,if the preparation is held for 20 hours before use, a major drop in their disease control effectiveness will occur at both acid and alkaline pH levels (Table 17-10).
3. Chlorothalonil (Daconil 2787™) is not affected by pH if it is used immediately after it is prepared for spraying. If allowed to stand in the spray tank for 20 hours before being used, regardless of the pH of

the preparation, its disease control effectiveness will be significantly reduced (Table 17-11).
4. If fenarimol (Rubigan™) is used at the time it is prepared, its disease control potential will not be affected by pH. Also, spray preparations of this material that are stored for 24 hours at pHs from 6.5 to 9.5 will retain their initial disease control effectiveness. However, if fenarimol is allowed to stand for 24 hours at pH 3.5, it can lose a significant amount of its potential for disease control.

The degree of pH stability of the active ingredient and the formulation as a whole should be known for each pesticide being used in the spray program. A properly ordered pesticide operation is one that includes monitoring the pH levels of the spray preparations. Measuring and keeping a record of the pH should be a standard procedure for every spray preparation. This means that owning a pH meter is not a luxury, it is a necessity if the pesticide spray program is to be carried out properly.

The pH of the water being used to prepare the sprays should be checked on a weekly basis. This information will enable the operator to assess the water's potential for hydrolyzing the various spray materials. The most important pH reading, however, is the one that is made on the pesticide preparation itself. The reason for this is that some formulations of pesticides contain buffering agents that offset the alkalinity that may exist in the water being used to prepare the spray. The decision of whether or not to acidify the preparation, should be made on the pH reading of the final spray mixture, not the pH of the water alone. If it does prove to be necessary to acidify the spray preparation, commercially prepared adjuvants are available for that purpose, and the use of these are to be preferred over muriatic acid.

Table 17-10. Effect of pH and tank storage time on the effectiveness of anilazine (Dyrene™) in the control of Sclerotinia dollar spot of creeping bentgrass (*Agrostis palustris*). *After Couch and Smith, 1987a.*

pH of Spray	Hours Stored in Sprayer	Percent Disease Control[a]
Non-Sprayed Check	—	0 a
6.5	20	35 b
9.5	20	46 bc
3.5	20	65 bcd
9.5	0	73 cd
6.5	0	84 d
3.5	0	84 d

[a]Means followed by the same letter are not significantly different (p = 0.05) from each other according to Duncan's multiple range test.

Table 17-11. Effect of pH and tank storage time on the effectiveness of chlorothalonil (Daconil 2787™) in the control of Sclerotinia dollar spot of creeping bentgrass (*Agrostis palustris*). *After Couch and Smith, 1987a.*

pH of Spray	Hours Stored in Sprayer	Percent Disease Control[a]
Non-Sprayed Check	—	0 a
3.5	20	1 a
6.5	20	1 a
9.5	20	27 a
9.5	0	77 b
3.5	0	84 b
6.5	0	100 b

[a]Means followed by the same letter are not significantly different (p = 0.05) from each other according to Duncan's multiple range test.

GUIDELINES FOR TANK MIXING SPRAY MATERIALS

Time and labor savings are two of the benefits of tank mixing of spray materials; however, there are certain factors that must be considered before making the decision to tank mix two or more pesticides, a pesticide and a fertilizer, or a pesticide and an adjuvant. An **adjuvant** is any substance that is used in combination with a pesticide in order to enhance its effectiveness. Examples of adjuvants are: (a) thickeners to reduce spray drift, (b) wetting agents to improve spreadability on leaf surfaces, (c) colorants to aid in making uniform spray applications (d) spreader-stickers to make the pesticide resistant to being dislodged from the surface of the plant, (e) acidifiers to move the spray mixture out of the alkaline range, and (f) spreader-extenders to increase the longevity of the pesticide.

Determine the Compatibility of the Components of the Mixture

One of the more important points to be established before preparing a spray tank mixture is whether or not the various components of the mixture are compatible. As it refers to pesticide usage, the term **compatible** means the ability of pesticides to be included in a tank mixture without impairment of their toxicity to the target organism, an alteration of their physical properties, or a resulting chemical reaction that produces a new compound that is toxic to the turfgrass. The basic types of incompatibility that apply to pesticides and pesticide combinations are: (a) physical, (b) chemical, (c) phytotoxic, and (d) placement.

Physical incompatibility leads to the production of an unstable mixture. It is commonly seen as excessive foaming, and/or precipitation of a sediment on the bottom of the sprayer tank. The physical compatibility of a pesticide mixture can be determined by the "jar test." Place one pint of water (500 ml) in a quart (1,000 ml) jar. Add each pesticide, or premix of a pesticide in water, one at a time and shake well with each addition. Use each product in the same proportion to carrier as it will be in the actual tank mixture. When all of the materials have been added, invert the jar 10 times, then inspect the mixture immediately and after it has been standing for 30 minutes. If a uniform mix cannot be made, or if nondispersable oil, sludge, or aggregates of solids form, then the components of the mixture are not physically compatible and should not be used as a companion spray.

Chemical incompatibility is a reaction in the tank that leads to the loss of toxicity to the target organism. As has been noted in the section on in-tank stability, some fungicides are unstable in alkaline and/or strongly acidic preparations. Therefore, compounds that cause the final spray preparation to either be alkaline or highly acidic should not be mixed with fungicides. Also, an adjuvant should never be added to a spray tank containing a pesticide until it has been learned from the pesticide's manufacturer that the combination is chemically compatible.

Phytotoxic incompatibility among the components of a tank mixture can stem from an interaction of the active ingredients of the pesticides in the mixture to form a compound that is injurious to the plants. It can also be brought on by the increased concentration of the carriers used in the individual formulations, or by the concurrent use of compounds with closely related biochemical modes of action.

Even when newly innovated pesticide tank mixes are tried on a small scale and no phytotoxicity is observed, one cannot be absolutely certain that injury will not occur at the time the entire area is sprayed. The reason for this is that phytotoxicity is determined by a complex of such interacting factors as (a) air temperature at the time the plants are sprayed, (b) plant genotype (some species and varieties are more prone to injury by certain fungicides than others) (c) the degree of dilution in the water carrier (concentrate sprays of some fungicides are more likely to cause plant injury), (d) level of plant nutrition at the time of application, and (e) the degree of soil moisture stress at the time the material is being used.

Compounds that are highly water soluble should not be tank mixed without label clearance or affirmation from the manufacturers that a phytotoxic interaction will not occur. Spray tank mixtures of emulsifiable concentrates (EC, E) have a heightened potential for phytotoxicity due to an accumulation of the carriers used in their formulation, therefore, either in-tank combinations or close sequential applications of two or more emulsifiable concentrate formulations should be avoided.

Because of certain similarities in biochemical modes of action, quintozene (Terraclor™) and chloroneb (Teremec SP™) have a high potential for phytotoxicity when used as companion treatments. Also, tank mixtures of chloroneb, chlorothalonil (Daconil 2787™) and iprodione (Chipco 26019™) can be phytotoxic to creeping bentgrass (*Agrostis palustris*) at the individual manufacturer's label rates (Couch and Smith, 1989).

The sterol inhibiting turfgrass fungicides, propiconazole (Banner™), triadimefon (Bayletyon™), and fenarimol (Rubigan™), and the turf growth regulators paclobutrazol (Scotts TGR Turf Enhancer™) and flurprimidol (Cutless™) are very closely related chemically. These compounds also have certain biochemical modes of action in common—the fungicides have some growth regulating capacity, and the growth regulators exhibit some fungicidal activity.

Paclobutrazol and flurprimidol are used to reduce frequency of mowing and/or to facilitate the gradual elimination of annual bluegrass (*Poa annua*). However, when they are used in conjunction with a sterol inhibiting fungicide, there can be a very high degree of phytotoxicity to the annual bluegrass in the sward (Tables 17-12, 17-13). At these times, there is no apparent injury to either Kentucky bluegrass (*Poa pratensis*), creeping bentgrass (*Agrostis palustris*), or perennial ryegrass (*Lolium perenne*) (Couch, Keating and Rieley, 1992). If either of these two growth regulators is being used under management conditions that are currently annual bluegrass-dependent, triadimefon, propiconazole, or fenarimol should not be used until 3–4 weeks after the last paclobutrozol or flurprimidol application.

Placement incompatibility occurs when each of the materials in the tank mixture must be placed in different zones to be effective. Examples of placement incompatibility are mixtures of a nematicide

Table 17-13. Phytotoxic interactions of paclobutrazol (Scotts TGR Turf Growth Enhancer™) and triadimefon (Bayleton™) on annual bluegrass (*Poa annua*). *After Couch, Keating and Rieley, 1992.*

Treatment	Rate Formulated Product per 1,000 ft^2 (93 m^2)[a]	Mean Injury Rating[b]
Triadimefon	4 oz (113.6 g)	0.8 a
Triadimefon	8 oz (227.2 g)	1.3 a
Paclobutrazol	0.2 oz (5.68 g)	3.8 b
Paclobutrazol	0.4 oz (11.4 g)	6.0 c
Paclobutrazol + triadimefon	0.2 oz (5.68 g) 8.0 oz (222.7 g)	6.8 cd
Paclobutrazol + triadimefon	0.4 oz (11.4 g) 4.0 oz (113.6 g)	7.3 cd
Paclobutrazol + triadimefon	0.2 oz (5.68 g) 4.0 oz (113.6 g)	8.2 e
Paclobutrazol + triadimefon	0.4 oz (11.4 g) 8.0 oz (227.2 g)	8.2 e

[a]Treatments applied on same day; plots rated for injury two weeks later.
[b]Rated on an injury scale of 1–10. 1–3 = 10–30 percent of annual bluegrass leaves chlorotic, 4–5 = 40–50 percent of annual bluegrass leaves chlorotic, and 6–10 = 60–100 percent of annual bluegrass leaves chlorotic.
[c]Duncan's multiple range groups based on p = 0.05. Means followed by the same letter are not significantly different from each other.

and a foliar fungicide, or a fertilizer and a contact foliar fungicide.

Use the Label-Designated Dosage Level for Each Fungicide in the Mixture

The dosage levels listed on the labels of the various fungicides have been worked out after extensive testing to assure adequate control of diseases over a wide range of levels of disease pressure and minimize the potential for phytotoxicity. These rates apply whether the materials are being used alone or in tank combination with other fungicides. Single component sprays should never be prepared at rates higher or lower than those listed on the label for control of the disease in question. Where multiple component spray preparations for control of more than one disease is concerned, each fungicide in the mixture should always be used at either its low or high label rates.

Unless there is documentation to show that the combination is synergistic, reduced low label rate mixtures of fungicides with different modes of action should never be used in attempts to control a single target disease. Sooner or later, such an approach will result in rapid and destructive outbreaks of the disease. Also, the continual use of suboptimal rates of fungicides can bring about the development of fungicide resistance. Therefore, it is extremely important

Table 17-12. Phytotoxic interactions of paclobutrazol (Scotts TGR Turf Growth Enhancer™) and propiconazole (Banner™) on annual bluegrass (*Poa annua*). *After Couch, Keating and Rieley, 1992.*

Treatment	Rate Formulated Product per 1,000 ft^2 (93 m^2)[a]	Mean Injury Rating[b]
Propiconazole	4 oz (113.6 g)	0.3 a
Propiconazole	8 oz (227.2 g)	0.5 a
Paclobutrazol + propiconazole	0.2 oz (5.68 g) 4.0 oz (113.6 g)	2.8 b
Paclobutrazol	0.2 oz (5.68 g)	3.8 b
Paclobutrazol	0.4 oz (11.4 g)	6.0 c
Paclobutrazol + propiconazole	0.4 oz (11.4 g) 4.0 oz (113.6 g)	7.3 d
Paclobutrazol + propiconazole	0.2 oz (5.68 g) 8.0 oz (227.2 g)	7.5 d
Paclobutrazol + propixonazole	0.4 oz (11.4 g) 8.0 oz (227.2 g)	8.0 d

[a]Treatment applied on same day; plots rated for injury two weeks later.
[b]Rated on an injury scale of 1–10. 1–3 = 10–30 percent of annual bluegrass leaves chlorotic, 4–5 = 40–50 percent of annual bluegrass leaves chlorotic, and 6–10 = 60–100 percent of annual bluegrass leaves chlorotic.
[c]Duncan's multiple range groups based on p = 0.05. Means followed by the same letter are not significantly different from each other.

to adhere exactly to the manufacturer's label dosage rates for each entry.

Make Certain that Spray Tank Agitation of the Mixture is Adequate

Thorough and continuous agitation of the tank preparation is essential. When mixing the materials in the sprayer, put two-thirds of the water in the tank first and then add each component one at a time and allow it to become thoroughly dispersed throughout the tank before adding the next item. Then finish filling the tank with water. All of the preparation should be used as soon as possible. This will reduce the likelihood of hydrolysis of the active ingredients, and also prevent possible separation, precipitation, or caking in the tank.

Spray tank preparations should undergo continual mixing. Keep agitation going at all times—on the way to the application site, during application and during stops for any reason. If it becomes necessary to halt the spraying operation for a period of time, the agitation system on the sprayer should be kept running.

EFFECT OF POSTSPRAY RAINFALL OR SPRINKLER IRRIGATION ON FUNGICIDE EFFECTIVENESS

The effective use of fungicides requires an understanding of their degree of vulnerability to being dislodged from the leaves by either rainfall or sprinkler irrigation. Modern foliar fungicide formulations usually contain one or more adjuvants. Both the numbers and types of adjuvants included in a given formulation will vary among the different classes of pesticides and their intended use patterns. However, the two adjuvants that are common to practically all spray formulations of turfgrass fungicides are wetting agents and stickers.

Turfgrass fungicides are often applied during periods of frequent rain showers. As a result, rain may occur shortly after the spraying operation has been completed. When this happens, the question arises as to whether a significant amount of the material has been washed off the plant surface. An on-the-spot decision must be made to either make an immediate second application or to delay further spraying until the next scheduled date.

The practice of spraying large areas such as golf fairways and sports fields raises an additional question regarding the effectiveness of sticking agents.

When applying fungicides to a large acreage, being able to use concentrated sprays in order to reduce the total amount of water needed to complete the operation has an obvious advantage. The question that is common to this type of operation is: Can the area be sprayed with a fungicide on a low volume basis, then as soon as the operation has been completed, turn on the irrigation system and complete the process of distributing the material over the entire plant surface?

Field research has been conducted to compare the levels of disease control provided by contact and penetrant fungicides when (a) rain occurs or irrigation is carried out before the spray dries on the leaves, (b) leaf washing occurs as the result of rainfall or overhead irrigation immediately after the spray dries, and (c) watering is withheld or rain does not develop until three days after the spray operation is completed. The fungicides included in this test were anilazine (Dyrene™), iprodione (Chipco 26019™), chlorothalonil (Daconil 2787™), fenarimol (Rubigan™), and triadimefon (Bayleton™) (Couch, 1985c). This study showed that the following:

1. If it rains or the sprinkler system is turned on in a treated area before the spray dries on the leaves, there will be a significant drop in the disease control effectiveness of contact and localized penetrant fungicides.
2. If the fungicide formulation contains an effective sticking agent, rainfall or sprinkler irrigation immediately after the spray dries on the leaves will not appreciably reduce the material's initial disease control effectiveness.
3. Acropetal penetrant and systemic penetrant fungicides are not as vulnerable as contact and localized penetrant fungicides to reduction in disease control effectiveness by rainfall or watering before the spray dries on the leaves. However, there can be a significant difference among these types of fungicides with respect to the degree of reduction of disease control efficiency by leaf washing before the spray dries. In the case of fenarimol, leaf washing before the spray dries significantly reduces both its initial control effectiveness and its longevity of control. With triadimefon, rainfall or sprinkler irrigation before the spray dries on the leaves does not significantly lower its initial disease control effectiveness nor does it reduce its longevity of control.

In conclusion, the basic effectiveness of a turfgrass fungicide in the control of foliar diseases is established by the initial amount of water used in its spray application. This principle has important implications in evaluating the merits of the practice of spraying large acreage with a low initial volume of a penetrant fungicide, and then after the operation is completed, turning on the irrigation system in an effort to obtain better distribution of the fungicide over the plant surface. If the formulation contains an effective sticking agent, then the moment the leaves dry, a significant amount of the fungicide cannot be dislodged by sprinkler irrigation and thus washed to the lower portions of the plants.

This means that if the sprinkler system is turned on before the spray dries on the leaves, the effectiveness of the penetrant fungicide will not be improved. In fact, in some cases, it may even be reduced. It also means that if sprinkler irrigation is employed after the spray has dried on the leaves, although the effectiveness of the penetrant fungicide will not be reduced, neither will it be improved.

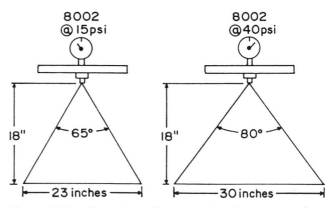

Figure 17-7. Illustration of how lowering the pressure from 40 to 15 psi (276 to 103 kPa) results in a smaller spray angle and a significant reduction in spray coverage of an 8002 flat fan spray tip. *Courtesy Spraying Systems Co., Wheaton, Illinois.*

PROCEDURES FOR MAKING ACCURATE AND UNIFORM FUNGICIDE APPLICATIONS

It has been estimated that throughout the United States, the extent of individual pesticide application errors average 25–35 percent. This means that because of either (a) inadequate sprayer calibration, (b) failure to cover the target area uniformly, or (c) improper spray tank preparations, over a billion dollars in labor and product cost is wasted annually. It is essential, then, that primary attention be given to calibration and maintenance of the spray equipment and to the development of accurate spraying procedures.

Configuration of the Broadcast Boom

Flat fan nozzles should be spaced on the boom to provide a 30–50 percent overlap of the spray pattern. In order to accomplish this, 80 degree flat fan nozzles should be spaced 20 inches (51 cm) apart on the boom, and should be operated 17 to 19 inches (43–48 cm) above the ground. When using flat fan nozzles with a spray angle other than 80 degrees, the manufacturer's specifications should be checked for proper spacing on the boom and the appropriate boom height. Depending on the nozzle size and type, the operating pressure can have a significant effect on spray angle and spray distribution. Lowering the pressure results in a smaller spray angle and a significant reduction in spray coverage (Figure 17-7). The viscosity of the spray preparation will also affect spray angle, the greater the viscosity of the liquid, as

created by more concentrate sprays, the smaller the spray angle.

For proper coverage, Raindrop™ nozzles should be tilted on the boom so that they are at a 45 degree angle to the turf surface. Their spacing on the boom should provide a 100 percent overlap of the spray pattern. This means that when RA-10 and RA-15 nozzles are spaced 30 inches (76 cm) apart on the boom, they should be operated 18 inches (46 cm) above the ground. If they are spaced 20 inches (51 cm) apart on the boom, they should be operated 12 inches (31 cm) above the ground.

Calibrating Sprayer Output

Before beginning the calibration operation, the sprayer should be rinsed with clean water. The nozzles should then be removed and cleaned. An old toothbrush, toothpick, or wood match is useful for cleaning nozzles and screens. Do not use a pocket knife or wire for cleaning. After this, start the sprayer and flush the system with clean water, then replace the nozzles.

Since pressure at the nozzle determines both the rate of delivery and the uniformity of spray distribution, it is extremely important to determine that pressure at the nozzles is identical across the entire width of the boom. Three pressure gauges should be mounted directly on the boom, one near each end and one in the center. Boom height should be measured to assure correct positioning above the ground and levelness across the boom. The sprayer pressure regulator should then be adjusted for pressure at the nozzles of 30–60 psi for flat fan nozzles and 40–60 psi for whirl chamber nozzles. Nozzles should be checked for individual flow rates across the entire boom.

The actual delivery rate of a sprayer per unit area of turfgrass surface is the product of nozzle pressure, nozzle size, and speed of the sprayer. Procedures for calibrating a power sprayer to deliver the desired amount of pesticide per 1,000 square feet of turfgrass are outlined in the catalogs of the major manufacturers of spray nozzles. These procedures call for measuring the output of one or more nozzles within the length of time required for the sprayer to move a predetermined distance, and then working this information through a mathematical formula.

Checking the Spray Pattern Provided by the Boom

It is very important that the boom's nozzle configuration provide a uniform distribution of spray across the entire width of the boom. The degree of uniformity of spray output within the boom's area of coverage cannot be determined by the flow-rate sampling procedures described above. Its measurement is best accomplished by the use of a special spray pattern analyzing pan of the type manufactured by Accu Tech Associates, 34290 East Frontage Road, Bozeman, Montana 59715. This pan is one component of a total spray analysis system known as Spray Chek™. It splits the spray into 2 inch (5 cm) increments across the width of the spray boom. The collections in the individual troughs flow into containers equipped with floats. When the collecting tray is set upright, the position of the float in each container provides an accurate assessment of how uniformly the material is being applied to the target area.

In addition to the collection tray for analyzing the actual deposition pattern of each nozzle within the boom, the Spray Chek™ system has a user friendly computer software program. Using such information as application rates, set-up details and sprayer performance data (e.g., nozzle spacing, nozzle pressure, nozzle flow rate, and desired delivery rate per unit area of turfgrass surface), the Spray Chek™ computer program analyzes the sprayer's actual performance and then compares it with what it should be. At this point, the sprayer speed needed to apply the material at the proper rate is also computed. Also, the software for the Spray Chek™ system can calculate the cost of a specific pesticide treatment when applied according to the procedures it has prescribed versus what it would have cost if the corrections had not been made.

Making Uniform Applications

Effective disease control requires avoiding skips and major overlaps in the spraying pattern. Regardless of how much time and effort have gone into planning and preparation, if the spray is not applied uniformly to the target area, more harm than good can result. Skips leave areas for disease to develop, while excessive overlaps are costly and can result in injury to the grass.

One system of identifying the outer border of the treated area during spray application is the use of a boom-mounted unit that deposits small areas of white foam at spaced intervals. Certain pesticides may become phytotoxic when sprayed onto foam marking deposits. Before being placed into general use, the potential for this occurrence should be determined by on-site tests in which the foam deposits are oversprayed with each of the materials being used in the pesticide program.

Another approach to assuring the uniformity of applications is the addition of a polymeric, nonstaining colorant to the spray preparation. Once the spraying equipment has been correctly set up and calibrated, a colorant helps the operator (a) maintain the proper amount of spray overlap between swaths, and (b) detect plugged nozzles or any other output irregularities across the boom that may occur during the spraying operation. When selecting a spray pattern indicator, one should verify that it is easy to use and clean up, compatible with the other components of the tank mixture, and safe for the spray operator and the environment.

USE OF GRANULAR FUNGICIDE FORMULATIONS

Granular formulations of turfgrass fungicides have the advantage of not needing on-site mixing with a diluent-carrier. Also, the equipment required for their application is both lighter and less expensive to purchase and maintain than that which is used for spray formulations. An additional consideration in deciding whether to use granular formulations as primary or secondary components of a turfgrass disease control program is their comparative effectiveness with spray formulations.

Field studies have been conducted at Virginia Tech with granular and spray formulations of the same active ingredients to determine (a) the amount of active ingredient required by each formulation type to provide the same level of disease control, (b) the comparative length of time granular and spray formulations take to bring the target disease under control, (c) how long the control lasts for each formulation type after applications have ceased, and (d) the effects of leaf wetness at the time of application, and mowing and/or irrigation soon after application, on the effectiveness of granular formulations. A total of nine contact, localized penetrant, and acropetal penetrant fungicides were tested, including selections from five different granular product lines (Table 17-14). The target diseases were Helminthosporium leaf spot of Kentucky bluegrass (*Poa pratensis*), Sclerotinia dollar spot of creeping bentgrass (*Agrostis palustris*), and Rhizoctonia blight of tall fescue (*Festuca arundinaecea*) (Couch, Garber and Jones, 1984).

These studies have shown that in the control of spring and summer foliar diseases of turfgrasses:

1. Acropetal penetrants have greater potential for use as granular formulations than either contact or localized penetrant fungicides.
2. Granular formulations of contact and localized penetrant fungicides require 2–3 times the active ingredient level of spray formulations to produce the same degree of disease control.
3. Granular formulations of contact and localized penetrant fungicides require a longer time to bring the target diseases under control, and they hold their established levels of control for a

shorter period than the same active ingredients as spray formulations.
4. There can be a significant difference in efficacy of disease control among various granular fungicide product lines of the same active ingredient.
5. Application of granular fungicides to wet leaves improves their disease control effectiveness.
6. Watering or rainfall immediately after the application of granular fungicides reduces their effectiveness in disease control. The extent of this reduction can vary among the various granular product lines.
7. Mowing and collecting the clippings immediately after the application of granular fungicides reduces their effectiveness in disease control. The extent of this reduction can vary extensively among the various granular product lines.

The first four principles are illustrated in the Sclerotinia dollar spot test results shown in Table 17-15.

For maximum effectiveness in the control of spring and summer foliar diseases with granular fungicides, (a) the turf should be mowed and watered if needed the day before application, (b) the fungicide

Table 17-14. Spray and granular formulations of the various fungicides used in the Virginia Tech comparative efficacy studies. *After Couch, Garber and Jones, 1984.*

Fungicide	Trade Names of Spray Formulations	Trade Names of Granular Formulations
Anilazine	Dyrene (Miles Corp.)	Proturf Fungicide III (O. M. Scott & Sons) Lawn Fungicide (Lofts Inc.) Professional Lawn Disease Control (Rockland Chem. Co.)
Benomyl	Tersan 1991 (DuPont)	Benomyl Turf Fungicide (Rockland Chem. Co.)
Chlorothalonil	Daconil 2787 (SDS Biotech)	Proturf 101-V Broad Spectrum Fungicide (O. M. Scott & Sons) Lawn Fungicide 2787 (Rockland Chem. Co.) Green Gold Turf Fungicide (Lebanon Chem. Co.)
Iprodione	Chipco 26019 (Rhone-Poulenc)	Proturf Fungicide VI (O. M. Scott & Sons)
Quintozene	Terraclor (Olin Corp.)	Lawn Disease Preventer (O. M. Scott & Sons) Turfcide (Olin Corp.)
Phenyl Mercury Acetate + Thiram	PMAS (Cleary Corp.) + Tersan 75 (DuPont)	Broad Spectrum Fungicide (O. M. Scott & Sons)
Thiophanate methyl	Fungo 50 (Grace Sierra Corp.)	Proturf Systemic Fungicide (O. M. Scott & Sons)
Triadimefon	Bayleton (Miles Corp.)	Proturf Fungicide 7 (O. M. Scott & Sons)

Table 17-15. Relative effectiveness of granular and spray formulation of chlorothalonil, iprodione, and triadimefon in the control of Sclerotinia dollar spot of 'Penncross' creeping bentgrass (*Agrostis palustris*). After Couch, Garber and Jones, 1984.

Fungicide[a]	Total Active Ingredient per 1,000 ft^2 (93 m^2)	Percent Disease Control[b]
Non-treated control	—	0 a
Chlorothalonil		
Daconil 2787 WP (S)	3.0 oz (84.9 g)	86 def
Proturf 101-V (G)	12.0 oz (339.6 g)	86 def
Lebanon Green Gold (G)	12.0 oz (339.6 g)	71 de
Rockland Lawn Fungicide (G)	12.0 oz (339.6 g)	47 cd
Lebanon Green Gold (G)	4.5 oz (127.4 g)	28 bc
Rockland Lawn Fungicide	4.5 oz (127.4 g)	18 ab
Proturf 101-V (G)	4.5 oz (127.4 g)	14 ab
Iprodione		
Chipco 26019 WP (S)	1.0 oz (28.3 g)	100 g
Proturf Fungicide VI (G)	2.0 oz (56.6 g)	100 g
Proturf Fungicide VI (G)	1.0 oz (28.3 g)	73 de
Triadimefon		
Bayleton WP (S)	0.5 oz (14.2 g)	95 g
Proturf Fungicide 7 (G)	0.5 oz (14.2 g)	100 g
Proturf Fungicide 7 (G)	1.0 oz (28.3 g)	100 g

[a](S) = spray application, (G) = granular application
[b]Means followed by the same letter are not significantly different (p = 0.05) from each other according to Duncan's multiple range test.

should be applied during the morning hours while the leaves are still wet from dew and guttation fluids, and (c) watering and mowing operations should then be postponed for as long as possible.

NONTARGET EFFECTS OF FUNGICIDES ON TURFGRASSES

The primary objective of field research with turfgrass fungicides is to identify both beneficial and detrimental effects on the total economy of the plants and exploit the one and minimize the other. In addition to data on effectiveness in the control of target diseases, these investigations provide information on such matters as the impact of fungicides on the severity of nontarget diseases, the potential of fungicides for enhancing disease resurgence, desirable and nondesirable hormonal effects fungicides may have on the treated plants, and impact of fungicides on nitrification and the formation of root mycorrhiza.

Increase in Severity of Nontarget Diseases

It has been shown that certain fungicides can bring about an increase in the severity of nontarget diseases. Late fall treatments of creeping bentgrass (*Agrostis palustris*) with chloroneb (Teremec SP™)

for control of Fusarium patch can foster an increase in the development of Rhizoctonia yellow patch (Smiley, 1981). Triadimefon (Bayleton™) can increase the severity of melting-out of Kentucky bluegrass (Dernoeden and McIntosh, 1991).

Outbreaks of Corticium red thread are more severe on perennial ryegrass (*Lolium perenne*) that has been treated continuously with benomyl (Tersan 1991™) (Dernoeden, O'Neill and J. J. Murray, 1985). The susceptibility of Kentucky bluegrass (*Poa pratensis*) to Helminthosporium leaf spot is greater in benomyl-treated turf (Jackson, 1970). Benomyl increases the severity of melting-out of Kentucky bluegrass (Dernoeden and McIntosh, 1991). The susceptibility of creeping bentgrass (*Agrostis palustris*) to the Pythium blight pathogen, *Pythium aphanidermatum*, is greater after treatments with benomyl (Warren, Sanders and Cole 1976). The incidence of rust (incited by *Puccinia coronata*) on 'Manhattan' perennial ryegrass (*Lolium perenne*) increases after applications of thiophanate methyl (Fungo 50™, Cleary 3336™) (Joyner and Couch, 1976).

Impact of Growth Regulators and Herbicides on Disease Development

Growth regulators can impact on disease development by restricting the plant's capacity to recover quickly from colonization by a pathogenic fungus.

For example, the application of plant growth retardants to turf can result in a significant increase in the severity of Corticium red thread (Chastagner and Vassey, 1979).

Herbicides have also been shown to affect the development of certain turfgrass diseases. Bensulide (Betasan™) and benefin (Balan™) increase the severity of Rhizoctonia blight and Sclerotinia dollar spot on bermudagrass (*Cynodon dactylon*) and Pythium blight (incited by *Pythium aphanidermatum*) on perennial ryegrass (*Lolium perenne*), but have no effect on Pythium blight on bermudagrass (Karr, Gudauskas and Dickens, 1979). Pythium blight is also unaffected by applications of DMPA (Zytron™) to turfgrass (Anderson, 1978).

Stripe smut of Kentucky bluegrass (*Poa pratensis*) is increased by applications of PCDP (Bandane™), calcium arsenate (Chipcal™), and linuron (Lorox™) (Altman and Campbell, 1977). The incidence and severity of Helminthosporium leaf spot of Kentucky bluegrass (*Poa pratensis*) is increased by applications of the chlorophenoxy herbicides 2,4-D, 2,4,5-T, MCPP (mecoprop), and dicamba (Banvel™), and decreased by 2,4,5-TP (silvex) (Hodges, 1980). The enhancement of Helminthosporium leaf spot by these materials is thought to be due to an acceleration of the rate of leaf senescence by the herbicides, thereby making the tissue more vulnerable to the pathogenic activities of the incitant (Madsen and Hodges, 1984).

Field tests with DCPA (Dacthal™), oxadiazon (Ronstar™), benefin (Balan™), bensulide (Betasan™), and napropamide (Devrinol™) have shown that these herbicides do not alter the severity of melting-out of Kentucky bluegrass (*Poa pratensis*). Treatments with DSMA (Methar™) significantly decrease the incidence of Sclerotinia dollar spot on creeping bentgrass (*Agrostis palustris*), whereas bensulide, siduron (Tupersan™), DCPA, and mixtures 2,4-D plus dicamba (Banvel™) and 2,4,5-T plus dicamba have no effect on the development of the disease (Couch and Garber, 1984).

Fungicide-Enhanced Disease Resurgence

Some diseases may return with increased severity in turf that has been previously treated with fungicides. This phenomenon is called **fungicide-enhanced disease resurgence**. Discontinuation of fungicide applications can ultimately bring about an increase in the development of Sclerotinia dollar spot. In field studies, 30 days after the last fungicide applications the incidence of Sclerotinia dollar spot in plots treated with either chlorothalonil (Daconil 2787™) or anilazine (Dyrene™) had increased to a level 2–3

times greater than that of the nontreated controls (Couch, Garber and Smith, 1981) (Table 17-16).

The reoccurrence of Rhizoctonia blight can be more severe on turf that has been treated with fungicides than in adjacent areas in which fungicides have not been applied. It has been observed that in late summer or early fall, when night temperatures begin to drop and the use of fungicides is diminished, a sudden return to warm nights can provide conditions for a greater buildup of the disease in turf which has been treated with fungicides (Dernoeden, 1992).

Hormonal Effects of Fungicides

Triazoles (Bayleton™, Banner™) and the benzimidazoles (Tersan 1991™, Fungo 50™, Cleary 3336™) have a cytokinin-like effect on plants (Dimond and Rich, 1977). Turfgrass treated with these materials tends to be darker green and the rate of leaf senescence of the younger leaves is delayed. Anilazine (Dyrene™) also increases the chlorophyll content of turfgrass plants. These increases in leaf chlorophyll could be due either to a stabilizing effect of the fungicide on the integrity of the chloroplast or an increased synthesis of chlorophyll. In addition to their antisenescent activity, triazoles (Banner™, Bayleton™) are also known to reduce water transpiration rates, which in turn lowers the wilting potential of the plants (Fletcher and Nath, 1984).

Impact of Fungicides on Carbohydrate Content and Accumulation of Nutrient Elements in the Leaves

Applications of anilazine (Dyrene™) can bring about a significant reduction in the carbohydrate content of creeping bentgrass (*Agrostis palustris*) leaves (Mazur and Hughes, 1976). Benomyl (Tersan 1991™) has been shown to increase the dry foliar weights of both Kentucky bluegrass (*Poa pratensis*) and creeping bentgrass (*Agrostis palustris*). Also, benomyl soil amendments can cause an increase in potassium and a decrease in phosphorous, calcium, magnesium, manganese, copper, boron, and sodium contents of creeping bentgrass leaves (Warren, Cole and Duich, 1974).

Effect of Fungicides on the Growth of Algae

Either chlorothalonil or mancozeb applied in a preventive program will restrict the development of blue green filamentous algae during prolonged wet periods.

Table 17-16. Impact of interruption of fungicide program on the incidence of Sclerotinia dollar spot of 'Penneagle' creeping bentgrass (*Agrostis palustris*). *After Couch, Garber and Smith, 1981.*

Fungicide[a]	Total Active Ingredient per 1,000 ft² (93 m²)	Disease Incidence[b,c] July 19	August 2	August 17
Non-treated control	—	61.7 a	53.3 a	15.0 b
Anilazine	2.0 oz (56.7 g)	13.3 b	50.0 a	31.7 a
Chlorothalonil	2.5 oz (71.9 g)	10.0 b	55.0 a	35.0 a
Iprodione	1.0 oz (28.4 g)	0.0 b	12.0 b	10.0 b
Triadimefon	0.25 oz (7.1 g)	0.0 b	0.0 b	1.7 b

[a]For a listing of representative trade names of each fungicide, see Appendix Table I.
[b]Last fungicide application date, July 14.
[c]Disease incidence based on percent blighted foliage per plot. Duncan's multiple range groups based on p = 0.05. Means followed by the same letter are not significantly different from each other.

Impact of Fungicides on Earthworm Populations

Benomyl and thiophanate methyl have been shown to be toxic to surface-feeding earthworms. The toxicity of these fungicides to earthworms is probably related to their anti-cholinesterase activity (Stringer and Wright, 1973; Wright and Stringer, 1973).

Effect of Fungicides on the Microbial Population of the Soil

The impact of fungicides on soil inhabiting microbes is variable. The results of a study on creeping bentgrass (*Agrostis palustris*) turf that had been treated four and five consecutive years with either anilazine (Dyrene™), mancozeb (Fore™), mixtures of mercurous and mercuric chlorides (Caloclor™), phenyl mercuric acetate (PMA™) and thiram (Tersan 75™), semesan and thiram (Tersan OM™), and cycloheximide (Actidione™) and thiram showed that there were no significant differences in the overall distribution of 23 genera of fungi in the soil of the treated and nontreated plots (Meyer *et al.*, 1971). On the other hand, repeated applications of benomyl (Tersan 1991™) have been found to affect the total numbers of bacteria and actinomycetes and may cause a shift in the makeup of genera of soil-inhabiting bacteria (van Faassen, 1974).

The most significant effect of fungicides used in turfgrass management on soil-inhabiting microbes appears to be on the growth and development of the fungi involved in the formation of mycorrhiza and the species of bacteria that affect nitrification.

Mycorrhiza is the symbiotic association of the mycelium of a highly specialized soil-borne fungus with the roots of plants. There are two basic types of mycorrhiza: ectomycorrhiza and endomycorrhiza. With ectomycorrhiza, most of the fungus body remains closely affixed to the root surface, producing distinctive clusters of short, thickened rootlets. Ectomycorrhiza occurs only in conifers and hardwoods. Endomycorrhiza develop on the roots of herbaceous plants, including turfgrasses. In contrast with ectomycorrhiza, endomycorrhiza do not alter the overall appearance of the roots. Endomycorrhizal fungi penetrate the root surface and colonize the underlying tissue. Throughout the colonization process an intricate balance in maintained between the activities of the invading fungus and the metabolic responses of the host. This leads to an accumulation of soluble carbohydrates in the root tissue which serve as a nutritional base for the fungus and the production of one or more metabolites which promote the growth of the plant. Turfgrasses with mycorrhiza develop more extensive root systems and the overall growth pattern of the plants is more vigorous.

Metalaxyl (Subdue™) does not appear to be detrimental to the development of mycorrhiza; however it has been shown that applications of label use rates of benomyl (Tersan 1991™), chlorothalonil (Daconil 2787™), quintozene (Turfcide™), triadimefon (Bayleton™), anailazine (Dyrene™), maneb (Dithane M-22™), chloroneb (Teremec SP™), and iprodione (Chipco 26019™, Rovral™) can significantly reduce the formation of mycorrhiza on creeping bentgrass (*Agrostis palustris*). The greatest impact of fungicides on restricting the development of mycorrhiza occurs in the spring while new roots are forming (Rhodes and Larsen, 1981).

Nitrification is the mechanism of converting ammonium ions via nitrite into nitrate ions which are readily utilized by green plants. The oxidation of ammonium ions is catalyzed by physiologically similar groups of bacteria belonging to the family *Nitrobacteraceae*. Species of *Nitrosomonas* oxidize ammonium ions into nitrite ions and then *Nitrobacter* species oxidize nitrite to nitrate.

Anilazine (Dyrene™), benomyl (Tersan 1991™), ethazole (Koban™), maneb (Dithane M-22™), quintozene (Turfcide™), and thiram (Spotrete™) can inhibit nitrification for several weeks to several months (Wainwright and Pugh, 1974; Dubey and Rodriguez-Kabana, 1970; Foster and McQueen, 1977; Mazur and Hughes, 1974). The activity of nitrifiers can be checked for several weeks to several months, depending on the fungicides used, dosages, and soil properties. When this happens, ammonia-nitrogen that has been added as an inorganic fertilizer will remain in the reduced form. For this reason, when ammonium sulfate is used as a nitrogen source, the nitrogen component of the fertilizer program should also include fertilizer that contains nitrate ions (Mazur and Hughes, 1976).

Relationship Between Fungicide Usage and Thatch Accumulation. Thatch accumulates in turfgrass when the annual production rate of senescent tissue exceeds the rate of decomposition. The rates at which these processes occur are affected by rate of plant growth, weather conditions, and microbial activity in the thatch. In a study on the relationship between fungicide usage and thatch formation, benomyl (Tersan 1991™), iprodione (Chipco 26019™), and mancozeb (Dithane M-45™, Manzate 200™) were found to be thatch-inducing in creeping bentgrass (*Agrostis palustris*), while anilazine (Dyrene™), chlorothalonil (Daconil 2787™), ethazol (Koban™), thiram (Tersan 75™), and quintozene (Terraclor™) had no effect on thatch accumulation. Comparisons of decomposition rates with thatch from plots treated with thatch-inducing fungicides showed no differences from those of nontreated controls. Based on this data and observations on the dynamics of plant growth in the treated and nontreated areas, it was concluded that the impact of these fungicides on the accumulation of thatch came from an increased rate of root and rhizome production in the surface 1.5 inches (4.5 cm) of the soil rather than reduction in the microbial population of the thatch itself (Smiley, 1981; Smiley *et al.*, 1985).

§ § §

Appendixes

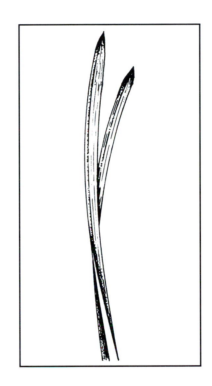

Table I. Profiles of Basic Fungicides and Nematicides Used for Control of Turfgrass Diseases

The following listing of fungicides and nematicides is arranged alphabetically according to the common (coined) name of each. The trade names included in each section have been selected only for the purpose of illustration. No discrimination is intended when the same chemical is marketed under other trade names, nor is endorsement by the author of the products bearing these names implied.

Trade Name	Dyrene™
Chemical Name	4,6-dichloro-N-(2-chlorophenyl)-1,3,5 triazine-2-amine
Group	Triazines
Manufacturer	Miles, Inc. Agriculture Division P.O. Box 4913 Kansas City, Missouri 64120 Telephone: (800) 842-8020
Formulations	50 WP, 4 F
Labeled for Control of	Sclerotinia dollar spot, Helminthosporium leaf spot, melting-out, Rhizoctonia blight, rust, Typhula blight, copper spot
Optimum Dilution Level	1–2 gallons (4.2–8.4 liters) of water per 1,000 ft^2 (93 m^2)
Optimum Nozzle Types and Sizes	Flat fan TeeJet™ (UniJet™) T-8002, T-8004, Delavan LF-2, LF-4, or Delavan Raindrop™ RA-10, RA-15
Optimum Pressure at the Nozzle	For nozzles listed above, 30–60 psi (207–414 kPa) for flat fan type and 40–60 psi (276–414 kPa) for Raindrop™
Resistance to Leaf Washing	Highly resistant to leaf washing after spray dries. Highly susceptible to leaf washing before spray dries.
In-Tank Stability	Unstable in both alkaline and acid pH ranges if stored in tank for 20 hours or more. Stable in alkaline pH ranges if sprayed immediately after preparation.
Toxicity	**Oral**: (rat) = 5,000 mg/kg **Dermal**: (rabbit) = >5,000 mg/kg **Inhalation**: (rat) = 2.764 mg/L air—4 hr **Signal word**: Danger
Modes of Action	**Topical**—Contact **Biochemical**—Ultimate sites of action of anilazine are not known. However, the material reacts quickly with amino groups and to some extent with thiols. It is likely, then, that it brings about the inhibition of a variety of cell processes by nonspecific combination with essential cell components.
Comments	Anilazine functions synergistically with propiconazole in the control of Sclerotinia dollar spot.

BENOMYL

Trade Name	Tersan 1991™
Chemical Name	methyl 1-(butylcarbamoyl)-2-benzimidazole-carbamate
Group	Benzimidazoles
Manufacturer	E. I. DuPont Co. Agricultural Products Walker's Mill, Barley Mill Plaza Wilmington, Delaware 19897 Telephone: (800) 759-2500

Formulation	50 DF
Labeled for Control of	Stripe smut, Fusarium patch, Sclerotinia dollar spot, Rhizoctonia blight, Fusarium blight
Optimum Dilution Level	No information, assume 2–3 gallons (8.2–12.6 liters) of water per 1,000 ft^2 (93 m^2)
Optimum Nozzle Types and Sizes	Flat fan TeeJet™ (UniJet™) T-8002, T-8004, Delavan LF-2, LF-4, or Delavan Raindrop™ RA-10, RA-15
Optimum Pressure at the Nozzle	For nozzles listed above, 30–60 psi (207–414 kPa) for flat fan type and 40–60 psi (276–414 kPa) for Raindrop™
Resistance to Leaf Washing	No information.
In-Tank Stability	No information.
Toxicity	**Oral**: (rat) = >10,000 mg/kg **Dermal**: (rabbit) = >10,000 mg/kg **Inhalation**: (rat) = >2 mg/L air—4 hr **Signal word**: Caution
Modes of Action	**Topical**—Acropetal penetrant **Biochemical**—Interferes with nuclear division (mitosis). Binds to protein, tubulin, which is a component of spindle fibers in cells undergoing mitosis as part of cell division.
Comments	Upon contact with water, breaks down to mehtyl-2-benzimidazole carbamate (MBC) which is the fungitoxic component. This is also the fungitoxicant component of thiophanate methyl (Fungo 50™ and Cleary 3336™).

CHLORONEB

Trade Names	Teremec™
Chemical Name	1,4-dichloro-2,5-dimethoxybenzene
Group	Aromatic Hydrocarbons (Substituted Benzenes)
Manufacturer	PBI/Gordon Corporation P.O. Box 4090 Kansas City, Missouri 64101 Telephone: (816) 421-4070
Formulations	65 WP
Labeled for Control of	Pythium blight, Typhula blight, Sclerotium blight, and Rhizoctonia blight
Optimum Dilution Level	4–5 gallons (16.8–21.0 liters) of water per 1,000 ft^2 (93 m^2)
Optimum Nozzle Types and Sizes	Flat fan TeeJet™ (UniJet™) T-8002, T-8004, Delavan LF-2, LF-4, or Delavan Raindrop™ RA-10, RA-15
Optimum Pressure at the Nozzle	For nozzles listed above, 30–60 psi (207–414 kPa) for flat fan type and 40–60 psi (276–414 kPa) for Raindrop™
Resistance to Leaf Washing	No information
In-Tank Stability	No information
Signal word	Caution
Modes of Action	**Topical**—Contact **Biochemical**—Is thought to affect DNA synthesis and block the activity of certain respiratory enzymes. Also prevents the development of cell wall membranes.
Comments	Tank mixtures of chloroneb and mancozeb are antagonistic in the control of Pythium blight incited by *Pythium aphanidermatum*.

CHLOROTHALONIL

Trade Name	Daconil 2787™
Chemical Name	tetrachloroisophthalonitrile
Group	Nitriles
Manufacturer	ISK Biotech Corporation 5966 Heisley Road P.O. Box 8000 Mentor, Ohio 44061-8000 Telephone: (216) 357-4105
Formulations	75 WP, 4.17 F
Labeled for Control of	Sclerotinia dollar spot, Helminthosporium leaf spot, melting-out, Rhizoctonia blight, gray leaf spot, Corticium red thread, stem rust of bluegrass, copper spot
Optimum Dilution Level	1 gallon of water (4.2 liters) per 1,000 ft² (93 m²)
Optimum Nozzle Types and Sizes	Flat fan TeeJet™ (UniJet™) T-8002, T-8004, Delavan LF-2, LF-4, or Delavan Raindrop™ RA-10, RA-15
Optimum Pressure at the Nozzle	For nozzles listed above, 30–60 psi (207–414 kPa) for flat fan type and 40–60 psi (276–414 kPa) for Raindrop™
Resistance to Leaf Washing	Highly resistant to leaf washing after spray dries. Highly susceptible to leaf washing before spray dries.
In-Tank Stability	Unstable in both alkaline and acid pH ranges if stored in tank for 20 hours or more. Stable in acid and alkaline pH ranges if sprayed immediately after preparation.
Toxicity	**Oral**: (rat) = 28,000 mg/kg **Dermal**: (rabbit) = >20,000 mg/kg **Inhalation**: (rat) = >0.54 mg/L air—4 hr **Signal word**: Danger
Modes of Action	**Topical**—Contact **Biochemical**—Reacts with glutathione, an important regulator of normal cell metabolism, to disrupt the regulation of cell functions. It also inhibits sulfur-dependent enzymes in the cell which then brings about a disruption of cell functions.
Comments	Volatilizes rapidly after application to foliage and is sensitive to ultraviolet light, which decreases its longevity. Functions synergistically with propiconazole in the control of Sclerotinia dollar spot.

CYPROCONAZOLE

Trade Name	Sentinel™ 40 WG Turf Fungicide
Chemical Name	a-(4-chlorophenyl)-a-(1-cyclopropylethyl)-1H-1,2,4-triazole-1-ethanol
Group	Demethylation Inhibitors (DMIs)
Manufacturer	Sandoz Agro, Inc. 1300 East Touhy Ave. Des Plaines, Illinois 60018 Telephone: (800) 435-8873
Formulations	40 WG
Labeled for Control of	Sclerotinia dollar spot, Rhizoctonia blight, Corticium red thread, anthracnose, rust, powdery mildew, stripe smut, summer patch, gray leaf spot, Fusarium patch, copper spot, Typhula blight, necrotic ring spot, Sclerotium blight

Optimum Dilution Level	2–5 gallons (8.4–21.0 liters) of water per 1,000 ft^2 (93 m^2)
Optimum Nozzle Types and Sizes	Flat fan TeeJet™ (UniJet™) T-8002, T-8004, Delavan LF-2, LF-4, or Delavan Raindrop™ RA-10, RA-15
Optimum Pressure at the Nozzle	For nozzles listed above, 30–60 psi (207–414 kPa) for flat fan type and 40–60 psi (276–414 kPa) for Raindrop™
Resistance to Leaf Washing	Susceptible to wash off before spray dries on leaf. After drying, highly resistant to wash off.
In-Tank Stability	No information, but generally considered stable for 24 hours.
Toxicity:	**Oral**: (rat) = 1,010 mg/kg **Dermal**: (rat) = >2,000 mg/kg **Inhalation**: Not determined **Signal word**: Caution
Modes of Action	**Topical**—Acropetal penetrant **Biochemical**—14a-Demethylation inhibition of ergosterol biosynthesis. Blocks cytochrome oxidase P-450, the enzyme which hydroxylates the 14a-methyl group.
Comments	Do not use on annual bluegrass (*Poa annua*) that has been treated with either paclobutrazol (Scotts TGR Turf Enhancer™) or flurprimidol (Cutless™) until 3–4 weeks after the last paclobutrozol or flurprimidol application.

ETHAZOL

Trade Names	Koban™
Chemical Name	5-ethoxy-3-trichloromethyl-1,2,4-thiadiazole
Group	Aromatic Hydrocarbons (Substituted Benzenes)
Manufacturer	Grace-Sierra Co. P.O. Box 4003 1001 Yosemite Drive Milpitas, California 95035 Telephone: (408) 263-8080
Formulations	30 WP, 1.3 G
Labeled for Control of	Pythium blight, damping off, and Pythium root rot and crown rot.
Optimum Dilution Level	4–5 gallons (16.8–21.0 liters) of water per 1,000 ft^2 (93 m^2)
Optimum Nozzle Types and Sizes	Flat fan TeeJet™ (UniJet™) T-8002, T-8004, Delavan LF-2, LF-4, or Delavan Raindrop™ RA-10, RA-15
Optimum Pressure at the Nozzle	For nozzles listed above, 30–60 psi (207–414 kPa) for flat fan type and 40–60 psi (276–414 kPa) for Raindrop™
Resistance to Leaf Washing	No information
In-Tank Stability	No information
Signal word	Caution
Modes of Action	**Topical**—Contact **Biochemical**—Is thought to affect DNA synthesis and block the activity of certain respiratory enzymes. Also prevents the development of cell wall membranes.
Comments	When using granular formulation, irrigate with ¼–½ inches (10–20 cm) water immediately after application.

ETHOPROP

Trade Name	Mocap™
Chemical Name	O-ethyl S, S-dipropyl phosphorodithioate
Group	Organophosphate nematicides
Manufacturer	Rhone-Poulenc AG Company 2 T. W. Alexander Drive P.O. Box 12014 Research Triangle Park, North Carolina 27709 Telephone: (800) 334-9745
Formulation	10 G
Labeled for Control of	Root parasitic nematodes on established turfgrass
Toxicity	**Oral**: 61.5 mg/kg (rat) **Dermal**: 2.4 mg/kg (rabbit) **Signal word**: Warning
Topical Mode of Action	**Contact**

Comments

Ethoprop is most effective against sting and spiral nematodes. This material is not absorbed and translocated in nematicidal amounts within the plant; therefore, it does not provide good control of endoparasites such as lance and rootknot nematodes. Ethoprop can be phytotoxic to some ornamental plants under certain conditions, because of this it should not be used within the drip lines of trees and shrubs. Also, ethoprop should not be applied to wet leaves, and it should not be used on newly seeded areas until the plants are well established.

Turfgrass mowed at ⅜ inch (10 mm) and lower is prone to injury by ethoprop at rates higher than 2.3 pounds (1 kg) of 10 percent active ingredient granular formulation per 1,000 square feet (93 m^2). Bentgrasses (*Agrostis* spp.) and ryegrasses (*Lolium* spp.) are more sensitive to ethoprop than other turfgrasses. Phytotoxicity is likely to occur when using the material on these two species at all cutting heights. The turf will normally outgrow this injury; however, if the risk of phytotoxicity is unacceptable, then ethoprop should not be used.

FENAMIPHOS

Trade Name	Nemacur™
Chemical Name	Ethyl 3-methyl-4-(methylthio)phenyl (1-methylethyl)
Group	Organophosphate nematicides
Manufacturer	Miles, Inc. Agriculture Division P.O. Box 4913 Kansas City, Missouri 64120 Telephone: (800) 842-8020
Formulation	10 G
Labeled for Control of	Root parasitic nematodes on established turfgrass
Toxicity	**Oral**: Approximately 3 mg/kg (rat) **Dermal**: Approximately 200 mg/kg (rabbit) **Signal word**: Danger Poison
Topical Mode of Action	**Systemic penetrant**

Comments	The residual activity of fenamiphos lasts for up to 12 weeks. Surface applications of the material eventually become effective at depths of 10–12 inches (25–30 cm); however, downward dispersal through the soil is rather slow. The reason for the slow movement is that fenamiphos has a strong polar property which causes it to disperse in such a manner that all valences in the soil become saturated from the surface downward. When it reaches the 10–12 inch (25–30 cm) depth, all of the product is bound to soil particles and therefore downward movement ceases. Because of its slow dispersal, optimum results are obtained with fenamiphos when it is applied on a preventive schedule—i.e., before the nematode population reaches a high level.

FENARIMOL

Trade Name	Rubigan™
Chemical Name	a-(2-chlorophenyl)-a-(4-chlorophenyl)-5- pyrimidinemethanol
Group	Demethylation Inhibitors (DMIs)
Manufacturer	Dow-Elanco Specialty Products Quad III: 9002 Purdue Road Indianapolis, Indiana 46268-1189 Telephone: (800) 352-6776
Formulations	50WP, 1 AS
Labeled for Control of	Sclerotinia dollar spot, copper spot, Rhizoctonia blight, necrotic ringspot, Fusarium blight, Fusarium patch, Typhula blight, Corticium red thread, take-all patch, spring dead spot of bermudagrass
Optimum Dilution Level	Not determined, assume 1–2 gallons (4.2–8.4 liters) of water per 1,000 ft² (93 m²) to be appropriate
Optimum Nozzle Types and Sizes	Flat fan TeeJet™ (UniJet™) T-8002, T-8004, Delavan LF-2, LF-4, or Delavan Raindrop™ RA-10, RA-15
Optimum Pressure at the Nozzle	For nozzles listed above, 30–60 psi (207–414 kPa) for flat fan type and 40–60 psi (276–414 kPa) for Raindrop™
Resistance to Leaf Washing	Fifty percent reduction in effectiveness if leaves are washed before spray dries. Highly resistant to leaf washing after spray dries.
In-Tank Stability	Highly stable in both alkaline and acid pH ranges.
Signal word	Warning
Modes of Action	**Topical**—Acropetal penetrant **Biochemical**—Inhibits sterol synthesis in sensitive fungi, thus restricting the development of cell membranes.
Comments	Do not use on annual bluegrass (*Poa annua*) that has been treated with either paclobutrazol (Scotts TGR Turf Enhancer™) or flurprimidol (Cutless™) until 3–4 weeks after the last paclobutrozol or flurprimidol application.

FLUTOLANIL

Trade Name	Prostar™
Chemical Name	N-[3-(1-methylethoxy) phenyl]-2-(tribluoromethyl)benzamide
Group	Carboximides
Manufacturer	AGREVO Corporation 3509 Silverside Road Wilmington, Delaware 19803 Telephone: (800) 992-9909

Formulation	50 WP
Labeled for Control of	Rhizoctonia blight, Corticium red thread, Limonomyces pink patch, Sclerotium blight, Rhizoctonia yellow patch, fairy ring, Typhula blight
Optimum Dilution Level	Not determined, assume 1–2 gallons (4.2–8.4 liters) of water per 1,000 ft^2 (93 m^2) to be appropriate
Optimum Nozzle Types and Sizes	Flat fan TeeJet™ (UniJet™) T-8002, T-8004, Delavan LF-2, LF-4, or Delavan Raindrop™ RA-10, RA-15
Optimum Pressure at the Nozzle	For nozzles listed above, 30–60 psi (207–414 kPa) for flat fan type and 40–60 psi (276–414 kPa) for Raindrop™
Resistance to Leaf Washing	No information
In-Tank Stability	No information
Toxicity	**Oral**: 10,000 mg/kg **Dermal**: >5,000 mg/kg **Signal word**: Caution
Modes of Action	**Topical**—Acropetal penetrant **Biochemical**—Interferes with respiration of the fungal cells by blocking the activity of certain respiratory enzymes.

FOSETYL AL

Trade Name	Aliette™
Chemical Name	aluminum tris(0-ethyl phosphonate)
Group	Phosphonates
Manufacturer	Rhone-Poulenc AG Company 2 T. W. Alexander Drive P.O. Box 12014 Research Triangle Park, North Carolina 27709 Telephone: (800) 334-9745
Formulations	80 WP
Labeled for Control of	Pythium blight
Optimum Dilution Level	2–4 gallons (8.4–16.8 liters/93 m^2) of water per 1,000 ft^2 (93 m^2)
Optimum Nozzle Types and Sizes	Flat fan TeeJet™ (UniJet™) T-8002, T-8004, Delavan LF-2, LF-4, or Delavan Raindrop™ RA-10, RA-15
Optimum Pressure at the Nozzle	For nozzles listed above, 30–60 psi (207–414 kPa) for flat fan type and 40–60 psi (276–414 kPa) for Raindrop™
Resistance to Leaf Washing	No information
In-Tank Stability	No information
Toxicity	**Oral**: 5,000 mg/kg (rat) **Dermal**: >2,000 mg/kg (rabbit) **Signal word**: Caution
Modes of Action	**Topical**—Systemic penetrant **Biochemical**—Biochemical mode of action is highly complex, involving both direct and indirect mechanisms. The degree of involvement of each factor most likely depends on the sensitivity of the fungus in question to direct inhibition by phosphonate and the host plant's defense response to the tissue being colonized.
Comments	Not compatible with flowable chlorothalonil or flowable mancozeb in a tank mixture. Functions synergistically with metalaxyl and propamocarb in the control of Pythium blight incited by Pythium aphanidermatum.

IPRODIONE

Trade Names	Chipco 26019™, Rovral Green™
Chemical Name	3-[3,5-dichlorophenyl]-N-[1-methyl]-2,4-dioxo-1- imidazolidinecarboxamide
Group	Dicarboximides
Manufacturer	*Chipco 26019™* Rhone-Poulenc AG Company 2 T. W. Alexander Drive P.O. Box 12014 Research Triangle Park, North Carolina 27709 Telephone: United States (800) 334-9745 Canada (905) 821-4450
Formulations	50 WP, FL (250 gm/liter)
Labeled for Control of	Sclerotinia dollar spot, Rhizoctonia blight, Helminthosporium leaf spot, melting out, Fusarium blight, Typhula blight, Fusarium patch, Corticium red thread
Optimum Dilution Level	0.5–4 gallons (2.1–16.8 liters of water per 1,000 ft^2 (93 m^2)
Optimum Nozzle Types and Sizes	Flat fan TeeJet™ (UniJet™) T-8002, T-8004, Delavan LF-2, LF-4, or Delavan Raindrop™ RA-10, RA-15
Optimum Pressure at the Nozzle	For nozzles listed above, 30–60 psi (207–414 kPa) for flat fan type and 40–60 psi (276–414 kPa) for Raindrop™
Resistance to Leaf Washing	Highly resistant to leaf washing after spray dries. Highly susceptible to leaf washing before spray dries.
In-Tank Stability	Highly stable in both alkaline and acid pH ranges.
Toxicity	**Oral**: (rat) = 5,000 mg/kg **Dermal**: (rabbit) = >2,000 mg/kg **Inhalation**: (rat) = >1.96 mg/L air—4 hr **Signal word**: Caution
Modes of Action	**Topical**—Localized penetrant **Biochemical**—Interferes with respiration by blocking the activity of certain respiratory enzymes.
Comments	Functions synergistically with propiconazole in the control of Sclerotinia dollar spot.

MANCOZEB

Trade Names	Fore™, Manzate 200 DF™
Chemical Name	62% ethylene bisdithiocarbamate, 10% manganese, 2% zinc
Group	Carbamates
Manufacturers	*Fore*: Rohm and Haas Co. Independence Mall West Philadelphia, Pennsylvania 19105 Telephone: (215) 592-3627
Manufacturers (*cont.*)	*Manzate 200 DF*: E. I. DuPont Co. Agricultural Products Walker's Mill, Barley Mill Plaza Wilmington, Delaware 19897 Telephone: (800) 759-2500

Formulations	50 WP, 4 F (Fore) 50 DF (Manzate 200)
Labeled for Control of	Helminthosporium leaf spot, melting out, Corticium red thread, Fusarium patch, Pythium blight, Sclerotinia dollar spot, copper spot, Rhizoctonia blight, Fusarium blight, rusts
Optimum Dilution Level	Not determined, assume 1–2 gallons (4.2–8.4 liters) of water per 1,000 ft^2 (93 m^2) to be appropriate
Optimum Nozzle Types and Sizes	Flat fan TeeJet™ (UniJet™) T-8002, T-8004, Delavan LF-2, LF-4, or Delavan Raindrop™ RA-10, RA-15
Optimum Pressure at the Nozzle	For nozzles listed above, 30–60 psi (207–414 kPa) for flat fan type and 40–60 psi (276–414 kPa) for Raindrop™
Resistance to Leaf Washing	No information
In-Tank Stability	No information
Toxicity	**Oral**: (rat) = >5,000 mg/kg **Dermal**: (rabbit) = >5,000 mg/kg **Signal word**: Caution
Modes of Action	**Topical**—Contact **Biochemical**—Fungitoxicity is thought to be due to chemical inactivation of important thiol containing systems, thus inhibiting enzyme activity within the fungal cell.
Comments	Mancozeb functions synergistically with metalaxyl and propamocarb in the control of Pythium blight incited by *Pythium aphanidermatum*. However, tank mixtures of chloroneb and mancozeb are antagonistic in the control of Pythium blight incited by *Pythium aphanidermatum*.

METALAXYL

Trade Names	Subdue™, Apron™
Chemical Name	N-2(2,6-dimethylphenyl)-N-(methoxyacetyl)alamine
Group	Phenylamides
Manufacturer	Ciba-Geigy Corporation P.O. Box 18300 Greensboro, North Carolina 27419 Telephone: (919) 632-6000
Formulations	2 EC, 2 G (Subdue™) 25 WP (Apron™)
Labeled for Control of	Subdue™: Foliar application for control of Pythium blight, yellow tuft, downy mildew Apron™: Seed treatment for control of seedling diseases incited by species of Pythium
Optimum Dilution Level	3–5 gallons of water per 1,000 sq. ft.
Optimum Nozzle Types and Sizes	Flat fan TeeJet™ (UniJet™) T-8002, T-8004, Delavan LF-2, LF-4, or Delavan Raindrop™ RA-10, RA-15
Optimum Pressure at the Nozzle	For nozzles listed above, 30–60 psi (207–414 kPa) for flat fan type and 40–60 psi (276–414 kPa) for Raindrop™
Resistance to Leaf Washing	No information
In-Tank Stability	No information.
Toxicity	**Oral**: (rat) = 1290–3000 mg/kg **Dermal**: (rabbit) = >2,010 mg/kg **Inhalation**: (rat) = >4.53 mg/L air—4 hr **Signal word**: Warning

Modes of Action	**Topical**—Acropetal penetrant **Biochemical**—Interferes with the ribonucleic acid (RNA) template complex of sensitive fungi, thus inhibiting ribosomal RNA synthesis.
Comments	Metalaxyl functions synergistically with mancozeb in the control of Pythium blight incited by *Pythium aphanidermatum*. With 2 G formulation, irrigate with ¼–½ inches (10–20 cm) water immediately after application.

PROPAMOCARB

Trade Name	Banol™
Chemical Name	propyl [3-(dimethylamino)propyl] carbamate monohydrochloride
Group	Carbamates
Manufacturer	AGREVO Corporation 3509 Silverside Road Wilmington, Delaware 19803 Telephone: (800) 992-9909
Formulations	6 F
Labeled for Control of	Pythium blight and Pythium damping off on turf
Optimum Dilution Level	2–4 gallons (8.4–16.8 liters/93 m²) of water per 1,000 ft² (93 m²)
Optimum Nozzle Types and Sizes	Flat fan TeeJet™ (UniJet™) T-8002, T-8004, Delavan LF-2, LF-4, or Delavan Raindrop™ RA-10, RA-15
Optimum Pressure at the Nozzle	For nozzles listed above, 30–60 psi (207–414 kPa) for flat fan type and 40–60 psi (276–414 kPa) for Raindrop™
Resistance to Leaf Washing	No information
In-Tank Stability	No information
Toxicity	**Oral**: (rat) = 2,000–8,500 mg/kg **Dermal**: (rabbit) = >3,920 mg/kg **Inhalation**: (rat) = >6.2 mg/L air—4 hr **Signal word**: Caution
Modes of Action	**Topical**—Localized penetrant **Biochemical**—Biochemical mode of action is thought to be based on alteration of fatty acid composition, which in turn alters the fluidity of the cell membranes.
Comments	Tank compatible with benomyl, iprodione, ethozol, chloroneb, triadimefon, chlorothalonil, and thiram. Functions synergistically with mancozeb and fosetyl Al in the control of Pythium blight incited by *Pythium aphanidermatum*.

PROPICONAZOLE

Trade Name	Banner™
Chemical Name	1-[(2-(2,4-dichlorophenyl)-4-propyl-1,3-dioxolan-2yl] methyl-1 H-1,2,4-triazole
Group	Demethylation Inhibitors (DMIs)
Manufacturer	Ciba-Geigy Corporation P.O. Box 18300 Greensboro, North Carolina 27419 Telephone: (919) 632-6000
Formulations	1.1 EC
Labeled for Control of	Sclerotinia dollar spot, Rhizoctonia blight, Corticium red thread, anthracnose, rust, powdery mildew, stripe smut, summer patch, gray leaf spot, Fusarium patch

Optimum Dilution Level	1–2 gallons (4.2–8.4 liters) of water per 1,000 ft² (93 m²)
Optimum Nozzle Types and Sizes	Flat fan TeeJet™ (UniJet™) T-8002, T-8004, Delavan LF-2, LF-4, or Delavan Raindrop™ RA-10, RA-15
Optimum Pressure at the Nozzle	For nozzles listed above, 30–60 psi (207–414 kPa) for flat fan type and 40–60 psi (276–414 kPa) for Raindrop™
Resistance to Leaf Washing	Susceptible to wash off before spray dries on leaf. After drying, highly resistant to wash off.
In-Tank Stability	No information
Toxicity	**Oral**: (rat) = 1,310 mg/kg **Dermal**: (rabbit) = >5,010 mg/kg **Inhalation**: (rat) = >2.45 mg/L air—4 hr **Signal word**: Warning
Modes of Action	**Topical**—Acropetal penetrant **Biochemical**—Inhibits sterol synthesis in sensitive fungi, thus restricting the development of cell membranes.
Comments	Bermudagrass (*Cynodon dactylon*) is sensitive to propiconazole. Do not exceed 4 fluid ounces (118.4 ml) per 1,000 ft² (93 m²) of 4 F formulated product on this species. Also, do not apply to bermudagrass golf greens when air temperatrures exceed 90° F (32° C). Also do not use on annual bluegrass (*Poa annua*) that has been treated with either paclobutrazol (Scotts TGR Turf Enhancer™) or flurprimidol (Cutless™) until 3–4 weeks after the last paclobutrozol or flurprimidol application. Functions synergistically with chlorothalonil, iprodione, vinclozolin, triadimefon, and anilazine in the control of Sclerotinia dollar spot.

QUINTOZENE (PCNB)

Trade Names	Terraclor™, Turfcide™, PCNB-10% Granular™
Chemical Name	pentachloronitrobenzene
Group	Aromatic Hydrocarbons (Substituted Benzenes)
Manufacturers:	*Terraclor™, Turfcide™* Uniroyal Chemical Co. Uniroyal Chemical Ltd. Benson Road 25 Erb Street Middlebury, Connecticut 06749 Elmira, Ontario N3B 3A3 Telephone (203) 573-3888 Telephone (800) 265-2157 *PCNB-10% Granular™* Lesco, Inc. 20005 Lake Road Rocky River, Ohio 44116 Telephone: (800) 321-5325
Formulations	75 WP (Terraclor™) 10 G (Turfcide™; PCNB-10% Granular™)
Labeled for Control of	Rhizoctonia blight, Helminthosporium leaf spot, Fusarium patch, Typhula blight
Optimum Dilution Level	Infomation not available
Optimum Nozzle Types and Sizes	Flat fan TeeJet™ (UniJet™) T-8002, T-8004, Delavan LF-2, LF-4, or Delavan Raindrop™ RA-10, RA-15
Optimum Pressure at the Nozzle	For nozzles listed above, 30–60 psi (207–414 kPa) for flat fan type and 40–60 psi (276–414 kPa) for Raindrop™
Resistance to Leaf Washing	No information

In-Tank Stability	No information
Toxicity	**Oral**: (rat) = >15000 mg/kg **Signal word**: Caution
Modes of Action	**Topical**—Contact **Biochemical**—Affects DNA synthesis and blocks the activity of certain respiratory enzymes. Also restricts the formation of chitin, which is a primary component of the cell walls of many of the fungi that are pathogenic to turfgrasses.
Comments	During warm growing conditions PCNB can be phytotoxic to cool season grasses—particularly creeping red fescue and bentgrasses. Refer to manufacturer's label for instructions concerning use limitations on cool season grasses.

THIOPHANATE METHYL

Trade Names	Fungo 50™, Cleary 3336™
Chemical Name	dimethyl 4,4-0-phenylenebis(3-thioallophanate)
Group	Benzimidazoles
Manufacturers	*Cleary 3336* W. A. Cleary Cemical Corp. 1049 Somerset Drive Somerset, New Jersey 08873 Telephone: (908) 247-8000 *Fungo 50* Grace-Sierra Co. P.O. Box 4003 1001 Yosemite Drive Milpitas, California 95035 Telephone: (408) 263-8080
Formulations	50 WP, 2 F
Labeled for Control of	Corticium red thread, stripe smut, Fusarium blight, Sclerotinia dollar spot, copper spot, Rhizoctonia blight, Fusarium patch, stripe smut
Optimum Dilution Level	1–2 gallons (4.2–8.4 liters) of water per 1,000 ft^2 (93 m^2)
Optimum Nozzle Types and Sizes	Flat fan TeeJet™ (UniJet™) T-8002, T-8004, Delavan LF-2, LF-4, or Delavan Raindrop™ RA-10, RA-15
Optimum Pressure at the Nozzle	For nozzles listed above, 30–60 psi (207–414 kPa) for flat fan type and 40–60 psi (276–414 kPa) for Raindrop™
Resistance to Leaf Washing	No information
In-Tank Stability	No information
Toxicity	**Oral**: 7500 mg/kg **Signal word**: Caution
Modes of Action	**Topical**—Acropetal penetrant. **Biochemical**—Interferes with nuclear division (mitosis). Binds to protein, tubulin, which is a component of spindle fibers in cells undergoing mitosis as a part of cell division.
Comments	Upon contact with water, breaks down to methyl-2- benzimidazole carbamate (MBC), which is the fungitoxic component. This is also the fungitoxic component of benomyl (Tersan 1991™).

TRIADIMEFON

Trade Name	Bayleton™
Chemical Name	1-(4-chlorophenoxy)-3,3-dimethyl-1-(1H-1,2,4-triazol-1,yl)-2-butanone
Group	Demethylation Inhibitors (DMIs)
Manufacturer	Miles, Inc. Agriculture Division P.O. Box 4913 Kansas City, Missouri 64120 Telephone: (800) 842-8020
Formulations	25 WP
Labeled for Control of	Sclerotinia dollar spot, Rhizoctonia blight (suppression), Fusarium blight, Corticium red thread, anthracnose, rust, powdery mildew, stripe smut, summer patch, copper spot, gray leaf spot, rusts, stripe smut, Typhula blight, Fusarium patch
Optimum Dilution Level	2 gallons (8.4 liters) of water per 1,000 ft² (93 m²)
Optimum Nozzle Types and Sizes	Flat fan TeeJet™ (UniJet™) T-8002, T-8004, Delavan LF-2, LF-4, or Delavan Raindrop™ RA-10, RA-15
Optimum Pressure at the Nozzle	For nozzles listed above, 30–60 psi (207–414 kPa) for flat fan type and 40–60 psi (276–414 kPa) for Raindrop™
Resistance to Leaf Washing	Leaf washing before spray dries does not appreciably reduce effectiveness.
In-Tank Stability	Highly stable in both alkaline and acid pH ranges.
Toxicity	**Oral**: (rat) = 812 mg/kg **Dermal**: (rabbit) = >2,000 mg/kg **Inhalation**: (rat) = >20 mg/L air—4 hr **Signal word**: Warning
Modes of Action	**Topical**—Acropetal penetrant **Biochemical**—Inhibits sterol synthesis in sensitive fungi, thus restricting the development of cell membranes.
Comments	Do not use on annual bluegrass (*Poa annua*) that has been treated with either paclobutrazol (Scotts TGR Turf Enhancer™) or flurprimidol (Cutless™) until 3–4 weeks after the last paclobutrozol or flurprimidol application. Functions synergistically with propiconazole in the control of Sclerotinia dollar spot.

VINCLOZOLIN

Trade Names	Vorlan™, Curalan™
Chemical Name	3-(3,5-dichlorophenyl)-5-ethenyl-5-methyl-2-4-oxazolidinedione
Group	Dicarboximides
Manufacturers	*Vorlan* Grace-Sierra Co. P.O. Box 4003 1001 Yosemite Drive Milpitas, California 95035 Telephone: (408) 263-8080 *Curalan* BASF Corporation P.O. Box 13528 Research Triangle Park, North Carolina 27709 Telephone: (919) 361-5300

Formulations	50 DF (Vorlan; Curalan) 41.3% FLO (Vorlan; Curalan)
Labeled for Control of	Sclerotinia dollar spot, Fusarium patch, Limonomyces pink patch, melting-out, Helminthosporium leaf spot, red leaf spot, Corticium red thread, Rhizoctonia blight
Optimum Dilution Level	1–2 gallons of water per 1,000 sq. ft.
Optimum Nozzle Types and Sizes	Flat fan TeeJet™ (UniJet™) T-8002, T-8004, Delavan LF-2, LF-4, or Delavan Raindrop™ RA-10, RA-15
Optimum Pressure at the Nozzle	For nozzles listed above, 30–60 psi (207–414 kPa) for flat fan type and 40–60 psi (276–414 kPa) for Raindrop™
Resistance to Leaf Washing	Highly resistant to leaf washing after spray dries. Highly susceptible to leaf washing before spray dries.
In-Tank Stability	Highly stable in both alkaline and acid pH ranges.
Toxicity	**Oral**: (rat) = 1,600 mg/kg **Dermal**: (rabbit) = >2,000 mg/kg **Inhalation**: (rat) = >1.17 mg/L air—4 hr **Signal word**: Caution
Modes of Action	**Topical**—Localized penetrant **Biochemical**—Inhibits spore germination. Interferes with respiration by blocking the activity of certain respiratory enzymes.
Comments	Functions synergistically with propiconazole in the control of Sclerotinia dollar spot.

Table II. Diseases of Turfgrasses Arranged According to Turfgrass Species Affected

Turfgrass	Disease, Pages

BAHIAGRASS
(*Paspalum notatum*)
	Fairy Rings, 181
	Nematodes, 217
	  burrowing, 227
	  dagger, 233
	  root knot, 235
	  lance, 234
	Sclerotinia Dollar Spot, 65
	Slime Molds, 135

BENTGRASS, Colonial
(*Agrostis tenuis*)
	Bacterial Wilt, 211
	Black Leaf Spot, 113
	Brown Stripe, 128
	Char Spot, 115
	Choke, 194
	Copper Spot, 69
	Cottony Snow Mold, 81
	Curvularia Blight, 159
	Ergot, 195
	Fairy Rings, 181
	Fusarium Blight, 42
	Fusarium Patch, 74
	Gray Leaf Spot, 111
	Leptosphaerulina Leaf Blight, 162
	Limonomyces Pink Patch, 39
	Nematodes, 217
	  cyst, 223
	  grass seed, 219
	  leaf gall, 222
	  spiral, 228
	Mastigosporium Leaf Spot, 130
	Oat Necrotic Mottle Virus, 207
	Take-all Patch, 28
	Pythium Blight, 51
	Ramularia Leaf Spot, 132
	Red Leaf Spot, 100
	Red Thread, 36
	Rhizoctonia Blight, 59
	Rust, 141
	Ryegrass Mosaic, 208
	Sclerotinia Dollar Spot, 65
	Sclerotinia Patch, 79
	Septoria Leaf Spot, 117
	Silver Top, 192
	Slime Molds, 135
	Smut, 149
	  flag, 152
	  stripe, 149
	Typhula Blight, 77

BENTGRASS, Creeping (*Agrostis palustris*)	Anthracnose, 156 Bacterial Wilt, 211 Blind Seed, 197 Bromegrass Mosaic, 209 Brown Stripe, 128 Char Spot, 115 Copper Spot, 69 Cottony Snow Mold, 81 Curvularia Blight, 159 Ergot, 195 Fairy Rings, 181 Fusarium Blight, 42 Fusarium Patch, 74

Turfgrass	Disease, Pages
BENTGRASS, Creeping (*cont.*)	Gray Leaf Spot, 111
	Helminthosporium Leaf Spot, 96
	Leptosphaerulina Leaf Blight, 162
	Limonomyces Pink Patch, 39
	Mastigosporium Leaf Spot, 130
	Necrotic Ring Spot, 25
	Nematodes, 217
	grass seed, 219
	Polymyxa Root Rot, 177
	Pseudocersporella Basal Rot, 179
	Pyrenochaeta Root Rot, 178
	Pythium Blight, 51
	Pythium Decline, 173
	Pythium Root Dysfunction, 171
	Ramularia Leaf Spot, 132
	Red Leaf Spot, 100
	Red Thread, 36
	Rhizoctonia Blight, 59
	Rhizoctonia Sheath Spot, 64
	Rhizoctonia Yellow Patch, 31
	Rust, 141
	Sclerotinia Dollar Spot, 65
	Sclerotinia Patch, 79
	Sclerotium Blight, 71
	Septoria Leaf Spot, 117
	Slime Molds, 135
	Smut, 149
	covered, 191
	flag, 152
	stripe, 149
	Summer Patch, 47
	Typhula Blight, 77
	White Patch, 73
	Zonate Eyespot, 106
BENTGRASS, Velvet (*Agrostis canina*)	Blind Seed, 197
	Char Spot, 115
	Copper Spot, 69
	Cottony Snow Mold, 81
	Curvularia Blight, 159
	Ergot, 195
	Fairy Rings, 181
	Fusarium Patch, 74
	Limonomyces Pink Patch, 39
	Nematodes, 217
	grass seed, 219
	Pythium Blight, 51
	Red leaf Spot, 100
	Rhizoctonia Blight, 59
	Rust, 141
	Sclerotinia Dollar Spot, 65
	Sclerotinia Patch, 79
	Slime Molds, 135
	Smut
	covered, 191
	Take-all Patch, 28
	Typhula Blight, 77
	Zonate Eyespot, 106
BERMUDAGRASS (*Cynodon dactylon*)	Anthracnose, 156
	Curvularia Blight, 159
	Fairy Rings, 181
	Fusarium Patch, 74
	Gaeumannomyces Decline, 175

Turfgrass	Disease, Pages
BERMUDAGRASS (*cont.*)	Gray Leaf Spot, 111
	Helminthosporium Stem and Crown Necrosis, 109
	Leaf Blotch, 108
	Limonomyces Pink Patch, 39
	Necrotic Ring Spot, 25
	Nematodes, 217
	burrowing, 227
	dagger, 233
	lance, 234
	ring, 231
	root lesion, 226
	spiral, 228
	sting, 230
	stubby root, 233
	Polymyxa Root Rot, 177
	Powdery Mildew, 139
	Pyrenochaeta Root Rot, 178
	Pythium Blight, 51
	Red Thread, 36
	Rhizoctonia Blight, 33, 59
	Rhizoctonia Sheath Spot, 64
	Rhizoctonia Yellow Patch, 31
	Rust, 141
	Sclerotium Blight, 71
	Sclerotinia Dollar Spot, 65
	Septoria Leaf Spot, 116
	Slime Molds, 135
	Smut
	loose, 192
	Spring Dead Spot, 85
	Zonate Eyespot, 106
BLUEGRASS, Annual (*Poa annua*)	Anthracnose, 156
	Bacterial Wilt, 211
	Cottony Snow Mold, 81
	Curvularia Blight, 159
	Ergot, 195
	Fairy Rings, 181
	Fusarium Blight, 42
	Fusarium Patch, 74
	Gray Leaf Spot, 111
	Leptosphaerulina Leaf Blight, 162
	Limonomyces Pink Patch, 39
	Melting-out, 93
	Necrotic Ring Spot, 25
	Nematodes
	lance, 234
	Ramularia Leaf Spot, 132
	Red Thread, 36
	Rhizoctonia Blight, 33, 59
	Rhizoctonia Sheath Spot, 64
	Rhizoctonia Yellow Patch, 31
	Rust, 141
	Sclerotium Blight, 73
	Sclerotinia Dollar Spot, 65
	Septoria Leaf Spot, 116
	Slime Molds, 135
	Smut
	blister, 153
	stripe, 149
	Summer Patch, 47
	Take-all Patch, 28
	Typhula Blight, 77

Turfgrass	Disease, Pages

BLUEGRASS, Canada
(*Poa compressa*)
	Anthracnose, 156
	Brown Stripe, 128
	Choke, 194
	Ergot, 195
	Fairy Rings, 181
	Helminthosporium Leaf Spot, 102
	Melting-out, 93
	Pythium Blight, 51
	Rhoizoctonia Blight, 59
	Rust, 141
	Septoria Leaf Spot, 116
	Slime Molds, 135
	Smut
	   blister, 153
	   flag, 152
	Take-all Patch, 28
	Zonate Eyespot, 106

BLUEGRASS, Kentucky
(*Poa pratensis*)
	Anthracnose, 156
	Ascochyta Leaf Spot, 126
	Bacterial Wilt, 211
	Barley Yellow Dwarf, 207
	Blind Seed, 197
	Bromegrass Mosaic, 209
	Brown Stripe, 128
	Choke, 194
	Cottony Snow Mold, 81
	Curvularia Blight, 159
	Ergot, 195
	Fairy Rings, 181
	Frost Scorch, 84
	Fusarium Blight, 42
	Fusarium Patch, 74
	Gray Leaf Spot, 111
	Helminthosporium Blight, 102
	Helminthosporium Leaf Spot, 96
	Leptosphaerulina Leaf Blight, 162
	Limonomyces Pink Patch, 39
	Melting-out, 93
	Necrotic Ring Spot, 25
	Nematodes
	   dagger, 233
	   lance, 234
	   pin, 232
	   ring, 231
	   root knot, 224
	   root lesion, 226
	   spiral, 228
	   stubby root, 233
	Oat Necrotic Mottle Virus, 207
	Powdery Mildew, 139
	Pseudocosporella Basal Rot, 179
	Pseudoseptoria Leaf Spot, 214
	Pyrenochaeta Root Rot, 178
	Pythium Blight, 51
	Red Thread, 36
	Rhizoctonia Blight, 33, 59
	Rhizoctonia Sheath Spot, 64
	Rhizoctonia Yellow Patch, 31
	Rust, 141
	Ryegrass Mosaic, 208
	Sclerotinia Dollar Spot, 65
	Sclerotinia Patch, 79

Turfgrass	Disease, Pages

BLUEGRASS, Kentucky (*cont.*)	Sclerotium Blight, 71
	 Sclerotinia Patch, 79
	 Selenophoma Leaf Spot, 124
	 Septoria Leaf Spot, 116
	 Silver Top, 192
	 Slime Molds, 135
	 Smut
	    blister, 153
	    flag, 152
	    loose, 192
	    stripe, 149
	 Spermospora Leaf Spot, 122
	 Stagonospora Leaf Spot, 119
	 Summer Patch, 47
	 Take-all Patch, 28
	 Typhula Blight, 77
	 Zonate Eyespot, 106

BLUEGRASS, Rough (*Poa trivialis*)	Blind Seed, 197 Brown Stripe, 128 Choke, 194 Fairy Rings, 181 Fusarium Patch, 74 Melting-out, 93 Rhizoctonia Blight, 59 Rust, 141 Selenophoma Leaf Spot, 124 Silver Top, 192 Slime Molds, 135 Smut stripe, 149 Take-all Patch, 28 Typhula Blight, 77
BLUEGRASS, Sandberg (*Poa secunda*)	Fairy Rings, 181 Pesudocercosporella Basal Rot, 179 Rust, 141 Slime Molds, 135
BLUEGRASS, Wood (*Poa nemoralis*)	Brown Stripe, 128 Fairy Rings, 181 Rhizoctonia Blight, 59 Rust, 141 Selenophoma Leaf Spot, 124 Slime Molds, 135

CENTIPEDEGRASS
 (*Eremochloa ophiuroides*)
	Anthracnose, 156
	 Fairy Rings, 181
	 Fusarium Blight, 42
	 Gray Leaf Spot, 111
	 Nematodes
	    dagger, 233
	    ring, 231
	    root lesion, 226
	    spiral, 228
	    stubby root, 233
	 Rhizoctonia Sheath Spot, 64
	 Slime Molds, 135

FESCUE, Chewings (*Festuca rubra* var. *commutata*)	Cottony Snow Mold, 81 Curvularia Blight, 159 Ergot, 195 Fairy Rings, 181 Fusarium Blight, 42 Fusarium Patch, 74

Turfgrass	Disease, Pages
FESCUE, Chewings (*cont.*)	Helminthosporium Blight, 102 Necrotic Ring Spot, 25 Powdery Mildew, 139 Ramularia Leaf Spot, 132 Red Thread, 36 Rhizoctonia Blight, 33 Silver Top, 192 Slime Molds, 135 Summer Patch, 47 White Patch, 73
FESCUE, Hard (*Festuca ovina* var. *duriuscula*)	Anthracnose, 156 Bacterial Wilt, 211 Fairy Rings, 181 Nematodes leaf gall, 222 Red Thread, 36 Silver Top, 192 Slime Molds, 135 Summer Patch, 47

FESCUE, Red
(*Festuca rubra*)
	Anthracnose, 156
	Ascochyta Leaf Spot, 125
	Bacterial Wilt, 211
	Barley Yellow Dwarf, 207
	Blind Seed, 197
	Brown Stripe, 128
	Choke, 194
	Cottony Snow Mold, 81
	Curvularia Blight, 159
	Ergot, 195
	Fairy Rings, 181
	Fusarium Blight, 42
	Fusarium Patch, 74
	Gray Leaf Spot, 111
	Helminthosporium Blight, 102
	Helminthosporium Leaf Spot, 96
	Leptosphaerulina Leaf Blight, 162
	Limonomyces Pink Patch, 39
	Necrotic Ring Spot, 25
	Nematodes
	   cyst, 223
	   pin, 232
	   stubby root, 233
	Powdery Mildew, 139
	Pseudoseptoria Leaf Spot, 214
	Pyrenochaeta Root Rot, 178
	Pythium Blight, 51
	Red Thread, 36
	Rhizoctonia Blight, 59
	Rust, 141
	Sclerotinia Dollar Spot, 65
	Sclerotinia Patch, 79
	Septoria Leaf Spot, 117
	Silver Top, 192
	Slime Molds, 135
	Smut
	   flag, 152
	Spermospora Leaf Spot, 122
	Stagonospora Leaf Spot, 119
	Summer Patch, 47
	Take-all Patch, 28
	Typhula Blight, 77
	White Patch, 73

Turfgrass	Disease, Pages
FESCUE, Shade (*Festuca rubra* var. *heterophylla*)	Fairy Rings, 181 Nematodes cyst, 223 Slime Molds, 135

FESCUE, Sheep
(*Festuca ovina*)
	Anthracnose, 156
	Ascochyta Leaf Spot, 126
	Barley Yellow Dwarf, 207
	Blind Seed, 197
	Choke, 194
	Cottony Snow Mold, 81
	Ergot, 195
	Fairy Rings, 181
	Fusarium Blight, 42
	Nematodes
	  leaf gall, 222
	Powdery Mildew, 139
	Pseudoseptoria Leaf Spot, 214
	Red Thread, 36
	Rhizoctonia Blight, 59
	Rust, 141
	Septoria Leaf Spot, 117
	Silver Top, 192
	Slime Mold, 135
	Smut
	  stripe, 149

FESCUE, Tall
(*Festuca arundinacea*)
	Anthracnose, 156
	Ascochyta Leaf Spots, 126
	Black Leaf Spot, 113
	Bacterial Wilt, 211
	Barley Yellow Dwarf, 207
	Blind Seed, 197
	Brown Stripe, 128
	Cercospora Leaf Spot, 121
	Cottony Snow Mold, 81
	Curvularia Blight, 159
	Ergot, 195
	Fairy Rings, 181
	Fusarium Blight, 42
	Fusarium Patch, 74
	Gray Leaf Spot, 111
	Helminthosporium Blight, 102
	Helminthosporium Leaf Spot, 96
	Leptosphaerulina Leaf Blight, 162
	Melting-out, 93
	Nematodes
	  cyst, 223
	  pin, 232
	  root lesion, 226
	  root knot, pseudo, 224
	  stubby root, 233
	Phleospora Leaf Spot, 129
	Pseudoseptoria Leaf Spot, 214
	Pythium Blight, 51
	Rhizoctonia Blight, 59
	Rhizoctonia Sheath Spot, 64
	Rhizoctonia Yellow Patch, 31
	Rust, 141
	Ryegrass Mosaic, 208
	Sclerotinia Patch, 79
	Septoria Leaf Spot, 117
	Silver Top, 192
	Slime Mold, 135

Turfgrass	Disease, Pages
FESCUE, Tall (*cont.*)	Smut stripe, 149 Stagonospora Leaf Spot, 119 Take-all Patch, 28 Typhula Blight, 77 Western Ryegrass Mosaic, 208 White Patch, 73

RYEGRASS, annual
(*Lolium multiflorum*)
	Anthracnose, 156
	Ascochyta Leaf Spot, 126
	Bacterial Wilt, 211
	Barley Yellow Dwarf, 207
	Blind Seed, 197
	Bromegrass Mosaic, 209
	Brown Stripe, 128
	Fairy Rings, 181
	Gray Leaf Spot, 111
	Helminthosporium Blight, 102
	Melting-out, 93
	Nematodes
	   cyst, 223
	   pin, 232
	   sting, 230
	Oat Necrotic Mottle Virus, 207
	Pythium Blight, 51
	Ramularia Leaf Spot, 132
	Rhizoctonia Blight, 59
	Rhynchosporium Leaf Blotch, 127
	Ryegrass Mosaic, 208
	Sclerotium Blight, 71
	Septoria Leaf Spot, 117
	Slime Molds, 135
	Spermospora Leaf Spot, 123
	Take-all Patch, 28
	Western Ryegrass Mosaic, 208

RYEGRASS, perennial
(*Lolium perenne*)
	Anthracnose, 156
	Ascochyta Leaf Spot, 126
	Bacterial Wilt, 211
	Barley Yellow Dwarf, 207
	Blind Seed, 197
	Bromegrass Mosaic, 209
	Brown Blight, 104
	Brown Stripe, 128
	Fairy Rings, 181
	Fusarium Blight, 42
	Gray Leaf Spot, 111
	Helminthosporium Leaf Spot, 96
	Leptosphaerulina Leaf Blight, 102
	Limonomyces Pink Patch, 39
	Melting-out, 93
	Necrotic Ring Spot, 25
	Nematodes
	   cyst, 223
	   pin, 232
	   spiral, 228
	   stubby root, 233
	Oat Necrotic Mottle Virus, 207
	Pythium Blight, 51
	Ramularia Leaf Spot, 132
	Red Thread, 36
	Rhizoctonia Blight, 59
	Rhizoctonia Yellow Patch, 31
	Rhynchosporium Leaf Blotch, 127

Turfgrass	Disease, Pages
RYEGRASS, perennial (*cont.*)	Rust, 141 Ryegrass Mosaic, 208 Ryegrass yellows, 213 Sclerotinia Patch, 79 Sclerotium Blight, 71 Septoria Leaf Spot, 117 Slime Molds, 135 Smut stripe, 149 Spermospora Leaf Spot, 123 Summer Patch, 47 Take-all Patch, 28 Typhula Blight, 77 Western Ryegrass Mosaic, 208

ST. AUGUSTINEGRASS
(*Stenotaphrum secundatum*)
	Cercospora Leaf Spot, 120
	Downy Mildew, 136
	Fairy Rings, 181
	Gray Leaf Spot, 111
	Nematodes
	   burrowing, 227
	   cyst, 223
	   cystoid, 224
	   dagger, 233
	   lance, 234
	   root knot, 224
	   ring, 231
	   root lesion, 226
	   spiral, 228
	   sting, 230
	Rhizoctonia Blight, 33
	Rhizoctonia Sheath Spot, 64
	Slime Molds, 135
	Smut
	   loose, 192
	St. Augustine Decline Virus, 205
	Take-all Root Rot, 176

ZOYSIA
(*Zoysia* spp.)
	Anthracnose, 156
	Black Leaf Spot, 113
	Curvularia Blight, 159
	Fairy Rings, 181
	Helminthosporium Crown and Root Rot, 110
	Nematodes
	   dagger, 233
	   lance, 234
	   ring, 231
	   root knot, pseudo, 224
	   root lesion, 226
	   spiral, 228
	   sting, 230
	   stubby root, 233
	Rhizoctonia Blight, 33
	Rhizoctonia Sheath Spot, 64
	Rhizoctonia Yellow Patch, 31
	Rust, 141
	Sclerotinia Dollar Spot, 65
	Slime Molds, 135

Table III. Grass Species Susceptible to Turfgrass Pathogens Listed by Common Name

Common Name	Scientific Name, Pages
Alkaligrass (marsh spikegrass, seashore saltgrass)	*Distichlis spicata* (L.) Greene, 196
Nutall	*Puccinellia airoides* (Nutt.) Wat. and Coult., 124, 125, 144, 146, 150, 192
Angletowngrass	*Andropogon nodosus* (Willem.) Nash, 94
Bahiagrass	*Paspalum notatum* Flugge, 67, 228, 234
Barley	
bobtail	*Hordeum jubatum* var. *caespitosum* (Scribn.) Hitchc., 30, 129, 140, 143, 192
bulbous	*H. bulbosum* L., 75, 98, 207
cultivated	*H. vulgare* L., 30, 35, 44, 45, 53, 54, 55, 61, 65, 72, 75, 78, 88, 89, 98, 106, 112, 119, 124, 126, 127, 129, 138, 140, 143, 172, 178, 179, 193, 197, 205, 206, 207, 209, 212, 213, 223, 225, 226, 227, 230, 232, 233, 234
four rowed	(see cultivated barley)
foxtail (squirrel-tailgrass)	*H. jubatum* L., 35, 44, 45, 53, 54, 61, 75, 85, 98, 114, 119, 126, 127, 129, 138, 143, 144, 147, 150, 153, 192, 193, 197, 209, 223, 225
little	*H. pusillum* Nutt., 30, 89, 119, 129, 140
meadow	*H. brachyantherum* Nevski, 35, 61, 75, 119, 126, 128, 140, 143, 147, 153, 192, 197, 207
Mediterranean	*H. hystrix* Roth, 35, 61, 89, 143, 198, 207
mouse	(see way barley)
squirreltail	(see foxtail barley)
way (way bentgrass, wall barleygrass, mouse barley)	*H. murinum* L., 30, 35, 53, 54, 61, 75, 89, 98, 126, 127, 140, 197, 223
Barleygrass, wall	(see way barley)
Barnyardgrass (cockspurgrass)	*Echinochloa crusgalli* (L.) Beauv., 35, 44, 53, 54, 61, 90, 98, 107, 112, 121, 143, 172, 178, 225
Beachgrass	
American (marran, psamma, sand reed)	*Ammophila breviligulata* Fernald, 142, 143, 150, 196
European (Marrangrass)	*A. arenaria* (L.) Link, 53, 54, 98, 142, 150, 196
Beardgrass	
annual (rabbitfootgrass)	*Polypogon monspeliensis* (L.) Desf., 140, 142, 144
prairie	(see little bluestem)
silver	(see silver bluestem)
yellow	(see Turkestan bluestem)
Bentgrass	
autumn	*Agrostis perennans* (Walt.) Tuckerm., 101, 143, 145, 155, 195
brown	(see velvet bentgrass)
Colonial	*A. tenuis* Sibth., 29, 35, 38, 44, 53, 54, 61, 67, 71, 75, 78, 80, 83, 89, 98, 101, 106, 112, 114, 115, 117, 122, 128, 131, 133, 138, 142, 143, 150, 152, 193, 195, 196, 208, 209, 212, 219, 225, 229, 231, 232, 234
creeping	*A. palustris* Huds., 27, 29, 33, 35, 38, 44, 50, 53, 54, 55, 61, 65, 67, 71, 72, 73, 75, 78, 80, 83, 87, 89, 98, 101, 106, 107, 112, 115, 117, 128, 131, 133, 138, 142, 143, 147, 150, 152, 172, 178, 179, 191, 193, 195, 196, 198, 209, 212, 219, 225, 229, 231, 232, 234
dune	*A. pallens* Trin., 147
fine	(see Colonial bentgrass)
Rhode Island	*A. capillaris* L., 219
spike (spike redtop)	*A. exarata* Trin., 35, 61, 75, 115, 117, 119, 128, 131, 140, 142, 150, 196, 219
Thurber	*A. thurberiana* Hitchc., 142
velvet	*A. canina* L., 29, 35, 38, 53, 55, 61, 67, 71, 75, 78, 80, 83, 89, 98, 101, 107, 115, 126, 131, 138, 143, 196, 198, 209, 219
way	(see way barley)
winter (ticklegrass, hairgrass)	*A. hiemalis* (Walt.) B.S.P., 84, 115, 117, 125, 128, 145, 196
Bermudagrass (wiregrass)	*Cynodon dactylon* (L.) Pers., 27, 33, 35, 38, 53, 55, 61, 65, 67, 71, 72, 75, 87, 88, 89, 91, 98, 107, 108, 109, 112, 114, 140, 143, 178, 207, 213, 225, 226, 227, 228, 229, 230, 233, 234

Common Name	Scientific Name, Pages
African, Uganda	*Cynodon transvaalensis* Burtt-Davy, 53, 88
Sunturf	*Cynodon magennisii* Hurcombe, 53
Billiondollargrass (Japanese millet)	*Echinochloa crusgalli* var. *frumentacea* (Roxb.) W. F. Wright, 44, 94, 112, 178, 206
Blowoutgrass	*Redfieldia flexuosa* (Thurb.) Vasey, 35, 53, 54, 62
Bluegrass	
alkali	*Poa juncifolia* Scribn., 33, 44, 54, 98, 117, 124, 129, 140, 143, 146, 150, 154, 197
Alpine	*P. alpina* L., 124, 129, 140, 145, 150, 219
annual (annual meadowgrass, low speargrass)	*P. annua* L., 27, 30, 33, 35, 38, 44, 45, 50, 53, 55, 62, 65, 67, 72, 75, 78, 83, 87, 89, 94, 98, 112, 114, 116, 138, 143, 145, 146, 150, 154, 172, 193, 197, 207, 208, 212, 219, 225, 226, 231, 234
Arctic	*P. arctica* R. Br., 75, 124, 150
big	*P. ampla* Merr., 35, 62, 75, 80, 94, 116, 117, 124, 129, 133, 140, 145, 146, 153, 197, 207
Bigelow	*P. bigelovii* Vasey and Scribn., 145, 146
bog	*P. leptocoma* Trin., 75, 140
bulbous (winter)	*P. bulbosa* L., 35, 62, 75, 94, 98, 126, 143, 195, 209
Canada (flat-stemmed meadowgrass, wiregrass)	*P. compressa* L., 30, 35, 53, 54, 55, 62, 80, 89, 94, 98, 107, 116, 117, 124, 129, 142, 143, 145, 150, 154, 179, 195, 197, 206, 207, 212
Canby	*P. canbyi* (Scribn.) Piper, 30, 55, 89, 116, 117, 140, 145, 146, 150, 153, 154, 197, 207
Chapman	*P. chapmaniana* Scribn., 143
Cusick	*P. cusickii* Vasey, 75, 116, 124, 140, 150
fowl (fowl meadowgrass)	*P. palustris* L., 35, 45, 53, 54, 62, 75, 78, 98, 117, 119, 140, 143, 145, 146, 150, 193, 197, 206, 209
Howell	*P. howellii* Vasey and Scribn., 143
inland	*P. interior* Rybd., 129, 140, 143, 145, 146, 207
Kentucky (smooth-stalked meadowgrass)	*P. pratensis* L., 27, 30, 33, 35, 38, 44, 45, 50, 53, 54, 55, 62, 65, 67, 72, 75, 78, 80, 83, 85, 87, 89, 94, 98, 103, 106, 107, 112, 115, 116, 117, 119, 124, 126, 129, 138, 140, 143, 145, 146, 150, 153, 154, 179, 192, 193, 195, 197, 198, 207, 208, 209, 212, 219, 225, 226, 227, 229, 231, 232, 233, 234
long tongue muttongrass	*P. longiligula* Scribn. and Will, 129, 133, 142, 197
muttongrass	*P. fendleriana* (Steud.) Vasey (*P. brevipaniculata* Scribn. and Williams, *P. longipedunculata* Scribn., *P. scabriuscula* Williams), 124, 142, 145, 146, 197
Nevada	*P. nevadensis* Vasey, 53, 54, 116, 117, 124, 129, 140, 143, 146, 154, 197
Pacific	*P. gracillima* Vasey, 116, 124, 126, 129, 140
pine	*P. scabrella* Thurb., 116, 140, 143, 146, 197
plains	*P. arida* Vasey, 94, 116, 124, 129, 140, 143, 145, 146, 197
rough (roughstalk bluegrass, roughstalked meadowgrass, trivialis)	*P. trivialis* L., 30, 35, 45, 53, 62, 75, 78, 80, 83, 94, 106, 112, 124, 129, 138, 144, 145, 146, 150, 195, 198, 208, 209, 212, 223, 225, 226
Sandberg	*P. secunda* Presl, 35, 53, 54, 55, 62, 75, 78, 94, 98, 116, 117, 124, 126, 129, 140, 143, 146, 150, 153, 154, 179, 192, 195, 197
Skyline	*P. epilis* Scribn., 124, 140
Texas	*P. arachnifera* Torr., 117, 129, 140, 142, 143, 145
Wheeler	*P. nervosa* (Hook.) Vasey, 116, 119, 124, 129, 140, 145, 146, 153, 197
winter	(see bulbous bluegrass)
wood (wood meadowgrass)	*P. nemoralis* L., 35, 45, 62, 114, 124, 129, 140, 145, 193, 197, 209, 212, 233
yellow	(see Turkestan bluestem)
Bluejoint	(see bluejoint reedgrass)
Bluestem	
big	*Andropogon gerardi* Vitman, also *A. furcatus* Muhl., 195, 196, 206, 209, 230, 234
little	*A. scoparius* Michx., 94, 126, 195, 196, 209, 226, 230, 234
sand (turkeyfoot)	*A. hallii* Hack., 98, 178

Common Name	Scientific Name, Pages
Bluestem (*cont.*)	
silver (silver beardgrass)	*A. saccharoides* Swartz, 196, 226, 229, 230, 232, 234
Turkestan (yellow beardgrass, yellow bluegrass)	*A. ischaemum* L., 226, 229, 234
Bluetop	(see bluejoint reedgrass)
Bottlebrush	*Hystrix patula* Moench, 36, 75, 89, 98, 112, 119, 124, 126, 129, 140, 143, 144, 150, 195, 197, 209, 225
Brachiaria	*Brachiaria platyphylla* (Griseb.) Nash, 196, 206
Bristlegrass	
green	*Setaria viridis* (L.) Beauv., 35, 45, 62, 98, 112, 138, 179, 194, 197, 208, 225
green foxtail	
knotroot	*S. geniculata* (Lam.) Beauv., 30, 89
plains (plains foxtail)	*S. macrostachya* H.B.K., 197
yellow (yellow foxtail)	*S. lutescens* (Weigel) Hubb., 35, 45, 53, 54, 62, 98, 112, 126, 138, 179, 193, 206, 208
Brome	
California	*Bromus carinatus* Hook. and Arn., 29, 35, 44, 53, 54, 55, 61, 75, 78, 89, 98, 115, 126, 127, 128, 133, 140, 145, 152, 178, 179, 196, 207
Canada	*B. purgans* L., 75, 114, 128, 143, 145, 209
downy	(see brome cheatgrass)
field	*B. arvensis* L., 29, 35, 53, 54, 55, 61, 89, 98, 127, 178, 208, 223
fringed	*B. ciliatus* L., 29, 85, 89, 114, 115, 128, 142, 143, 145, 150, 152, 196, 208
Japanese	(see Japenese chess)
meadow	*B. erectus* Huds., 29, 35, 53, 54, 55, 61, 75, 80, 89, 98, 114, 140, 178, 196, 207
mountain	(see California brome)
nodding	*B. anomalus* Rupr., 114, 142, 143, 145
rescue	(see rescuegrass)
smooth	*B. inermis* Leyss., 29, 35, 44, 45, 53, 54, 55, 61, 75, 78, 80, 83, 89, 90, 98, 107, 109, 112, 114, 122, 126, 127, 128, 133, 138, 140, 142, 150, 178, 179, 193, 196, 207, 208, 209, 225, 227, 232, 233
Bromegrass	
barren	*Bromus sterilis* L., 29, 38, 89, 145, 179, 207, 208, 223
soft	(see soft chess)
wood	*Brachypodium sylvaticum* (Huds.) Beauv., 114, 223
wood false	(see wood bromegrass)
Brookgrass	*Catabrosa aquatica* (L.) Beauv., 140, 143
Broomsedge	*Andropogon virginicus*, 150, 196, 206
Browntop	(see Colonial bentgrass)
Buffalograss	*Buchloe dactyloides* (Nutt.) Engelm., 35, 61, 94, 140, 143
Bunchgrass	
feather	(see green needlegrass)
green mountain	(see greenleaf fescue)
Canarygrass	*Phalaris canariensis* L., 142, 197, 213
California	*P. californica* Hook. and Arn., 143
Carolina	(see also Maygrass) *P. caroliniana* Walt., 142, 143
large	*P. tuberosa* L., 35, 62, 98, 207
reed	*P. arundinacea* L., 30, 35, 53, 54, 62, 89, 98, 106, 107, 124, 125, 126, 127, 138, 140, 142, 143, 150, 197, 207, 225
Cane	
giant	*Arundinaria gigantea* (Walt.) Muhl., 128
small	*A. tecta* (Walt.) Muhl., 128
Carpetgrass	
common	*Axonopus affinis* Chase, 35, 55, 61
Cat's-tail	(see timothy)
Centipedegrass	*Eremochloa ophiuroides* (Munro) Hack., 27, 35, 44, 61, 65, 87, 112, 205, 230, 234
Cheat	(see brome chess)
Cheatgrass	
brome	*Bromus tectorum* L., 29, 35, 44, 53, 54, 61, 65, 75, 78, 89, 98, 126, 143, 145, 179, 206, 207, 208, 212, 225
downy	(see brome cheatgrass)

Common Name	Scientific Name, Pages
Goatgrass (*cont.*)	
jointed	*A. triuncialis* L., 53, 54, 179, 205, 207
Goldentop	*Lamarckia aurea* (L.) Moench, 142, 143
Goosegrass	*Eleusine indica* (L.) Gaertn., 35, 61, 107, 108, 112, 138, 206, 225, 227
Grama	
blue	*Bouteloua gracilis* (H.B.K.) Lag., 35, 45, 53, 54, 55, 61, 98, 127, 143, 178, 193, 195, 196
hairy	*B. hirsuta* Lag., 229
side-oats	(see mesquitegrass)
Guineagrass	*Panicum maximum* Jacq., 107, 121, 197, 205, 227, 228
Hairgrass	(see also Winter bentgrass)
annual	*Deschampsia danthonioides* (Trin.) Munro ex Benth., 29, 89, 119, 124, 125, 128, 140, 143, 147, 207
crested	(see prairie Junegrass)
long-awned	(see hair lawn muhly)
mountain	*D. atropurpurea* (Wahl.) Scheele, 35, 61, 119, 125, 128, 150
silver	*Aira caryophyllea* L., 198
slender	*Deschampsia elongata* (Hook.) Munro ex Benth., 78, 126, 128, 143, 147
tufted	*D. caespitosa* (L.) Beauv., 29, 89, 119, 122, 125, 128, 131, 142, 143, 145, 147, 150, 196, 198, 207
Hardinggrass	*Phalaris tuberosa* var. Stenoptera (Hack.) Hitchc. (*P. stenoptera* Hack.), 107
Harestailgrass	*Lagurus ovatus* L., 142, 143
Herdsgrass	(see red top and timothy)
Holygrass (sweetgrass)	*Hierochloe odorata* (L.) Beauv., 35, 61, 112, 126, 142, 197
Indiangrass	
yellow	*Sorghast rum nutans* (L.) Nash, 53, 54, 97, 197
Johnsongrass	*Sorghum halepense* (L.) Pers., 44, 55, 71, 94, 126, 179, 206, 208, 227, 230, 233, 234
Junegrass	
prairie (crested hairgrass)	*Koeleria cristata* (L.) Pers., 35, 75, 98, 124, 129, 140, 143, 150, 153, 179, 195, 197, 207, 223
Jungle-rice	*Echinochloa colonum* (L.) Link, 35, 61, 112, 225, 227
Lawngrass	
Japanese	(see Zoysiagrass)
Korean	(see Zoysiagrass)
Lovegrass	
Boer	*Eragrostis chloromelos* Steud., 55
India	*E. pilosa* (L.) Beauv., 98
Lehmann	*E. lehmanniana* Nees, 55
purple	*E. pectinacea* (Michx.) Nees, 107, 138, 225
sand	*E. trichodes* (Nutt.) Wood, 35, 61
weeping	*E. curvula* (Schrad.) Nees, 35, 53, 55, 61, 98, 112
Lymegrass	
sand	(see European dunegrass)
Maidencane	*Panicum hemitomon* Schult., 228
Maize	
corn	*Zea mays* L., 35, 44, 45, 53, 54, 55, 62, 71, 90, 98, 112, 138, 179, 194, 206, 208, 209, 212, 230, 231, 233
Indian corn	(see corn)
Manilagrass	*Zoysia matrella* (L.) Merr., 113, 146, 230, 231, 234
	Z. pungens Willd., 146
Mannagrass	
American	*Glyceria grandis* S. Wats., 85, 119, 128, 143, 146, 197
eastern	*G. septentrionalis* Hitchc., 128, 195, 197
floating	(see Eastern mannagrass)
fowl (fowl meadowgrass)	*G. striata* (Lam.) Hitchc., 85, 119, 128, 140, 142, 143, 153, 195, 197
nerved	(see fowl mannagrass)

Common Name | Scientific Name, Pages

Mannagrass (*cont.*)
  northern — *G. borealis* (Nash) Batchelder, 128, 197, 198
  pale — *G. pallida* (Torr.) Trin., 154
  rattlesnake (rattlesnakegrass) — *G. canadensis* (Michx.) Trin., 195, 197
  tall — *G. elata* (Nash) Hitchc., 115, 119, 128, 142, 143
Marram — (see American beachgrass)
Marramgrass — (see European beachgrass)
Marshgrass
  salt — (see saltmeadow cordgrass)
Maygrass — *Phalaris caroliniana* Walt., 142, 143
(see also Carolina canarygrass)
Meadowgrass
  annual — (see annual bluegrass)
  flat-stemmed — (see Canada bluegrass)
  fowl — (see fowl mannagrass and fowl bluegrass)
  rough-stalked — (see rough-bluegrass)
  smooth-stalked — (see Kentucky bluegrass)
  wood — (see wood bluegrass)
Melic
  California — *Melica imperfecta* Trin., 124, 153
  false — *Schizachne purpurascens* (Torr.) Swallen, 114, 119, 126, 142
  Harford — *Melica harfordii* Boland, 124
  Smith — *M. smithii* (Porter) Vasey, 123, 129
Mesquitegrass (side-oats grama) — *Bouteloua curtipendula* (Michx.) Torr., 35, 45, 53, 54, 61, 98, 114, 125, 127, 143, 178, 193, 196, 207, 230, 232, 234

Millet
  browntop (browntop panicum) — *Panicum ramosum* L., 226, 229, 230
  cattail — (see pearl millet)
  foxtail — *Setaria italica* (L.) Beauv., 53, 54, 55, 98, 112, 179, 205
  Japanese — (see billiondollargrass)
  pearl (cattail) — *Pennisetum glaucum* (L.) R. Br., 71, 94, 109, 138, 205, 206, 232, 233
  proso (hog millet, broomcorn millet) — *Panicum miliaceum* L., 35, 45, 53, 54, 55, 62, 98, 112, 138, 179, 193, 205
  Texas (Coloradograss) — *P. texanum* Buckl., 112
Milletgrass
  spreading — *Milium effusum* L., 129, 140, 143
  tall — (see spreading milletgrass)
Moorgrass — *Molinia caerulea* (L.) Moench, 143
Muhlenbergia
  marsh — *Muhlenbergia racemosa* (Michx.) B.S.P., 35, 45, 53, 54, 62, 98, 112, 125, 129, 193, 209
  wood — *M. sylvatica* (Torr.) Torr., 129
Muhly
  alkali — (see scratchgrass)
  max — *M. richardsonis* (Trin.) Rydb., 35, 62
  plains — *M. cuspidata* (Torr.) Rydb., 125, 143
  pull-up — *M. filiformis* (Thurb.) Rydb., 129
  spike — *M. wrightii* Vasey, 94
  Texas — *M. texana* Buckl., 98
  wirestem — *M. frondosa* (Poir.) Fernald, 209
Muscarenegrass — *Zoysia tenuifolia* Willd., 67, 146, 234
Muttongrass — *Poa fendleriana* (Steud.) Vasey, 124, 142, 145, 146, 197
  longtongue — *P. longiligula* Scribn. and Will., 129, 133, 142, 197
Napiergrass (elephantgrass) — *Pennisetum purpureum* Schumach., 71, 112
Natalgrass (rubygrass) — *Rhynchelytrum roseum* (Nees) Stapf and Hubb., 112, 228
Needle-and-thread — *Stipa comata* Trin. and Rupr., 35, 54, 62, 75, 98, 124, 126, 129, 144, 179, 197

Needlegrass
  California — *Stipa pulchra* Hitchc., 98
  Columbia — *S. columbiana* Macoun, 75, 124, 129, 197

Common Name	Scientific Name, Pages
Needlegrass (*cont.*)	
desert	*S. speciosa* Trin. and Rupr., 129
green (feather bunchgrass, green stipa)	*S. viridula* Trin., 35, 55, 62, 95, 98, 119, 124, 126, 129, 144, 179, 197
Lemmon	*S. lemmon* (Vasey) Scribn., 75, 124, 129
Letterman	*S. lettermani* Vasey, 123, 129, 197
nodding	*S. cernua* Stebbins and Love, 55
purple	(see Califonia needlegrass)
Richardson	*S. richardsoni* Link, 124
Thurber	*S. thurberiana* Piper, 129
western	*S. occidentalis* Thurb., 126, 129
Williams	*S. williamsii* Scribn., 129, 179
Nimblewill	*Muhlenbergia schreberi* Gmel., 107, 206
Nitgrass	*Gastridium ventricosum* (Gouan) Schinz and Thell., 143, 207
Oat	
slender	*Avena barbata* Brot., 142, 143, 145, 206, 207
wild	*A. fatua* L., 35, 44, 53, 54, 61, 98, 138, 140, 142, 143, 145, 206, 207, 208, 225
Oatgrass	
California	*Danthonia californica* Boland, 35, 61, 124, 128, 198, 207
common wild	*D. spicata* (L.) Beauv., 124, 127, 143, 195, 196
golden	(see yellow trisetum)
Parry	*Danthonia parryi* Scribn., 196
poverty	(see common wild oatgrass)
tall	*Arrhenatherum elatius* (L.), 29, 35, 53, 54, 55, 61, 72, 80, 89, 115, 119, 124, 126, 128, 133, 142, 143, 196, 212, 223, 225, 227
timber	*Danthonia intermedia* Vasey, 150
tuber	*Arrhenatherum elatius* var. *bulbosum* (Willd.) Spenner, 128
wild	(see wild oat)
yellow	(see yellow trisetum)
Oats	
animated	*Avena sterilis* L., 29, 35, 61, 89, 98, 112, 206, 207, 223
common	*A. sativa* L., 27, 29, 33, 35, 44, 45, 50, 53, 54, 55, 61, 65, 72, 75, 78, 87, 89, 98, 109, 112, 119, 124, 126, 128, 138, 140, 142, 143, 145, 178, 179, 193, 196, 205, 206, 207, 208, 209, 212, 223, 225, 226, 227, 230, 231, 232, 233, 234
cultivated	(see common oats)
narrow false	(see spike trisetum)
seed	*Uniola paniculata* L., 230
Oniongrass	*Melica bulbosa* Geyer, 119, 123, 126, 129, 195
Alaska	*M. subulata* (Griseb.) Scribn., 129
Geyer	*M. geyeri* Munro, 129, 146
purple	*M. spectabilis* Scribn., 123, 129, 150
Orchardgrass (cocksfoot)	*Dactylis glomerata* L., 35, 44, 45, 53, 54, 55, 61, 75, 78, 80, 98, 112, 124, 126, 127, 128, 131, 138, 140, 143, 145, 146, 150, 152, 172, 178, 193, 195, 196, 206, 207, 208, 209, 212, 223, 225, 227, 229, 231, 232, 233, 234
Ozarkgrass	*Limnodea arkansana* (Nutt.) L. H. Dewey, 143
Panic	
beaked	*Panicum anceps* Michx., 107
blue (giant panicgrass)	*P. antidotale* Retz., 55, 94
Panicgrass	
giant	(see blue panic)
Panicum	
brown top	(see browntop millet)
fall	*P. dichotomiflorum* Michx., 107, 112, 121, 154, 205, 206
Paspalum	
brown seed	*Paspalum plicatulum* Michx., 112, 142
sand	*P. stramineum* Nash, 112
Pinegrass	(see Arizona fescue)
Plumegrass, silver	*Erianthus alopecuroides* (L.) Ell., 197
Porcupinegrass	*Stipa spartea* Trin., 35, 54, 62, 98, 124, 197, 209
Povertygrass (red three awn)	*Aristida longiseta* Steud., 125

Common Name	Scientific Name, Pages
Psamma	(see American beachgrass)
Purpletop	*Tridens flavus* (L.) Hitchc., 144, 206
Quakegrass (Couchgrass)	*Agropyron repens* (L.) Beauv., 29, 35, 38, 53, 54, 55, 61, 83, 89, 98, 107, 114, 115, 119, 124, 126, 127, 128, 130, 133, 138, 140, 142, 143, 144, 149, 152, 178, 196, 209, 212, 225
Quakinggrass	
big	*Briza maxima* L., 143, 205
little	*B. minor* L., 143
perennial	*B. media* L., 38
smaller	(see little quakinggrass)
Rabbitfootgrass	(see annual beardgrass)
Rattlesnakegrass	(see rattlesnake mannagrass)
Red Top (herdsgrass)	*Agrostis alba* L., 29, 35, 38, 53, 54, 55, 61, 67, 75, 83, 84, 89, 98, 101, 114, 115, 117, 122, 126, 127, 128, 131, 133, 140, 142, 143, 145, 147, 152, 155, 195, 196, 207, 212, 219, 225
Oregon	*A. oregonensia* Vasey, 128, 133
spike	(see spike bentgrass)
Reed	
common	(see common reedgrass)
giant	*Arundo donax* L., 112, 124
Reedgrass	
bluejoint	*Calamagrostis canadensis* (Michx.) Beauv., 75, 85, 114, 119, 125, 126, 127, 128, 131, 133, 140, 142, 143, 195, 196
common	*Phragmites communis* Trin., 55, 124, 125, 129, 197, 209
giant	(see big sandreed)
northern	*Calamagrostis inexpansa* A. Gray, 114, 115, 125, 128, 142, 143, 196
Pacific	*C. nutkaensis* (Presl) Steud., 142, 196
plains	*C. montanensis* Scribn., 35, 61, 125, 142, 150
prairie	(see prairie sandreed)
purple	*C. purpurascens* R. Br., 142
sand	(see prairie sandreed)
Scribner	*C. scribneri* Beal, 122, 125, 150
sweet	(see drooping woodreed and stout woodreed)
Rescuegrass (rescue brome)	*Bromus catharticus* Vahl, 35, 61, 98, 112, 128, 133, 140, 145, 207, 226, 230
Rhodesgrass	*Chloris gayana* Kunth, 90, 94, 207
Ribbongrass	*Phalaris arundinacea* var. *picta* L., 107, 197
Rice	*Oryza sativa* L., 27, 35, 53, 54, 55, 62, 64, 72, 87, 88, 90, 112, 138, 154, 207, 208, 212, 224, 226, 227, 231
Indian	(see annual wildrice)
wild	(see annual wildrice)
Ricegrass	
Bloomer	*Oryzopsis bloomeri* (Boland) Ricker, 75
Indian	*O. hymenoides* (Roem. and Schult.) Ricker, 35, 53, 54, 62, 75, 98, 119, 129, 179, 194
Ripgutgrass	*Bromus rigidus* Roth, 35, 61, 75, 140, 143, 145, 207
Rivergrass	*Fluminea festucacea* (Willd.) Hitchc., 146
Rubygrass	(see Natalgrass)
Rushgrass	
long leaved (meadow tall dropseed, tall dropseed)	*Sporobolus asper* (Michx.) Kunth, 124, 144, 209
rough	*S. clandestinus* (Bieler) Hitchc., 124
sand dropseed	*S. cryptandrus* (Torr.) A. Gray, 35, 53, 54, 55, 62, 115, 124, 144
small	*S. neglectus* Nash, 35, 62, 138
Rye	
beach wild (American dunegrass)	*Elymus mollis* Trin., 124, 128, 145, 197
beardgrass, wild	*E. triticoides* Buckl., 114, 115, 127, 128, 140, 142, 143, 144, 145, 150, 192, 197
blue wild	*E. glaucus* Buckl., 29, 35, 53, 54, 61, 75, 78, 89, 98, 119, 124, 126, 127, 128, 133, 140, 143, 144, 145, 150, 152, 197
Canada, wild	*E. canadensis* L., 29, 35, 53, 54, 55, 61, 75, 80, 89, 98, 114, 119, 124, 126, 127, 128, 130, 140, 142, 143, 144, 145, 150, 152, 178, 192, 195, 196, 206, 226, 227, 229, 230, 234

Scientific Name	Common Name, Pages
Bromus arvensis L.	field brome, 29, 35, 53, 54, 55, 61, 89, 98, 127, 178, 208, 223
Bromus asper Murray	114
Bromus breviaristatus Buckl. (*B. subvelutinus* Shear)	140, 145
Bromus brizaeformis Fisch. and Meyer	chess, rattlesnake, 53, 54, 207
Bromus carinatus Hook. and Arn. (*B. carinatus* var. *hookerianus* Shear)	California brome, mountain brome, 29, 35, 44, 53, 54, 55, 61, 75, 78, 89, 98, 115, 126, 127, 128, 133, 140, 145, 152, 178, 179, 196, 207
Bromus catharticus Vahl	rescue brome, rescuegrass, 35, 61, 98, 112, 128, 133, 140, 145, 207, 226, 230
Bromus ciliatus L. (*B. richardsoni* Link)	fringed brome, 29, 85, 89, 114, 115, 128, 142, 143, 145, 150, 152, 196, 208
Bromus commutatus Schrad.	hairy chess, upright chess, 75, 126, 138, 140, 145, 207
Bromus erectus Huds.	meadow brome, upright chess, 29, 35, 53, 54, 55, 61, 75, 80, 89, 98, 114, 140, 178, 196, 207
Bromus frondosus (Shear) Woot. and Standl.	127, 128
Bromus grandis (Shear) Hitchc.	145
Bromus hordeaceus L.	soft bromegrass, soft chess, 143
Bromus inermis Leyss.	smooth brome, 29, 35, 44, 45, 53, 54, 55, 61, 75, 78, 80, 83, 89, 90, 98, 107, 109, 112, 114, 122, 126, 127, 128, 133, 138, 140, 142, 150, 178, 179, 193, 196, 207, 208, 209, 225, 227, 232, 233
Bromus japonicus Thunb.	Japanese chess, Japanese brome, 29, 35, 53, 54, 61, 73, 89, 98, 126, 138, 143, 179, 207
Bromus laevipes Shear	128, 145
Bromus madritensis L.	29, 35, 53, 54, 61, 89, 98, 145
Bromus marginatus Nees	145, 152
Bromus mollis L.	soft bromegrass, soft chess, 35, 38, 44, 55, 61, 75, 128, 140, 145, 207, 208
Bromus orcuttianus Vasey	29, 89, 128
Bromus pacificus Shear	128
Bromus polyanthus Scribn.	Spencergrass, 142, 143, 145
Bromus pumpellianus Scribn.	35, 53, 54, 61, 127, 142, 143, 145, 196
Bromus purgans L.	hairy woodchess, Canada brome, 75, 114, 128, 143, 145, 209
Bromus racemosus L.	29, 35, 61, 75, 89, 140, 145, 198, 207, 208
Bromus rigidus Roth (*B. villosus* Forssk.)	ripgutgrass, 35, 61, 75, 140, 143, 145, 207
Bromus rigidus var. *gussonei* (Parl.) Coss. and Dur. (*B. villosus* var. *guussonii* Aschers. and Graebn.)	145
Bromus rubens L.	foxtail chess, 145, 207
Bromus scoparius	145
Bromus secalinus L.	cheat, chess, chess brome, 29, 35, 61, 75, 89, 127, 128, 140, 143, 145, 196, 207, 208, 225
Bromus sitchensis Trin.	112, 128, 145
Bromus sterilis L.	barren bromegrass, 29, 38, 89, 145, 179, 207, 208, 223
Bromus syriaci	114
Bromus tectorum L.	cheatgrass, cheatgrass brome, downy brome, downy cheat, downy chess, 29, 35, 44, 53, 54, 61, 65, 75, 78, 89, 98, 126, 143, 145, 179, 206, 207, 208, 212, 225
Bromus tectorum var. *nudum* Mert. and Koch	143
Bromus tomentellus Boiss.	207
Bromus trinii Desv. (*B. eximius* Piper)	Chilean chess, 114
Bromus vulgaris (Hook.) Shear	29, 89, 122, 128, 140
Buchloe dactyloides (Nutt.) Engelm.	buffalograss, 35, 61, 94, 140, 143
Calamagrostis breweri Thurb.	shorthair, 75
Calamagrostis canadensis (Michx.) Beauv.	bluejoint, bluejoint reedgrass, bluetop, 75, 85, 114, 119, 125, 126, 127, 128, 131, 133, 140, 142, 143, 195, 196
Calamagrostis canadensis var. *scabra* (Presl) Hitchc.	115, 128, 131, 150, 152
Calamagrostis hyperborea Lange	142, 143
Calamagrostis inexspansa A Gray (*C. elongata* Rydb.)	Northern reedgrass, 114, 115, 125, 128, 142, 143, 196
Calamagrostis koelerioides Vasey	125, 142
Calamagrostis montanensis Scribn.	plains reedgrass, 35, 61, 125, 142, 150
Calamagrostis neglecta (Ehrh.) Gaertn. Mey. and Schreb.	85, 142, 196

Scientific Name	Common Name, Pages
Calamagrostis nutkaensis (Presl) Steud. (*C. aleutica* Trin.)	Pacific reedgrass, 142, 196
Calamagrostis pickeringii A. Gray	150
Calamagrostis purpurascens R. Br.	purple reedgrass, 142
Calamagrostis rubescens Buckl.	pinegrass, 115, 122, 125, 140, 142
Calamagrostis scopulorum Jones	142
Calamagrostis scribneri Beal	Scribner reedgrass, 122, 125, 150
Calamovilfa gigantea (Nutt.) Scribn. and Merr.	big sandreed, giant reedgrass, 195
Calamovilfa longifolia (Hook.) Scribn.	prairie sandgrass, prairie sandreed, prairie reedgrass, sand reedgrass, 53, 54, 98, 124, 143, 178
Catabrosa aquatica (L.) Beauv.	brookgrass, 140, 143
Cenchrus brownii R.S.	107
Cenchrus echanitus L.	107
Cenchrus pauciflorus Benth.	field sandbur, sandbur, 35, 53, 54, 61, 98, 178
Chloris castillpoama Lillo and Par.	114
Chloris gayana Kunth	Rhodesgrass, 90, 94, 207
Chloris radiata (L.) Swartz	114
Chloris verticillata Nutt.	windmillgrass, 98
Cinna arundinacea L.	stout woodreed, wood reedgrass, 106, 114, 128, 140, 142, 143, 145, 195, 196
Cinna latifolia (Trevir.) Griseb.	drooping woodreed, wood reedgrass, sweet reedgrass, 119, 128, 142, 143, 145
Cladium jamaicense Crantz	112
Cocos nucifera L.	107
Coix lacryma-jobi L.	205
Commelina elegans H.B.K.	107
Commelina erecta L.	112
Cynodon dactylon (L.) Pers.	bermudagrass, wiregrass, 27, 33, 35, 38, 53, 55, 61, 65, 67, 71, 72, 75, 87, 88, 89, 90, 98, 107, 108, 109, 112, 114, 140, 143, 178, 207, 213, 225, 226, 227, 228, 229, 230, 233, 234
Cynodon magennisii Hurcombe	Sunturf bermudagrass, 53
Cynodon transvaalensis Burtt-Davy	African bermudagrass, Uganda bermudagrass, 53, 88
Cynosurus cristatus L.	crested dog's-tail, crested dogtail, dogstailgrass, 128, 131, 198, 207, 208, 212
Cynosurus echinatus L.	198, 207
Cynosurus pratensis	131
Dactylis glomerata L.	orchardgrass, cocksfoot, 35, 44, 45, 53, 54, 55, 61, 75, 78, 80, 98, 112, 124, 126, 127, 128, 131, 138, 140, 143, 145, 146, 150, 152, 172, 178, 193, 195, 196, 206, 207, 208, 209, 212, 223, 225, 227, 229, 231, 232, 233, 234
Dactyloctenium aegyptiacum Willd.	crowfootgrass, 205, 225
Danthonia californica Boland	California oatgrass, 35, 61, 124, 128, 198, 207
Danthonia intermedia Vasey	timber oatgrass, 150
Danthonia parryi Scribn.	Parry oatgrass, 196
Danthonia spicata (L.) Beauv.	common wild oatgrass, poverty oatgrass, 124, 127, 143, 195, 196
Deschampsia atropurpurea (Wahl.) Scheele	mountain hairgrass, 35, 61, 119, 125, 128, 150
Deschampsia caespitosa (L.) Beauv.	hairgrass, tufted hairgrass, 29, 89, 119, 122, 125, 128, 131, 142, 143, 145, 147, 150, 196, 198, 207
Deschampsia danthonioides (Trin.) Munro ex Benth.	annual hairgrass, 29, 89, 119, 124, 125, 128, 140, 143, 147, 207
Deschampsia elongata (Hook.) Munro	slender hairgrass, 78, 126, 128, 143, 147
Deschampsia holciformis Presl	143
Digitaria cillaris (Rentz.) Koeler	southern crabgrass, 112
Digitaria decumbens Stent.	112
Digitaria horizontalis Willd.	112
Digitaria ischaemum (Schreb.) Schreb. ex Muhl.	smooth crabgrass, 107, 112, 138
Digitaria sanguinalis (L.) Scop.	crabgrass, fingergrass, hairy crabgrass, large crabgrass, 35, 61, 98, 107, 112, 128, 138, 140, 205, 206, 207, 225, 228
Digitaria serotina (Walt.) Michx.	112
Distichlis maritima Raf.	115
Distichlis spicata (L.) Greene	alkalingrass, marsh spikegrass, seashore saltgrass, 196
Distichlis stricta (Torr.) Rydb.	178, 192
Echinochloa colonum (L.) Link	jungle-rice, 35, 61, 112, 225, 227

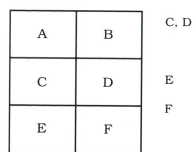

Plate 28 - St. Augustinegrass Decline and Slime Molds

A, B   Overall views of symptoms of St. Augustinegrass decline.

C, D   Close views of individual leaf symptoms of St. Augustinegrass decline. The form and color of these symptoms are similar to those of downy mildew of St. Augustinegrass (see Plate 27-B).

E   Overall view of slime mold on the leaves of Kentucky bluegrass.

F   Close view of fruiting bodies of slime mold fungus growing on the surface of Kentucky bluegrass leaves.

Photos C, D courtesy of Robert Haygood.

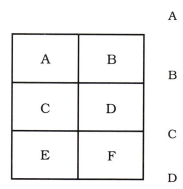

Plate 29 - Fairy Rings and Anaerobiosis

A   Fairy ring showing early Type I symptoms. (There is a zone of stimulated grass and the fruiting structures [sporophores] of the pathogen are evident).

B, C   Fairy rings showing advanced Type I symptoms. (The plants in the former zone of stimulated grass have died.)

D   Profile of greens mixture showing anaerobiosis at the black layer stage of development.

E   Profile of greens mixture showing anaerobiosis at black layer stage of development and illustrating the beneficial effects of aerification. Note the absence of the black layer in the areas penetrated by the aerifier tines.

F   Profile of a sand trap showing anaerobiosis at the black layer stage of development.

Photo B courtesy of Leon Lucas; photos D, E, F courtesy of Jonathan Scott.

Plate 30 - Centipedegrass Decline, Localized Dry Spots, and Nematodes Damage

A   Symptoms of centipedegrass decline. This disease is caused by the same virus that incites St. Augustinegrass decline. See Plate 28-B for a comparison of leaf symptoms.

B   Soil plugs removed from localized dry spot on a creeping bentgrass golf green illustrating the complete absence of soil moisture in and below the root zone.

C   Overall view of damage to creeping bentgrass putting green due to localized dry spots.

D   Sting nematode damage to centipedegrass.

E   Sting nematode damage to bermudagrass.

F   Lance and stunt nematode damage to creeping bentgrass under putting green management.

Photos A, D courtesy Robert Haygood, photos B, C, E courtesy of Leon Lucas, photo F courtesy of Robert Wick.

PLATE 1

PLATE 2

PLATE 3

PLATE 4

PLATE 5

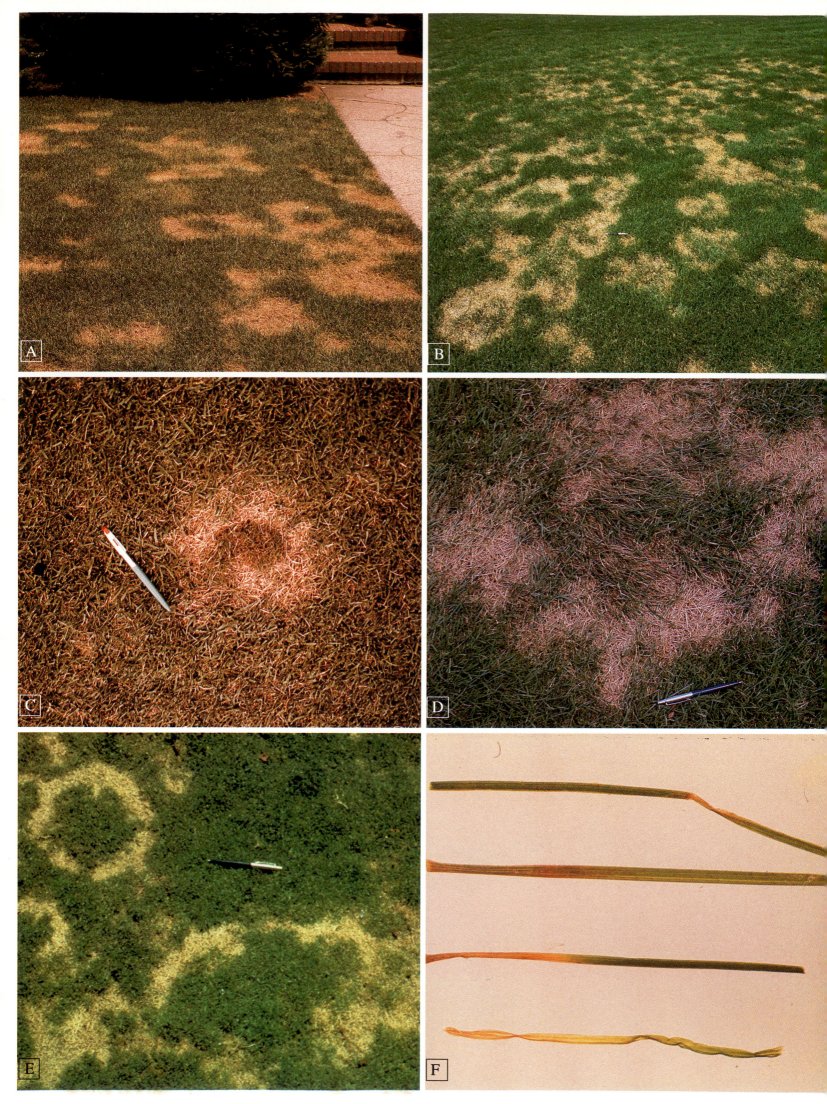

PLATE 6

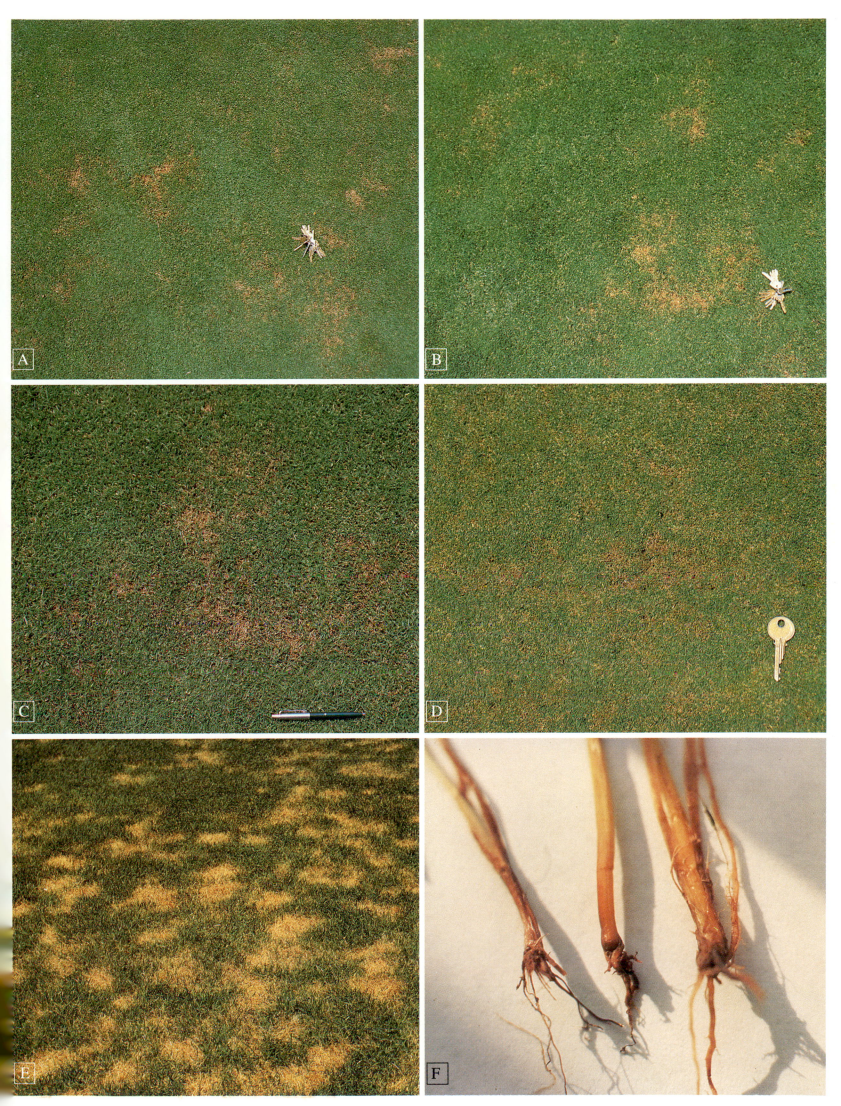

PLATE 7

PLATE 8

PLATE 9

PLATE 10

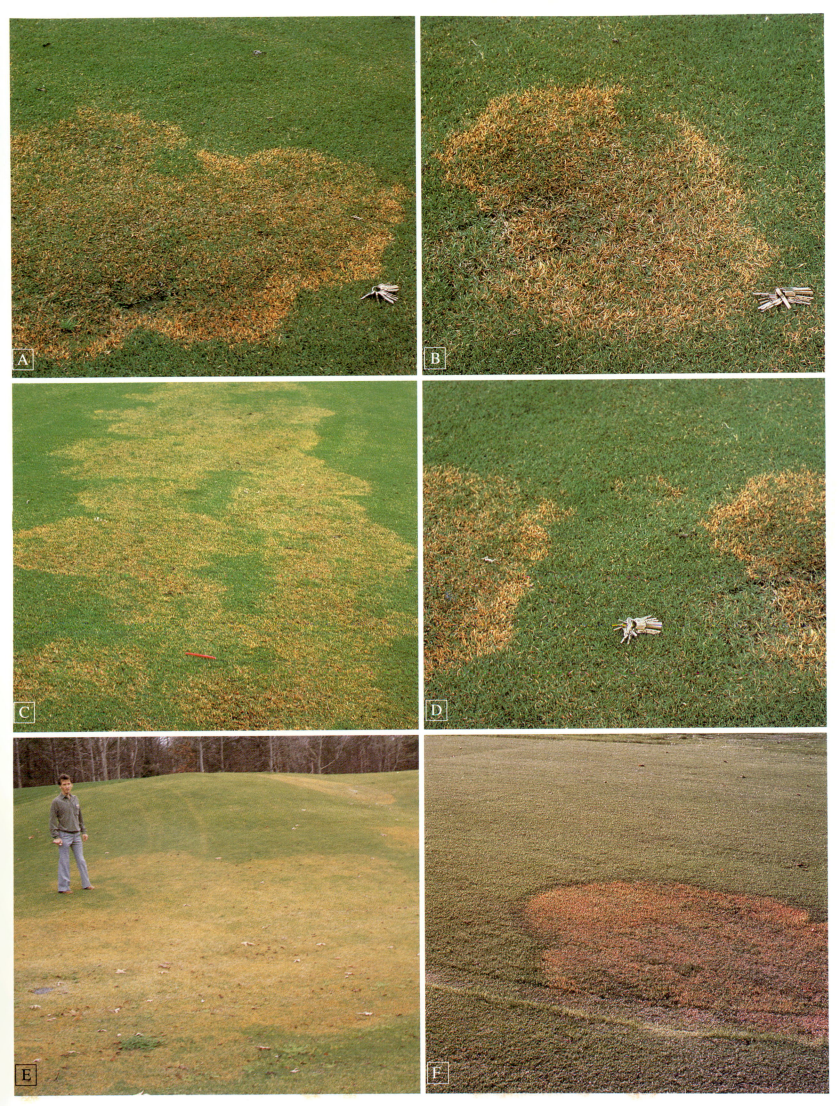

PLATE 11

PLATE 12

PLATE 13

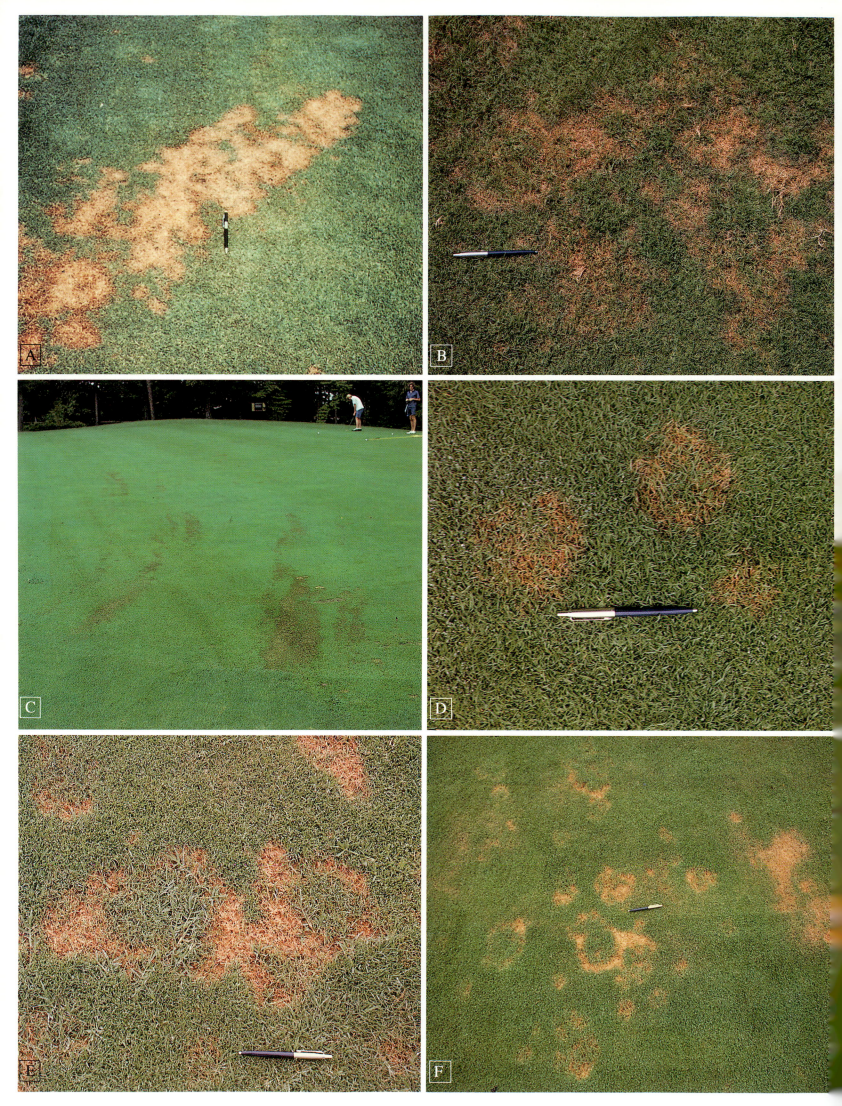

PLATE 14

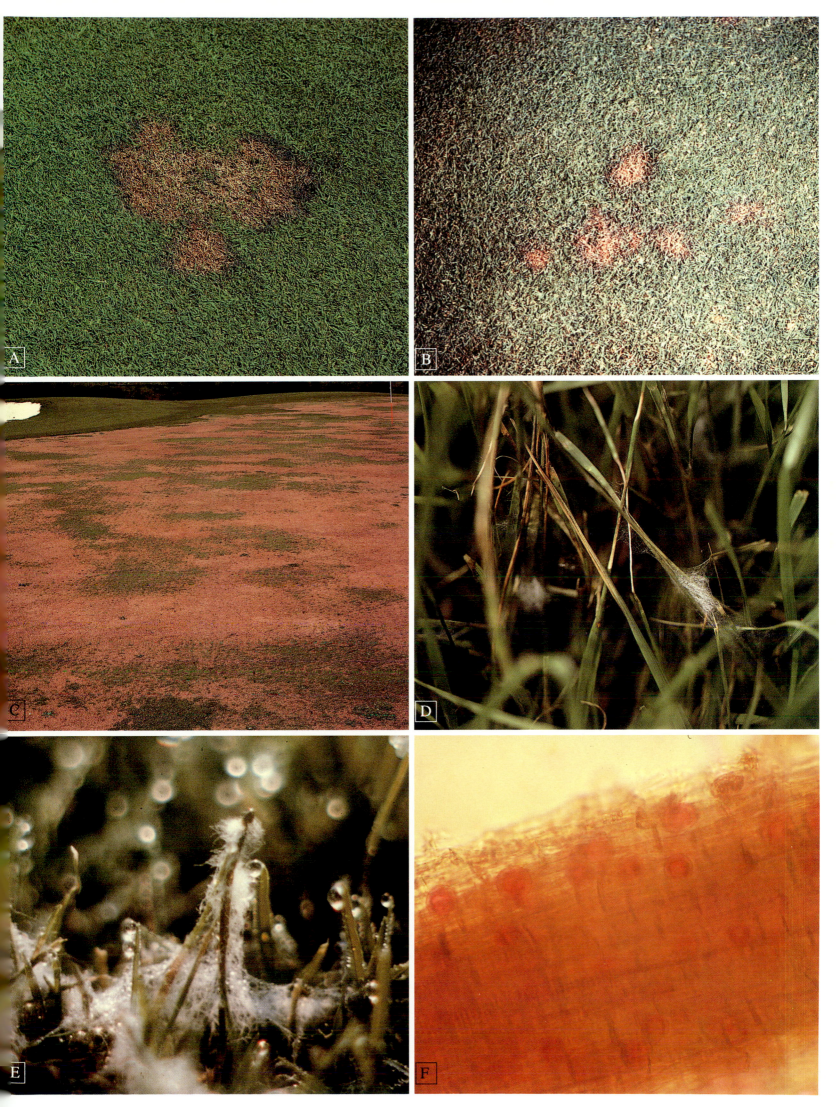

PLATE 15

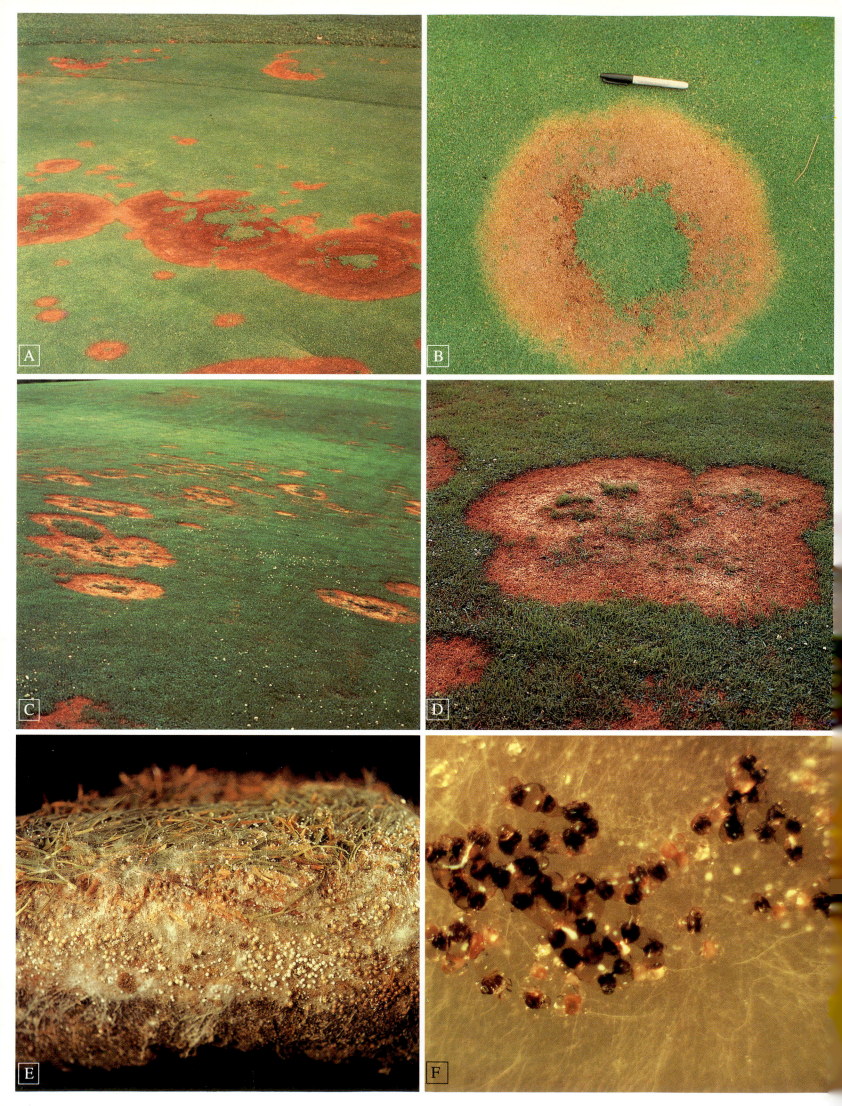

PLATE 16

PLATE 17

PLATE 18

PLATE 19

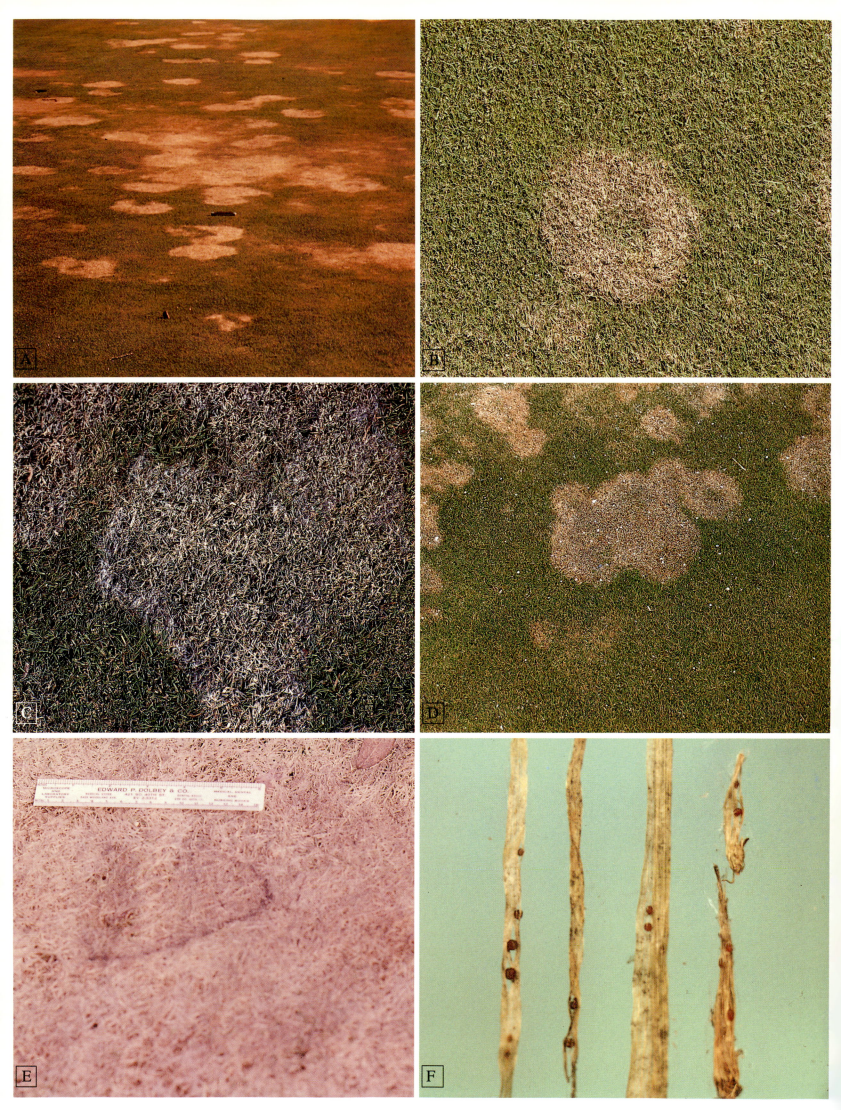

PLATE 20

PLATE 21

PLATE 22

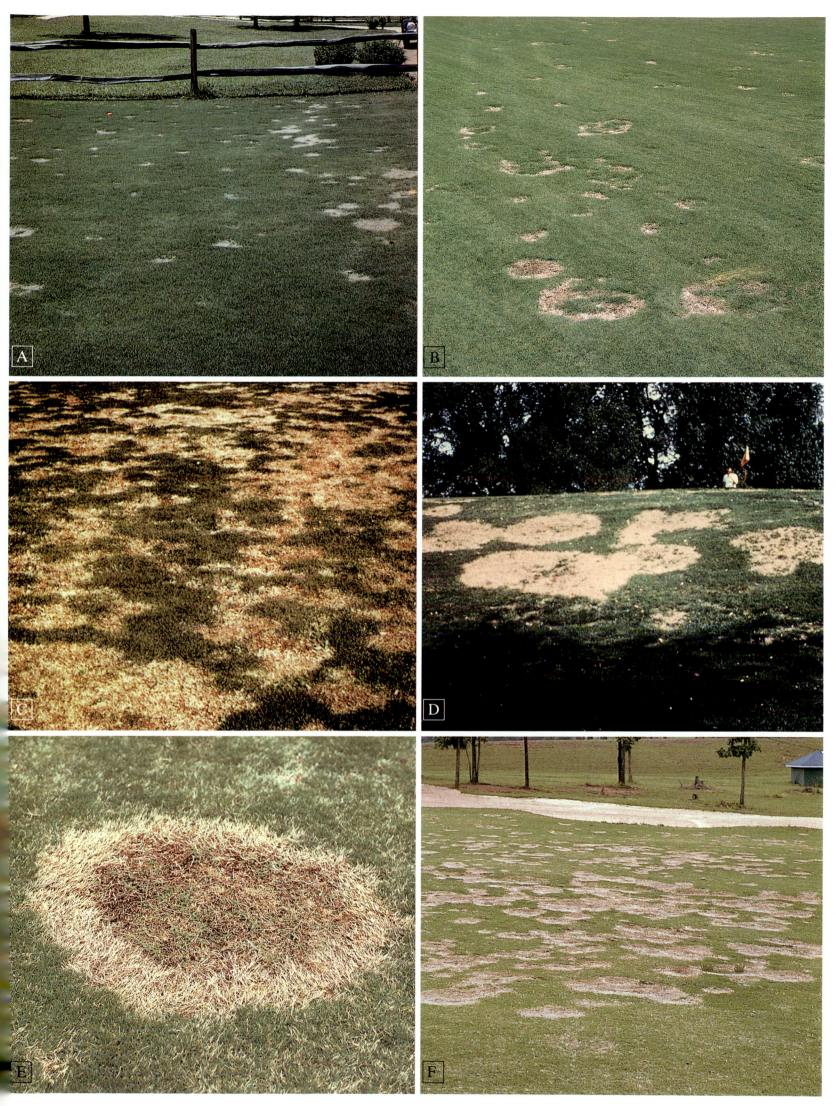

PLATE 23

PLATE 24

PLATE 25

PLATE 26

PLATE 27

PLATE 28

PLATE 30

Glossary

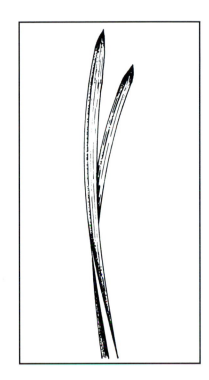

PESTICIDES AND PESTICIDE USAGE

ABSORPTION—Absorption pertains to the uptake of substances by the skin, respiratory system and gastrointestinal tract.

ACROPETAL MOVEMENT—The upward movement of a pesticide within a plant.

ACROPETAL PENETRANT—A chemical compound that when applied to the surface of a plant passes into the underlying tissue in quantities that are phytotoxic to the target organism and then moves upward in the plant. Triadimefon (Bayleton™) and metylaxyl (Subdue™) are examples of fungicides that are acropetal penetrants.

ACTIVATOR—A material added to a pesticide to either directly or indirectly increase its toxicity.

ACTIVE INGREDIENT (ai)—The chemical compound in a product responsible for the desired effects, or in the case of an economic poison, the ingredient or ingredients which are capable, in themselves, of preventing, destroying, repelling, or mitigating insects, fungi, rodents, weeds, or other pests. Commonly abbreviated ai.

ACUTE TOXICITY—A measure of the amount of a substance, as a single dosage or concentration, required to kill test animals of several species.

ADDITIVE EFFECT—The level of pest control provided by the cooperative action of two or more pesticides which is equal to the response predicted by taking into account the response of each material applied singly. Additive control is not the direct sum of the efficacy levels of the respective components of the mixture. If the reduced rate mixture of a pesticide is only additive (i.e., not synergistic), the control potential of the joint application will be less than that of the full label rate of the most efficacious component used alone.

ADHERENCE—The property of a substance to adhere or stick to a given surface.

ADJUVANT—Any component of a formulation which modifies the mixture beneficially.

ADSORBED—Held or bound in such a manner (a surface phenomenon) that the chemical is rendered inactive or only slowly available. Clay and inorganic colloids exhibit adsorption properties.

ADULTERATED—By law, applied to any economic poison if its strength or purity falls below the professed standard of quality as expressed on its labeling or under which it is sold or if any substance has been substituted wholly or in part for the article or if any valuable constituent of the article has been wholly or in part abstracted.

AEROSOL—A suspension of liquids or solids in air. Aerosol-sized droplets or particles measure 100 microns ($\frac{1}{100}$ mm) or less in diameter.

ANIONIC SURFACTANT—A surface-active additive to a pesticide having a negative surface charge. Anionic surfactants perform better in cold, soft water. Most wetting agents are of this class.

ANTAGONISM—The level of control provided by the joint action of two or more pesticides which is less than that of the predicted control.

ANTIBIOTICS—Chemical substances produced by certain living cells such as bacteria, yeasts and fungi that are damaging to the growth the cells of other organisms. Streptomycin is an example of an antibiotic used in plant protection.

ANTIDOTE—A practical immediate treatment for the purpose of alleviating the effects of poisoning.

ANTIOXIDANT—A substance capable of chemically protecting other substances against oxidation or spoilage.

AQUEOUS—Indicating the presence of water in a solution.

AQUEOUS SUSPENSION (AS)—A water suspension of microdroplets of a liquid pesticide that has been surrounded by oil.

AUXILIARY SOLVENTS—Solvents added in addition to the primary solvent to keep a formulation as a solution under conditions of relatively low temperatures.

AVERAGE PARTICLE SIZE—(i) The arithmetic mean diameter, (ii) the diameter of particles of average surface, (iii) the diameter of particles of average volume, (iv) the diameter of particles of the same specific surface as the powder. Statements referring to average particle size should designate which of these four possible diameters is actually measured.

BACTERICIDE—A chemical that kills bacteria.

BASAL TREATMENT—A treatment applied to the stems or trunks of plants at and just above the ground line.

BASIPETAL MOVEMENT—The downward movement of a pesticide within a plant.

BIOACTIVITY—Pertains to the property of affecting life.

BIOASSAY—The qualitative or quantitative determination of a substance by the systematic measurement of the response of living organisms as compared to measurement of the response to a standard or standard series of tests.

BIOCIDE—Synonymous with pesticide.

BRAND—The name, number, trademark or designation applied to an economic poison of any particular description by the manufacturer, distributor, importer or vendor. Each economic poison differing in the ingredient statement, analysis, manufacturer or distributor, name, number or trademark is considered legally to be a distinct and separate brand.

CARCINOGEN—A substance or agent capable of producing cancer.

CARCINOGENIC—The term used to describe the cancer producing property of a substance or agent.

CARRIER—The liquid or solid material added to a chemical compound to facilitate its field application. An inert material which when used with toxic compound improves the physical dispersion of the toxicant.

cfs—Cubic feet per second of flow.

CHEMICAL NAME—One that indicates the chemical composition and/or chemical structure of the compound under consideration.

CHOLINESTERASE—Abbreviation for the term acetylcholinesterase. An enzyme capable of influencing the rate of hydrolysis of acetylcholine, thereby limiting the activity of the nerve impulses.

CHRONIC TOXICITY—The results produced in test animals by lifetime exposure to a dose or concentration estimated to approximate the exposure to be encountered through use of the test substance in a prescribed manner.

COLORATION—Certain white or colorless pesticides must be treated with a coloring agent which will produce a uniformly colored product not subject to change in color beyond the minimum requirements during ordinary conditions of marketing, storage and use. Seed treatment materials are examples of pesticides which have been colored to indicate upon visual inspection that seed have been treated.

COMMON NAME—The name given to a pesticide by a recognized committee. e.g., American Standards Association Sectional Committee on Common Names for Pest Control Chemicals, The International Committee of the USDA, etc. Example: chlorothalonil is the common name of tetrachloroisopthalonitrile (Daconil 2787™).

COMPATIBLE—Capable of acting together. Chemicals that can be mixed and applied as a single treatment without the loss of their effectiveness against the intended pests or becoming phytotoxic.

CONCENTRATION—Refers to the amount of active ingredient or acid equivalent in a given volume or weight of diluent.

CONTACT FUNGICIDE—A fungicide which is only effective against fungi that are present on the external parts of the plant.

DEFLOCULATING AGENT—A material added to a suspension to prevent settling. A substance which aids in the production or maintenance of a dispersion of a solid within a liquid.

DEGRADATION—The process by which a chemical compound is reduced to a less complex compound.

DEPOSIT—Synonym: Spray Residue. The amount of dry pesticide deposited per unit area of plant, plant part or other surface at any given time. Initial Deposit = the amount deposited initially.

DERMAL—Of or pertaining to the skin.

DERMAL TOXICITY—Toxic effects brought on by the passage of the material into the body through the skin.

DILUENT—Any liquid or solid material serving to dilute or carry an active ingredient in the preparation of a formulation.

DIRECTED APPLICATION—An application to a restricted area such as a row, bed, or at the base of plants.

DISINFECTANT—An agent that kills or inactivates organisms after they have entered plant tissue.

DISINFESTANT—An agent that kills or inactivates organisms present on the surface of the plant or plant part or in the immediate environment.

DISPERSING AGENT—A material that reduces the cohesive attraction between like particles. Dispersing and suspending agents are added during the preparation of wettable powders to facilitate wetting and suspension of the toxicants.

DOSE, DOSAGE—Quantity of a toxicant applied per unit of area, plant, or soil.

DOSE RATIO—Ratio between successively increasing doses.

DRIFT—The movement of droplets or particles of sprays and dusts by wind and air currents from the target area to an area not to be treated (outside the target area).

DRY FLOWABLE (DF) (WDG)—A dry pesticide formulation consisting of uniformly sized microgranules from an aqueous suspension of a wettable powder. The finished product is free of dust, can be measured volumetrically, and disperses readily when placed in water.

EMULSIFIABLE CONCENTRATE (EC) (E) (LC)—Produced by dissolving the toxicant and an emulsifying agent in a petroleum based solvent. The strength of the formulation is usually stated in pounds of toxicant per gallon of concentrate.

EMULSIFICATION—A process of breaking up large particles or liquids into smaller ones which remain suspended in another liquid. Emulsification may be accomplished by either mechanical or chemical means.

EMULSIFY—To make into an emulsion. When small drops of one liquid are finely dispersed (distributed) in another liquid, an emulsion is formed. The drops are held in suspension by an emulsifying agent, which surrounds each drop and makes a coating around it.

EMULSIFYING AGENT—A material which facilitates the suspending of one liquid in another; for example, oil dispersed in water.

EMULSION—A mixture of two or more liquids that are not soluble in one another. One is suspended as small droplets in the other.

ESCAPE—A plant or section of a treated area that missed treatment or failed to respond to treatment in the same manner as other treated plants.

FILLER—A diluent in powdered form.

FLOWABLE (F) (FL) (FLO)—A suspension of microfine particles of dry technical ingredient in a water base to which a thickener has been added. (Water base paint is formulated by this same procedure).

FORMULATION—The form in which a pesticide is offered for sale (e.g., emulsifiable concentrate, wettable powder, dust, granules, solution, etc.).

FORTIFIED—The pesticidal properties of one product may be enhanced by fortifying with another.

FUMIGANT—A chemical toxicant employed in a volatile form.

FUNGICIDAL—Possessing the ability to kill fungi.

FUNGICIDE—A chemical that kills fungi.

FUNGISTAT—Possessing the ability to inhibit the germination of fungus spores or the development of mycelium while in continued contact thus ultimately leading to their death.

GERMICIDE—A substance that kills microorganisms.

GRANULAR (G)—A type of formulation for dry application with spreading equipment in which a pesticide is absorbed, mixed with, or impregnated into a generally inert carrier in such a way that the final product consists of small granular particles. The mesh size of the particles of individual formulations will vary from fine (10-14 mesh) to coarse (7-10 mesh) depending on the type of carrier, the nature of the pesticide and the type of area to be treated.

GROWTH REGULATOR (PGR)—An organic substance effective in minute amounts for modifying plant growth processes.

HAZARD—The probability that injury will result from use of a substance in a prescribed quantity and manner.

HYDROGEN-ION CONCENTRATION (pH)—A measure of the acidity of a chemical solution. The greater the concentration of hydrogen-ions (atoms of hydrogen with positive charges), the more acid the solution is. The hydrogen-ion concentration is expressed in terms of the pH of the solution.

HYDROLYSIS—The decomposition of a chemical compound into smaller units with the resulting addition of water elements. Certain pesticides will hydrolyze under strongly acid or alkaline conditions while others are highly stable through a wide pH range.

INERT INGREDIENT—All ingredients which are not "active". See Active Ingredient.

INGREDIENTS—The simplest constituents of the economic poison which can reasonably be determined and reported.

INTRADERMAL—Within the skin.

INVERT EMULSION—An emulsion having the water suspended as small droplets in oil. See Emulsion.

LABEL—All written, printed or graphic matter either on, or attached to the economic poison, or the immediate container thereof, and the outside container or wrapper to the retail package of the economic poison.

LABELING—All information and other written, printed or graphic matter upon the economic poison on any of its accompanying containers or wrappers to which reference is made on the label or in supplemental literature accompanying the economic poison.

LABILE—Easily destroyed.

LATENT—Dormant. Delayed.

LC_{50}—A means of expressing the toxicity of a compound present in air as a dust, mist, gas or vapor. The LC_{50} is the statistical estimate of the dosage necessary to kill 50 percent of a very large population of the test species, through toxicity on inhalation under stated conditions, or, by law, the concentration which is expected to cause death in 50 percent of the test animals treated. When referring to dust or mist, it is expressed as micrograms per liter as a dust or mist. In the case of a gas or vapor the LC_{50} value is given as parts per million (ppm).

LD_{50}—A common method of expressing the toxicity of a compound. The test is conducted by either applying the candidate chemical to the skin (dermal), injecting it intravenously, or administering it orally in the test animal's food. Dermal toxicities ore often slightly less than the oral values while intravenous toxicities are higher than the oral figures. The degree of toxicity determined by these tests is generally recorded as the LD_{50} value. This is the dose required to kill 50 percent of the population of test animals and is expressed in milligrams per kilogram (mg/kg) body weight. The smaller the LD_{50}, the more toxic the chemical. The gradation of dermal toxicities of pesticides based on LD_{50} values is as follows:

	Category	LD_{50} (mg/kg)
1.	Extremely toxic	1
2.	Highly toxic	1–50
3.	Moderately toxic	50–100
4.	Slightly toxic	500–5000
5.	Practically nontoxic	5000–15,000
6.	Practically harmless	>15,000

LEACHING—Movement of a substance downward in water through the soil.

LIQUID CONCENTRATE (LC)—See Emulsifiable Concentrate.

LOCALIZED PENETRANT—A chemical compound that when applied to the surface of a plant passes into the underlying tissue and remains in quantities that are toxic to the target organism and remains in the tissue at the points of entry (i.e., is not moved to other locations within the plant). Iprodione (Chipco 26019™) is an example of a fungicide that is a localized penetrant.

MISCIBLE—When two or more liquids are blended together to form a uniform mix, they are said to be miscible.

MISCIBLE LIQUIDS—Two or more liquids capable of being mixed, and will remain mixed under normal conditions.

NEMATICIDAL—The ability of a chemical to have lethal effects on nematodes.

NEMATICIDE—A chemical that kills nematodes.

NEMATISTAT—Possessing the ability to significantly inhibit the metabolism of a nematode while in contininued contact, thus ultimately leading its death.

NO RESIDUE—As the term applies to pesticides, the act of registration of an economic poison on the basis of the absence of a residue at time of harvest on the raw agricultural product when the economic poison is used as directed.

ORAL TOXICITY—Toxic effects brought on by the passage of the material into the body through the mouth.

PARTS PER MILLION (ppm)—An expression of concentration or the relative content of an item or substance in another. (e.g., 1 ppm is 0.0001 percent, and 1 percent is 10,000 ppm).

PENETRANT—A chemical compound that when applied to the surface of a plant passes into the underlying tissue in quantities that are toxic to the target organism. Some penetrants remain in place—i.e., are not translocated to other locations within the plant. These are referred to as "**localized penetrants**" [e.g., iprodione (Chipco 26019™)]. Other penetrants move only upward in the plant after penetration. These are referred to as "**acropetal penetrants**" [e.g., Fenarimol (Rubigan ™) and thiophanate methyl (Fungo 50™)]. While other penetrants are translocated uniformly throughout the plant after penetration. These are referred to as "**systemic penetrants**" [e.g., fosetyl Al (Aliette™)].

PEST—By law, forms of plant and animal life and viruses when they exist under circumstances that make them injurious to plants, people, domestic animals, other useful vertebrates, useful invertebrates or other articles or substances.

PESTICIDES—Chemical substances used to kill pests. The pests may be weeds, insects, rats and mice, algae, nematodes, and other destructive forms of life.

PHYTOCIDAL—Possessing the ability to kill or injure higher plants or plant parts.

PHYTOTOXIC—Pertaining to the property of killing or injuring higher plants or plant parts.

PHYTOTOXICITY, ACUTE—The immediate, dramatic impact of an agrochemical on the well being of the plant or plant part in question.

PHYTOTOXICITY, CHRONIC—The continuous, low order impact of an agrochemical on the well being of the plant or plant part in question.

PLANT GROWTH REGULATOR (PGR)—A substance intended to alter the growth patterns of plants through physiological rather than physical action. The term does not include substances intended solely for use as nutrients or fertilizers.

POSTEMERGENCE—After the emergence of specified plant.

POTENTIATE—To augment, increase or improve the activity, utility or effectiveness of a compound for a given purpose.

PREPLANTING—Any time before the crop is planted.

PROTECTIVE VALUE—Ability to prevent infection of the plant or plant part.

psi—Pressure measured in pounds per square inch.

RATE—The amount of active ingredient of a pesticide applied per unit area (i.e., 1,000 square feet). Rate is preferred to the occasionally used terms, dosage and application.

RESIDUE—That amount of material which remains on the treated plant or plant part.

RESISTANCE—The ability of the target organism to remain relatively unaffected by the pesticide. There are two types of pesticide resistance, phenotypic (tolerance) and permanent. (i) **Phenotypic resistance** is a transient condition. It is the consequence of an unusually high level of disease pressure brought on by climatic and/or management situations that favor severe outbreaks of a disease. When this situation develops, either the approved dosage levels for the fungicide may fail to give satisfactory control of the disease or the longevity of control may be significantly reduced. However, when the conditions that heightened the development of the disease no longer exist, the basic control level of the fungicide is once again restored. (ii) **Permanent resistance** is a continuing event brought on by alterations in the genetic makeup of the target organism that governs certain physiological or structural characteristics which in turn reduce its vulnerability to the pesticide in question. These characteristics are inherited, and thus are perpetuated in successive generations of the pathogen.

RESPIRATORY TOXICITY—Intake of pesticides through nasal and throat passages into the lungs. Pesticides may reach the lungs as vapor or as extremely fine droplets or particles. Most compounds are more toxic by this route.

SAFENER—A material added to a pesticide to eliminate or reduce phytotoxic effects.

SELECTIVE PESTICIDE—A chemical that is more toxic to some pest species than to others.

SLURRY—A watery mixture or thick suspension of an insoluble pesticide.

SOIL APPLICATION—Application of chemical made primarily to the soil surface rather than to vegetation.

SOIL INCORPORATION—Mechanical mixing of the pesticide with the soil.

SOIL INJECTION—Mechanical placement of the pesticide beneath the soil surface with a minimum or mixing or stirring.

SOIL STERILANT—A chemical that prevents the growth of plants or microorganisms when present in the soil.

SOLUBLE POWDER (SP)—A powder formulation that dissolves and forms a solution in water.

SPOT TREATMENT—The application of pesticide to a selected location within an area or to selected individual plants.

SPRAY DRIFT—The movement of airborne spray particles from the intended application area.

SPREADER—A substance which increases the area that a given volume of liquid will cover on a solid or on another liquid.

STICKER—A substance which when added to a spray solution increases the capacity of the active ingredient to adhere to the treated surface.

SUBACUTE TOXICITY—Results produced in test animals of various species by long term exposure to repeated doses or concentrations of a substance.

SURFACTANT—A material which facilitates and accentuates the emulsifying, dispersing, spreading, wetting and other surface-modifying properties of the formulations.

SUSPENSION—A system consisting of very finely divided solid particles dispersed in solid, liquid or gas.

SYNERGISM—The phenomenon which results in a cooperative action of discrete agents such that the total effect is greater than the sum of the two components taken separately.

SYNTHESIS—A coming together of two or more substances to form a new material.

SYSTEMIC PENETRANT—A pesticide that passes through the surface of a plant in quantities that are toxic to the target organism and is translocated uniformly throughout the entire plant. Fosetyl Al (Aliette™) is an example of a systemic fungicide.

TENACITY (ADHERENCE)—The resistance of a pesticide deposit when subjected to prescribed washing techniques.

TENACITY INDEX—A ratio of the residual deposit over the initial deposit when subjected to prescribed washing techniques.

TOXICANT—An agent capable of exhibiting toxicity; a poison.

TOXICITY—The degree to which a substance is injurious or poisonous to plants, animals or human beings. The toxicological properties of all pesticides as they relate to animals and human beings must be evaluated before they can be marketed. The acute toxicity is determined by testing the candidate chemical against various mammals, generally rats and mice. For an explanation of how these measurements are made, see LD_{50} and LC_{50}.

TRADE (BRAND) NAME—The proprietary name given to a product by the manufacturer or formulator to distinguish it as an item produced or sold by him.

WATER DISPERSABLE GRANULES (WDG)—See Dry Flowable.

WETTABLE POWDER (WP)—A powder formulation which, when added to water forms a suspension used for spraying.

WETTING AGENT—A material which reduces the contact angle of a liquid on a given surface. Limited to wetting pesticides and not leaves or other surfaces. A compound which when added to a spray solution causes it contact plant surfaces more thoroughly.

Bibliography

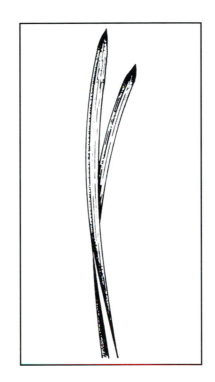

Bibliography

Abad, Z. G., H. D. Shaw, L. T. Lucas and K. J. Jones. 1992. Taxonomy and pathology of *Pythium* species associated with decline of bentgrass in North Carolina. Phytopathology 82:1123. (Abstr.)

Abbott, E. V. and R. L. Tippett. 1964. Additional hosts of sugarcane mosaic virus. Plant Disease Reptr. 48: 443–445.

Ainsworth, G. C. 1981. Introduction to the History of Plant Pathology. Cambridge University Press: New York. 315 p.

Allen, W. W., R. A. Kilpatrick and E. C. Bashaw. 1966. A technique for screening St. Augustine grass for tolerance to *Rhizoctonia solani*. Plant Disease Reptr. 50: 622–623.

Altman, J. and C. L. Campbell. 1977. Effects of herbicides on plant diseases. Ann. Rev. Phytopathology 15: 361–385.

Anderson, J. R. 1978. Pesticide effects on non-target soil microorganisms. *In*: Pesticide Microbiology, I. R. Hill and S. J. L. Wright, Ed. Academic Press: London. 844 p. (313–354).

Anderson, J. W. and K. S. Rowen. 1965. Activity of peptidase in tobacco leaf tissue in relation to senescence. Jour. Biochem. 97:741–746.

Apt, W. J., H. M. Austenson and W. D. Courtney. 1960. Use of herbicides to break the life cycle of the bentgrass nematode, *Auguina agrostis* (Steinbuck 1799) Filipjev 1936. Plant Disease Reptr. 44:524–526.

Arsvoll, K. 1976. *Sclerotinia borealis*, sporulation, spore germination and pathogenesis. Meld. Norg. Landbrhogsk. 54(9). 49 p.

Arsvoll, K. and A. Larsen. 1977. Effects of nitrogen, phosphorus and potassium on resistance to snow mold fungi and in freezing tolerance in *Phleum pratense*. Meld. Norg. Landbrhogsk. 56(29). 14 p.

Arsvoll, K. and J. D. Smith. 1978. *Typhula ishikariensis* and its varieties, var. *idahoensis* comb. nov. and var. *canadensis* var. nov. Canadian Jour. Bot. 56:348–364.

Arthur, J. C. 1929. The Plant Rusts. Chapman-Hall: London. 446 p.

Ashbaugh, F. M. and P. O. Larsen. 1983. Evaluation of fungicides for curative control of red thread (1982). Fungicide Nematicide Tests: 38. Amer. Phytopath. Soc., Minneapolis. p. 200.

Atilano, R. A. 1983. Susceptibility of St. Augustinegrass germ plasm to *Pyricularia grisea*. Plant Disease 67: 782–783.

Aycock, R. 1966. Stem rot and other diseases caused by *Sclerotium rolfsii*. North Carolina Agric. Expt. Sta. Tech. Bull. 174. 202 p.

Bahuon, A. 1985. Factors in the infectious development and impregnation characteristics of *Corticium fuciforme* (Berk.) Wakef., the pathological agent responsible for red thread disease in turf grasses. *In*: Proc. 5th Int. Turfgrass Conf. F. Lemaire, Ed. INRA Publications, Versailles, France. 870 p. (569–577).

Bain, D. C. and C. W. Edgerton. 1943. The zonate leaf spot, a new disease of sorghum. Phytopathology 33: 220–226.

Bain, D. C., B. N. Patel and M. V. Patel. 1972. Blast of ryegrass in Mississippi. Plant Disease Reptr. 56:210.

Ballion, P. 1906. Recherches sur Les Cerceles Myceliens (Ronds de Fees). Actes Soc. Linn Bordeaux 61:62–88.

Banttari, E. E. 1966. Grass hosts of aster yellows virus. Plant Disease Reptr. 50:17–21.

Batemen, D. F. 1970. Pathogenesis and disease. *In*: Biology and Pathology of *Rhizoctonia solani*. J. R. Parmiter, Jr., ed. Univ. California Press, Berkeley. 255 p. (161–171)

Bayless-Elliot, J. S. 1926. Concerning "fairy rings" in pastures. Annals Appl. Biol. 13:277–288.

Bean, G. A. 1966. Observations on Fusarium blight of turfgrasses. Plant Disease Reptr. 50:942–945.

Bean, G. A. 1969. The role of moisture and crop debris in the development of Fusarium blight of Kentucky bluegrass. Phytopathology 59:479–481.

Bean, G. A. and R. D. Wilcoxson. 1964a. Helminthosporium leaf spot of bluegrass. Phytopathology 54:1065–1070.

Bean, G. A. and R. D. Wilcoxson. 1964b. Pathogenicity of three species of Helminthosporium on roots of bluegrass. Phytopathology 54:1084–1085.

Beard, J. B., J. M. Vargas and P. E. Rieke. 1973. Influence of nitrogen fertility on *Tricholoma* fairy ring development in Merion Kentucky bluegrass (*Poa pratensis* L.). Agronomy Jour. 65:994–995

Becker, G. 1953. La vie privee des champignons. Paris: Stock. 198 p.

Bell, A. A. 1967. Fungi associated with root and crown rots of *Zoysia japonica*. Plant Disease Reptr. 51:11–14.

Bennett, F. T. 1935. *Corticium* disease of turf. Journ. Board Greenkeeping Res. 4:32–39.

Bennett, F. T. 1937. Dollarspot disease of turf and its causal organism, *Sclerotinia homoeocarpa* n. sp. Annals Appl. Biol. 24:236–257.

Berkeley, M. J. 1873. Australian fungi. Jour. Linn. Soc. 12:175.

Berkeley, M. J. 1855. Vibrio forming excrescences on the roots of cucumber plants. Gardners Chronicle (April):220.

Bloom, J. R. and H. B. Couch. 1960. Influence of environment on diseases of turfgrasses. I. Effect of nutrition, pH, and soil moisture on Rhizoctonia brown patch. Phytopathology 50:532–535.

Boerema, G. H. and A. A. Verhoeven. 1977. Check-list for scientific names of common parasitic fungi. Series 2b: Fungi on field crops: cereals and grasses. Neth. Jour. Plant Path. 83:165–204.

Bollard, E. G. 1950a. Studies in the genus *Mastigosporium*. I. General account of the species and their host ranges. Trans. British Mycol. Soc. 33:250–264.

Bollard, E. G. 1950b. Studies in the genus *Mastigosporium*. II. Parasitism. Trans. British Mycol. Soc. 33:265–275.

Bolton, A. T. and W. E. Cordukes. 1981. Resistance to *Colletotrichum graminicola* in strains of *Poa annua* and reaction of other turfgrasses. Canadian Jour. Plant Path. 3:94–96.

Booth, C. 1971. The Genus Fusarium. Commonwealth Mycological Institute. Kew, Surrey, England. 237 p.

Bosewinkel, H. J. 1977. New plant disease records in New Zealand: records in the period 1969–76. New Zealand Jour. Agric. Res. 20:583–589.

Boyle, L. W. 1961. The ecology of *Sclerotium rolfsii* with emphasis on the role of saprophytic media. Phytopathology 51:117–119.

Brauen, S. E., R. L. Goss, C. J. Gould and S. P. Orton. 1975. The effects of sulphur in combinations with nitrogen, phosphorous and potassium on colour and Fusarium patch disease of Agrostis putting green turf. Jour. Sports Turf. Res. Inst. 51:83–91.

Braverman, S. W. 1954. Studies on *Sclecotrichum graminis* Fckl. M.S. Thesis. The Pennsylvania State University. University Park. 49 p.

Bridge, J. and N. G. M. Hague. 1974. The feeding behavior of *Tylenchorhynchus* and *Merlinius* species and their effect on growth of perennial ryegrass. Nematologica 20:119–130.

Britton, M. P. and G. P. Cummins. 1959. Subspecific identity of the stem rust fungus of Merion bluegrass. Phytopathology 49:287–289.

Britton, M. P. and D. P. Rogers. 1963. *Olpidium brassicae* and *Polymyxa graminis* in roots of creeping bent putting greens. Mycologia 55:758–763.

Broadfoot, W. C. 1936. Experiments on the chemical control of snowmold of turf in Alberta. Sci. Agric. 16:615–618.

Broadfoot, W. C. 1941. A low-temperature Basidiomycete causing early spring killing of grasses and legumes in Alberta. Phytopathology 31:1058–1059.

Brodie, B. B. and G. W. Burton. 1967. Nematode population reduction and growth response of Bermuda turf as influenced by organic pesticide applications. Plant Disease Reptr. 51:562–566.

Brown, G. E., H. Cole, Jr. and R. R. Nelson. 1972. Pathogenicity of *Curvularia* sp. to turfgrass. Plant Disease Reptr. 56:59–63.

Bruehl, G. W. and B. Cunfer. 1971. Physiological and environmental factors which affect the severity of snow mold of wheat. Phytopathology 61:792–799.

Bruehl, G. W. and H. V. Toko. 1957. Host range of two strains of the cereal yellow-dwarf virus. Plant Disease Reptr. 41:730–734.

Bruehl, G. W., H. V. Toko and H. H. McKinney. 1957. Mosaics of Italian ryegrass and orchardgrass in western Washington. Phytopathology 47:577. (Abstr.)

Bruton, B. D. 1979. Etiology of *Sclerophthora macrospora* on St. Augustinegrass. Ph.D. Dissertation. Texas A & M University. College Station. 103 p.

Bruton, B. D. and R. W. Toler. 1980. Influence of time and temperature on inoculation and infection of St. Augustinegrass by *Sclerophthora macrospora*. Phytopathology 70:565. (Abstr.)

Bruton, B. D., R. W. Toler and M. P. Grisham. 1986. Preventive and curative control of downy mildew of St. Augustinegrass by metalaxyl. Plant Disease 70:413–415.

Bugnicourt, F. 1950. Les speces du genre Curvularia isolees des semences de Ris. Rev. gen. Bot. 57:65–77.

Bunt, J. A. 1975. Effect and mode of action of some systemic nematicides. Mided. Landhouwnogesch. Wageningen. 128 p.

Burpee, L. L. 1980a. Identification of Rhizoctonia species associated with turfgrass. *In*: Advances in Turfgrass Pathology, B. G. Joyner and P. O. Larsen, Ed. Harcourt Brace Jovanovich: Duluth. 197 p. (25–28).

Burpee, L. L. 1980b. *Rhizoctonia cerealis* causes yellow patch of turfgrasses. Plant Disease 64:1114–1116.

Burpee, L. L. 1988. Preventive control of cold weather diseases. Golf Course Management 56(8):62–68.

Burpee, L. L. 1992. Assessment of resistance to *Rhizoctonia solani* in tall fescue. Plant Disease 76:1065–1068.

Burpee, L. and A. Anderson. 1988. Particle size analyses of root zone mixes in golf greens suffering from black layer. Greenmaster 28(8):12–13.

Burpee, L. L. and J. H. Bouton. 1993. Effects of eradication of the endophyte *Acremonium coenophialum* on epidemics of Rhizoctonia blight of tall fescue. Plant Disease 77:157–159.

Burpee, L. L. and L. G. Goulty. 1984. Suppression of brown patch disease of creeping bentgrass by isolates of nonpathogenic *Rhizoctonia* spp. Phytopathology 74:692–694.

Burpee, L. L. and L. G. Goulty. 1986. Influence of foliar-applied nitrogen on the severity of dollarspot. The Greenmaster 22(8):19.

Burpee, L. L., L. M. Kaye, L. G. Goulty and M. B. Lawton. 1987. Suppression of gray snow mold on creeping bentgrass by an isolate of *Typhula phaecorrhiza*. Plant Disease 71:97–100.

Burpee, L. L. and M. W. Lawton. 1990. Biological control of Typhula blight. Golf Course Management 58(11): 76–78.

Burpee, L. L. and S. B. Martin. 1992. Biology of Rhizoctonia species associated with turfgrass. Plant Disease 76: 112–117.

Burpee, L. L., A. E. Mueller and D. J. Hannusch. 1990. Control of Typhula blight and pink snow mold of creeping bentgrass and residual suppression of dollarspot by triadimefon and propiconazole. Plant Disease 74:687–689.

Burpee, L. L., P. L. Sanders, H. Cole, Jr. and R. T. Sherwood. 1980. Pathogenicity of *Ceratobasidium cornigerum* and related fungi representing five anastamosis groups. Phytopathology 70:843–846.

Burrill, T. J. 1881. Bacteria as a cause of diseases in plants. American Naturalist 15:527–531.

Cahill, J. V., J. J. Murray, N. R. O'Neill and P. H. Dernoeden. 1983. Interrelationships between fertility and red thread fungal disease of turfgrass. Plant Disease 67:1080–1083.

Calvert, E. L. and A. E. Muskett. 1945. Blind-seed diseases of ryegrass (*Phialea temulenta* Prill and Delacr.). Annals Appl. Biol. 32:329–343.

Carr, A. J. H. 1975. Diseases of herbage crops—some problems and progress. Annals Appl. Biol. 81:235–279.

Carrier, L. 1922. Control of brown patch with Bordeaux mixture. Bulletin U. S. Golf Association Green Section. Vol. 2. p. 301–305.

Carrow, R. N. 1992. Cultivation has changed. USGA Green Section Record 30(1):5–9.

Chastagner, G. 1986. Necrotic ring spot update. Proc. 40th Northwest Turfgrass Conf. p. 197–198.

Chastagner, G. 1987. Management of necrotic ring spot. Northwest Turfgrass Topics 30(1):8–9.

Chastagner, G. and W. Vassey. 1979. Turfgrass disease research report. Proc. 33rd Northwest Annual Turfgrass Conf. p. 111–115.

Cheesman, J. H., E. C. Roberts and L. H. Tiffany. 1965. Effects of nitrogen level and osmotic pressure of the nutrient solution on incidence of *Puccinia graminis* and *Helminthosporium sativum* infection in Merion Kentucky bluegrass. Agronomy Jour. 57: 599–602.

Chen, C. T., C. S. Lee and M. J. Chen. 1972. Mycoplasmalike organisms in *Cynodon dactylon* and *Brachiaria distachya* affected by white leaf disease. Rep.Taiwan Sugar Exp. Sta. 56:49–55.

Chen, C. T., H. J. Su, B. C. Raju and H. C. Huang. 1977. A new spiroplasma isolated from bermuda grass (*Cynodon dactylon* (L.) Pers). Proc. Amer. Phytopathol. Soc. 4:231. (Abstr.)

Chitwood, B. G. 1955. Partial host list of economically plant pathogenic nematodes. Unprocessed mimeograph of the Florida State Plant Board.

Christensen, M. J. 1979. Rhizoctonia species associated with diseased turfgrasses in New Zealand. New Zealand Jour. Agric. Res. 22:627–629.

Christie, J. R. 1936. The development of root-knot nematode galls. Phytopathology 26:1–22.

Christie, J. R. 1959. Plant Nematodes—their Binomics and Control. Univ. Fla. Agr. Expt. Sta., Gainesville, 256 p.

Clarke, B. B., P. M. Halisky, C. R. Funk and R. E. Engel. 1985. Preventative control of red thread and pink patch in perennial ryegrass. Phytopathology 75:1286. (Abstr.)

Coker, W. C. and J. N. Couch. 1928. The Gastromycetes of the Eastern United States and Canada. Univ. North Carolina Press: Chapel Hill. 201 p.

Colbaugh, P. F. and R. M. Endo. 1974. Drought stress: an important factor stimulating the development of *Helminthosporium sativum* on Kentucky bluegrass. *In*: Proc. 2nd Int. Turfgrass Conf. Eliot Roberts, Ed. Madison, Wis., American Soc. Agron. 602 p. (328–334).

Colby, S. R. 1967. Calculating synergistic and antagonistic responses of herbicide combinations. Weeds 15:20–22.

Cole, H., Jr. 1976. Factors affecting Fusarium blight development. Weeds, Trees and Turf. Vol. 15, No. 7. p. 35–37.

Cole, H., Jr., S. W. Braverman and J. Duich. 1968. Fusaria, and other fungi from seeds and seedlings of Merion and other turf-type bluegrasses. Phytopathology 58: 1415–1419.

Cole, H., Jr., L. L. Burpee, P. L. Sanders and J. M. Duich. 1978. Stripe smut control with a single spring dormant season application of fungicide, 1977. *In*: Fungicide Nematicide Tests 33:142. Minneapolis, Minn., American Phytopath. Society.

Cole, H., Jr., C. G. Warren and P. L. Sanders. 1974. Fungicide tolerance—a rapidly emerging problem in turf grass disease control. *In*: Proc. 2nd Int. Turfgrass Conf. Eliot Roberts, Ed. Madison, Wis., American Soc. Agron. 602 p. (344–349).

Cormack, M. W. 1948. Winter crown rot or snow mold of alfalfa, clover, and grasses in Alberta. I. Occurrence, parasitism, and spread of the pathogen. Canadian Jour. Agr. Res. 26:71–85.

Cormack, M. W. 1952. Winter crown rot or snow mold of alfalfa, clovers or grasses in Alberta. II. Field studies on host and varietal resistance and other factors related to control. Canadian Jour. Botany 30:537–548.

Couch, H. B. 1957. The control of bluegrass and fescue diseases. Bull. 58, New York State Turf Association: 223–225.

Couch, H. B. 1962. Diseases of Turfgrasses. Reinhold: New York. 288 p.

Couch, H. B. 1964. Fusarium blight of turfgrass. Bulletin 77, New York State Turfgrass Association. p. 297–298.

Couch, H. B. 1966. Relationship between soil moisture, nutrition and severity of turfgrass diseases. Jour. Sports Turf. Res. Inst. 11:54–64.

Couch, H. B. 1971. Turfgrass disease control in the twentieth century. Golf Superintendent. Vol. 39, No. 10. p. 23–26.

Couch, H. B. 1976. Fursarium blight of turfgrasses—an overview. Weeds, Trees and Turf 15(7):8–9, 34–35.

Couch, H. B. 1979a. Heat stress, not anthracnose is scourge of *Poa annua*. Weeds, Trees and Turf 18(6):41–50, 54–56.

Couch, H. B. 1979b. Turfgrass diseases: past, present, future. *In*: Advances in Turfgrass Pathology (B. G. Joyner and P. O. Larsen, Ed.). Harcourt Brace Jovanovich: Duluth. 197 p. (15–23).

Couch, H. B. 1980. Relationship of management practices to the incidence and severity of turfgrass diseases. *In*: Advances in Turfgrass Pathology, B. G. Joyner and P. O. Larsen, Ed. Harcourt Brace Jovanovich: Duluth. 197 p. (65–72).

Couch, H. B. 1981. The nature and control of decline and dying-out of Toronto C-15 bentgrass. USGA Green Section Record 19(6):4–7.

Couch, H. B. 1983. Recent insights on the nature and control of Corticium red thread. USGA Green Section Record 21(6):8–11.

Couch, H. B. 1984. Precision in turfgrass disease nomenclature: Standard names for turfgrass diseases. Golf Course Management 52(2):8–25.

Couch, H. B. 1985a. Common names for turfgrass diseases. *In*: Common Names for Plant Diseases, J. D. Hansen, Ed. Plant Disease 69:649–676.

Couch, H. B. 1985b. Patch diseases of turfgrasses: Facts, fallacies, fads and fantasies. Golf Course Management 53(8):6–7, 12–20.

Couch, H. B. 1985c. Turfgrass fungicides II: Dilution rates, nozzle size, nozzle pressure and disease control. Golf Course Management 52(8):73–76, 78–80.

Couch, H. B. 1985d. Turfgrass fungicides III: Effect of post-spray rainfall or irrigation on the effectiveness of fungicides. Golf Course Management 53(2):50–58.

Couch, H. B. 1986. The patch diseases. Weeds, Trees and Turf 25(4):86–96.

Couch, H. B. 1988. Sorting out the patch diseases. Golf Course Management 56(7):46–54.

Couch, H. B. 1991. Results of 1991 Virginia Tech Turfgrass Disease Control Trials. Ann. Rept. Turfgrass Pathology Lab., Virginia Tech, Blacksburg, Va. 70 p.

Couch, H. B. and E. R. Bedford. 1966. Fusarium blight of turfgrasses. Phytopathology 56:781–786.

Couch, H. B. and J. R. Bloom. 1960. Influence of soil moisture stresses on the development of the root knot nematode. Phytopathology 50:319–321.

Couch, H. B. and J. R. Bloom. 1968. Influence of environment on diseases of turfgrasses. II. Effect of nutrition, pH, and soil moisture on Sclerotinia dollar spot. Phytopathology 50:761–763.

Couch, H. B. and J. M. Garber. 1984. Results of 1981 turfgrass disease control trials. Report Turfgrass Pathology Laboratory, Virginia Tech, Blacksburg, Virginia.

Couch, H. B., J. M. Garber and J. A. Fox. 1979. Relative effectiveness of fungicides and nematicides in Fusarium blight control. Golf Business Magazine 53(7):12–16.

Couch, H. B., J. M. Garber and D. Jones. 1984. Turfgrass

fungicides: Application methods and effectiveness. Golf Course Management 52(7):40–52.

Couch, H. B., J. M. Garber and B. D. Smith. 1981. Results of 1981 turfgrass disease control trials. Report Turfgrass Pathology Laboratory, Virginia Tech, Blacksburg, Virginia.

Couch, H. B., and B. G. Joyner. 1976. Interactions among fungicide treatments and nitrogen fertilization in the control of rust on Manhattan ryegrass. Phytopathology 77:1733. (Abstr.)

Couch, H. B., P. Keating and E. Rieley. 1992. Results of 1992 turfgrass disease control trials. Report Turfgrass Pathology Laboratory, Virginia Tech, Blacksburg, Virginia.

Couch, H. B., L. T. Lucas and R. A. Haygood. 1990. The nature and control of Rhizoctonia blight. Golf Course Management 58(6):48–58.

Couch, H. B. and L. D. Moore. 1971. Influence of nutrition and total nonstructural carbohydrate content on *Helminthosporium sativum*-incited leaf spot of Kentucky bluegrass. Phytopathology 61:888. (Abstr.)

Couch, H. B., L. D. Moore and J. F. Shoulders. 1974. Relationship of mowing height to carbohydrates and protein contents and susceptibility of Kentucky bluegrass cultivars to *Helminthosporium sorikinianum*. Agronomy Abstracts. p. 97.

Couch, H. B., L. H. Purdy and D. W. Henderson. 1967. Application of soil moisture principles to the study of plant disease. Bulletin 4. Research Division, Virginia Polytechnic Inst., Blacksburg. 23 p.

Couch, H. B. and B. D. Smith. 1987a. Results of 1987 Virginia Tech Turfgrass Disease Control Trials. Ann. Rept. Turfgrass Pathology Lab., Virginia Tech, Blacksburg, VA. 37 p.

Couch, H. B. and B. D. Smith, 1987b. Relationship of suspect nutrition, air temperature, and duration of leaf wetness to the development of Helminthosporium leaf spot of creeping bentgrass. Phytopathology 77 (12):1733. (Abstr.)

Couch, H. B. and B. D. Smith. 1989. Results of 1989 Virginia Tech Turfgrass Disease Control Trials. Ann. Rept. Turfgrass Pathology Lab., Virginia Tech, Blacksburg, VA. 81 p.

Couch, H. B. and B. D. Smith. 1990. Results of 1990 Virginia Tech Turfgrass Disease Control Trials. Ann. Rept. Turfgrass Pathology Lab., Virginia Tech, Blacksburg, VA. 75 p.

Couch, H. B. and B. D. Smith. 1991a. Synergistic and antagonistic interactions of fungicides against *Pythium aphanidermatum* on perennial ryegrass. Crop Protection 10:386–390.

Couch, H. B. and B. D. Smith. 1991b. Increase in incidence and severity of target turfgrass diseases by certain fungicides. Plant Disease 75:1064–1067.

Coursen, B. W. and W. R. Jenkins. 1958. Host-parasite relationships of the pin nematode, *Paratylenchus projectus* on tobacco and tall fescue. Phytopathology 48:460. (Abstr.)

Coursen, B. W., R. W. Rhode and W. R. Jenkins. 1958. Additions to the host lists of the nematodes, *Paratylenchus projectus* and *Trichodorus christiei*. Plant Disease Reptr. 42:456–460.

Courtney, W. D. and H. B. Howell. 1952. Investigations on bentgrass nematode *Auguina agrostis* (Steinbuch 1799) Filipjev 1936. Plant Disease Reptr. 36:75–83.

Courtney, W. D., D. V. Peabody, Jr. and H. M. Austenson. 1962. Effect of herbicides on nematodes in bentgrass. Plant Disease Reptr. 46:256–257.

Crahay, J. N., P. H. Dernoeden and N. R. O'Neill. 1988. Growth and pathogenicity of *Leptosphareia korrae* in bermudagrass. Plant Disease 72:945–949.

Cullimore, D. R. 1990. Monitoring and managing black plug layering problems in golf courses. Newsletter Saskatchewan Turfgrass Assoc. No. 5. p. 4.

Cullimore, D. R., S. Nilson, S. Taylor and K. Nelson. 1990. Structure of a black plug layer in a turfgrass putting sand green. Jour. Soil and Water Conservation 45(6): 657–659.

Cunningham, P. C. 1965. *Cersosporella herpotrichoides* Fron. on gramineous hosts in Ireland. Nature 207: 1414–1415.

Cutright, N. J. and M. B. Harrison. 1970. Some environmental factors affecting Fusarium blight of 'Merion' Kentucky bluegrass. Plant Disease Reptr. 54:1018–1020.

Dahl, A. S. 1934. Snowmold of turfgrasses as caused by *Fusarium nivale*. Phytopathology 24:197–214.

Dale, J. L. 1966. Infection of St. Augustinegrass with virus causing maize dwarf mosaic. Plant Disease Reptr. 50: 441–442.

Dale, J. L. 1972. A spotting and discoloration condition of dormant bermudagrass. Plant Disease Reptr. 56: 355–357.

Dale, J. L. 1978. Atypical symptoms of Rhizoctonia-infection on zoysia. Plant Disease Reptr. 62:645–647.

Dale, J. L. and M. C. McDaniel. 1982. St. Augustinegrass decline in Arkansas. Plant Disease 66:259–260.

Dale, J. L. and C. L. Murdoch. 1969. *Polymyxa* infection of Bermuda grass. Plant Disease Reptr. 53:130–131.

Davis, D. B. and P. H. Dernoeden. 1991. Summer patch and Kentucky bluegrass quality as influenced by cultural practices. Agronomy Journal 83:670–677.

Davis, R. F., H. T. Wilkinson and R. T. Kane. 1993 Nematodes in creeping bentgrass and annual bluegrass. Golf Course Management (May). p. 54–56.

Davis, W. H. 1933. Snow mold and brown patch caused by *Sclerotium rhizoides*. Phytopathology 23:8. (Abstr.)

Deacon, J. W. 1973a. Factors affecting the occurrence of Ophiobolus patch disease of turf and its control by *Phiolophora radicicola* [*graminicola*]. Plant Pathology 22:149–155.

Deacon, J. W. 1973b. *Phialophora radicicola* [*graminicola*] and *Gauemannomyces graminis* on roots of grasses and cereals. Trans. British Mycological Soc. 61:471–485.

Dean, J. L. 1966. Zonate leafspot of sorghum. Ph.D. Dissertation. Louisiana State University, Baton Rouge. 89 p.

De Cleene, M., F. Leyns, M. Van Den Mooter, J. Swings and J. De Ley. 1981. Reaction of grass varieties grown in Belgium to *Xanthomonas campertris* pv. *graminis*. Parasitica 37:29–34.

Dernoeden, P. H. 1987. Management of take-all patch of creeping bentgrass with nitrogen, sulfur, and phenyl mercury acetate. Plant Disease 71:226–229.

Dernoeden, P. H. 1992. The side effects of fungicides. Golf Course Management (July). p. 90–98.

Dernoeden, P. H. and N. Jackson. 1980. Infection and mycelial colonization of gramineous hosts by *Sclerophthora macrospora*. Phytopathology 70:1009–112.

Dernoeden, P. H. and M. S. McIntosh. 1991. Disease enhancement and Kentucky bluegrass quality as influenced by fungicides. Agronomy Journal 83:322–326.

Dernoeden, P. H. and N. R. O'Neill. 1983. Occurrence of Gaeumannomyces patch disease in Maryland and growth and pathogenicity of the causal agent. Plant Disease 67:528–532.

Dernoeden, P. H., N. R. O'Neill and J. J. Murray. 1985. Nontarget effects of fungicides on turfgrass growth and enhancement of red thread. *In*: Proc. 5th Int. Turfgrass Conf. F. Lemaire, Ed. INRA Publications, Versailles, France. 870 p. (579–593).

Detweiler, A. R., J. M. Vargas, Jr. and T. K. Danneberger. 1983. Resistance of *Sclerotinia homoeocarpa* to iprodione and benomyl. Plant Disease 67:627–630.

de Waard, M. A. 1988. Interactions of fungicide resistance. *In*: Fungicide Resistance in North America, C. J. Delp, Ed. APS Press, St. Paul. 133 p. (98–100).

Dewan, M. M. and K. Sivasithamparam. 1988. *Pythium* spp. in roots of wheat and ryegrass in Western Australia and their effect on root rot caused by *Gaeumannomyces graminis* var. *tritici*. Soil Biol. Biochem. 20: 801–808.

Dickerson, O. J. 1966. Some observations on *Hypsoperine graminis* in Kansas. Plant Disease Reptr. 50:396–398.

Dickinson, L. S. 1932. The effect of air temperature on the pathogenicity of *Rhizoctonia solani* parasitizing grasses on putting green turf. Phytopathology 20:597–608.

Dimond, A. E. and S. Rich. 1977. Effect of physiology on the host and host/pathogen interactions. *In*: Systemic Fungicides (2nd ed.), R. W. Marsh, Ed., Longman, London. 115 p.

DiPaola, J. M., J. B. Beard and H. Brawand. 1982. Key events in the seasonal root growth of bermudagrass and St. Augustinegrass. Hortscience 17:829–831.

Distribution of plant-parasitic nematodes in the South. 1960. Report of U.S.D.A. Regional Project S-19. Southern Cooperative Series Bull. 74.

Drechsler, C. 1922. A new leaf spot of Kentucky bluegrass caused by an undescribed species of Helminthosporium. Phytopathology 12:35. (Abstr.)

Drechsler, C. 1923. Some graminicolus species of Helminthosporium: I. Jour. Agric. Res. 24:641–740.

Drechsler, C. 1929a. Leaf spot and root rot of bluegrass. U.S. Golf Assoc. Green Sect. Bulletin 9:120–123.

Drechsler, C. 1929b. Occurrence of the zonate-eyespot

fungus, *Helminthosporium giganteum*, on some additional grasses. Jour. Agr. Res. 39:129–135.

Drechsler, C. 1935. A leaf spot of bentgrass caused by *Helminthosporium erythrospilum*, n. sp. Phytopathology 25:344–361.

Dubey, H. D. and R. Rodriguez-Kabanna. 1970. Effect of Dyrene and maneb on nitrification and ammonification and their degradation in soils. Proc. Soil Science Society America 34:435–439.

Dunlap, A. A. 1944. *Pleospora* on lawn grass in Texas. Plant Disease Reptr. 28:168.

Dunn, R. A. and J. W. Noling. 1993. 1993 Florida nematode control guide. Publication SP-54, Institute of Food and Agricultural Sciences, University of Florida, Gainesville. 45 p.

Eggens, J. L., C. P. M. Wright and K. Carey. 1989. Nitrate and ammonium nitrogen effects on growth of creeping bentgrass and annual bluegrass. Hort. Science 24: 952–954.

Egli, T. and D. Schmidt. 1982. Pathogenic variation among causal agents of bacterial wilt of forage grasses. Phytopath. Zeit. 104:138–150.

Egli, T., M. Goto and D. Schmidt. 1975. Bacterial wilt, a new forage grass disease. Phytopath. Zeit. 82:111–121.

Eighmy, T. T., D. Maratea and P. L. Bishop. 1983. Electron microscope examination of waste water biofilm formation and structural components. Applied and Environmental Microbiology 45:1921–1931.

Elliott, M. L. 1991a. A selective medium for *Gaeumannomyces*-like fungi. Plant Disease 75:1075.

Elliott, M. L. 1991b. Determination of an etiological agent of bermudagrass decline. Phytopathology 81:1380–1384.

Elliott, M. L. 1993a. Association of *Gaeumannomyces graminis* var. *graminis* with a St. Augustinegrass root rot disease. Plant Disease 77:206–209.

Elliott, M. L. 1993b. Bermudagrass decline: Transmission of the causal agent *Gaeumannomyces graminis* var. *graminis* by vegetative planting material. International Turfgrass Society Res. Jour. 7:329–334.

Elliott, M. L. and J. L. Cisar. 1989. Control of gray leaf spot (*Magnaporthe grisea*) on St. Augustinegrass in a newly established sod field. *In*: Turfgrass Research in Florida: A Technical Report. Institute of Food and Agricultural Sciences, University of Florida, Gainesville. 169 p. (63–66).

Elliott, M. L. and T. E. Freeman. 1992. Bermudagrass decline. Florida Coop. Ext. Serv. Fact Sheet PP-31. 4 p.

Elliott, M. L., A. K. Hagan and J. M. Mullen. 1991. Association of *Gaeumannomyces graminis* var. *graminis* with St. Augustinegrass root rot disease. Plant Disease 77:206–209.

Elliott, M. L. and P. L. Landschoot. 1991. Fungi similar to *Gaeumannomyces* associated with root rot of turfgrasses in Florida. Plant Disease 75:238–241.

Endo, R. M. 1963. Influence of temperature on rate of growth of five fungus pathogens of turfgrass and on rate of disease spread. Phytopathology 55:857–861.

Endo, R. M. 1966. Control of dollar spot of turfgrass by nitrogen and its probable basis. Phytopathology 56: 877. (Abstr.)

Endo, R. M., R. Baldwin, S. Cockerham, P. F. Colbaugh, A. H. McCain and V. H. Gibeault. 1973. Fusarium blight, a destructive disease of Kentucky bluegrass and its control. California Turfgrass Culture 23(1):1–2.

Endo, R. M. and P. F. Colbaugh. 1974. Fusarium blight of Kentucky bluegrass in California. Proc. 2nd International Turfgrass Conf. Madison, Wis., American Soc. Agron. 602 p. (325–327).

Endo, R. M. and I. Malca. 1965. Morphological and cyto-histological responses of primary roots of bentgrass to *Sclerotinia homoeocarpa* and D-Galactose. Phytopathology 55:781–789.

Endo, R. M., I. Malca and E. M. Krausman. 1964. Degeneration of the apical meristem and apex of bentgrass roots by a fungal toxin. Phytopathology 54:1175–1176.

Endo, R. M., H. D. Ohr and E. M. Krausman. 1985. *Leptosphaeria korrae*, a cause of spring dead spot in California. Plant Disease 69:235–237.

Erwin, L. E. 1941. Pathogenicity and control of *Corticium fuciforme*. Univ. Rhode Island Agr. Expt. Sta. Bull. 278.

Eshed, N. and A. Dinoor. 1981. Genetics of pathogenicity in *Puccinia coronata*: The host range among grasses. Phytopathology 71:156–163.

Faloon, R. E. 1976. *Curvularia trifolii* as a high temperature turfgrass pathogen. New Zealand Jour. Agric. Res. 19:243–248.

Faris, J. A. 1933. Influence of soil moisture and soil temperature on infection of wheat by *Urocystis tritici*. Phytopathology 23:10–11.

Farr, D. F., G. F. Bills, G. P. Chamuris and A. Y. Rossman. 1989. Fungi on Plants and Plant Products in the United States. APS Press: St Paul. 1252 p.

van Faassen, H. B. 1974. Effect of the fungicide benomyl on some metabolic processes, and on numbers of bacteria and actinomycetes in the soil. Soil Biol. Biochem. 6: 131–133.

Feder. W. A. and J. Feldmesser. 1957. Additions to the host list of *Radopholus similis*, the burrowing nematode. Plant Disease Reptr. 41:33.

Feldmesser, J. and A. M. Golden. 1972. Control of nematodes damaging home lawngrasses in two counties in Maryland. Plant Disease Reptr. 56:476–480.

Fenstermacher, J. M. 1970. Variation within Sclerotinia homoeocarpa F. T. Bennett. M. S. Thesis, Univ. Rhode Island, Kingston. 68 p.

Fenstermacher, J. M. 1980. Certain features of dollar spot disease and its causal organism. *In*: Advances in Turfgrass Pathology, B. G. Joyner and P. O. Larsen, Ed. Harcourt Brace Jovanovich: Duluth. 197 p. (49–53).

Ferguson, M. H. and F. V. Grau. 1949. The history and development of controls for major diseases of bentgrass on putting greens. Timely Turf Topics of the USGA Green Section. Spring, 1949.

Filer, T. H., Jr. 1965a. Parasitic aspects of a fairy ring

fungus, *Marasmius oreades*. Phytopathology 55:1132–1134.

Filer, T. H., Jr. 1965b. Damage to turfgrasses caused by cyanogenic compounds produced by *Marasmius oreades*, a fairy ring fungus. Plant Disease Reptr. 49:571–574

Filer, T. H., Jr. 1966a. Effect on grass and cereal seedlings of hydrogen cyanide produced by mycelium and sporophores of *Marasmius oreades*. Plant Disease Reptr. 50:264–266.

Filer, T. H., Jr. 1966b. Red thread found on Bermuda grass. Plant Disease Reptr. 50:525–526.

Fischer, G. W. 1940. Fundamental studies of the stripe smut of grasses (*Ustilago striaeformis*) in the Pacific Northwest. Phytopathology 30:93–118.

Fischer, G. W. 1953. Manual of the North American Smut Fungi. Ronald Press: New York. 343 p.

Fischer, G. W. and C. S. Holton, 1957. Biology and Control of the Smut Fungi. Ronald Press: New York. 622 p.

Fischer, G. W., R. Sprague, H. W. Johnson and J. R. Hardison. 1942. Host and pathogen indices to the diseases observed on grasses in certain Western States during 1941. Plant Disease Reptr. Suppl. 137:87–144.

Fletcher, R. A. and V. Nath. 1984. Triadimefon reduces transpiration and increases yield in water stressed plants. Physiol. Plant. 62:422–425.

Ford, R. E., H. Fagbenle and W. N. Stoner. 1970. New hosts and serological identity of bromegrass mosaic virus from South Dakota. Plant Disease Reptr. 54:191–195.

Forer, L. B. 1977. *Longidorus breviannulatus* associated with a decline of bentgrass in Pennsylvania. Plant Disease Reptr. 61:712.

Foster, M. G. and D. J. McQueen. 1977. The effects of single and multiple applications of benomyl on nontarget soil bacteria. Bull. Environ. Contam. Toxicol. 17:477–481.

Franklin, M. T. 1951. The cyst-forming species of Heterodera. Commonwealth Agr. Bur., England. 74–80.

Freeman, T. E. 1959. A leafspot of St. Augustine Grass caused by *Cercospora fusimaculans*. Phytopathology 49:160–161.

Freeman, T. E. 1960. Effects of temperature on cottony blight of ryegrass. Phytopathology 50:575. (Abstr.)

Freeman, T. E. 1963. Age of ryegrass in relation to damage by *Pythium aphnidermatum*. Plant Disease Reptr. 47:844.

Freeman, T. E. 1964a. Helminthosporium diseases of Bermudagrass. Golf Course Reptr. 32(5):24–26.

Freeman, T. E. 1964b. Influence of nitrogen on severity of *Piricularia grisea* infection of St. Augustine grass. Phytopathology 54:1187–1189.

Freeman, T. E. 1965. Rust of Zoysia spp. in Florida. Plant Disease Reptr. 49:382.

Freeman, T. E. 1967. Diseases of southern turf grasses. Florida Agric. Exp. Sta. Tech. Bull. 731. 31 p.

Freeman, T. E. 1969. Influence of nitrogen sources on growth of *Sclerotinia homoeocarpa*. Phytopathology 59:114.

Freeman, T. E. 1970. A seed disorder of Bermuda grass caused by *Helminthosporium spiciferum*. Plant Disease Reptr. 54:358–359.

Freeman, T. E. 1972. Seed treatment for control of Pythium blight of ryegrass. Plant Disease Reptr. 56:1043–1045.

Freeman, T. E. 1980. Seedling diseases of turfgrasses incited by Pythium. *In*: Advances in Turfgrass Pathology, B. G. Joyner and P. O. Larsen, Ed. Harcourt Brace Jovanovich: Duluth. 197 p. (41–44)

Freeman, T. E. and G. C. Horn. 1963. Reaction of turfgrasses to attack by *Pythium aphanidermatum* (Edson) Fitzpatrick. Plant Disease Reptr. 47:425–427.

Freeman, T. E. and G. W. Simone. 1988. Turfgrass diseases and their control. Florida Coop. Ext. Ser. Cir. 221-H. 13 p.

Fushtey, S. G. 1980. Chemical control of snow mold in bentgrass turf in southern Ontario. Canadian Plant Disease Survey 60:25–31.

Fushtey, S. G. and D. K. Taylor. 1977. Blister smut in Kentucky bluegrass at Agassiz, B.C. Canadian Plant Disease Survey 57:29–30.

Gaskin, T. A. 1965a. Varietal reaction of creeping bentgrass to stripe smut. Plant Disease Reptr. 49:268.

Gaskin, T. A. 1965b. Varietal reaction of Kentucky bluegrass to Septoria leaf spot (*Septoria macropoda*). Plant Disease Reptr. 49:802.

Gaskin, T. A. 1965c. Varietal resistance to flag smut in Kentucky bluegrass. Plant Disease Reptr. 49:1017.

Gaskin, T. A. 1965d. Susceptibility of bluegrass to root-knot nematodes. Plant Disease Reptr. 49:89–90.

Gibeault, V. A., R. Auto, S. Spaulding and V. B. Younger. 1980. Mixing turfgrasses controls Fusarium blight. California Agriculture. October. p. 11–12.

Giblin-Davis, R. M., J. L. Cisar and F. G. Bilz. 1988. Evaluation of three nematicides for the control of phytoparasitic nematodes in 'Tifgreen II' bermudagrass. Annals Applied Nematology 2:46–49.

Giblin-Davis, R. M., J. L. Cisar, F. G. Bilz and K. E. Williams. 1992. Host status of different bermudagrasses (*Cynodon* spp.) for the sting nematode, *Belonolaimus longicaudatus*. Jour. Nematology 24(4S):749–756.

Gibson, R. W. and R. T. Plumb. 1976. The transmission and effect on yield of ryegrass mosaic virus in a filtered air environment. Annals Appl. Biol. 82:79–84.

Gill, C. C. 1967. Oat necrotic mottle, a new virus in Manitoba. Phytopathology 57:302–307.

Gill, C. C. 1976. Oat necrotic mottle virus. *In*: Descriptions of Plant Viruses No. 169. Commonwealth Mycol. Inst./ Assoc. Appl. Biol.: Kew, Surrey, England. 4 pp.

Gockel, J. F. 1987. Looking for light in all the right places. Golf Course Management 55(7):26–32.

Godfrey, G. H. 1925. Experiments with the control of brown-patch with chlorophenol mercury. Prof. Paper No. 1. Boyce Thompson Institute for Plant Research. 5 p.

Godfrey, G. H. 1929. A destructive root disease of pineapple and other plants due to *Tylenchus brachurus* n. sp. Phytopathology 19:611–629.

Golden, A. M. and N. A. Minton. 1970. Description and larval herromorphism of *Hoplolaimus concaudamuvencus* n. sp. (Nematoda: Hoplolaimidae). Jour. Nematology 2:161–166.

Good, H. M., J. R. Christie and G. C. Nutter. 1956. Identification and distribution of plant parasitic nematodes in Florida and Georgia. Phytopathology 46:13. (Abstr.)

Good, J. M., N. A. Minton and C. A. Jaworski. 1965. Relative susceptibility of selected cover crops and coastal Bermudagrass to plant nematodes. Phytopathology 55:1026–1030.

Good, J. M., A. E. Steele and T. J. Ratcliffe. 1959. Occurrence of plant parasitic nematodes in Georgia turf nurseries. Plant Disease Reptr. 43:236–238.

Goodey, T. 1927. On *Tylenchus graminis* (Hardy 1850) Marcinoroski 1909. Jour. Helminth. 5:163–170.

Goodey, T. 1930. On *Tylenchus agrostis* (Steinbuch, 1799). Jour. Helminth. 8:197–210.

Goodey, T. 1933. *Anguillulina graminophila* n. sp., a nematode causing galls on the leaves of fine bentgrass. Jour. Helminth. 11:45–56.

Goodey, T. 1934. On gall formation due to the nematode, *Anguillulina graminis*. Jour. Helminth. 12:119–122.

Goodey, T. and M. T. Franklin. 1956. The nematode parasites of plants catalogued under their host. Commonwealth Bur. of Agr. Parasitology (Helminthology), England. 139 p.

Goss, R. L. 1968. The effects of potassium on disease resistance. *In*: The Role of Potassium in Agriculture (V. J. Kilmer, S. E. Younts, and N. C. Brady, Eds.). American Society of Agronomy: Madison, Wis. p. 221–241.

Goss, R. L. and C. J. Gould. 1971. Inter-relationships between fertility levels and Corticium red thread disease of turfgrasses. Jour. Sports Turf. Res. Inst. 47: 48–53.

Goss, R. L. and C. J. Gould. 1967. Some inter-relationships between fertility levels and Ophiobolus patch disease in turfgrass. Agron. Jour. 59:149–151.

Goto, M. 1990. Fundamentals of Bacterial Plant Pathology. Academic Press: New York. 342 p.

Gough, F. J. and M. E. McDaniel. 1969. Zoysia rust in Texas. Plant Disease Reptr. 53:232.

Gould, C. J. 1957. Turf diseases in western Washington in 1955 and 1956. Plant Disease Reptr. 41:344–347.

Gould, C. J. 1976. A cool weather strain of Rhizoctonia brown patch? Northwest Turfgrass Topics 19(1): p. 3, 8.

Gould, C. J., S. E. Brauen and R. L. Goss. 1977. Entyloma blister smut on *Poa pratensis* in the Pacific Northwest. Proc. American Phytopath. Soc. 4:205–206. (Abstr.)

Gould, C. J., R. L. Goss and M. Eglitis. 1961. Ophiobolus patch disease of turf in western Washington. Plant Disease Reptr. 45:296–297.

Gould, C. J., R. L. Goss and V. L. Miller. 1961. Fungicidal tests for control of Fusarium patch disease of turf. Plant Disease Reptr. 45:112–118.

Gould, C. J., V. L. Miller and R. L. Goss. 1965. New experimental and commercial fungicides for control of Fusarium patch disease of bentgrass turf. Plant Disease Reptr. 49:923–927.

Gould, C. J., V. L. Miller and D. Polley. 1955. Fairy ring disease of lawns. Golf Course Reptr. 23(8):16–20.

Grafton, K. F., J. M. Poehlman and D. T. Sechler. 1982. Tall fescue as a natural host and aphid vectors of barley yellow dwarf in Missouri. Plant Disease 66:318–320.

Graham, T. W. 1951. Nematode root rot of tobacco and other plants. South Carolina Agr. Exp. Sta. Bull. 390.

Graham, J. H. and E. S. Luttrell. 1961. Species of *Leptosphaerulina* on forage plants. Phytopathology 51: 680–693.

Gregory, P. H. 1982. Fairy rings; free and tethered. Bull. British Mycol. Soc. 16:161–163.

Griffin, G. D. 1984. Nematode parasites of alfalfa, cereals, and grasses. *In*: Plant and Insect Nematodes, W. R. Nickle, Ed. Marcel Dekker: New York. 925 p.

Griffiths, M. A. 1924. Experiments with flag smut of wheat and the causal fungus, *Urocystis tritici* Kcke. Jour. Agr. Res. 27:425–449.

Groves, J. W. and C. A. Bowerman. 1955. *Sclerotinia borealis* in Canada. Canadian Jour. Botany 33:591–594.

Groves, J. W. and A. J. Skolko. 1945. Notes on seed-borne fungi. III. Curvularia. Canadian Jour. Sci., C, 23: 94–104.

Gudauskas, R. T. 1962. Stem and crown necrosis of coastal Bermuda grass caused by *Helminthosporium spiciferum*. Plant Disease Reptr. 46:498–500.

Gudauskas, R. T. and S. M. McCarter. 1966. Occurrence of rust on zoysia species in Alabama. Plant Disease Reptr. 48:418.

Hagan, A. K. 1980. Epidemiological studies of melting-out of Kentucky bluegrass and development of a fungicide bioassay. Ph.D. Dissertation. Ohio State University, Columbus. 149 p.

Hagan, A. K. and P. O. Larsen. 1985. Source and dispersal of conidia of *Drechslera poae* in Kentucky bluegrass turf. Plant Disease Reptr. 69:21–24.

Hagemeyer, J. W. 1951. A new stage in the life cycle of the golden nematode, *Heterodera rostochiensis* Wollenweber. Proc. Helminth. Soc. Wash. 18:112–114.

Halisky, P. M. and C. R. Funk. 1966. Environmental factors affecting growth and sporulation of *Helminthosporium vagans* and its pathogenicity to *Poa pratensis*. Phytopathology 56:1294–1296.

Halisky, P. M., C. R. Funk and P. L. Babinsky. 1969. Chemical control of stripe smut in "Merion" Kentucky bluegrass. Plant Disease Reptr. 53:286–288.

Halisky, P. M., C. R. Funk and S. Bachelder. 1966. Stripe smut of turf and forage grass—its prevalence, pathogenicity, and response to management practices. Plant Disease Reptr. 50:294–298.

Halisky, P. M., C. R. Funk and R. E. Engel. 1966. Melting-out of Kentucky bluegrass varieties by *Helminthosporium vagans* as influenced by turf management. Plant Disease Reptr. 50:703–706.

Hall, J. 1989. An agronomic perspective on black layer. Parks and Ground Management 42(3):20–22.

Hall, T. J., P. O. Larsen and A. F. Schmitthenner. 1980. Survival of *Pythium aphanidermatum* in golf course turfs. Plant Disease 64:100–1103.

Hardison, J. R. 1942. Grass diseases in Michigan in 1941. Plant Disease Reptr. 26:67–75.

Hardison, J. R. 1943. Specialization of pathogenicity in *Erysiphe graminis* on wild and cultivated grasses. Phytopathology 34:1–20.

Hardison, J. R. 1945a. Specialization in *Erysiphae graminis* for pathogenicity on wild and cultivated grasses outside the tribe *Hordeae*. Phytopathology 35:394–405.

Hardison, J. R. 1945b. Specialization of pathogenicity in *Erysiphae graminis* on *Poa* and its relation to bluegrass improvement. Phytopathology 35:62–71.

Hardison, J. R. 1948. Field control of blind seed disease of perennial ryegrass in Oregon. Phytopathology 38:404–419.

Hardison, J. R. 1949. Blind seed disease of perennial ryegrass. Oregon State College Agr. Ext. Expt. Sta. Cir. 177.

Hardison, J. R. and R. Sprague. 1943. A leaf spot of grasses caused by a new species of *Phleospora*. Mycologia 35:185–188.

Haygood, R. A. and O. W. Barnett. 1988. Occurrence of Panicum mosaic virus on St. Augustine grass in South Carolina. Phytopathology 78:627–628. (Abstr.)

Haygood, R. A., R. M. Lippert, A. R. Mazur and L. C. Miller, 1989. Influence of pH and water stress on the susceptibility of centipede grass to *Rhizoctonia solani*. Phytopathology 79:373. (Abstr.)

Haygood, R. A. and S. B. Martin. 1990. Characterization and pathogenicity of species of Rhizoctonia associated with centipedegrass and St. Augustinegrass in South Carolina. Plant Disease 74:510–514.

Heald, C. M. and G. W. Burton. 1968. Effect of organic and inorganic nitrogen on nematode populations of turf. Plant Disease Reptr. 52:46–48.

Heald, C. M. and A. M. Golden. 1969. *Meloidodera charis*, a cystoid nematode infection of St. Augustinegrass. Plant Disease Reptr. 53:527.

Heald, F. D. and F. A. Wolf. 1911. New species of Texas fungi. Mycologia 3:5–22.

Healy, M. J., M. P. Britton and J. D. Butler. 1965. Stripe smut damage on 'Pennlu' creeping bentgrass. Plant Disease Reptr. 49:710.

Heard, A. J. and E. T. Roberts. 1975. Disorders of temporary ryegrass swards in south-east England. Annals Appl. Biol. 81:240–243.

Hendrix. F. G., Jr. and W. A. Campbell. 1973. Pythiums as plant pathogens. Annual Review Phytopathology 11:77–98.

Hesling, J. J. 1958. The efficiency of certain grasses as hosts of cereal root eelworm. Plant Pathology 7:141–143.

Hims, M. J., C. H. Dickinson and J. T. Fletcher. 1984. Control of red thread, a disease of grasses caused by *Laetisaria fuciformis*. Plant Pathology 33:513–516.

Hodges, C. F. 1970. Influence of temperature on growth of stripe smutted creeping bentgrass and on sorus development of *Ustilago striiformis*. Phytopathology 60:665–668.

Hodges, C. F. 1972. Interaction of culture age and temperature on germination and growth of *Curvularia geniculata* and on virulence. Canadian Jour. Bot. 50:2093–2096.

Hodges, C. F. 1976a. Comparative primary infection characteristics of *Ustilago striiformis* and *Urocystis agropyri* on cultivars of *Poa pratensis*. Phytopathology 66:1111–1115.

Hodges, C. F. 1976b. Development of healthy shoots from Poa pratensis systemically infected by *Ustilago striiformis* and *Urocystis agropyri*. Plant Disease Reptr. 60:120–121.

Hodges, C. F. 1978. Postemergent herbicides and the biology of *Drechslera sorokiniana*: influence on severity of leaf spot on *Poa pratensis*. Phytopathology 68:1359–1363.

Hodges, C. F. 1980a. Postemergent herbicides and pathogenesis by *Drechslera sorokiniana* on leaves of *Poa pratensis*. *In*: Advances in Turfgrass Pathology, B. G. Joyner and P. O. Larsen, Ed. Harcourt Brace Jovanovich: Duluth. 197 p. (101–112).

Hodges, C. F. 1980b. Interaction of sequential leaf senescence of *Poa pratensis* and pathogenesis by *Drechslera sorokiniana* as influenced by postemergent herbicides. Phytopathology 70:628–630.

Hodges, C. F. 1985a. *Pythium*-induced root dysfunction of secondary roots of *Agrostis palustris*. Plant Disease 69:336–340.

Hodges, C. F. 1985b. *Pythium*-induced root dysfunction of creeping bentgrass on high sand content greens. USGA Green Section Record 23(5):11–13.

Hodges, C. F. 1989. Another look at black layer. Golf Course Management 57(3):56–58.

Hodges, C. F. and M. P. Britton. 1969. Infection of Merion bluegrass, *Poa pratensis*, by stripe smut, *Ustilago striiformis* Phytopathology 59:301–304.

Hodges, C. F. and M. P. Britton. 1970. Directional growth and the perennial characteristics of *Ustilago striiformis* in *Poa pratensis*. Phytopathology 60:849–851.

Hodges, C. F. and J. P. Madsen. 1978. The competitive and synergistic interactions of *Drechslera sorokiniana* and *Curvularia geniculata* on leaf spot development on *Poa pratensis*. Canadian Jour. Bot. 56:1240–1247.

Hodges, C. F. and D. P. Taylor. 1966. Host-parasite interactions of a root-knot nematode and creeping bentgrass, *Agrostis palustris*. Phytopathology 56:88–91.

Holcomb, G. E. 1985. A mosaic disease of centipedegrass and crowfootgrass. Phytopathology 75:500. (Abstr.)

Holcomb, G. E. and R. E. Motsinger. 1967. Zoysia rust in Louisiana. Plant Disease Reptr. 56:726.

Holcomb, G. E., K. S. Derrick, R. B. Carver and R. W. Toler. 1972. St. Augustine decline virus found in Louisiana. Plant Disease Reptr. 56:69–70.

Homeyer, B. and K. Wagner. 1981. Mode of action of phenamiphos and its behaviour in soil. Nematologica 27:215–219.

Horsfall, J. G. 1930. A study of meadow-crop diseases in New York. Cornell Univ. Agr. Expt. Sta. Mem. 130.

Horst, G. 1991. Another look—turf and salinity. USGA Green Section Record 29(4):11–13.

Hosotsuji, T. 1977. Control of diseases, insect pests and weeds of turf. Japan Pesticide Information Leaflet No. 33.

Howard, F. L., J. B. Rowell and H. L. Keil. 1951. Fungus diseases of turfgrasses. Univ. Rhode Island Agr. Expt. Sta. Bull. 308.

Hsiang, T., X. Liu, K. Carey and J. Eggens. 1991. Effects of Ringer and other lawn amendments on turfgrass. 1991 Research Report, Guelph Turfgrass Institute. University of Guelph, Ontario, Canada. p. 21–28.

Hull, R. J., N. Jackson and C. R. Skogley. 1979. Nutritional implications of stripe smut severity in Kentucky bluegrass turf. Agronomy Journal 71:553–555.

Hungerford, C. W. 1923. A serious disease of wheat caused by *Sclerotium rhizodes*. Phytopathology 13:463–464.

Hurd, B. and M. P. Grisham. 1983. *Rhizoctonia* spp. associated with brown patch of St. Augustinegrass. Phytopathology 73:1661–1665.

Ichitani, T., T. Tani and T. Umakoshi. 1986. Identification of *Pythium* spp. pathogenic on Manilla grass (*Zoysia matrella* Merr.). Trans. Mycol. Soc. Japan 27:41–50.

Index of Plant Diseases in the United States. 1960. U.S.D.A. Agriculture Handbook No. 165. 531 p.

Ivanowski, D. 1892. Ueber die Moasikkrankheit der Tabakspflanze. St. Petersb. Acad. Imp. Sci. Bull. 35. Ser. 4, Vol. 3:67–70. (Translated into English by J. Johnson as Phytopathological Classics No. 7, 1942, American Phytopathological Society: St. Paul).

Jackson, N. E. 1958. Ophiobolus patch disease fungicide trial, 1958. Jour. Sports Turf. Res. Inst. 9:459–461.

Jackson, N. E. 1970. Evaluation of some chemicals for control of stripe smut in Kentucky bluegrass turf. Plant Disease Reptr. 54:168–170.

Jackson, N. E. 1973. Apothecial production in *Sclerotinia homoeocarpa* F. T. Bennett. Jour. Sports Turf Res. Inst. 49:58–63.

Jackson, N. E. 1984. A new cool season patch disease of Kentucky bluegrass turf in the northeastern United States. Phytopathology 74:812. (Abstr.)

Jackson, N. E. 1980a. Yellow tuft. *In*: Advances in Turfgrass Pathology, B. G. Joyner and P. O. Larsen, Ed. Harcourt Brace Jovanovich: Duluth. 197 p. (135–137).

Jackson, N. E. 1980b. Yellow tuft disease of turf grasses. A review of recent studies conducted in Rhode Island. *In*: Proc. 3rd Int. Turfgrass Conf. J. B. Beard, Ed. American Soc. Agron., Madison, Wis. p. 265–270.

Jackson, N. E. and P. H. Dernoeden. 1979. Fall fungicide application for control of stripe smut and leaf spot, 1977. *In*: Fungicide Nematicide Tests 34:307. Minneapolis, Minn., American Phytopath. Society.

Jackson, N. E. 1982. Yellow tuft. Grounds Maintenance 17(9):36, 56.

Jackson, N. E. and P. H. Dernoeden. 1980. *Sclerophthora macrospora*: the incitant of yellow tuft disease of turf grasses. Plant Disease 64:915–916.

Jackson, N. E. and J. M. Fenstermacher. 1973. A patch disease of two bentgrasses caused by *Drechslera gigantea*. Plant Disease Reptr. 57:84–85.

Jackson, N. E. and V. J. Herting. 1985. *Colletotrichum graminicola* as an incitant of anthracnose/basal stem rotting of cool season turfgrasses. *In*: Proc. 5th International Turfgrass Conf., Avignon, France, F. Lamire (Ed.). p. 647–656.

Jakobsen, J. 1975. Nematoder pa graes. Nord. Jordbrugsforsk 57:514–515.

Jensen, H. J. 1953. Experimental greenhouse host range studies of two root-lesion nematodes, *Pratylenchus vulnus* and *Pratylenchus penetrans*. Plant Disease Reptr. 37:382–387.

Jensen, H. J., H. B. Howell and W. D. Courtney. 1958. Grass seed nematode and production of bentgrass seed. Oregon Agr. Exp. Sta. Bull. 565.

Jepson, S. B. 1987. Identification of root-knot nematodes. C. A. B. International: Wallingford, Oxon. 265 p.

Johnson, A. W. 1970. Pathogenicity and interaction of three nematode species on six Bermudagrasses. Jour. Nematology 2:36–41.

Johnson, A. W. and W. M. Powell. 1968. Pathogenic capabilities of a ring nematode, *Criconemoides lobatum*, on various turf grasses. Plant Disease Reptr. 52:109–113.

Jones, B. L. and J. Amador. 1969. Downy mildew, a new disease of St. Augustinegrass. Plant Disease Reptr. 53:852–854.

Joyner, B. G. and H. B. Couch. 1976. Relation of dosage rates, nutrition, and suscept genotype to side effects of fungicides on turfgrasses. Phytopathology 66:806–810.

Joyner, B. G. and P. O. Larsen. 1980. Advances in Turfgrass Pathology. Harcourt Brace Jovanovich: Duluth. 197 p.

Joyner, B. G., R. E. Partyka and P. O. Larsen. 1977. Rhizoctonia brown patch of Kentucky bluegrass. Plant Disease Reptr. 61:749–752.

Juhnke, M. E., D. E. Mathre and D. C. Sands. 1983. A selective medium for *Gaeumannomyces graminis* var. *tritici*. Plant Disease 68:233–236.

Kackley, K. E., P. H. Dernoden and A. P. Grybauskas. 1989. Effect of fungicides on the occurrence and growth *in vitro* of Basidiomycetes associated with superficial fairy rings in creeping bentgrass. Plant Disease 73:127–130.

Kackley, K. E., A. P. Grybauskas, R. L. Hill and P. H. Dernoeden. 1990a. Influence of temperature-soil water status interactions on the development of summer patch. Phytopathology 80:650–655.

Kackley, K. E., A. P. Grybauskas, P. H. Dernoeden, and R. L. Hill. 1990b. Role of drought stress in the development of summer patch in field-inoculated Kentucky bluegrass. Phytopathology 80:655–658.

Kallio, A. 1966. Chemical control of snow mold (*Sclerotinia borealis*) on four varieties of bluegrass (*Poa pratensis*) in Alaska. Plant Disease Reptr. 50:69–72.

Kaplan, J. D. and N. Jackson. 1982. Variations in growth and pathogenicity of fungi associated with red thread disease of turf grass. Phytopathology 72:262. (Abstr.)

Karr, G. W., Jr., R. T. Gudauskas and R. Dickens. 1979. Effects of three herbicides on selected pathogens and diseases of turfgrasses. Phytopathology 69:279–282.

Kaufman, C. H. 1918. The Agaricaceae of Michigan. Michigan Geological and Biological Survey Pub. 26, Biological Ser. 5. Vol. I. 924 p.

Keil, H. L. 1946. "White-heads" of grasses. Ph.D. Dissertation. The Pennsylvania State University, University Park. 37 p.

Kelsheimer, E. G. and A. J. Overman. 1953. Notes on some ectoparasitic nematodes found attacking lawns in the Tampa Bay area. Proc. Fla. State Hort. Soc. 66:301–303.

Kirby, E. J. M. 1961. Host-parasite relations in the choke disease of grasses. Trans. British Mycological Soc. 44: 493–503.

Kirby, R. S. 1922. The take-all disease of cereals and grasses. Phytopathology 12:66–68.

Kline, D. M. and R. R. Nelson. 1963. Pathogenicity of isolates of *Cochliobolus sativus* from cultivated and wild gramineous hosts of the Western Hemisphere to species of the *Gramineae*. Plant Disease Reptr. 47: 890–894.

Klomparens, W. J. 1953. A study of *Helminthosporium sativum* P. K. & B. as an unreported parasite of *Agrostis palustris* Huds. Ph.D. Dissertation. Michigan State University, East Lansing. 77 p.

Kobriger, K. M. and D. J. Hagedorn. 1981. A simplified technique for production of *Pythium* oospores. Phytopathology 71:232. (Abstr.)

Koehane, J. A. 1967. Environmental studies of Fusarium blight in Merion Kentucky bluegrass. M.S. Thesis. University of Massachusetts, Amherst, Mass. 116 p.

Kohlmeyer, J. and E. Kohlmeyer. 1974. Distribution of *Epichloe typhina* (Ascomycetes) and its parasitic fly. Mycologia 66:77–86.

Kohn, L. M. 1979. Delimitation of the economically important plant pathogenic *Sclerotinia* species. Phytopathology 69:881–886.

Kohn, L. M. and D. J. Greenville. 1989. Anatomy and biochemistry of stromatal anamorphs in the Sclerotiniaceae. Canadian Jour. Bot. 67:371–393.

Kouyeas, V. and H. Kouyeas. 1963. Notes on species of *Pythium*. Annals Institute Phytopathologique Benaki 5:207–227.

Kozelnicky, G. M. 1969. First report of stripe smut of bluegrass in Georgia. Plant Disease Reptr. 53:580.

Kozelnicky, G. M. and W. N. Garrett. 1966. The occurrence of zoysia rust in Georgia. Plant Disease Reptr. 50:839.

Kreitlow, K. W. 1942. *Sclerotium rhizodes* on grasses in Pennsylvania. Plant Disease Reptr. 26:360–361.

Kreitlow, K. W. 1943. *Ustilago striaeformis*. II. Temperature as a factor influencing development of smutted plants of *Poa pratensis* L. and germination of fresh chlamydospores. Phytopathology 33:1055–1063.

Kreitlow, K. W. 1947. Seed transmission and suggested control measures for stripe smut of timothy. Phytopathology 37:13. (Abstr.)

Kreitlow, K. W. and F. V. Juska. 1959. Susceptibility of Merion and other Kentucky bluegrass varieties to stripe smut (*Ustilago striiformis*). Agronomy Journal 51:596–597.

Kreitlow, K. W., F. V. Juska and R. T. Haard. 1965. A rust on *Zoysia japonica* new to North America. Plant Disease Reptr. 49:185–186.

Krusberg, L. R. 1956. Studies on the tesselate stylet nematode. Phytopathology 46:18. (Abstr.)

Kuhn, J. G. 1858. Die Krankheiten der Kulturgewachse, ihre Ursachen und ihre Verhuting. Berlin. 321 p.

LaMonde, J. L. and R. L. Wick. 1991. Occurrence of *Heterodera iri* in putting greens in Northeastern United States. Plant Disease 76:643.

Lancashire, J. A. and G. C. M. Latch. 1966. Some effects of crown rust (*Puccinia coronata* Corda) on the growth of two ryegrass varieties in New Zealand. New Zealand Jour. Agr. Res. 9:628–640.

Lancashire, J. A. and G. C. M. Latch. 1970. The influence of nitrogen fertilizer on the incidence of crown rust (*Puccinia coronata* Corda) on two ryegrass cultivars. New Zealand Jour. Agr. Res. 13:287–293.

Lacey, J. 1967. Mastigosporium leaf fleck of perennial ryegrass. Plant Pathology 16:48.

Landschoot, P. J. and N. Jackson. 1987. A *Magnaporthe* sp. with a *Phialophora* conidial state causes summer patch disease of *Poa pratensis* and *Poa annua*. Phytopathology 77:1734. (Abstr.)

Landschoot, P. J. and B. B. Clarke. 1989. Evaluation of fungicides for control of summer patch on annual bluegrass. 1989 Fungicide Nematicide Test Results. American Phytopath. Soc., Minneapolis, Minn. p. 245.

Landschoot, P. J. and N. Jackson. 1989. *Magnaporthe poae* sp. nov., a hyphopodiate fungus with a *Phialophora* anamorph from grass roots in the United States. Mycological Research 93:59–62.

Landschoot, P. J. and B. F. Hoyland. 1992. Gray leaf spot of perennial ryegrass turf in Pennsylvania. Plant Disease 76:1280–1282.

Landschoot, P. J., B. B. Clarke, and N. Jackson. 1989. Summer patch in the Northeast. Golf Course Management 57(8):38–42.

Lane, L. C. 1977. Brome mosaic virus. *In*: Descriptions of Plant Viruses No. 180. Commonwealth Mycol. Inst./ Assoc. Appl. Biol.: Kew, Surrey, England. 4 pp.

Large, E. C. 1962. Advance of the Fungi. Dover Pub. Co.: New York. 488 p.

Larsen, P. O., A. K. Hagan, B. G. Joyner and D. A. Spilker. 1981. Leaf blight and crown rot on creeping bentgrass a new disease caused by *Drecshlera catenaria*. Plant Disease 65:79–81.

Latch, G. C. M. 1964. *Ramularia pusilla* Ung. and *Ramulariaspera holci-lanati* (Cav.) Lind. in New Zealand. New Zealand Jour. Agr. Res. 7:405–416.

Latch, G. C. M. 1966. Fungus diseases of ryegrasses in New Zealand. New Zealand Jour. Agr. Res. 9:394–409.

Latham, J. M. 1987. The agronomics of sand in construction and topdressing. USGA Green Section Record 25(5): 1–4.

Laughlin, C. W. and J. M. Vargas. 1972. Pathogenic potential of *Tylenchorhynchus dubius* on selected turfgrass. Jour. Nematology 4:277–280.

Lautz, W. 1958. Chemical control of nematodes parasitic on turf sweet corn. Proc. Florida Hort. Soc. 71:38–40.

Lawton, M. B. and L. L. Burpee. 1990. Effect of rate and frequency of application of *Typhula phacorrhiza* on biological control of Typhula blight of creeping bentgrass. Phytopathology 80:70–73.

Leach, J. G., C. V. Lowther and M. A. Ryan. 1946. Stripe smut (*Ustilago striaeformis*) in relation to bluegrass improvement. Phytopathology 36:57–72.

Leach, J. G. and M. Pierpoint. 1948. *Rhizoctonia solani* may be transmitted with seed of *Agrostis tenuis*. Plant Disease Reptr. 42:240.

Lebeau, J. B. 1964. Control of snow mold by regulating winter soil temperature. Phytopathology 54:693–696.

Lebeau, J. B. 1966. Pathology of winter injured grasses and legumes in western Canada. Crop Science 6:23–25.

Lebeau, J. B. 1976. Fall management of fine turfgrass. Research Highlights, Agriculture Canada Research Station, Lethbridge, Alberta. p. 6–8.

Lebeau, J. B. and M. W. Cormack. 1961. Development and nature of snow mold damage in western Canada. *In*: Recent Advances in Botany. Univ. Toronto Press. Vol. 1, Sect. 5. p. 544–549.

Lebeau, J. B. and J. G. Dickson. 1955. Physiology and nature of disease development in winter crown rot of alfalfa. Phytopathology 45:667–673.

Lebeau, J. B. and E. J. Hawn. 1961. Fairy rings in Alberta. Canadian Plant Disease Surv. 41:317–320.

Lebeau, J. B. and E. J. Hawn. 1963a. Formation of hydrogen cyanide by the mycelial stage of the fairy ring fungus. Phytopathology 53:1395–1396.

Lebeau, J. B. and E. J. Hawn. 1963b. A simple method for the control of fairy ring caused by *Marasmius oreades*. Jour. Sports Turf. Res. Inst. 11(39):23–25.

Lebeau, J. B. and C. E. Logsdon. 1958. Snow mold of forage crops in Alaska and the fungus *Laetisaria arvalis* Burdsall and Yukon. Phytopathology 48:148–150.

Lebeau, J. B. and C. E. Logsdon. 1968. Pink snow mold in southern Alberta. Canada Plant Disease Surv. 48:130–131.

Lee, T. A., Jr. 1973. Isolation, purification and characterization of the virus causing St. Augustine decline. Ph.D. Dissertation. Texas A & M University, College Station. 65 pp.

Lees, E. 1869. On the formation of fairy rings and the fungi that inhabit them. Trans. Woolhope Nat. Field Club, 1868:211–229.

Lefebvre, C. L. and A. G. Johnson. 1941. Collections of fungi, bacteria, and nematodes of grasses. Plant Disease Reptr. 25:556–579.

Libbey, R. O. 1938. *Corticium* disease. Jour. Board Greenkeeping Res. 5:269–270.

Lindenbach, S. K. and D. R. Cullimore. 1989. Preliminary *in vitro* observations on the bacteriology of the black plug layer phenomenon associated with the biofouling of golf greens. Jour. Applied Bacteriology 67:11–17.

Linford, M. B. 1939. Attractiveness of roots and excised shoot tissues to certain nematodes. Proc. Helminth. Soc. Wash. 6:11–18.

Lordello, L. G. E. and T. M. Filho. 1969. Mais tres capins hospedeiros de nematoides migraderes. Rev. Agric. Piracicaba 45:78.

Lucas, L. T. 1976. *Sclerotium rolfsii* on bentgrass in North Carolina. Plant Disease Reptr. 60:820–822.

Lucas, L. T. 1980a. Control of spring dead spot of bermudagrass with fungicides in North Carolina. Plant Disease 64:868–870.

Lucas, L. T. 1980b. Spring deadspot of bermudagrass. *In*: Advances in Turfgrass Pathology, B. G. Joyner and P. O. Larsen, Ed. Harcourt Brace Jovanovich: Duluth. 197 p. (183–187).

Lucas, L. T. 1982. Southern blight. Grounds Maintenance 17(5):40–42.

Lucas, L. T. 1990. Diseases of bentgrass on high-sand-content golf greens. North Carolina Agr. Ext. Serv. Turfgrass Diseases Information Note No. 4:75–78.

Lucas, L. T., C. T. Blake and K. R. Barker. 1974. Nematodes associated with bentgrass golf greens in North Carolina. Plant Disease Reptr. 58:822–824.

Lucas, L. T. and W. B. Gilbert. 1979. Managing dormant bermudagrass. Golf Course Management 47(9):14–23.

Ludwig, F. 1906. Pilzingel und Pilzwurzeln. Promethesis 17(865):522–526.

Lukens, R. J. 1960. Chemical control of stripe smut of *Poa pratensis* with nabam. Plant Disease Reptr. 44:672.

Lukens, R. J. 1966. Urea, an effective treatment for stripe smut on *Poa pratensis*. Plant Disease Reptr. 49:361.

Lukens, R. J. 1967. Infection of inflorescence of *Poa pratensis* by *Helminthosporium vagans*. Plant Disease Reptr. 51:752.

Lukens, R. J. 1968. Low light intensity promotes melting-out of bluegrass. Phytopathology 58:1058.

Lukens, R. J. 1970. Melting-out of Kentucky bluegrass, a low sugar disease. Phytopathology 60:1276–1278.

Luttrell, E. S. 1951. Diseases of tall fescue grass in Georgia. Plant Disease Reptr. 35:83–85.

MacGarvie, Q. D. and C. J. O'Rourke. 1969. New species of *Spermospora* and *Cersosporella* affecting grasses and other hosts in Ireland. Irish Jour. Agr. Res. 8:151–167.

Madsen, J. P. and C. F. Hodges. 1980. Nitrogen effects on the pathogenicity of *Drechslera sorokiniana* and *Curvularia geniculata* on germinating seed of *Festuca rubra*. Plant Disease 70:1013–1016.

Madsen, J. P. and C. F. Hodges. 1984. Effect of chlorophenoxy herbicides on free amino acids in sequentially senescent leaves of *Poa pratensis* and on pathogenesis by *Bipolaris sorokiniana*. Phytopathology 74:1407–1411.

Mai, W. F. and B. Lear. 1953. The golden nematode. Cornell Univ., Agr. Expt. Sta. Ext. Bull. 870.

Mai, W. F., H. W. Crittenden and W. R. Jenkins. 1960. Distribution of stylet-bearing nematodes in the northeastern United States (Rept. Tech. Comm. N. E. Reg. Project. N.E.-34). New Jersey Agr. Expt. Sta. Bull. 795.

Malca, I. and R. M. Endo. 1965. Identification of galactose in cultures of *Sclerotinia homoeocarpa* as the factor toxic to bentgrass roots. Phytopathology 55:775–780.

Malca, I. and J. H. Owen. 1957. The gray-leaf spot disease of St Augustine grass. Plant Disease Reptr. 41:871–875.

Malca, I. and A. J. Ulstrup. 1962. Effects of carbon and nitrogen nutrition on growth and sporulation of two species of *Helminthosporium*. Bulletin Torrey Bot. Club 89:240–249.

Marion, D. F. 1974. Leaf surface fluid composition of velvet bentgrass as affected by nitrogen fertility and its relationship to inoculum viability of *Gloeocerspora sorghi* and severity of copper spot. Ph.D. Dissertation. University of Rhode Island, Kingston. 91 p.

Markland, F. E., E. C. Roberts and L. R. Frederick. 1969. Influence of nitrogen fertilizers on Washington creeping bentgrass, *Agrostis palustris* Huds. II. Incidence of dollar spot, *Sclerotinia homoeocarpa*, infection. Agronomy Jour. 61:701–705.

Marsenowski, K. 1909. Parasitische und semiparasitische an Pflanzen lebenden Nematoden. Arb. Kaisenlichen Biol. Anstalt Lanu-u. Fonst. Berlin 7:1–192.

Martin, S. B., C. L. Campbell and L. T. Lucas. 1983. Horizontal distribution and characterization of *Rhizoctonia* spp. in tall fescue turf. Phytopathology 73:1064–1068.

Martin, S. B. and L. T. Lucas. 1984. Characterization and pathogenicity of *Rhizoctonia* spp. and binucleate *Rhizoctonia*-like fungi from turfgrasses in North Carolina. Phytopathology 74:170–175.

Massart, J. 1910. Sur Les Ronds de Sorciere de *Marasmius oreades* Fries. Ann. Jard. Bot. Buitenzorg Sup. 3, Part 2:583–586.

Massie, L. B. and H. Cole, Jr. and J. Duich. 1968. Pathogen variation in relation to disease severity and control of Sclerotinia dollar spot of turfgrass by fungicides. Phytopathology 58:1616–1619.

Mathur, S. P. 1970. Degradation of soil humus by the fairy ring mushroom. Plant and Soil 33:717–720.

Matocha, J. E. and L. Smith. 1980. Influence of potassium on *Helminthosporium cynodontis* and dry matter yields of 'Coastal' bermudagrass. Agronomy Journal 72:565–567.

Matsumoto, M. and T. Araki. 1982. Field observation of grasses under snow cover in Sapporo. Res. Bulletin Hokkaido National Agr. Exp. Sta. 135:1–10.

Mayer, A. 1886. Ueber die Mosaikkrankheit des Tabaks. Die Landw. Vers. Stat. 32:451–467. (Translated into English by J. Johnson as Phytopathological Classics No. 7, 1942. American Phytopathological Society: St. Paul).

Mazur, A. R. and T. D. Hughes. 1974. Nitrogen transformation in soil as affected by the fungicides benomyl, Dyrene, and maneb. Agronomy Journal 67:755–758.

Mazur, A. R. and T. D. Hughes. 1976. Chemical composition and quality of Penncross creeping bentgrass as af-

fected by ammonium nitrate, and several fungicides. Agronomy Journal 68:721–723.

McAlpine, D. 1906. A new hymenomycete—the so-called *Isaria fuciformis* Berk. Annales Mycologica 4:541–551.

McBeath, J. H. 1985. Pink snow mold on winter cereals and lawn grasses in Alaska. Plant Disease 69:722–723.

McCarter, S. M. and R. H. Littrell. 1968. Pathogenicity of *Pythium myriotylum* to several grass and vegetable crops. Plant Disease Reptr. 52:179–183.

McCarty, L. B. and L. T. Lucas. 1989. *Gaeumannomyces graminis* associated with spring dead spot of bermudagrass in the southeastern United States. Plant Disease 73:659–661.

McCarty, L. B., L. T. Lucas and J. M. DiPaola. 1990. Spring dead spot of bermudagrass. Golf Course Management 58(10):36–40.

McCoy, R. E. 1973. Relation of fertility level and fungicide application to incidence of *Cercospora fusimaculans* on St. Augustinegrass. Plant Disease Reptr. 57:33–35.

McCoy, N. L., R. W. Toler and J. Amador. 1969. St. Augustine decline (SAD)—a virus disease of St. Augustine grass. Plant Disease Reptr. 53:955–958.

McGlohon, N. E., J. N. Sasser and R. T. Sherwood. 1961. Investigations of plant-parasitic nematodes associated with forage crops in North Carolina. North Carolina Agric. Exp. Sta. Tech. Bull. 148.

Meredith, D. S. 1963. Further observations on the zonate eyespot fungus, *Drechslera gigantea*, in Jamaica. Trans. Brit. Mycol. Soc. 46:201–207.

Meyer, W. A. and J. B. Sinclair. 1970. *Pyrenochaeta terrestris*, a root pathogen on creeping bentgrass. Plant Disease Reptr. 54:506–507.

Meyer, W. A. and A. J. Turgeon. 1975. Control of red leaf spot on 'Toronto' creeping bentgrass. Plant Disease Reptr. 59:642–645.

Meyer, W. A., M. P. Britton, L. E. Gray and J. B. Sinclair. 1971. Fungicide effects on fungal ecology in creeping bentgrass. Mycopathologia et Mycologia Applicata 43:309–315.

Middleton, J. T. 1943. The taxonomy, host range, and geographic distribution of the genus Pythium. Torrey Bot. Club Mem. 20(1):1–171.

Miller, P. W. and F. P. McWhorter. 1948. The use of vapor-heat as a practical means of disinfecting seeds. Phytopathology 38:89–101.

Miller, R. H. and J. F. Wilkinson. 1977. Nature of organic coating on sand greens of non-wettable golf greens. Soil Sci. Soc. Am. Proc. 41:1203–1204.

Minton, N. A. and H. Ivey. 1967. The pseudo root-knot nematode on Bermudagrass in Alabama. Plant Disease Reptr. 51:148.

Misra, A. P., O. M. Prakash and R. A. Singh. 1972. *Helminthosporium catenarium* incitant of a new leaf blight disease of barley in India. Indian Phytopathology 24:582–583.

Misra, A. P. and R. A. Singh. 1972. Hitherto an unrecorded disease of wheat incited by *Helminthosporium catenarium* in India. Indian Phytopathology 24:803–804.

Monteith, J. 1933. A Pythium disease of turf. Phytopathology 23:23–24. (Abstr.)

Monteith, J. and A. S. Dahl. 1932. Turf diseases and their control. The Bulletin, U.S. Golf Assoc. 12:8–126.

Moore, L. D. and H. B. Couch. 1961. *Pythium ultimum* and *Helminthosporium vagans* as foliar pathogens of Gramineae. Plant Disease Reptr. 45:616–619.

Moore, L.D., H. B. Couch and J. R. Bloom. 1963. Influence of environment on diseases of turfgrasses. III. Effect of nutrition, pH, and soil temperature, air temperature, and soil moisture on Pythium blight of Highland bentgrass. Phytopathology 53:53–57.

Moore, L. D., H. B. Couch and J. R. Bloom. 1968. Influence of calcium nutrition on pectolytic and cellulolytic enzyme activity of extracts of Highland bentgrass foliage blighted by *Pythium ultimum*. Phytopathology 58: 833–838.

Morgan, J. V. and H. B. Tukey, Jr. 1964. Characterization of leachate from plant foliage. Plant Physiology 39: 590–593.

Moss, M. A. and L. E. Trevathan. 1987. Environmental conditions conducive to infection of ryegrass by *Pyricularia grisea*. Phytopathology 77:863–866.

Mower, R. G. 1962. Histological studies of suscept-pathogen relationships of *Helminthosporium sativum* P. K. and B., *Helminthosporium vagans* Dreshs. and *Curvularia lunata* (Wakk.) Boed. on leaves of Merion and of common Kentucky bluegrass (*Poa pratensis*). Ph.D. Dissertation. Cornell Univ., Ithaca, N.Y., 150 p.

Muchovej, J. J. 1987. *Drechslera gigantea* on *Eleusine indica* in Brazil. Fitopathol. Bras. 12:405–406.

Muchovej, J. J. 1986. Definition of leaf health in *Agrostis palustris* at the time of infection and clonization by *Curvularia lunata*. Annals Applied Biology 109: 249–258.

Muchovej, J. J. and H. B. Couch. 1985. Curvularia blight of turfgrasses: A historical perspective. Rasen-Turf-Gazon 16(3):88–92.

Muchovej, J. J. and H. B. Couch. 1987. Colonization of bentgrass turf by *Curvularia lunata* after clipping and heat stress. Plant Disease 71:873–875.

Muller, E. 1951. On the development of *Pleospora gaeumannii* nov spec. Ber. Schweitz Bot. Ges. 61:165–174.

Mulligan, T. E. 1960. The transmission by mites, host range and properties of ryegrass mosaic. Annals Appl. Biol. 48:575–579.

Murdoch, C. L., W. J. Apt and H. Tashiro. 1977. Effects of nematicides on root-knot nematodes in bermudagrass putting greens in Hawaii. Plant Disease Reptr. 61: 978–981.

Muse, R. R. 1971. Chemical control of Fusarium blight of 'Merion' Kentucky bluegrass. Plant Disease Reptr. 55: 333–335.

Muse, R. R. 1974. Influence of nutrition on the development of Helminthosporium red leaf spot on Seaside bentgrass, *Agrostis palustris*. Physiological Plant Pathology 4:99–105.

Muse, R. R. and H. B. Couch. 1965. Influence of environment on diseases of turfgrasses. IV. Effect of nutrition and soil moisture on Corticium red thread of creeping red fescue. Phytopathology 55:507–510.

Muse, R. R., H. B. Couch, L. D. Moore and B. Muse. 1972. Pectolytic and cellulolytic enzymes associated with Helminthosporium leaf spot on Kentucky bluegrass. Canadian Jour. Microbiology 18:1091–1098.

Muse, R. R., A. F. Schmitthenner and R. E. Partyka. 1974. *Pythium* spp. associated with foliar blighting of creeping bentgrass. Phytopathology 64:252–253.

Myers, D. F. and W. E. Fry. 1978. The development of *Gloeocercospora sorghi* on sorghum. Phytopathology 68:1147–1155.

Nelson, E. B. and C. M. Craft. 1991a. Identification and comparative pathogenicity of *Pythium* spp. from roots and crowns of turfgrasses exhibiting symptoms of root rot. Phytopathology 81:1529–1536.

Nelson, E. B. and C. M. Craft. 1991b. Introduction and establishment of strains of *Enterobacter cloaceae* in golf course turf for the biological control of dollar spot. Plant Disease 75:510–514.

Nelson, E. B. and C. M. Craft. 1992. Suppression of dollar spot on creeping bentgrass and annual bluegrass turf with compost-amended topdressings. Plant Disease 76:954–958.

Niblett, C. L. and A. Q. Paulsen. 1975. Purification and further characterization of Panicum mosaic virus. Phytopathology 65:1157–1160.

Niblett, C. L., A. Q. Paulsen and R. W. Toler. 1977. Panicum mosaic virus. *In*: Descriptions of Plant Viruses No. 177. Commonwealth Mycol. Inst./Assoc. Appl. Biol.: Kew, Surrey, England. 4 pp.

Niehaus, M. H. 1968. Relative amounts of stripe and flag smut on Merion Kentucky bluegrass. Plant Disease Reptr. 52:633–634.

Nishihara, N. 1972. A new disease of *Festuca elatior* caused by *Phleospora graminearum*. Bull. Nat. Grassland Res. Inst. (Japan) 1:1–5.

Nishimura, S. and M. Sabaki. 1963. Isolation of the phytotoxic metabolites of *Pellicularia filamentosa*. Annals Phytopathol. Soc. Japan 28:228–234.

Noble, R. J. 1923. Studies on *Urocystis tritici* Koern., the organism causing flag smut of wheat. Phytopathology 13:127–138.

Norton, D. C. 1959. Relationship of nematodes to small grains and native grasses in north and central Texas. Plant Disease Reptr. 43:227–235.

Novak, L. A. and L. M. Kohn. 1991. Electrophoretic and immunological comparisons of developmentally regulated proteins in members of the Sclerotiniaceae and other sclerotial fungi. Appl. Environ. Microbiol. 57: 525–534.

Nutter, G. C. and J. R. Christie. 1959. Nematode investigations on putting green turf. U.S.G.A. Jour. and Turf Mgt. 11(7):24–28.

Nutter, F. W., H. Cole, Jr. and R. D. Schein. 1982. Conidial sampling of *Drechslera poae* to determine the role of mowing in spore dispersal. Plant Disease 66:721–723.

Nutter, F. W., H. Cole, Jr. and R. D. Schein. 1983. Disease forecasting system for warm weather Pythium blight of turf grass. Plant Disease 67:1126–1128.

Oakley, R. A. 1924. Brown patch investigation. The Bulletin, Green Section, U.S. Golf Assoc. 4:87–92.

Odvody, G. N., L. D. Dunkley and L. K. Edmunds. 1974. Zonate leaf spot in the northern sorghum belt. Plant Disease Reptr. 58:267–268.

O'Neill, N. R. 1980. Southern blight of cool season grasses. Phytopathology 70:691. (Abstr.)

O'Neill, N. R. and J. J. Murray. 1985. Etiology of red thread and pink patch diseases in the United States. *In*: Proc. 5th Int. Turfgrass Conf. F. Lemaire, Ed. INRA Publications, Versailles, France. 870 p. (595–607).

Ormund, D. J., E. C. Hughes and R. A. Shoemaker. 1970. Newly recorded fungi from Colonial bentgrass in coastal British Columbia. Canadian Plant Dis. Surv. 50:111–112.

Orr, O. H., W. A. Humphery and M. J. Henry. 1977. *Sclerotium rolfsii* on turf in California. *In*: Proc. Turf. Landscape Institute, Anaheim, California. University of California, Riverside. p. 12–13.

Orton, C. R. 1944. Graninicolous species of Phyllachora in North America. Mycologia 36:18–53.

Orton, C. R. and E. Strazza. 1928. "Drum-head" brown patch. Misc. Paper, Boyce Thompson Institute for Plant Research, Yonkers, N.Y. 7 p.

Osborne, D. J. 1959. Control of leaf senescence by auxins. Nature 183:1459–1460.

Ostergaard, H. 1983. Predicting development of epidemics on cultivar mixtures. Phytopathology 73:166–172.

Parbery, D. G. 1967. Studies on graminicolus species of *Phyllachora* Nke. in Fckl. V. A taxonomic monograph. Australian Jour. Bot. 15:271–375.

Parbery, D. G. 1971. Studies on graminicolous species of *Phyllachora* Nke. in Fckl. VI. Additions and corrections to Part V. Australian Jour. Bot. 19:207–235.

Parmeter, J. R., Jr. and H. S. Whitney. 1965. Taxonomy and nomenclature of the imperfect state. *In*: Rhizoctonia solani: Biology and Pathology, J. R. Parmeter, Jr., Ed. Univ. Calif. Press: Berkeley. 255 p. (7–19).

Parris, G. K. 1957. Screening Mississippi soils for plant parasitic nematodes. Plant Disease Reptr. 41:705–706.

Partyka, R. E. 1976. Factors affecting Fusarium blight in Kentucky bluegrass. Weeds, Trees and Turf 15(7): 37–38.

Paul, A. R. 1972. *Pyrenophora erythrospila* sp. nov., the perfect stage of *Drechslera erythrospila*. Trans. Brit. Mycol. Soc. 51:707–710.

Pelhate, J. 1968. Recherche des besoins en eau chez quelques moisissures des grains. Mycopathol. et Mycol. Appl. 36:117–128.

Pennypacker, B. W., P. L. Sanders and H. Cole, Jr. 1982. Basidiomycetes associated with a patterned midsummer wilt of bluegrass. Plant Disease 66:419–420.

Perry, V. G., H. M. Darling and G. Thorne. 1959. Anatomy, taxonomy and control of certain spiral nematodes attacking blue grass in Wisconsin. Univ. Wisconsin Agr. Expt. Sta. Res. Bull. 207.

Perry, V. G. and G. C. Horn. 1969. The nematode parasites of warm season turf grasses. *In*: Proc. 1st International Turfgrass Research Conference. Sports Turf. Res. Inst.: Bingley, Yorkshire. 610 p. (330–336).

Perry, V. G. and K. M. Maur. 1969. The pseudo root-knot nematode of turf grasses. The Golf Supt. 37(10): 30–32.

Pirone, T. P. 1972. Sugarcane mosaic virus. *In*: Descriptions of Plant Viruses No. 88. Commonwealth Mycol. Inst./ Assoc. Appl. Biol.: Kew, Surrey, England. 4 pp.

Piper, C. V. and H. S. Coe. 1919. Rhizoctonia in lawns and pastures. Phytopathology 9:89–92.

Pitt, D. L. and A. Bainbridge. 1983. Dispersal of *Pseudocercosporella herpotrichoides* spores from infected wheat straw. Phytopathol. Zeit. 106:214–215.

Punithalingam, E. 1979. Graminicolous Ascochyta Species. Mycol. Paper 12. Commonwealth Mycological Institute. Kew, Surrey, England. 215 p.

Punja, Z. K. and R. G. Grogan. 1981a. Eruptive germination of sclerotia of *Sclerotium rolfsii*. Phytopathology 71:1092–1099.

Punja, Z. K. and R. G. Grogan. 1981b. Mycelial growth and infection without a food base by eruptively germinating sclerotia of *Sclerotium rolfsii*. Phytopathology 71:1099–2003.

Punja, Z. K. and R. G. Grogan. 1982a. Chemical control of *Sclerotium rolfsii* on golf greens in Northern California. Plant Disease 65:108–111.

Punja, Z. K. and R. G. Grogan. 1982b. Effects of inorganic salts, carbonate-bicarbonate anions, ammonia, and the modifying influence of pH on sclerotial germination of *Sclerotium rolfsii*. Phytopathology 72:635–639.

Purchio, A. F. and J. J. Muchovej. 1991. Pyricularia diseases of grasses: A historical overview. Rasen-Turf-Gazon 22:63–69.

Radewald, J. D., L. Pyeatt, F. Shibuya and W. Humphrey. 1970. *Meloidogyne naasi*, a parasite of turfgrass in southern California Plant Disease Reptr. 54:940–942.

Ramsbottom, J. 1953. Mushrooms and Toadstools. Collins: London. 306 p.

Rasmussen, S. L. and M. E. Stanghellini. 1988. Effect of salinity stress on the development of Pythium blight in *Agrostis palustris*. Phytopathology 78:1495–1497.

Ratanaworabhan, S. and G. C. Smart, Jr. 1969. The ring nematode, *Criconemoides ornatus*, on peach and centipedegrass. Jour. Nematology 2:204–208.

Rau, G. J. 1958. A new species of sting nematode. Proc. Helminth. Soc. Wash. 25:95–98.

Razin, S. 1969. Structure and function of mycoplasma. Ann. Rev. Microbiology 23:317–356.

Rea, C. 1922. British Basidiomycetae. Cambridge University Press: London. 799 p.

Redhead, S. A. and J. D. Smith. 1981. A North American

Smith, J. D. 1953b. Fungi and turf diseases. (3). Fusarium patch disease. Jour. Sports Turf. Res. Inst. 8:230–252.

Smith, J. D. 1954. A disease of *Poa annua*. Jour. Sports Turf. Res. Inst. 8:344–353.

Smith, J. D. 1955. Fungi and turf diseases. (5). Dollar spot disease. Jour. Sports Turf. Res. Inst. 9:35–59.

Smith, J. D. 1956. Fungi and turf diseases. (6). Ophiobolus patch. Jour. Sports Turf. Res. Inst. 9:180–202.

Smith, J. D. 1957a. Fungi and turf diseases (7). Fairy rings. Jour. Sports Turf. Res. Inst. 9:324–352.

Smith, J. D. 1957b. Seed dressing trails, 1956. Jour. Sports Turf. Res. Inst. 9:244–250.

Smith, J. D. 1958. The effect of lime application on the occurrence of Fusarium patch disease on a forced *Poa annua* turf. Jour. Sports Turf. Res. Inst. 9:467–470.

Smith, J. D. 1959a. Turf diseases in the north of Scotland. Jour. Sports Turf. Res. Inst. 10:42–46.

Smith, J. D. 1959b. Fungal Diseases of Turfgrasses. The Sports Turf Res. Inst.: Bingley, Yorkshire. 90 p.

Smith, J. D. 1965. Fungal Diseases of Turfgrasses. The Sports Turf Res. Inst.: Bingley, Yorkshire. 97 p.

Smith, J. D. 1969. Snow molds on lawns in Saskatoon. Canadian Plant Disease Survey 49:141.

Smith, J. D. 1975. Resistance of turfgrasses to low-temperature basidiomycetes snow mold and recovery from damage. Canadian Plant Disease Survey 55:147–154.

Smith, J. D. 1976. Snow mold control in turfgrasses with fungicides in Saskatchewan. 1971–74 Canadian Plant Disease Survey 56:1–8.

Smith, J. D. 1980. Snow molds of turfgrasses: Identification, biology and control. *In*: Advances in Turfgrass Pathology, B. G. Joyner and P. O. Larsen, Ed. Harcourt Brace Jovanovich: Duluth. 197 p. (75–80).

Smith, J. D. 1981. Snow molds of winter cereals: guide for diagnosis, culture and pathogenicity. Canadian Jour. Plant Pathology 3:15–25.

Smith, J. D. 1987. Winter-hardiness and overwintering diseases of amenity turfgrasses with special reference to the Canadian Prairies. Agriculture Canada Res. Branch Tech. Bull. 1987–12E. 192 p.

Smith, J. D. 1988. Black plug layer on Saskatchewan golf courses. Greenmaster 24(8):6–11, 21.

Smith, J. D. and D. A. Cooke. 1978. Dormie Kentucky bluegrass. Canadian Jour. Plant Science 58:291–292.

Smith, J. D., N. Jackson and A. R. Woolhouse. 1989. Fungal Diseases of Amenity Turf Grasses. E. & F. N. Spong: London. 401 p.

Smith, J. D. and K. Mortensen. 1981. Fungicides for snow mold control in turf grass. Saskatchewan tests, 1979/1980. Greenmaster 17:6–8.

Smolik, J. D. and R. B. Malek. 1973. Effect of *Tylenchorhynchus nudus* on growth of Kentucky bluegrass. Jour. Nematology 5:272–274.

Southards, C. J. 1967. The pseudo-root knot nematode of Bermuda grass in Tennessee. Plant Disease Reptr. 51:455.

Spilker, D. A. and P. O. Larsen. 1985. Characterization and host range of *Drechslera catenaria*, the pathogen of leaf blight and crown rot of creeping bentgrass. Plant Disease 69:331–333.

Sprague, R. 1946. Rootrots and leafspots of grains and grasses in the Northern Great Plains and western states. Plant Disease Reptr. Suppl. 163:101–268.

Sprague, R. 1950. Diseases of Cereals and Grasses. Ronald Press: New York. 538 p.

Sprague, R. 1962. Some leafspot fungi on western Gramineae—XVI. Mycologia 54:593–610.

Sprague, R. and C. J. Rainey. 1950. Studies in the life-history of Typhula spp. on winter wheat in Washington. Phytopathology 40:969. (Abstr.)

Stahl, E. 1900. Der Sinn Der Mycorhizenbildung. Jarb. Wiss. Bot. 34(4):539–668.

Stalpers, J. A. and W. M. Loerakker. 1982. *Laetisaria* and *Limonomyces* species (Corticiaceae) causing pink diseases in turf grasses. Canadian Jour. Bot. 60:529–537.

Stedman, O. J. 1980. Observations on the production and dispersal of spores, and infection by *Rhynchosporium secalis*. Annals Applied Biol. 95:163–175.

Steinbuch, J. G. 1799. Das Grasalchen, *Vibrio agrostis*. Naturforscher, Halle 28:233–259.

Stem, M. 1992. White leaf: A new disease infects bermudagrass in Southeast Asia. Golf Course Management (March). p. 86–89.

Stienstra, W. C. 1980. Snow molds on Minnesota golf greens. *In*: Proc. 3rd Int. Turfgrass Conf. J. M. Beard, Ed. Madison, Wis., American Soc. Agron., p. 271–274.

Stirrup, H. H. 1932. *Sclerotium rhizoides* Auersw. in England. Trans. Brit. Mycol. Soc. 14:308.

Stout, A. B. 1911. A sclerotium disease of blue joint and other grasses. Univ. Wisc. Res. Bull. 18:207–261.

Stringer, A. and M. A. Wright. 1973. The effect of benomyl and some related compounds on *Lumbricus terrestris* and other earthworms. Pesticide Science 4:165–170.

Subirats, F. J. and R. L. Self. 1972. Fusarium blight of centipede grass. Plant Disease Reptr. 56:42–44.

Summer, D. L. and D. K. Bell. 1982. Root diseases induced in corn by *Rhizoctonia solani* and *Rhizoctonia zeae*. Phytopathology 72:86–91.

Sutker, E. M. and L. T. Lucas. 1987. Biocontrol of *Rhizoctonia solani* in tall fescue turfgrass. Phytopathology 77:1721.

Tarr, S. A. J. 1962. Diseases of Sorghum, Sudan Grass and Broom Corn. Commonwealth Mycological Institute. Kew, Surrey, England. 380 p.

Thirumalachar, M. J. and J. G. Dickson. 1949. Chlamydospore germination, nuclear cycle and artificial culture of *Urocystis agropyri* on red top. Phytopathology 39:333–339.

Thirumalachar, M. J. and J. G. Dickson. 1953. Spore germination, cultural characters and cytology of varieties of *Ustilago striiformis* and the reaction of hosts. Phytopathology 43:527–535.

Thomas, F. 1905. Die Wachtumgesch windikeit Eines Pilzkreeses von *Hydnum suavolens* Scop. Ber. Deutch. Bot. Gesell. 23(9):476–478.

Thompson, D. C., B. B. Clarke, J. R. Hackman and J. A.

Murphy. 1993. Influence of nitrogen source and soil pH on summer patch development in Kentucky bluegrass. International Turfgrass Society Res. Jour. 7:317–323.

Thompson, D. C., M. C. Fowler and R. W. Smiley. 1982. Recognizing Nigrospora blight. Plant Disease 66:265.

Tisserat, N. A. and J. C. Pair. 1989. *Ophiosphaerella herpotricha*, a cause of spring dead spot of bermudagrass in Kansas. Plant Disease 73:933–937.

Todd, T. C. and N. Tisserat. 1990. Occurrence, spatial distribution, and pathogenicity of some phytoparasitic nematodes on creeping bentgrass putting greens in Kansas. Plant Disease 74:660–663.

Todd, T. C. and N. Tisserat. 1993. Understanding nematodes and reducing their impact. Golf Course Management (May). p. 38–52.

Toler, R. W. 1973. 'Floritam'—a new disease resistant St. Augustinegrass. Texas Agr. Expt. Sta. L:1146. 5 pp.

Toler, R. W. 1983. Downy mildew of St. Augustinegrass. Grounds Maintenance 18(2):98, 104.

Toler, R. W., B. D. Bruton and M. P. Grisham. 1983. Evaluation of St. Augustinegrass accessions and cultivars for resistance to *Sclerophthora macrospora*. Plant Disease 67:1008–1010.

Toler, R. W., R. W. McCoy and G. C. Horne. 1972. Resistance in St. Augustinegrass, *Stenotaphrum secundatum*, to St. Augustine decline. Phytopathology 62:807. (Abstr.)

Tomiyama, K. 1955. Studies on the snow blight disease of winter cereals. Hokkaido National Agric. Expt. Sta. Rept. 47:224–234.

Townshend, J. L., J. L. Eggens and N. K. McCollum. 1973. Turf grass hosts of three species of nematodes associated with forage crops. Canadian Plant Disease Survey 53:137–141.

Traquair, J. A. 1980. Conspecificity of an unidentified snow mold basidiomycete and a *Coprinus* species in the section *Herbicolae*. Canadian Jour. Plant Path. 2:105–115.

Trevathan, L. E. 1982. Pathogenicity on ryegrass and cultural variability of Mississippi isolates of *Pyricularia grisea*. Plant Disease 66:592–594.

Troll, J. and R. A. Rohde. 1966. The effects of nematicides on turfgrass growth. Plant Disease Reptr. 50:489–492.

Troll, J. and A. C. Tarjan. 1954. Widespread occurrence of root parasitic nematodes in golf course greens in Rhode Island. Plant Disease Reptr. 38:342–344.

Tucker, M. C. and J. L. Dale. 1967. Rust on zoysia in Arkansas. Plant Disease Reptr. 51:893.

Tuite, J. 1969. Plant Pathological Methods: Fungi and Bacteria. Burgess Publishing Company, Minneapolis. 239 p.

Turgeon, A. J. 1976. Effects of cultural practices on Fusarium blight incidence in Kentucky bluegrass. Weeds, Trees and Turf. Vol. 15, No. 7. p. 39–41.

Tyson, J. 1936. Snowmold injury to bent grasses. Quart. Bull. Michigan Agr. Expt. Sta. 19:87–92.

Ulstrup, A. J. 1952. Observations on crazy top of corn. Phytopathology 42:675–680.

Ulstrup, A. J. 1955. Crazy top on some wild grasses and the occurrence of the sporangial stage of the pathogen. Plant Disease Reptr. 39:839–841.

Vaartnou, H. and C. R. Elliott. 1969. Snowmolds on lawns and lawngrasses in northwest Canada. Plant Disease Reptr. 53:891–894.

Van de Bogart, F. 1976. The genus *Coprinus* in western North America. Part I: Section Coprinus. Mycotaxon 4:233–275.

Van Den Mooter, M., J. Swings, M. De Cleene, F. Leyns and J. De Ley. 1981. Isolation and identification of *Xanthomonas campestris* pv. *graminis* from forage grasses in Belgium. Parisitica 37:23–28.

Vanterpool, T. C. and R. Sprague. 1942. *Pythium arrhenomanes* on cereals and grasses in the northern great plains. Phytopathology 32:327–328.

Vargas, J. M. and J. B. Beard. 1970. Chloroneb, a new fungicide for the control of Typhula blight. Plant Disease Reptr. 54:1075–1077.

Vargas, J. M., Jr., R. Detweiler, C. W. Laughlin and S. Worrall. 1973. 1973 turfgrass fungicide research report. Plant Disease Report No. 25. Michigan State Univ., East Lansing, p. 21–30.

Vittum, P. J., R. L. Wick and S. R. Swier. 1987. Nematodes on New England putting greens. Golf Course Management 55(8):60–62.

Voorhees, R.K. 1934. Sclerotial rot of corn caused by *Rhizoctonia zeae* n. sp. Phytopathology 24:1290–1303.

Wadsworth, D. F. and H. C. Young, Jr. 1960. Spring dead spot of Bermudagrass. Plant Disease Reptr. 44:516–518.

Wagner, R. E. and P. M. Halisky. 1981. Influence of thatch accumulation on disease incidence and fungicidal effectiveness in Kentucky bluegrass turf. Phytopathology 71:565. (Abstr.)

Wainwright, M. and G. J. F. Pugh. 1974. The effects of fungicides on certain chemical and microbial properties. Soil Biol. Biochem. 6:263–265.

Walker, J. 1980. *Gaeumannomyces*, *Linocarpon*, *Ophiobolus* and several other genera of scolecospored ascomycetes and *Phialophora* conidial states, with a note on hyphopodia. Mycotaxon 11:1–129.

Walker, J. and A. M. Smith. 1972. *Leptosphaeria narmari* and *L. korrae* spp. nov., two long-spored pathogens of grasses in Australia. Trans. Brit. Mycol. Soc. 58:459–466.

Wallace, H. R. 1955. The influence of soil moisture on the emergence of larvae from cysts of the beet eelworm, *Heterodera schachtii* Schm. Ann. Appl. Biol. 43:477–484.

Wallace, H. R. 1956. Soil aeration and the emergence of larvae from cysts of the beet eelworm, *Heterodera schachtii* Schm. Ann. Appl. Biol. 44:57–66.

Wallace, G. B. and M. M. Wallace. 1949. Plant diseases of economic importance in Tanganyika Territory. Mycol. Paper Commonwealth Mycological Institute, 26.

Wallis, A. R. 1873. A new disease among ryegrass. Report of the Society for Agriculture, Victoria Appendix (P) p. 242–244.

Warren, C. G., H. Cole and J. M. Duich. 1974. Influence of benzimidazole fungicides on growth and foliar element accumulation of *Agrostis palustris* Huds. and *Poa pratensis* L. Soil Science and Plant Analysis 5: 413–425.

Warren, C. G., P. L. Sanders and H. Cole, Jr. 1974. *Sclerotinia homoeocarpa* tolerance to benzimidazole-configuration fungicides. Phytopathology 64:1139–1142.

Warren, C. G., P. L. Sanders and H. Cole, Jr. 1976. Increased severity of Pythium blight associated with use of benzimidazole fungicides on creeping bentgrass. Plant Disease Reptr. 60:932–935.

Warren, C. G., P. L. Sanders and H. Cole, Jr. 1977. Relative fitness of benzimidazole and cadmium tolerant populations of *Sclerotinia homoeocarpa* in the absence and presence of fungicides. Phytopathology 67:704–708.

Weerapat, P., D. T. Sechler and J. M. Poehlman. 1972. Host study and symptom expression of barley yellow dwarf virus in tall fescue (*Festuca arundinacea*). Plant Disease Reptr. 56:167–168.

Wehmeyer, L. E. 1955. The development of the ascocarp in *Pseudoplea gaeumannii*. Mycologia 47:163–176.

Weihing, J. L., S. G. Jenson and R. I. Hamilton. 1957. *Helminthosporium sativum*, a destructive pathogen of bluegrass. Phytopathology 47:744–746.

Wells, H. D. 1959. Annual ryegrass, *Lolium multiflorum*, host for *Sclerotium rolfsii*. Plant Disease Reptr. 43:834.

Welty, R. E. and M. E. Mellbye. 1989. *Puccinia graminis* subsp. *graminicola* identified on tall fescue in Oregon. Plant Disease 73:775.

Wernham, C. C. and St. J. P. Chilton. 1943. Typhula snow-mold of pasture grasses. Phytopathology 33:1157–1165.

Wernham, C. C. and R. S. Kirby. 1941. A new turf disease. Phytopathology 31:24. (Abstr.)

West, E. 1961. *Sclerotium rolfsii*, history, taxonomy, host range and distribution. Phytopathology 51:108–109.

Western, J. H., and J. J. Cavitt. 1959. The choke disease of cocksfoot (*Dactylis glomerata*) caused by *Epichloe typhina* (Fr.) Tul. Trans. British Mycol. Soc. 42:298–307.

Wick, R. L. 1982. Occurrence of Melanotus white patch on red and Chewings fescue. Plant Disease 72:268.

Wilkins, P. 1973. Infection of *Lolium multiflorum* with *Rhynchosporium* species. Plant Pathology 22:107–111.

Wilkins, P. W. and P. L. Catherall. 1977. Variation in reaction to barley yellow dwarf virus in ryegrass and its inheritance. Annals Appl. Biol. 85:257–263.

Wilkins, P. W. and J. K. Exley. 1977. Bacterial wilt of ryegrass in Britain. Plant Pathology 26:99.

Wilkinson, H. T. 1987. Yellow ring on *Poa pratensis* caused by *Trechispora alnicola*. Plant Disease 71:1141–1143.

Wilkinson, H. T. and D. Pedersen. 1993. *Gaeumannomyces graminis* var. *graminis* infecting St. Augustinegrass selections in southern California. Plant Disease 77:536.

Wilkinson, J. F. and R. H. Miller. 1978. Investigation and treatment of localized dry spots on sand golf greens. Agronomy Journal 70:299–304.

Williams, D. W., A. J. Powell and P. C. Vincelli. 1993. Response of dollar spot to dew removal from creeping bentgrass. Agronomy Abstracts: 1993 Annual Meetings. American Soc. Agron., Madison, Wisc. p. 165.

Winchester, J. A. and E. O. Burt. 1964. The effect and control of sting nematodes on Ormond Bermuda grass. Plant Disease Reptr. 48:625–628.

Winslow, R. D. 1954. Provisional list of host plants of some root eelworms (*Heteroda* spp.). Ann. Appl. Biol. 41: 591–605.

Wolff, E. T. 1947. An experimental study of *Colletotrichum graminicolum* on fine turf. Ph.D. Dissertation. The Pennsylvania State University, University Park. 79 p.

Wollaston, W. H. 1807. "On fairy rings." Phil. Trans. Roy. Soc. London, Part 2, 133–138.

Wong, P. T. W. and T. R. Siviour. 1979. Control of Ophiobiolus patch in *Agrostis* turf using avirulent fungi and take-all suppressive soils in pot experiments. Ann. Appl. Biol. 92:191–197.

Worf, G. L. 1988. Evaluating snow mold control. Golf Course Management 56(8):70–80.

Worf, G. L., J. S. Stewart and R. C. Avenius. 1986. Necrotic ring spot of turfgrass in Wisconsin. Phytopathology 70:453–458.

Wright, M. A. and A. Stringer. 1973. The toxicity of thiabendazole, benomyl, methyl benzimidazol-2-yl carbamate and thiophanate-methyl to the earth worm, *Lumbricus terrestris*. Pesticide Science 4:431–432.

Zeiders, K. E. 1976. A new disease of reed canarygrass caused by *Helminthosporium catenarium*. Plant Disease Reptr. 60:556–560.

Zelcer, A., M. Bar-Joseph, Z. Fleischer, M. Klein, S. Cohen and G. Lobenstein. 1972. *In*: Mycoplasmalike organisms associated with plant disease in Israel. Summ. 3rd Israel Cong. Plant Pathol. 21–22 February, Rehovot. 94 p. (p. 13).

Zummo, N. and A. G. Plakidas. 1958. Brown patch of St. Augustinegrass. Plant Disease Reptr. 42:1141–1147.

Index

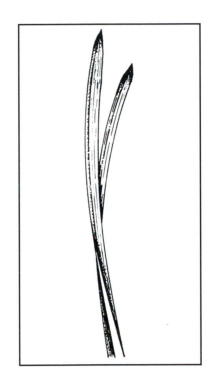

Index

Abacarus hystrix, 209
Acremonium typhinum (see *Epichloe typhina*)
Acti-dione™
    first use on turf, 7–8
Additive fungicide mixtures (*see* fungicide mixtures)
Algae, role in anaerobiosis, 169–170
Aliette™
    first use on turf, 10
    profile, 291
Allogenesis, 13
Ammonium nitrate
    effects on disease, 250
Ammonium sulfate
    effects on disease, 250
Anaerobiosis, 165–170
    diagnostic features, 165
    disease profile, 165–169
    control, 169–170
Anerobic decomposition
    products of, 168
Anguina agrostis, 219
Anguina graminis, 222
Anilazine
    first use on turf, 8
    profile, 285
Antagonistic fungicide mixtures (*see* fungicide mixtures)
Anthracnose, 156–158
    symptoms, 156
    the pathogen, 156
    disease profile, 157–158
    control, 158
Antibodies 244
Aphids
    vectors of yellow dwarf virus, 208
Appressorium
    function, 23
    illustrated, 23
Arlington Turf Gardens, 6
Aromatic hydrocarbons, 261
Ascochyta desmazieresii
    description, 125
    turfgrass hosts, 125
Ascochyta hordei
    description, 125–126
    hosts
        turfgrasses, 126
        all gramineous species, 126

Ascochyta leaf spots, 125–126
    symptoms, 125–126
    the pathogens, 125–126
    disease profile, 125
    control, 126
Asocochyta sorghi
    description, 126
    isolation and culture, 126
    hosts
        turfgrasses, 126
        all gramineous hosts, 126
Autogenesis, 13

Bacteria
    nature of, 211
    diagram of cell, 212
Bacterial wilt, 211–213
    symptoms, 211–212
    the pathogen, 212
    disease profile, 212–213
    control, 213
Banol™
    first use on turf, 10
    profile, 294
Barley yellow dwarf virus
    nature of, 207
    hosts
        turfgrasses, 207
        all gramineous species, 207–208
Bayleton™
    first use on turf, 10
    profile, 297
Belonolaimus gracilis, 230
    turfgrass host, 230
Belonolaimus longicaudatus, 230
    hosts
        turfgrass, 230
        all gramineous species, 230
Benomyl
    first use on turf, 10
    profile, 285
Bentgrass summer decline (*see* Pythium root dysfunction, Pythium decline)
Benzimidazoles
    first use on turf, 10
    profile, 261, 285, 296
Biological control
    concepts, 253
    methods
        use of known microbes, 253–255

Biological control (*cont.*)
    use of natural organic products, 255–257
Biotrophy defined, 22
Bipolaris cynodontis
    description, 108
    hosts
        turfgrasses, 108
        all gramineous species, 108
Bipolaris sorokiniana
    description, 97
    isolation and culture, 97
    hosts
        turfgrasses, 97–98
        all gramineous species, 98
Biopolaris spicifera
    description, 109
    hosts
        turfgrasses, 109
        all gramineous species, 109
Bipolaris stenospila, 109
Bipolaris tetramera
    description, 110
    isolation and culture, 110
    hosts
        turfgrasses, 110
        all gramineous species, 110
Black leaf spot, 113–115
    symptoms, 113
    the pathogens, 113–114
    disease profile, 115
    control, 115
Blind seed, 197–199
    symptoms, 197
    the pathogen, 198
    disease profile, 198–199
    control, 199
Blister smut, 153–154
    symtpoms, 153
    the pathogen, 153
    control, 154
Board of Greenkeeping Research, 6
Bordeaux Mixture
    early use on turf, 4
British Sports Turf Research Institute, 6
Bromegrass mosaic, 209
    symptoms, 209
    the virus, 209
    hosts
        turfgrasses, 209

Bromegrass mosaic (*cont.*)
  all gramineous species, 209
  disease profile, 109
Brown blight 104–105
  symptoms, 104
  the pathogen, 104
  disease profile, 105
  control, 105
Brown patch, "drumhead," 4 (*see also*
      Rhizoctonia blight)
Brown stripe, 128–129
  symptoms, 128
  the pathogen, 128
  disease profile, 129
  control, 129

Cadminate
  first use on turf, 7
Cadmium succinate
  first use on turf, 7
Calcium nutrition
  effects on disease, 249
Calomel
  first use on turf, 6
Carbamates, 261
Carboximides, 261
Centipedegrass decline (*see* St.
      Augustinegrass/centipedegrass
      decline)
Ceratobasidium cereale (see *Rhizoctonia
      cerealis*)
Cercosperella herpotrichoides (see
      Pseudocercosperella herpotrichoides)
Cercospora festucae
  description, 121–122
  hosts
    turfgrasses, 122
    all gramineous species, 122
Cercospora fusimaculans
  description, 121
  isolation and culture, 121
  hosts
    turfgrasses, 121
    all gramineous species, 121
Cercospora leaf spots, 120–122
  symptoms, 120–121
  the pathogens, 120
  disease profile, 121
  control, 121
Cercosporidium graminis
  description, 128
  isolation and culture, 128
  hosts
    turfgrasses, 128
    all gramineous species, 128–129
Char spot, 115
  symptoms, 115
  the pathogen, 115
  disease profile, 115
  control, 115
Cheilaria agrostis
  description, 115
  hosts
    turfgrasses, 115
    all gramineous species, 115

Chipco 26019™
  first use on turf, 10
  profile, 292
Chloroneb
  first use on turf, 8
  profile, 286
Chlorophenol mercury
  first use on turf, 6
Chlorothalonil
  first use on turf, 10
  profile, 287
Choke, 194–195
  symptoms, 194
  the pathogen, 194
  disease profile, 195
  control, 195
Claviceps purpurea
  description, 196
  hosts
    turfgrasses, 196
    all gramineous species, 196–197
Cochliobolus geniculatus (see *Curvularia
      geniculata*)
Cochliobolus intermedius (see *Curvularia
      intermedia*)
Cochliobolus lunatus (see *Curvularia
      lunata*)
Cochliobolus spicifer (see *Bipolaris
      spicifera*)
Colletotrichum graminicola
  description, 156–157
  isolation and culture, 157
  turfgrass hosts, 152
Colonization
  concept of, 15–16
Copper spot, 69–71
  symptoms, 69–70
  the pathogen, 70
  disease profile, 71
  control, 71
Copper stearate
  first use on turf, 5
  Copper sulfate
  first use on turf, 5
Coprinus kubickae, 185
Coprinus psychromorbidus
  description, 82
  isolation and culture, 82–83
  hosts
    turfgrasses, 83
    all gramineous species, 83
Corrosive sublimate
  first use on turf, 6
Corticium fuciforme (see *Laetesaria
      fuciformis*)
Corticium red thread, 36–39
  symptoms, 36–37
  the pathogen, 37
  disease profile, 38
  control, 39
Cottony snow mold, 81–84
  symptoms, 81–82
  the pathogen, 82
  disease profile, 83
  control, 83–84

Couch, H. B., 8
Covered smut, 191–192
  symptoms, 191
  the pathogens, 191
  disease profile, 191
  control, 191–192
Criconemella curvata, 232
  turfgrass hosts, 232
Criconemella cylindricum, 232
  hosts
    turfgrasses, 232
    all gramineous species, 232
Criconemella cylindricus (see *Criconemella
      ornata*)
Criconemella lobatum (see *Criconemella
      rustica*)
Criconemella ornata, 232
  hosts
    turfgrasses, 232
    all gramineous species, 232
Criconemella rustica, 232
  turfgrass hosts, 232
Criconemella typica, 232
  turfgrass hosts, 232
Curvularia blight, 159–162
  symptoms, 159
  the pathogens, 159–161
  disease profile, 161
  control, 161–162
Curvularia geniculata
  description, 159
  isolation and culture, 161
  turfgrass hosts, 159
Curvularia inaequalis
  description, 159
  isolation and culture, 161
  turfgrass hosts, 159
Curvularia intermedia
  description, 159
  isolation and culture, 161
  turfgrass hosts, 160
Curvularia lunata
  description, 160
  isolation and culture, 161
  turfgrass hosts, 160
Curvularia protuberata
  description, 160–161
  isolation and culture, 161
  turfgrass hosts, 161
Curvularia trifolii
  description, 161
  isolation and culture, 161
  turfgrass hosts, 161
Cycloheximide
  first use on turf, 7–8

Daconil 2787™
  first use on turf, 10
  profile, 287
Dahl, Arnold S, 6
Damping off
  defined, 187
  seed transmitted pathogens, 189
DBCP
  first use on turf, 8

Demethylation inhibitors (DMIs), 261
Deoxyribonucleic acid, 203, 211, 243
Desulfuromonas spp.
    role in anaerobiosis, 167
Dexon™
    first use on turf, 8
Diagnostic procedures
    collecting samples for laboratory
        workups, 246
    complicating factors in diagnosis, 243
    field procedures
        use of immunoassay kits, 243
        determining the cause of root
            declines, 246
    laboratory procedures
        use of slide mounts, 243
        plating techniques, 243
        nucleic acid probe, 243
        "ooze-test," 212
        use of diaphanoscope, 197
    maintaining records of diagnoses and
        control procedures, 247
Diazoben
    first use on turf, 8
Dicarboximides, 262
Disease control
    use of integrated disease control
        strategies, 249–257
    evolution of practices, 4–11
    fundamentals of, 243–257
    selection and use of fungucides, 257
    use of resistant turfgrasses, 252
Disease defined, 14
Disease dynamics, 14–16
Disease nomenclature, 16–17
Diseases of the inflorescence, 191–199
Dithane M-22™
    first use on turf, 8
Ditylenchus graminophila, 222
DNA (*see* Deoxyribonucleic acid)
Dolichodorus spp., 235
    turfgrass hosts, 235
Downy mildew (yellow tuft), 136–139
    symptoms, 137
    the pathogens, 137
    disease profile, 138–140
    control, 140
Drechslera catenaria
    description, 105–106
    isolation and culture, 106
    hosts
        turfgrasses, 106
        all gramineous species, 106
Drechslera dictyoides
    description, 102–103
    isolation and culture, 103
    hosts
        turfgrasses, 103
        all gramineous species, 103
Drechslera erythrospila
    description, 101
    isolation and culture, 101
    hosts
        turfgrasses, 101
        all gramineous species, 101

Drechslera gigantea
    description, 107
    hosts
        turfgrasses, 107
        all gramineous species, 107
Drechslera leaf blight, 105–106
    symptoms, 105
    the pathogen, 105
    disease profile, 106
    control, 106
Drechslera poae
    description, 93
    isolation and culture, 93–94
    hosts
        turfgrasses, 94
        all gramineous species, 95
Drechslera rostrata (see *Setosphaeria*
    rostrata)
Drechslera siccans
    description, 104
    isolation and culture, 104
    hosts
        turfgrasses, 104
        all gramineous species, 104
Drechslera triseptata, 110
Dry spots, localized, 186
Dyrene™
    first use on turf, 8
    profile, 285

Entolomya crastophylum (see *Entolomya*
    dactylidis)
Entolomya dactylidis
    description, 153–154
    hosts
        turfgrasses, 154
        all gramineous species, 154
Entolomya oryzae (see *Entolomya*
    dactylidis)
Enzymes, pectolytic
    role in disease development, 57, 99
Epichloe typhina
    description, 194–195
    hosts
        turfgrasses, 195
        all gramineous species, 195
Ergot, 195–197
    symptoms, 195–196
    the pathogen, 196
    disease profile, 197
    control, 197
Erysiphae graminis
    description, 139–140
    hosts
        turfgrasses, 140
        all gramineous species, 140
Ethazol
    first use on turf, 8
    profile, 288
Ethoprop
    use as a postplant nematicide, 239–
        240
    profile, 289
Evapotranspiration
    role in anaerobiosis, 167

Fairy rings, edaphic 3, 181–185
    symptoms, 181–182
    the pathogens, 183
    hosts, 182
    disease profile, 182–184
    control, 184–185
Fairy rings, "false," "superficial" (*see* Fairy
    rings, lectophilic)
Fairy rings, lectophilic, 185–186
    symptoms, 185
    the pathogens, 185
    hosts, 185
    disease profile, 186
    control, 186
Fairy rings, types of, 181
Fenamiphos
    use as postplant nematicide, 239
    profile, 289
Fenarimol
    first use on turf, 10
    profile, 290
Flag smut, 152–153
    symptoms, 152
    the pathogen, 152
    disease profile, 153
    control, 153
Flea beetles
    vectors of bromegrass mosaic, 209
Fore™
    first use on turf, 8
    profile, 292
Formalin
    first use on turf, 5–6
Fosetyl Al
    first use on turf, 10
    profile, 291
Frost scorch, 84–85
    symptoms, 84
    the pathogen, 84
    disease profile, 85
    control, 85
Fungi
    nature of, 21–25
Fungicidal resistance, 264–267
    forms of
        cross, 266
        monogenic, 265
        polygenic, 265
    potential among specific fungicides, 266
    tactics for reducing occurrence, 266–267
Fungicide
    dilution rates, 267–268
    formulations
        aqueous suspension, 262
        dry flowable, 262
        dispersable granules, 263
        emulsifiable concentrate, 262
        flowable, 263
        granular, 263
        water soluble, 263
        wettable powder, 263
    leaf washing, impact on effectiveness,
        274–275
    spray combinations
        additive combinations, 263–264

Fungicide (*cont.*)
    antagonistic combinations, 263–264
    phytotoxic combinations, 272–273
    synergistic combinations, 263–264
    tank mixing guidelines, 272–274
    uniform applications of, 275–276
    use of granular formulations, 275–278
Fungicide, modes of action, 259–261
    biochemical, 260–261
    topical
        contact, 259–260
        penetrant
            acropetal, 260
            localized, 260
            systemic, 260
Fungicide, nontarget effects, 278–281
    on algal growth, 279–280
    on disease resurgence, 279
    on earthworm populations, 280
    hormonal effects, 279
    interaction with herbicides
        and growth regulators, 278–279
    on mychorrizal development, 280
    on severity of nontarget diseases, 278
    on soil microbes, 280–281
    on thatch accumulation, 281
Fungicide groups, 261–262
    aromatic hydrocarbons, 261
    benzimidazoles, 261
    carbamates, 261
    carboximides, 261
    demethylation inhibitors (DMIs), 261
    dicarboximides, 262
    nitriles, 262
    phenylamides, 262
    phosphonates, 262
    substituted benzenes, 261
    triazoles, 262
Fungicide nomenclature, 259
Fungicides
    history of development, 5–11
    total sales for turf, 11
    profiles of (*see* Appendix Table I)
Fungo 50™
    first use on turf, 10
    profile, 296
Fusarium, nonpathogenic species, 43
Fusarium blight, 42–47
    symptoms, 42–43
    the pathogens, 43, 44
    disease profile, 45–46
    control, 46–47
Fusarium culmorum, 43, 188
    description, 43
    isolation and culture, 43
    hosts
        turfgrasses, 44
        all gramineous species, 44
Fusarium damping off, 188–189
    symptoms, 188
    the pathogens, 188
    disease profile, 188
    control, 189
Fusarium nivale (see *Michrodochium
    nivale*)

Fusarium patch, 74–77
    symptoms, 74
    the pathogen, 74
    disease profile, 75–76
    control, 76–77
Fusarium poae, 44, 193
    description, 44
    hosts
        turfgrasses, 44
        all gramineous species, 44–45
Fusarium roseum f. sp. *cerealis* (see
    Fusarium poae)
Fusarium roseum f. sp. *culmorum* (see
    Fusarium culmorum)

Gaeumannomyces decline of
    bermudagrass, 175–176
    symptoms, 175
    the pathogen, 175
    all gramineous species, 175
    disease profile, 175–176
    control, 176
Gaeumannomyces graminis var. *avenae*,
    28
    description, 28
    isolation and culture, 29
    hosts
        turfgrasses, 29
        all gramineous species, 29–30
Gaeumannomyces graminis var. *graminis*,
    88, 175, 176
    description, 88
    isolation and culture, 88
    hosts
        turfgrasses, 88–89
        all gramineous species, 89
Gloeocercospora sorghi
    description, 70
    isolation and culture, 70–71
    hosts
        turfgrasses, 71
        all gramineous species, 71
Gloeotinia granigena
    description, 198
    isolation and culture, 198
    hosts
        turfgrasses, 198
        all gramineous species, 198
Glomerella graminicola (see
    Colletotrichum graminicola)
Glycocalyx, 166
Gray leaf spot, 111–113
    symptoms, 111
    the pathogen, 111
    disease profile, 112
    control, 112–113
Gray snow mold (*see* Typhula blight)

Haustorium
    function, 24
    displayed, 23
Helicotylenchus cornurus, 228
    turfgrass hosts, 229
Helicotylenchus digonicus, 229
    turfgrass hosts, 229

Helicotylenchus erythrinae, 229
    hosts
        turfgrasses, 229
        all gramineous species, 229
Helicotylenchus melancholicus, 229
    turfgrass host, 229
Helicotylenchus microlobus, 229
    turfgrass host, 229
Helicotylenchus nannus, 229
    hosts
        turfgrasses, 229
        all gramineous species, 229
Helicotylenchus platyurus, 229
    turfgrass host, 229
Helicotylenchus pseudorobustus, 229
    turfgrass host, 229
Helicotylenchus pumilis, 229
    turfgrass host, 229
Helminthosporium blight, 102–104
    symptoms, 102
    the pathogen, 102–103
    disease profile, 103
    control, 103–104
Helminthosporium catenarium (see
    Dreschslera catenaria)
Helminthosporium crown and root rot, 110
    symptoms, 110
    the pathogen, 110
    disease profile, 110–111
    control, 111
Helminthosporium cynodontis (see
    Biopolaris cynodontis)
Helminthosporium dictyoides (see
    Drechslera dictyoides)
Helminthosporium erythrospilum (see
    Drechslera erythrospila)
Helminthosporium giganteum (see
    Dreschlera gigantea)
Helminthosporium-incited diseases, 93–
    111
Helminthosporium leaf spot, 96–100
    symptoms, 96–97
    the pathogen, 97
    disease profile, 98–99
    control, 99–100
Helminthosporium siccans (see *Drechslera
    siccans*)
Helminthosporium sorokinianum (see
    Bipolaris sorokiniana)
Helminthosporium spiciferum (see
    Bipolaris spicifera)
Helminthosporium tetramera (see
    Bipolaris tetramera)
Helminthosporium vagans (see *Drechslera
    poae*)
Hemicycliophora spp., 235
    turfgrass hosts, 235
Heterodera iri, 224
    turfgrass hosts, 224
Heterodera leuceilyma, 223
    turfgrass host, 223
Heterodera major, 223
    hosts
        turfgrasses, 223
        all gramineous species, 223–224

Heterodera punctata, 224
  turfgrass host, 224
Hoplolaimus concaudajuvencus, 234
  turfgrass hosts, 234
Hoplolaimus galetus, 234
  turfgrass host, 234
Hoplolaimus tylenchiformis, 234
  hosts
    turfgrasses, 234
    all gramineous species, 234
Hybridomas, 244
Hydrogen cyanide
  role in disease development, 83, 184
Hypha
  description, 21
  illustrated, 22, 23
Hypsoperine graminis (see *Meloidogyne graminis*)

Immunoassay (ELISA)
  use in diagnosis
    description of procedure, 243–245
    use of kits, 244, 246
Incitants of disease
  abiotic, 13
  biotic, 13
Infection cushion
  described, 23
  illustrated, 23
Infection defined, 15, 22
Infection peg
  described, 23
  illustrated, 23
Infiltrometer, field, 169
Iprodione
  first use on turf, 10
  profile, 292

Jackson, Noel, 8
Joyner, B. G., 8

Koban™
  first use on turf, 8
  profile, 288

Laetesaria fuciformis
  description, 37
  isolation and culture, 38–39
  hosts
    turfgrasses, 38
    all gramineous species, 38
Lanzia sp. (see *Sclerotinia homoeocarpa*)
Larsen, P. O., 8
Leaf blotch, 108–109
  symptoms, 108
  the pathogen, 108
  disease profile, 108
  control, 108–109
Leafhoppers
  vectors of turfgrass pathogens, 213–214
Leaf smuts, 149–154
Leaf wetness
  effects on disease, 252
Leptosphaeria avenaria (see *Stagonospora avenae*)

Leptosphaeria korrae
  description, 27, 86
  isolation and culture, 27, 86–87
  hosts
    turfgrasses, 27, 87
    all gramineous species, 27, 87
Leptosphaeria narmari
  description, 87–88
  isolation and culture, 88
  hosts
    turfgrasses, 88
    all gramineous species, 88
Leptosphaerulina australis
  description, 162
  isolation and culture, 161
  turfgrass hosts, 162
Leptosphaerulina leaf blight, 162–163
  symptoms, 162
  the pathogens, 161–162
  disease profile, 161
  control, 163
Leptosphaerulina trifolii
  description, 163
  isolation and culture, 163
  turfgrass hosts, 163
Limonomyces pink patch, 39–42
  symptoms, 39–40
  the pathogen, 40
  disease profile, 41–42
  control, 42
Limonomyces roseipellis
  description, 40–41
  isolation and culture, 41
  hosts
    turfgrasses, 41
    all gramineous species, 41
Localized dry spots, 186
Longidorus breviannulatus, 234
  turfgrass host, 234
Longidorus elongatus, 235
  turfgrass host, 235
Longidorus sylphus, 235
  turfgrass host, 235
Loose smuts, 192
  symptoms, 192
  the pathogens, 192

Macrosteles fascifrons
  ryegrass yellows vector, 213
Macrosiphum avenae, 208
Macrosiphum dirhodum, 208
Magnaporthe grisea (see *Pyricularia grisea*)
Magnaporthe poae
  description, 49
  isolation and culture, 50
  rapid detection with nucleic acid probe, 243
  hosts
    turfgrasses, 50
    all gramineous species, 50
Mancozeb
  first use on turf, 8
  profile, 292
Marasmius oreades
  mechanism of pathogenesis, 184

Marasmius siccus, 185
Mastigosporium album
  description, 131
  isolation and culture, 131
  hosts
    turfgrasses, 131
    all gramineous hosts, 131
Mastigosporium leaf spot, 130–132
  symptoms, 130
  the pathogens, 130–131
  disease profile, 132
  control, 132
Mastigosporium rubricosum
  description, 130
  isolation and culture, 131
  hosts
    turfgrasses, 130
    all gramineous hosts, 130–131
Mastigosporium rubricosum var. *agrostidis*
  (see *Mastigosporium rubricosum*)
Mat (*see* Thatch)
Melanotus phillipsii
  description, 73
  isolation and culture, 73
  turfgrass hosts, 73
Melanotus white patch, 73–74
  symptoms, 73
  the pathogen, 73
  disease profile, 73–74
  control, 74
Meloidodera charis, 224
  turfgrass host, 224
Meloidogyne arenaria, 224
  turfgrass hosts, 224
Meloidogyne graminicola, 224
  hosts
    turfgrasses, 224
    all gramineous species, 224–225
Meloidogyne graminis, 225
  hosts
    turfgrasses, 225
    all gramineous species, 225
Meloidogyne hapla, 225
  turfgrass hosts, 225
Meloidogyne incognita, 225
  turfgrass hosts, 225
Meloidogyne marylandi, 225
  turfgrass hosts, 225
Meloidogyne microtyla, 225
  hosts
    turfgrasses, 225
    all gramineous species, 225
Meloidogyne naasi, 225
  hosts
    turfgrasses, 225
    all gramineous species, 225–226
Melting-out of Kentucky bluegrass, 93–96
  symptoms, 93
  the pathogen, 93
  disease profile, 95–96
  control, 96
Meptam-sodium
  use as preplant nematicide, 239
Mercuric chloride
  first use on turf, 6

Mercuric cyanide
  first use on turf, 6
Mercuric sulfate
  first use on turf, 6
Mercuric sulfide
  first use on turf, 6
Mercurous chloride
  first use on turf, 6
Mercurous nitrate
  first use on turf, 6
Metalaxyl
  first use on turf, 10
  profile, 293
Methyl bromide
  procedure for use, 184–185
Michrodochium nivale, 74, 188
  description, 74
  isolation and culture, 74–75
  hosts
    turfgrasses, 75
    all gramineous species, 75
Mites
  vectors of pathogenic fungi and viruses,
    194, 208–209
Mocap™ (*see* Ethoprop)
Mollerodiscus sp. (see *Sclerotinia*
    homoeocarpa)
Mollicutes, nature of, 211
Monographella nivalis (see
    Michrodochium nivale)
Monteith, John, 6
Mowing height, effects on disease, 251
Mucilago spongiosa
  description, 135
Mycelium
  description, 21
  illustrated, 22, 23
Mycoplasma, aster yellows
  cultural characteristics, 213
  hosts
    turfgrasses, 213
    all gramineous species, 213
Mycoplasma, nature of, 211
Myriosclerotinia borealis
  description, 80
  isolation and culture, 80
  hosts
    turfgrasses, 80
    all gramineous species, 80

Necrotic mottle, 207
  symptoms, 207
  the virus, 207
Necrotic ring spot, 25–28
  symptoms, 25–27
  the pathogen, 27
  disease profile, 27–28
  control, 28
Necrotrophy
  defined, 22
Nemacur™ (*see* fenamiphos)
Nemagon™
  first use on turf, 8
Nematode control, 235–240

Nematode control (*cont.*)
  cultural practices, 235
  use of resistant grasses, 235–237
  use of nematicides, 235–239
  use of preplanting soil fumigants, 239
  use of nonfumigant nematicides, 239
  maximizing nematicide effectiveness,
    240
Nematodes
  assay procedures, 237–239
  characteristics of life cycles, 217
  damage threshold levels, concept of,
    235–237
  damage threshold levels, specific, 238
  diseases caused by, 217–240
  methods of feeding, 217–218
  requirements for pathogenicity, 218
  symptoms of feeding, 218–219
Nematodes, floral and foliar feeding forms
  grass seed
    symptoms, 218
    the nematode, 219
    turfgrass hosts, 219
    disease profile, 219–221
    control, 221–222
  leaf gall
    symptoms, 222
    the nematodes, 222
    turfgrass hosts, 222
    disease profile, 222
Nematodes, root feeding forms
  Ectoparasites
  awl nematodes
    symptoms, 235
    the nematodes, 235
  cyst nematodes
    the nematodes, 223–224
    disease profile, 224
  cystoid nematodes
    the nematode, 224
  dagger nematodes, 233
    symptoms, 233
    the nematode, 234
  lance nematodes, 234
    symptoms, 234
    the nematodes, 234
  needle nematodes, 234
    symptoms, 234
    the nematodes, 234–235
    disease profile, 235
  pin nematodes, 232
    symptoms, 232
    the nematodes, 232
  ring nematodes, 231
    symptoms, 231
    the nematodes, 232
  sheath nematodes, 235
    the nematodes, 235
  spiral nematodes, 228
    symptoms, 228
    the nematodes, 228–229
    disease profile, 229–230
  sting nematodes, 230
    symptoms, 230

Nematodes, root feeding forms (*cont.*)
    the nematodes, 230
    disease profile, 230
  stubby root nematodes, 233
    symptoms, 233
    the nematodes, 233
  stunt nematodes, 230
    symptoms, 230
    the nematodes, 230–231
    disease profile, 231
  Endoparasites
  burrowing nematode, 227
    symptoms, 227
    the nematode, 228
    disease profile, 227
  rootknot nematodes, 224
    symptoms, 224
    the nematodes, 224–225
    disease profile, 226
  root lesion (meadow) nematodes, 226
    symptoms, 226
    the nematodes, 226–227
    disease profile, 227
Nitriles, 262
Nitrogen nutrition
  effects on disease, 249–250
Nozzle
  flat fan, 268
  whirl chamber, 269
  flood jet, 269
Nozzle pressure
  impact on fungicide effectiveness, 268–269
Nozzle types
  impact on fungicidal effectiveness, 268–269
Nutrition
  effects on disease, 249–250

Oat necrotic mottle virus
  nature of, 207
  hosts
    turfgrasses, 207
    all gramineous species, 207
Ophiobolus graminis var. *avenae* (see
    Gaeumannomyces graminis var.
    avenae)
Ophiobolus graminis var. *graminis* (see
    Gaeumannomyces graminis var.
    graminis)
Ophiobolus herpotrichus (see
    Ophiosphaerella herpotricha)
Ophiosphaerella herpotricha
  description, 89
  isolation and culture, 89–90
  hosts
    turfgrasses, 90
    all gramineous species, 90
Organic products, natural
  list of, 257

Panicum mosaic virus, 205
  nature of, 205
  hosts
    turfgrasses, 205
    all gramineous species, 205

Paratrichodorus christiei, 233
  hosts
    turfgrasses, 233
    all gramineous species, 233
Paratrichodorus primitivus, 233
  hosts
    turfgrasses, 233
    all gramineous species, 233
Paratrichodorus proximus, 233
  turfgrass host, 233
Paratylenchus hamatus, 232
  turfgrass hosts, 232
Paratylenchus nanus, 232
  turfgrass hosts, 232
Paratylenchus projectus, 232
  hosts
    turfgrasses, 232
    all gramineous species, 232–233
Parzate C™
  first use on turf, 9
Patch diseases, 25–91
  list of, 26
  spring and fall, 25–42
  summer, 42–74
  winter, 74–91
Pathogenesis defined, 15
Pediculopsis graminum, 194
Penicillin, 211
Peptidoglycan, 211
pH
  soil
    effects on disease development, 250
  spray solution
    effect on fungicide stability, 270–
      271
Phenylamides, 262
Phenylmercury acetate
  first use on turf, 8
Phialophora graminicola, 47, 48
Phleospora graminearum
  description, 129–130
  hosts
    turfgrasses, 130
    all gramineous hosts, 130
Phleospora leaf spot, 129–130
  symptoms, 129
  the pathogen, 129–130
  disease profile, 130
  control, 130
Phosphonates, 262
Phosphorous nutrition
  effects on disease, 249
Phyllachora bulbosa
  description, 113
  hosts
    turfgrasses, 113
    all gramineous speciess, 113
Phyllachora cynodontis
  description, 113–114
  hosts
    turfgrasses, 114
    all gramineous species, 114
Phyllachora fuscens
  description, 114

Phyllachora fuscens (*cont.*)
  hosts
    turfgrasses, 114
    all gramineous species, 114
Phyllachora graminis
  description, 114
  hosts
    turfgrasses, 114
    all gramineous species, 114
Phyllachora silvataca
  description, 114
  hosts
    turfgrasses, 114
    all gramineous species, 115
Physarum cinereum
  description, 135
Phytotoxic fungicide mixtures (*see*
    fungicide mixtures)
Pink snow mold (*see* Fusarium patch)
Piper, Charles V., 4–5
Pleospora gaumannii (see
    Leptosphaerulina australis)
PMAS™
  first use on turf, 8
Poa semilatent virus, 206
  nature of, 206
  hosts
    turfgrasses, 206
    all gramineous species, 206
Polymyxa graminis
  description, 178
  hosts
    turfgrasses, 178
    all gramineous species, 178
Polymyxa root rot, 177–178
  symptoms, 177
  the pathogen, 177
  disease profile, 178
Potassium nutrition
  effects on disease, 249
Powdery mildew, 139–141
  symptoms, 139
  the pathogen, 139
  disease profile, 140
  control, 141
Pratylenchus brachyurus, 226
  turfgrass hosts, 226
Pratylenchus hexincisus, 226
  hosts
    turfgrasses, 226
    all gramineous species, 226–227
Pratylenchus neglectus, 227
  turfgrass hosts, 227
Pratylenchus penetrans, 227
  hosts
    turfgrasses, 227
    all gramineous species, 227
Pratylenchus pratensis, 227
  hosts
    turfgrasses, 227
    all gramineous species, 227
Pratylenchus zeae, 227
  hosts
    turfgrasses, 227

Pratylenchus zeae (*cont.*)
  all gramineous species, 227
Prokaryotes
  diseases caused by, 211–214
Propamocarb
  first use on turf, 10
  profile, 294
Propiconazole
  first use on turf, 10
  profile, 294
Pseudocercosperella basal rot, 179–
    180
  symptoms, 179
  the pathogen, 179
  disease profile, 179
Pseudocercosperella herpotrichoides
  description, 179
  hosts
    turfgrasses, 179
    all gramineous species, 179
Pseudoplea gaumannii (see
    Leptosphaerulina australis)
Pseudoseptoria donacis
  description, 124
  hosts
    turfgrasses, 124
    all gramineous species, 124
Pseudoseptoria everhartii
  description, 125
  hosts
    turfgrasses, 125
    all gramineous species, 125
Pseudoseptoria leaf spot, 124–125
  symptoms, 124
  the pathogens, 124–125
  disease profile, 125
  control, 125
Puccinia coronata
  description, 141
  hosts
    turfgrasses, 141–142
    all gramineous species, 142
Puccinia crandallii
  description, 142
  hosts
    turfgrasses, 142
    all gramineous species, 142
Puccinia cynodontis
  description, 142
  hosts
    turfgrasses, 142
    all gramineous species, 142
Puccinia festucae
  description, 142–143
  hosts
    turfgrasses, 143
    all gramineous species, 143
Puccinia graminis f. sp. *agrostidis*
  description, 143
  hosts
    turfgrasses, 143
    all gramineous species, 143–144
Puccinia montanensis
  description, 144

Puccinia montanensis (*cont.*)
  hosts
    turfgrasses, 144
    all gramineous species, 144
Puccinia pattersoniana
  description, 144
  hosts
    turfgrasses, 144
    all gramineous species, 144
Puccinia piperi
  description, 144–145
  hosts
    turfgrasses, 145
    all gramineous species, 145
Puccinia poae-sudeticae
  description, 145
  hosts
    turfgrasses, 145
    all gramineous species, 145
Puccinia rubigo-vera
  description, 145
  hosts
    turfgrasses, 145
    all gramineous species, 145–146
Puccinia zoysiae
  description, 146
  hosts
    turfgrasses, 146
    all gramineous species, 146
Pyrenochaeta root rot, 178–179
  symptoms, 178
  the pathogen, 178
  disease profile, 178
Pyrenochaeta terrestris
  description, 178
  isolation and culture, 178
  hosts
    turfgrasses, 178
    all gramineous species, 178–179
Pyricularia grisea
  description, 111
  isolation and culture, 111
  hosts
    turfgrasses, 111
    all gramineous species, 112
Pythium aphanidermatum, 52, 171, 188
  description, 52–53
  isolation and culture, 56
  hosts
    turfgrasses, 53
    all gramineous species, 53
Pythium aristosporium, 171, 172, 188
  description, 172
  isolation and culture, 173
  hosts
    turfgrasses, 172
    all gramineous species, 172–173
Pythium arrhenomanes, 53, 171, 188
  description, 53
  isolation and culture, 56
  hosts
    turfgrasses, 53
    all gramineous species, 53–54
Pythium blight, 51–59
  symptoms, 52

Pythium blight (*cont.*)
  the pathogens, 52, 53, 54, 55
  disease profile, 56–58
  control, 58–59
Pythium damping off, 187–188
  symptoms, 187
  the pathogens, 187, 188
  disease profile, 187–188
  control, 189
Pythium decline, 173–175
  symptoms, 173
  the pathogens, 171
  disease profile, 174
  control, 174
Pythium graminicola, 54, 171, 188
  description, 54
  isolation and culture, 56
  hosts
    turfgrasses, 54
    all gramineous species, 54
Pythium irregulare, 171, 188
Pythium myriotylum, 54, 171, 188
  description, 54–55
  isolation and culture, 56
  hosts
    turfgrasses, 55
    all gramineous species, 55
Pythium patch, 91
Pythium root dysfunction, 171–173
  symptoms, 171
  the pathogens, 171–172
  disease profile, 173
  control, 173
Pythium species
  pathogenic to roots and crowns, 171
  pathogenic to seedlings, 188
Pythium tardecrescens, 171, 188
Pythium torrulosum, 171, 188
Pythium ultimum
  description, 55
  isolation and culture, 56
  hosts
    turfgrasses, 55
    all gramineous species, 55
Pythium ultimum var. *sporangiiferum*, 171,
  188
Pythium ultimum var. *ultimum*, 171, 188
Pythium vanterpoolii, 171, 188

Quintozene (PCNB)
  first use on turf, 8
  profile, 295

Radopholus similus, 228
  hosts
    turfgrasses, 228
    all gramineous species, 228
Ramularia leaf spot, 132
  symptoms, 132
  the pathogen, 132
  disease profile, 133
  control, 133
Ramularia pusilla
  description, 132–133
  isolation and culture, 133

Ramularia pusilla (*cont.*)
  hosts
    turfgrasses, 133
    all gramineous hosts, 133
Red leaf spot, 100–102
  symptoms, 100–101
  the pathogen, 101
  disease profile, 101–102
  control, 102
Rhizoctonia blight of cool season
    turfgrasses, 59–64
  symptoms, 60
  the pathogen, 60
  disease profile, 62–63
  control, 63–64
Rhizoctonia blight of warm season
    turfgrasses, 33–36
  symptoms, 34
  the pathogen, 34
  disease profile, 35
  control, 35–36
Rhizoctonia cerealis
  description, 32
  isolation and culture, 32
  hosts
    turfgrasses, 32
    all gramineous species, 33
Rhizoctonia damping off, 188–189
  symptoms, 188–189
  the pathogen, 189
  disease profile, 189
  control, 189
Rhizoctonia oryzae
  description, 65
  hosts
    turfgrasses, 65
    all gramineous species, 65
Rhizoctonia sheath spot, 64–65
  symptoms, 64
  the pathogens, 64, 65
  disease profile, 65
  control, 65
Rhizoctonia solani, 34, 60, 189
  description, 34, 60
  isolation and culture, 34, 60–61
  hosts
    turfgrasses, 34, 61
    all gramineous species, 35, 61–62
Rhizoctonia yellow patch, 31–33
  symptoms, 31
  the pathogen, 32
  disease profile, 33
  control, 33
Rhizoctonia zeae
  description, 64
  hosts
    turfgrasses, 64
    all gramineous species, 64–65
Rhopalosiphum maidis, 208
Rhopalosiphum prunifoliae, 208
Rhynchosporium leaf blotch, 127–128
  symptoms, 127
  the pathogens, 127
  disease profile, 127–128
  control, 128

Rhynchosporium orthosporum
  description, 127
  isolation and culture, 127
  hosts
    turfgrasses, 127
    all gramineous hosts, 127
Rhynchosporium secalis
  description, 127
  isolation and culture, 127
  hosts
    turfgrasses, 127
    all gramineous hosts, 127
Ribonucleic acid, 203, 211
RNA (*see* Ribonucleic acid)
Rotylenchus erythrinae (see
    Helicotylenchus erythrinae)
Rubigan™
  first use on turf, 10
  profile, 290
Rusts, 141–149
  symptoms, 141
  the pathogens, 141–146
  disease profile, 147–148
  control, 148–149
Ryegrass leaf mottle, 206
  symptoms, 206
  the virus, 206
  disease profile, 206
Ryegrass mosaic, 208
  symptoms, 208
  the virus, 208
  hosts
    turfgrasses, 208
    all gramineous species, 208
  disease profile, 208–209
Ryegrass yellows, 213
  symptoms, 213
  the pathogen, 213
  disease profile, 213

SAR (sodium absorption ratio), 174
Sclerophthora macrospora
  description, 137
  detection in tissue, 137
  hosts
    turfgrasses, 137–138
    all gramineous species, 138
Sclerospora macrospora (see *Sclerophthora*
    macrospora)
Sclerotia
  described, 21
  illustrated (Plates 16-E, F; 20-F; 21-D, E, F)
Sclerotinia borealis (see *Myriosclerotinia*
    borealis)
Sclerotinia dollar spot, 65–69
  symptoms, 66
  the pathogen, 66
  disease profile, 67–68
  control, 68–69
Sclerotinia homoeocarpa
  description, 66
  review of taxonomic position, 66–67
  isolation and culture, 66
  hosts
    turfgrasses, 67

Sclerotinia homoeocarpa (*cont.*)
    all gramineous species, 67
Sclerotinia patch, 79–81
  symptoms, 79–80
  the pathogen, 80
  disease profile, 80–81
  control, 81
Sclerotinia snow mold (*see* Sclerotinia patch)
Sclerotium blight, 71–73
  symptoms, 72
  the pathogen, 72
  disease profile, 72–73
  control, 73
Sclerotium rhizodes
  description, 84
  isolation and culture, 84
  hosts
    turfgrasses, 84
    all gramineous species, 84–85
Sclerotium rolfsii
  description, 72
  isolation and culture, 72
  hosts
    turfgrasses, 72
    all gramineous species, 72
Scolecotrichum graminis (see
    Cercosporidium graminis)
Seedling diseases, 187–190
Seed transmitted pathogens, list of, 189
Selenophoma everhartii (see
    Pseudoseptoria everhartii)
Selenophoma donacis (see *Pseudoseptoria*
    donacis)
Semesan™
  first use on turf, 6
Senectopathic disorders, 155–163
  concept of, 155
Senescence
  concept of, 155
  condition of leaves during, 155
Septogloeum oxysporum (see *Cheilaria*
    agrostis)
Septoria avenae (see *Stagonospora avenae*)
Septoria calamagrostidis
  description, 117
  hosts
    turfgrasses, 117
    all gramineous species, 117
Septoria leaf spots, 116–118
  symptoms, 116, 117, 118
  the pathogens, 116, 117, 118
  disease profile, 118
  control, 118
Septoria loligena
  description, 118
  hosts
    turfgrasses, 118
    all gramineous species, 118
Septoria macropoda
  description, 116
  hosts
    turfgrasses, 116
    all gramineous species, 116
Septoria macropoda var. *grandis*
  description, 116

Septoria macropoda var. *grandis* (*cont.*)
  hosts
    turfgrasses, 116
    all gramineous species, 116
Septoria macropoda var. *septulata*
  description, 116
  hosts
    turfgrasses, 116
    all gramineous species, 116
Septoria oudemansii
  description, 116–117
  hosts
    turfgrasses, 117
    all gramineous species, 117
Septoria tenella
  description, 117
  hosts
    turfgrasses, 117
    all gramineous species, 118
Septoria triseti
  description, 117
  hosts
    turfgrasses, 117
    all gramineous species, 117
Septoria tritici
  description, 118
  hosts
    turfgrasses, 118
    all gramineous species, 118
Setosphaeria rostrata, 109
Silver top, 192–194
  symptoms, 192–193
  the pathogen, 193
  disease profile, 194
  control, 194
Slime molds, 135–136
  symptoms, 135
  the pathogens, 135
  disease profile, 135–136
  control, 136
Smith, J. D., 8
Soil moisture
  effects on disease, 251–252
Soluble salts
  in root and crown disease, 174
Southern blight (*see* Sclerotium
    blight)
Spermospora ciliata
  description, 122
  isolation and culture, 122
  hosts
    turfgrasses, 122
    all gramineous species, 122–123
Spermospora leaf spots, 122–124
  symptoms, 122, 123
  the pathogens, 122, 123
  disease profile, 124
  control, 124
Spermospora lolii
  description, 123
  hosts
    turfgrasses, 124
    all gramineous species, 124
Spermospora subulata f. *ciliata* (see
    Spermospora ciliata)

Sphaerulina trifolii (see *Leptosphaerulina trifolii*)
Spiroplasma, nature of, 211
Spiroplasma, white leaf
  characteristics of, 214
  isolation and culture, 214
  hosts
    turfgrasses, 214
    all gramineous species, 214
Spore
  defined, 21
  illustrated, 22, 23
Spring dead spot of bermudagrass, 85–91
  symptoms, 85–86
  the pathogens, 85–90
  disease profile, 90
  control, 90–91
Stagonospora avenae
  description, 119
  hosts
    turfgrasses, 119
    all gramineous species, 119–120
Stagonospora leaf spot, 119–120
  symptoms, 119
  the pathogen, 119
  disease profile, 120
  control, 120
St. Andrews, Royal and Ancient Golf
    Club, 3
St. Augustinegrass/centipedegrass decline,
    205–206
  symptoms, 205
  the virus, 205
  disease profile, 205
  control, 205
St. Augustinegrass leaf mottle, 206
  symptoms, 206
  the virus, 206
  disease profile, 206
Stem and crown necrosis, 109
  symptoms, 109
  the pathogen, 109
  disease profile, 109
  control, 109
Stripe smut, 149–152
  symptoms, 149
  the pathogen, 149
  disease profile, 150–151
  control, 151–152
Subdue™
  first use on turf, 10
  profile, 293
Substituted benzenes, 261
Sugarcane mosaic virus, 206
  nature of, 206
  hosts
    turfgrasses, 206
    all gramineous species, 206
Sulfur
  first use on turf, 5
  role in anaerobiosis, 167
Summer decline (*see* Pythium root
    dysfunction, Pythium decline)
Summer patch, 47–51
  symptoms, 48–49

Summer patch (*cont.*)
  the pathogen, 49–50
  disease profile, 50–51
  control, 51
Symptomatology
  terminology, 16
Synergy, fungicide, 263

Take-all patch, 28–31
  symptoms, 28
  the pathogen, 28–29
  disease profile, 30
  control, 30–31
Take-all root rot of St. Augustinegrass,
    176–177
  symptoms, 176
  the pathogen, 176
  disease profile, 177
  control, 177
Terraclor
  first use on turf, 8
  profile, 295
Tersan 1991™
  first use on turf, 10
  profile, 285
Tersan OM™
  first use on turf, 6
Tersan SP™
  first use on turf, 8
  profile, 286
Tetracycline, 211, 213
Thanatephorous cucumeris (see
    Rhizoctonia solani)
Thatch
  pseudo, 250
  profile of, 250
  management effects on disease, 250–251
Thiophanate ethyl
  first use on turf, 10
Thiophanate methyl
  first use on turf, 10
  profile, 296
Thiram
  first use on turf, 6
Tilletia decipiens
  description, 191
  turfgrass host, 191
Tilletia pallida
  description, 191
  hosts
    turfgrasses, 191
    all gramineous species, 191
Toxoptera graminum, 208
Trechispora alnicola, 185
Triadimefon
  first use on turf, 10
  profile, 297
Triazoles, 262
Trichodorus obtusus (see *Paratrichodorus
    primitivus*)
Tricholoma sordidum
  effect of nitrogen on pathogenicity of,
    184
Turfgrass culture
  development of, 3–4

Tylenchorhynchus acutus, 230
  hosts
    turfgrass, 230
    all gramineous species, 230
Tylenchorhynchus claytoni, 230
  hosts
    turfgrass, 230
    all gramineous species, 231
Tylenchorhynchus dubius, 231
  hosts
    turfgrass, 231
    all gramineous species, 231
Tylenchorhynchus lamelliferus, 231
  turfgrass host, 231
Tylenchorhynchus martini, 231
  hosts
    turfgrass, 231
    all gramineous species, 231
Tylenchorhynchus nudus, 231
  turfgrass host, 231
Typhula blight, 77–79
  symptoms, 77
  the pathogens, 77–78
  disease profile, 78–79
  control, 79
Typhula incarnata
  description, 77–78
  isolation and culture, 78
  hosts
    turfgrasses, 78
    all gramineous species, 78
Typhula ishikariensis
  description, 78
  hosts
    turfgrasses, 78
    all gramineous species, 78
Typhula itoana (see *Typhula incarnata*)

United States Golf Association, 4
Upsulum
  first use on turf, 6
Uromyces dactylidis
  description, 146
  hosts
    turfgrasses, 146
    all gramineous hosts, 146
Uromyces jacksonii
  description, 146
  hosts
    turfgrasses, 146
    all gramineous hosts, 147
Ustilago affinis
  description, 192
  turfgrass host, 192
Ustilago agropyri
  description, 152
  isolation and culture, 152
  hosts
    turfgrasses, 152
    all gramineous species, 152–153
Ustilago cynodontis
  description, 192
  turfgrass host, 192
Ustilago festucae (see *Ustilago agropyri*)

Ustilago poae (see *Ustilago agropyri*)
Ustilago striiformis
    description, 149
    isolation and culture, 149
    hosts
        turfgrasses, 149
        all gramineous species, 149–150
Ustilago trebouxii
    description, 192
    hosts
        turfgrasses, 192
        all gramineous species, 192
Ustilago tritici (see *Ustilago agropyri*)

Vapam™ (*see* Meptam-sodium)
Vinclozolin
    first use on turf, 10
    profile, 297
Viruses
    form and composition, 203–204
    mechanisms of pathogenicity, 203
Virus-incited diseases, 203–208
Vorlan™
    first use on turf, 10

Vorlan™ (*cont.*)
    profile, 297

Water table
    perched, 166
Western ryegrass mosaic, 208
    symptoms, 208
    the virus, 208
    hosts
        turfgrasses, 208
        all gramineous species, 208
    disease profile, 208
White heads (*see* Silver top)
White leaf of bermudagrass
    symptoms, 214
    the pathogen, 214
    disease profile, 214
White top (*see* Silver top)
Winter crown rot (*see* Cottony snow mold)
Woolhouse, A. R., 8

Xanthomonas campestris pv. *graminis*
    description, 212
    isolation and culture, 212

Xanthomonas campestris pv. *graminis*
        (*cont.*)
    hosts
        turfgrasses, 212
        all gramineous species, 212
Xiphinema americanum, 234
    hosts
        turfgrasses, 234
        all gramineous species, 234

Yellow dwarf, 207–208
    symptoms, 207
    the virus, 207
    disease profile, 208
Yellow tuft (*see* Downy mildew)

Zineb
    first use on turf, 9
Zonate eyespot, 106–108
    symptoms, 107
    the pathogen, 107
    disease profile, 107–108
    control, 108

NOTES